SCHOPENHAUER: A BIOGRAPHY

Arthur Schopenhauer (1788–1860) was one of the most original and provocative thinkers of the nineteenth century. He spent a lifetime striving to understand the meaning of living in a world where suffering and death are ubiquitous. In his quest to solve "the ever-disquieting riddle of existence," Schopenhauer explored almost every dimension of human existence, developing a darkly compelling worldview that found deep resonance in contemporary literature, music, philosophy, and psychology.

This is the first comprehensive biography of Schopenhauer written in English. Placing him in his historical and philosophical contexts, David E. Cartwright tells the story of Schopenhauer's life to convey the full range of his philosophy. He offers a fully documented portrait in which he explores Schopenhauer's fractured family life, his early formative influences, his critical loyalty to Kant, his personal interactions with Fichte and Goethe, his ambivalent relationship with Schelling, his contempt for Hegel, his struggle to make his philosophy known, and his reaction to his late-arriving fame. The Schopenhauer who emerges in this biography is the complex author of a philosophy that had a significant influence on figures as diverse as Samuel Beckett, Jorge Luis Borges, Emile Durkheim, Sigmund Freud, Thomas Hardy, Thomas Mann, Friedrich Nietzsche, and Ludwig Wittgenstein.

David E. Cartwright is professor of philosophy and religious studies at the University of Wisconsin – Whitewater. He has published numerous articles on Schopenhauer and nineteenth-century German philosophy, translated and edited several of Schopenhauer's books, and is the author of the *Historical Dictionary of Schopenhauer's Philosophy*.

Schopenhauer
A Biography

David E. Cartwright

University of Wisconsin – Whitewater

CAMBRIDGE
UNIVERSITY PRESS

CAMBRIDGE UNIVERSITY PRESS
Cambridge, New York, Melbourne, Madrid, Cape Town, Singapore,
São Paulo, Delhi, Dubai, Tokyo

Cambridge University Press
32 Avenue of the Americas, New York, NY 10013-2473, USA

www.cambridge.org
Information on this title: www.cambridge.org/9780521825986

First published 2010

Printed in the United States of America

A catalog record for this publication is available from the British Library.

Library of Congress Cataloging in Publication data

Cartwright, David E.
Schopenhauer : a biography / David E. Cartwright.
p.   cm.
Includes bibliographical references and index.
ISBN 978-0-521-82598-6 (hardback)
1. Schopenhauer, Arthur, 1788–1860.   2. Philosophers – Germany –
Biography.   I. Title.
B3147.C26   2010
193–dc22
[B]   2009036874

ISBN 978-0-521-82598-6 Hardback

Was man in der Jugend wünscht,
hat man im Alter die Fülle.
Goethe, Dichtung und Wahrheit

Contents

Preface

Arthur Schopenhauer continues to be one of the most widely read philosophers outside of academe, and it is only a slight exaggeration to say that academics have paid him more attention in the last thirty years than they have in any period following the publication of his philosophical masterpiece, *The World as Will and Representation*, which appeared in December 1818. This remark, however, is not an exaggeration at all if it is restricted to Anglo-American scholars. Schopenhauer's broad popularity is relatively easy to understand, as is the resurgence of interest among scholars. In addition to addressing traditional topics in aesthetics, epistemology, ethics, logic, and metaphysics in the rigorous and specialized forms favored by philosophers, his fifty-year quest to discover and explain the meaning of the totality of experience led him to investigate almost every significant aspect of human experience. Ever the perennialist, he dealt with universal themes concerning the human condition, such as love, sex, suffering, death, the meaning and value of life, and redemption. He also explored phenomena neglected by many philosophers, including colors, genius, homosexuality, humor, madness, the metaphysics of music, the moral status of animals, mysticism, paranormal phenomena, and weeping. Always committed to the truth, he trailed its spurs wherever its track steered. Seldom worrying about writing to please, he stated the truth as he saw it. His voracious curiosity and cosmopolitan sensibilities made him the first major Western philosopher to seriously consider Eastern thought. In addition to his stressing commonalities between Eastern and Western perspectives, Hinduism and Buddhism helped shape his philosophy, and he recognized ways in which Eastern thought transcended that of the West.

Yet it is not simply his vast array of topics that draw readers to Schopenhauer. He loathed obscurantism of any kind, and he viewed the torturous styles of many of his contemporaries as displaying a poverty of thought that they attempted to conceal by incomprehensible jargon wrapped in ponderous sentence structures. Compared to his contemporaries and compared to most philosophers, he wrote wonderfully and clearly. He philosophized from the heart, from a genuine astonishment about the world, and not simply from a puzzlement about what other philosophers had said. He wrote with wit, irony, and sarcasm; polemically and provocatively; with grace and beauty. At times, reading Schopenhauer is an aesthetic experience of the first order. His works abound with personal observations based on his travels, his experiences of great works of art, and his keen attention to human behavior. He was as likely to quote from Goethe as he was from Kant. To illustrate a point, or to clarify an idea, he would draw from world literature and religion, from poetry and philosophy, and from the natural sciences.

Schopenhauer's original and darkly compelling worldview, with its expressive and inviting style and its emphasis on instinctive drives and nonrational forces directing not only human behavior, but everything in the world, has had a remarkable history of influence. Some scholars have detected the imprint of his thought in the work of figures as diverse as Jacob Burckhardt, Paul Deussen, Emile Durkheim, Albert Einstein, Sigmund Freud, Carl Jung, Erwin Schrödinger, Swami Vivekānanda, and Wilhelm Wundt. Others have heard him in the music of Johannes Brahms, Antonín Dvorák, Gustav Mahler, Arnold Schönberg, and Richard Wagner. Still others have read him in Charles Baudelaire, Samuel Beckett, Jorge Luis Borges, Joseph Conrad, Afanasij Fet, Gustav Flaubert, Theodor Fontane, André Gide, George Gissing, Thomas Hardy, Friedrich Hebbel, Hermann Hesse, Henrik Ibsen, Thomas Mann, William Somerset Maugham, Guy de Maupassant, Herman Melville, Edgar Allan Poe, Marcel Proust, Wilhelm Raabe, August Strindberg, Leo Tolstoy, Ivan Turgenev, Virginia Woolf, and Emile Zola. Moreover, there are those who have noted his mark on the philosophies of Henri Bergson, Eduard von Hartmann, Max Horkheimer, Friedrich Nietzsche, Ludwig Marcuse, Max Scheller, Richard Taylor, Hans Vaihinger, and Ludwig Wittgenstein.

The resurgence of interest in Schopenhauer by scholars has been driven, in part, by his rich *Wirkungsgeschichte*. He claimed that we have learned some things from him that we will never forget. And, although this is true, it is as if scholars are recovering the memory of the author of those things. For decades, Schopenhauer had been viewed by Anglo–American analytic philosophers as a source for pointedly poignant observations on human life and as a figure of literary and not philosophical interest. But the tide has changed. Kant scholars, at first interested in Schopenhauer's critique of the Kantian philosophy, have also come to appreciate the philosophical power of his thought. Philosophers first drawn to him in order to understand Schopenhauer's formative influence on Nietzsche and Wittgenstein have also come to appreciate the rigor and power of his work. Now even a dyed-in-the-wool, hardline analytical philosopher has come to appreciate the explanatory power of his philosophy. But what about the thinker himself, about whom it was once said that students knew more about him than about his philosophy?

Although Schopenhauer has been called an arch-pessimist, misanthrope, misogynist, cynic, irrationalist; a friendless, godless philosopher of will; unloved, loveless, arrogant, mother-despising, an academic failure; a fierce advocate of a contradictory worldview; even a seamstress-beating, Hegel-hating hurler of ad hominems – although Schopenhauer has been called all these, many of which are true, few know more about him. For Schopenhauer was also a master of German prose, a poodle-loving, flute-playing Rossini devotee, a polyglot, an Upanishads-reading Buddhist, and a Plato-esteeming, Kant-admiring, Goethe-revering, mission-driven philosopher of the body, of sexual love, of art, of tranquility, of compassion, and of redemption. In fact, Arthur Schopenhauer was, in many senses, a singular philosopher. But what is the thing in itself behind these many appearances?

Acknowledgments

With a deep sense of gratitude, I offer my thanks to those who have either directly or indirectly enabled me to write this book. I have benefitted substantially from the work of earlier biographers, especially from studies by Patrick Bridgwater, Wilhelm Gwinner, Arthur Hübscher, and Rüdiger Safranski. Ulrike Bergmann's biography of Johanna Schopenhauer and Gabriele Büch's biography of Adele Schopenhauer considerably aided my understanding of Schopenhauer's relationships with his mother and sister. My interpretation of Schopenhauer's philosophy has been informed by the writings of Urs App, John E. Atwell, Arati Barua, Douglas Berger, Dieter Birnbacher, Patrick Gardiner, George Goedert, D. W. Hamlyn, Dale Jacquette, Christopher Janaway, Yauso Kamata, Matthias Koβler, P. F. H. Lauterman, Ludger Lütkehaus, Bryan Magee, Rudolf Malter, G. Steven Neeley, Moria Nicholls, Alfred Schmidt, Ivan Soll, Volker Spierling, F. C. White, Robert Wicks, Julian Young, and Günter Zöller. These scholars and their works have been an immense help in my understanding of Schopenhauer's life and philosophy.

I would be remiss if I were not to mention the support provided to me by my colleagues at the University of Wisconsin – Whitewater. In particular, I must thank Edward E. Erdmann for many satisfying conversations as we labored through our translations of Schopenhauer, *nämlich*, *hingegen*, and *eben* aside. My colleagues in the Department of Philosophy and Religious Studies, Richard Brooks, Wade Dazey, Crista Lebens, Ann Luther, and David Simmons, willingly discussed Schopenhauer with me without resignation, often displaying the patience of a saint as I spoke almost ad nauseum about the philosopher. The University of Wisconsin – Whitewater generously supported my research for this book through a sabbatical during the spring semester of 2006. The Steven Shelton Schopenhauer Collect, housed in my department's library, provided immediate access to valuable primary and secondary literature. For helping me understand Schopenhauer's disposition toward amateur botanizing and for aiding me with plant identification, I owe a debt to my friend, Richard Larson of The Dawes Arboretum

This book would not have seen the light of day without the careful work of Vickie Schmidt. She transformed my messy, hardscrabble, handwritten heap of pages into a readable text, improving my work in countless ways. Elyse Smithback and Carol Lohry Cartwright also played a crucial in this transformation. Eden Lohry Smithback was almost along for the ride.

I must also acknowledge Dover Publications for permission to use E. F. J. Payne's translation of Schopenhauer's *The World as Will and Representation*, Berg Publishers for the use of Payne's translation of *Arthur Schopenhauer: Manuscript Remains in Four Volumes*, and Oxford University Press for the use of extracts from Payne's translation of Schopenhauer's *Parerga and Paralipomena*.

The late Terence Moore invited me to engage in this project, something that I would never have considered on my own. Without his encouragement, this book would not have been written. I must also thank Beatrice Rehl for her guidance and patience.

I dedicate this book to my loving wife, Carol Lohry Cartwright.

Notes on the Text

The goals of this book are to tell the story of Arthur Schopenhauer's life, to describe how he came to his philosophy, and to provide a general account of his philosophical thought. I have composed this work, however, to serve readers with diverse interests. I assume that all readers are interested in Schopenhauer's life. After all, why else would one read a biography about Schopenhauer? Moreover, since Schopenhauer lived for philosophy, as he repeatedly asserted, a major theme of his life also involves how he came to his philosophy, and to understand his life, it is important to understand the genesis of his philosophy. Nevertheless, some readers are likely to be more interested in his life than in particular areas of his philosophy. To accommodate readers with different interests, I have kept biographical materials as distinct as possible from accounts of his particular books, so that readers may ignore discussions of particular books without loss of the narrative of Schopenhauer's life, and so that readers may also focus on specific areas of his philosophy. Consequently, discussions of Schopenhauer's books occur under chapter sections titled by the name of the particular book; when appropriate, I use subsections to denote particular topics in that book. Then I either continue the chapter with a new section that continues biographical materials, or conclude the chapter. For example, in Chap. 5, I discuss under the section "On the Fourfold Root of the Principle of Sufficient Reason" Schopenhauer's dissertation, including the significant revisions that it received thirty-four years later in its second edition, and then I continue the story of his life in the following section, "Weimar." I conclude Chap. 7 with a discussion of his principal work under the section "The World as Will and Representation," which includes the subsections "Epistemology," "Metaphysics of Nature," "Metaphysics of Art," and "Metaphysics of Morals," which correspond to the four major divisions of this book.

Chronology of Schopenhauer's Life and Works

1788 February 22: Arthur Schopenhauer born in Danzig to the patrician merchant Heinrich Floris Schopenhauer and Johanna Schopenhauer (born Trosiener), later a popular writer and novelist.

1793 March: The Schopenhauers move to Hamburg, to avoid the Prussian annexation of Danzig.

1797 June 12: Schopenhauer's only sibling, Louise Adelaide (Adele), is born.

July: Travels to France with his father, remaining in Le Havre for two years with the family of a business associate of his father.

1799 August: Returns from France and enrolls in Dr. Runge's private school, an institution designed to educate future merchants.

1800 July: Accompanies his parents on a three-month trip to Hannover, Karlsbad, Prague, and Dresden.

1803 May: The Schopenhauers, minus Adele, begin a tour of Holland, England, France, Switzerland, Austria, Silesia, and Prussia; the tour is Schopenhauer's reward for agreeing to continue his training as a merchant and for foregoing preparation for attendance at a university.

June 30: Attends the Reverend Lancaster's school in Wimbledon for twelve weeks.

1804 August: Conclusion of European tour; Schopenhauer receives confirmation in Danzig.

September–December: Serves as an apprentice to a Danzig merchant.

1805 January: Begins apprenticeship with a Hamburg merchant.

April 20: Heinrich Floris dies; his wife and son believe that his death is a suicide.

1806 September: After liquidating the family business, Johanna moves to Weimar with Adele. Schopenhauer remains as an apprentice in Hamburg.

1807 May: With his mother's encouragement, Schopenhauer ends his apprenticeship.

June: Attends a gymnasium at Gotha.

December: Terminates his studies at Gotha, after being rebuked for writing a lampoon of an instructor; relocates to Weimar, but lives separately from his family.

1808 To prepare for the university, takes private studies in Latin and Greek and studies mathematics and history on his own.

1809 February: Upon reaching the age of majority, receives his inheritance, one-third of his father's estate.

October: Matriculates as a medical student at the University of Göttingen.

1810 Winter semester: Studies philosophy with Gottlob Ernst Schulze, whose recommended reading of Plato and Kant introduces Schopenhauer to his two favorite philosophers; begins reading Friedrich Wilhelm Joseph von Schelling.

1811 September: Enrolls in the University of Berlin to study philosophy.

Winter semester: Attends Johann Gottlieb Fichte's lectures, becoming increasingly disenchanted with Fichte's philosophy. He continues studying Schelling and continues reading Fichte.

1812 Spring–Summer: Concludes private studies of Fichte and Schelling; continues private study of Kant and Plato; and reads Francis Bacon and John Locke.

Summer semester: Attends Friedrich Ernst Schleiermacher's lectures.

Winter: Regularly observes psychiatric patients at the Berlin Charité.

1813 May: Fearing military conscription and an attack by Napoleon, Schopenhauer leaves Berlin for a short stay at Weimar.

June: Retires to Rudolstadt to write his dissertation.

October: *On the Fourfold Root of the Principle of Sufficient Reason* earns Schopenhauer a doctorate in philosophy, in absentia, from the University of Jena; his dissertation is published.

November: Returns to Weimar; Goethe, who received a dedicated copy of Schopenhauer's dissertation, interests the young philosopher in color theory, a subject they will discuss periodically for the next few months.

December: Begins to borrow volumes of the *Asiatisches Magazin* from the ducal library in Weimar.

1814 **March**: Schopenhauer borrows a Latin translation of the *Upanishads* from the ducal library in Weimar; this Latin translation, the *Oupnek'hat*, would become his "Bible."

May: After a series of vicious quarrels with his mother, Schopenhauer moves to Dresden; the philosopher will never see his mother again, either dead or alive.

1816 **May**: The fruit of Schopenhauer's work with Goethe on color theory, *On Vision and Colors*, is published.

1818 **March**: Schopenhauer completes his principal work, *The World as Will and Representation*.

September: First trip to Italy.

December: Appearance of his principal work, which bears a publication date of 1819.

1819 **Spring**: While Schopenhauer is in Italy, his daughter is born in Dresden; the child dies late that summer.

July: Returns to Germany to address a family financial crisis caused by the failure of the banking house of Muhl.

December: Applies to the University of Berlin to qualify as a *Privatdozent*, an unsalaried lecturer; expresses his desire to teach at the same time as Hegel's principal lectures.

1820 **March**: Schopenhauer receives a passing grade on his test lecture, during which he and Hegel engage in a minor dispute.

Summer semester: Offers and convenes lectures for the first and only time and does not complete the course; Schopenhauer's lectures are listed in Berlin's prospectus of lectures in 1820–22 and in 1826–31.

1821 Begins an on-and-off, decade-long affair with Caroline Richter, later "Medon."

August: Schopenhauer allegedly assaults the seamstress Caroline Marquet, an event that would lead to a series of lawsuits, lasting for more than five years.

Fall: Inquires about an academic position at Gießen.

1822 **May**: Second Italian tour.

1823 **May**: Schopenhauer returns to Germany; overwinters in Munich, suffering through various illnesses and depression.

1824 Schopenhauer lives in Gastein (Switzerland), Mannheim, and Dresden.

November: Attempts to secure contracts to translate David Hume's *Natural History of Religion* and *Dialogues Concerning Natural Religion* into German, and Giordano Bruno's *della Causa, principio ed Uno* into Latin.

1825 **January**: Attempts to secure a contract to translate Laurence Sterne's *Tristram Shandy* into German.

May: Returns to Berlin and begins to study Spanish.

1826 Discovers the first edition of Kant's *Critique of Pure Reason*.

1827 **May**: Final, negative, judgment against Schopenhauer in the Marquet case.

September: Inquires about an academic position at Würzburg.

1828 **February**: Inquires about an academic position at Heidelberg.

1829 **May**: Attempts to secure a contract to translate Gracián's *Oráculo manual arte de prudencia* into German.

December: Attempts to secure a contract to translate Kant's principal works into English.

1830 **June**: Schopenhauer's Latin revision of his color theory, "*Commentatio undecima exponens Theoriam Colorum Physiologcam eandemque primariam*" is published in *Scriptores Ophthalmologici minores*.

1831 **August**: Schopenhauer flees from Berlin to Frankfurt am Main, due to the cholera epidemic.

1832 **Beginning of the year**: A depressed Schopenhauer isolates himself in his rooms for two months.

April: Completes his Gracián translation and once more attempts to have it published; the translation is published posthumously in 1862.

July: Moves to Mannheim.

1833 **July**: Permanently moves to Frankfurt, where he will live for the remainder of his life.

1835 It is likely that a second daughter, who dies in infancy, is born in Frankfurt.

1836 **March**: *On the Will in Nature* is published.

1837 **August**: Schopenhauer begins a letter exchange with the editors of Kant's collected works and convinces them to publish the first edition of Kant's *Critique of Pure Reason* and to relegate the changes in its second edition to an appendix.

1838 **April 17**: Johanna Schopenhauer dies in Bonn; Schopenhauer does not attend his mother's funeral.

1839 **January**: Schopenhauer's prize-essay "On the Freedom of the Human Will" receives the gold medal from the Royal Norwegian Society of Sciences in Trondheim; a Norwegian translation is published the next year.

1840 **January**: Despite being the only entry, the prize-essay "On the Foundation of Morality" is refused the crown by the Royal Danish Society of Sciences in Copenhagen.

September: Schopenhauer's two prize-essays are published as *The Two Fundamental Problems of Ethics* (bearing a publication date of 1841); he includes a lengthy preface in which he berates the Royal Danish Society and Hegel.

1841 **Spring**: Unsuccessfully tries to persuade Charles Lock Eastlake, the translator of Goethe's color theory, to translate *On Vision and Colors* into English.

1842 Caroline Marquet dies.

Summer: Meets with his sister Adele in Frankfurt, their first personal meeting in twenty years.

1844 **March**: The second edition of *The World as Will and Representation* appears in two volumes.

July: Beginning of letter exchange with Johann August Becker.

1845 **Summer**: Begins work on *Parerga and Paralipomena*.

1846 **July**: First personal meeting with Julius Frauenstädt.

1847 **December**: A significantly revised second edition of *The Fourfold Root of the Principle of Sufficient Reason* appears.

1848 **March**: Street fighting in Frankfurt disrupts Schopenhauer's life.

1849 **March**: Last meeting with his sister.

April 25: Death of Adele Schopenhauer in Bonn; Schopenhauer does not attend the funeral.

December: Laments the loss of his white poodle Atma; soon thereafter acquires a brown poodle, also called Atma.

1851 **November**: *Parerga and Paralipomena* appears.

1853 **April**: An anonymous review (by John Oxenford) "Iconoclasm in German Philosophy," appears in the *Westminster Review*.

May: The *Vossische Zeitung* publishes a German translation of Oxenford's review.

1854 **September**: Second edition of *On the Will in Nature*.

December: Second edition of *On Vision and Colors*; Richard Wagner sends Schopenhauer a dedicated copy of *The Nibelung's Ring*.

1855 **October**: The philosophy faculty at the University of Leipzig sponsors an essay contest for the exposition and criticism of the Schopenhauerian philosophy.

1857 First lectures on Schopenhauer are delivered at the universities in Bonn and Breslau.

1859 **November**: The third edition of *The World as Will and Representation* appears.

1860 **September**: The second edition of *The Two Fundamental Problems of Ethics* appears.

September 21: Arthur Schopenhauer dies in Frankfurt am Main.

I

The Affirmation of the Will

ARTHUR SCHOPENHAUER VIEWED himself as homeless. This sense of homelessness became the leitmotif of both his life and his philosophy. After the first five years of his life in Danzig, where he was born on 22 February 1788, his family fled the then free city to avoid Prussian control. From that point on, he said, "I have never acquired a new home."[1] He lived in Hamburg on and off for fourteen years, but he had his best times when he was away from that city. When he left Hamburg, he felt as if he were escaping a prison. He lived for four years in Dresden, but he would only view this city as the birthplace of his principal work, *The World as Will and Representation*. More than a decade in Berlin did nothing to give him a sense of belonging. He would angrily exclaim that he was no Berliner. After living as a noncitizen resident in Frankfurt am Main for the last twenty-eight years of his life, and after spending fifty years attempting to understand the nature and meaning of the world, he would ultimately conclude that the world itself was not his home. If one were to take this remark seriously, then even Danzig had not been his home. He was homeless from birth. But being homeless from birth did not mean that there was no point to his life. Schopenhauer would also conclude that from birth he had a mission in life.

[1] Arthur Schopenhauer, *Gesammelte Briefe*, ed. Arthur Hübscher (Bonn: Bouvier Verlag Herbert Grundmann, 1987), p. 48. This remark is found in Schopenhauer's *curriculum vitae*, which he included in his request to lecture and do his habilitation at the University of Berlin (31 December 1819). The *curriculum vitae* was in Latin and it, as well as a German translation, is also given in *Gesammelte Briefe*, pp. 47–55, 647–56. Arthur Hübscher has observed that the *curriculum vitae* is the most important source of knowledge for the first three decades of Schopenhauer's life; see his "Arthur Schopenhauer: Ein Lebensbild," in *Arthur Schopenhauer: Sämtliche Werke*, 4th ed., 7 vols., ed. Arthur Hübscher (Mannheim: F. A. Brockhaus, 1988), Vol. 1, p. 141. The *curriculum vitae* is Schopenhauer's lengthiest autobiographical reflection.

He was almost deprived, however, of being born in Danzig. During a tour of England, Heinrich Floris Schopenhauer discovered that his wife was pregnant. Johanna, as a first-time mother, naturally and reasonably wanted to return to the house of her parents to give birth under her mother's care. Heinrich Floris insisted otherwise. He wanted his child and hoped-for son to be born in England, thereby acquiring the rights of English citizenship, which would be useful credentials for a future merchant. Johanna acquiesced to her husband's will: "[After a] difficult struggle with myself that I completely endured . . . I succeeded in conquering my inner opposition [to staying in London]."[2] Overcoming an initial resistance, and embracing the situation and warm reception "by loving friends," she came to look "towards the future calmly."[3]

Johanna's calm soon became shattered, however. The foggy days and gloomy London nights triggered her husband's anxiety, a dim expression of the depression and melancholy that would become increasingly pronounced during the remaining eighteen years of his life. The immediate object of Heinrich Floris's free-floating anxiety during her pregnancy became his wife's well-being. In an odd move, he decided they should return to Danzig, even though traveling through northern Germany in the fall and early winter would be arduous. He did, however, have his wife examined by a well-known London surgeon, John Hunter, who assured the nervous couple that the continual motion of the trip should have a salutary effect on a woman in Johanna's condition.

The Schopenhauers disembarked from Dover at the end of November and reached Danzig on New Year's Eve 1787. Johanna would later claim that it was her desire that motivated the return, but she also knew it was her husband's anxious concern for her health that prompted him to haul her back to native grounds, because she had already been prepared to give birth in England. Although Schopenhauer's father dragged his mother back to Danzig, at least Arthur was not dragged into the world through the use of forceps. So in a twofold sense, he was unlike Gotthold Ephraim Lessing's son, a figure whose wisdom Arthur would later laud by saying that "because this son had absolutely declined to come into the world, he

---

[2] Johanna Schopenhauer, *Jugendleben und Wanderbilder*, ed. Willi Drost (Barmstedt Holstein: Velox-Verlag, 1958), p. 214.
[3] Ibid., p. 215.

had to be dragged forcibly into life by means of forceps; but hardly was he in it, when he had hurried away from it."[4]

Danzig

Arthur's birthplace had been populated by Schopenhauers since the late seventeenth century. His great-grandfather, Johann Schopenhauer, was a successful merchant, as was his son, Arthur's paternal grandfather, Andreas (1720–94), who was also an art dealer and the owner of an impressive collection of paintings.[5] Arthur's paternal grandmother, Anna Renata (1726–1804), was the daughter of a Dutch merchant and shipowner, Hendrick Soersmans, who had come to Danzig, serving as the Dutch Minister-Resident of the region from 1754 to 1775.[6]

Schopenhauer's paternal grandparents were prolific. Anna Renata gave birth fifteen times, but several of her offspring possessed the wisdom of Lessing's son. Of the eleven children who lived past the first few days, there were six sons and five daughters. Two of these sons died young, and two more made it into middle age. Arthur's uncle and godfather, Johann Friedrich, died at the age of forty-five in 1794, and Karl Gottfried, who also became Heinrich Floris's business partner, died at the age of thirty-four in 1795. Only Heinrich Floris, who was born in 1747, and his youngest brother, Michael Andreas (1758–1813), lived into their fifties. The fate, however, of the five daughters was even worse. Only Maria Renata (1750–1807) survived into adulthood. She married a merchant, Christian Gottfried Tietz, in 1779, and they provided Arthur with his only cousin, Karl Gottfried Tietz (1781–1833).[7]

---

[4] Arthur Schopenhauer, *The World as Will and Representation*, 2 vols., trans. E. F. J. Payne (New York: Dover, 1969) Vol. 2, p. 579/*Sämtliche Werke*, Vol. 3, p. 665.]

[5] See Hübscher, "Lebensbild," *Sämtliche Werke*, Vol. 1, p. 32.

[6] See Patrick Bridgwater, *Arthur Schopenhauer's English Schooling* (London/New York: Routledge, 1988), p. 3.

[7] For Schopenhauer's genealogy, see Hermann Haßargen, "Die Danziger Vorfahren Arthur Schopenhauers," *Heimatblätter des Deutschen Heimatbundes* (Danzig, 1928, 4); Walther Rauschenberger, "Schopenhauers Ahnen," *Jahrbuch der Schopenhauer-Gesellschaft*, Vol. 21 (1934), pp. 131–49 and "Nachträge zu Schopenhauers Ahnentafel," *Jahrbuch der Schopenhauer-Gesellschaft*, Vol. 24 (1937), p. 153; Arthur Hübscher, "Drei Tanten Schopenhauers," *Schopenhauer-Jahrbuch*, Vol. 61 (1980), pp. 127–50; and Kurt Asendorf, "Altes und Neues zur Schopenhauer-Genealogie," *Schopenhauer-Jahrbuch*, Vol. 69 (1988), pp. 609–13.

Heinrich Floris would have the good fortune of inheriting his father's business savvy and connections. Unfortunately, what he inherited from his mother would prove disastrous. Anna Renata possessed a "pathological nature."[8] She was given to severe bouts of depression and anxiety, and she was said to have a violent disposition. Because of her mental disorders, she was placed under the care of trustees after her husband's death. Her youngest son, Michael Andreas, was considered "an imbecile" since birth, and Karl Gottfried became "half mad" prior to his death.[9] Heinrich Floris would also show increasingly odd behavior prior to his death; his depression, anxiety, and tendency toward violent verbal outbursts all seemed to have their roots in the Dutch side of the family. Arthur would recognize his own tendencies toward depression, anxiety, and melancholy as descending from his father: "Inherited from my father is the anxiety which I myself curse . . . and combat with all the force of my will."[10] Later, when he was asked whether his pessimism resulted from something he suffered in his early childhood, he responded, "Not at all; rather I was always very melancholy as a youth."[11] He would later theorize that one inherited one's will from one's father. Contrary to this theory, it seemed as though Heinrich Floris had inherited his will from his mother.

Andreas Schopenhauer educated Heinrich Floris to ensure his success as a merchant. In addition to studies in Danzig, Heinrich Floris lived for many years abroad, accumulating practical experiences of the world, sharpening his business skills, and developing important business connections with future trading partners. In Bordeaux, he clerked in the firm of Bethmann. While in France, he developed a passion for Voltaire and

---

[8] Hübscher, "Lebensbild," p. 32. Also see Johanna's account of madness in Heinrich Floris's family in a letter to Arthur, 22 July 1835, in Ludger Lütkeaus (ed.), *Die Schopenhauers: Der Familien Briefwechsel von Adele, Arthur, Heinrich Floris und Johanna Schopenhauer* (Zurich: Haffmans Verlag, 1991), pp. 355–6.

[9] Ibid., p. 32.

[10] Arthur Schopenhauer, *Manuscript Remains in Four Volumes*, trans. E. F. J. Payne, ed. Arthur Hübscher (Oxford/New York/Munich: Berg, 1988–90), Vol. 4, "Εἰς ἑαυτόν," #28.

[11] Arthur Hübscher (ed.), *Arthur Schopenhauer: Gespräche* (Stuttgart/Bad Cannstatt: Frommann-Holzboog, 1971), p. 131. It is curious to note that Schopenhauer never referred to his philosophy as "pessimism" in any of the books that he prepared for publication, although, as Rudolf Malter has noted, this is the term most frequently used to describe his philosophy (along with "irrationalism"; and "voluntarism," which are also terms that he did not use to describe his philosophy), see his *Arthur Schopenhauer: Transcendentalphilosophie und Metaphysik des Willens* (Stuttgard/Bad Cannstatt: Frommann, 1991), p. 151. As this incident illustrates, he did not object to being called a pessimist.

for light French literature, including that of a decidedly erotic nature. Johanna alluded to this in her memoirs: "The French novels which he put in my hands taught me that, during his stay of many years in that country, he must have had many an experience that was not apt to elevate my sex in his eyes."[12] This taste for "French novels" was soon transferred to Johanna, who strove, after her husband's death, to keep Jean-Baptiste Louvert de Couvray's erotic six-volume *Amorous Adventures of the Chevalier de Faublas* [*Les amours du chevalier du Faublas*] out of Arthur's hands. She was worried that such writings would transfer her husband's views of women to her son. It is not known whether she was successful in her endeavor to keep the books out of her son's hands. Even if she was, she appeared to have been completely unsuccessful in preventing her son from sharing his father's attitudes toward her sex.

Besides living in France, Heinrich Floris also lived in England, although less is known about the length of time he lived there. He was in England in 1773, and he may have remained there until 1780.[13] During his time in London, he developed a profound appreciation of the liberties afforded British citizens, and of England's progressive constitution, as well as its institutions. He became an unabashed Anglophile who would continue throughout his life to read the London *Times*. Arthur would also come to harbor a lifelong love for England, which tended to counterbalance his deep loathing for the narrow-minded religious bigotry he would come to always associate with England. And like his father, he would grow up to read the *Times* daily. When Heinrich Floris returned to Danzig, he received on 19 November 1780, in conjunction with his brother Karl Gottfried, who was also fluent in French and English, the right to conduct business under the title Shipping Company and Commissions – Brothers Schopenhauer [*Reederei und Kommissionen – Gebrüder Schopenhauer*]. The brothers were shipping agents, but they also engaged in some banking and brokering, along with exchanging grain and raw materials from the Baltic for British manufactured goods.

Heinrich Floris was not a handsome man. Perhaps he was just the reverse. He had a square and muscular frame, a round head, a broad face, a prominent under jaw, puffy blue eyes, and a wide mouth framed with thick lips. Unfortunately, neither Arthur nor his sister Adele would

[12] Johanna Schopenhauer, *Jugendleben*, p. 147.
[13] See Bridgwater, *Arthur Schopenhauer's English Schooling*, pp. 5–6.

escape the imprint of their father's appearance. Still, despite his uninviting appearance, there must have been something about him that would cause him to stand out in a crowd – at least in a crowd in 1773 in Berlin. Friedrich II (Frederick the Great), upon his return from a trip, spotted Heinrich Floris among a group of spectators. He stopped and asked him where he lived. Heinrich Floris told him he was a merchant from Danzig. For some unknown reason, the Prussian king then asked him whether he had a spaniel. He replied in the affirmative, which must have pleased the King, because he invited Heinrich Floris to visit him at six o'clock the next morning. The King was impressed with Schopenhauer's dog, but more so with the man himself. He invited him to settle in Prussia, after informing him that Danzig's independence would have no future. And as could have been anticipated by anyone familiar with Heinrich Floris's loyalties, the staunch republican declined the Royal invitation.[14]

This incident with Friedrich II signified Heinrich Floris's attitude toward political authority, and especially toward the Prussian monarchy. This attitude was captured in the Schopenhauer family motto: "*Point de bonheur sans liberté*" [Without liberty there can be no happiness]. Heinrich Floris's independent spirit, which bordered on obstinacy, can be sensed in a cherished family story about an event that occurred during the Prussian blockade of Danzig about a decade later in 1783. Schopenhauer's grandfather Andreas was forced to billet Prussian troops in his estate. As an act of good will, General Friedrich von Raumer offered free importation of forage for Heinrich Floris's prize stud horse. Heinrich Floris politely refused Raumer's generosity, while adding, "I thank the Prussian General for his good will . . . and when my fodder is gone, I will have my horses put to death."[15]

As his business prospered, and as was customary for a man of his age and station, Heinrich Floris desired a wife. Perhaps this was only a secondary concern. What he wanted was an heir. It is not known what particularly attracted him to Johanna Henriette Trosiener. Certainly, she had youth on her side, and she came from a respectable family, even though her father's business and political loyalties clashed with those of her future husband. Her father, Christian Heinrich Trosiener (1730–97), was a less successful merchant than Heinrich Floris. He was the

[14] Hübscher, *Gespräche*, p. 224.
[15] Johanna Schopenhauer, *Jugendleben*, p. 147.

son of a shoemaker and street peddler, Christian Trosiener, who came to Danzig from the village of Altschottland. His father, Christoph Trosiener, who was Johanna's great-grandfather, was a farmer from East Prussia. Johanna's father was known as a forceful man, both intellectually and physically. He was a member of the council of St. Johanna Church and became one of the four quartermasters for the Fishing Quarters. As such, he belonged to Danzig's corporate middle class, the "Third Estate," whose business interests clashed, at times, with those of the city's patricians such as Heinrich Floris, and with the independent status of Danzig. For a short period, he was a city councilor, and approximately a month before the birth of his first grandchild, Arthur, he foolishly proposed, as a means for enhancing trade to the Baltic countries, that Danzigers should become citizens of Prussia and pledge allegiance to its king. Although there is no record of Heinrich Floris's reaction to this move of his in-law, it is reasonable to imagine that such a loyal republican would have found it fitting that Trosiener was forced to resign from the city council and, ultimately, to sell his business and move his family to the domain of Stutthof. The fortunes of the Trosieners greatly declined, and after Christian Heinrich's death, the Schopenhauers supported them.

Johanna's mother, Elisabeth (née Lehmann, 1745–1818), was the daughter of a merchant and druggist, Georg Lehmann, and Susanna Concordia Lehmann (née Neumann). Arthur's maternal grandparents were less prolific than his paternal grandparents, but they were more successful at raising their children into adulthood. Their first child and only son, Heinrich, who was baptized in 1765, died in youth. Johanna, born on 9 July 1766, was the eldest of three daughters. She was followed by Arthur's godmother, Charlotte Elisabeth (1768–1828), and Juliane Dorothea (1773–1849).[16] A stillborn daughter had also been born in 1771.

As a female in the mid-eighteenth century, Johanna's planned course in life was fixed by her gender. Ideally, she would become a wife and mother. Although her father knew French, Polish, and Russian from his business travels, her parents were not well educated. Nonetheless, they did allow Johanna to receive a broader education than most girls of her time. Certainly, she was schooled in deportment and household management, and she learned to play the piano and speak French, a language required for polite society. Around the age of three or four, she attended a nearby

[16] See Arthur Hübscher's "Drei Tanten Schopenhauers," pp. 127–50.

school for young girls that was operated by the mother and two sisters of the well-known painter and engraver Daniel Chodowiecki.[17] She was taught deportment there, as well as elementary French.[18] Later, she was also able to observe Chodowiecki in his studio. Both the art and the artist enchanted the young girl. Johanna reported in her memoirs that this experience inspired her to become a painter and woke in her young soul a deep appreciation of art. Using language that one could have thought had come from her son, she reported that from that moment and throughout her entire life, art was "my comfort and joy; through it I was released."[19]

Johanna's remarks about the significance of art describe her experiences at around the age of seven, the same age at which she was tutored at home in German, history, and geography by a candidate for a theology degree named Kuschel, who oddly had been referred to by his aspirations as "Kandidate" Kuschel. In any case, when Johanna was thirteen, the tutor made a proposal of marriage to the recently confirmed young woman, a proposition that was ignored by both Johanna and her parents. Perhaps Kuschel had become infatuated with Johanna, or maybe he was simply trying to improve his lot by marrying his employer's daughter. Kuschel, however, was also forward in a beneficial way. He subscribed to the Enlightenment ideal that ignored the differences between a proper education for a boy and what was more appropriate for a girl. Kuschel's sentiment was also apparent in Richard Jameson, a man whom Johanna credits with having the greatest influence on her early life. As she would later reflect, "Every child has a guardian angel: thanks to mine . . . for entrusting me to such a man as Jameson . . . the charge of preparing me for the checkered life that awaited me."[20]

---

[17] Chodowiecki's most famous book is *Sketchbook of a Trip from Berlin to Danzig* [*Skizzenbuch einer Reise vom Berlin nach Danzig*]. It includes Plate 24, "Chodowiecki Greets His Mother" [*Chodowiecki begrüßst seine Mutter*], which shows the interior of his mother's school.

[18] It was likely that Johanna learned to speak Polish, due to her Polish nurse, before she spoke German. Later, she would perfect her French, a language required by her social status, at the school of Mamsell Ackermann, the Société des Jeunes Dames; see Ulrike Bergmann's *Johanna Schopenhauer: 'Lebe und sei so glücklich als du kannst'* (Leipzig: Reclam, 2002), pp. 35, 41.

[19] Johanna Schopenhauer, *Jugendleben*, p. 33.

[20] Ibid., p. 54. Johanna frequently referred to Jameson as "Dr. Jameson" in *Jugendleben*; see, for example, p. 28. Jameson, however, left the University of Edinburg without receiving the Doctor of Divinity degree; see Bridgwater, *Schopenhauer's English Schooling*, pp. 29–94 for a well-documented account of Jameson's life.

Jameson, who hailed from Scotland, came to Danzig in 1764 at the age of forty to serve as the Anglican chaplain, ministering to the "English" community, which had been flourishing there since the last half of the sixteenth Century.[21] The English chapel stood at Heilige Geistgasse 80, between the Trosieners' home and the house of the Shipmasters Guild. Because the chapel shared a continuous terrace with the Trosiener place, Jameson and Johanna's parents became fast friends. Jameson knew Johanna from birth, and he took a lively interest in her education. It was due primarily to him that she became fluent in English, which made her uneasy at one point: "A girl and learning English! For what on earth would you use that? This question was repeated daily by friends and relatives, because this was unheard of at that time in Danzig. I began to feel ashamed at my knowledge of the English language and therefore I resolutely refused to learn Greek."[22] Under Jameson's gentle guidance, Johanna became familiar with English literature, including John Milton, Thomas Young, Shakespeare, and Pope's translation of Homer. Jameson also helped instill in the young girl a love for all things English, a trait that would provide a common interest between Johanna and her future husband.

It is not known when and how Heinrich Floris met Johanna. Although it is also not known why he wanted to marry her in particular, she did come from a respectable family and she was properly finished. She was not a bad-looking woman, but the blue-eyed, brown-haired Johanna was likely not considered a beauty either. She did possess a cheerful personality; she was vivacious, charming, and sociable, which were character traits lacking in her husband, and which would provide useful support for the proper household and societal needs of a gentleman merchant. Johanna also shared her future husband's republican ideals and his Anglophilia, and like him, she spoke French and English.

When Heinrich Floris approached Christian Trosiener for permission to propose marriage to Johanna, as was traditional and customary, the entire family was surprised. Her parents, of course, were flattered that a rich patrician wanted to marry one of their daughters. In her memoirs,

---

[21] Ironically, the "English" community was composed primarily of Scots, whose main emigration to Danzig took place from the mid-sixteenth to the end of the seventeenth century. The Scottish community flourished throughout the eighteenth century, until the second partition of Poland and the Prussian occupation of Danzig in 1793; see Bridgwater, *Schopenhauer's English Schooling*, pp. 1–3.

[22] Johanna Schopenhauer, *Jugendleben*, p. 56.

Johanna claimed that her parents did not pressure her into marriage and it was simply up to her to decide whether to accept the marriage proposal, which she did, although she also noted that she did not feel ardent love for Heinrich Floris, and he did not expect it.[23] Arthur would later account for the lack of his mother's passion in his highly misogynistic essay, "On Women." Women, he claimed, are passionately attracted to "young, strong, and handsome men," an unconscious expression of the will of the species that ensures the healthy propagation of humankind.[24] At best, Heinrich Floris was strong. But given Johanna's family situation and the social expectations of a young woman, perhaps his strength, coupled with the promise of social status and wealth, compensated for her husband's lack of youth and attractiveness. With two younger, unmarried sisters at home, the ramifications of living in her father's home after rejecting what would be considered a good match would probably be such that one could safely conclude that Johanna really had no choice but to accept Heinrich Floris's proposal. The thirty-eight-year-old rich merchant married the eighteen-year-old woman on 16 May 1785 in the old, small church, All of God's Angels, in Danzig.

The newly married couple lived in a townhouse in Danzig during the winter. Summers were spent at the family estate, Polanki, which was near Oliva, a small village that was an enclave of summer homes owned by wealthy Danzigers. Oliva was located about four miles northwest of Danzig. Their house was replete, as Johanna described it, "with every English comfort."[25] She enjoyed the beauty and pastoral charm of the setting – the English garden, the small lake with a boat, the eight pet lambs, each of which wore a bell set to ring in a different octave. Inside she was surrounded by artwork – paintings, engravings, and casts of antique sculptures. The library contained a rich assortment of English and French literature.

During the week, Heinrich Floris remained in Danzig, leaving Johanna with her servants at Polanki. Despite the beauty of the setting and the opulence of her abode, she adopted a solitary mode of life, avoiding visits

---

[23] Ibid., p. 151.
[24] Arthur Schopenhauer, *Parerga and Paralipomena*, trans. E. F. J. Payne (Oxford: Clarendon Press, 1974; reprint 2001), Vol. 2, p. 618/*Sämtliche Werke*, Vol. 6, p. 654.
[25] Johanna Schopenhauer, *Jugendleben*, p. 159.

to her neighbors. She took short pleasure drives in her carriage and long walks in the surrounding meadows, forests, and fields, far out of range of the highway. Johanna had adopted a state of existence meant to still Heinrich Floris's suspicions about her faithfulness. She was directed to do so, she said, by following "a certain inner voice, which I have all my life been directed to follow, as on the rare occasions when I acted against it I invariably found cause to regret it bitterly."[26] Although there is no record regarding the function of Johanna's *daimōn* concerning Heinrich Floris' marriage proposal, it appears to have set a theme for her relationship to her husband – that of behaving in a way that would serve her husband's will.

The weekends brought some cheer to Johanna's cloistered existence, however. Her husband frequently returned with guests, and still other guests would arrive on Sundays, thus providing her with opportunities to exercise her social graces and display her skills as a hostess. In addition to visits from her beloved mentor, "Dr." Jameson, other members of the British colony who were business associates of Heinrich Floris would frequent the home. Naturally, family members would visit regularly, as did some minor luminaries, such as Abbe Georg Joseph Vogler, the organist and composer of church music, and the French balloonist Blanchard, who in 1785 floated over the English Channel in a hot air balloon.

Heinrich Floris became anxious and restless in the late spring of 1787, at least more so than normal. Fearing Prussia's design on Danzig and, perhaps, sensitive to the *ennui* of his young wife, he decided that they would travel to England to explore the site for a possible relocation of his home and business. Johanna was overjoyed by the prospect of travel and the opportunity to experience a country she had worshipped from afar. The couple departed Danzig on St. John the Baptist's Day, 24 June. Unknown to both, Arthur traveled with them. They slogged through the troublesome sand and passed through many poor towns and villages in their richly provisioned carriage until they arrived in Berlin. Johanna thought that Berlin, with its many newly constructed buildings, looked like a theater set. From Berlin, the Schopenhauers journeyed to Hanover. Heinrich Floris had been experiencing difficulty with his hearing, a problem that would later trouble his son, so he sought the advice of the doctor

---

[26] Ibid., p. 162.

and philosopher Johann Georg Ritter von Zimmermann.[27] The fashion-able doctor, who was once the personal physician of the British royal family, and who had been ennobled by Friedrich II, recommended that Heinrich Floris visit the spa at Bad Pyramont. At Pyramont, Zimmermann frequently visited the Schopenhauers, as did the raconteur and friend of Lessing Christoph Friedrich Nicolai, who published a parody of Goethe's *The Sufferings of Young Werther* [*Die Leiden des jungen Werther*, 1774], which he called *The Joys of Young Werther* [*Die Freuden des jungen Werther*], in 1775.

After Bad Pyramont, the Schopenhauers journeyed to Kassel, Frank-furt am Main, Ghent, Antwerp, Lille, Brussels, and Paris, where they vacationed for four weeks. After departing from Calais for London, they discovered Johanna's pregnancy, which eventually became the origin of that hasty trip back to Danzig in preparation for their first child's birth. Although the return to Danzig defeated Heinrich Floris's desire for his son to enjoy British citizenry, with the rights attached to and the advan-tages resulting from such a favored birthplace, he may have realized some consolation from naming his son Arthur, a name spelled the same in both English and French, signifying Heinrich Floris's esteem for both countries.[28] And, in a very non–Germanic fashion, he decided not to give his son a middle name. Friedrich Nietzsche, whose father was of a much different mindset, having given his son the middle name of Wilhelm, would later drop the nationalistic middle name, much in the Schopen-hauerian fashion.

---

[27] Zimmerman was a passionate opponent of the Enlightenment and a good friend of the poet Christoph Martin Wieland. Johanna had read his *Concerning Solitude* [*Über die Einsamkeit*, 1784/1785] when they met in 1787. It is likely that it was Johanna's copy of the book that remained in Schopenhauer's posthumous library. He referred to this book twice in his philosophical writings. In the first edition of *The World as Will and Representation* he cited it as providing a possible case of death by starvation, an example of a form of suicide against which Schopenhauer could find no moral objections; see *Faksimilenachdruck der I. Auflage der Welt als Wille und Vorstellung*, ed. Rudolf Malter (Frankfurt am Main: Insel, 1987), p. 575, and *The World as Will and Representation*, Vol. 1, p. 401/*Sämtliche Werke*, Vol. 2, p. 475, which are of the third edition, 1859. In the prize-essay, *On the Basis of Morality*, he quotes Zimmerman: "Reflect deeply till your dying day that nothing is so rare as a good judge," *On the Basis of Morality*, E. F. J. Payne (trans.) (Indianapolis: Hackett, 1997), p. 43/*Sämtliche Werke*, Vol. 4, II. *Die beiden Grundprobleme der Ethik*, p. 111. Unfortunately, Zimmerman lost the capacity to be a good judge toward the end of his life. He died after suffering years of severe depression in 1795 – in solitude.

[28] Johanna Schopenhauer, *Jugendleben*, p. 225; also see Schopenhauer, *Gespräche*, p. 264, fn 433.

In her memoirs, Johanna recalled that "in the days as well as the nights I had scarcely a thought other than that of my son Arthur."[29] Many years later, to reconcile herself to her unhappy son, she told him that he was her only hope and "the most beautiful joy of my life."[30] Although these remarks might have been sincere, it is doubtful that Arthur would have been willing to believe them. He considered Johanna a "bad mother" [*mauvaise mere*].[31] It may be easy to imagine that he had Johanna in mind when he wrote, "As in animals, so in humans, the original maternal love is partly *instinctive* and therefore ceases with the helplessness of the children. In its place, there should then appear one based on habit and reasoning; but often it fails to appear, especially when the father does not love the mother. The father's love for his children is of a different kind and is more enduring. It rests on his again recognizing in them his own innermost self and is thus of metaphysical origin."[32]

Perhaps Heinrich Floris did not love his wife. We know that she lacked "ardent love" for her husband and that he did not expect it. By her own account, she felt maternal love for Arthur, recalling in her memoirs that she was like all young mothers. "No more beautiful, innocent, and, for his age, clever child than mine lives on God's earth," she thought.[33] Johanna and young Arthur spent their summers in Polanki. Periodically, they would visit the Trosieners in Stutthof. These visits to Arthur's maternal grandparents, and visits by Johanna's sisters, as well as Heinrich Floris's weekend returns, often accompanied by guests, would break the tedium of Johanna's routine. There was, however, at least one surprising weekday visit from her husband. On a hot July evening in 1789, Heinrich Floris rode on horseback to his estate, flush with excitement and joy. The Bastille had been stormed. Johanna shared her husband's delight, and the couple would continue to read developing stories about the French Revolution in various newspapers enthusiastically.

The spring of 1793 brought a significant and not unexpected change in the Schopenhauers' life course. Prussia and Russia started to carve up sovereign Polish territory, and Prussia annexed the once Polish-protected

---

[29] Ibid., p. 225.
[30] Lütkehaus, *Die Schopenhauers*, p. 164, Johanna to Arthur, 28 April 1807.
[31] Schopenhauer, *Gesammelte Briefe*, p. 159, Schopenhauer to Anthime Grégoire de Blésimaire, 10 December 1836.
[32] Schopenhauer, *Parerga and Paralipomena*, Vol. 2, p. 625/*Sämtliche Werke*, Vol. 6, p. 662.
[33] Johanna Schopenhauer, *Jugendleben*, p. 225.

free cities of Danzig and Thorn. When the city council unanimously passed a resolution to place Danzig under Prussian sovereignty on 11 March 1793, the feisty republican Heinrich Floris immediately resolved to abandon Danzig, as did a number of anti-Prussian families. The move was financially costly. The family lost one-tenth of its wealth to taxes. Thus the Schopenhauers unwittingly contributed to Prussia's military opposition to revolutionary France. Later, Arthur claimed to have paid an even greater cost through his lifelong sense of homelessness: "Thus I was already homeless in tender childhood. I was in my fifth year at that time."[34] It is difficult, however, to understand his attachment to Danzig. He retained his citizenship in Danzig, so he was not legally homeless. Unlike his father, who resolved never to return to Danzig, which he never did, Arthur did return to visit relatives. He served his first, brief apprenticeship there, and he was confirmed there. He could have decided to live in Danzig, but even after the demise of his wanderlust, when he sought permanent location, the possibility of relocating to Danzig seemed not to have been factored into his decision. The magnetic charm of Danzig appears to be its absence in Arthur's life. Perhaps it symbolized a location in which he imagined Johanna's instinctive maternal love had been drawn to his helplessness, and with his loss of helplessness, he could not imagine love in Danzig.

Hamburg

The Schopenhauers retreated to Hamburg. It is not known why they did not relocate to London. Heinrich Floris scouted it twice for that purpose, and he had various acquaintances and trading partners there. Hamburg, however, was a logical choice for a merchant with republican sensibilities. As Danzig had once been, it was a free, Hanseatic city, a republic that adopted a constitution in 1772, one that achieved a delicate balance between the patricians and the middle class. It was also a seaport with a trading pattern much like that of Danzig. But, and more importantly, it appeared to be secure from Prussian aggression, because its autonomy was protected by the Netherlands and England, and it had strong trading ties to France. Hamburg was also a no-nonsense, practical, merchant's

---

[34] Schopenhauer, *Gesammelte Briefe*, p. 48, *Vitae Curriculum Arthurii Schopenhaueri*, Phil: Doct, 31 December 1819.

town in which Heinrich Floris could feel at home, although it lacked the cosmopolitanism of Danzig. Hamburg would be the location of most of Arthur's development through his eighteenth year, and his experiences there, as well as his two years in France and two years on a European pleasure tour, would shape his character and attitudes in fundamental ways. It would be the city in which his only other sibling was born. It would also be the place where his mother would cultivate and hone her skills as a hostess, which she would later employ with great success in Weimar. Last, it would become the site of Heinrich Floris's death.

Upon their arrival in Hamburg, the Schopenhauers rented an apartment at Neuer Weg 76, a curious name for a street in the *Altstädter* or "Old City." After three years of hard work and concentrated effort, Heinrich Floris reestablished his business. Although it never achieved the same success as its predecessor in Danzig, it prospered sufficiently to allow the Schopenhauers to buy a new home in the affluent part of town. The compound at Neuer Wandrahm 92 housed both the business and the family's living quarters. The rear of the structure backed up to the canal, which eased the receiving and shipping of commodities. It contained the stockrooms and storage, as well as the business office or "counting house," where business functions, such as recordkeeping, accounting, and correspondence, were conducted. There was an inner courtyard, enclosed by a carved wooden gallery. At the front of the compound was the residence, consisting of two main rooms and eight smaller chambers. The home included an extensive picture gallery, a well-stocked library, and an elaborately appointed ballroom, which could accommodate more than 100 guests.

The Schopenhauers' new address placed them in proximity to Hamburg's merchant elite – Jenisch, Parish, Godeffroy, Voght, and Sieveking. The fact that they circulated in the society of the Sievekings, in particular, demonstrated that they enjoyed the best of Hamburg's social life. Georg Heinrich Sieveking, "Hamburg's Rothschild," was among the most influential men in northern Germany. His wife Johanna ("Hannchen") was the daughter of the polymath Dr. Johann Albert Heinrich Reimarus. Sieveking was an unabashed admirer of the French Revolution, perhaps even more so than his fellow Hamburgers. Of course, as with his contemporaries, his support diminished as the Revolution played out to terror. In 1796, he spearheaded a delegation to Paris, and he managed to overcome significant business and political problems between France and Hamburg, an act that earned widespread praise and erased some of the suspicion that he was a Jacobin. And, as was expected of a man of his station, he sponsored scholars and artists and supported French *émigrés* and Hamburg's poor.

By running among Hamburg's business elite, the Schopenhauers also ran with Hamburg's cultural and intellectual luminaries, the brightest of whom was the poet Friedrich Gottlieb Klopstock, who was already famous when he moved to Hamburg in 1770. Despite the fact that his emotional and religious sensibilities cut against the practical and utilitarian orientation of the Hamburgers, Klopstock enjoyed, in tautological fashion, celebrity status immediately upon his arrival – fame itself was sufficient to be famous in Hamburg. Johanna, who most likely met the old poet at the Sievekings' residence, had already read him in her youth. Arthur, who never mentioned any personal interactions with Klopstock, something he was inclined to do with any well-known person whose life intersected with his own, would later recommend him, along with Christoph Martin Wieland, Goethe, and Friedrich Schiller, to contemporary "ink-slingers" as models for the proper use of the German language.[35]

The Schopenhauers also circled in the orbit of Hannchen Sieveking's father, Dr. Reimarus. He was a friend of Lessing, who edited and published a work by Dr. Reimarus's father, Hermann Samuel, which was *On the Purpose of Jesus and His Early Followers* [*Von dem Zwecke Jesu und seiner Jünger*, 1778].[36] Dr. Reimarus was a man of wide-ranging interests and talents. In addition to contributing to medicine, including work on the treatment of smallpox and the use of belladonna during eye operations, he wrote tracts on natural religion, philosophy, and animal physiology. His commitment to the improvement of society led him to become one of

[35] Schopenhauer, *Parerga and Paralipomena*, Vol. 2, p. 533, fn/*Sämtliche Werke*, Vol. 6, p. 566, fn.

[36] Schopenhauer referred to *Concerning the Purpose of Jesus and His Early Followers* as an "eminently readable book" and he accepted Reimarus's contention that the Gospels were based on some materials written during Jesus' life. Reimarus supported this claim by noting that the Gospels contained prophecies that were promised to be fulfilled during the lifetimes of some of Jesus' contemporaries. Had the Gospels been written some hundred years later, he argued, these obviously unfulfilled and embarrassing prophecies would not have appeared; see Schopenhauer, *Parerga and Paralipomena*, Vol. 2, p. 384/*Sämtliche Werke*, Vol. 6, p. 407. Schopenhauer's posthumous library contained three books by Herman Samuel Reimarus and four by Johann Albert Heinrich Reimarus; see *Der handschriftliche Nachlaß*, Vol. 5, pp. 134–6, 278.

the founders of the Hamburg Society for the Promotion of the Arts and Trades [*Hamburgischer Gesellschaft zur Förderung der Künste und Gewerbe*]. The Society was not, however, exactly true to its name, where the arts were mentioned before the trades, because it actually put support for the trades above that for the arts. To be sure, it supported artists and scholars, but it preferred sponsoring research on techniques for eliminating wood-gnawing sea worms, a threat to ships, to supporting starving artists, who likely would have eaten wood if they could.

The Schopenhauers were also familiar with the Baron de Staël-Holstein, the husband of Madame de Staël and onetime Swedish diplomat, who despite his rich wife periodically relied on the financial aid of the Sievekings.[37] Other notables associating with Arthur's parents were Count Karl Friedrich Reinhard, who was ennobled by Napoleon and who enjoyed a robust diplomatic career; the painter Wilhelm Tischbein, who accompanied Goethe on his Italian tour in 1786; Canon Lorenz Meyer, art patron and father of one of Arthur's youthful friends; Professor August Gottlieb Meißner, a well-known author of bombastic novels; the Reverend John Knipe, English chaplain to Hamburg;[38] the actress Madame Chevalier, star of the French theater in Hamburg; Count Friedrich Adolf von Kalckreuth, a Prussian field marshal, who would later try to comfort Johanna prior to Napoleon's October 1806 occupation of Weimar;[39] and Professor J. G. Büsch.

The French Revolution brought numerous aristocratic *émigrés* and their sympathizers to Hamburg. Oddly, they were welcomed in a city that embraced, although in reserved terms, the Revolution, that had deeply republican commitments, and that practiced an English way of life, right down to the style of dress. Still, there was the attraction of opposites, and the emigrants' lambent spirits and *joie de vivre* penetrated the sober and sensible atmosphere of this merchants' town. There was more

---

[37] Schopenhauer reported that Goethe faulted Madame de Staël for exaggerating the honesty of the Germans in *De l'Allemagne*, something, Goethe feared, that would mislead and harm visitors; see Schopenhauer, *On the Will in Nature*, trans. E. F. J. Payne (New York/Oxford: Berg, 1992), p. 32f/*Sämtliche Werke*, Vol. 4, p. 17. De Staël's book also helped promote the image of Germans being apolitical.

[38] Knipe would later accompany one of Schopenhauer's youthful friends, Charles Godeffroy, on a trip to England; see Arthur Hübscher's "Zwei Hamburger Jugendfreunde," *Schopenhauer-Jahrbuch*, Vol. 51 (1970), p. 38.

[39] See Johanna's letter to Arthur, 18 October 1806, in Lütkehaus, *Die Schopenhauers*, pp. 82–3.

merriment – dancing, gambling, drinking, and loving, both free and for a fee. French cafés appeared in many quarters and a French theater was established. But as the money of the *émigrés* diminished, and many of them were forced by circumstances to teach French, dance, and fencing, so did their novelty, and instead of transforming Hamburg's cultural life, they were transformed. France, however, was about to play an analogous role in Arthur's life, but in reverse, when he went to France. And unlike the *émigrés*, whose luster tarnished over time in Hamburg, Arthur's time in France would brighten with the passage of time. His years spent in France were "the most joyful part of my childhood," he wrote in 1819.[40] A powerful statement, because these were the only years of his youth during which he did not live with his parents.

Le Havre

It was customary for fathers to become close to their children once they reached the age of eight. After one year of taking a more concentrated interest in his son's development, Heinrich Floris's idea of becoming close to his son was to put him at a distance. He placed him in the home of a business associate, Andre Charles Grégoire de Blésimaire, in Le Havre, France for two years. In his *curriculum vitae* from 1819, Arthur claimed that it was his father's desire that he become "a successful merchant and, at the same time, a man of the world and with fine manners."[41] Heinrich Floris was attempting to duplicate the same sort of experiences in his son that Andreas Schopenhauer provided to him. The parallel between these experiences, both of which sought to groom liberal and cosmopolitan attitudes in a son who would be well connected to various trading partners, breaks down in a telling detail. Unlike Andreas Schopenhauer, who let a mature Heinrich Floris live and work abroad, Heinrich Floris took a nine-year-old boy to live abroad. If a five-year-old Arthur felt "homeless" after his family fled Danzig, it is easy to imagine the effect this had on him, especially because he was a child who feared abandonment. In an entry to his private diary, dating to around 1833, Arthur reflected critically on his

---

[40] Schopenhauer, *Gesammelte Briefe*, pp. 48/649. This remark is from the Latin *curriculum vitae* Schopenhauer sent to the Philosophy Faculty at the University of Berlin, 31 December 1819. The first page reference is to the Latin original and the second to a German translation.
[41] Ibid.

character: "Nature has done more than is necessary to isolate my heart, in that she endowed it with suspicion, sensitiveness, vehemence and pride in a measure that is hardly compatible with the *mens aequa* of a philosopher." But after noting the conflict between his character and the equanimity of a philosopher, he notes an example of the terrible grip of anxiety, which he attributes to an inheritance from his father: "Even as a six-year-old child, my parents, returning home one evening from a walk, found me in the depths of despair since I suddenly imagined myself to be forever abandoned by them."[42] Given Schopenhauer's youthful experiences of being raised by parents who failed to express love between one another, it may be the case that Schopenhauer's observation is one of mistaken causality. It was likely that his early family life colored his character as much as did his "nature."

Father and son set out for France shortly after the birth of Arthur's only sibling, a sister named Louise Adelaide Lavinia (Adele), who was born on 12 June 1797. Arthur was unable to recall fifty-two years later whether Adele was born in June or July, although he claimed, "to this day, I still have a lively recollection of her birth."[43] Heinrich Floris's decision to take Arthur to France one month after the birth of his daughter allowed him to escape the hectic household scene, to return to visit France, and to free Johanna from the demands of both a young son and an infant – demands that were mitigated, however, by the family maid, Sophie Duguet.[44] It was also a time of relative political tranquility, and Heinrich Floris exploited the end of the First Coalition War, which had ended earlier that year, because northern Germany once more was in a state of neutrality.

After spending two weeks sightseeing in Paris and meeting with business associates, Heinrich Floris left Arthur with the Grégoire family, in whose home he experienced an intimacy that was lacking in his own. The Grégoires treated him as a "second son."[45] Their "first son," Jean Anthime, who was approximately one year older than Arthur, became

---

[42] Schopenhauer, *Manuscript Remains*, Vol. 4, "Εἰς ἑαυτόν," #28.

[43] Schopenhauer, *Gesammelte Briefe*, p. 237, Schopenhauer to Sibylle Mertens-Schaaffhausen, 7 September 1849.

[44] In her novel, *Anna: Ein Roman aus der nächsten Vergangenheit* (1845), Adele had both Sophie and her husband, Johannes Duguet, appear as servants. Adele's novel was published by F. A. Brockhaus, Johanna's and Arthur's publisher.

[45] Schopenhauer, *Gesammelte Briefe*, pp. 48, 649, Schopenhauer to the Faculty of the University of Berlin, 31 December 1819.

his friend. In the greater context of his life, he may have been the most intimate friend Schopenhauer ever had, if one bears in mind that he lived a life with few truly intimate friends. As a youth, Anthime possessed a kindred soul. Years later, as they lay down to rest one day during a hike in an oak forest near Trittau in Holstein, Arthur began brooding about the wretchedness of life. It is so short, frail, and transitory, Arthur averred, that it does not even pay to trouble oneself by trying to undertake anything that requires great effort. Anthime replied that he knew all of that, while adding that he had to become a merchant, which seemed to him "completely stupid and useless."[46]

A tutor named Durand instructed the boys in French, elementary Latin, and French literature. Arthur excelled in French, so much so that when he would finally return to his family's home, his father would be delighted to hear him speak as if he were French, and Arthur would report that he had to relearn his German.[47] In addition to light French literature, the boys read Voltaire's epic poem *Le Henriade*, which roundly criticized religious fanaticism. Both Heinrich Floris and Johanna held Voltaire in great esteem – *Candide* was Heinrich Floris's favorite book – and both approved of Voltaire's stance against religious intolerance. Arthur also would come to venerate Voltaire. He was a member of the aristocracy of the intellect, he opined, who "should be given a place at the table where monarchs and their princes sit."[48] In the nurturing atmosphere of the Grégoires' home, Arthur also was encouraged to develop his sensitivities to the suffering of others. Later, the ideals of religious tolerance and compassion for the misfortunes of others would be reinforced by his experiences and instruction in Dr. Runge's school.

Anthime would reappear during various stages in Schopenhauer's life. With each appearance, the two friends became more distant, until Anthime disappeared for good after 1845. Arthur's French "brother" traveled to

---

[46] Ibid., p. 156, Schopenhauer to Anthime, 10 December 1836. Schopenhauer corresponded with Grégoire in French, and used the familiar "*tu*" in writing to his "French brother."

[47] Ibid., pp. 48, 649.

[48] Schopenhauer, *Parerga and Paralipomena*, Vol. 1, p. 431/*Sämtliche Werke*, Vol. 5, p. 460. Like his father, Schopenhauer esteemed the "immortal *Candide* of the Great Voltaire," although it was not his favorite book, as it was for Heinrich Floris; see Schopenhauer, *The World as Will and Representation*, Vol. 2, 582/*Sämtliche Werke*, Vol. 3, p. 668. Schopenhauer also prefaced his "Criticisms of the Kantian Philosophy" with a quotation from Voltaire's *Siècle de Louis XIV*, Chap. 32: "It is the privilege of true genius, and especially of the genius who opens up a new path, to make great mistakes with impunity," ibid., Vol. 1, 412/ibid., Vol. 2, p. 488.

Hamburg at the end of May 1806. His goal was to continue to prepare for his business career by learning German. He would have lived with the Schopenhauers, but by the time Anthime arrived, the family had been shattered. Heinrich Floris was dead; the compound at Neuer Wandrahm 92 was on the market; the business was being liquidated; Johanna was exploring Weimar to secure a new home for herself and Adele; and Arthur was suffering through his apprenticeship with city senator Martin Johann Jenisch and boarding with an insurance agent named Gysbert Willink. Johanna arranged, however, for Anthime to board with Pastor Hübbe in nearby Allermöhe. Later, in January 1807, the nineteen-year-old Anthime moved in with his German "brother."

Besides lamenting their apparent fates in the forest at Trittau – with Anthime not escaping his "completely stupid and useless" merchant's destiny – the two "brothers" engaged in activities common to young men of their social status. They attended balls and parties, went to the theater, and tried to seduce women of lower social status, namely, chorus girls, actresses, and maids. Occasionally, they even paid for their pleasures.[49] Schopenhauer, whose philosophy was colored and shaped deeply through his reflections on his own experiences, would finally muster the nerve in 1844 to include his masterful, daring, and, at times, ludicrous essay, "The Metaphysics of Sexual Love," in the second edition of *The World as Will and Representation*. Writing without a philosophical predecessor to either build upon or refute, and stressing the omnipresence of sexuality in human affairs well before Sigmund Freud, he notes his ambivalence to the role of *erōs* in his own life:

Next to love of life, it [sexual impulse] shows itself here as the strangest and most active of all motives, and incessantly lays claim to half the powers and thoughts of the younger portion of humankind. It is the ultimate goal of almost all human effort. . . . It does not hesitate to intrude with its trash, and to interfere with the negotiations of statesmen and the investigations of the learned. It knows how to slip its love-notes and ringlets even into ministerial portfolios and philosophical manuscripts. Every day it brews and hatches the worst and most perplexing quarrels and disputes, destroys the most valuable relationships, and breaks the strongest bonds. It demands the sacrifice

---

[49] Anthime wrote Arthur, remembering how they enjoyed the "embraces of an industrious whore," during his time in Hamburg; see Paul Hoffmann, "Schopenhauer und Hamburg," *Jahrbuch der Schopenhauer-Gesellschaft*, Vol. 19 (1932), p. 217; cited in Rüdiger Safranski, *Schopenhauer and the Wild Years of Philosophy*, trans. Ewald Osers (Cambridge, MA: Harvard University Press, 1990), p. 66.

sometimes of life or health, sometimes of wealth, position, and happiness. Indeed, it robs of all conscience those who were previously honorable and upright, and makes traitors of those who have previously been loyal and faithful.[50]

More than half the powers and thoughts of the two young men were likely claimed by sexual desire, with this probably being neither odd nor unusual. But in his escapades with Anthime, Schopenhauer engaged in a contest that he was bound to lose. His friend was charming and sociable, and Arthur had inherited not only his father's will, but also his aspect. He moreover lacked the magnetic personality that would compensate for his lack of physical attractiveness. Still, even in contexts in which he did not compete directly for female affection with a friend, Schopenhauer believed he was a loser in a game he wanted to win. In an entry to his private diary from around 1831, Schopenhauer quotes one of his heroes, Lord Byron: "The more I see of men, the less I like them; if I could say the same of women too, all would be well."[51] Many years later, the old philosopher confessed to Carl Georg Bähr that "as far as women are concerned, I was fond of them – had they only wanted to have me."[52] This summarizing reflection on his relationships with women by the sixty-eight-year-old Schopenhauer reveals one of the significant bases for his misogyny. The disrupting "trash" of sexuality moved him to philosophically trash women in his infamous essay, "On Women," which is found in the work that ultimately won him an audience, *Parerga and Paralipomena* (1851).[53] He devalued what he desired but could not have.

Anthime disappeared from Schopenhauer's life after the latter failed to reply to one of Anthime's letters in 1817. Then, in 1836, he reappeared. Grégoire read about one of Johanna's novels in a newspaper. He purchased and read *The Aunt* [*Die Tante*, 1823]. Believing that Adele was its author, he wrote to her and inquired about the fate of his "dear brother."[54] Adele forwarded Grégoire's letter to her brother, remarking, "he appears to

[50] Schopenhauer, *The World as Will and Representation*, Vol. 2, p. 544f./*Sämtliche Werke*, Vol. 3, p. 610f.

[51] Schopenhauer, *Manuscript Remains*, Vol. 4, p. 502/*Der handschriftliche Nachlaß*, Vol. 4, 2, p. 117.

[52] Schopenhauer, *Gespräche*, p. 239.

[53] Schopenhauer, *Parerga and Paralipomena*, Vol. 2, pp. 614–26/*Sämtliche Werke*, Vol. 6, pp. 650–63.

[54] See Schopenhauer, *Gesammelte Briefe*, p. 526, notes to letter 152.

have much love for you."[55] At this time, Schopenhauer was approaching forty-nine and Grégoire was fifty.

Schopenhauer's letter to Grégoire contains an intimate gloss on the intervening nineteen years since their last correspondence. The letter, written in French, addresses Anthime as if he were a brother, using the familiar "*tu*" instead of the formal "*vous*." It is prefaced by a short poem:

> A good little man
> lives still –
> closer to you
> than you believe.
>
> [*Petit bon-homme*
> *Vit encomme –*
> *Plus près de toi*
> *que tu ne crois.*][56]

He closes the letter with a postscript that corrects Anthime's mistaken impression about the author of *The Aunt*, praises Johanna's literary skills, and slams her skills as a mother: "It is not my sister, but my mother, who writes novels. She has become famous and has experienced the second edition of her 24 volume collected works. She is a good novelist, but a very bad mother. I have not seen her since 1814. She lives in Bonn with my unmarried sister."[57]

The candor of the postscript is remarkable, and his positive assessment of Johanna's literary skills shows that Schopenhauer thought his mother would not have the opportunity to read it. He would have been indifferent, however, about Johanna being able to read the statement about her being a very bad mother. He had let her know on numerous occasions about his feelings on that. Conversely, he never let her know about his estimation of her skills as a writer. In fact, he told her just the opposite. In 1813, shortly after the publication of his dissertation, *On the Fourfold Root of the Principle of Sufficient Reason* [*Über die vierfache Wurzel des Satzes vom Zureichenden Grunde*], he engaged her in one of the many heated arguments that led to his resolute decision in 1814 never to see Johanna again. After Johanna

---

55 Lütkehaus, *Die Schopenhauers*, p. 390, Adele to Arthur, 2 December 1836.
56 Ibid, p. 156, Schopenhauer to Anthime Grégoire de Blésimaire, 10 December 1836.
57 Ibid, p. 159. Johanna Schopenhauer's twenty-four-volume collected works [*Sämtliche Schriften*] appeared in 1830–31 through the Leipzig publisher F. A. Brockhaus. The second edition appeared in 1834.

asked sarcastically – she could hurl barbs as skillfully as her son – whether his book was for pharmacists, Arthur retorted that it would still be read when scarcely a single copy of her writings could be found in a junk yard. Johanna, however, mastered the situation, terminating the confrontation by stating, "Of yours the entire printing will still be available."[58]

It may appear strange that Schopenhauer would praise his mother's literary skills behind her back, but his radical alienation from his mother is sufficient to explain why he would not pay her this compliment to her face. Besides, he viewed her as a "very bad mother," and at two levels, he believed that being a good mother was a more important accomplishment for a woman. Personally, he believed that he suffered from Johanna's lack of mothering skills. He also maintained that she was a poor wife, as will be seen later. Theoretically, she also failed her mission as a female, for whom, he argued, her sad lot in life was to be a good wife and mother. In "On Women," he quoted with approval the following lines from Byron's *Sardanapalus* to articulate his view:

> The very first
> Of human life must spring from woman's breast,
> Your first small words are taught you from her lips,
> Your first tears quench'd by her, and your last sighs
> Too often breathed out in a woman's hearing,
> When men have shrunk from the ignoble care
> Of watching the last hour of him who led them.[59]

Schopenhauer's treatment of Johanna's death would later comport with Byron's generalization, whereas Adele would fulfill her role.

Schopenhauer had multiple reasons for praising his mother's ability as a writer. There were the inescapable facts of Johanna's success. She was for a decade the most successful female author in Germany, and her considerable body of writings received a second edition. For years, moreover, Schopenhauer himself was known not as the philosopher Arthur Schopenhauer, but as the son of the novelist Johanna Schopenhauer. Although this rankled him considerably, in his competition with Grégoire, he could use Johanna's notoriety to brag about himself. To recognize his mother's literary merits was to recognize his own. By 1836, he was already

---

[58] Schopenhauer, *Gespräche*, p. 17, reported by Wilhelm Gwinner.
[59] Schopenhauer, *Parerga and Paralipomena*, Vol. 2, p. 614/ *Sämtliche Werke*, Vol. 6, p. 650. He quoted Byron's original English. The quotation is from *Sardanapal*, act 1, scene 2.

philosophically vested in the theory that children inherited their intellects from their mothers. Thus, to recognize Johanna's intelligence was to recognize his own in a way that attributed an even greater intellect to himself, because "on account of the generally weaker nature of the female sex, these [intellectual] faculties never reach in the woman the degree to which in favorable circumstances, they subsequently rise in their sons."[60]

Schopenhauer continues this line of thought by making a claim that, if he thought of his own case, would seem to give his mother more credit than he wanted to give to her: "but as for woman herself, we have to estimate her achievements more highly in this very connection."[61] This claim, however, did not mean that Johanna's work trumped Arthur's. He regarded his work as a work of genius, and he believed that women have never produced a work of genius. His inheritance from his mother, his intellect, had the good luck of finding a male skull that would provide room for the development of a larger brain, a necessary but not sufficient condition for genius. Women just had heads that were too small for intellectual greatness; ones that could, at best, contain talent.[62]

There were also vestiges of Arthur's sexual competition with Anthime in this letter. After bragging about his physical fitness and his wrinkle-free, rosy complexion, despite the fact that his whiskers and hair were almost white, he remarked that he still had to have an occasional "*petite liaison*," and had sired two children out of wedlock, both of whom died young—"*2 batards, que j'avois, sont morts jeunes.*"[63] For years, he added, he had a secret affair with a woman whom he loved greatly. It ended badly, he continued, when she failed to keep her promise to follow him when he left Berlin. This caused him much sorrow, because "she was the only

---

[60] Schopenhauer, *The World as Will and Representation*, Vol. 2, p. 522f./*Sämtliche Werke*, Vol. 3, p. 598.

[61] Ibid., p. 523/ibid., p. 599.

[62] See Schopenhauer, *The World as Will and Representation*, Vol. 2, p. 392/*Sämtliche Werke*, Vol. 3, pp. 448–9 and *Parerga and Paralipomena*, Vol. 2, p. 620/*Sämtliche Werke*, Vol. 6, p. 656 for some of Schopenhauer's curious remarks about brains, size, and the sexes.

[63] Schopenhauer, *Gesammelte Briefe*, p. 159, Schopenhauer to Anthime Grégoire de Blésimaire, 10 December 1836. While he was on a vacation in Italy in the summer of 1819, the maid of a Dresden family gave birth to Schopenhauer's daughter, who died later that summer. The second daughter was born sometime in 1835 or early 1836 in Frankfurt am Main. Like his earlier child, she also died very young. Adele alludes to this second child in letters to Ottilie Wilhelmine Ernestine Henriette von Goethe, 16 January 1836 and 6 June 1836; see Gabriele Büch, *Alles Leben ist Traum: Adele Schopenhauer, eine Biographie* (Berlin: Aufbau Taschenbuch Verlag, 2002), p. 226.

being to which I was genuinely bound."[64] Time, he assured Anthime, had
eventually eased this pain.

To reestablish the intimacy between the two dear brothers, Schopenhauer also entrusted Grégoire with a secret that was even unknown to
his family. In 1826, on the advice of some associates, Schopenhauer
invested a considerable sum of money in Mexican bonds. Contrary to
their assurances, the investment proved costly, reducing Schopenhauer's
yearly income by one-third. He hoped to recover his money, he told
Anthime, but feared that the independence movement in Texas, which
was provoked by the Americans, "a nation of rogues and cheats," would
thwart the recouping of his investment.[65] Schopenhauer's financial affairs
certainly evoked Grégoire's interest, and two years later, when Schopenhauer sought his advice concerning an investment in a Paris life insurance
company, he proposed managing Schopenhauer's money. Contrary to
Grégoire's advice, Schopenhauer invested in the Paris company, a move
that led to the termination of their correspondence, until seven years later,
when Grégoire wrote that he would be traveling to Frankfurt am Main
with his daughter. Schopenhauer arranged for their stay at the Englischer
Hof. The two old friends had different reactions to their reunion. Grégoire
was twice married with children, an ex-merchant who had become almost
like his father. Schopenhauer was unmarried and a philosopher who was
not at all like his father. Grégoire reported that their mealtime conversations were pleasant.[66] But thirteen years later, in 1858, the much older
Schopenhauer told Carl Georg Bähr that he had been disappointed. Bähr
reports him saying that "one 'diverges' more and more, the older one
becomes. Finally, one is completely alone."[67]

This reflection of the old philosopher articulates Schopenhauer's stance
as a man who stands alone. Meanwhile, we return to examine the eleven-
year-old boy who is preparing to leave France and the only home in which
he felt he had a loving family. After two years of the happiest period of
his youth, Arthur departed from Le Havre in August 1799, traveling by
himself to Hamburg. His parents arranged for him to take the seaward,

[64] Schopenhauer, *Gesammelte Briefe*, p. 159, Schopenhauer to Anthime Grégoire de Blésimaire,
  10 December 1836. Schopenhauer is referring to Caroline Medon.
[65] Ibid., p. 159.
[66] See Schopenhauer, *Gespräche*, p. 15f.
[67] Ibid., p. 264. Bähr reports that the conversation took place on 15 May 1858 in Frankfurt am
  Main.

rather than the overland route, because they feared the resumption of hostilities between France and Britain, along with their allies. Although Schopenhauer reported upon his return that he had to struggle to regain his mother tongue, "My good father jumped with joy when he heard me chatter away as if I were French."[68]

Runge's Private School

Heinrich Floris continued grooming Arthur for a successful business career by enrolling him in Dr. Johann Heinrich Christian Runge's private school, an institution designed to train the scions of great merchants to follow in the footsteps of their parents. Runge's school enjoyed a reputation as the best school of its kind in Hamburg, and Arthur would spend four years there (1799–1803). Runge was a progressive educator and a charismatic figure. Educated at the Johanneum and the Akademisches Gymnasium in Hamburg, he ultimately took his degree in theology at the University of Halle, the academic hotspot for Pietism, a reform movement in the Lutheran Church that strove to reinvigorate the devotional ideal in Lutherism during the seventeenth and eighteenth centuries.

Runge's professor, August Hermann Niemeyer (1754–1828), was a great-grandson of August Hermann Francke (1663–1727), who challenged the theological orthodoxy of the Lutheran Church, which was naturally embraced by the landed gentry. Francke, supported by Friedrich Wilhelm I, spread Pietistic ideals throughout Prussia. By 1794, however, the absolutism of the King and religious orthodoxy were once more allied, and Niemeyer and his colleague at Halle, Johann August Rösselt, as well as Johann Gustav Reinbeck at Frankfurt and Immanuel Kant at Königsberg, were conjured by Friedrich Wilhelm II as renegade professors. Runge expressed the same humane attitudes as Niemeyer, but in a way that reduced religion to ethics and personal conduct.

Runge was not able to secure a ministry after his graduation from Halle, a fate not uncommon to his peers. Consequently, he became a teacher and established a school at Katharinenkirchhof. The school enrolled approximately forty students, who were divided into two classes. In his *curriculum vitae*, Schopenhauer claimed that in Runge's school, "I learned

---

[68] Schopenhauer, *Gesammelte Briefe*, pp. 48/649, Schopenhauer's *curriculum vitae*, 31 December 1819.

everything that was fundamental and of use for a merchant."[69] A sense of Schopenhauer's educational experiences, and what would be considered to be fundamental and useful for a merchant, can be gleaned from one of Runge's publications, *Report on My School to the Parents of My Students* [*Bericht über meine Schulanstalt an die Eltern meiner Schülers*, 1808], and the diaries of one of Arthur's chums, Lorenz Meyer.[70]

Runge's institution had two classes, the lower school and the upper school. The two classes had a shared curriculum. In the lower school, two hour blocks per week were scheduled for Latin, French, German, intellectual exercises [*Denkübungen*], and natural history. Four hours per week were devoted to religion and six to geography and topography. In the upper school, English replaced topography and mathematics replaced intellectual exercises.[71] The study of language, geography and topography, and mathematics was geared to the demands of students' future careers. The ability to write letters and read orders in French, German, and English was of great practical significance. The knowledge of trade routes, trade centers, and imports and exports and the ability to draft bills and calculate assets were basic tools for the merchant. More specific and practical instruction would come later, when the students would be apprenticed to merchants. Within this sensible and practical education, the inclusion of Latin appears to be a duck out of water. But the instruction was perfunctory, providing at best the ability to pronounce Latin words. As Schopenhauer noted, Latin instruction was "not serious and dedicated only to appearance."[72]

---

[69] Ibid., pp. 48/649.

[70] In his *curriculum vitae*, Schopenhauer mentioned that Runge was the author of a pedagogical writing (ibid., p. 49/649). In addition to the one mentioned in the text, Runge published at least two additional works: *Pedagogical Home Table or Necessary Rules of Conduct for Parents for the Dutiful Education of their Children* [*Pädagogische Haustafel oder notwendige Verhaltungsmassregln für Eltern zur pflichtmässigen Erziehung ihrer Kinder*, 1800] and *Primer for the Religious Instruction for My Maturing Students* [*Leitfaden zum Religious-Unterricht für meine reiferen Schüler*, 1804].

[71] See Patrick Bridgwater, *Arthur Schopenhauer's English Schooling*, pp. 282–3; Rüdiger Safranski, *Schopenhauer and the Wild Years of Philosophy*, pp. 32–3; Hildegard von Machtaler's "Lorenz Meyers *Tagebücher*," *Schopenhauer-Jahrbuch*, Vol. 49 (1968), pp. 95–111 and, foremost, Arthur Hübscher's "Ein vegessener Schulfreund Schopenhauers," *Schopenhauer-Jahrbuch*, Vol. 46 (1965), pp. 130–52, for discussions of Lorenz Meyer and the schedule of courses in Runge's school.

[72] Schopenhauer, *Gesammelte Briefe*, pp. 49/649. This remark about Latin instruction at Runge's school is accurate, but it was still too much for Schopenhauer. His mother mentioned his

Religious instruction for four hours per week was second only to that in geography and topography. If Lorenz Meyer's diary were a reliable guide, it would be better to think of this as moral instruction. There were no devotional services, religious *Schwärmerei*, or disharmonious signing of hymns. Instead the boys were taught about various moral duties, such as sparing others' feelings, duties toward siblings and servants (curiously, nothing on duties to one's parents), and improving the lives of others. Various needs or requirements are emphasized. One needs to avoid tempting others, backbiting, and gossip. What needs to be expressed is friendship, kindness, compassion, generosity, charitability, and helping others in business. There is no justification, the students were told, for the white lie; honesty and truth were always required.[73] Although Schopenhauer would jettison the idea of duty from his ethics, and he would express an ambivalent attitude toward white lies, the orientation of Runge's ethics, which is always in relationship to one's treatment of others, remained constant in his moral thought.

Heinrich Floris also directed Arthur's moral development, but from a distance. He presented him with a small sixteen-page pamphlet by Matthias Claudius. It bore the intimate title *To My Son H – [An meinen Sohn H –*, 1799]. On the title page, Heinrich Floris wrote his own son's name in pencil, as if Claudius spoke for him. Claudius was the feature writer and editor of the *Wandsbecker Messenger [Wandsbecker Bothen]*, a journal that featured poems, book reviews, and essays in a straightforward, folksy, and chatty language. Claudius himself wrote under the pseudonym "Asmus." Curiously, "Asmus" played an oblique role in Schopenhauer's intellectual life, one that became only partially apparent late in his philosophical career, when he referred to and quoted him. Later yet, in his Frankfurt am Main apartment, his picture would share a frame with one of Kant. Claudius decried religious orthodoxy, rejected dogmatism, and was equally suspicious of the emotional enthusiasm expressed in the mystical effusions of early Pietism. Religion is to transform the personality so that it can escape that which ties and enslaves a person to the world, according to Asmus, and by doing so, it moves one into contact with

difficulty in learning Latin, based on his Runge experience, as one of her concerns later, when Arthur wanted to prepare for a university education.

73 See Patrick Bridgwater, *Arthur Schopenhauer's English Schooling*, p. 283, which summarizes Lorenz Meyer's account of religious instruction at Runge's school.

the good and eternal. But this assimilation of Claudius would occur only later. It is not clear what the young Schopenhauer took from his father's gift. He did, however, underline two of its Pietistic rules for life: "Consider yourself too good to do evil," and "Always have something good in mind."[74] Perhaps both connote correctives for how he actually thought of himself and what he often had in mind.

Boys will be boys, however, and Arthur and his fellows engaged in the usual sorts of horseplay and mischief common to adolescents. On more than one occasion, Runge had to lecture his students about respecting the day teachers, who represented a lower rung on the social ladder. (It appears that his moral instructions should have included duties to one's teachers.) There were squabbles and fights. For an unknown reason, blindman's bluff was a favorite game. Arthur possessed a pair of fine pistols, and it was reported that he got carried away with some experiments with gunpowder, which led to some minor burns. His friend, Charles Godeffroy, suffered worse in a mishap with phosphorus.[75] They smoked cigars and drank alcohol. They practiced fencing and rode horses. Arthur, who started to play the flute as early as 1799, would continue to play it – an activity that moved Friedrich Nietzsche to challenge Schopenhauer's pessimism.[76]

At night, the boys would attend parties, balls, and masquerades, enjoying the social benefits of their class and honing their social skills and manners. It is not known, however, whether Arthur ever attended any of the celebrations held during the visit of Lord Horatio Nelson, Lady Emma Hamilton, and her cuckold husband, Sir William Hamilton.[77] The

---

[74] See *Der handschriftliche Nachlaß*, Vol. 5, p. 404 for Schopenhauer's highlighted passages from Claudius's *To My Son H.* He also owned Claudius's *Collected Works of the Wandsbecker Messenger* [*Sämtliche Werke des Wandsbecker Bothen*, 1775–90]. In a letter to Johann August Becker, 25 October 1853, Schopenhauer wrote that he found Claudius's history of conversion especially noteworthy; see Schopenhauer, *Gesammelte Briefe*, p. 325. In the third edition of *The World as Will and Representation* (1859) he added a number of references to Claudius (Asmus), Vol. 1, pp. 394, 395, 398, 403/*Sämtliche Werke*, Vol. 2, pp. 466, 467, 471, 477.

[75] Letter from Charles Godeffroy to Schopenhauer, 8 September 1803, quoted in Patrick Bridgwater, *Arthur Schopenhauer's English Schooling*, p. 250; see p. 252 for the phosphorus incident.

[76] In a letter to Schopenhauer from Johanna, 8 April 1799, she wrote, "Your father permits you to purchase the ivory flute for 1 *Louisd'or* . . . ," Lütkehaus, *Die Schopenhauers*, p. 49. Nietzsche challenges Schopenhauer's pessimism in the third essay, section 7 of *On the Genealogy of Morality*, and his remark about Schopenhauer's flute-playing is found in section 186 of *Beyond Good and Evil*.

[77] In *The Lady and the Admiral* [*Die Lady und die Admiral*, 1933], Hans Leip provided a fictional account of a twelve-year-old Schopenhauer chatting away precociously with Nelson and the

citizens of Hamburg were giddy over their visit. The old Klopstock was moved to write a poem, *Die Unschuldigen* [*The Innocents*], inspired by the not-so-innocent beauty of Lady Hamilton, who was Nelson's mistress, and who would bear him a daughter, Horatia, one year later. Nelson and his party arrived in Hamburg on 21 October and stayed until 31 October 1800. The English merchants sponsored a grand gala at the bowling green to honor Nelson, who was warmly received at all of his public appearances. Johanna mentioned Lord Nelson and Lady Hamilton in the outline of her memoirs, and it is likely that the Schopenhauers met both figures. Nelson, whose body was slowly whittled away in war – he had lost an eye and an arm – would surrender the remainder of his body at the battle of Trafalgar five years later. The *cachet* of the name Nelson was likely one of the factors that would later lead the Schopenhauers to enroll Arthur in the Reverend Lancaster's Wimbledon School.

Dr. Runge took an active interest in his students, and he encouraged their parents to treat their children reasonably but firmly and to avoid the hypocrisy of inconsistently applied standards and the arbitrary exercise of authority. Although it may be safe to say that Arthur's dread at becoming an apprentice merchant was shared by most of his peers, Runge sensed Arthur's desire to become a scholar. Schopenhauer credits Runge with the ability to ascertain that he also had the intellectual wherewithal required for the life of the mind. Runge joined Arthur in his pitches to his father that he should attend a gymnasium: "Dr. Runge bore witness for me, that I possessed other and higher intellectual capabilities than those needed by a merchant."[78] Perhaps to avoid arbitrary authority and to give Arthur the guidance of his own heart, Heinrich Floris set aside his plans for his son and yielded to Arthur's request, but he did so in a way that sought to protect his son from the poverty both he and Johanna associated with the lives of scholars and artists. He sought to purchase a benefice from the Cathedral Chapter, but the price of establishing this endowment was too costly.[79]

Heinrich Floris's willingness to act to realize Arthur's scholarly desires softened his hard image, especially in his son's eyes. Trying to secure a

Hamiltons. Patrick Bridgwater, *Arthur Schopenhauer's English Schooling*, pp. 20–22, has a good discussion of this fraud.

[78] Schopenhauer, *Gesammelte Briefe*, pp. 49/649.

[79] Safranski estimates the amount of the benefice at 20,000 *Taler*. Heinrich Floris's estate was valued at 57,000 *Taler* in 1805; see *Schopenhauer and the Wild Years of Philosophy*, p. 37.

Hamburg prebend was an act of "fatherly love" that put his son's well-being before everything else. He did so, Arthur thought, because his father viewed poverty as inseparable from a scholarly life.[80] Arthur, however, was oblivious to his father's specific attitude toward his son. He might have been receptive to the idea that his son possessed intellectual abilities far greater than those useful to a merchant, but his attitudes also implied that Arthur's abilities were not sufficient to earn him a good life. Still, he did not force Arthur to abandon his desires. To accomplish this, and to achieve his will, Heinrich Floris engineered a situation that would make Arthur concede to his wishes through his own will. Consequently, he gave Arthur a choice in early 1803. He and Johanna would be taking a lengthy pleasure tour of Europe that spring. Arthur could remain in Hamburg and learn Latin to prepare for a scholarly career, or he could join them, provided he would promise to prepare to become a merchant. It is not clear what Johanna thought about this choice. Years later, she would tell Arthur that his desire to become a scholar was her "warmest wish," but that her voice carried little weight. Thus, she did not speak on his behalf, but repressed her wish.[81] Johanna was well practiced in subordinating her desires to her husband's will, and in this case, she was a dutiful wife and not a loving mother.[82]

Arthur recognized years later that his father dangled an irresistible lure for a fifteen-year-old, one that allowed his own desires to trap him in a life he detested. His *curriculum vitae* provides an uneasy analysis of his alleged choice. His father, he wrote, had not forced him to forego a formal education, due to Heinrich Floris's "innate respect for the freedom of each human."[83] But respecting a person's freedom obviously did not entail ignoring or exploiting that which would lead his son to betray himself. He noted that his father knew he was eager to see the world

[80] Schopenhauer, *Gesammelte Briefe*, pp. 49/649.

[81] Lütkehaus, *Die Schopenhauers*, p. 164, Johanna to Arthur, 28 April 1807.

[82] Schopenhauer thought that there were natural tensions between husbands and wives, because the wives favor their children over their husbands, due to their unconscious concern for the future generation; see *Parerga and Paralipomena*, Vol. 2, p. 618/*Sämtliche Werke*, Vol. 6, p. 654f. Had Schopenhauer applied this generalization to his mother – and it is hard to think that he had not – this would have become another measure of Johanna's failure as a mother. For some reason, Schopenhauer never seriously considered how being a good wife, which he would have believed Johanna had been by submitting to her husband's will, could also become the basis upon which he judged her a bad mother.

[83] Schopenhauer, *Gesammelte Briefe*, pp. 49/649.

and that he had a lively longing to revisit Le Havre. (Heinrich Floris, of course, raised this possibility.) He knew, moreover, that the trip was something a young heart could not forego. Arthur chose the trip instead of pursuing his education as a scholar, and he promised his father that upon his return, he would prepare for the life of a merchant. He took this pledge seriously. Even after his father's death, he toiled away as an apprentice merchant for two more years. It was only after the business was liquidated and after the encouragement of his mother that he would enter a gymnasium, a college preparatory school.

2

A Tour for a Trade

ARTHUR'S DECISION TO take the grand pleasure tour continued his father's strategy of having his son, as Arthur would later tell Carl Georg Bähr, "read from the book of the world."[1] This "reading" was designed to enable the young Schopenhauer to prepare for the life of an international merchant. Direct familiarity with other countries, the opportunity to hone his language skills, and personal interaction with his father's business associates and their acquaintances all supported the development of the cosmopolitan attitudes, knowledge, connections, and values that Heinrich Floris viewed as practicable for business success. This early and unconventional form of education played a formative role in Schopenhauer's intellectual development as a philosopher. It is almost as if reading from the book of the world became the keystone of Schopenhauer's philosophical methodology and one of the central bases for his critique of his philosophical hero, Immanuel Kant, whom he found to be working from judgments about things and not from the things in themselves. It was as if Kant tried to determine the height of a tower by measuring its shadow, Schopenhauer analogized, whereas his philosophy measured the tower itself.[2] Even the drive itself to philosophize must spring from astonishment about the world, he claimed, and only a pseudo-philosopher is prompted to do so based on what some other philosopher has said.[3] Thus he would become doubly upset with the philosophy of one of his future teachers, Johann Gottlieb Fichte, who was prompted, he claimed, to become a philosopher due to his astonishment about what Kant

---

[1] Schopenhauer, *Gespräche*, p. 264.
[2] See Schopenhauer, *The World as Will and Representation*, Vol. 1, pp. 452–3/*Sämtliche Werke*, Vol. 2, p. 537.
[3] See ibid., Vol. 2, p. 170/ibid., Vol. 3, p. 188.

said, especially about what he had said about the thing in itself.[4] Fichte's work was no more than the distorted shade of a shadow.

Both Arthur and Johanna kept journals of their travels. Johanna would publish her journal as *Reminiscences of a Tour in the Years 1803, 1804, and 1805* [*Erinnerungen von einer Reise in den Jahren 1803, 1804, und 1805*] in 1813/1814. Later, its second edition would appear in 1818 as *Tour through England and Scotland* [*Riese durch England und Schottland*], which was published by F. A. Brockhaus, the future publisher of Arthur's *The World as Will and Representation*. The contrasts between the travel diaries of the mother and the son are instructive. Johanna, ever the socialite, was more interested in describing people, the fashions of the country, and social affairs. Her love of English gardens was effusive, a love that harkens back to Oliva. She described the splendors of the grand houses of the aristocracy, but she retained her class loyalties and republican sensibilities. She had "nothing to say about the everyday life of the great and noble: in no country do they truly reflect the nation but rather resemble each other everywhere, in Russia as in France, in England as in Germany.... In our travels we have always sought to get to know the customs of the real people of the country being visited, and for this one has to look neither too high nor too low, for it is nowadays preserved only in the middle classes."[5] Naturally, she carefully described the various museums and theaters visited by her family, as well as the architecture of various cities and towns. The socialite, however, was also the *Frau* of an important merchant, and she toured a number of places unusual for a "Lady" to visit: coal mines, a mint, a steel factory, a brewery, and an armament factory.

Johanna's travel diaries express neither the sensibilities of a contemporary feminist nor those of a more progressive figure of her age. Indeed, she used her sex to diminish her readers' expectations in the second introduction to her journal: "It contains a woman's simple tales of what she has seen and observed, written to entertain pleasantly, not to instruct deeply."[6] It is as if her book itself was to fulfill a woman's function. Still, she was sensitive to the ways in which social conventions restricted women's possibilities.

---

[4] See ibid., Vol. 1, p. 32/ibid., Vol. 1, p. 38.

[5] Johanna Schopenhauer, *A Lady Travels: The Diaries of Johanna Schopenhauer*, trans. Ruth Michaelis and Willy Merson (London: Routledge, 1988), p. 146.

[6] Ibid., p. xi.

Thus, she noted the tedium experienced by women at the conclusion of a
London dinner party. The sexes segregated themselves; men to one room,
and women to another. The men continued to drink wine as they smoked
cigars; they told risqué jokes, and discussed politics. This left the women
"to sit around a fireplace . . . staring at each other stifling a yawn."[7] The
vivacious Johanna would have preferred the company of the men. Later,
she observed a ball at a girls' boarding school, which was located in the
small town of Southwark, near London. She found the formal part of the
program a bore, and she noted the indifference expressed in the young
girls' mechanical performances. But then some of the foreign boarders
performed country dances, and the merriment shown by the girls led her
to reflect in a manner similar to the later style of her son: "Their bright
eyes were full of expectations for the future, confident that it, too, was to be
a dance of joy. It may well be that now those same eyes are filled with tears
of longing as they remember these carefree days, irretrievably lost. We
thought of their future with foreboding and took leave of them in the midst
of their happiness, with silent prayers for their well-being."[8] Unlike her
son, however, it was not the wretchedness of life that prompted Johanna's
sense of the girls' unhappy futures. It was that they were to become wives
and mothers – an autobiographical reflection.

Johanna kept her travel diary to ultimately transform it into a book.
Arthur kept his own due to his parents' insistence. It was not that they
wanted him to share his observations. Instead, they viewed it as the means
through which their son could improve his writing skills and develop a
good, clear writing hand. Given that the primary audience for Arthur's
reflections was his parents, it is easy to imagine that he would be less than
totally forthcoming, and that he would only write that which he felt was
appropriate for his parents' eyes. Consequently, his travel diary is not a
record of his deepest thoughts and most intimate secrets. Much of the
diary is mundane. He duly recorded the family's arrivals and departures
from various locales, the travails of travel, the weather, and the quality
of the accommodations of numerous inns – "bad," "fair," "good," and
"really good." He mentioned people the family visited and notables they
met. He was more sophisticated, however, when he criticized the quality
of architecture and city design, the production of plays, the skills of

[7] Ibid., p. 159.
[8] Ibid., pp. 197–8.

the actors, and the art galleries and museums. He recorded the thrills of various hikes, and he delighted in climbing mountains. The bird's-eye vistas, the looking down to survey great stretches of territory and observe human affairs from a distance, gave him the sense of adopting a universal perspective, one that suggested a comprehensive view of the totality of things. This was an experiential foreshadowing of the theoretical aspirations of his philosophy, which sought to produce a totalizing account of all possible experience. And as the tour progressed, so did his awareness of the doleful consequences of choosing to accept the tour: a mercantile career. The brooding his mother would later criticize becomes clearer as he becomes increasingly sensitive to human misery and poverty – encounters that would provide later material for his observations on the vanity of life.

In many ways, Arthur was a sophisticated and precocious boy, but he was a boy nonetheless. He delighted in bashing the various aristocrats whom the family encountered by noting how common they appeared.[9] He was captivated by a ventriloquist's act in London, where he was also astonished by an attraction in Leicester Square called the "Invisible Girl," where for two shillings and a sixpence, one could ask a question of a glass globe that was suspended by a ribbon from the ceiling.[10] Four trumpets protruded from the globe, and one could hear a girl's voice answer through one of the trumpets. Music would also project from the globe, and the disembodied voice would describe the questioner and reply in English, German, and French. Arthur was baffled: "This strange trick, which has found the greatest applause, was incomprehensible to me as it is still today to everyone else."[11] At St. Feriol, by the basin of the Lanquedoc Canal, the terrifying roar of the opening of the underground water gates

---

[9] See Arthur Schopenhauer, *Reisetagebücher aus den Jahren* 1803–4, ed. Charlotte von Gwinner (Leipzig : F. A. Brockhaus, 1923), pp. 59, 258.

[10] See ibid., p. 44. The entry for 8 June 1803 describes the ventriloquist, and on p. 65, the entry for 7 October 1803 describes the encounter with the Invisible Girl.

[11] Ibid., p. 65. Schopenhauer was so taken by this experience that fifteen years later, in the first edition of *The World as Will and Representation*, he wrote that when we try to become conscious of ourselves independent of objects of cognition and willing, we fail. When we introspect and try to do the impossible, to become aware of ourselves as subjects of cognition per se, "We lose ourselves in a bottomless void; we find ourselves like a hollow glass globe, from the emptiness of which a voice speaks. But the cause of this voice is not to be found in the globe, and since we want to comprehend ourselves, we grasp with a shudder nothing but a wavering and unstable phantom." Vol. 1, p. 278 fn./*Sämtliche Werke*, Vol. 2, p. 327.

moved him. The sound was deafening.[12] Later, in Hirschberg, he awoke one morning and looked in the mirror. He was yellow in color and his ears were swollen. Still, he went for a stroll; "When I went a short way down the street, I saw with horror my shadow, from which two long ears projected from under my hat. Shuddering, I thought of the cry of King Richard III: 'Shine out fair sun! till I brought a glass,/That I may see my Shadow as I pass!'"[13] This minor incident perhaps captures concisely the young Schopenhauer. He was moved to understand a strange and temporary affliction by quoting Shakespeare – in English.

The Schopenhauers commenced their carefully planned European tour on Tuesday, 3 May 1803, after sending the almost six-year-old Adele and her nursemaid to Johanna's parents in Danzig. After a four-hour delay, due to contrary winds on the Elbe, they arrived at Hamburg, where they picked up their coach. They made their way to Lüneburg that evening, traveling with a servant and with a rich store of provisions, including wine and pâté. They departed at four o'clock the next morning, arriving that evening in Bremen. Arthur visited the lead cellars, a local tourist attraction, which boasted a collection of mummified corpses. He was relatively unreflective about the mummified remains, and noted their odorlessness, their possession of hair, and their "still perceptible features."[14] His confrontation of the leathery dead did not provoke him to philosophize about the ephemeral state of human existence. Later, in London, he was also not philosophical about the fleshy dead he witnessed at a hanging. It was only in regard to the great and heroic dead in Westminster Abbey and the distant and imagined dead he associated with the ruins of a Roman amphitheatre at Nîmes that he would exhibit a glint of his belief that "Death is the real inspiring genius or Musagetes of philosophy. . . . "[15] That evening, he and his parents attended a performance of August Friedrich Ferdinand von Kotzebue's *Armut und Edelsinn*. The troupe was fair, he wrote, but Madame Breda, who appeared in a guest role, was "excellent."[16] He would continue to play his own role as critic for all the plays and performances

---

[12] See Schopenhauer, *Reisetagebücher*, p. 131, entry for 28 March 1804.

[13] Ibid., p. 302, entry for 2 August 1804. The quotation is from Shakespeare's *Richard III*, Act 1, Scene 2.

[14] Ibid., p. 20, entry for 5 May 1803.

[15] Schopenhauer, *The World as Will and Representation*, Vol. 2, p. 463/*Sämtliche Werke*, Vol. 3, p. 528.

[16] Schopenhauer, *Reisetagebücher*, p. 20, entry for 5 May 1803.

that he attended throughout the tour. Seldom, if ever, did he have a bad word to say about actresses.

From Bremen the family traveled through dreary Westphalia. They reached the Dutch border on 8 May and the village of Amersfoort the next day. There they read about the possible resumption of hostilities between England and France in a Dutch newspaper, which caused them to abandon their plan to tour France. They journeyed to Amsterdam, the Hague, Rotterdam, Bergen Op Zoom, and Antwerp and crossed the French border on 20 May 1803. Three days later, the Schopenhauers arrived at the northwestern French seaport of Calais and prepared to cross to Dover. Ill winds postponed the crossing of the Straits of Dover until two o'clock in the morning. Arthur became seasick almost immediately: "I was one of the most sick and passed a wretched night."[17] There were others more wretched than he, however. After four hours, with Calais still in sight, three rowboats deposited passengers from a French packet-boat, which had not been permitted to disembark due to the resumption of the war. Arthur felt compassion for these poor souls who were not even allowed to take their luggage, and he noted the fear of the women and children as they climbed aboard the pitching and rolling ship. And almost as if he'd channeled his father, he noted that each person had to pay the fare and had to give two guineas to the sailors who rowed them to the ship: "I assume [they paid the fare] also aboard the French packet-boat. Generally, one is overcharged here [in France] in every possible way."[18] After an eleven-hour crossing, the Schopenhauers landed in Dover.

From Dover they journeyed to Canterbury. The following morning they took breakfast in Rochester and lunch at Shooter's Hill, which was twenty-six miles from London. Shooter's Hill, which Arthur called "Schooting Hill," was famous for its overview of London and for the various scoundrels and highwaymen who haunted its vicinity and preyed upon both the locals and tourists. A gallows lay at the foot of the hill to swiftly dispatch these bandits, whose corpses were displayed at the summit. Arthur does not mention whether anyone was hanging around during the day his family visited the hill, but his journal contains a curious remark: "One has a magnificent view of London and the surrounding

[17] Ibid., p. 35, entry for 23 and 24 May 1803.
[18] Ibid., p. 35.

region from here, but we could not see it because of the thick fog."[19] There is nothing like an unseen magnificent view!

The Schopenhauers reached London in the afternoon of 25 May 1803. Arthur was impressed by the City: "I found my expectations actually exceeded by London. I had not imagined it to be quite *so*, and I saw with astonishment the beautiful, grand houses, the wide streets, and the rich shops that one finds in a colorful variety in the front of each house, in every street."[20] London would become the standard by which he measured other cities. Paris did not measure up to London, he later noted. It was not as well paved, clean, and safe for pedestrians.[21] Although London was large, housing more than one million souls, and its streets teamed with carriages and its walkways were vibrant with foot traffic, Arthur appreciated the orderliness of its traffic flow and the rational design of the city, making it easy, he claimed, for tourists to make their way around town. Frequently he noted in his journal with pride that he had no difficulty strolling around on his own.

The nature of Heinrich Floris's business connections in London was impressive. The first person the family visited was Lady Dorothy Anderson, the wife of Sir John William Anderson, who was born in Danzig and, like Heinrich Floris, was the son of a Danzig merchant. Anderson succeeded both financially and politically in England. He was Lord Mayor of London in 1797, and he was three times elected to Parliament. His business, Sir John Wm Anderson Drewe and Co., was the elder Schopenhauer's trading partner and agent. Anderson's business partner, Samuel Drewe, would later become Governor of the Bank of England (1828–30).[22] Drewe called upon the Schopenhauers shortly after their arrival, and he would serve as a conduit for Arthur's allowance during his time in Wimbledon School, and Anderson Drewe and Co. would serve as the collection point for the family's letter exchanges. Other notable business associates were Isaac Solly, head of Isaac Solly and Sons and later chair for twenty years of the London Dock Company, and Sir Claude Scott, Director of the Royal Exchange Assurance and a cofounder of London University.[23]

---

[19] Ibid., p. 36, entry for 25 May 1803.
[20] Ibid., p. 36.
[21] See ibid., pp. 81–2, entry for 30 November 1803.
[22] See Patrick Bridgwater, *Arthur Schopenhauer's English Schooling*, p. 120, fn. 4.
[23] Ibid., p. 126, fn. 20.

Johanna ignored describing the aristocracy in her writings, due to their self-sameness in every land. Although not dwelling on his encounters with them in any great detail, Arthur perceived their commonness in a different sense. Like his reflections on the various cities, buildings, gardens, art galleries, museums, theaters, and tourist attractions, Schopenhauer's *a priori* anticipations gauged his descriptions of the nobles. One Sunday afternoon the Schopenhauers joined the crowd at Windsor to witness the promenade of the royal family. The King was a good-looking old man, Arthur thought, but the Queen and her daughters were a different story: "The Queen is ugly and not at all ladylike. All the princesses are not pretty and are showing their age."[24] Later, the Austrian royal couple received a reversed judgment. The Emperor had a "stupid face" and reminded Schopenhauer of a tailor. The Empress, although "not pretty," was perceived by him to have the advantage over her husband, because she looked "clever."[25]

Wimbledon School

On 30 June 1803, after roughly five weeks on tour, Arthur became a special boarder at the Reverend Thomas Lancaster's academy, which was called Wimbledon School for Young Noblemen and Gentlemen. His twelve weeks at Wimbledon School were the unhappiest of his travels, and they may have been among the most unpleasant of his youth. It is

---

[24] Ibid., p. 59, entry for 26 June 1803. It is odd that Schopenhauer had less to say about the family's visit to Sir William Herschel's home than he did about the British royal family. Herschel, who hailed from Hamburg, was already famous for his work in astronomy at the time of the visit. Arthur simply noted the extraordinary size of his telescopes, which were mounted on house-high platforms in his garden. Unlike her son, Johanna, who carried a letter of introduction to Herschel, provided a concise history of his life, and she told the story of his rise from poverty in Hamburg to securing a royal sponsorship in England; see her *A Lady Travels*, pp. 237–40. Herschel's son, John Herschel, who was also knighted, continued his father's work and distinguished himself in his own right. In *On the Will in Nature* [*Über den Willen in der Natur*, 1836], Schopenhauer cited a passage from John Herschel's *A Treatise on Astronomy* (London: Longman, Rees, Orme, Brown, Green, and Longman, 1833) to support the thesis that gravity expressed a will inherent in bodies; see *On the Will in Nature*, trans. E. F. J. Payne (New York/Oxford: Berg, 1992), pp. 85–6/*Sämtliche Werke*, Vol. 4, pp. 80–82. Later, in the second edition of his main work, he cited the Herschels to illustrate his claim that diligence and perseverance, rather than great intellectual ability, are sufficient for excelling in some branches of knowledge; see *The World as Will and Representation*, Vol. II, p. 522/*Sämtliche Werke*, Vol. 3, p. 598.

[25] Schopenhauer, *Reisetagebücher*, p. 258, entry for 25 June 1804.

likely that it was his experiences there that would move him to write to his young friend Lorenz Meyer that he had come "to hate the entire [British] nation."[26] But why was he so negatively affected? It is unfortunate that his extant travel diary only includes entries concerning the day he journeyed to the school and the day when he left. He made both trips alone. Moreover, the letters he wrote to his parents, sister, and friends no longer exist. It is not clear, however, that he kept his journal during this time. One nevertheless suspects that he did, because Johanna later used his journal to help prepare her own for publication, which included a harsh description of Wimbledon School.[27] It is also reasonable to believe that Arthur's diary recorded his displeasure in unreserved terms, and his parents, who read his journal, knew the extent of his despair. If that were the case, they may have destroyed these entries due to their dark content.

When Schopenhauer made his potentially self-defeating decision to forego the life of the mind for the pleasures of the grand European tour, it is likely that his choice was made without knowing he would spend three months in an English boarding school for boys as his parents, free from the cares of tending to a child, enjoyed a tour of England and Scotland. There is nothing in the historic record, however, that expresses his feelings of being tricked or betrayed by his parents due to this enrollment. He stated very simply in his *curriculum vitae* that the purpose of this detour was to learn the English language thoroughly, which he was able to do.[28] Heinrich Floris championed the goal of his son's learning English, but with specific objectives in mind. He wanted his son "to write in a fluent and masculine hand" and to develop "the best and clearest penmanship," both of which were serviceable skills for a merchant and characteristics he demanded that Arthur display in his required weekly letters.[29] Schopenhauer consistently failed to write in a fashion that pleased his father, who constantly provided recommendations for improvement, such as avoiding fancy flourishes in his penmanship and observing his capital letters more carefully. He advised Arthur to copy his mother's letters and to learn "to hold the pen in such a way that one can move it just with the fingers without moving

[26] Schopenhauer, *Gesammelte Briefe*, p. 1, Schopenhauer to Lorenz Meyer, September 1803.
[27] Johanna provides an unflattering description of Wimbledon School in *A Lady Travels*, pp. 198–200.
[28] See Schopenhauer, *Gesammelte Briefe*, pp. 49, 649.
[29] Lütkehaus, *Die Schopenhauers*, p. 61, Heinrich Floris to Arthur, 25 August 1803.

the hand, and wield it lightly."[30] This, he claimed, is the entire secret of writing with a good, clear hand.

Heinrich Floris's letters to Arthur during his enrollment in Wimbledon School are far different in tone from those he sent to his young son in Le Havre. The latter have some warmth. He even signed one, "your good father Schopenhauer," and none of the three extant letters contain the fussy criticisms found in each and every one of the six Wimbledon letters.[31] Both sets of letters share a common characteristic. They were short. This difference in tone may be a simple function of Arthur's age and Heinrich Floris's expectations. He was eleven years old during his last year in France and fifteen in England. Thus, Heinrich Floris could have been striving to be a good father in both instances, and due to Arthur's age, have adopted different means to fulfill this role. He was tender to a boy and hard on an adolescent who was on the cusp of preparing to make his way in a difficult world. Still, even if Heinrich Floris was attempting to serve Arthur's future well-being, his niggling criticisms seem more of an expression of his own increasing mental instability. Johanna seems to allude to this in one of her letters to Arthur: "You know that your father manufactures worries when there are no real ones."[32] Arthur himself, who increasingly deified his father after his death, recognized that his father had his well-being in mind, but as he confided to an acquaintance, "I did, to be sure, have to suffer a great deal in my education, due to the hardness of my father."[33]

Heinrich Floris's litany of worries and complaints, imagined or not, dominated his Wimbledon letters. In addition to his problems with Arthur's writing skills and penmanship, and the mailing costs and the lack of timeliness of his son's letters, he also worried about the dangers and usefulness of his swimming lessons, and the cost of his education. He even suggested that Arthur should try to beat his singing master out of his one guinea fee, and "meanwhile, your piano lessons will help you progress in singing on your own."[34] Then there was the issue of Arthur's posture. He must have had a tendency to slouch, because his father wrote, "Your mother expects, as I do, that you will not need to be reminded to walk

[30] Ibid., p. 62.
[31] Ibid., p. 51, Heinrich Floris to Arthur, 9 August 1799.
[32] Ibid., p. 63, Johanna to Arthur, 13 September 1803.
[33] Schopenhauer, *Gespräche*, p. 230, reported by Julius Frauenstädt.
[34] Lütkehaus, *Die Schopenhauers*, p. 63, Heinrich Floris to Arthur, 17 September 1803.

upright like other well-raised people, and [she] sends her love."[35] The phrase, "your mother expects," or "your mother is not satisfied with your last letters," represents a common ploy of Arthur's parents. The dissatisfactions of Heinrich Floris are also those of Arthur's mother. Johanna's longer and more intimate letters to her son reiterate her husband's concerns, but more gently: "In any case, I am rather satisfied with everything you write. Your father is very pleased that you have asked for two hours of writing, and I also think that this is the cleverest thing you could do."[36] Together, Arthur's parents presented a united front.

The weight of his parents' criticisms did little to improve his posture – or his writing skills. A little more than a year after he escaped Wimbledon School, Arthur began to prepare for a mercantile career by training in Danzig. Heinrich Floris once again became obsessed with the figure of his slouching son:

> My dear Son,
>
> Since you have now given me your written vow to learn to write well and fluently, and to learn to calculate sums perfectly, I will rely on you to do so, with the request that you walk straightly, as other people do, so that you do not develop rounded shoulders, which look ghastly. Good posture at the writing desk is as equally necessary as it is in everyday life, since if, when one is dining out, one sees another stooping, one takes him as a disguised tailor or cobbler. . . .
>
> Should you acquire better deportment through sound instruction in the riding school, or through physical exercise by a good trainer, I will also be happy to pay for its costs. . . . [37]

One wonders whether Heinrich Floris's derisive reference to his son's appearing like a disguised tailor harkened back to the recollection of Arthur's describing the Emperor as looking common, like a tailor, in his travel journal. But even if he was attempting to pay his son back with his own coin, in order to hit upon a posture-reshaping sense of the betrayal of his social standing, he failed to achieve an immediate effect. Walking and writing constitute the subjects of his final letter to his son: " . . . in regard to walking and sitting upright, I advise you to request of anyone you are with to give you a blow, when you are caught inattentive of this great matter. Thus the children of princes have experienced this and

---

[35] Ibid., p. 63.
[36] Ibid., p. 56, Johanna to Arthur, 4 August 1803.
[37] Ibid., p. 64, Heinrich Floris to Arthur, 23 October 1804.

have not been shy about this short-term pain, simply so that they do not appear as louts their entire lives. . . . I still find, here and there, the capital letters of your scribbling to be genuine monstrosities, especially in your German, which, as your mother tongue, must not show a single mistake in your handwriting."[38] Arthur never developed a clear writing hand, but he did develop a good gait. At least, he thought so. The almost forty-nine-year-old philosopher would later report to his youthful friend Anthime Grégoire de Blésimaire that "My carriage and gait are sure and quick. I still usually walk faster than all others."[39]

Heinrich Floris's letters could almost be characterized in the terms Thomas Hobbes used to describe life in a state of nature. But instead of being "nasty, brutish, and short," his letters were only "nasty, fussy, and short." Johanna's letters were very different – to a degree. Fulfilling her role as his mother, she addressed her son's concerns, but she did so in a way that privileged her role as a dutiful wife. Her letters express a playful and, at times, a cheerful tone, but there is also an egocentric intimacy that casts the spotlight back on the author and the ways in which she was superior to her son. Of course, she reinforces her husband's complaints, and she articulates her own, even while identifying herself with Arthur's suffering from his father's will.

In his first letter to his parents while at Wimbledon School, Arthur must have complained about his inability to establish any meaningful friendships with his classmates and about feeling further isolated and alienated due to the rigid and formal atmosphere of the school. Johanna, unlike Heinrich Floris, addressed her son's loneliness and offered what appears, at first glance, to be good advice. He should be more forthcoming and take the initiative in establishing comradery with the other boys. Referring to his two years at Le Havre, Johanna reminds him that he has had experience at an early age of living with foreigners, whereas his English peers have had none. She understands, moreover, why Arthur would find the formality of the school odd, and she confesses that she does not like starchiness and rigid formality, but this, she said, is often necessary for decorum. She directs him to look at himself as part of the problem, because he has a tendency to be smug and self-satisfied, "as I

[38] Ibid., p. 65f., Heinrich Floris to Arthur, 20 November 1804.
[39] Schopenhauer, *Gesammelte Briefe*, p. 157, Schopenhauer to Grégoire de Blésimaire, 10 December 1836.

have often noticed to my annoyance."[40] She wishes that this experience would reform his character: "I am glad that you must live with people of a different stamp, even though they stray, perhaps, to the other extreme. I will be very pleased if I would observe upon my return [to London] that you have assumed something of this 'complimentary nature,' as you call it; that you will carry this too far I do not fear."[41]

Johanna could sympathize with Arthur's feelings of loneliness and confinement. She also knew the weight of conforming to her husband's will. Drawing on her own experiences on the family estate near Oliva, she tells her son, "Drawing, reading, playing your flute, fencing, and going for walks is still quite a variety of activities. For years I knew almost no other activities and joys of life, and I fared very well."[42] Because he is just beginning life, he must understand how to live, she continues, and his stay at Wimbledon will enable him to later enjoy all of life's pleasures. Soon, however, the iron fist behind the velvet glove appears:

I think we will return to London in about six weeks. If you desire to join and then accompany us on our tour, I advise you, in a friendly way, to make it the case that, upon our return, your father will be satisfied by your handwriting; otherwise, in all seriousness, expect nothing. If I were in your place, I would spend all of my time and strain every nerve to reach this goal. You are reasonable enough, if you reflect on it, to see how necessary it is for your future success to write well, quickly, and clearly. I cannot conceive how, with due care and much practice, learning such a mechanical skill should become so difficult! One can do everything that one seriously wants; of that I am absolutely convinced from my own experience. Thus, if you do not write well, it is your fault, and you must suffer the consequences, since it is our duty and our will to use everything in our powers that contributes to your improvement, the manner and means we use to do it cannot be measured by your approval.[43]

Johanna's message was clear. Arthur's parents would do whatever they thought would lead to his development, even if he found his experiences disagreeable. She then mentions the remarkable and beautiful mansions, parks, and gardens and the wild and wonderful landscapes that she and Heinrich Floris enjoyed on their tour without him. It almost seems that her concern is not to inform her son about his parents' experiences, nor does it appear that she is providing Arthur with a sense of what he missed. Instead,

[40] Lütkehaus, *Die Schopenhauers*, p. 52, Johanna to Arthur, 19 July 1803.
[41] Ibid.
[42] Ibid., pp. 52–3.
[43] Ibid., p. 54.

it looks as if she wanted Arthur to have a sense of what he could expect, if he rejoined the tour; that is, if his handwriting improved. She also dropped a curious remark. After claiming that they had not stayed long in one place, which kept her from having company, Johanna provided an explanation: "You know that your father does not like to meet people."[44] The fruit did not fall far from the tree. Arthur's standoffish attitude to his classmates mirrored his father's. Johanna overcame her husband's antisocial stance by enjoying the constantly changing scenery and by diligently working on her diary. She transcended Arthur's unpleasant character by enjoying his absence, by criticizing him at a distance, and by making both appear to be the will of his father. She closed her letter with a note of strangely worded warmth: "*Adieu*, dear Arthur, I am sorry for your sake that you are not with us, but at least you are using your time profitably, if not also agreeably. Take to heart everything that I have written and follow my advice. Take my word that through this you will live well. Your father expects letters from you soon, but on better paper."[45]

Both Heinrich Floris and Johanna complained about the tardiness of their son's letters. From Edinburgh the former wrote that he was "surprised," even "worried," about Arthur's failure to write one per week.[46] He was also annoyed with Arthur's handwriting. A little more than a week later, from Glasgow, Johanna conjectured that he failed to keep his writing schedule, because he was waiting for a response from his parents. They had no obligation to do so, she wrote, but "you are obligated to give us a report of how you use your time and to render an account of all your activities and actions."[47] She was not displeased with the appearance of Arthur's letters, but she was concerned with their content: "Still I must provide you some advice about your writing, dear Arthur, which does not concern the outward form of your writing, but about the more important part of it, the content. Make it a rule never, even when in a hurry, to send a letter or even the most insignificant note, without reading through it, word for word, and carefully. If you do not do this, I predict that you will often bitterly regret it, and besides, this is the only way to improve your style and to rectify mistakes."[48]

[44] Ibid., p. 54f.
[45] Ibid., p. 55.
[46] Ibid., p. 55, Heinrich Floris to Arthur, 26 July 1803.
[47] Ibid., p. 56, Johanna to Arthur, 4 August 1803.
[48] Ibid., p. 57.

Johanna decided to give him a lesson. Arthur had used the Voltairean phrase, "infamous bigotry," to describe a pervasive attitude that he experienced at Wimbledon School. This is a turn of phrase, she wrote, that no civilized and educated person would even let slip into his or her speech, even in a heated argument. In regard to this bigotry, he wished that "the truth should burn through the Egyptian darkness in England with its torch."[49] Unable to find an appropriate German term to refer to her son's brave desire, she used an English one: "bombast." Worse, it was nonsense: "How can you expect the truth to do such a thing? As far as I know, darkness can be illuminated, but burn, my son, burn it cannot truthfully do."[50] Although Schopenhauer tended to be somewhat grandiloquent in his philosophical writings, and he remained ever inclined to use phrases civilized and educated people avoided in heated arguments, he weighed his word choices carefully. Nine years later, while a student at the University of Berlin, Schopenhauer would derisively reflect on Fichte's claim concerning the intelligibility of Kant's moral principle, the categorical imperative: "*Intelligibility of the categorical imperative!* An absurd and preposterous idea! Egyptian darkness!"[51] One can imagine that Johanna would have also found this remark unintelligible. Darkness obscures vision, not thought!

Johanna's Glasgow letter is an especially rich document. It reveals some of Arthur's "extra" studies at Wimbledon, aspects of his earlier readings and education, and it dispenses advice that is designed to reconcile him to his mercantile career. It also expresses her own resignation to her life as wife and mother. She encouraged Arthur to work diligently on his

---

[49] Ibid., p. 59. The letter fragment in the *Gesammelte Briefe*, p. 1, Arthur to Johanna 25 July 1803, was gleaned from Johanna's letter.

[50] Ibid.

[51] Schopenhauer, *Manuscript Remains*, Vol. 2, p. 401/*Der handschriftliche Nachlaß*, Vol. 2, p. 349. Friedrich Nietzsche quoted Schopenhauer's remark about the incomprehensibility of the categorical imperative in Sect. 142 of his *Daybreak: Thoughts on the Prejudices of Morality* [*Morgenröthe*, 1881; trans. R. J. Hollingsdale. Cambridge: Cambridge University Press, 1982], without citing the source of the quotation. It is likely that he took it from Wilhelm Gwinner's *Arthur Schopenhauer Depicted from Personal Acquaintance* [*Arthur Schopenhauer aus persönlichem Umgange dargestellt*], ed. Charlotte von Gwinner (Leipzig: Brockhaus, 1862) to which Nietzsche refers in *On the Genealogy of Morals* [*Zur Genealogy der Moral*] (1887) third treatise, Sect. 20. Schopenhauer might have recalled Johanna's criticism of his metaphor when he wrote, "Whatever torch we light, and whatever space it may illuminate, our horizon will always remain encircled by the depth of night," *The World as Will and Representation*, Vol. 2, p. 185/*Sämtliche Werke*, Vol. 3, p. 206 – No burning truths, just light and darkness!

drawing, one of her own passions as a young girl, because it is likely that he will never again have much time for it. Still, she warned that he must not neglect playing his flute in favor of his drawing. She wondered about his progress in his singing lessons, and she raised a question that evokes a strange image of the future philosopher: When he sings *God Save the King*, can he sing "in a soprano voice, like a woman?"[52] It is not known how Arthur responded to this question. One hopes, however, that at the age of fifteen, he did not. In response to her previous letter, Arthur must have mentioned that he was able to establish friendships only with boys from Germany. Johanna endorsed his sticking with his fellow countrymen, because the English boys were not used to someone like him.

Arthur must have also mentioned in a letter to Johanna that he was reading Friedrich Schiller's tragedies in his spare time. Johanna counseled against such extracurricular readings. He was at Wimbledon to improve his English, and reading his native language would thwart this goal. She was, however, not simply upset with the language of Arthur's readings. She also found the content problematic. Reading too much poetry would also make her son's career in business even more dreadful. Therefore, she recommended that he forego poetry for a time and concentrate on more serious readings. Johanna adopted a twofold strategy to bring Arthur to his senses. She identified with her son's enthusiasm for literature, and she turned Schiller against himself. She knew, Johanna wrote, how agreeable it is to immerse oneself in the works of artistic genius, but this could rob a person of the ability to appreciate more serious works. Schiller, she noted, had said that "life is serious, art carefree," and he had remarked that he would not have become himself if he had only read poetry in his youth.[53] She reminded Arthur that he was about to enter the serious side of life, and she warned him that too much cheerful reading would only make his life more intolerable. Life is serious business and it is time to get serious. At fifteen, she wrote, he had read the best German and French poets, as well as some of the English ones, but he had not read a single

[52] Lütkehaus, *Die Schopenhauers*, p. 57, Johanna to Arthur, 4 August 1803.

[53] Ibid., p. 58. Arthur had met Schiller in the summer of 1800 at a park in Weimar. He did little, however, other than note that he and his parents had met him; see "Journal of a Trip from Hamburg to Karlsbad, and from There to Prague; Return Trip to Hamburg" ["Journal einer Reise vom Hamburg nach Carlsbad, und vom dort nach Prag; Rückreise nach Hamburg"], 1800, in Wilhelm Gwinner's *Arthur Schopenhauer*, p. 224, entry for 30 July 1800.

prose work, except for some novels, and no more history than what Dr. Runge required. This, she told him, is not right!

Johanna then drew on her own resignation to motivate Arthur to prepare for the serious business of life by becoming serious about business:

> You know that I have a feeling for beauty, and I am pleased that you perhaps inherited this from me, but this feeling cannot serve us now as a guide to the world as it is. It must be preceded by what is useful, and I would prefer to see you become anything other than a so-called *Bellesprit*. These gentlemen speak of poetry, actors, composers, and painters as though one lived only to go to the theater and concerts. They pride themselves and their ability to throw around a few easy to learn technical terms and fashionable words, and they look down with scorn and contempt on the hard-working, prosaic merchant, who ultimately pays for their celebrated artists and probably must ultimately provide this wise, pompous enthusiast with a corner of his desk, so that he has something to eat along with his enthusiasm for art – unless something in his papa's soul had been so unpoetic in nature as to earn the money for the pictures and books of his wiser son. You will never go that far, but at the end of your letter to me you finally forced me to smile.[54]

It is likely that Johanna's Glasgow letter made a deep and lasting impression on Schopenhauer, but not the one she hoped to make. Near the end of his life, in a conversation with an acquaintance, he used phrases that seem to hearken back to this letter to describe his parents. He mentioned that his father, "the prosaic merchant from Danzig," encouraged and supported his flute-playing and that "my poetic mother, the beautiful soul [*Schöngeist*] of Weimar, was opposed to my wish."[55] Thus he endorsed Johanna's claims that hard-working merchants supported their sons' artistic aspirations and that the so-called *bel esprit* expressed self-absorbed aesthetic attitudes antithetical to the arts. Although Arthur, as his mother predicted, never became the *bel esprit* that she described in her letter, in Arthur's eyes his mother personified the very creature she reviled in her letter. Heinrich Floris's labors as a merchant prepared the grounds for Johanna's rich cultural life in Weimar, but only after his death. Johanna's insistence that he abandon enjoying the works of artistic genius to prepare for a useful vocation, in order to fulfill the serious business of

---

[54] Ibid., p. 58–9. Perhaps Arthur's "bombast" about truth burning through the Egyptian darkness of England brought the smile to Johanna's face.

[55] Schopenhauer, *Gespräche*, p. 223f, reported by Robert von Hornstein. Schopenhauer must have forgotten Johanna's advice to not sacrifice his flute playing for drawing.

life, must have ultimately signified to him his mother's hypocrisy, because in Weimar, she became a *bel esprit*.

Johanna may have been accurate about her son's deployment of his sense of beauty to transcend the tedious routines of Wimbledon School and his father's constant nagging to master his penmanship. And if he had not inherited his sensitivity to art from his mother, the very atmosphere of Arthur's home in Hamburg, where he was surrounded by fine art and literature, could have been sufficient for the cultivation of his aesthetic tastes. The European tour itself, which included regular and frequent attendance at plays and concerts, visits to museums and art galleries, explorations of gardens and natural areas, and sightseeing of magnificent architecture in some of Europe's greatest cities, was structured also to provide Arthur with a first-rate aesthetic education. If Schopenhauer the boy was guilty of misusing art, as his mother warned, and was thereby making himself more vulnerable to a fate he dreaded, the aesthetics of Schopenhauer the philosopher would align the enjoyment of the works of artistic genius with the most serious side of life, the release from a world steeped, by its very essence, in suffering and destruction. Moreover, unlike his mother, whom he viewed as living the superfluous life of a *bel esprit*, which was made possible by the hard work of a prosaic merchant, he considered his inheritance "as a consecrated treasure which is entrusted to me simply for the purpose of being able to solve the problem set to me by nature and to be for myself and humankind what nature intended me to be."[56]

It would be eleven years after his experiences at Wimbledon School before Schopenhauer would view art as a preparation for and not as a distraction from the serious business of life. But while he was at Wimbledon School, he was just fifteen and taking solace from Schiller at the time of the lesson from his mother. One might ask why his parents selected Wimbledon School for Arthur's training. Certainly, there were many other schools where he could have just as well cultivated his knowledge of English while also freeing his parents to enjoy their tour without the burdens of traveling with a child. Why would his experiences there lead him to say that he had come to hate the entire nation? He was an Anglophile before he traveled to England, and he did remain one throughout his life,

---

[56] Schopenhauer, *Manuscript Remains*, Vol. 4, p. 503/*Der handschriftliche Nachlaß*, Vol. 4, 2, p. 118.

but what did he sense as a deep flaw in the British character, and why did he sense it due to his time at Reverend Thomas Lancaster's school?

It is not known what led Schopenhauer's parents to choose Wimbledon School. The family could have heard about the school from Heinrich Floris's business associates prior to the European tour. Lorenz Meyer, one of Arthur's youthful friends from Dr. Runge's school, who corresponded with Arthur during the tour, was apprenticed under Martin Albert Rücker, whose brother lived on the same road on which Wimbledon School was located. Meyer himself spent the summer of 1802 in the home of John Arthur Rucker (who dropped the umlaut from his name) in nearby Wandsworth.[57] Meyer's principal was a business associate of Heinrich Floris, and he knew Meyer's father, also named Lorenz, well. However, Samuel and Mary Percival, with whom the Schopenhauers frequently socialized in London and with whom Arthur dined when he traveled to London while he was in school, may have induced them to select the school. The Percivals' son, George, who was roughly Arthur's age, had shown Arthur the sights of London.[58] They also accompanied the Schopenhauers on their visit to the school on 27 June 1803, three days prior to Arthur's attendance. Johanna noted in her published travel journal that Wimbledon School was among the best of its kind and that "Lord Nelson had two of his nephews educated there."[59] She may have received this impression of the school from the Reverend Thomas Lancaster himself. Although Lancaster knew and associated obliquely with Nelson, and would in 1805 rename the school "Nelson House," it is unlikely that Nelson's nephews attended the school.[60] It is more likely the name of Nelson lured the Schopenhauers to his school, because Johanna certainly prided herself on meeting Nelson and Lady Hamilton in 1800 in Hamburg.

The physical structure of Wimbledon School for Young Noblemen and Gentlemen would have itself appealed to the Schopenhauers. Surrounded

---

[57] See Bridgwater, *Arthur Schopenhauer's English Schooling*, p. 261 and pp. 238–41, Lorenz Meyer's letter to Schopenhauer, 22 July 1803.

[58] Johanna mentioned the Percivals to Arthur in a letter from 19 July 1803 (see Lütkehaus, *Die Schopenhauers*, p. 53) and Schopenhauer mentions the young Percival twice in his travel diary; see Schopenhauer, *Reisetagebücher*, pp. 40–41, the entries for 3 and 6 June 1803.

[59] Johanna Schopenhauer, *A Lady Travels*, p. 198.

[60] See Bridgwater, *Arthur Schopenhauer's English Schooling*, p. 205. Bridgwater suggests that several of Nelson's nephews may have visited Lancaster socially and that he may have dropped the name "Nelson" in such a way as to suggest that they had been his students. This would have appealed to the snobbery of Johanna.

by spacious gardens and an orchard, the grand mansion, which was constructed in 1613 in the Dutch-Jacobean style, was originally the home of a prosperous merchant, Robert Bell, a member of the Managing Committee of the East India Company and the Master of the Girdlers Company of London.[61] After changing hands during the next century and one half, including a stint as an unsuccessful inn, it was purchased in 1789 by the Anglican minister Thomas Lancaster, who was the vicar of St. Mary the Virgin Church in the nearby village of Merton Park. It was through this position that Lancaster became acquainted with Lord Nelson, who lived in Merton for eighteen months between 1801 and 1803. When Schopenhauer attended the school, there were about sixty students between the ages of six and sixteen. These students were "unruly simpletons," as Schopenhauer must have described them to Lorenz Meyer.[62] The school had four fulltime resident teachers and several part-time teachers, with the latter taking responsibility for the educational extras that were available for additional fees, such as dancing, drawing, fencing, music, and singing. According to Lancaster's *A Plan of Education*, the regular subjects taught in his academy included elocution, reading, writing in Latin, French, and Greek, arithmetic, "merchants accounts," mathematics, geography, history, and biography.[63] Johanna noted that the curriculum of Wimbledon School completely ignored "other subjects worth knowing, such as we teach our children in Germany."[64] Although she did not say what these subjects were, the sciences such as physics and astronomy are conspicuous by their absence.

The students were divided into two groups: regular and special boarders. The latter paid three times the amount of the former, according to Johanna. Quite naturally, Arthur was a special boarder, a distinction that his mother noted spared him the poor dinner fare of the regular students and afforded him the privilege of recreation in the pleasure gardens and

---

[61] The mansion has been restored and renamed Eagle House. It serves now as the home of the Al-Furgan Islamic Heritage Foundation, something that would have upset both the Reverend Lancaster and Schopenhauer, but for very different reasons.

[62] Lorenz Meyer refers to Arthur's fellow students as "unruly simpletons" in a letter, as if he was repeating what Arthur had already written; see Bridgwater, *Arthur Schopenhauer's English Schooling*, p. 247.

[63] See ibid., pp. 288–300 for a comparison between Lancaster's educational plan and those of more progressive English institutions. Lancaster's *A Plan of Education* first appeared in 1794 and received a second publishing in 1797.

[64] Johanna Schopenhauer, *A Lady Travels*, p. 198f.

orchard, whereas the other students were confined to the "dreary courtyard and were beaten pitilessly should they sneak into those forbidden
regions."[65] All of the students, however, had well-to-do parents, but she
also observed that the regular students received an extra lesson by being
excluded from the privileged playgrounds; namely, "money should be
the goal towards which to strive."[66] Because Arthur was not an ordinary
student, it would appear that Johanna was subconsciously depriving her
son of this lesson. This, however, may not have been the case. Arthur's
status as the son of a wealthy merchant, as well as Johanna's keen sense of
social status, probably mandated that her son receive the best of the best
available, despite Heinrich Floris's complaints about the costs. Besides,
she may have hoped that the other students' envy of Arthur's status would
serve to awaken her son's aspiration for wealth.

Instruction at Wimbledon School was of a kind common to most
English academies, and it was far from the progressive spirit of Dr.
Runge's school and the few progressive institutions in England. Runge
strove to avoid brutal authoritarianism and to instill a humane spirit and
rational attitude in his students. The method of instruction at Wimbledon
School was mechanical, by rote, and always motivated by threat of the rod.
Johanna called it "an extremely pedantic form of education . . . [it] robs the
Englishman at an early age of any chance of achieving an independent view
of life."[67] Despite the advantages Arthur enjoyed as a special boarder, the
staid and uninspired atmosphere of Wimbledon School must have been
particularly difficult. He was disposed to being boisterous, independent,
and curious, and he had a propensity for entering into quarrels, both intellectual and physical. It is difficult to imagine that his character would have
suffered transformation into that of a quiet, demure, and obedient student.
It is likely, therefore, that he suffered the rod on more than one occasion,
and Johanna's account of the disciplinary practices at Wimbledon School
were derived from Arthur's personal experiences. If a student failed to
learn a lesson or misbehaved at play, the punishment was to memorize a
page of Latin or Greek. If the student failed in this task, he was sent to

[65] Ibid., p. 199.

[66] Ibid.

[67] Johanna Schopenhauer, *Sämmtliche Schriften*, 24 vols. (Leipzig/Frankfurt am Main: F. A.
Brockhaus, 1st ed. 1830–31; 2nd ed., 1834), Vol. 16, p. 118, cited in Bridgwater, *Arthur
Schopenhauer's English Schooling*, p. 316.

Lancaster's office, where he received seven or eight stout blows with the cane. This was done, Johanna observed, "with no regard as to whether the boy was six or sixteen, and in a most disgraceful manner."[68] The same sort of punishment was meted out to a student accused by one of his peers of some offense. As long as the accused denied the offense, no punishment would be exacted, but the accuser would then line up a series of witnesses and "even if he and they were obviously lying, the accused would be punished, unless he in turn could call other witnesses to prove his innocence. It was all coldly formal, as in the English court. No thought was given to getting to know the character of the child, his sense of appreciation of right or wrong, or to encouraging a love of true justice."[69]

It is easy to understand Schopenhauer's failure to establish friendships with his English classmates. At fifteen he was among the older students at Wimbledon, and he was more cosmopolitan and sophisticated than his British peers. He was alienated by the dull routines of the school and the ease with which his fellow students complied with them. He must have been amused by Lancaster's insistence that his young gentlemen speak French during the period between their morning and evening prayers. Vicesimus Knox, one of England's more progressive educators of that time, reported that this practice led to two undesirable results. The boys either learned to speak "a barbarous broken French" or would "condemn themselves to silence."[70] Schopenhauer was fluent in French, and he must have viewed contemptuously the other boys' fragmented French or stupid silence. It is likely that he taunted these poor souls, given his tendency toward mischief. It is also likely that they retaliated. Johanna mentioned the loss of a tie pin, pencil, and penknife she had sent as presents. Presumably, they were stolen.[71] Schopenhauer's unhappiness seems to have stemmed from the combination of the stifling atmosphere at Wimbledon School, its dull and mechanical mode of education, the uncongenial natures of its students, his parents' carping about his

---

[68] Johanna Schopenhauer, *A Lady Travels*, p. 200.
[69] Ibid., Johanna's description of punishment at Wimbledon School strongly suggests that Arthur felt the rod – perhaps on more than one occasion.
[70] Vicesimus Knox, *Liberal Education* (9th ed., 1788) Vol. 1, p. 186; quoted in Bridgwater, *Arthur Schopenhauer's English Schooling*, p. 296.
[71] See Lütkehaus, *Die Schopenhauers*, p. 53, Johanna to Arthur, 19 July 1803. She promised her son that she would give him an even finer tiepin when he rejoined her in London.

penmanship, and Johanna's cheerful accounts of her experiences in Scotland. Yet what appears to have moved him to state his hatred for the entire nation to his Hamburg friend Lorenz Meyer was his experience of the shallow religiosity displayed by the English observance of the Sabbath. Each day commenced and closed with prayers, but Arthur found Sundays to be even worse. Lancaster began the day by subjecting his students to a practice run of the sermon that he would deliver later at his nearby church in Merton. Then the boys, dressed in their Sunday best, were marched by their teachers to a two-hour sermon at the church in Wimbledon. In the afternoon and in the evening, they were compelled to attend additional services. During the times between services they were allowed either to read the Bible or to stroll with their instructors. Any boy who deviated from this routine was shown the error of his ways by the good Reverend's cane. It is easy to imagine that Arthur had some personal experience with the consequences of such deviations.

It was in regard to his dreadful experiences of the Sabbath that prompted Schopenhauer to articulate his hope, so roundly criticized by his mother, that the truth would burn through the "Egyptian darkness in England with its torch." After complaining about the bombast of her son's language, Johanna playfully chided Arthur: "I must be allowed to laugh a bit too. Do you know how many wars I had with you this winter and previously, when you wanted to undertake nothing proper on Sundays and holidays, because it was your duty to rest? Now you have had enough of your every Sunday day of rest."[72] Certainly, Arthur took no solace in his mother's response. It is doubtful that he appreciated the irony that made his mother laugh.

In her published travel diary, Johanna also complained about "the fanatical pedantry with which the sanctity of the Sabbath is guarded here, surpassing even that of the Jews who prohibit only work, not play."[73] She was also sensitive to the toll it took on the young: "Children, alas, fare badly, as special schools have been set up for them on Sunday evenings. They are marched there in a procession, after having to recite the rather senseless and dull liturgy of the Church of England twice at church and once at home."[74] It is interesting to notice how closely Johanna's

---

[72] Ibid., p. 59, Johanna to Arthur, 4 August 1803.
[73] Johanna Schopenhauer, *A Lady Travels*, p. 162.
[74] Ibid., p. 163.

pejorative language will foreshadow Arthur's, but it is more interesting to notice that her last remark described Sundays at Wimbledon
School.[75] Like her son, she loathed the British Sabbath. Yet, instead
of sympathizing with her son's misery, she laughed at it. To be fair to
Johanna, these remarks were published ten years after the fact, and it
could have been the case that she was persuaded to Arthur's perspective
later. Yet this is not a credible explanation if one accepts the veracity of her
reminiscences, for she also delighted in recalling how she had shocked her
British acquaintances by relating how in Germany they played cards on
Sunday, and "sometimes for a lot of money."[76] Certainly, the light-hearted
and playful Johanna could have expressed her sympathy for Arthur's complaints about the Sabbath, but she chose to exploit the opportunity to her
advantage. His experiences at Wimbledon School should teach him that
she had been right about Sundays and holidays in Hamburg. He had
now received in England what he thought he wanted in Germany, and
he found this to be undesirable. This should show him that mother knew
best. Moreover, Johanna suggested that by placing him in Wimbledon
School, his parents also had his best interests in mind, even though they
were contrary to his current wishes. It was unlikely, however, that Arthur
drew this inference. When he read Johanna's published travel journal,
it is likely that Arthur felt that his mother was amused by her son's
despair.

Schopenhauer would forget neither the narrow-minded religiosity nor
the Reverend. With an uncanny ability to relive and recast his scorn
decades after the fact, he condemned in unrestrained terms what he
regarded as the pernicious effects of the Anglican Church and ministers
on the national character of the British. Some of his diatribes occur
in unexpected places. Thus forty-eight years after his experiences in
England, within the essay, "Sketch of a History of the Doctrine of the Ideal
and Real," from the first volume of *Parerga and Paralipomena*, he provided
a summary of European philosophy from the French philosopher René
Descartes to his own on what he regarded as one of the two most difficult
problems for modern philosophy, accounting for the relationship between
human experiences of things (the ideal) and things in themselves (the

---

[75] It has been frequently claimed that Johanna used Arthur's travel journal to refresh her memory
   when she was writing *A Lady Travels*. This very well may be a case in point.
[76] Ibid., p. 162.

real).[77] Although his aims in this essay were to situate his philosophy within the mainstream of European modern philosophy and to claim that his philosophy was the first to solve this central problem, he mentioned John Locke's admission that it was possible for the mind to be material and how "in his own day it exposed him to the malicious attacks of an artful Anglican priest, the Bishop of Worcester."[78] Schopenhauer then provided a lengthy footnote:

There is no Church that dreads the light more than does the English just because no other has at stake such great pecuniary interests, its income amounting to 5,000,000 pounds sterling, which is said to be 40,000 pounds more than the income of the whole of the remaining Christian clergy of both hemispheres taken together. On the other side, there is no nation which is so painful to see methodically stupefied by the most degrading blind faith than the English, who surpass all others in intelligence. The root of the evil is that there is no ministry of public instruction and hence that this has hitherto remained entirely in the hands of the parsons. These have taken good care that two-thirds of the nation will not be able to read and write; in fact, from time to time, they even have the audacity with the most ludicrous presumption to yelp at the natural sciences. It is, therefore, a human duty to smuggle into England, through every conceivable channel, light, liberal-mindedness, and science, so that the best-fed of all priests may have their business brought to an end. When English people of education display on the Continent their Jewish sabbatarian superstition and other stupid bigotry, they should be treated with undisguised derision, *until they are shamed into common sense* [Schopenhauer's English], for such things are a scandal to Europe and should no longer be tolerated. Therefore even in the ordinary course of life, we should never make the least concession to the superstition of the English Church, but should at once stand up to it in the most caustic and trenchant manner whenever it puts in an appearance. For no arrogance exceeds that of Anglican parsons; on the Continent, therefore, this must suffer humiliation; so that a portion thereof is taken home, where there is lack of it. For the audacity of Anglican parsons and of their slavish followers is quite incredible, even at the present time; it should, therefore, be confined to the island and, when it ventures to show itself on the Continent, it should be made to play the role of owl by day.

Schopenhauer's rant against the Anglican Church and "Anglican parsons" continued in *Parerga and Paralipomena*. This time, instead of occurring in a footnote, it intrudes into an idealistic analysis of occult

---

77 The second problem concerned the freedom of the will. With his characteristic lack of modesty, Schopenhauer claimed to have solved both problems; see his *Prize Essay on the Freedom of the Will*, trans. E. F. J. Payne (Cambridge: Cambridge University Press, 1999).

78 Schopenhauer, *Parerga and Paralipomena*, Vol. 2, p. 16/*Sämtliche Werke*, Vol. 6, p. 16. Schopenhauer is referring here to Edward Stillingfleet (1635–99), Bishop of Worcester, who attacked Locke, especially for "undermining the trinity," in *Vindication of the Doctrine of the Trinity* (1696).

phenomena, such as spirit-seeing, clairvoyance, animal magnetism, and telekinesis, in "Essay on Spirit Seeing and Everything Connected Therewith." There he diagnosed the cause of the tremendous financial support for the church: "The law of primogeniture is the real source of the scandalous English obscurantism that hoaxes the people, namely the law that makes it necessary for the aristocracy (taken in the widest sense) to provide for their younger sons. If they are not fit for the Navy or Army, the 'Church Establishment' (characteristic term) with its revenue of five million [pounds sterling] a year affords them a *charitable institution*. Thus for a young country gentleman a 'living' is procured (also a characteristic expression) either through favor or for money."[79] Naturally, he condemned this practice: "It is the most shameless simony in the world."[80] This was especially true when this practice is contrasted with the wretched state of affairs in Ireland, where "thousands of whose inhabitants die of starvation, must, in addition to her own Catholic clergy voluntarily paid for from her own resources, maintain an ideal army of Protestant clergy with an archbishop, twelve bishops, and a host of deans and rectors, although not directly at the expense of the people, but from church property."[81] The moral hypocrisy of the church rankled Schopenhauer even more deeply, given the demoralizing effects of the parsons' views of the Sabbath: "When parsons tell the people a pack of lies by saying that half the virtues consist in spending Sundays in idleness and blabbing in church, and that one of the greatest vices, paving the way to all others, is '*Sabbathbreaking*' [Schopenhauer's English]; that is, not spending Sundays in idleness. And so those papers that give accounts of criminals under sentence of death, they explained their whole career of crime from the shocking vice of 'Sabbathbreaking'."[82]

The preaching of moral nonsense concerning the virtues of keeping the Sabbath had especially ruinous effects, Schopenhauer argued, because it enabled its practitioners to engage in some of the most morally reprehensible behavior with a good conscience:

Surely the ordinary man must believe that, if only, as his spiritual guides impress on him, he follows "*a strict observance of the holy Sabbath and a regular attendance on divine service*" [Schopenhauer's English], in other words, if only on Sundays he idles away

---

[79] Ibid., Vol. 1, p. 270/ibid., Vol. 5, p. 287.
[80] Ibid., Vol. 1, p. 271/ibid., Vol. 5, p. 288.
[81] Ibid., Vol. 1, p. 272/ibid., Vol. 5, p. 289.
[82] Ibid., Vol. 1, p. 272f./ibid., Vol. 5, p. 289.

his time inviolably and thoroughly and does not fail to sit in church for two hours to hear the same litany for the thousandth time and to rattle it off *a tempo* – that if only he does all this, he can reckon on some indulgence with regard to one thing or another which he occasionally permits himself to do. Those devils in human form, the slave-owners and slave-traders in the free states of North America (they should be called the Slave States), are, as a rule, orthodox and pious Anglicans who would regard it as a grave sin to work on Sundays and who, confident of this and of their regular attendance at church, hope for eternal happiness.[83]

Sabbath-keeping devils in human form, of course, could also practice, in good faith, even worse deeds: "Then think of the Christians in America whose inhabitants were for the most part, and in Cuba, entirely exterminated."[84] Slaves and Native Americans, however, did not keep the Sabbath, so they were guilty of the vice of "Sabbathbreaking."

Schopenhauer's scathing indictment of Anglican parsons utilized terms parallel to those he used to blast post-Kantian, German philosophers, especially his favorite targets for abuse, Johann Fichte, Friedrich Schelling, and Georg Hegel, each one of whom he also accused of having "bread-winning" motivations, of being obscurants, and of producing a corrupting influence on his audience. Depending on his point of emphasis, the crimes of his philosophical contemporaries were often graver than those of the Anglicans. Sometimes, however, the reverse was the case. Thus he found both sets guilty of being motivated by self-serving and pecuniary interests, but the post-Kantians denigrated a more noble calling by living from philosophy, whereas the British parsons abused religion. Yet the Anglicans affected a more intelligent public, he held, but the German idealists despoiled Kant, and by erasing the important insights of Germany's greatest philosopher, they returned the level of philosophical understanding to that of the British, who were ignorant of the Kantian philosophy. And if the idealists had made Kant passé in Germany, he thought that Kant and others could be exported to England as a means to overcome the Church: "On the whole, it is high time that missions of reason, enlightenment, and anti-clericalism were sent to England with von Bohlen's and Strauss' biblical criticisms in one hand and the *Critique of Pure Reason* in the other, in order to stop the business of those self-styled *reverend* parsons, the most arrogant and impudent in the world and put an

[83] Ibid., Vol. 2, p. 355f./ibid., Vol. 6, p. 376f.
[84] Ibid., Vol. 2, p. 356/ibid., Vol. 6, p. 377.

end to the scandal."[85] Schopenhauer could entertain this hope about the British, and he would try to bring Kant's first critique to England, because the Church of England had darkened the Enlightenment by repressing only science and philosophy, and German obscurantism functioned by more insidious means. The post-Kantians' convoluted and cumbersome writing styles did more than hide the poverty of their thought via incomprehensible language wrapped in ponderous sentence structures; they had a mind-numbing effect on a generation of Germans. They learned to speak all day without saying a thing, and they were rendered incapable of recognizing clearly stated truths, such as those expressed by his philosophy.[86]

If Schopenhauer's three months at Wimbledon School, and his additional three months in England, produced a lasting bitterness toward England, it was only directed toward the Church of England and what he found to be its strangling effects on elements of that nation's social and intellectual life. He was an anglophile his entire life. He continued to believe that the English were the most intelligent of all Europeans; he read the London *Times* throughout his life; and he had a deep and abiding respect for English writers and philosophers. His own writing style, moreover, bears a greater resemblance to those of John Locke, George Berkeley, and David Hume than it does to those of his much beloved Kant and many of his philosophical contemporaries. Twenty-seven years after his time in England, when he may have been attempting to hand

---

[85] Ibid., Vol. 1, p. 269f./ibid., Vol. 5, p. 287. Schopenhauer is referring to Peter von Bohlen (1796–1840), orientalist and author of *Genesis: Historically-Critically Explained* [*Die Genesis, historisch-kritisch erläutert*, 1835], and David Friedrich Strauss (1808–73), theologian and biblical critic, best known for his *The Life of Jesus Critically Examined*, 2 vols. [*Das Leben Jesu Kritisch bearbeitet*, 1835–6]. Both of these authors tended to reject elements of Christianity that ran counter to science and to interpret Christian documents in their historical context, understanding Christian beliefs in anthropological and secular terms. Strauss attempted to refute Schopenhauer's pessimism in his *The Old and New Faith* [*Der alte und der neue Glaube*] (Stuttgart, 1872), an attack that raised Nietzsche's hackles in one of his "Untimely Meditations," "David Strauss, the Confessor and Writer" ["David Strauss, der Bekenner und Schriftsteller," 1873; in Untimely Meditations, trans. R. J. Hollingdale. Cambridge: Cambride University Press, 1983], Sects. 6, 7.

[86] He accused Hegel, in particular, of having "had on philosophy and thus on German literature generally, an extreme stupefying, one might say pestilential, influence." The problem was that Hegel's convoluted and cumbersome style was imitated by others, he thought, and simply allowed people to speak all day without saying a thing; see *On the Basis of Morality*, p. 14/*Sämtliche Werke*, Vol. 4, *Die beiden Grundprobleme der Ethik*, p. xvii.

Kant to the British – although he did not have von Bohlen's and Strauss' biblical criticisms in his other hand – he wrote, in English, the following to an anonymous editor: "As to my knowledge of the English language I owe it chiefly to have received part of my education in England – where I was even for a while a parlour boarder at the Revd Mr. Lancasters in Wimbledon, in 1803, – further to a good deal of English reading ever since, lastly to having lived very much in English company on the continent. My English accent is such as to have made me very frequently been mistaken [sic.] by Englishmen for their countryman at first acquaintance, though I confess that usually in the course of half an hour they would be undeceived."[87]

All of these reflections came years later, well after the fact. At this point in his life, Schopenhauer is a boy savoring his hatred for the entire nation and dreaming of blazing truths setting the darkness afire. Still, these early experiences help reveal the genius behind Schopenhauer's philosophical method. An initial affective response calls attention to a problem. Subsequent experience gives rise to an explanation, which is followed by a recognition of the means for eliminating that which gave rise to the emotion in the first place. What makes all of this possible is the truth. With the exception of his responses to the beautiful and the sublime, whether in nature or in great works of art, Schopenhauer's beginning philosophical prompts are negative in tone. Even his account of the drive itself to philosophize, prompted by astonishment, is based on the recognition of the ubiquity of suffering and death, and the satisfaction of philosophical desire is the truth, an explanation and a solution for the "ever-disquieting riddle of existence."[88] Ultimately, he would find that the truth itself brought consolation. But for now, it is Arthur's liberation from the disquietude of Wimbledon School that is needed.

The journal entry for Arthur's release from Wimbledon School, 20 September 1803, is surprisingly flat. Whereas one would have expected it to include some unhappy slams at the good Reverend Lancaster and Arthur's dull classmates, or some expressions of joy, he simply noted that he traveled to London alone, where he rejoined his parents, who had been

---

[87] Schopenhauer, *Gesammelte Briefe*, p. 119, Schopenhauer to the "Author of Damiron's Analysis", 21 December 1829.

[88] Schopenhauer, *The World as Will and Representation*, Vol. 2, p. 171/*Sämtliche Werke*, Vol. 3, p. 189.

there for two weeks. It rained incessantly that day, and Arthur arrived at his destination soaked to the bone. The rain continued the next day, spoiling the family's plan to attend the horse races at Enfield. Four days later, he continued his journal, noting that he had not included entries those days, because the family had already viewed all of London's significant sights during their earlier stay. Indeed, the Schopenhauers found themselves in London longer than they originally anticipated, because renewed hostility between England and France had made travel from Dover to Calais impossible.

Seeing the World

The Schopenhauers revisited earlier attractions, toured grand homes, visited museums, and dined with family friends to pass the time. While in London, they attended a number of performances of Shakespeare, including *Much Ado about Nothing* at Drury Lane and *Hamlet* and *Richard III* at Covent Garden. It is obvious that Arthur was already familiar with Shakespeare, and his journal focused on the quality of the performances rather than the content of the plays. He did, however, complain about the performance of *Richard III*, because it had altered the script, making it difficult to recognize the play. Still, Arthur praised the actor Cooke's interpretation of King Richard, crediting him with surpassing "all English acting I have seen. I far prefer him to Kemble. He had only erred in not sufficiently disfiguring himself, since his ugliness and deformity is alluded to during the entire play."[89] Johanna was also taken by Mr. Cooke, "a great and true actor," and like her son, she was taken by Cooke's Richard: "Never before was that part played as he played it, nor will it ever be again."[90]

Shakespeare, or more specifically his tomb, had already made a deep impression on the young Schopenhauer. Like countless tourists before and after them, the Schopenhauers toured Westminster Abbey during the first layover in London. Arthur was struck by the serious mien of the statue of Shakespeare, which stood over his tomb, and by the "beautiful"

---

[89] Schopenhauer, *Reisetagebücher*, p. 65, entry for 3 October 1803. Arthur incorrectly referred to Cooke as "Cook." Kemble was Cooke's rival as the great tragedic actor of that time.

[90] In *A Lady Travels*, p. 178, Johanna mentioned Cooke's critics' complaint that one could observe his Richard in all other parts he played. She also complained about the tendencies of actors to alter Shakespeare's scripts (p. 179).

lines about the ephemeral nature of life, from *The Tempest*, which were written on parchment and to which the stony bard points. Naturally, these lines find their way into Arthur's journal:

> The cloud-capp'd towers, the gorgeous palaces,
> The solemn temples, the great globe itself,
> Yea, all which it inherits, shall dissolve
> And, like this insubstantial pageant faded,
> Leave not a rack behind. We are such stuff
> As dreams are made on, and our little life
> Is rounded with sleep.[91]

This sad reflection was supplemented in Arthur's journal by his notice of John Gay's quip, which was recorded below his bust:

> Life is a jest, and all things show it:
> I thought so once, and now I know it.[92]

Three years later, Arthur used Gay's lines within a letter in response to his mother's descriptions of the horrors of the battle of Weimar.[93] In reply, Johanna chided her son's lament concerning the wretchedness of life, and she seems to recommend her reaction as a model: "I now live completely after my heart's wishes; quite calmly, loved by splendent people. . . . "[94] Arthur's heart aches at the suffering of others; his mother's heart beats to realize her own desires. Trying circumstances can bring out the best in people, she suggested, and remaining aloof from life's woes can become the means to deprive them of their sting. Eventually, Arthur too would live completely after his heart's wishes, and he would remain aloof from life's tribulations and woes by philosophically reflecting on them. However, he would not do so surrounded by splendent people who loved him.

Johanna also quoted the same lines from Shakespeare's *The Tempest* in her travel journal, but unlike her son, she did not reflect philosophically on the human condition. The tombs of kings, heroes, and poets united in a single place those who were separated by social standing, space, and time, Arthur noted. Death was the great leveler. Arthur wondered what these

---

[91] Schopenhauer, *Reisetagebücher*, p. 50, entry for 14 June 1803.
[92] Ibid.
[93] Schopenhauer, *Gesammelte Briefe*, p. 1, Schopenhauer to Johanna, 9 November 1806.
[94] Lütkehaus, *Die Schopenhauers*, p. 116, Johanna to Schopenhauer 14 November 1806.

great men took with them. He answered his own question: "The Kings left behind crown and scepter, heroes their weapons, poets their reputation; but the great spirits among them, whose distinction came from themselves and not from things external to them, take their greatness with them. They take everything they had here."[95] Johanna, however, reflected on and criticized the architecture, the organization, and the shabby conditions of the Abbey. She found the wax effigies of England's Kings and Queens particularly off-putting: "Veritable scarecrows [that] should have been destroyed long ago for the only interest is in the clothes they wore in life. If Queen Elizabeth, in particular, knew what a hideous picture she presents here to posterity, that vanity, which was so characteristic of her life, would not let her rest easily in her grave."[96] Arthur, however, failed to notice that the Kings and Queens left their clothing behind.

Finally, after a two-week delay, each day of which Arthur had hoped would be the day of their departure, the Schopenhauers left London. After traveling for two days, they reached Harwich, a town Arthur found to be small, dirty, and lacking in anything worth seeing. They were stuck in this miserable place for another day, as the family waited for a decent wind for their sea crossing to Rotterdam. After a wretched, stormy forty-hour crossing, they arrived at Maalvis and traveled the three miles in coach to Rotterdam. Arthur, who was never able to gain his sea-legs, was thoroughly miserable, and he was sick in bed during the crossing. His parents fared only slightly better. On their sojourn through Holland, they paused in Gorkum, where Arthur observed the Gothic church where his maternal great-great-grandfather had been a preacher. The Schopenhauers then traveled through Breda, Antwerp, Malines, Brussels, Bergen, Péronne, and Senlis and they arrived at Paris on 27 November 1803.

Paris disappointed Arthur, who found it wanting in comparison to London. Outside of the main boulevards, Paris was dirty and poorly lighted. Foot travel was dangerous in its narrow streets, where one had to be on watch for carriages and wagons. Even its best boutiques paled next to those of London. The family enjoyed the typical tours of the well-to-do, which included locations associated with the Revolution and its aftermath.

[95] Schopenhauer, *Reisetagebücher*, p. 51f., entry for 14 June 1803.
[96] Johanna Schopenhauer, *A Lady Travels*, p. 225. She also complained that the family failed to locate the tombs of Swift, Pope, and her and Arthur's beloved Lawrence Sterne.

The location of the Bastille, whose storming had sent an excited Heinrich Floris scurrying back on a weekday to his country estate to share the good news with Johanna, moved Arthur to reflect on the "eternal misery, the silent laments, and the hopeless misery of the imprisoned."[97] The young Schopenhauer marveled at the curious collection of animals at the Jardin des Plantes, especially the elephants, but he failed to sympathize with the plight of these captives. Naturally, the family visited the Louvre, and on more than one occasion. Arthur was overwhelmed by the quality and magnitude of its collections. He also had the good fortune to observe a number of art treasures recently "liberated" by Napoleon, such as the Laocoon, the Vatican Apollo, the Venus of Medici, and the Dying Gladiator. Nine days earlier, he had observed this red-fingered patron himself at the Theatre des Français. The First Consul's entrance at the theater was announced by a thunderous round of applause, which immediately inclined Arthur to move closer for a better look at his face. His physiognomic quest failed, however. The theater was too dark. Still, he was impressed with the simplicity of Bonaparte's uniform and the fact that he was accompanied only by two officers; "otherwise he was completely alone."[98]

Approximately six weeks later, on 15 January 1804, Schopenhauer caught a second glimpse of the First Consul in Tulleries Plaza. This time he was mounted on a magnificent white horse, reviewing 6,000 Italian troops. Arthur observed the spectacle from a comfortable window seat in a nearby hotel. But once again, he was disappointed. Although he could clearly observe Napoleon's figure and movements, he still could not perceive his facial features. Finally, the next evening in the Theatre Faideau, he got a closer look at the soon to be self-crowned Emperor of the French: "The First Consul was there. I was seated so that I was able to see him well during the entire performance."[99] Curiously, Schopenhauer did not record his impressions of Napoleon's face.

Schopenhauer's later philosophical *bête noire*, G. W. F. Hegel, also encountered a mounted, troop-reviewing Napoleon some thirty months later. On 13 October 1806, the day before the Battle of Jena, where the French quickly routed the Prussian troops and thereby ended any German

[97] Schopenhauer, *Reisetagebücher*, p. 92, entry for 12 December 1803.

[98] Ibid., p. 81, entry for 28 November 1803.

[99] Ibid., p. 108, entry for 16 January 1804.

hope to reestablish the Holy Roman Empire, which Napoleon had put to death three months earlier by maneuvering sixteen of its member states to form the paper giant, the Confederation of the Rhine, Hegel observed, "I saw the Emperor – this world soul (*Weltgeist*) – riding out of the city on reconnaissance. It is indeed a wonderful sensation to see such an individual, who, concentrated here in a single point, astride a horse, reaches out over the world and masters it. . . . "[100] While Hegel was scrambling to safeguard and finish the *Phenomenology of Spirit* [*Phänomenologie des Geistes*, 1807], due to the mischief of this horse-riding "world soul," he found it impossible not to admire Napoleon. But once Hegel subjected this "wonderful feeling" to philosophical contemplation, he realized that it was not the world soul that he observed that day in Jena. Instead, it was a "world historic individual," whose passions and ambitions did the bidding of spirit and helped drive history to its next stage, toward spirit's coming to knowledge of itself.[101]

Hegel's initial response to Napoleon, the "wonderful feeling" that resulted from seeing the world soul on horseback, was more sophisticated than Schopenhauer's, even though Hegel himself regarded feelings as the lowest form of cognition. He was, however, thirty-six years old, a lecturer at Jena, and in the process of laying the foundations for his system of philosophy. Schopenhauer was a teenager, drawn to Napoleon's celebrity without any curiosity about his historic significance. Yet after the War of Liberation in 1813 and the subsequent invasion of France, which sent a defeated Napoleon, still maintaining his title of Emperor, to exile on the island of Elba, Schopenhauer was in Dresden beginning his labors on *The World as Will and Representation*. Although many were calling for Napoleon's head, this ersatz world soul became an object for his philosophical reflection. Napoleon, he wrote, was no more culpable than numerous other individuals who would have done the same, had they had his greater powers of reasoning and understanding, his courage, and his historic opportunities. He was just driven by his egoism, as are most people, and he, as they, pursued his own interests at the expense

---

[100] Hegel, *The Letters*, trans. Clark Butler and Christiane Seiler (Bloomington: Indiana University Press, 1984), p. 114. This is a letter from Hegel to his friend and promoter, Friedrich Immanual Niethammer.

[101] Hegel, *The Philosophy of History*, trans. J. Sibree (New York: Dover, 1956), p. 31, where Napoleon is mentioned as a world historical individual, along with Alexander the Great and Julius Caesar.

of others. Had others had Napoleon's power, they would have done the
same. But Napoleon's rare power also

> . . . revealed the whole malice of the human will; and the suffering of his age, as the
> necessary other side of the will, revealed the misery that is inseparably united with
> the evil will, whose total appearance is the world. But this is just the purpose of the
> world; that it will recognize the unspeakable misery with which the will to life is bound
> and is, strictly speaking, one. Bonaparte's appearance thus contributes greatly to this
> purpose. The purpose of the world is not to be an insipid fool's paradise; rather, it is
> to be a tragedy in which the will to life recognizes itself and turns away from itself.
> Bonaparte is only a powerful mirror of the human will to life.
> The difference between the person who causes suffering and the person who suffers
> is only in the world of appearance. All of this is the one will to life which is identical
> with great suffering, and through cognition of this, it can turn away from itself and
> end itself.[102]

There is a curious parallel between Hegel's and Schopenhauer's analyses of Napoleon's significance. Both viewed him as an extraordinary individual, and both connected him to the purpose of the world. For Hegel he was a world historical individual whose ambitions and passions served to move history to its goal, just as Alexander the Great and Julius Caesar had done during their time. Each played a vital role in spirit's progress through time. For Schopenhauer, he was a man with unique abilities and courage, rare powers that enabled him to bring to the world stage the terrible spectacle of the will to life at war with itself, the grounds for the denial of the will.

The parallels, however, are partial, and they move to radically distinct standpoints. Napoleon advances history toward its goal. Hegel is keenly aware, moreover, of the "slaughter-bench" of history, but makes light of this by contemplating the "final purpose, destiny, or the nature and concept of Spirit." He uses this contemplation to keep himself from indulging in sentimental reflections and depressing emotions directed at the fact that men such as Napoleon "may treat other great and even sacred interests inconsiderately – a conduct which indeed subjects them to moral reprehension. But so mighty a figure must trample down many an innocent flower, crush to pieces many things in its path."[103] The

---

[102] Schopenhauer, *Manuscript Remains*, Vol. 1, p. 222/*Der handschriftliche Nachlaß*, Vol. 1, pp. 202–3.

[103] Hegel, *Reason in History*, trans. Robert S. Hartman (Indianapolis/New York: Bobbs-Merrill, 1953), p. 27.

phenomenon of Napoleon does not make things better in this world, according to Schopenhauer. It repeats merely the same – the will to life feasting on itself.[104] Alexander and Caesar had done likewise. There is nothing new about Napoleon on the stage of world history. It is the same story told in a different form. It is also one that can be seen at any time, at any place, provided one has sufficient vision to see it. Moreover, even if things work out in the end, Schopenhauer argued, it never undoes what has been done. Bloody means are not redeemed by noble ends. And it is the depressing emotions and the sentimental feelings occasioned by "trampled flowers" that provide the means for ascertaining the purpose of the world. As he continued to work out the first impression of his philosophy in Dresden, these general claims would receive more detail, but not in a manner directed against Hegel's views. Hegel was completely outside Schopenhauer's philosophical consciousness at that time. He would only become Schopenhauer's "black beast" after the failure of the product of his labor in Dresden.

Let us return to the teenaged Schopenhauer. After spending eighteen days in Paris, Arthur escaped his parents by sating the very ardent desire that led him to betray his own better hope to become a scholar and that seemed to destine him to become the future head of his father's business. He traveled by stagecoach for two days to Le Havre, and so great was his joy at renewing his acquaintance with the Grégoire de Blésimaires that he even thought that the motley crew of his fellow travelers was "entirely very good." Arthur felt as if he were dreaming, and when he arrived, "I could scarcely convince myself that I was actually in Havre."[105] At his arrival, Arthur had the type of experience that is common to anyone revisiting a scene of youth. The city seemed smaller than he remembered, but after a short while, he felt as if he had never been away. He managed to see all of his earlier acquaintances and he experienced again everything that he viewed as significant in the city. Although he spent eight days in Le

---

[104] In 1850, however, Schopenhauer's view of Napoleon is more harsh that it was in 1814, forgetting, as it were, his function of bringing to the world stage the spectacle of the will to life at war with itself: ". . . the predatory incursions of French hordes under the leadership of Bonaparte and the great efforts that were subsequently necessary to expel and punish that gang of robbers, had brought about a temporary neglect of the sciences and thus a certain decline in the general dissemination of knowledge," *Parerga and Paralipomena*, Vol. 2, pp. 346–7/*Sämtliche Werke*, Vol. 6, p. 367.

[105] Schopenhauer, *Reisetagebücher*, p. 95, entry for 15 December 1803.

Havre, his journal entry for those days is brief and merely a continuance of
that from the day he left Paris. It does not record anything that he would
not have wanted his parents to read, and there is no mention of what
he did with his "French brother" Anthime, which certainly would have
had some mischievous moments, and perhaps some imaginary amorous
advantages. He did note, however, that he was able to fulfill all of his
wishes, as he probably could not have done in London. He departed Le
Havre to rejoin his parents in Paris on Christmas Sunday.

The family spent approximately another month in Paris. They went
to the Louvre several more times and visited Notre Dame, which did
not measure up to Arthur's anticipations. He found it to be smaller and
less beautiful than Westminster Abbey, although he was impressed by its
great rose window. Naturally, they were drawn to visit Versailles, which
still bore the scars of the Revolution. Still, like countless others, Arthur
was overwhelmed and complained that he lacked the time to take in all of
it. Just as during their time in London, the family visited art galleries and
museums and attended plays and concerts.

Schopenhauer's parents, especially Johanna, despite her earlier fears
that Arthur might become a *bel esprit*, encouraged and directed the development of his aesthetic sensitivities. The European tour contributed significantly to his art education. He was exposed to numerous examples of
all kinds of works of great art, and his direct experiences with the arts
would later inform his aesthetics and lead him to develop a more elaborate
and heartfelt philosophy of art than the majority of his contemporaries.
He took great pride in his direct experiences of great works of art, and he
would use this against Kant's aesthetics, whose artificiality he attributed to
the fact that he " . . . probably never had the opportunity to see an important work of art."[106] And although he believed that Kant had performed
a lasting service to aesthetics by directing attention away from objects
referred to as "beautiful" and from the search for characteristics or properties of those objects, and by bringing it back to the person who made the
judgment that something was beautiful, his lack of personal experience of
beauty led him "not to start from the beautiful itself, from the intuitively
immediate beautiful, but from the *judgment* concerning the beautiful, the

---

[106] Schopenhauer, *The World as Will and Representation*, Vol. 1, p. 529/*Sämtliche Werke*, Vol. 1,
     p. 627.

so-called, and very badly so-called, judgment of taste."[107] He likened
Kant's theory to a theory of colors developed by an intelligent blind person who had to work from the accurate statements that others made about
color.[108] Thanks to his parents, and to the European tour, Schopenhauer
was never in this awkward position.

The Schopenhauers departed Paris after a two-month stay. Problems
occurred from the start. Even before they left the city limits, a wheel fell
from their carriage. Travel to Bordeaux was rough. Rugged mountain
roads and rain made additional repairs of the carriage necessary. One
can imagine that Arthur thought their travel efforts repaid themselves,
because he judged Bordeaux "the most beautiful city in France."[109] They
remained in Bordeaux for eight weeks, before they continued their travels
through southern France. In Montpellier, Arthur took in the gardens of
the perfumer, Ryban, where he lamented the fact that he was a month
too early to savor the fragrance and enjoy the colors of the thousands of
rose bushes. This perception of a lost opportunity to enjoy the beauty of
Ryban's gardens points to a curious feature of Arthur's aesthetic tastes.
The perfumer's gardens were utilitarian, designed for the efficient collection of rosebuds and petals; but throughout his journal, Schopenhauer
tended to express a greater sensitivity to natural beauty than the beauty
of works of art. And although this may simply be due to his age, natural
beauty in his aesthetics would turn out to be logically prior to that of great
works of art. Thus it serves as the basis for the beauty in art. But natural
beauty will turn out in the final analysis to be nonnatural, because it is
the genius of the artist who sees the universal in the particular, and who
intuits what will turn out to be a very un-Platonic Platonic Idea. It is not
the case that beauty, natural or artistic, resides in some set of properties
of some object, nor is it the case that beauty lies simply in the eyes of
the beholder; rather, the experience of the beautiful is a function of both
the observer and the observed, including the contemplation of a Platonic
Idea, in which the perceiver loses a sense of her or himself and becomes
one with the object. Everyday ways of experiencing things as the possible
means for sating or thwarting desires vanish, and time seems to stand still.

---

[107] Ibid., p. 531/ibid., p. 629.
[108] Ibid., p. 531/ibid., p. 629.
[109] Schopenhauer, *Reisetagebücher*, p. 120, entry for 5 February 1804.

Still, the aesthetic analysis of the enjoyment of the beautiful lies in the future. While on tour, the young Schopenhauer is still accumulating experiences of nature and art that would provide the material for his philosophy of the beautiful. To be sure, he employs the terms "beauty," "beautiful," and "sublime" within his travel diary, but only as a somewhat sophisticated teenager who lacks the more formal and classical education he would have received in a gymnasium. His experiences of ordinary states of affairs, those available to everyone, supply the basis for the future insights of the philosopher. In Austria, for example, his enjoyment of the beauty of nature was rudely disturbed: "Something that interrupts, in the most unpleasant and annoying manner, the stranger who comes to Lauterbrunn to observe the most sublime beauty, are the children of the farmers, who follow and surround him, begging incessantly. How completely different it is in Chamouny, where, excepting the *Crétins*, everyone would be ashamed to beg from a stranger."[110] In prescient form the young Schopenhauer recognized here the problem of aesthetics. Aesthetic enjoyment of both the beautiful and the sublime – the philosopher Schopenhauer would never write about "sublime beauty" – only temporarily silences the stings of the urges of the will.[111] There are always needy farmers' children whose begging returns us to the world as will. Aesthetic escape is, sadly, temporary.

Arthur encountered worse than annoying beggars during the tour, however. He witnessed the execution of three criminals in London:

This morning I attended a sad spectacle: I saw three humans hanged. It always remains the most shocking sight to see humans brought to a violent end. Nevertheless, an English hanging of this type is still not as gruesome as some executions. The

---

[110] Ibid., p. 210, entry for 29 May 1804.

[111] Both the feelings of the beautiful and the sublime involve a transition from normal cognition, which views objects as means to satisfy or thwart desire, to a state in which a person becomes a pure, will-less, painless, and timeless subject of cognition, a state in which the observer loses all sense of self and seems to become lost in the object of contemplation. The essential difference between these feelings concerns the transition from ordinary, interested cognition to that of becoming this pure subject; ". . . what distinguishes the feeling of the sublime from that of the beautiful is that, with the beautiful, pure cognition has gained the upper hand without struggle . . .," *The World as Will and Representation*, Vol. 1, p. 202/ *Sämtliche Werke*, Vol. 2, p. 238. Objects that prompt the feeling of the sublime are those that are threatening or hostile to a person, such as a raging storm at sea, whereas those related to the beautiful are unthreatening, like a sunny, colorful, tree-lined mountain valley. More will be said about this later.

unfortunate man certainly suffers less than half a minute: as soon as the scaffold drops, he does not move. One does not see his face, over which a white hood is pulled. I believe that the quick death does not occur from strangulation; rather the force of the fall breaks his neck, due to a knot in the rope. What confirms this is that all of their heads hang to the same side. This scene here is less horrible than elsewhere, since it is not done so ceremoniously. There are no pealing bells here for the poor sinners, execution shirt, and the like; the scaffold stands before the prison gates, and the crowd of spectators is not as large, because there are regular hangings every six weeks. I was at a window across from the prison, so close that I could discern the facial features of the delinquents. I shuddered when the rope was placed around their necks. This was a horrible moment. Their souls already appeared to be in the next world, and it was as if they did not notice anything. A clergyman was with them on the scaffold; he spoke continuously to one of them in particular. It was a piteous sight to see the anxiety that moved these men to prayer in their last moments. One of them moved his hands up and down as he prayed, and he made the same motion a couple of times after he had fallen.[112]

It appears that Schopenhauer had observed executions in his own country, because he found the British rituals less ceremonious than those of other places. His reactions also seem to support this conjecture. Although he viscerally reacted to the spectacle – he "shuddered" when the nooses were drawn around the necks of the condemned – he also was keen to observe the entire deadly scene. Just as he would with respect to Napoleon's face later in Paris, he carefully observed the faces of the criminals. Despite the fact that he found the praying man's gestures "piteous," and he judged the entire event to be a "sad spectacle," he distanced himself by analyzing the cause of death: a broken neck rather than strangulation. This was confirmed, he thought, by the fact that the neck of each of the men hung to the same side. He judged that the men had a quick death; it took less than half a minute.

The very evening of the execution, Schopenhauer attended the performance of a ventriloquist. Oddly, he devoted approximately as many words to the evening's entertainment as he did to the morning's. Unlike the execution, which just appeared to be a variation on something he had experienced before, this was a new experience: "I have never watched anything

---

[112] Schopenhauer, *Reisetagebücher*, pp. 43–4, entry for 8 June 1803. It is likely that the execution took place at Newgate Prison and that Schopenhauer and his parents had paid for a window seat for the hanging at the pub called Magpie and Stump; see Bridgwater, *Schopenhauer's English Schooling*, p. 125, fn. 18.

with as much astonishment and admiration as this ventriloquist."[113] From the sight of men dangling from the ends of ropes to the sound of another pitching his voice in different directions, Arthur does not recognize that both events were treated as forms of entertainment. The hanging allowed him to enjoy fear and pity, and the ventriloquist brought wonder and delight. Had the ventriloquist been at the execution, perhaps he could have thrown his voice into the dangling men, thus providing him with a truly extraordinary experience. And just as his parents purchased his entry for the performance by the ventriloquist, they also paid for his window seat at the execution.

Arthur's reflections on the freshly dead criminals were not profound. At most, the observations were clever about the cause of their deaths. At least he did recognize, in the case of the great dead at Westminster Abbey, that death was the great equalizer. Still, he identified with neither the lowly nor the exalted dead. This would change eleven months later, however, when the family would visit the ruins of a Roman amphitheater at Nîmes:

It was a strange sensation as I found myself on the same seats from which the Romans first watched their plays. I saw half-obliterated characters and letters carved in many seats, which were probably the names of those who sat here more than two thousand years ago. On other stones, names and coats of arms were carved with years and centuries, which make the inscriptions noteworthy as antiques, something that the tourist who was here in the 1500s and 1600s had likely not thought. The traces of the different centuries, which the gray stones have seen, soon leads one's reflections to the thousands of long decomposed humans who, throughout these many centuries, had walked across these ruins in their own day, just as I was doing today. If the duration of humans can be called brief, it is so in comparison with the duration of their works.[114]

The young man's reflections on the passing of generations expressed a melancholy mood and connoted a dim sense of his own mortality, a response he had neither to the deaths of the executed prisoners nor to the celebrated dead entombed in Westminster Abbey. As he walked along the ruins, he viewed his own activity in the same terms as those early attendees of the theater and the more recent tourists of the sixteenth and seventeenth centuries. His observations of the graffiti, the fading inscriptions from the Romans and the still legible names of the tourists, prompts his

---

[113] Ibid., p. 44, entry for 8 June 1803.
[114] Ibid., pp. 139–40, entry for 6 April 1804.

realization that the works of humans outlast flesh and blood, and that the more enduring works, like the amphitheater itself, outlast the scratching on the works by others. Schopenhauer's identification with those who came before him, "those long decomposed humans," evokes a "strange sensation," which is curiously not described in his writing. Just as his travel diary failed to articulate a philosophical explanation of his experience of the beautiful, it also failed to provide a philosophical analysis of the sublime: "Many objects of our perception excite the impression of the sublime; by virtue of their . . . great antiquity, and therefore their duration in time, we feel ourselves reduced to nothing in their presence, and yet revel in the pleasure of beholding them."[115] Schopenhauer, however, would have to read Kant before he could turn his experiences into the material for his aesthetics.

From Nîmes the family traveled to Marseilles, which, like Bordeaux, Arthur judged to be "the most beautiful city in France," due to the tastefully constructed stone houses in the new section of the city.[116] In this regard, he paid Marseilles the ultimate compliment: it was "actually similar to London."[117] Schopenhauer would vividly recall the next leg of the family's journey forty-six years later: "Insofar as inorganic nature does not consist of water, it has a very sad and even depressing effect on us when it manifests itself without anything organic. Instances of this are the districts that present us with merely bare rocks, particularly the long rocky valley without any vegetation, not far from Toulon, through which passes the road to Marseilles."[118] Toulon, however, contained something sadder and more depressing than an arid, rocky valley. Its grand arsenal included a prison whose inmates were displayed for the public like animals in an inhumane zoo. Naturally, the Schopenhauers were drawn to this popular tourist attraction.

The prisoners, the infamous "galley slaves," did all of the hard labor in the arsenal. Arthur was shocked by the wretched conditions in which the convicts served their time. The galley slaves were divided into three classes, based on the severity of their offenses and, if not in a perfectly retributive sense, their punishments were coordinated to an analogous

---

[115] Schopenhauer, *The World as Will and Representation*, Vol. 1, p. 206/*Sämtliche Werke*, Vol. 2, p. 245.

[116] Schopenhauer, *Reisetagebücher*, p. 146, entry for 8 April 1804.

[117] Ibid., p. 147, entry for 8 April 1804.

[118] Schopenhauer, *Parerga and Paralipomena*, Vol. 2, p. 425/*Sämtliche Werke*, Vol. 6, p. 453.

degree of severity. The first class of prisoners, army deserters and insubordinate soldiers, served the least amount of time and received the least severe punishment. They were allowed to walk freely around the arsenal, although each had a heavy iron ring placed around one leg. Members of the second class had committed worse crimes, although Schopenhauer does not mention their crimes or those committed by members of the third class. Those in the second class were forced to work and live while chained to another miscreant, but members of the third class, those guilty of the worst crimes, had the worst fate. They were chained to the benches of old and decrepit ships, which were not fit for service. The benches served both as their work stations and as their living quarters. These poor souls were fed bread and water, and their hopelessness, misery, and despair became palpable for Schopenhauer as he sympathized with their horrid existence: "Can one think of a more terrible feeling than that of one of these unfortunates as he is chained to the bench in the dark galley and from which nothing but death can separate him?"[119] This cruel sentence, he reflected, is even sometimes made worse, because many of the prisoners had the inseparable company of other men on each side of their bench.

The hellish conditions of the arsenal led Arthur to speculate on the fate of the few prisoners who, after ten, twelve, or even twenty years of confinement, were released into society. What is to become of a lost soul such as this? He answered his own question: "He returns to the world to which he had been dead for ten years: the prospects he might have had, when he was ten years younger, have vanished; no one will accept anyone coming from the galley, and ten years of punishment have not cleared him of a moment of crime. He must become a criminal for a second time and end up on the gallows."[120] Schopenhauer was stunned to learn that there were six thousand galley slaves. But he overcame this response by returning to a facial theme in his journal: "The faces of these humans could provide appropriate subject-matter for physiognomical reflections."[121]

Dangling criminals with broken necks, the great and celebrated dead of Westminster Abbey, begging children of farmers, the bloody remains and destruction of the Revolution and Terror, and the pitiable galley slaves of Toulon provide a counterbalance to Schopenhauer's experiences

[119] Schopenhauer, *Reisetagebücher*, p. 155, entry for 8 April 1804.
[120] Ibid., p. 156, entry for 8 April 1804.
[121] Ibid., p. 156.

of natural beauty and art. The scales measuring this balance of the terrible and the delightful began to tip to the darker side of life for the young Schopenhauer. The ubiquity of suffering and death will become the troubling phenomenon that will eventually drive his quest to explain a world seeped in evil and to determine the significance of living in such a despairing domain. But in this stage of his life, Schopenhauer attempted to transcend his emotional response to life's horrors by moving toward a scientific understanding of the phenomena that evoked these feelings. Hanging did not strangle, but instead broke the necks of the executed men; that their heads all hung to one side confirmed that the force of the fall and the hitch of the noose broke their necks. To understand the nature of these criminals, their faces might provide the key, just as Napoleon's face and those of the galley slaves are profound objects for physiognomic explanations. Later, during his unhappy apprenticeship in Hamburg, he would steal away to attend lectures on phrenology by Franz Joseph Gall, thereby directing his gaze away from the face to the skull. Later still, he would matriculate as a medical student at the University of Göttingen. And much later, he would discover that science stayed at the surface of things. He wanted to go to the core.

During the family's excursions around the regions of Marseilles and Toulon, Arthur saw the Château d'If, the state prison in which Louis XIV had confined for many years the mysterious *Masque de Fer*, the Man in the Iron Mask. Years later, Schopenhauer would blur his experiences of the galley slaves and Louis' unfortunate prisoner within the context of an analogy between a penitentiary and the world. He did this, moreover, in a way that included the results of his physiognomic reflections: " . . . one of the evils of a penitentiary is also the society we meet there. What this is like will be known by anyone who is worthy of a better society without my telling him. The beautiful soul, as well as the genius, will sometimes feel in the world like a noble state-prisoner in the galleys among common criminals; and they, like him, will therefore attempt to isolate themselves. Generally speaking, however, the above-mentioned way of looking at things will enable us to regard without surprise and certainly without indignation the so-called imperfections, that is, the wretched and contemptible nature of most men both morally and intellectually, which is accordingly stampt on their faces."[122] The "above-mentioned

---

[122] Schopenhauer, *Parerga and Paralipomena*, Vol. 2, p. 303/*Sämtliche Werke*, Vol. 2, p. 322.

way of looking at things" is to view the world and human existence as something that should not be, a claim that implied for Schopenhauer that both the fate of humankind and the behavior of most is miserable. Even the person of a fine nature and the genius is included in this description and, as such, is in reality a fellow prisoner. So, despite the drive to isolate themselves from one another, the noble and the base, the genial and the common, all are condemned prisoners whose proper address to one another should be " . . . instead of *Sir, Monsieur*, and so on, *Leidengefährte, socii malorum, compagnon de misères*, my *fellow sufferer*. However strange this might sound, it accords with the facts, puts the other person in the most correct light, and reminds us of the most necessary things, tolerance, patience, forbearance, and love of one's neighbour, which everyone needs and each of us, therefore, owes to another."[123]

But to see the world as a penal colony, and each person as a fellow criminal, would take Schopenhauer some time. It would even take the distance of almost three decades before he would articulate the *aperçu* of the European tour, although by that time it had already been expressed in *The World as Will and Representation* some fourteen years earlier. Nevertheless, after fleeing Berlin and its cholera epidemic for the safety of Frankfurt in 1831, he recorded in the darkly titled notebook, the *Cholera Book*, the fundamental world-altering result of the tour: "In my seventeenth year, without any learned school education, I was affected by the *wretchedness of life*, as was the Buddha when in his youth he caught sight of sickness, old age, pain, and death. The truth, which the world clearly and loudly proclaimed, soon vanquished the Jewish dogma that had been imprinted in my mind, and the result for me was that this world could not be the work of an all-good being, but rather that of a devil who had summoned into existence creatures, in order to gloat over the sight of their agony."[124]

---

[123] Ibid., Vol. 2, p. 304/ibid., Vol. 2, p. 323.

[124] Schopenhauer, *Manuscript Remains*, Vol. 4, p. 119/*Der handschriftliche Nachlaß*, Vol. 4, I, p. 96. One of the reasons that Nietzsche was drawn to Schopenhauer concerned his sensitivity to and honest dealing with the problem of suffering and evil. Another point of contact was their affinity for attempting to understand the meaning and value of living in a world dominated by woe and death. Nietzsche also described an experience comparable to Schopenhauer's Buddha-like experience: "In fact, the problem of the origin of evil haunted me as a thirteen-year-old lad . . . and as to my "solution" to the problem back then, well, I gave the honor to God, as is fitting, and made him the father of evil," Friedrich Nietzsche, *On the Genealogy of Morality*, trans. Maudemarie Clark and Alan J. Swensen (Indianapolis/Cambridge:

The young Schopenhauer's behavior during this period of his life, how-ever, did not exhibit any changes compatible with his demonization of the creator. There is no record of objection to or reservation about his confir-mation, which took place in Danzig after the conclusion of the European tour. Although it is true that the Schopenhauers were not deeply religious by any standards, Arthur adhered to his confession as a young man, until he was twenty-four.[125] But even when he rejected the possibility of the existence of a God, in either the singular or plural, he maintained a curi-ously ambivalent stance toward religion, which is dramatically expressed in his well-known essay, "On Religion." There, within a dialogue between Demopheles, "friend of the people," and Philalethes, "friend of the truth," he allows both disputants the opportunity to express his own views, much in the manner in which David Hume had done in one of Schopenhauer's favorite philosophical books, *Dialogues Concerning Natural Religion* (2nd ed., London: 1779). And although he hoped for the slow death of reli-gion, the "euthanasia of religion," and thereby sided as he always would with the truth rather than with what would please people, he argued that this good death could only be administered by truths expressed clearly and in a form intelligible to the people, since religion served as truth's deputy.[126] Later, both Nietzsche and Freud would parlay elements of Schopenhauer's analysis of religion into their own insights.[127]

From the inhumane human zoo in Toulon, the Schopenhauers returned to Marseilles, and from there they set out for Switzerland. They went first

Hackett, 1998), preface, Sect. 3, p. 2. This remark also suggests one of the reasons that the young Nietzsche would turn against Schopenhauer as his philosophy matured. The young Schopenhauer demonized the creator for producing evil, whereas the young Nietzsche deified evil by making it the work of God; see my "Nietzsche's Use and Abuse of Schopenhauer's Moral Philosophy for Life," in *Willing and Nothingness: Schopenhauer as Nietzsche's Educator*, ed. Christopher Janaway (Oxford: Clarendon Press, 1998), pp. 128–31.

[125] Arthur Hübscher observed that "One must not forget that Schopenhauer up to the twenty-fourth year of his life was an adherent of his Church," *The Philosophy of Schopenhauer in Its Intellectual Context*, p. 8.

[126] Schopenhauer, *Parerga and Paralipomena*, Vol. 2, p. 119/*Sämtliche Werke*, Vol. 2, p. 119.

[127] See, for example, Nietzsche, *The Gay Science* [*Die fröhliche Wissenschaft*] (1882; trans. Walter Kaufmann. New York: Vintage, 1974.), Sect. 357, where he praises Schopenhauer as the first admitted atheist among Germans, for his "honest atheism," and for his recognition of the "ungodliness of existence." In *Freud: The Mind of the Moralist* (Chicago: University of Chicago Press, 1979), pp. 295–9, David Rieff argues that Freud's *The Future of an Illusion* (1928) closely follows Schopenhauer's essay from *Parerga and Paralipomena*, Vol. 2, "Dialogues on Religion."

to Aix, then to Avignon, Montèlmar, Tain, Valence, and St. Vallier, and to Lyon, where they crossed into Switzerland. They reached Pont d'Ain on the evening of May 10 and Geneva on the next evening. Outside Geneva, during an excursion to the gardens of the recently deceased uncle of Mme. de Staël-Holstein, Arthur was overwhelmed by the view of Mont Blanc, which at 15,781 feet stood as the highest peak in the Alps. And although the young Schopenhauer found himself lacking the words to describe the mountain's grandeur, it would leave an indelible impression that the older philosopher would use as a metaphor for the melancholy and serenity of the genius: "The gloomy disposition of highly gifted minds, so frequently observed, has its emblem in Mont Blanc, whose summit is often hidden in the clouds. But when on occasion, especially in the early morning, the veil of clouds is rent, and the mountain, red in sunlight, looks down on Chamonix from its celestial height above the clouds, it is then a sight at which the heart of everyone is most deeply stirred. So also does the genius, who is often melancholy, display at times that characteristic serenity ..., which is possible in him alone, and [which] springs from the most perfect objectivity of the mind."[128]

If the ruins of Nîmes and the galley slaves at the great arsenal at Toulon stimulated Schopenhauer's gloomy and melancholy reflections, then the mountains themselves brought the young man cheerfulness and serenity. By gazing upward at the rugged and ragged lines formed above the horizon, Schopenhauer experienced a dim sense of something permanent looming over the changing landscape below, which included his own ephemeral nature. But he preferred the experience of looking down from mountaintops to that of looking up at that which would outlast the spectator. At least on three occasions he climbed mountains during the tour – the Chapeau (May 16), Mount Pilatus (June 6), and Schneekoppe (July 30) – and each time he was transformed and transfixed by the grand vistas that blended all small and particular things into a colorful panorama. Climbing mountains, and better yet hiking mountains, thrilled the young Schopenhauer, as it did and continues to do to countless others. Becoming lost in the enjoyment of vision from a height gave the future philosopher fundamental experiences for his very personal analysis of natural beauty and deep appreciation for wild and uncultivated areas that were fortunate to escape the hands of human beings.

---

[128] Schopenhauer, *The World as Will and Representation*, Vol. 2, p. 383/ *Sämtliche Werke*, Vol. 3, p. 438f.

The Schopenhauers continued their journey in Switzerland from Geneva to Avenches, and on to Bern and then to Burgdorf, where Arthur recorded, "We went immediately after our arrival to see the institute of the famous Pestaluzzi [sic.] about whose new educational method so much has been said and written."[129] The Swiss-born Johann Heinrich Pestalozzi (1746–1827) had established a school in 1799 in the Castle of Burgdorf, where he taught local children free of charge. He had become well known in German-speaking lands for his novel *Leonard and Gertrude* [*Lienhard und Gertrud*, 1781], which expressed many of his ideas about social reform and education, and his more direct treatise on education, *How Gertrude Teaches Her Children* [*Wie Gertrud ihre Kinder lehrt*, 1801]. Inspired by Rousseau's *Emile*, Pestalozzi advocated educating the total child – hands, heart, and head. Foregoing rote memorization of materials, to be reinforced by the rod, he attempted instead to establish a cooperative, supportive, and loving family-like atmosphere in his school, an atmosphere that focused on a child's intuitions and direct, concrete experiences as the basis of learning. Words were never employed by Pestalozzi when the student could hear, see, smell, or touch an object, and he encouraged his students to actively experience things, to describe their experiences, and to follow their own natural curiosity. Later, both Alexander von Humboldt and Fichte would praise "Pestalozzianism," and Pestalozzi's educational methods would play a formative role in the school system of Prussia, and in a modified form in England, and in the United States of America through one of his assistants, Joseph Neef, who opened a school in Philadelphia.[130]

The family was disappointed to discover, however, that the renowned pedagogue would not be teaching that day. Nevertheless, they spent several hours observing instruction in geometry, arithmetic, reading, and language. They were impressed by the eight-year-old students' skills in drawing geometrical figures without the aid of a ruler or compass.

---

[129] Schopenhauer, *Reisetagebücher*, pp. 213–14, entry for 31 May 1804.

[130] See William Kilpatrick's *The Education of Man – Aphorisms* (New York: Philosophical Library, 1951), for a summary of Pestalozzi's educational principles; and K. Silber's *Pestalozzi: The Man and His Work* (London: Routledge & Kegan Paul, 1965). For a biographical and historical treatments of Pestalozzi, his teaching methodology, and historical effects, see Peter Stadler's *Pestalozzi: Gerschichte Biographie von der alten Ordnung zur Revolution* (1746–97) (Zurich: Neu Zürcher Zeitung, 1988), and Hermann Levin Goldschmidt, *Pestalozzis unvollendete Revolution: Philosophie Dank der Schweiz von Rousseau bis Turel* (Vienna: Passagen, 1995).

Likewise, Arthur was amazed by their ability to solve mathematical problems without the aid of a pen and paper. He recorded an example: "How many times does 'eight times two' go into 'four times, twelve times one'? Answer: 'three times'."[131] He was unimpressed by the way the children used slips of paper to count, which they did not do in the customary manner of saying "one, two, three," but by uttering "one times one, two times one, three times one." This is so mechanical, Schopenhauer thought, that the student realized no more than a student who counted straightforwardly, and that to say "three times one," the student already had the concept of three. Yet, many years after the fact, he recalled the students' multiplication exercises to help support his claim that arithmetic is based on the pure intuition of time: "But simple counting itself is multiplication by one, and for this reason in Pestalozzi's educational establishment the children have always to multiply thus: 'two times two are four times one.'"[132]

Arthur also noted that the students learned to read not by first studying the alphabet, but by learning to recognize syllables and whole words. He did not record what he thought about this method for teaching reading, but he did find the language instruction "most curious." The teacher would line the students into rows. One boy would touch a part of his body and say its name in German and then in French. The other boys would then do likewise. Arthur approved of this method of language instruction, noting that the teacher "always endeavors to provide them [the students] with a sensible representation of the thing that was named."[133] Although the young Schopenhauer did not realize it at the time, the ideas of "intuition [*Anschauung*]" and "sensible representation [*sinnliche Vorstellung*]" would play foundational roles in his philosophical methodology. He would argue that all substantive knowledge claims must ultimately be based on intuition and that sensible representations are the basis of our knowledge of the world. Like Pestalozzi, Schopenhauer would always insist that the direct experience of the thing itself is prior to any abstract, conceptual knowledge.[134] He would claim, however, that " . . . the fund and substance

---

[131] Schopenhauer, *Reisetagebücher*, p. 215, entry for 31 April 1804.

[132] Schopenhauer, *The World as Will and Representation*, Vol. 2, p. 35/ *Sämtliche Werke*, Vol. 3, p. 40.

[133] Schopenhauer, *Reisetagebücher*, p. 216, entry for 31 April 1804.

[134] Schopenhauer's posthumous library contained Pestalozzi's *My Researches on the Course of Nature in the Development of the Human Race, by the Author of Leonard and Gertrude* [*Meine*

of all our knowledge lies in the comprehension of the world through *intuition* [*Anschauung*]. But this can be gained only from ourselves; it cannot be *instilled* into us in any way. Therefore, our worth, both moral and intellectual, does not come to us from without, but proceeds from the very depths of our own nature; and no Pestalozzian pedagogies can turn a born simpleton into a thinker; never!"[135] A thinker, for Schopenhauer, was born so.

The family had just returned to their room at the inn when Pestalozzi himself paid them a visit. Arthur thought that he looked old – he was fifty-eight – but he was taken by his "extraordinary liveliness." Still, he was put off by the pedagogue's poor pronunciation of German and French, his stuttering, and his appearing to be at a loss for words. (Schopenhauer did not say whether Pestalozzi searched for some object to which he could point.) He also derisively remarked that his teachers and students also spoke the same poor Swiss German. It is surprising that Schopenhauer did not remark on the kind and supportive role of Pestalozzi's new method of instruction, especially after his recent, bitter experiences at Lancaster's Wimbledon School. He did, however, note that although he did not have sufficient time to gain a complete understanding of this method of instruction, its success, when compared to other methods, had to be measured by its results. The local villagers, however, were more suspicious about Pestalozzi's new educational method, and he was forced to close his school and leave Burgdorf shortly after the Schopenhauers' visit.

The journey continued to Lucern, Zurich, Schaffhausen, Konstanz, Augsberg, Munich, Braunau, and then to Vienna, where Arthur found it almost impossible to understand the German dialect spoken by the common folk. From Vienna the family traveled to Schmiedelberg, where Arthur hired a guide for a two-day climb of the Schneekoppe. Before ascending to the summit, he and his guide spent the evening in a small chalet. He reached the peak the next morning as the rising sun illuminated the crown of the mountain while the countryside below remained cloaked in darkness, and from that vantage point "one sees the world in chaos beneath oneself."[136] He remained on the peak for approximately one hour

---

Nachforschungen über den Gang der Natur in der Entwickelung des Menschengeschlechts vom Verfasser von Lienhard und Gertrud, 1797]. Hübscher does not report any annotations by Schopenhauer; see *Der handschriftliche Nachlaß*, Vol. 5, p. 123.

[135] Schopenhauer, *Parerga and Paralipomena*, Vol. 2, p. 479/*Sämtliche Werke*, Vol. 6, p. 510.

[136] Schopenhauer, *Reisetagebücher*, p. 298, entry for 30 July 1804.

before the wind and cold prompted him to return to the world. Descending to the chaos below, Schopenhauer took some solace by engaging in some amateur botanizing, allowing the colors and fragrances of *Geun montanum* and *Anemone alpine* to serve as momentary diversions.

Schopenhauer hiked down to Hirschberg to meet his parents. He was exhausted. He complained that he had never been so hot and so tired. The wind, the sun, and the lengthy walk produced the strange effect mentioned earlier. The next morning he was shocked by the image that confronted him in the mirror. His skin appeared golden and his ears had ballooned to monstrous proportions. Nevertheless, he kept an appointment for an early morning promenade through the village. It was as if Schopenhauer sensed that his return to the world and the chaos below had transformed the young traveler into a monster, a merchant's apprentice.[137]

From Hirschberg the Schopenhauers returned to Schmiedeberg, and then to Landshut, Waldenberg, and Breslau, through the deep sands to Hainau, and on to Dresden, where they spent ten days. Finally, they reached Berlin. The entries in Schopenhauer's travel diary for the last three weeks are short, amounting to a little more than five pages in a journal that covered approximately sixteen months and roughly three hundred pages.[138] It is as if Arthur resigned himself to his fate after descending the Schneekoppe. His last entry, dated 25 August, is flat; "This afternoon we finally reached Berlin."[139] His youth is spent. Now comes the serious business of life. A more fitting ending for the tour, however, occurs at the end of the first of three copybooks that constituted Schopenhauer's travel diary. After listing his assessment of the various inns along the tour, he quotes from Shakespeare's *Richard II*:

> From all evils, that befall us may
> The worst is death – and death must have its day.

Beneath this cheerful remark, he concludes: "*In coelo quies, tout finis bas* [In heaven calm, down here all is ending]."[140]

---

[137] Ibid., p. 302, entry for 2 August 1804.
[138] These exclude his three months at Wimbledon School, for which there are no journal entries.
[139] Schopenhauer, *Reisetagebücher*, p. 310.
[140] Ibid., p. 18, Charlotte von Gwinner's introduction.

3

A Father's Death; A Philosopher's Birth

F ROM BERLIN, HEINRICH FLORIS returned to Hamburg, and Johanna and Arthur went to Danzig, where they would stay for three months. While in Danzig, Johanna retrieved Adele, visited her family, and was entertained by her friends. Arthur went to Danzig to be confirmed, to suffer the dire consequences of his self-defeating decision of selecting the European pleasure tour over his deeper desire to become a scholar, and to once again receive the same sort of tedious and carping letters from a distant father. Indeed, his father's letters to Danzig were almost carbon copies of those Arthur received during his three-month sentence at Wimbledon School. No matter what Arthur promised about living up to his father's expectations, nor what good reports he received about his son, Heinrich Floris found a way to find fault. Thus he wrote Arthur about his mother's report that he had become a fine young gentleman, and her remark about how others had commented on his orderly behavior, but he used this only to make yet another demand: "let this orderliness also prevail in your room and luggage, because that event in Braunau was very annoying."[1] In response to yet another of his son's promises to improve his writing and calculating skills, instead of encouraging him to do so, he demanded that he walk erect, "like other people do, so that you will not get round shoulders, which look horrible. Good posture at the stand-up writing-desk is equally important as it is in everyday life; since if, when dining out, one observes another sitting with a bent back, one assumes him to be a cobbler or a tailor in disguise."[2] The tight-fisted Heinrich Floris

---

[1] Lütkehaus, *Die Schopenhauers*, p. 64, 23 October 1804. It is not known what difficulties Schopenhauer had with his traveling gear in Braunau, and perhaps Heinrich Floris is referring to a minor altercation Arthur had with the police in regard to receiving a pass to leave the city gates; see Schopenhauer, *Reisetagebücher*, pp. 254–5. 19 June 1804.
[2] Ibid., p. 64.

became so upset with the prospects that his son might be mistaken for a tradesman that he offered to pay for exercise lessons, provided Arthur could find a good trainer.

While in Danzig, Arthur served a brief three-month apprenticeship with a business associate and friend of his father, Jakob Kabrun. His father's desire was for his son to learn to write proper business letters in German, French, and English, so that upon his return to Hamburg, he would not approach his next principal as a complete novice. Heinrich Floris also hoped that Arthur would learn to make himself more agreeable to other people and to improve his social skills. In his last letter to his son, he articulated these concerns, and he hammered away at Arthur's sloppy penmanship and his poor deportment. The only warmth exhibited in the letter followed a common pattern. Approval led to a demand for something better: "It is completely good that you will be confirmed in Danzig, but here [in Hamburg] you will still attend Mr. Runge's morning lectures in theology."[3] The elder Schopenhauer never appears satisfied with his son.

Johanna and her children returned to Hamburg in mid-December 1804. Almost immediately, in January of the new year, Arthur received a new master, Senator Martin Jenisch, a family friend and business associate of Heinrich Floris. Not because Senator Jenisch was a harsh taskmaster, but because a life in commerce rubbed against his nature, the young Schopenhauer loathed his position. Later he would complain that "never was there a poorer student of business than I. My entire nature strove against this occupation."[4] Arthur resorted to sneaking books into work so that he could read on the sly, and he also read in the evenings in his room, seeking to stimulate his imagination and his thinking in ways neglected in the counting house. When the famous phrenologist Franz Joseph Gall delivered a series of lectures, he sought to sate his physiognomic curiosity through the use of a bit of deception and cunning, which he was more than capable of managing. He tricked his principal into giving him some time off, and if Heinrich Floris expected his son to make himself more agreeable to others, Arthur recognized that his unhappy life was making him act just the opposite. The costs of his choice to take the European tour quickly

---

[3] Ibid., p. 66, 20 November 1804. Schopenhauer was confirmed on 25 August 1804 at St. Mary's Church, the same church in which he was baptized.

[4] Schopenhauer, *Gesammelte Briefe*, p. 651.

became clear. His choice had brought him "an odious occupation and the worst type of slavery... more and more I come to the realization that I had agreed to the wrong journey through life – a mistake I completely doubted to be able to once again make good."[5]

As Arthur was slogging along a path of life that he found odious, Heinrich Floris's life was hurling toward its end. Ever since his marriage, his unfortunate inheritance from his maternal lineage had gradually expressed itself. To be sure, there was the normal sort of physical decline as he entered the fifth decade of his life. Frequently during the European tour, he excused himself from the more rigorous and demanding hikes that were enjoyed by his wife and son. In addition to the diminution of his physical vigor, he became increasingly hard of hearing.[6] He also suffered some unspecified illness after the family's return to Hamburg. Many years later, Arthur's recollection of this malady bashed his mother specifically and women generally: "I am acquainted with women. They consider marriage only as an institution for their care. As my own father was sick and miserably confined to his wheel chair, he would have been abandoned had it not been for an old servant who performed the so-called duty of love. My Frau mother gave parties while he was wasting away in solitude and amused herself while he was suffering bitter agonies. That is the love of women!"[7]

Heinrich Floris's Death

Traces of Heinrich Floris's impending psychological decline appeared very early in his marriage. His unfounded worries about Johanna's fidelity, which led her to virtually isolate herself in the family summer house in Oliva, and the dark panic that compelled him to drag his very pregnant wife from London to Danzig in the dead of winter began to signify difficulties with his mental health. Then there were Johanna's complaints

---

[5] Ibid., p. 651.

[6] Heinrich Floris must have suffered hardness of hearing for many years. A well-known anecdote concerns the announcement to his employees of Arthur's birth. One of them is alleged to have said to the gathering: "If he will come to resemble his father, he will become a fine baboon." He did not respond; see Schopenhauer, *Gespräche*, p. 381. Schopenhauer was said to have related this story to his friend, Wilhelm Gwinner.

[7] Schopenhauer, *Gespräche*, p. 152. This was said by Schopenhauer to one of his young, earlier followers, Adam Ludwig von Doß, as part of his attempt to discourage him from marrying – unless his future wife was rich.

during the European tour: the social isolation that she often experienced due to her husband's desire not to meet new people, and her confidence to Arthur that his father was inclined to manufacture worries when there were no real ones. The very fact that Heinrich Floris would abandon his business for eighteen months for a pleasure tour of Europe would suggest, perhaps, a loss of interest in the very thing he desired his son to serve. The darkening of his mood was also expressed in his niggling and nagging letters to his son. Once back home in Hamburg, he was inclined to loud outbursts and strange behavior. He would pace his room at night. He became mistrustful of his employees and he would often pore over the account books. When he was found floating in the icy waters of the canal behind the family compound on 20 April 1805, both Johanna and Arthur viewed his death as a suicide, although it was possible that instead of jumping out of the warehouse loft, he may have fallen.

Schopenhauer was devastated by his father's death. He reported in his *curriculum vitae* that a guilty conscience at the prospects of breaking his pledge to his father, as well as the inertia of his grief, kept him serving his apprenticeship with Jenisch, even though nothing stood in his way if he were to abandon his position. He also claimed that as a result of his bereavement, "the darkening of my spirit so greatly intensified that it was close to becoming an actual melancholy."[8] Even five months after the fact, his friend Anthime Grégoire told him to buck up and face his grief "more philosophically."[9]

Schopenhauer never analyzed his grief or depression philosophically, but the issue of suicide engaged him philosophically his entire life. Seven years after his father's death, while he was a student at the University of Berlin, he recorded his first reflections in a note "against suicide." Life is a joke, he wrote, because all of its pleasures and pains do not touch a person's inner and better self. There are those, however, who fail to realize this, and they take life too seriously. So when misfortune occurs, some live a life full of vices and thereby seek to abuse their inner and better selves. Others show that by committing suicide, they cannot take a joke: "Therefore as a *mauvais joueur* he does not bear the loss with composure,

---

[8] Schopenhauer, *Gesammelte Briefe*, p. 651.
[9] *Der Briefwechsel Arthur Schopenhauer*, ed. Carl Gebhart (Munich: R. Piper, 1929), Vol. xvi, p. 19. Quoted in Rüdiger Safranski, *Schopenhauer and the Wild Years of Philosophy*, p. 55.

but when bad cards are dealt to him he peevishly and impatiently refuses to go on playing, throws down the cards, and breaks up the game."[10]

Was his father simply a "*mauvais joueur*," a bad sport? Did he take life too seriously? Could he not take a joke? It is difficult to believe that when he wrote about suicide, he was not thinking of his father. Still, there is nothing in his observations that suggests anything personal. Two years later, as he labored on *The World as Will and Representation* in Dresden, he began to arrive at the view he would articulate in its fourth book: "The ordinary suicide from dissatisfaction, failure, and discontent is nothing but the most glaring expression of the inner variance with itself which is essential to life. . . . The suicide cannot give up willing, but he ceases to live; he destroys the appearance of willing through willing instead of abolishing willing itself. The suicide is therefore the greatest contradiction."[11] Suicide is a will not to will.

Schopenhauer's reflections on suicide continue to mature. Three years later, as he still labored in Dresden, he recognized an ethical incentive as a possible restraint on suicide: "I will not avoid suffering so that it may contribute to the abolition of the will to life, whose appearance is so fearful. For it strengthens my knowledge of the essential nature of the world which has already dawned on me, so that it may become the quieter of my will."[12] Finally, Schopenhauer folded together these observations, among others, into the sixty-ninth chapter of *The World as Will and Representation*, and he adduced this point as "the reason why almost all ethical systems, philosophical as well as religious systems, condemn suicide, though they cannot state anything but strange and sophistical arguments for doing so."[13]

---

[10] Schopenhauer, *Manuscript Remains*, Vol. 1, p. 33/*Der Handschriftliche Nachlaβ*, Vol. 1, p. 32.

[11] Ibid., Vol. 1, para. 275; see Arthur Schopenhauer, *Die Welt als Wille und Vorstellung: Faksimiledruck der ersten Auflage*, pp. 572–7. Later editions of *The World as Will and Representation* leave his treatment of suicide virtually unchanged. The minor changes consist of additional references to cases of voluntary deaths by starvation.

[12] *Manuscript Remains*, Vol. 1, p. 530/*Der Handschriftliche Nachlaβ*, Vol. 1, p. 479/*Sämtliche Werke*, Vol. 2, p. 473.

[13] Schopenhauer, *The World as Will and Representation*, Vol. 1, p. 399. Schopenhauer recognized a type of voluntary death that was immune to his moral reason against suicide, that is, voluntary death by starvation, and because he recognized many different intermediate stages between this type of suicide and ordinary suicides driven by despair, he found it difficult to arrive at an explanation of suicide. Thus he claimed, "human nature has depths, obscurities,

Schopenhauer, however, would not publish anything about suicide for another twenty years. Still, he brooded about the issue within his notebooks. As he did so, the ghost of his father assumed greater significance. Around 1828, he hoped for a second edition of *The World as Will and Representation*, and he sketched a number of prefaces for the new edition. The first of these is found immediately after a discussion of suicide in which he concluded that the hereditary nature of suicide demonstrates that it is the nature of the individual that is the dominant factor in suicide rather than the external circumstances of a person's life. He then composed the following:

Dedication to the second edition: to the manes of my father Heinrich Floris Schopenhauer, the merchant

Noble, splendid spirit whom I thank for all I am and that I fulfilled, your active care has sheltered and borne me not merely through the helplessness of childhood and the indiscretions of youth, but also into man's estate right up to the present day. For by putting in the world a son like me, you at the same time provided that he would be able to exist and to develop as such in a world like this.... To you I therefore dedicate my work which could arise only under the shade of your protection and which to this extent is also *your work*; and I express to you in the grave the thanks which I owe solely to you and to no one else:

... That I was able to develop and apply the powers, given to me by nature, to that for which they were destined; that I was able to follow my inborn impulse and to think and work for innumerable people, whereas no one did anything for me; for all of this I thank you, my father, I thank your activity, your good sense, your thrift and thoughtfulness for the future. Therefore, my father, let me extol you! And everyone who in my works finds some pleasure, consolation, or instruction shall be aware of your name and know that, if H.F.S. had not been the man he was, A.S. would have been ruined a hundred times. And so let my gratitude do the only thing it can do for you who have finished; let it carry your name as far as my name is able to carry it.[14]

But what was it that H.F.S. did for A.S.? He provided him with the financial means to live for philosophy. By living frugally and by managing his money well, he did not have to support his philosophy by laboring for a living. He did not have to grind lenses like Spinoza, nor did he have to have a university position like Kant. Consequently, he had time to

and intricacies, whose elucidation and unfolding are of the very greatest difficulty"; see Schopenhauer, *The World as Will and Representation*, Vol. 1, p. 402/*Sämtliche Werke*, Vol. 2, p. 476.

[14] Schopenhauer, *Manuscript Remains*, Vol. 3, p. 413f./*Der Handschriftliche Nachlaß*, Vol. 3, p. 379.

devote to his work without having to please customers or the Church and State.

But Heinrich Floris only supplied the means for his son's philosophical life by dying. Schopenhauer knew this; as a means for overcoming his feelings of guilt, he invested the utmost value in his father's sacrifice: "I regard my inheritance as a consecrated treasure which is entrusted to me simply for the purpose of being able to solve the problem set by my nature and to be for myself and humankind what nature intended me to be. I regard it as a charter without which I would be useless to humankind and would have the most wretched existence a man of my nature had ever had. I would therefore regard it as the most ungrateful and unworthy misuse of so rare a fate, if I were to spend possibly half of my income on tailors, milliners, and dealers in fancy goods in the expectation, so often disappointed, of living a life that is more enjoyable."[15] As he continued drafting prefaces promising that Heinrich Floris's name would be continued by the work of his son, it was almost as if Schopenhauer thought that a philosophy bearing the family name would appease his father as well as would a business holding the name "Schopenhauer." He never, however, published any version of the prefaces that honored his father.[16]

Some twenty years after his initial publication of his views on suicide in *The World as Will and Representation*, Schopenhauer would revisit the subject in his unsuccessful prize essay, "On the Foundation of Morality" [*Über das Fundament der Moral*].[17] In this case, he decided to bash the claim of his beloved Kant, which was that suicide violates a duty to oneself. Without even rehearsing Kant's argument, Schopenhauer simply called it "paltry and not even worth an answer. We are forced to laugh when we think that such reflections could have wrested the dagger from the hands of Cato, Cleopatra, Cocceius Nerva (Tacitus, *Annals* VI. 26), or Arria

---

[15] Ibid., Vol. 4, p. 507/ibid., Vol. 4, p. 118f. Hübscher dates this entry "about 1831."

[16] As Schopenhauer continued to draft prefaces, there is a shift from the earlier dedications to his father to the later condemnations of his philosophical contemporaries, especially Hegel; see, for example, *Manuscript Remains*, Vol. 3, "Advesaria," para. 120; Vol. iv, "Pandectae II," para. 51, and "Spicilegia," para. 82, 94, 96, 97, 98, 100, 103. Schopenhauer's *Der Handschriftliche Nachlaβ*, Vol. 3 follows the same divisions.

[17] This is the original title of the essay. When it was published in 1841, within *The Two Fundamental Problems of Ethics* [*Die beiden Grundprobleme der Ethik*], it was retitled "Prize Essay On the Basis of Morality" ['Preisschrift über die Grundlage der Moral"]. Nevertheless, Schopenhauer gave its original title on the title page of *The Two Fundamental Problems of Ethics*.

wife of Paetus (Pliny, *Letters* III. 16)."[18] Later, Schopenhauer claims that suicide is automatic in certain cases: "For it is quite certainly a universal rule that a human actually resorts to suicide as soon as the immensely strong, inborn drive to the preservation of life is definitely overpowered by great suffering; daily experience shows this."[19]

Schopenhauer resumed his bashing of those who condemned suicide some forty-five years after his father's death in his lengthiest discussion of the issue in the essay "On Suicide," found in the second volume of *Parerga and Paralipomena.* In particular, he attacked the British criminalization of suicide: "As I have said, suicide is even accounted a crime and connected with this, especially in vulgar and bigoted England, are an ignominious burial and the confiscation of legacies; for which reason a jury almost invariably brings in a verdict of insanity."[20] Moral feeling should decide the matter, he continued, and unlike genuine crimes such as murder, fraud, theft, and assault, which evoke in us lively feelings of indignation, resentment, and a desire for revenge, the report of suicide evokes our feelings of sadness, compassion, and, perhaps, some admiration for that person's courage.[21] Then he appeals to what he takes as his

---

[18] Schopenhauer, *On the Basis of Morality,* trans. E. F. J. Payne (Indianapolis: Hackett, 1997), p. 59/*Sämtliche Werke,* Vol. 4, p. 127. Schopenhauer is referring to Kant's *Groundwork for the Metaphysics of Morals* [*Grundlegung zur Metaphysik der Sitten,* 1785; trans. H. J. Paton, New York: Harper &Row, 1964] AK. 422. (All references to Kant will refer to the pagination found in the respective volume of Kant's *Gesammelte Schriften,* edited by the Prussian Academy [Berlin: Walter de Gruyter, 1902–]. All good translations of Kant will include the Prussian Academy's pagination.)

[19] Ibid., 93/ibid., Vol. 4, p. 159f. Here Schopenhauer is directly challenging Kant's argument at *Groundwork* AK. 422. There Kant had argued that the maxim "From self-love I make it my rule to shorten my life if its continuance threatens more pain than it promises" cannot become a universal law of nature, because it is self-contradictory; namely, it converts a feeling whose function is to further life into one that ends it. Therefore, Kant concludes we have a duty not to commit suicide. Schopenhauer challenges Kant's claim that this maxim is self-contradictory by claiming that it is a universal law that in certain instances, great suffering defeats the innate drive for self-preservation. Schopenhauer will jettison the Kantian idea of duty, and indeed of any prescriptive form of ethics, from his moral philosophy, as we will see.

[20] Schopenhauer, *Parerga and Paralipomena,* Vol. 2, p. 306/*Sämtliche Werke,* Vol. 6, p. 325.

[21] Moral feelings, or better, affective responses toward actions, are the bases for Schopenhauer's account of moral values. Actions that evoke the approbation of an impartial witness and the doer of the deed possess moral worth; those that evoke the disapprobation of an impartial witness and the doer of the deed are morally reprehensible; and those that evoke neither approbation nor disapprobation are morally indifferent or neutral. Schopenhauer's clearest statement of this can be found in a letter to Johann August Becker, dated 10 December 1844; see Schopenhauer, *Gesammelte Briefe,* p. 220.

readers' common experience: "Who has not had acquaintances, friends, and relatives who have voluntarily departed from the world? And should we all regard these with abhorrence as criminals? *Nego ac pernego* [I say no, certainly not]! I am rather of the opinion that the clergy should be challenged once and for all to tell us with what right they stigmatize as a *crime* an action that has been committed by many who were honored and beloved by us."[22] The clergy, he also claimed, cannot cite biblical authority for this stigmatization, nor do they have valid philosophical arguments.

After claiming in his essay "On Suicide" that David Hume had refuted all the current arguments against suicide, Schopenhauer referred his readers to Chapter 69 of his main work and, saving them the trouble of going to that work, he provides them with his view.[23] But instead of a "moral incentive" that restrains against suicide, he writes of "the only valid moral reason against suicide. It lies in the fact that suicide is opposed to the attainment of the highest moral goal since it substitutes for the real salvation from this world of woe and misery one that is merely apparent." Still, even though there is a moral reason against suicide, Schopenhauer claims that this does not entail that suicide is a crime, as the Christian clergy would have it. At best, he continued, Christianity opposes suicide, because it recognizes that suffering is the real purpose of life, but it takes a higher moral standpoint to condemn it: "That reason against suicide is, however, ascetic and therefore applies to an ethical standpoint much higher than that which European moral philosophers have ever occupied. But if we descend from this view, there is no longer any valid moral reason for

---

[22] Schopenhauer, *Parerga and Paralipomena*, Vol. 2, p. 307f/ *Sämtliche Werke*, Vol. 6, p. 326.

[23] In this essay, Schopenhauer referred to David Hume's "Of Suicide," and credits him with refuting the current arguments against suicide. In "Of Suicide," Hume had argued that suicide is not a transgression against our duties to God, our neighbor, or ourselves, and that it had to be a transgression of a duty to be criminal: "If suicide be criminal, it must be a transgression of our duty, either to God, our neighbors, or ourselves." See Hume's *Essays Moral, Political and Literary* (Indianapolis: Library Fund, 1987), p. 580. Instead of arguing, as Hume did, that God had equipped humans with the means for them to terminate a horrible life, Schopenhauer claimed that nature had given humans that privilege – as we have seen. Schopenhauer, following Hume, quotes Pliny's remark from *Historia naturalis* that "Not even God is capable of everything. For even if he wanted to, he cannot come to a decision about his own death. Yet with so much suffering in life, such a death is the best gift he has granted to man"; see Schopenhauer, *Parerga and Paralipomena*, Vol. 2, p. 307/ *Sämtliche Werke*, Vol. 6, p. 326, and Hume, *Essays*, p. 589.

condemning suicide."[24] This higher moral standpoint is his theory of the denial of the will, which he also claimed was recognized in Buddhism and Hinduism.

Ultimately it appears that Schopenhauer's analysis of suicide served to both defend and condemn his father. Although European clergy and philosophers would condemn Heinrich Floris, they had no sound arguments to support this condemnation. This could only be mounted from an ethical standpoint higher than that which prevailed in Europe. To do so, they would have to recognize that suffering has a potentially sanctifying dimension insofar as it could lead to the denial of the will. Schopenhauer, of course, recognized this standpoint. Therefore he could condemn suicide. Perhaps "condemn" is too strong a term. It is not as if knowledge of this ethical standpoint could have deterred Heinrich Floris. The moral reason against suicide would not have moved someone who was "driven to suicide through a purely morbid deep depression."[25] Because this is a matter of will and not reason, such people could not have done otherwise, once they had overcome the fear of death. The problem with suicide is that it is an act of will and not the denial of will; it short-circuits the possibility of salvation. On a more mundane level, the suicide focuses only on his or her own suffering, failing to realize that this is also the plight of all others who are left in the lurch.

If the young Schopenhauer struggled with his father's death, how did Johanna react? She published an odd sort of notification in the *Staats-und Gelehrten Zeitung des Hamburgischen unparteiischen Corrrespondenten* on 24 April 1805, four days after her husband's unanticipated death: "I hereby do my sad duty to announce to my relatives and friends the death of my husband, Mr. Heinrich Floris Schopenhauer, which was caused by an unfortunate accident. Expressions of condolences are not requested; they would only increase my grief."[26] Was Johanna so grief-stricken that

---

[24] Schopenhauer, *Parerga and Paralipomena*, Vol. 2, p. 309/*Sämtliche Werke*, Vol. 6, p. 328.

[25] Ibid., Vol. 2, p. 310/ibid., Vol. 6, p. 330. For some recent studies on Schopenhauer's views on suicide, see Dieter Birnbacher, "Schopenhauer und die ethische problem des Selbstmordes," *Schopenhauer-Jahrbuch*, Vol. 66 (1985), pp. 115–30, and Dale Jacquette, "Schopenhauer on the Ethics of Suicide," *Continental Philosophy Review*, Vol. 33 (2000), pp. 43–58 and *The Philosophy of Schopenhauer* (Chesham: Acumen, 2005), pp. 132–43.

[26] Quoted in Ulrike Bergmann's *Johanna Schopenhauer: 'Lebe und sei so glücklich als du kannst'* (Leipzig: Reclam, 2002), p. 111. My understanding of Johanna Schopenhauer was greatly enhanced by Bergmann's work.

expressions of sympathy would increase rather than lessen her pain, or did she not wish to be reminded of something she had already put behind her? It is likely to be the latter. Johanna tended to look forward and not backward. Besides her own financial liberation – she inherited one-third of her husband's estate – she also had two children under her care.

Johanna's Rebirth

Johanna sold the family home four months after her husband's death and moved the family to temporary lodging on the opposite side of Hamburg, Kohlhöfen 87. There were just too many sad memories haunting the mansion on Neuer Wandrahm, not the least of which were the memories conjured by the sight of the place of Heinrich Floris's death. Having neither the interest nor the skills to run the family business, and having two children depending on her care, she liquidated the firm, with the help of a business associate of her husband, Wilhelm Ganslandt. She now had the financial means to strike out on her own. Had she followed tradition, she would have returned to Danzig, because her mother and sisters still resided there, as did Heinrich Floris's relatives. But in the absence of her husband's will, traditional expectations lost their power. She longed for something more exciting. After the customary year of mourning, she set out for Weimar, the "German Athens," to scout for a new home for herself and Adele. Arthur would remain in Hamburg, serving in his unhappy apprenticeship.

   Johanna's sensibilities and tastes made Weimar a natural choice for her relocation. Weimar, the "city of poets," and the cultural and intellectual center of the Germanic lands, would provide her with a milieu for which she had longed. As she had once confessed in a letter to her son while he suffered through the rigid and tedious demands of Wimbledon School, she knew the delights of immersing herself in the works of artistic genius. She had identified with her son's deep feelings for the beautiful. Nevertheless, she recommended that he repress those yearnings, because they fettered one's ability to confront the serious side of life.[27] Johanna had also needed to repress her own deep wishes in order to fulfill her role as wife and mother, and like her son, she had to deal with a demanding and depressed Heinrich Floris. His death and her inheritance freed her from her own

---

[27] See Johanna's letter to Arthur, 4 August 1803; see Lütkehaus, *Die Schopenhauers*, pp. 56–60.

serious business, as they eventually would free Arthur from business. Therefore, Johanna resigned from her own resignation. She would leave it for the heroines of her future novels. Once she settled in Weimar, she would tell her son that "I now live completely after my heart's wishes."[28]

But there were more than the works of genius in Weimar. There were the geniuses themselves. Since 1775, it had been Goethe's place of residence. He had been brought to the city by Carl August, who was the son of the dowager Duchess Anna Amalia, and who would later become the Duke of Saxony-Weimar-Eisenach. Goethe served in a variety of political offices within Carl August's courts; ultimately his role was that of Carl August's "Privy Councilor." Goethe drew Friedrich Schiller to Weimar; Schiller made it his home from 1799 until his death in 1805. Together, Goethe and Schiller organized the Weimar theater. Johann Gottlieb Herder was summoned to Weimar to reform the educational system of the duchy, with Goethe and Christoph Martin Wieland helping to pull some strings, but ultimately, Goethe's strained friendship with Herder collapsed when Herder, who could be merciless and tactless, told Goethe, who often treated Herder poorly, that he preferred his natural son to Goethe's play, *The Natural Daughter* [*Die natürliche Tochter*].[29] Wieland, the poet and translator of Shakespeare, had himself arrived in Weimar in 1772 to tutor Anna Amalia's sons.

Weimar was also thick with lesser lights and flashing stars. The Weimar-born, prolific, and reactionary playwright, August von Kotzebue, who would be stabbed to death by a theology student in 1819 in Mannheim, tried unsuccessfully to merge into Weimar's cultural life. When Johanna first arrived in Weimar, she rented rooms from Kotzebue's sister, who wrote simple moralistic novels for women, such as *Luise or the Unfortunate Results of Carelessness* [*Luise oder die unseligen Folgen des Leichtsinns*], under the penname Amalie Berg.[30] The flamboyant and half-mad Zacharias Werner made a momentary splash. In the winter of 1807, Arthur was reading his *Martin Luther or the Sanctity of Power* [*Martin Luther oder Weihe der Kraft*] and recommended it to his mother. Johanna followed Arthur's advice and found the play to be overdone and not to her taste. She

---

[28] Ibid., p. 116: letter from Johanna to Arthur, 14 November 1806.

[29] See A. Gillies, "Herder and Goethe," in *German Studies: Presented to Leonard Ashley Willoghby by Pupils, Colleagues and Friends* (Oxford: Basil Blackwell, 1952), p. 83.

[30] See Ulrike Bergmann's *Johanna Schopenhauer*, p. 118.

wrote to Arthur that she wished that Werner would come to study with Goethe to cultivate his "great talent."[31] Johanna's wish became partially satisfied. Goethe brought Werner to Weimar, but not so Werner would study with him. Instead, it was a show to his colleagues that he could still summon to his court the next big thing, who many, including Madame de Staël, thought would fill Schiller's shoes. Although Goethe maintained an ironic distance from Werner, he produced Werner's *Wanda, Queen of Sarmatia* [*Wanda, Königin der Sarmaten*] in early 1808. Arthur thought highly of both the play and its author:

He [Werner] was a friend of my youth and certainly influenced me, and that is, in a positive way. In my adolescence I was enthusiastic about his works, and when I was in my 20th year, I was able to enjoy my association with him to the fullest in the house of my mother in Weimar. He was well-inclined towards me and often spoke with me, even on serious and philosophical topics. His memory is still precious to me and has left its trace. I could tell you much about him verbally. He wrote *Wanda* at that time, and it was produced for the first time on the birthday of the Grand Duchess. I have seen the play often, but I have never read it. I still know by heart the "Song of the Virgins in the Grey Mist." Despite their subjective coloring, his dramas are still incomparably better than anything else that has been accomplished in that style. The previous winter I had read his *Luther*.[32]

Arthur and Adele remained under the care and supervision of their French servants, Johannes and Sophie Duguet, as Johanna struck out to Weimar. Much to Arthur's displeasure, she did not travel alone. Accompanying her was Felix Ratzky, who had recently appeared in Hamburg for a change of luck. Ratzky, who has been described as an indiscrete and reckless man – a "bad man," as Johanna would later claim – had scandalized the Trosieners. Johanna's younger sister and Arthur's godmother, Charlotte Elisabeth, had moved in with the still married Ratzky after her divorce from Fritz Reyser. When Ratzky's wife died, she married him.[33] In any case, Ratzky provided security for a woman traveling alone, and he was her sister's husband.

---

[31] Lütkehaus, *Die Schopenhauers*, p. 151, letter from Johanna to Arthur, 10 March 1807.

[32] Schopenhauer, *Gesammelte Briefe*, p. 328, letter from Schopenhauer to Johann August Becker. Schopenhauer's remark about his ability to tell Becker a great deal about Werner verbally may allude to an incident in which a maid claimed Werner tried to rape her. Nevertheless, Werner was an odd sort of person, inclined toward delusions of grandeur. Ultimately, he converted to Catholicism and became a priest.

[33] See Arthur Hübscher's "Drei Tanten Schopenhauers," p. 129.

Johanna arrived at Weimar on 14 May 1806. Along the way, she had become so enchanted with Gotha that she considered living there. Still, she was drawn by the cultural life of Weimar and she decided that spending two weeks there would solve her quandary – Gotha or Weimar. As befitted her social status, she had a number of acquaintances in Weimar. The first person whom she visited was Johannes Daniel Falk, who also hailed originally from Danzig. Falk was a philanthropist, private tutor, writer of satires, and friend of Goethe.[34] She also called upon Friedrich Justin Bertuch, whom she had met with her husband in 1800, during a trip to Karlsbad. Bertuch, a merchant, a dabbler in the arts, and a publisher, was also Councilor, administrator of the privy purse, and legal advisor for Carl August. He also founded the well-known *Jenaische Allgemeine Litteraturzeitung*, a periodical that would publish a lukewarm review of Arthur's dissertation, which, coincidentally, was published by Bertuch's *Commission der Hof-Buch-und Kunsthandlung*. Johanna also met with the son of a Hamburg Senator, Cornelius Johann Ridel, whose wife Amalie was the sister of Charlotte Buff, the model for Lotte in Goethe's *The Sufferings of Young Werther*, the work in which Goethe shot Werther to save himself. Goethe himself remained elusive, however. He was scheduled to give Johanna a tour of the library, but he cancelled, due to sickness. She did, however, have the good fortune to be introduced to Carl Ludwig Fernow, professor of philosophy at Jena, art connoisseur, and librarian. Fernow would play a decisive role in the lives of the two Schopenhauers. Johanna also became acquainted with Wieland. She wrote to her son that the entire night prior to her meeting Wieland, she would be thinking, and here she wrote in English, "O Lord O Lord what an honour is this."

Johanna's experiences in Weimar eliminated the possibility of relocating to Gotha. Twelve days in the city of poets were sufficient to return her to her initial resolve. In the very same letter in which she revealed her giddiness about meeting Wieland, she articulated her reasons in favor of Weimar: "Society appears very agreeable here and not very expensive. It will be easy to assemble around my tea table the first-rate heads in Weimar, and perhaps in Germany, at least once a week and to lead a thoroughly pleasant life. The region around Weimar is not remarkably beautiful, but it is very pretty. Still, the park is actually very beautiful. I hope for a great

---

[34] Falk founded an orphanage in Weimar, the Homeland Mission.

enjoyment from the theater. I have attended it three times and it is quite excellent. We have scarcely a shadow of it in Hamburg."[35]

Johanna's confidence about her success was reasonable. She had the personal connections, the well-practiced skills as a hostess, which she had honed in Hamburg, and the financial means to establish a salon. She spoke French and English, painted and sketched, played the piano, and loved literature, and her extensive traveling provided a wealth of stories. Personally, she was energetic, cheerful, and attentive to her guests. Also, she had a title. She would become known as "Hofrätin Schopenhauer" by using a hereditary Polish title of her late husband, but one that Heinrich Floris never used. Nevertheless, there was a particular mania for titles in Weimar. In this fashion, she could be like Privy Councilor Goethe and Court Councilor Wieland. Once established, Johanna had her tea parties twice a week – Thursdays and Sundays.

After arranging for her lodgings in Weimar, Johanna hurried back to Hamburg to tie up loose ends, to bid farewell to her friends and acquaintances, to collect the nine-year-old Adele and her servants, and to leave Arthur behind. She departed Hamburg on 21 September without bidding Arthur a personal good-bye. Instead, she left him a proxy farewell in the form of a letter that her son discovered the day that she left: "You have just departed, I can still smell the smoke of your cigar, and I knew that I will not see you for a long time. We spent the evening together joyfully; let that be our good-bye. Farewell my good, dear Arthur. When you receive these lines, I will presumably no longer be here; but even if I am, do not come to see me, I cannot bear farewells. Instead, we can see one another when we want; I hope it will not be too long before reason will permit us to do as we will. Farewell, this was the first time I ever deceived you. I ordered the horses for half past six. I hope that my deception will not give you pain; I did it for my sake, since I know how weak I am in such moments, and I know how much any violent emotion affects me."[36] Johanna's feelings were spared. By the time Arthur read the letter, she had vanished.

There is an interesting parallel between Johanna's farewells to her husband and son. In Heinrich Floris's death notice, she declined expressions

---

[35] Lütkehaus, *Die Schopenhauers*, p. 73, Johanna to Arthur, 4 June 1806.

[36] Ibid., p. 74, Johanna to Arthur, letter dated simply "Sunday Evening." Johanna left for Weimar on the morning of Monday, 20 September 1806.

of sympathy to spare herself grief. In her farewell letter to Arthur, she stole away in the early hours of the morning to spare herself distress. Although there may be something authentic in these overly dramatic expressions of her sensitivities, it is likely that this was more the case concerning her departure from her son than it was concerning the death of her husband. Although Arthur was also liberated by his father's death, his grief and feelings of guilt conspired against his true wishes. This was not the case for Johanna, who followed her heart's desire after yielding to the customary period of mourning. It may have been the case that what she feared first and foremost about a personal farewell to her son was not her own sadness, but her worries over dealing with a son who might make a scene. Still, she was his mother and he her son, and she did care about his well-being. Her son's unhappy life would trouble Johanna and she would eventually play a vital role in freeing Arthur from the trap of his own inertia. Still, the smell of Arthur's cigar probably also reminded her of Heinrich Floris.[37]

While Johanna dashed to Weimar, her son remained mired in his apprenticeship, boarding with the insurance broker Gysbert Willinck. Only his extracurricular readings and the weekend visits by his "French brother," Anthime Grégoire, who had arrived at the end of May to perfect his business knowledge of German, and who was boarding with Pastor Hübbe in nearby Deichdorf Allermöhe, brought Arthur consolation. Johanna traveled to Weimar completely oblivious to the political situation. During the European tour, the Schopenhauers kept a keen eye on Napoleon's mischief, which they carefully avoided through travel delays or changing their plans. Johanna's enthusiasm for her relocation kept her from realizing that she was approaching the eye of a storm. A month prior to Johanna's trip, Napoleon tried to come to terms with the British by offering them the return of Hanover, an offer that also aimed at weakening Prussia's position in northern Germany. This naturally irritated King Friedrich Wilhelm III of Prussia, who then allied Prussia with Russia. This provoked Napoleon to deploy French troops east of the

---

[37] Heinrich Floris also smoked cigars. It is curious to note that Arthur could not remember the month of his sister's birth – fifty-two years after the fact – but he could vividly recall his father announcing Adele's birth, "through smoke swirling under his nose"; see Schopenhauer, *Gasammelte Briefe*, p. 237, Schopenhauer to Sibylle Mertens-Schaaffhausen.

Rhine. Prussia counteracted this deployment by demanding Napoleon's withdrawal as well as the abolition of the Confederation of the Rhine. The dogs of war were straining at their leashes as Johanna reached Weimar on 28 September. Friedrich Wilhelm III declared war on France on 9 October.

Contrary to the recommendation of Privy Councilor Goethe, Carl August unwisely cast his lot with Prussia. Early October brought the encampment of one hundred thousand Prussian and Saxon soldiers around Weimar. Friedrich Wilhelm III and Queen Louise arrived in Weimar around 10 October. Johanna was anxious and considered fleeing Weimar. On 11 October she learned that an old friend from Danzig and a frequent guest at her Hamburg parties, Field Marshall Friedrich von Kalckreuth, was in town. She sent her servant Johannes Duguet with a note to the Prussian commander, who promised to call on her that night, but was unable to do so and postponed his visit until the next evening. Meanwhile she sought advice about her plight. She was assured by her friends that she should be safe in Weimar, because the fighting was likely to take place near Leipzig. Still, she would have fled had she been able to secure horses. On 12 October, however, a visitor even more esteemed than Kalckreuth arrived: "A stranger was announced to me; I entered into the anteroom and saw a handsome, serious man dressed in black, who bowed low and said with much decorum: 'Allow me to present to you the Privy Councilor Goethe.' I looked around the room to see where Goethe was, since after this stiff description that had been given to me of him, I could not recognize him as this man."[38] Oddly, she did not recognize how stiff it was for Goethe to refer to himself in the third person. Naturally, she was overjoyed, especially when Goethe grasped both of her hands with his and reassured her about the future. Goethe's stay was brief, but he promised that he would call on her again. That evening, Field Marshall Kalckreuth arrived. He was dissatisfied with the way events were unfolding, but told Johanna that she would not be at risk by staying in Weimar. Still, Kalckreuth was ambivalent. If she wished to leave Weimar, she could travel to Erfurt and from there to Magdeburg. Johanna decided to stay, but still attempted in vain to secure horses in case it became necessary to flee. She even went to see the Grand Duchess for horses. Anna Amalia had none to

---

[38] Lütkehaus, *Die Schopenhauers*, p. 82, Johanna to Arthur, 19 October 1806.

spare. When her lady-in-waiting was fleeing on the next day, she invited Johanna and Adele to join her.[39] Johanna declined, because she did not want to leave her loyal servants behind.

Johanna returned home after her audience with the Grand Duchess. That afternoon, Kalckreuth visited her for a third time. Johanna was touched by the old General's concern, and she was filled with anxiety about his fate, as he was preparing to join his troops. The activities of the day left her longing for some solitude. Consequently, she sent Adele and Sophie to an evening performance of Kotzebue's comedy, *Fanchon*. Still, Johanna did not remain home long, and had Duguet take her through the busy streets to visit the Ridels. The visit proved comforting, because they decided the reports that the French would be engaged at Leipzig were true. She returned home to find Adele and Sophie made merry by the play. They went to sleep that night, she said, without any concerns: the night was as still as the grave. The next morning, on the fourteenth, cannons could be heard in the distance, and despite reports of Prussian success, Johanna prepared for the worst. She hid her valuables, bought as much food as possible, brought her wine from the cellar to her apartment – because if the French came, this was what they would want first – and gathered with her neighbors and landlady, making bandages. As they did so, Hegel madly scrambled in Jena to safeguard the manuscript for the *Phenomenology of Spirit*, as his horse-mounted world spirit made short work of a coalition of Prussian and Saxon forces there and as Marshall Davout routed the main Prussian army at Auerstädt.

False reports of Prussian and Saxon success on the battlefield continued to circulate around Weimar. A friend rapped on Johanna's windows and shouted that there was a complete victory. Her neighbors, the Contas, her landlady, Adele, Sophie and her husband, and Johanna fell rejoicing into each other's arms. Still, Johanna sensed that something was wrong. Her intuition proved accurate, because Prussian soldiers soon were scrambling through the streets, hastily fleeing for their lives. Within minutes, screams of "the French are coming" filled the air. Johanna's window-knocking friend had been correct. There had been a complete victory, but the

---

[39] Johanna had met the Grand Duchess's lady-in-waiting, Fraülein von Göchausen, previously, and she arranged a half-hour meeting between Anna Amalia and Johanna. Wilhelm Tischbein had given Johanna letters of introduction to both Göchausen and Goethe. Tischbein was a painter and a frequent attendee at Johanna's parties in Hamburg. He accompanied Goethe on his tour of Italy.

celebrants drew the invalid inference that the victory had gone to the Prussians. Soon booming cannons rattled the same windows as Johanna's friend; a ball struck harmlessly within fifty paces of Johanna's home; bullets whistled and hissed through the air as several structures soon caught fire – one column of fire soared as high as Mount Blanc, Johanna wrote to Arthur. It was Weimar's good fortune that there were no winds that night, because the entire city could have gone up in flames; Napoleon would not permit the inhabitants of Weimar to extinguish the flames. The roaring cannons fell quiet and their noise was replaced by the sharp reports of muskets as the French executed a mop-up action in the streets, which soon became littered with wounded and dying men. Johanna resigned herself to fate. She gathered Adele on her lap as she sat on a sofa: "I hoped that a single bullet would kill us both; at least one would not have to grieve for the other. Never had the thought of death been more present to me, never had it been less frightful to me."[40]

The rout of the Prussian and Saxon forces left the citizens of Weimar to deal with the aftermath. To field a rapid and highly mobile army, Napoleon traveled lightly, without magazines and supply trains for provisions. This meant that his men needed to live off the land, as it were, thus requiring the locals to meet their material needs.[41] Although Napoleon officially forbade looting by his troops, he was not disinclined to teach his enemies a lesson. So he turned a blind eye to the actions of his infantry, who treated Weimar as their wartime reward. Johanna was fortunate that the first wave of soldiers who descended on her home were members of the cavalry, "hussars," as she called them. One of these men was a countryman of Johanna's maid Sophie, and Sophie's good cheer and cooking, and Johanna's wine, won them over. It also helped that Johanna herself spoke flawless French. In time, they developed a rapport with these "hussars," and their presence in her home gave it some protection. When things calmed down after one night and day of chaos, one of these men accompanied Johanna and Adele to speak to Prince Murat. The Prince refused to talk to Johanna, but would talk to the soldier, who arranged for a *Commissaire des Guerres* to return to her quarters for her protection. In time, one of her hussars brought to her house for shelter a well-known

---

[40] Lütkehaus, *Die Schopenhauers*, p. 88, Johanna to Arthur, 19 October 1806.
[41] See Robert B. Holtman, *The Napoleonic Revolution* (Philadelphia/New York/Toronto: Lippincott, 1967), pp. 40–41.

lapidary, his nursing wife, a newborn and two children, and a maid. The family had been driven by bayonet from their home. Eventually, the house was filled with displaced souls, representing all strata of Weimar's society, except for the nobility. They had all fled, except for the Duchess, who arranged with Napoleon an end to the hostilities. Weimar-Saxony pledged to return to neutrality between France and Prussia.

The good spirits and hospitality of Sophie, the sweetness of the young Adele, and Johanna's familiarity with French customs and her ability to speak French established a connection with the French soldiers who sought provisions and quarters at Hofrätin Schopenhauer's home. She almost moved a rough hussar to tears by offering him a small chest of gold if he demanded it: "*Si vous la demandez il faut que je vous la donne.*" Instead of the chest itself, the soldier took a small piece of gold. Ultimately, the presence of the *Commissaire des Guerres* ensured that Johanna's abode would be one of the few to escape the dire effects of Napoleon's lesson. Before the war, Weimar had slightly more than 7,500 inhabitants, and many evacuated the city during the preparation for war. Once the French occupied Weimar, many people fled to the nearby woods and fields. One of Johanna's hussars estimated the number of marauding French soldiers at 50,000, and she identified the looters as members of the infantry. In her letter to Arthur, she viewed the cavalry as gentlemen, and the infantry as barbarians: "The first bear all of the stamps of culture, the last are wild people, hardened to everything."[42] Earlier, in the same letter, she described members of the infantry as "wild, bloody humans, whom I cannot call soldiers, in torn, white blouses, murder and death in their eyes." These bloody wild men, she continued, managed much mischief, singing, "Let us eat, drink, plunder and burn all houses down." Any vacant home was plundered, with any portable item of value stolen, and windows and furniture smashed. Inhabitants less fortunate than Johanna were driven from their homes and their homes were then treated as if they were vacant. Certainly, there were a few others who escaped the madness. The Bertuchs were spared in virtue of their quartering the French General Berthier, and Wieland received protection because he was a member of the National Institute. But those who were spared were more than counterbalanced by those who were damned. Herder's widow was robbed and all of her husband's manuscripts were

---

[42] Lütkehaus, *Die Schopenhauers*, p. 99, Johanna to Arthur, 19 October 1806.

destroyed. The Ridels lost everything except a tea machine that the looters failed to recognize as silver. Even the great Goethe was not spared indignities. He would have been roughed up, or worse, had not Christiane Vulpius, Goethe's lover and "housekeeper," and others intervened to save him.[43]

Johanna's relatively good fortune put her in a position to shine. It was almost as if she set out to be a good hostess to all of Weimar. She sent her linens to the wounded for bandages; she supplied food and wine for the unfortunate. Even Goethe followed her lead and opened his wine cellar to the recovering warriors. There is nothing like a disaster to bring people together. As she wrote her son, "My existence here will be agreeable; people have become better acquainted with me in ten days than otherwise in ten years. Goethe told me today that I have become a Weimarian through a baptism of fire."[44] Goethe even told her that he wanted to meet during the winter to brighten its dreary days. In order to cheer herself and keep up her own spirits, every day she gathered her acquaintances and gave them tea and buttered bread, a feat more difficult to arrange than it appears, as she told Arthur. The Swiss painter and art scholar Johann Heinrich Meyer, the Old Fernow, and Goethe himself, were regular attendees at these gatherings; Wieland promised regular visits.

The events in Weimar moved Goethe to embrace convention by making an honest woman out of Christiane. He had been living with her in a quasi-open fashion for eighteen years, although she was technically his housekeeper. In 1789 she bore his son, August, whom Goethe gave his name. But on 19 October 1806, he married her. Johanna reported that the great man told her that "in times of peace one may well by-pass the law, in

---

[43] It is odd that Napoleon did not send protectors to Goethe's home. He was certainly a fan of Goethe, and he claimed to have read *The Sufferings of Young Werther* seven times. It may have been the case that Napoleon also wanted to teach Goethe a lesson due to the many political offices he held in Carl August's court. Almost two years after the occupation of Weimar, in September 1808, Napoleon summoned Goethe to the Prince's Congress in Erfurt – perhaps a reverse Faustian summoning. Goethe was alleged to have asked the Emperor whether a tragedy could still be based around the idea of fate. Napoleon was said to have replied: "What do we want with fate now? Politics is our fate." James Sheehan's *German History: 1720–1866* (Oxford: Oxford University Press, 1989), p. 358. Schopenhauer traveled to this conference with Johannes Falk, where Schopenhauer was reported to have made scandalous remarks about the ladies of the court, who had moved from viewing Napoleon as a monster to viewing him as the most charming man on earth; see *Gespräche*, p. 21 for Falk's report.

[44] Lütkehaus, *Die Schopenhauers*, p. 102, Johanna to Arthur, 19 October 1806.

times like ours one must honor it."[45] It would be Johanna's acceptance of
Christiane at her tea parties that led Goethe to favor her parties, because
others continued to look down their noses at Frau Geheimratin Goethe.
He felt that Johanna would be more liberal in attitude toward his wife
because she was a stranger who lived in large cities. Johanna's explanation
was more straightforward: "I think that if Goethe could give her his
name, we indeed could give her a cup of tea."[46] Goethe's presence at her
tea parties gave Johanna's gatherings a magnetic atmosphere that drew
numerous significant personalities to her home, along with her, at that
time, insignificant son. Goethe would come to play a significant role in
both her children's lives.

On the day Goethe wed, Johanna wrote to Arthur a massive letter
of approximately eight thousand words in which she described her war
experiences in melodramatic terms.[47] It was peppered with numerous
references to its reader: "Oh dear Arthur," "Oh my son," "Dear, dear
Arthur," and it was salted with an equal share of exclamations to the Lord:
"Oh God," "Good God," and "Oh my God." The letter was not meant for
Arthur's eyes only. She asked him to share it with Tischbein, Gansland,
Willink, and others in Hamburg. When he was done with it, he was
instructed to send it to her sister Juliane in Danzig. It was, Johanna said,
too lengthy for her to copy. Still, copies of the letter were widely circulated.
One could say that it marks Johanna's debut as an author.[48] Although
Johanna described the wretched conditions in Weimar, she also told her
son that "One has only a concept of the horrors of war if one sees it
close-up as I; I could tell you things that would make your hair stand on
end, but I will not, since I recognize how fond you are of brooding about
human misery."[49]

Johanna's letters neither moved Arthur to take up arms to oppose
the French, nor did Napoleon's victory stir a desire in the young man for

[45] Ibid, p. 107, Johanna to Arthur, 24 October 1806. Although they married on 19 October,
Goethe had the ring inscribed 14 October, the day of the battles of Jena and Auerstedt.

[46] Ibid, p. 107.

[47] See ibid., pp. 80–103, Johanna to Arthur, 19 October 1806. Johanna's reactions to the occupation of Weimar, given above, were taken from this letter. She also described conditions in
Weimar in letters from 20, 24, 26 October 1806; see ibid., pp. 103–10.

[48] I owe this point to Ulrike Bergmann. She also observed that Johanna "stylized herself as a
heroine of a historic drama." *Johanna Schopenhauer*, p. 127. Sophie, Adele, and the younger
Conta were given their due also in this letter.

[49] Lütkehaus, *Die Schopenhauers*, p. 100, Johanna to Arthur, 19 October 1806.

German unity, a yearning that was common to many men of his generation. Odds are that he would not have been keen to attend Fichte's delivery of *Addresses to the German Nation* [*Reden an die deutsche Nation*], which were given in the winter of 1807–8 in French-occupied Berlin and which were denied publication by the Prussian censors. Heinrich Floris had succeeded in cultivating within his son a cosmopolitan attitude, an attitude that even transcended Nietzsche's later idea of the "good European" and made Arthur open to Eastern thought.[50] Nor did his mother's letters lead Schopenhauer to sympathize with the sad plight of the Weimarians in general or Johanna and Adele in particular. Instead, he interpreted his mother's attempt to cheerfully craft an agreeable life as predicated on forgetting all of the horrors of France's defeat of the Prussian and Saxon army:

Forgetting doing in despair: This is such a strange trait of human nature; one would not believe it if one did not see it. Tieck expressed it marvelously in approximately these words: "We stand and wail and ask the stars who has been more unhappy than we, while behind our backs the scoffing future stands and laughs at the transitory pain of humans." But certainly it must be so: nothing is bound to hold fast in a transitory life; no unending pain, no eternal joy, no enduring sensation, no lasting enthusiasm, no higher decision that could hold good for life. Everything is annulled by the passage of time. The minutes, the countless atoms of small details into which every action decays, are the worms that consume everything great and bold. The monster, ordinary life, pushes down everything that strives upwards. There is nothing serious in life, because the dust is not worth the trouble. How could there be an eternal passion in consequence of this wretchedness?[51]

Arthur's reply to Johanna's war report dimly shows features of his later philosophical reflections on the vanity of life. As Thomas Mann remarked in response to Schopenhauer's elegant descriptions of the wretchedness of life: "Everyone realizes that when this commanding spirit and great writer

[50] See Nietzsche's *The Gay Science*, Sect. 357, where he claims that Schopenhauer posed the question of the meaning of existence as a "good European."

[51] Lütkehaus, *Die Schopenhauers*, p. 116, Arthur to Johanna, 8 November 1806. Schopenhauer's quotation from "The Marvels of Music" is not very precise. The original is, "When a brother of mine has died and, at such an event of life, I appropriately display deep sorrow, sit weeping in a narrow corner, and ask all the stars who has ever been more grieved than I, – then, – while the mocking future already stands behind my back and laughs about the quickly fleeting pain of the human being. . . ." See Wilhelm Heinrich Wackenroder, *Confessions and Fantasies*, trans. Mary Hurst Schubert (University Park/London: The Pennsylvania State University Press, 1971), p. 181.

speaks in general of the suffering of the world, he speaks of yours and mine, and all of us feel triumph at being avenged by the heroic word."[52] It is unlikely that Johanna would have agreed fully with Mann's judgment. She would have recognized Arthur's letter as another expression of her son's severely depressive and critical spirit. On the one hand, he was accusing Johanna of exhibiting that strange trait of human nature – forgetting despair. On the other hand, he was also trying to undermine Johanna's cheerfulness – it, like pain, is transitory and not worth the effort. Her cheerfulness was also vulnerable in more immediate ways. In the very letter to which he responded, Johanna noted his tendency to brood about human misery, and she claimed to have avoided telling him things that would have made his hair stand on end. Arthur knew, moreover, that Johanna attributed this disposition to his patrilineal inheritance, and both mother and son believed that Heinrich Floris took his own life. Perhaps Arthur's letter was designed to suggest that he was on the verge of doing likewise – after all, there is nothing "serious in life" that makes it "worth the trouble." Indeed, after a series of letters lamenting his position in Hamburg, Johanna wrote of "the melancholy brooding that you received as the inheritance from your father," in the letter that would prepare the stage for Arthur's liberation.[53] Either Johanna's compassion or guilt would defeat his mother's happiness. Still, the actual effect of this letter, at this time, was to reinforce her belief about her son's disagreeable personality – he sure could spoil the fun. In four short years, however, the depressed young man would find something to take seriously and that was worth the trouble.

Although Schopenhauer's letter possessed clear attempts to manipulate his mother, it did express authentic distress. His family life was shattered by his father's death and even though his earlier life was far from ideal, it provided stability and security for a young man who worried about abandonment throughout his entire life. Now he was living on his own in Hamburg, playing at becoming a merchant. He wanted to join his mother, his sister, and the Duguets in Weimar. Still, he remained frozen in Hamburg. Reflecting on that period of his life, he said that nothing forced him to remain in his apprenticeship; he was his own master, "so-to-say." His father was dead and his mother did not stand in his way.

[52] Thomas Mann, *Schopenhauer* (Stockholm: Bermann-Fischer Verlag, 1938), p. 27.
[53] Lütkehaus, *Die Schopenhauers*, p. 164, Johanna to Arthur, 28 April 1807.

Still, he remained, "in part because I made it a matter of conscience not to annul the decision of my father so soon after his death."[54] Yet it was not the ghost of a dead man, nor a nonexistent family business to run, that chained him to the counting house. It was his own conscience. In life and death, Heinrich Floris tended to put him in a double bind. First, there was the choice of the European tour or the life of a scholar. Second, he had to choose between maintaining his pledge to his father or breaking it. Arthur betrayed himself with his decisions. He had decided for the immediate, short-term pleasures of the tour, rather than pursuing his deeper desires. Now, to maintain a bond with his father's desires and to avoid a guilty conscience, it was his own sense of obligation that defeated his deeper desire for a life of the intellect. He wanted Johanna to bail him out. Perhaps quoting "Tieck" and drawing out what he found as the implications of this view would also show his mother that he was destined to be something greater than a businessman.

Arthur's reply also mirrored the language and mood of the author whose lines he quoted from memory. Yet he misattributed the quotation to Ludwig Tieck, the poet, novelist, literary critic, and editor and co-author of *Fantasies on Art for Friends of Art* [*Phantasien über die Kunst, für Freunde der Kunst*, 1799].[55] Schopenhauer's quotation is from an essay found in that work, "On the Marvels of Music" ["*Über die Wunder der Tonkunst*"], written by Wilhelm Heinrich Wackenroder, who had the misfortune of dying from typhus at the age of twenty-five, but who also had the good fortune of Tieck's friendship, because he would publish Wackenroder's essays as *Fantasies on Art*, "partly with confidence, partly with anxiety," as a legacy to his deceased friend.[56] Wackenroder, like Tieck, was one of the Early German Romantics, a cadre of men and (some) women,

---

[54] Schopenhauer, *Gesammelte Briefe*, p. 651.

[55] Schopenhauer's posthumous library included *Fantasies on Art* as well as Wackenroder's *Confessions for the Heart of an Art-Loving Friar* (*Herzenergiessungen eines Kunstliebenden Klosterbruders*), which appeared anonymously in the fall of 1796 (although it bore a publication date of 1797). Schopenhauer met Tieck in the winter of 1824–5 in Dresden. In one account, they were said to have become involved in an argument about various philosophical systems, during the course of which Tieck referred to God, a remark that caused Schopenhauer to leap from his seat, as if he were stung by a tarantula, repeating with mocking laughter, "What? You need a God?" Wilhelm Gwinner, Schopenhauer's friend, executor of his will, and his first biographer, reported that the basis of the quarrel concerned Schopenhauer's criticisms of Friedrich Schlegel, a friend from Tieck's youth; see Schopenhauer, *Gespräche*, p. 53.

[56] Wackenroder, *Confessions and Fantasies*, p. 163, Tieck's "Preface" to *Fantasies on Art*.

philosophers, theologians, literary critics, writers, and poets, who set out to disturb the cool, calculating rationality of the Enlightenment, and who aimed to replace its rigidly mechanical view of nature with a conception of nature as a teleologically structured, dynamic, organic whole, which is self-generating and self-organizing. These Early Romantics promoted the cultivation of one's feelings and imagination as the means of knowledge, fostered an idiosyncratic form of individuality, self-consciously employed mythology, loved fairy tales and the Orient, glorified art – especially music – and sought to transcend all finiteness, limitation, and dualism through identification with some greater whole. Tieck would eventually live for a time in Jena, which housed many of the Early Romantics since the mid-1790s: the Schlegels, (Carl Wilhelm) Friedrich and his later wife Dorothea, and August Wilhelm and Caroline; Novalis (Friedrich Leopold Freiherr von Hardenberg); Friedrich Hölderlin; Friedrich Joseph Wilhelm von Schelling; and others.[57]

The function of time in Schopenhauer's letter suggests another essay from the *Fantasies on Art*, "A Wondrous Oriental Tale of a Naked Saint" ["*Ein wonderbares morgenländisches Märchen von einem nackten Heiligen*"]. In this quintessentially romantic tale the naked saint becomes obsessed with the relentless grinding of the wheel of time until he can do little more than act as if he were turning the wheel, and when someone wandered by his cave, "... he tended to burst out laughing hysterically over the fact that someone was still able to think of these trivial earthly concerns amidst the frightful rolling on of time; at such moments he bounded from his cave in a single, tiger-like leap and, if he could snatch the unfortunate one, he smashed him to the ground dead in a single motion. He then jumped quickly back into the cave and turned the Wheel of Time more violently than before; however, he raged on for a long time and scorned in disjointed utterances how it was possible for human beings to work at something else, to take on a *tactless* occupation."[58] The saint continued turning the wheel in despair, except at times when the moon would appear before his cave, and he would stop, haunted by an all-consuming desire for some unknown, beautiful thing that he could seize and to which he

[57] See Ameriks, Karl, *The Cambridge Companion to German Idealism* (Cambridge: Cambridge University Press, 2000), p. xiv, for a map of Jena, showing the residences of various notable figures in the early 1800's.
[58] Wackenroder, *Confessions and Fantasies*, p. 176.

could cling. Years passed and then one beautiful, moonlit summer night two lovers floated in a skiff up the river that raced before the saint's grotto, and while they gave expression to their tender feelings, "Ethereal music floated up from the skiff into the open heavens; sweet bugles and I know not what other enchanting instruments brought forth a floating world of sounds and, in the harmonies which were drifting up," the lovers began to sing.[59] The lovers' song stilled the Wheel of Time, and the saint shed his naked body and his spirit was drawn upward, in a dancing motion, to disappear into the infinite firmament.

Schopenhauer's letter expressed the same sense of despair as that of Wackenroder's nude holy man. The relentless march of time rendered trivial all earthly concerns: they could not be taken seriously; they were not worth the trouble. Behind Schopenhauer's nihilistic pronouncement, however, one can sense a longing for something that would lift him beyond the "scoffing future." Shortly after this letter, he fired off another that continued his Wackenroderean theme. Music comes to the rescue: "And still a compassionate angel has pleaded on our behalf for the heavenly flower, and it rises tall in full magnificence, rooted in the soil of wretchedness. – The pulsations of divine music have not ceased beating through the centuries of barbarism, and a direct echo of eternity has remained with us as a result of it, intelligent to each receptive mind and elevated above all vice and virtue."[60] Schopenhauer would always retain a link with Early German Romanticism with his exaltation of music, and when he would develop his hierarchy of the arts, music would stand at the top of the scale. And, with the possible exception of Schelling, he would develop an aesthetics grander in scope and richer in detail than that of his philosophical contemporaries. In 1812, in the notes to his study of Schelling's *Philosophy and Religion* [*Philosophie und Religion*, 1804], he jotted: "Philosophy is art, and its material is the understanding. For that reason it is prose throughout."[61] He would extend this insight specifically regarding the expressive power of music. Philosophy is like art, because it replicates the world conceptually, and music does the same in tones.[62]

[59] Ibid., p. 177.

[60] Lütkehaus, *Die Schopenhauers*, pp. 125–6, Arthur to Johanna, November 1806.

[61] Schopenhauer, *Manuscript Remains*, Vol. 2, p. 337/*Der Handschriftliche Nachlaß*, Vol. 2, p. 325.

[62] See Schopenhauer, *The World as Will and Representation*, Vol. 2, p. 533/*Sämtliche Werke*, Vol. 3, p. 610.

It is likely, however, that the young Schopenhauer would have found something perplexing and problematic about Wackenroder's wondrous oriental tale. The naked saint was liberated from both the Wheel of Time and his body by ethereal music and the lovers' song:

> Sweet thrills of expectation
> Flow away o'er field and stream
> Moonbeams make the preparation
> For the lover's sensual dreams.
> How the waves whisper, O how they call
> And reflect in their dark depths the heavenly all.[63]

At this stage in his life, Schopenhauer found a different direction to the tug of love. In a poem, written sometime between 1804 and 1806, his attitude toward sensuality is decidedly not Wackenroderean:

> Voluptuous pleasure, infernal delight,
> Love insatiable and invincible!
> From the heights of heaven
> Thou hast dragged me down
> And cast me in fetters
> Into the dust of this earth.
> How shall I aspire and soar
> To the throne of the eternal,
> Or to be reflected in the imprint
> Of the thought supreme
> Or be cradled in fragrance
> Or fly through space illimitable,
> Wholly devout and filled with awe,
> With outbursts of mirth,
> Or wrapt in humility,
> Or hearing only harmony?
> How shall I forget
> The vileness of this dust,
> Or refrain from scolding fools,
> From envying the great,
> From mocking the infirm,
> From seeing the vicious?
> How shall I see and adore
> The master in his work or
> In the body the mind?
> Yet, bond of weakness,

---

[63] Wackenroder, *Confessions and Fantasies*, p. 177.

Thou draggest me down and
Thy threads and webs
Hold me firmly in their grasp.
All my efforts to rise
Are abortive and vain.[64]

Later, Schopenhauer would maintain that "all amorousness is rooted in the sexual impulse alone" and that "it does not hesitate to intrude with its trash and to interfere with the negotiations of State and the investigations of the learned."[65] Sexuality ties one to the world governed by restless time and binds one to that world, having a quite opposite effect from elevating one beyond the wretched world. Nor could sexuality be the source of the music that moves its consumer to salvation. The naked saint could – at best – be a voyeur, enthralled by the sex play of the lovers, and consumed by its trash.

A Magnificent Mama?

Johanna had hoped that Anthime's presence in Hamburg would bring some brightness to Arthur's drab life, and she was delighted when he moved in to live with Arthur at the insurance broker Willink's home: "I imagine that now you will lead a very joyous life with your friend; take pleasure in that in the meantime and be of good cheer."[66] Although Schopenhauer took some comfort in the company of his friend – they shared readings lists, indulged in lamenting their senseless fates as merchants, attended parties and concerts – their amorous adventures provided Arthur with more despair than delight. Anthime was more of the ladies' man, and his success emphasized Arthur's failure. His desires, moreover, controlled him and sating his desires seemed often not to have been the goal of women whose affections he could not purchase. Thus the trash of sexuality dragged him down and those with whom he wanted to get down only humiliated him by their rejections. But ultimately, he would go down on women in unrestrained terms in the essay "On Women," in the second volume of *Parerga and Paralipomena*.

---

[64] Schopenhauer, *Manuscript Remains*, Vol. 1, pp. 1–2 / *Der Handschriftliche Nachlaβ*, Vol. 1, pp. 2–3.

[65] Schopenhauer, *The World as Will and Representation*, Vol. 2, p. 533 / *Sämtliche Werke*, Vol. 3, p. 610.

[66] Lütkehaus, *Die Schopenhauers*, p. 143, Johanna to Arthur, 30 January 1807.

Johanna's letters to her despondent son did little to lift his spirits. She encouraged him to cheer up, to take the adverse situation and triumph over it – as she did – saying that adversity can bring out the best in people. She expressed concern over his chronic hearing problems: "it is the only thing that now hinders my complete happiness . . . courage and composure are indeed our only weapons against all of the evils of the world."[67] To distract and to make him useful, she sent him on errands – delivering letters, fetching her books, crayons, and a straw hat. Twice she recommended that he should become acquainted with the painter Phillip Otto Runge, of whom Goethe thought highly and with whom he had been corresponding. This, however, was an impossible task. Runge had left Hamburg some seven months before Johanna's recommendations.[68] She sends Adele's and Sophie's greetings. She says little, however, about Arthur's sister. She is taking piano lessons. Goethe likes to visit her in her room, amusing her with puppet shows. She reports family squabbles in Danzig, and she mentions that his first master in Danzig, Jakob Kabrum, was forced to quarter eight Prussian soldiers; "the poor man, certainly you have compassion for him."[69] She was having her portrait done by an up-and-coming painter, Caroline Bardua, who had painted Goethe and Wieland, but only because Johanna was pestered into it. The painting captured her, but not Adele. The portrait, which has Johanna sitting before an easel and with a palette of colors in her hand, has a melancholy Adele leaning with folded hands on the back of her chair, gazing at the unseen work on canvass, which made for an appropriate allegory for Adele's life, watching behind the scenes of her mother's life. Johanna is depicted as staring at whoever looks at the painting, as if she is noticing those who notice her, rather than looking at the painting under her hand. It is not a masterpiece, she tells Arthur, but it was done gratis. She would send it to him in the spring. She informs Arthur about some of the playful antics at her tea parties, activities that would draw the derision of the very

---

[67] Ibid., p. 132, Johanna to Arthur, 19 December 1806.

[68] In *On Vision and Colors*, trans. E. F. J. Payne, ed. with an intro. David Cartwright (Oxford: Berg, 1994), p. 28/*Sämtliche Werke*, Vol. 1, p. 28, Schopenhauer praised Runge's "ingeniously contrived color sphere" for clearly representing the maximum purity and freedom from white and black of each color and for showing how various colors gradually transition from one to another. He also praised Runge's arabesques for representing "the palpably unnatural and impossible, but from which a deep meaning is nevertheless expressed." *Parerga and Paralipomena*, Vol. 2, p. 363/*Sämtliche Werke*, Vol. 6, p. 386.

[69] Lütkehaus, *Die Schopenhauers*, p. 130, Johanna to Arthur, 22 December 1806.

sensible and practical people of Hamburg, and she does so while citing Tieck: " . . . to prudent and reasonable people our activities would almost appear to be foolish. If a senator or burgomaster saw me gluing slips of paper together with Meyer, as Goethe and others were standing by and eagerly giving advice, he would have genuine Christian pity for our poor childish souls; but that is just the divinity of art, says your dear Tieck, if I am not mistaken."[70]

Johanna quite naturally had to describe the brilliant successes of her tea circle. Bardua, Fernow, Meyer, the Contas, the Ridels, the Falks, and the Bertuchs were constant attendees. The old poet Wieland, for whom Johanna felt genuine affection, would only visit when he knew that Goethe would not be present. She attributed this to Wieland feeling oppressed by the weight of Goethe's gravitas, but she also knew that as a member of Anna Amalia's "Court of the Muses," the old man associated with a cultural clique antagonistic to Goethe and his crew. Anna Amalia and Schiller's widow, Charlotte, were visited by Johanna and they would visit her. Goethe, of course, was the star attraction at her parties and everything tended to revolve around his moods. Goethe could be convivial and charming or distant and even petulant. Goethe, however, knew he was GOETHE! Johanna carefully arranged her parties in such a way that Goethe, who tended to make his entrances self-consciously, would find something that would lead him to feel graciously at home:

I put a table in the corner with drawing materials for him. His friend Meyer gave me this idea. What a being is this Goethe, so great and so good. Since I never know when he will arrive, I am startled every time he enters the room. It is as if he were of a higher nature than all of the others, since I see clearly that he produces the same impression on everyone, even those who have known him longer and who are far closer to him than I. He himself is always a little silent and in a way self-conscious when he arrives, until he has taken a good look to see who is present, and then he sits down close to me, a little behind me, so that he can support himself on the backrest of my chair. I would then begin a conversation with him, and he would come to life and be indescribably charming. He is the most perfect being I know, also in his appearance; a tall fine figure, holding himself very straight, very carefully dressed, always completely in black or dark blue, his hair very tastefully coifed and powdered as befits his age, and a very magnificent face with two clear, brown eyes, mild and piercing at the same time. When he speaks he becomes unbelievably beautiful, and I cannot see enough of him. He is now around fifty years old; what must he have been when he was younger.[71]

---

[70] Ibid., p. 141, Johanna to Arthur, 30 January 1807.
[71] Ibid., p. 123, Johanna to Arthur, 28 November 1806.

Once Goethe warmed to the room and sensed that he could be himself, he would frequently become the star on the stage, instead of a celebrity in the audience. Sometimes, he would do so softly. Johanna wrote to Arthur about an instance of this in which she compared Goethe to his father: "Goethe began to speak about his approaching old age, and with a softness of tone, with a very noble self-consciousness, that touched us all deeply. At the same time he firmly held my hand, as he did frequently, and he vividly reminded me then of your father, who would also hold me firmly at such times."[72] Sometimes, Goethe would be highly animated, raucous, and playful. He would read poems, letters, and stories, vigorously acting out the moods of the pieces with wild gestures and loud shouts. Once he began with such spirited marching around the room that Johanna's landlady complained about the noise. On several visits, he read scenes from August Schlegel's translation of the seventeenth-century playwright Pedro Calderón de la Barca's *El príncipe constant* [*The Constant Prince*]. Goethe owned the German stage rights to the play and would produce it and direct it on 30 January 1811. Schopenhauer would attend its first performance and become greatly affected by the play, and he would become a life-long fan of Calderón.[73] On occasion, Goethe would also play the glass harmonica.

Whenever Goethe did not deliberately claim center stage, Johanna made sure that her friends would be entertained. Sometimes they sat at

---

[72] Ibid., p. 165, Johanna to Arthur, 28 April 1807. Because Johanna destroyed all of her son's letters, we do not know how he responded, or if he responded, to his mother's comparison of Goethe to Heinrich Floris. Schopenhauer always regarded his mother as flirtatious, and he always feared that his mother would remarry. It is doubtful, however, that he would have worried about the recently married Goethe, and his awe of Goethe was so great that he may have been impressed that his mother was on such good terms with the great man.

[73] Schopenhauer would later learn to read Spanish in order to read Calderón in the original. The play itself would have a profound effect on him. In *The Constant Prince*, Calderón depicts a martyr of the faith who stoically bears a life-long imprisonment and obtains a state of antipathy to all of life's pleasures and pains, until death frees him from death itself. This play helped ingrain the themes of the transitory nature of human existence, overcoming the world, and death as the goal of life, with death signifying a return to something eternal; see Arthur Hübscher's *The Philosophy of Schopenhauer in Its Intellectual Context: Thinker Against the Tide*, trans. Baer, Joachim and David E. Cartwright (Lewiston, N.Y.: Edwin Mellen Press, 1989), p. 27. Schopenhauer regarded Shakespeare and Calderón as the greatest dramatic poets of modern times; see Schopenhauer, *Parerga and Paralipomena*, Vol. 1, p. 369/*Sämtliche Werke*, Vol. 5, p. 393. Schopenhauer's ranking of Calderón with Shakespeare may have been prepared by Goethe. Johanna mentioned that after finishing *The Constant Prince*, Goethe said that "One could mention by name Calderón next to Shakespeare," Lütkehaus, *Die Schopenhauers*, p. 156, Johanna to Arthur, 23 March 1807.

separate tables, sketching, gluing slips of paper together, and discussing recent concerts and plays. Other times, Johanna would play her new piano or have Adele's piano teacher entertain the crowd. Conta and Bardua were inclined to sing duets, and Conta would sing solo, accompanying himself on the guitar. Occasionally, a visiting opera singer would bring a more professional performance to the tea party. Of course, there was the usual sort of gossiping, joke-telling, and discussions of the best places to vacation and travel. Johanna, of course, also served up tea and buttered bread. She would reiterate to Arthur that her parties were not costly.

Schopenhauer's contribution to the correspondence with his mother does not survive. She destroyed his letters after their final separation less than a decade later. Still, the content of Johanna's letters clearly indicates that Arthur continued to lament his Hamburg life and his preparation for a career in business. Likewise, he must have continued to articulate his desire to attend the university, and more importantly, he must have confided to Johanna his doubts about qualifying for the university. His education was a training to become an international businessman. Had he been able to attend a gymnasium, he would have studied Greek and Latin. In his *curriculum vitae*, Schopenhauer gave three reasons that he did not quit his apprenticeship after his father's death. There was the inertia based on his deep grief. There was the prospect of a guilty conscience for rescinding his promise to his father. "Last," he wrote, "I believed that I was at a too advanced age to still be able to learn the classical languages."[74]

Johanna discussed with Goethe Arthur's concern about his being too old to learn classical languages. She told him about the difficulty Arthur had studying Latin as a youth, although she also told Goethe that he had quite easily mastered English and French. It would not surprise him, Goethe replied, if Arthur found it exceedingly difficult to master Latin. Johanna inferred that she should discourage Arthur's desires, but Goethe told her not to do that and to tell Arthur that "if you still wanted to do it, that would be very good and useful, although you would not be able to bring it to perfection."[75] It now appeared that both Schopenhauers became concerned about Arthur's ability to pursue his education. The topic must have become an item of discussion among members of Hofrätin

---

74 Schopenhauer, *Gesammelte Briefe*, p. 50, Arthur to the Philosophy Faculty of the King Friedrich Wilhelms University at Berlin, 31 December 1819.
75 Lütkehaus, *Die Schopenhauers*, p. 133, Johanna to Arthur, 22 December 1806.

Schopenhauer's tea circle. Approximately, three months later, Johanna sent another mixed message to her son:

I think of you often and with genuine love for you. I frequently wish that you were with me, and when Fernow and St[ephan] Schütze tell me how late they started their studies, and I now see what the two have become, many a project flies through my mind, but of course both brought school knowledge and hard-earned, self-acquired knowledge to the academy, which you lack, given the refined education that you received and which in our position you had to receive. Both of them were born into a very restricted mediocrity in a small locality, and they were able to forgo many a pleasure, the kind of pleasure you are bound to think indispensable, at least in the future, so you will probably have to remain in that career you have chosen.[76]

Johanna also diagnosed the cause of her son's despair and, as if he were an attendee at one of her tea parties, she attempted to bring him some cheer. She had known for a long time that he was discontented with his lot in the world, but this did not worry her, she wrote, because this was an attitude in common with young men his age. You will reach an understanding of yourself, she continued, and then you will be pleased by the world. Johanna also recognized that Arthur may have a more difficult transition into living an effective life than others, due to his isolation in Hamburg, but he had her support: "My poor, dear Arthur . . . perhaps I alone understand you and could listen to you patiently and advise you and comfort you. . . ."[77] "Your problem is that you do not know how to decide; you vacillate, and you do not know what will suit you," she wrote, demonstrating her understanding of her son. She offered advice; be patient, you will change, and you will discover your true desires. And to console her melancholy son, she predicted that once he arrived at an understanding of himself, his indecision would disappear, and he would live well and be happy. It is only natural to think that she is wrong, Johanna wrote in anticipation of Arthur's response, but after reading her lines in another year or so, he will discover that she was correct. It was as if Johanna was proposing an alliance with her son; one that would supersede the pact he had with Heinrich Floris, but an alliance that would keep him in Hamburg, pursuing his father's plan.

Perhaps to move Schopenhauer beyond the indecisive state of complaining about his condition and to bring him to a decision to take

---

[76] Ibid., p. 149, Johanna to Arthur, 10 March 1807.
[77] Ibid., p. 151, Johanna to Arthur, 10 March 1807.

command over his life, she told him about a heartfelt and intimate conversation she had with "Father" Wieland: "He spoke a great deal about
himself, about his youth. No one recognized his talent or understood
him. . . . He was not born a poet, only circumstances and not the force of
his genius brought him to it. He had missed his true career: he should
have studied philosophy or mathematics, since that would have brought
something great out of him."[78] He had to study law, Johanna continued,
and he had to become a municipal administrator in a small town, writing
verse to escape the wretchedness of his bureaucratic tasks. "Never," he
said, "had I a friend with whom I could share or discuss my work. I
was always alone. No one understood me and no one came close to my
heart." Wieland's sad confession knifed against the praise of moderation
central to most of his writings, but it did occasion an ironic response from
Schopenhauer's mother: "Dear Arthur, to hear an old man, almost 80
years old, speak like this is truthfully depressing, and he is called the 'Poet
of the Graces.'"[79] Johanna tried to comfort the old poet's sense of loss of
his creative drives and his sense of his impending death by mentioning
the example of Voltaire. He was flattered, Johanna wrote, by the comparison to Voltaire, but said that Voltaire was a completely different man
than he, because he could still write something worthwhile in his old age,
whereas he no longer possessed any imagination. Consequently, his only
joy now was to occasionally translate Cicero. Johanna closed her letter
with a postscript in which she wrote that she was sending Arthur a sketch
of Goethe: "Am I not a magnificent mama?"

[78] Ibid., p. 153, Johanna to Arthur, 10 March 1807.
[79] Ibid., p. 154, Johanna to Arthur, 10 March 1807. Johanna's reference to Wieland as "the Poet
of the Graces," alludes to his *Musarion, or the Philosophy of the Graces* [*Musarion, oder die
Philosophy der Grazien*, 1768] which is often viewed as the most successful example of his verse
narratives and as a work that achieves a balance of the author's aesthetic and didactic intent.
Wieland promotes the virtue of moderation in *Musarion* against the extremes of enthusiasm
and indifference. As a young man, Goethe was greatly impressed with the work: "*Musarion* had
the most effect upon me; and I can yet remember the place and the very spot where I got sight
of the first proof-sheet. . . . Here it was that I believed I saw antiquity again living and fresh.
Everything that is plastic in Wieland's genius here showed itself in its highest perfection." *The
Autobiography of Johann Wolfgang von Goethe*, trans. John Oxenford (Chicago and London:
University of Chicago Press, 1974), Vol. 1, p. 291 [the original title was *Aus meinem Leben:
Dichtung und Wahrheit*, 1811 et al.] Also see Elizabeth Boas, "Wieland's *Musarion* and the
Rococo Verse Narrative," in *Periods in German Literature*, ed. James M. Ritchie (London:
Wolff, 1968), Vol. 2, pp. 23–41; and for overviews of Wieland's writings, see Jutta Hecker,
Wieland: Die Geschichte eines Menschen in der Zeit (Stuttgart: Mellinger, 1971) and John A
McCarthy, *Christoph Martin Wieland* (Boston: Twayne, 1979).

Arthur's Release

On 28 March 1807, Arthur wrote a letter that Johanna called long and serious. He followed this letter with another note, which she answered on 13 April, the same day that she received it. She was not prepared, however, to provide him with a correspondingly serious reply; that would come later. She assured him that she had reflected on his letters with great concern and that his satisfaction laid close to her heart. Arthur's despair and her anguish for her son's future led her to state a bitter regret. Had only her voice carried greater weight concerning her son's fate, he would not have been in his present state of misery. Last, she promised her unhappy, complaining, and indecisive son that she would provide him with a serious reply, one that would demonstrate how much she loved him.

Fifteen days later, on 28 April, Johanna composed a letter of approximately three thousand words. When she finished it, she said her fingers hurt. It was an earnest letter that did not deliver what the languishing apprentice merchant desired. She knew that Arthur wanted her to resolve his life-altering dilemma – should he continue his training for a merchant's life or should he prepare for a university education? His future hung in the balance. This was also a decision too weighty for the cheerful widow. She knew that Arthur expected her to decide, so she explained why she would not and what she would do. Arthur's situation was too foreign to hers, making it too difficult for her to think her way into it, and even if she could, she also realized that she was a person very different from her son. Indeed, she wrote that in important matters she displayed the fault opposite to that of her son. He was too indecisive and she was perhaps too rash and unconventional. Consequently, she made it clear that he had to decide, and that once he made a decision, she would support it and provide concrete advice.

Yet Johanna adopted a strategy her husband had employed when Arthur made the potentially life-wrecking decision to tour Europe, but unlike Heinrich Floris, she moved Arthur to choose what he ultimately desired, instead of leading him to select a short-term pleasure at the cost of his long-term well-being. She knew what her son truly wanted to do, and she simply made it possible for him to do so. She did this in a letter in which she displayed her knowledge of her son and in which she told her own story about her role in Arthur's life. In heartfelt and sincere terms, she also articulated her concern for his future and her love for her troubled son. She knew, she confessed, what it was to live a life repugnant to one's inner nature, and she promised to do whatever was necessary to spare him that misery. Once again she lamented how little her voice counted in his life, and she added how her desires had been thwarted: "What you wish now was indeed my warmest wish; how hard I strove to make it occur, despite everything set against me. Still I thought that I had succeeded, but we both were deceived in a cruel way, about which we preferred to remain silent, our later complaints helped nothing."[80] Although Johanna did not say it, indeed they both remained silent about it, perhaps the cruel deception was the decision Heinrich Floris forced upon his son. She returned to this theme later in the letter, where she claimed that everything she did was for Arthur's well-being, and this included attending Runge's and Lancaster's schools: "All of this is my work . . . and had my plan not been so unmercifully destroyed, you would now have a canon and would be at a university. . . . Only a cruel ruse could defeat my plan. In his own mind, your father could not be wrong; he also wanted the best for you, and he knew only one thing, perhaps it's also the best thing."[81]

Although Johanna was attempting to shift the blame to her husband concerning Arthur's sad situation, it is doubtful that he failed to catch the inconsistencies in her letter. In addition to implying that Heinrich Floris alone was responsible for his current situation, she also mentioned that his disposition for melancholy was a sad share of his inheritance from his father, something she could do nothing about and which she thought time would erase. Still, if her voice carried so little weight, Arthur must have wondered how her plan succeeded in the cases of his attending Runge's and Lancaster's schools. Moreover, the letters that he had received from his mother at Wimbledon School reiterated the messages of his father, but in more intimate and less gruff language. Even if Johanna subordinated her hopes and wishes for her son by adopting the role of dutiful wife, from the nature of her letters it would have been difficult for her son to have realized that this was the case. But had Arthur even drawn this conclusion, it is likely that he would have seen this as a failure of his mother, because

[80] Lütkehaus, *Die Schopenhauers*, p. 164, Johanna to Arthur, 28 April 1807.

[81] Ibid., p. 164, Johanna to Arthur, 28 April 1807. Lütkehaus rejects, without reason, Heinrich Floris's offer to Arthur of the European tour and the life of merchant or a scholarly life as the "cruel deception" that destroyed Johanna's plan; see ibid., p. 171fn.

fit mothers put the interests of their children over their husband's, he later philosophized; mothers unconsciously act as if thinking "the constitution, and consequently the welfare, of the species are placed in our hands and entrusted to our care by means of the next generation coming from us."[82] A good mother would have naturally sought the well-being of her child, even if it led to tensions and discord between her and her husband.

But Johanna had legitimate concerns about Arthur's happiness if he were to pursue a life of the mind. She imagined that he would have a family and she knew that his share of Heinrich Floris's estate would not be sufficient to support his family in the manner to which her son had become accustomed. She also had seen the fate of many well-educated men who had to serve either the rich or the noble to support themselves. Consequently, she attempted to mount a case for Arthur remaining in the life path determined by his father. She did not mount a strong case, however, perhaps because she knew that she would be unable to convince her son, or perhaps because there was not a strong case to be made for it. In any case, she complimented Arthur's progress in his apprenticeship, and she envisioned that he had the capacity to become a merchant in what she called the best sense of the term. If he were to become rich, she said, he could do innumerable good things and lead a life of greater freedom than others. She recommended that he read a work by Raynal, whose title she could not recall.[83] He could establish a family, gain a good reputation, and live in a big city. Moreover, he could support her in her old age and she could die without worrying about Adele's well-being.

To provide Arthur with a sense of his prospects if he were to pursue a university education and a life founded on his studies, Johanna went beyond her own experiences and she solicited the counsel of a man who could provide an insider's view of such a life. Thus she consulted Fernow, whom she had already described to Arthur as her "best friend," and a man, she said, Arthur would love and respect if he were to know him.[84] His

---

[82] Schopenhauer, *Parerga and Paralipomena*, Vol. 2, p. 618/*Sämtliche Werke*, Vol. 6, p. 654.

[83] Johanna's reference is to the French *abbé* Guillaume-Thomas-François Raynal (1713–96). Lütkehaus suggests that the title was *Mémoires de politique de l'Europe*; see *Die Schopenhauers*, p. 171. Schopenhauer owned Raynal's *Esprit de Guillaume-Thomas Raynal, recveil également nécessaire à ceux qui commandent et à ceux qui obéissent*, 1782.

[84] The Schopenhauers' beloved Fernow was diagnosed in the summer of 1807 with arteriolar sclerosis, a virtual death sentence at that time. Shortly after the diagnosis he began writing his autobiography and sharing the story of his life with Johanna. When his wife died in September

judgment and discretion could be trusted, she wrote, and so she read him the portions of Arthur's letters that were relevant to the situation at hand. She also enclosed a separate letter from Fernow with her own in which the old writer on art and aesthetics addressed Arthur's situation. Although Fernow did not tell Arthur what to do, he found his remarks about finding oneself and planning one's life so powerfully moving that in recounting its effect on him some forty-seven years later, he said that when he held it in his hands, "he experienced a shudder in his innermost being as he never had again and broke out in a flood of tears."[85]

Fernow erased Arthur's doubts about his ability to learn Latin and to succeed in school. He was older than Schopenhauer when he started his studies (although Johanna mentioned that Fernow knew Latin and possessed a better educational background than Arthur), and Fernow mentioned a young man who started at Arthur's age and succeeded in becoming a significant scholar. If he possessed an indefatigable drive for knowledge and the fortitude to endure an arduous preparation for his matriculation, both Johanna and Fernow concurred, then he was likely to succeed. But Arthur needed to determine for himself whether his desire to go to the university stemmed from the core of his innermost being and not simply from his deep dissatisfaction with his present circumstances. This self-examination was of the utmost importance, he was advised, because without this innate drive for an intellectual life, he could discover the same dissatisfaction and boredom with his new career. This could be ruinous, causing him to mistrust himself and to lack the courage to forge a new path in life and the commitment to travel it.

If he were to decide to prepare for the university, Johanna told Arthur that she would arrange for a tutor in Latin. He could not, however, move to Weimar. She would arrange for him to live nearby; there were too many distractions in Weimar, and he would need to study his Latin night and

---

1808, the very sick man moved in with Johanna. He died in her home that December, an event that deeply saddened the normally cheerful widow. Later, Johanna enriched and expanded her confidant's writings into *Carl Ludwig Fernow's Life* [*Carl Ludwig Fernow's Leben*, 1810]; see Bergmann, *Johanna Schopenhauer*, pp. 157–62.

[85] Schopenhauer, *Gespräche*, p. 482, reported by Wilhelm Gwinner, from a conversation with Schopenhauer sometime in 1854. In his *curriculum vitae* Schopenhauer credited Fernow's letter more than his mother's assistance as providing him with the resolve to quit his apprenticeship. He referred to Fernow as a man "with quite excellent talents" and he mentioned being moved to tears by his letter; see Schopenhauer, *Gesammelte Briefe*, pp. 50–1, 651.

day for two years. Afterward, she recommended a year at a gymnasium and
suggested the one in Gotha. Still, she wanted him to consider his decision
very carefully. The life of an accomplished scholar is not charming. It is
a demanding, laborious, and difficult life, one that does not bring wealth;
often it is even difficult to earn enough to meet one's basic needs. She
recommends that he become either a doctor or a lawyer. Better to be a
lawyer, she continued, because lawyers have more freedom than doctors,
because the latter are restricted by the demands of their patients. Best, she
suggested, is to become a professor of law, because he could escape the
tedium of daily practice, and if he accomplished something extraordinary
in law, he would earn honors. To make it as a writer, she observed, you
need to produce something excellent. Fernow does this, but he is already
at his desk by five in the morning, and he labors until noon. Then he
returns to the writing desk for a couple of hours each night. This he does,
day in and day out. Why does he do it? Only for the joy in his work. This
life exacted a toll on her friend. His hair was already snow white at forty-
two; he looked like an old man, and he had ruined his health, she wrote.
Still, he was naturally merry and good spirited due to the suitability of his
vocation. (When Schopenhauer would eventually enroll at the University
of Göttingen, he would go there to study medicine.)

Johanna also reassured Arthur that he was free to do as he wanted and
that she would place no obstacles in his path to happiness. Once he made
the decision he should stand resolute and persevere. That would bring
him to his goal: "Choose what you want . . . but with tears in my eyes I
implore you not to cheat yourself. Treat yourself seriously and honorably;
this concerns the well-being of your life. This concerns the joys of my old
age, since only you and Adele, I hope, can replace my lost youth."[86] Once
he has decided, she wrote, she would offer her advice and he should not
hurt her feelings by rebelling against her. In a possible reference to both
her dead husband and son, she claims "you know that I am not stubborn;
that I know to give in to reason and that I will never demand something
from you that I cannot support with reasons."[87] Arthur, however, would
seldom find that she had sufficient reason for many of her demands, and
when she did, he was not persuaded.

---

[86] Lütkehaus, *Die Schopenhauers*, p. 168, Johanna to Arthur, 28 April 1807.
[87] Ibid., p. 168, Johanna to Arthur, 28 April 1807.

Johanna closed her letter with some chatter about her social life, "bon-bons," as she referred to such reports in earlier letters. It was as if she needed to return to her own world after spending so much time on Arthur's. Goethe had been sick – near death – and she had not seen him for two weeks. Tomorrow, he should visit, and she would have her final tea party for the season. Summer was approaching and people would be traveling. She saw a performance of *Don Carlos*, to which Schiller had made changes shortly before his death. She did not enjoy it; it was too unusual. She mentions Fernow, Ridel, and Tischbein. Dwelling on these "trifles" threatens to make her miss posting the letter. She finished with a request for a quick reply.

It is not clear when Johanna received Arthur's reply, but it was as she anticipated, and almost immediately after she received it, she wrote Jenisch and Willink that Arthur would be leaving Hamburg. It was as if once she received a decisive answer from an indecisive son, she would burn the bridges to bar a return to his earlier life. There is no time for regrets, she wrote Arthur; they could come later. Johanna, for whom it was difficult to reflect on the past, tells Arthur that "now there is just one way for us and it goes forward."[88] She also praised Arthur's coming to a quick decision, something that would have troubled her had it come from someone else, but that it came from him led her to conclude that it was "the power of natural instincts that drives you."[89] Johanna arranged and organized Arthur's move to the ducal town of Gotha, some twenty miles from Weimar. She was following the advice of Fernow, to whom she read Arthur's reply, and who expressed his approval of the decision and promised to provide additional advice and help.

Schopenhauer departed from Hamburg at the end of May, leaving behind a city whose economic health had been steadily declining since the turn of the century. When he left, it was nearing rock bottom. In the previous November, it was occupied by the French, and the mandatory hospitality expected by the French was costly. After the crushing defeat of Prussia, and as Napoleon prepared to confront Russia, his last serious threat in Europe, he issued the Berlin Decree as an economic counterpoint to the British, who had declared the entire coast of Europe from the Elbe

[88] Ibid., p. 171, Johanna to Arthur, 14 May 1807.
[89] Ibid.

River to Brest under blockade. Because trade with Britain was a robust source of Hamburg's wealth, the effect of the Berlin Decree was disastrous. Hamburg would only begin to recover with Napoleon's ultimate defeat.

It is unlikely that the economic woes of Hamburg troubled Schopenhauer. Judging from the content of Johanna's replies to his letters, he never said anything sufficient to provoke her comment. And if Hamburg's problems had an impact on his life, he probably used them as more fodder for his "melancholy broodings" on the wretchedness of life, another example of his taking the particular and folding it into the universal. The only thing that seems to have been particularly troubling to him was his own despair. Johanna's worry about her son's regretting his decision was idle insofar as it concerned leaving Hamburg. Indeed, later in his life, when he considered putting down roots, he never considered Hamburg.

Schopenhauer was accepted on 16 July in the *Selekta*, a special class of students at Gotha who attended lectures in German. He lodged with one of the teachers at the gymnasium, Karl Gotthold Lenz, and he received daily two-hour instruction in Latin from the director of the school, Friedrich Wilhelm Doering. Schopenhauer reported that his previous knowledge of Latin was so thin that he had to learn declension and conjugation. Nevertheless, he made such astonishing progress in his studies that Doering predicted that he would achieve highly praiseworthy results.[90] Doering's praise helped to erase Schopenhauer's earlier fears about being "too old" to learn the classical languages, but Johanna did not take Doering's prophecy seriously, and she let her son know it. One of her acquaintances, Franz Ludwig Karl Friedrich Passow, who taught at the gymnasium in Weimar, had told her that Doering was notorious for "blowing the trumpet" of his students.[91] Doering's students doing well reflected on his skills as a teacher and it also pleased their parents, who were paying for their sons' educations. Curiously, Johanna suspended her skepticism concerning Passow's report, and she accepted Passow's word at face value. She may have realized that Passow and Doering were competitors, and that Passow might also have a professional and financial interest in criticizing his colleague. When Arthur later reported that Fernow's friend, the philologist Christian Friedrich Jacob, praised the quality of his essays in his mother tongue, Johanna wrote that this did not surprise her, because

[90] See Schopenhauer, *Gesammelte Briefe*, pp. 51, 651–2.
[91] Lütkehaus, *Die Schopenhauers*, p. 179, Johanna to Arthur, 12 August 1807.

this should be easy for someone with his talent. She expected that Arthur would do well, but she warned that if he were to accomplish anything serious, he needed to transcend the common sort of dilettantism found even among barbers' apprentices.[92]

Although Schopenhauer's writings in German drew Jacob's praise, the young scholar had no words of praise for the native German speakers whose lives unfolded beneath the impressive Friedenstein Castle. He found Gotha peopled by men and women smugly conventional in temperament, conscious of rank and status, and insensitive to all higher culture, to art, to literature, and to philosophy. It did not cost him much time to look down his nose at the court officials, merchants, and farmers, whom he viewed as having their noses in everyone's business, keenly conscious of how someone might advance their own interests. Moved by a wickedly supercilious muse, he set to verse his assessment of the solid citizens of Gotha:

> They spy, listen, and pay attention
> To everything that happens.
> What moves each, what each does,
> What each says, aloud or softly,
> Nothing escapes them.
> Through windows they keep watch.
> Their ears pressed against doors,
> No event is unobserved,
> No cat can walk upon the roof
> Without them knowing about it.
> Of a person's mind, thought, and worth
> They do not prick up their ears.
> How much he consumes each year,
> And whether he rightly belongs,
> To the town's dignitaries,
> Whether he must be greeted first
> Whether "Lord" or gracious,
> Whether councilor or clerk,
> Lutheran or Roman Catholic,
> Married or single.
> How large his house, how fine his clothes,
> Is profoundly considered.
> Yet: can he be of use to us?
> This question they of course prefer

---

[92] See ibid.

To considerations great and small.
Or else they ask what thinks he of us?
What are his thoughts and words?
They ask of every Smith and Jones
And carefully weigh their every word,
And they screw up their eyes.[93]

Schopenhauer's behavior in Gotha, however, qualified him as a subject of its citizens' prying curiosity and, by the criteria suggested by his poem, a fellow philistine. He spent money freely, running through 150 *Taler* in a five-week period, the monthly salary of a senior civil servant, and during a day trip to Liebenstein, he spent 10 *Taler*, the equivalent of the monthly income of a tradesman.[94] He was also infatuated with the nobility, and he bragged to his mother about his associations with barons and countesses. Quite naturally, Arthur's prodigality and associations with nobility caused Johanna great concern. She always stressed the frugality of her own lifestyle and her economical use of her resources. Almost *ad infinitum* she told Arthur that the costs of her twice-weekly tea parties were small – she only served tea and buttered bread. And when she sought summer lodging in Jena, she emphasized how little it cost. Now his mother was accusing him, and rightly so, of doing what he accused his mother of doing – living a lavish lifestyle. She was also bothered about her son's infatuation with the nobles: "You belong to the bourgeois world, remain in it, and recall that you assured me that you wanted to renounce all splendor if you could only live for knowledge, and that this would bring you more honor than to chase after frippery and appearance."[95] Naturally, she also told him not to drink too much. A glass of beer at dinner and a glass of wine or two later in his room would be appropriate. She did not want to preach, she told him, but young people do not know how to celebrate properly, and in her youth, she had seen men for whom it was habitual to drink too much.[96] She probably had her own father in mind.

---

93 Schopenhauer, *Manuscript Remains*, Vol. 1, p. 3f./ *Der handschriftliche Nachlaß*, Vol. 1, p. 3.
94 See Rüdiger Safranski, *Schopenhauer and the Wild Years of Philosophy*, p. 88.
95 Lütkehaus, *Die Schopenhauers*, p. 181, Johanna to Arthur, 12 August 1807.
96 See ibid., pp. 175–6, Johanna to Arthur, 15 July 1807. The subject of drinking arose due to Arthur's landlord serving water and not wine at his meals. It seems that Lenz did not drink wine. Johanna told Arthur that it would not be unreasonable for him to request beer with his dinner, because he paid enough money for his lodgings.

Arthur's good times in Gotha were relatively short-lived, however, as he dramatically put it in his *curriculum vitae*, "But, Oh misfortune! I still had not learnt to cease my dangerous jokes, which ruined me."[97] His "dangerous joke" was a satirical poem he wrote about one of the instructors, Christian Ferdinand Schulze, a fellow he said he could not even recall seeing:

> Pulpit luminary, delight of the chair,
> Town announcer and mouthpiece of the lodge,
> Perfect Christian, thorough Jew, gentile
> Who hears tomes in the morning and talents at night,
> Master of the seven liberal arts,
> A man who knows and can do all,
> The bloom and acme of all fine minds,
> Who thousands of friends has – and names.[98]

The faculty soon became aware of the poem and headmaster Doering felt compelled to punish Arthur. He therefore ceased providing private Latin lessons to him, even though he told Arthur that he enjoyed doing so. He could remain in the gymnasium, but he would have to find another instructor to continue his private lessons. Schopenhauer claimed that he did not want to do this, so he decided to leave Gotha.

Schopenhauer left Gotha on 23 December 1807, and his mother did not see his arrival as an early Christmas present or as the harbinger of a happy new year. And unlike her son, who viewed his departure as voluntary, Johanna held that his prank led to his expulsion. In the same letter as she pronounced this as the reason for the end of his career in Gotha, she decided that she would analyze his character in unreserved terms and in terms that revealed why she had welcomed distance between her and "dear Arthur":

You are not an evil human; you are not without intellect and education; you have everything that could make you a credit to human society. Moreover, I am acquainted with your heart and know that few are better, but you are nevertheless irritating and unbearable, and I consider it most difficult to live with you. All of your good qualities become obscured by your super-cleverness and are made useless to the world merely

---

[97] Schopenhauer, *Gesammelte Briefe*, pp. 51, 652.
[98] Schopenhauer, *Manuscript Remains*, Vol. 1, p. 4/*Der handschriftliche Nachlaß*, Vol. 1, p. 4. He also composed at this time a favorable poem for his teacher, Friedrich Jacobs, who had left Gotha, and a satirical poem, based on the Lord's Prayer, addressed to "Our Father Homer"; see ibid., Vol. 5, p. 377.

because of your rage at wanting to know everything better than others; of wanting to improve and master what you cannot command. With this you embitter the people around you, since no one wants to be improved or enlightened in such a forceful way, least of all by such an insignificant individual as you still are; no one can tolerate being reproved by you, who also still show so many weaknesses yourself, least of all in your adverse manner, which in oracular tones, proclaims this is so and so, without ever supposing an objection. If you were less like you, you would only be ridiculous, but thus as you are, you are highly annoying.[99]

Johanna knew that her description of Arthur's character was harsh, but she tried, as she had done before, to put her iron fist within a velvet glove. Her description was a mirror she held before him so that he could see how he appeared to the world. It was a warning, she said, that he would ruin his life, unless he reformed his behavior. Thus it was an act of love, Johanna thought, and if he did not believe that she loved him, she recommended that Arthur should think of all the things she had done for him. Johanna's assessment was brutal, and it was honest. In a number of ways, it was also true. She captured something central to Schopenhauer's nature concerning his mania for knowing things better than others and in his propensity for improving and enlightening others in a manner that was embittering, especially because it came from a young man who had no record of accomplishment. Less than a decade later, when he worked on color theory with Goethe, Johanna's description of her son would prove to be prophetic. Even Schopenhauer's philosophical relationship to Goethe's "giant brother," Kant, would express many elements of his character about which Johanna was duly alarmed.[100] Of course, Kant was dead, and so he could not become embittered about Arthur's oracular pronouncements, but Goethe was not dead. He responded, however, not as Johanna predicted. And if Johanna was inclined to see Heinrich Floris in her son, and as Arthur would philosophize about inheriting one's character from one's father, something both Schopenhauers overlooked was that Arthur shared his mother's disposition toward brutal honesty, speaking his truths even if they displeased others.

---

[99] Lütkehaus, *Die Schopenhauers*, pp. 187–8, Johanna to Arthur, 6 November 1807.

[100] Schopenhauer, *The World as Will and Representation*, Vol. 1, p. 529/*Sämtliche Werke*, Vol. 1, p. 529. Schopenhauer made the "giant brother" remark within an analysis of Kant's *Critique of the Power of Judgment* and with the observation that Kant probably had no knowledge of Goethe, "the only person of his century and country fit to be placed by his side as his giant brother."

There were, however, a number of decisions that had to be made before Schopenhauer left Gotha. How would he continue his education? Where? Various gymnasia were considered. The one at Munich, however, was too expensive, and Göttingen's had a poor Latin program. The Karolinum at Braunschweig was for cavaliers, and the Schulpforta, Nietzsche's future grammar school, was too monastic. Altenberg, some eight miles from Weimar, had a good gymnasium, as did Weimar. But it would not be possible to enroll in Weimar, Johanna wrote, because its director, Christian Ludwig Lenz, the brother of Arthur's Gotha landlord, was aware of the Gotha prank and would fight "body and soul" against his enrollment. Johanna, consequently, suggested that he matriculate at nearby Altenberg. If he did not want to attend Altenberg, the best that she could arrange for him would be private instruction in the classical languages for six hours a week, and he would have to study other subjects on his own. In any case, Johanna estimated that if his studies unfolded well, he could attend the University of Göttingen in two years. Johanna had hoped that Arthur would choose to go to Altenberg. Naturally, he chose to go to Weimar.

Johanna could not understand her son's decision, and she attributed it to something more sinister than his desire to reunite with his family. She feared that his goal was to assume charge of the family, to occupy the position vacated by his late father. She knew that he thought her "lavish" life-style would exhaust his father's estate and that he dreaded the idea that his mother might remarry. She probably thought that her constant emphasis on the frugality of her way of life should have extinguished this idea, and although she had playfully mentioned several suitors, she had tried to make it clear that she had no inclination to return to the role of wife. She had been married and to be married was to be dominated by one's husband. She desired not to be subordinated to either husband – or son. Johanna also recognized that the constant "bonbons" she sent Arthur, her stories about her parties, glamorized these affairs, and she recognized Goethe's magnetic charm. Still, she told Arthur that he would be the only young person at the salon; that he would be found too insignificant to be given any attention by other attendees, especially Goethe; and that if he attended the gymnasium at Altenberg, he still could attend her parties. Naturally, she feared that Arthur would manifest all of those negative character traits she described in her letter and thereby ruin the calm, easy-going milieu enjoyed by the beautiful spirits of her salon.

Johanna accepted Arthur's decision, but she set strict terms and conditions for his life in Weimar before she allowed him to slink away from his defeat in Gotha. She had good reasons for doing so, because Arthur had been a disruptive force during earlier visits to Weimar. During these visits, mother and son clashed frequently and violently. Johanna did not record the specifics of these arguments, but they were such that she told Arthur that she would rather make any sacrifice than live with him. She loved him, she said to reassure her son, and she knew that he had his good points and that she was not repelled by his innermost being. The problem was his "exterior," his views, judgments, habits, and ill-humor that put her off. His behavior depressed her; it ruined her serenity. She told him she could not tolerate his "scowling face, your bizarre judgments spoken by you like oracular dicta not allowing any kind of objection," and she said that these aspects of this exterior had "oppressed me . . . I now live very calmly, for many years I have had not one unpleasant moment that I did not owe to you. I am at peace with myself, no one contradicts me, I contradict no one, not a loud word is heard in my household . . . When you grow older, dear Arthur, and see many things more brightly, we will also be in better harmony with each other, and perhaps I will live in your house, with your children, as is fitting for an old grandmother."[101] Until that time, she continued, and to reach that time of harmony, they had to live apart. He could visit her home, but he would be a guest and as such would have no say about domestic matters such as Adele's education and the duties of the servants. He could come to her home daily at one o'clock and stay until three. He could attend her tea parties on Thursdays and Sundays, and on those days he could dine with her. On other days, she would arrange for his meals at his own lodgings. When, however, he was a guest in her home, she demanded that Arthur would "abstain from tiresome arguing etc., which also makes me angry, as well as all lamentations about the stupid world and human misery, because this always gives me a bad night and ugly dreams, and I like to sleep well."[102]

Arthur accepted his mother's conditions, because he had no choice if he were to come to Weimar. It must have been extremely difficult for the nineteen-year-old to have been told by his mother that "It is necessary for my happiness to know that you are happy, but not to be a witness

---

[101] Lütkehaus, *Die Schopenhauers*, p. 199, Johanna to Arthur, 13 December 1807.Ibid., p. 200.
[102] Ibid., p. 200.

to it."[103] Arthur had struggled his entire life to overcome his feelings of abandonment, and now his mother made distance a condition for his drawing close to his family. Worse, his mother had told him virtually everything about him was repugnant, except his inner nature, a nature that had done nothing, as far as his mother was concerned, to express itself. He was to behave as if he were a guest in her home, and her letter, despite her claims of love and concern, did nothing to make Arthur feel as if he were an invited guest. He may have also found it ironic that his mother looked forward to spending her final years in his home, surrounded by her grandchildren – a lodger and not a guest.

Johanna arranged for Arthur to board in the same lodgings as his private language instructor, the colleague-bashing Passow, who was a scant nineteen months older than his student. In his *curriculum vitae* Schopenhauer was less than forthright concerning the reason he provided for not living with his mother; living in the same house as his teacher made him always ready at hand. Goethe had recommended Passow to the gymnasium at Weimar in 1807. He would remain until 1810, when he joined the Conradinum at Danzig, and in 1815, he became a professor of some renown at the University of Breslau. Originally, Passow instructed Schopenhauer in Latin and Greek, but soon he focused on Greek, and Arthur studied Latin privately with the director of the Weimar gymnasium, Lenz, who would not accept the terrible Gotha prankster in his school, but found no difficulty in being paid for private lessons. Arthur worked diligently on both languages and made excellent progress toward mastering both. By the time he entered the university, Schopenhauer claimed that he knew the classical languages better than his peers and better than some of the "philologists."[104] Due to their instruction, Schopenhauer always felt a debt of gratitude to his instructors Passow and Lenz. In addition to his private language studies, Schopenhauer also engaged in self-directed studies of the classics, mathematics, and history. By the fall of 1809, he was qualified to attend a university.

In his *curriculum vitae*, Schopenhauer reported that his thirst for knowledge drove him to study into the middle of the night, a claim that one

---

[103] Ibid., p. 198.
[104] Schopenhauer, *Gesammelte Briefe*, pp. 51, 652. Pleticha (ed.), *Das Klassische Weimar: Texte und Zeugnisse* (Munich, 1983); quoted in Safranski, *Schopenhauer and the Wild Years of Philosophy*, p. 98.

would expect in a document that sought to gain him the right to habilitate at a university. His life in Weimar, however, also had its diversions. He attended balls, masquerades, and the theater, sometimes three times a week. He continued playing the flute and toyed with playing the guitar. Fernow introduced him to the Italian poets. In the winter he enjoyed sleigh rides. Then, twice a week, there were his mother's tea parties, which he assiduously attended whenever he heard that Goethe would make an appearance. Goethe maintained a cool distance from the young Schopenhauer, just as Johanna had predicted. Perhaps Johanna had warned him about Arthur's depressive and combative disposition, which would have rankled Johanna's role model for the virtues of a tranquil and serene life. Perhaps, however, Goethe's aloofness was a function of Arthur's association with Passow, who had alienated the great man by criticizing Schiller in the same breath in which he denounced the Early Romantics. The affront made Passow a *persona non grata* at Johanna's parties, and she barred her son's tutor from her gatherings. Naturally, Passow resented this exclusion, referring to the attendees at Johanna's affairs as "the common bipeds," which became one of Schopenhauer's favorite descriptions of the vast majority of humans.[105]

Schopenhauer was even moved during this time to write his only known love poem:

> The carolers pass through lanes and streets,
> We stand before your house;
> My sorrow for me would turn to joy
> If at the window you'd stand and see.
> In the streets the carolers sing
> In the downpour and in snow
> Wrapped in a cloak of whitish tint
> I look up at your window.
> The sun is shrouded in clouds,
> And yet on this wintry morning
> The light and gleam of your eyes
> Infuse in me celestial warmth.
> The curtain hides your window from view;
> On a cushion of silk you dream
> Of the happiness of love to come,
> Do you discern the sport of fate?

---

[105] Pleticha (ed.), *Das Klassische Weimar: Texte und Zeugnisse* (Munich, 1983); quoted in Safranski, *Schopenhauer and the Wild Years of Philosophy*, p. 98.

> The carolers pass through lanes and streets,
> My eyes linger longingly in vain;
> Your curtain masks the sun and
> My destiny and fate are overcast.[106]

The muse for Schopenhauer's limping poem was the actress and famous beauty Caroline Jagemann, who also was the mistress of Carl August, Duke of Weimar-Saxony. Schopenhauer was struck poetic after attending a grand masked ball at Weimar's city hall shortly before his twenty-first birthday. This grand affair, staged by Goethe and Falk, moved Schopenhauer to dress as a fisherman and he managed to move close to the stunning Jagemann. Later, he told his mother that "I would take her home, though I found her breaking stones in the street."[107] Jagemann, however, never went into road work, but instead was ennobled by her lover, the Duke. Some twenty-three years after Arthur's empty fishing excursion, he ran into "Frau von Heygendorf" from "the glorious Weimar period," and told her the parable of the porcupines:[108] "One cold winter's day, a number of porcupines huddled together quite closely in order through their natural warmth to prevent themselves from being frozen. But they soon felt the effects of their quills on one another, which made them again move apart. Now when the need for warmth once brought them together, the drawback of quills was repeated so that they were tossed between two evils, until they had discovered the proper distance from which they could best tolerate one another."[109] We do not know Jagermann's response to this parable. Schopenhauer enjoyed telling it to her even though she still was not sufficiently cold to be drawn close to Schopenhauer's quills.

Schopenhauer turned twenty-one on 22 February 1809. Upon reaching the age of majority, he was entitled to his share of Heinrich Floris's estate, which he had parceled out in equal shares to Johanna, Arthur, and Adele. Johanna would have preferred to manage Arthur's share, and she made a feeble and futile attempt to do so: "It's hard to bargain with you. Are not our interests the same?"[110] Her son, however, had different interests

---

[106] Schopenhauer, *Manuscript Remains*, Vol. 1, p. 6/*Der handschriftliche Nachlaß*, Vol. 1, p. 6.

[107] Schopenhauer, *Gespräche*, p. 17.

[108] Schopenhauer, *Gesammelte Briefe*, p. 273, letter from Schopenhauer to Julius Frauenstädt, 2 January 1852. The meeting with the former Jagemann occurred some 18 years prior to this letter. By 1852, Frau von Heygendorf had been dead for four years.

[109] Schopenhauer, *Parerga and Paralipomena*, Vol. 2, p. 621/*Sämtliche Werke*, Vol. 6, p. 640.

[110] Lütkehaus, *Die Schopenhauers*, p. 206, Johanna to Arthur, September 1809.

and the only shared interest was their mutual worry about the other's free spending. Arthur would receive 19,000 *Taler*, an amount that would yield approximately 950 annual interest. As his mother noted, their inheritance did not make them rich, but it was sufficient for living well. The annual interest itself was more than double the salary for a well-paid professor at the nearby University of Jena. Johanna also tried to convince her son to invest his money with the Danzig banker Abraham Ludwig Muhl, who promised an eight percent return. Always cautious, and skeptical of his mother's advice, Schopenhauer invested only 6,000 *Taler* with Muhl, preferring to put the remainder of his funds in more conservative government bonds. A decade later, Johanna would find both her and Adele's money in serious peril.

4

The University Years

S CHOPENHAUER MATRICULATED AS a student of medicine at the
University of Göttingen on 9 October 1809. He left behind no record
of his reason for going to Göttingen. At first blush, the nearby University
of Jena would have appeared to be a natural choice. Goethe oversaw the
university and took a lively role in its development. By the turn of the
nineteenth century, it was the axis around which German intellectual life
revolved, and it was peopled with a cadre of influential writers, poets,
and philosophers such as had never before been witnessed in Germany.
Goethe induced Schiller to teach there in 1787, and he taught there
until he moved to Weimar in 1793. It became the foremost center for
Kant's philosophy, eclipsing even Kant's home institution at Königsberg.
Christian Gottfried Schütz began lecturing on Kant's philosophy as early
as 1784 – Kant's *Critique of Pure Reason* appeared in 1781 – and Schütz
founded the most important vehicle for the dissemination and discussion
of Kantian philosophy, the journal *Allgemeine Litteratur Zeitung*. The
great popularizer and proponent of Kant's philosophy, Carl Leonhard
Reinhold, arrived in 1787, and when he departed in 1794, Goethe brought
in Fichte as his replacement. Schelling arrived in 1798 and Hegel in
1801. Jena also became the home ground for many of the most significant
figures in Early German Romanticism. Friedrich Schlegel moved to Jena
in 1799, and he was soon followed by his brother August. Friedrich
von Hardenberg (Novalis), the death-intoxicated author of the *Hymns to
the Night*, appeared on the scene, as did Schopenhauer's beloved Ludwig
Tieck. Even a still lucid Johann Christian Friedrich Hölderlin put in a brief
appearance (1793–5) in the city to be close to his fellow Württenbergian
Schiller. Hölderlin, however, had vanished by the time of the arrival of
his dear friends from the Tübingen seminary, Schelling and Hegel.

A miniature from this time, painted in Weimar by Karl Friedrich Kaaz, a friend of Schiller and Goethe, shows the twenty-one-year-old future university student sporting the hairstyle in popular fashion.[1] Loosely curled hair cascades obliquely down the center of his forehead, making its breadth no longer apparent. The hair on the sides of his head is swept forward above the ears, reaching toward the exterior ends of his eyebrows, which arch over clear, deep blue eyes, which were so wide apart that they could not be spanned by a standard pair of eyeglasses. His hair appears to be red, but this is only due to the fading of a green pigment used to mix the color of his hair, which is ash blond. His face is round, and above his small mouth with full lips is a small reddish-blond mustache, which rests below a well-formed, slightly bulbous nose. He wears a black dress coat, stylish at the time, but he would have his coats copied from the same pattern throughout his life, regardless of changes in fashion. A high white collar breaks high on his neck, and its corners sweep up, over his coat, and tip down at their ends. He is lacking his white cravat, which would later become a standard, and which would cover his rather short, stout neck. He is said to have been of medium height. His figure is square, like his father's. His head is large, like his mother's.

The glory days of Jena had been eclipsed, however, by the time Schopenhauer was qualified to attend the university. Fichte, who presumed to schedule lectures on Sundays at the same time as local church services, who declared that the ethical basis of religion required only practical postulates about God's existence, and whom some accused of having Jacobin tendencies, was branded an atheist and removed from his professorship in 1799. Schelling also found it expedient to quit Jena after becoming embroiled in scandal. The twenty-three-year-old philosopher fell in love with a thirty-five-year-old married woman, August Schlegel's wife, Caroline, about whom vicious rumors circulated that she killed her fifteen-year-old daughter from a previous marriage to have Schelling for herself. When a new university was organized in Würzberg, Schelling was happy to relocate there in 1803. In the same year, Schütz transferred to

---

[1] See Arthur Hübscher, *Schopenhauer-Bildnisse: Eine Ikonographie* (Frankfurt am Main: Kramer, 1968), p. 39. In 1851, two years after he received the miniature, following the death of Adele, he framed it with a note in Latin, explaining why his hair appears red. Upon Schopenhauer's death, it was passed on to the executor of his will, Wilhelm Gwinner. It was donated in 1960 to its current possessor, the Arthur Schopenhauer-Archiv (Frankfurt am Main), by Gwinner's granddaughter, Charlotte von Wedel.

the University of Halle, taking his journal with him. By the time Napoleon arrived on the scene, none of the Early Romantics remained to see him push that which was already tumbling. After the Battle of Jena, much of the city was looted, and most of the university was burned down. Only its good reputation prevented Napoleon from closing it, as he had done elsewhere.[2] Hegel, who was a struggling *Privatdozent*, and who therefore received no salary from the university, had to collect fees from students attending his lectures. He was broke, the recent father of an illegitimate son, a nervous would-be author of the *Phenomenology of Spirit*, and he was happy to leave Jena for Bamberg to become the editor of the *Bamberger Zeitung* in 1807. Ironically, Napoleon would also lead Schopenhauer to receive his doctorate from Jena, but *in absentia*.

There may have been more personal reasons for Schopenhauer's decision not to enroll at Jena, however. Goethe, who had been cool to him at Johanna's parties, although he had great affection for Adele, might not have wanted him at Jena. After all, Johanna had painted a terrible image of her combative and moody son, and his closeness to Passow might have further soured Goethe. In the summer of 1808, both Johanna and Arthur traveled to Jena and requested a letter of recommendation for Arthur. Goethe never wrote one. Johanna may not have encouraged Arthur to go to Jena because she wished a greater distance between her and her son, a feeling that Arthur may also have shared. After two years, moreover, the luster of Johanna's tea parties could have rubbed thin. Later, he would tell his friend Julius Frauenstädt that he always felt strange and lonely around his mother and her circle and that they had been unsatisfied with him.[3]

Schopenhauer was vaguely familiar with Göttingen. In the summer of 1800, he had journeyed with his parents from Hamburg to Prague via Karlsbad and Göttingen. He visited the museum and the botanical gardens, which had been established by Albrecht von Haller, who had also established a maternity hospital and the library, and brought renown to Halle through his work in physiology.[4] The young Schopenhauer was impressed by the library, which held, according to his cautious estimate,

---

[2] See Max Steinmetz (ed.), *Geschichte der Univesität Jena* (Jena: VEB Gustav Fischer, 1958), pp. 240–43.

[3] See Schopenhauer, *Gespräche*, p. 130.

[4] See Schopenhauer's "Journal of a Trip from Hamburg to Karlsbad," appended to Wilhelm Gwinner's *Arthur Schopenhauer aus personlichen Umgange dargestellt*, pp. 214–16.

twenty thousand volumes – at the midpoint of the nineteenth century, it held more than three hundred thousand volumes, compared to the sixty thousand at Jena.[5] Still, it is unlikely that these youthful impressions served substantially to guide his decision. It is more likely that Göttingen's progressive reputation and its preeminence in the sciences appealed to Schopenhauer. In particular, it appears that he took his mother's advice seriously about enrolling in a study for the purpose of earning a living, a *Brotstudium*, literally a "bread study." Although she had pitched the study of law over medicine, the study of medicine was a natural choice for a young man who had deep curiosity about Napoleon's physiognomy and an apprentice merchant who would steal away to attend the lectures of the phrenologist Gall.

Göttingen was a relatively "new" German university, founded by the Hanoverian princes in 1737, and due to their connections to the English royal family, the university and city had an English ambiance, a feature that appealed to Schopenhauer's anglophile sensibilities. More importantly, the university was well supported by the nobility, and it paid a relatively high salary compared to other universities, something that drew strong faculty. The university was committed to modern principles and it demoted the study of theology, which was the central discipline in most German universities. This safeguarded the faculty from sectarian difficulties such as those that beset Halle in 1723, when the Pietists convinced King Friedrich Wilhelm I to remove Christian Wolff, who was then Germany's leading philosopher, from his post. It also sought to enroll nobles, who paid higher fees and who were otherwise inclined to attend a "knightly academy" (*Ritterakadmie*), where they aspired to become Renaissance gentlemen. To do so, Göttingen expanded its curriculum to include not only law, but also dancing, fencing, riding, music, and modern languages.[6] The presence of nobility would not have deterred the young Schopenhauer, who had distressed his mother by his predilection to socialize with the nobles in Gotha.

It is not surprising that Schopenhauer scheduled a set of classes heavy in the sciences during his first semester, the winter semester of 1809–10.

[5] See Arthur Hübscher's *The Philosophy of Schopenhauer in Its Intellectual Context*, p. 483, note 2.
[6] See Charles E. McCleland's *State, Society, and University in Germany: 1700–1914* (Cambridge: Cambridge University Press, 1980), pp. 32–45.

He attended the lectures on mathematics by Bernhard Friedrich Thibaut, who also stood surety for Schopenhauer's borrowing privileges at the library. Curiously, he also attended Arnold Heeren's lectures on the "History of the European States from the Barbarian Invasions up to the Most Recent Times." Heeren took an interdisciplinary or "universal" approach to history, using economic, political, and geographical considerations to explain the customs and institutions of a country. Schopenhauer, however, appeared to be more interested in the details of Heeren's lectures than in his methodology. Schopenhauer would later recall Heeren's vivid description of the sadistic murder of Edward II in the second edition of *The World as Will and Representation*, although he could not bring himself to repeat Heeren's description, which is found in Schopenhauer's notebook, because the murder was "too horrible for me to mention."[7] But unmentionable details of historical events were much to his taste. In his second semester, the summer semester of 1810, Schopenhauer was in the audience for Heeren's lecture series on the "History of the Main Events in the Middle Ages, Especially of the Crusades." Later, Schopenhauer would reject the idea that history was a science and conclude that history only showed that which was, is, and always will be the same.[8] In the summer of 1811, his last semester, Schopenhauer enrolled in Heeren's course of lectures on ethnography. This was an especially fateful and fortuitous choice, because these lectures may have led Schopenhauer to become interested in Eastern thought at the same time as he was inspired to study philosophy. Heeren was deeply interested in India, and as Schopenhauer attended his lectures, Heeren was laboring on the third edition of his *Ideas Concerning the Politics, Commerce, and Trade of the Most Distinguished People of the Old World* [*Ideen über die Politik, den Verkehr und den Handel der vernehmsten Völker der alten Welt*, 1791, 1795] by expanding the section on India, which appeared in its second edition (1804–5). In his notes to the lectures on Japan, Schopenhauer placed emphasis on Japanese sexual

---

7 Schopenhauer, *The World as Will and Representation*, Vol. 2, p. 520/*Sämtliche Werke*, Yol. 3, p. 593. He recorded Heeren's description of the murder of Edward II of England as follows: "A red-hot tube was thrust up his rectum which burnt his intestines, so that the body bore no traces of murder," *Manuscript Remains*, Vol. 2, p. 4/*Der handschriftliche Nachlaß*, Vol. 2, p. 4.

8 "*Eudem, sed aliter* [the same, but different]," should be the motto for history, Schopenhauer would argue, and that "If someone has read Herodotus, he has, for philosophical purposes, already studied enough history"; see *The World as Will and Representation*, Vol. 2, p. 444/*Sämtliche Werke*, Vol. 3, p. 508.

practices – as one might have expected – and noted that Buddhism reigned in Burma.[9]

The most significant professor Schopenhauer encountered during his first year was Johann Friedrich Blumenbach, who had an illustrious career for more than three decades at Göttingen. The *"Magister Germaniae* of the natural sciences," who pioneered the study of comparative anatomy in Germany and founded modern anthropology, delivered four courses of lectures to the aspiring student of medicine.[10] In his first semester, Schopenhauer attended two of Blumenbach's cycles of lectures: natural history and mineralogy. In his third semester, the winter semester of 1810–11, Schopenhauer enrolled in his lectures on comparative anatomy and physiology, and in his last, the summer of 1811, he took Blumenbach's course on physiology. Thirty-four years after this final course, Schopenhauer recalled, "When I was a student at Göttingen, Blumenbach in his lectures on physiology spoke very seriously to us about the horrors of vivisection and pointed out to us what a cruel and shocking thing it was. He therefore said that it should very rarely be resorted to and only in the case of very important investigations that were of direct use. But it must be done with the greatest publicity in the large lecture-hall after an invitation has been sent to all the medical students, so that the cruel sacrifice on the altar of science may be of the greatest possible use."[11] Blumenbach's

---

9 Schopenhauer's notes for Heeren's lectures on eastern, northern, and southern Asia included: "They [the Japanese] have *monogamy. Unmarried girls are not bound to chastity,* and marry after they had been, for a long time, in one of many *bordellos.* In marriage, however, they must be faithful [Schopenhauer's emphases]"; and "The ancient religion of the country [Japan] is that of Shinto. Its leader is the Dairo. In addition, the religion of the Buddha [Schopenhauer's marginal note – "which reigns among the Burmese"] has become established. It should also be regarded as the philosophical-religious sect. They have printing presses and books like the Chinese. Still, nothing of its literature is translated." Urs App's "Notizen Schopenhauer zu Ost-, Nord- und Südostasien vom Sommersemester 1811," *Schopenhauer-Jarhbuch,* Vol. 84 (2003), p. 39. App's article includes Schopenhauer's lecture notes for Heeren's lectures on ethnography, pp. 21–39.
10 Arthur Hübscher, "Introduction," *Manuscript Remains,* Vol. 2, p. viii / *Der handschriftliche Nachlaß,* Vol. 2, p. viii.
11 Schopenhauer, *Parerga and Paralipomena,* Vol. 2, p. 373 / *Sämtliche Werke,* Vol. 2, p. 396f. In a manner like Peter Singer, Schopenhauer continues to describe cruel, repetitive, and unnecessary experiments conducted on nonhuman animals; see Singer's *Animal Liberation: A New Ethics for Our Treatment of Animals* (New York: Avon Books, 1975). As will be discussed later, one of the very contemporary-sounding dimensions of Schopenhauer's ethics concerns his attribution of moral standing to nonhuman animals. Like Jeremy Bentham and Peter Singer, he will argue that sentience is a sufficient condition for a being having moral status;

anti-vivisection stance would help move Schopenhauer to his own views concerning the moral standing of nonhuman animals.

Other than his views on vivisection and a command of many anatomical and physiological facts, Blumenbach did not affect Schopenhauer's philosophy in any directly detectable ways. He had introduced the idea of the "formative drive [*Bildungstriebes*]" into physiology, the idea of an active formative drive that operates unconsciously in organic nature parallel to the mechanical formative force inherent in matter that operates within the inorganic realm. Kant praised Blumenbach's notion of the formative drive in his *Critique of the Power of Judgment* [*Kritik der Urtheilskraft*, 1790], but Goethe was less impressed. He thought that it failed to elucidate the dark basis of organic nature, but succeeded at giving it an anthropomorphic name.[12] Years later, Schopenhauer sided with Goethe. It was one of many names, along with "natural force" or "vital force," that signified the meaningful end of scientific explanations of the world, endpoints – and here he sided with Kant – that require a metaphysical explanation.[13] Schopenhauer respected Blumenbach's erudition, and when he entertained establishing an academic life, he wrote to Blumenbach to inquire about the possibility of habilitating at Göttingen, that is, of qualifying to teach at the university. And although flattery greases the wheels of favor's request, there was something genuine in Schopenhauer's description of Blumenbach as "one of the most valuable" of all of the university's distinguished scholars.[14]

In addition to Blumenbach's lectures, Schopenhauer enrolled in a substantial set of courses within the natural sciences. He attended chemistry lectures offered by the physician and professor of chemistry and

---

but unlike Bentham and Singer, Schopenhauer is not a utilitarian. Curiously, Schopenhauer conducted experiments concerning the distillation of ferrous potassium cyanide in 1825 at Berlin. In these experiments, he tested the poison on two young cats, both of which died. It is not at all clear why the philosopher was engaged in this exercise, and he appeared to be unaffected by the quick and apparently painless deaths of his animal subjects; see *Manuscript Remains*, Vol. 3, pp. 242–3/ *Der handschriftliche Nachlaß*, Vol. 3, pp. 221–2.

[12] See Arthur Hübscher's "Introduction" to the second volume of Schopenhauer's *Manuscript Remains*, pp. viii–ix/ *Der handschriftliche Nachlaß*, Vol. 2, p. ix, and *The Philosophy of Schopenhauer in Its Philosophical Context*, pp. 160–62.

[13] See Schopenhauer, *On the Will in Nature*, p. 21/ *Sämtliche Werke*, Vol. 4, p. 4.

[14] Schopenhauer, *Gesammelte Briefe*, p. 43, Schopenhauer to Johann Friedrich Blumenbach, early December 1819. Blumenbach's reply on 15 December 1819 was not encouraging, and Schopenhauer eliminated Göttingen as a possibility for academic employment.

pharmacy Friedrich Stromeyer, the discoverer of cadmium; botany, taught by Heinrich Adolf Schrader, who served as the "guarantor" for Schopenhauer's library borrowing privileges during his second and third semesters and with whom he boarded at Schrader's residence in the very botanical gardens he had toured in 1800; and physics, given by the mathematician and physicist Johann Tobias Mayer. Each of these courses was taken during Schopenhauer's second semester. In his third semester, the winter semester of 1810–11, he took another lecture cycle from Mayer, physical astronomy and meteorology. Sometime during his time at Göttingen, he also attended lectures by the anatomist and surgeon Conrad Johann Martin Longenbeck, and lectures on "Anatomy of the Human Body," offered by Adolf Friedrich Hempel.[15]

In his final semester Schopenhauer attended "History of the Empire," offered by the quixotic challenger of statistics August Ferdinand Lueder, who came to Göttingen after the University of Helmstedt, founded in 1576, closed in 1809, a fate shared by more than half of the German universities during the Napoleonic period.[16] Although Göttingen's gain in this case was not Helmstedt's loss – Lueder left unceremoniously for Jena around 1814 – his fellow refugee from Helmstedt, Gottlob Ernst Schulze, was a definite, positive addition, because his arrival in the summer of 1810 doubled Göttingen's philosophy faculty, whose other member was Friedrich Bouterwek. Schopenhauer took his first philosophy courses from Schulze in the 1810–11 winter semester, specifically, metaphysics and psychology, and he took a third, logic, in his final semester, summer 1811. Schopenhauer's exposure to Schulze was a life-transforming experience. In a short biographical notice he wrote for *Development of German Speculation since Kant* (*Entwicklung der deutschen Spekulation seit Kant*, 1853), Schopenhauer stated, "When I was in the 2nd semester [at Göttingen], I was awakened to philosophy through the lectures of G. E. Schulze, Aenesidemus. He provided me with the wise advice to first direct my private studies exclusively to Plato and Kant and, until I had mastered

---

[15] In his *curriculum vitae*, Schopenhauer mentions Langenbeck and Hempel without saying when he attended their lectures, and in a letter to Frauenstädt, 30 September 1850, he mentions Langenbeck "whose lecture on anatomy I attended in 1809. . . . " If Schopenhauer's recollection is correct, this would have been his first semester; see Schopenhauer, ibid., p. 249.

[16] See Theodore Ziolkowski's *German Romanticism and Its Institutions* (Princeton, NJ: Princeton University Press; 1990), p. 228.

these, not to look at others; namely, Aristotle or Spinoza." By following this advice, Schopenhauer added, "I have done very well."[17]

Schopenhauer's reference to Schulze as "Aenesidemus" was not idiosyncratic, nor was it a matter of confusing him with the first-century Greek skeptic by the same name. Rather, Schulze had published a book anonymously in 1792 with the title *Aenesidemus, or on the Foundations of the Elemental Philosophy Offered by Mr. Professor Reinhold in Jena. Together with a Defense of Skepticism against the Pretensions of the Critique of Reason* [*Aenesidemus, oder, über die Fundamente der von dem Herrn Professor Reinhold in Jena gelieferten Elementar-Philosophie: nebst einer Vertheidung des Skeptizismus gegen die Anmaassungen der Vernunftkritik*, 1792]. Schulze, whose identity was soon discovered, was henceforth tagged with the name of the book's protagonist, Aenesidemus, who throughout the book launches into a Humean-style attack on Hermias, a Kantian-style philosopher. Schulze's primary target was Carl Leonhard Reinhold, a man with a private life that was more chameleon-like than Schelling's philosophy. He was a Jesuit novice-master, who lost his faith in Catholicism, became a Freemason, converted to Protestantism, became a professor at Jena, married Wieland's daughter, and worked with Wieland on his important journal, the *Teutscher Merkur*, in which, between 1786 and 1787, Reinhold published four articles that greatly popularized Kant's philosophy, which he revised and published with new "letters" from 1790 to 1799 as *Letters on the Kantian Philosophy* [*Briefe über die kantische Philosophie*] (Leipzig: Georg Joachim Göschen, 1790). Reinhold, however, decided that Kant's attempt in the *Critique of Pure Reason* to put metaphysics on the path of becoming a science was simply that, and he claimed that he would actually make it so with his "elementary philosophy [*elementar Philosophie*]." What we needed to do, Reinhold said, was to recast Kant's critical philosophy into the form of a deductive system based on an indubitable and certain first principle, the "principle of consciousness."[18]

---

[17] Schopenhauer, *Gesammelte Briefe*, pp. 260–61, Schopenhauer to Johann Eduard Erdmann, 9 April 1851.

[18] See Reinhold's *Versuch einer neuen Theorie des Menschlichen Vorstellungsvermögens* (Darmstadt: Wissenschftliche Buchgesellschaft, 1963: photomechanical reprint of the 1781 edition, Widtmann and Mauke, Prague and Jena) and *Über das fundament des Philosophischen Wissens* (Hamburg: Felix Meiner, 1978; photomechanical reprint of the 1790 edition, Mauke, Jena). Also see Terry Pinkard's *German Philosophy 1760–1860: The Legacy of Idealism* (Cambridge: Cambridge University Press, 2002), pp. 98–106.

Aenesidemus was an ambitious work and it managed to make a name for Schulze, although the name was "Aenesidemus" instead of "Gottlob." He revived a criticism of Kant that was advanced by the religious enthusiast and vigorous opponent of the Enlightenment Friedrich Heinrich Jacobi, who argued that Kant's hyperrationalism leads to nihilism, a word he has been credited with coining.[19] Both Reinhold and Kant, Schulze argued, contradicted a basic tenet of the critical philosophy, that is, Kant's philosophy, by claiming that our experiences of things, or representations of objects in the world, are caused by objects existing independent of our experiences, that is, by things in themselves. The problem was that both philosophers held that causality is one of the *a priori* forms of human cognition that structures our experiences of things and is only valid within the realm of our experiences. Consequently, it makes no sense to attribute a causal role to things in themselves. Against Reinhold's elementary philosophy, Schulze charged that his principle of consciousness failed to provide a certain and indubitable foundation for the critical philosophy, because his account of the principle of consciousness could never touch firm ground. All consciousness is intentional, that is, it always is of something. A self-conscious subject, then, has to have a representation of itself that it relates to itself, but this requires the subject to relate the representation of itself to itself once more to itself, *ad infinitum*.

Schulze was not content to demonstrate the problems with Reinhold's and Kant's theoretical philosophy. He found Kant's practical or moral philosophy problematic, especially Kant's moral theology. In the *Critique of Practical Reason* [*Kritik der praktischen Vernunft*; trans. Lewis White

[19] Jacobi provoked the infamous "pantheism controversy [*Pantheismusstreit*]" in the mid-1780s by claiming that Gotthold Ephraim Lessing, one of the most esteemed figures of the German Enlightenment, had confessed to being a Spinozist, shortly before his death. This was a shocking assertion for many, because Spinoza was generally viewed as an atheist and a fatalist. Among others, the German philosopher Moses Mendelssohn was provoked to defend his dead friend, and he battled Jacobi through a series of uncivil publications. Of course, Jacobi loathed the Enlightenment's deification of reason, finding it nihilistic, that is, denying anything supernatural such as freedom, the immortality of the soul, and God. Jacobi seemed to love controversy. He also helped fuel the charge of atheism against Fichte and argued that Schelling was a pantheist. For concise descriptions of the Jacobi–Mendelssohn exchange, see Lewis White Beck's "From Leibniz to Kant," in *The Age of German Idealism*, eds. Robert C. Solomon and Kathleen M. Higgins (London/New York: Routledge, 1993), pp. 28–33, and Paul Franks's "All or Nothing: Systematicity and Nihilism in Jacobi, Reinhold, and Maimon," in *The Cambridge Companion to German Idealism*, ed. Karl Ameriks (Cambridge: Cambridge University Press, 2000), pp. 95–100.

Beck, Indianapolis: Bobbs-Merrill, 1788] Kant had argued that if his ethics were valid, we had good reason for accepting his postulates of practical reason; that is, although we cannot know, because we have no relevant experiences, we could, nevertheless, think that humans are free, the soul is immortal, and there is a God. The second Aenesidemus found Kant's reasoning here to be weak, because it was obvious to theoretical reason that thinking that something is so does not make it so. Ultimately, Schulze maintained that Hume's skepticism was not refuted by either Reinhold or Kant; that we do not know that every event has a cause, that there is a self or thinking substance, that there is a world beyond our constantly changing and fleeting perceptions, or that there is a God.[20]

Schopenhauer's student notebooks for Schulze's lectures on metaphysics and psychology from the winter semester 1810–11 are interesting documents. In addition to copying Schulze's dictations, they are punctuated by his own observations and reflections. His references to Reinhold, Kant, and Plato show that he was following his professor's recommendation concerning the latter two philosophers. Reinhold was an exception.[21] He was likely stimulated to read Reinhold because he had met him in June 1809 in his mother's salon, when Reinhold traveled with his wife to Weimar to visit his father-in-law, Wieland. Schopenhauer's observations on Schulze's lectures demonstrate the supercleverness (*Superklugheit*) his mother had noted as an off-putting dimension of his character. Perhaps a better word for it would be "smart-aleckiness." In response to Schulze's observation that there is never an event so horrid

---

[20] Later, Schopenhauer would find Kant's postulates of practical reason problematic. He would also agree with Schulze's claims about God and the existence of a self or thinking substance, but he would return to Kant's claim that every change has a cause and that the external world is empirically real.

[21] Library circulation records at the University of Göttingen show that Schopenhauer was checking out philosophical books prior to his auditing Schulze's summer 1810 lecture. These included Schelling's *On the World Soul* [*Von der Weltseele*, eine Hypothese der höhern Physik zur Erklärung des allegeinen Organismus (Hamburg: Friedrich Perthes, 1798)] and *Ideas for a Philosophy of Nature* [*Ideen zu einer Philosophie der Natur*, 1797], trans. Errol E. Harris and Peter Heath (Cambridge: Cambridge University Press, 1988) and Plato's *Dialogues*. It is likely that he started reading Kant during Schulze's lectures on metaphysics during the winter semester 1810–11, guided by his instructor's *Critique of the Theoretical Philosophy* [*Kritik der theoretischen Philosophie*, 1801], and his first notes on Kant may stem from that time; see Arthur Hübscher, *The Philosophy of Schopenhauer in Its Intellectual Context*, pp. 162, 181; and Schopenhauer, *Manuscript Remains*, Vol. 1, pp. 10–13/*Der handschriftliche Nachlaß*, Vol. 1, pp. 11–13.

that someone fails to find something beneficial in it, the novice philosophy student penned the verse "Oh Lord, Oh Lord/Have mercy on the gentleman."[22] Sarcastically, he refers to his teacher as "the sophist Schulze" and "Gottlob." Once he referred to the professor as "the blockhead [*Rindvieh*] Schulze" for claiming that the reason young people prefer tragedies and older people comedies is due to the joy in risk-taking engaged in by the young and the older people's need to laugh after experiencing real tragedy. The young, Schulze declared, are also capable of quickly shaking off sadness. Schopenhauer observes, "But why am I abusive today, since every day I suffer in silence once more," and he then quotes Homer: "Endure to the end, my heart, harder things you have suffered already" – but in the Greek![23] Still, contrary to Schulze, the young Schopenhauer could not quickly quit sadness, although he would always prefer tragedies.

Schopenhauer read *Aenesidemus* sometime between 1810 and 1811.[24] It seemed to convince him, as it did Fichte, to abandon the idea of the thing in itself.[25] Unlike Fichte, however, Kant's great unknown always hovered in the back of his mind, and Fichte would help him to return to it. Indeed, one of the enduring struggles of his philosophy would turn on his seeking clarity and closure about this central Kantian concept. It would only be with the publication of the second edition of Schopenhauer's principal work in 1844 that he would credit Aenesidemus Schulze with exposing Kant's defective deduction of the thing in itself, and still later, with *Parerga and Paralipomena* in 1851, that he would give more than passing reference to his first philosophy professor's most famous work.[26] In both cases, however, and with the second more than the first, he was striving to draw an audience to his books, and one of his strategies was to situate himself within the history of Western philosophy and to distance himself from post-Kantian German idealists. Prior to this effort, Schulze received scant

---

[22] Schopenhauer, *Manuscript Remains*, Vol. 1, p. 10/*Der handschriftliche Nachlaß*, Vol. 1, p. 9.

[23] Ibid., pp. 12, 14/ibid., pp. 12, 14.

[24] See Hübscher, *The Philosophy of Schopenhauer in Its Intellectual Context*, p. 189.

[25] Fichte reviewed *Aenesidemus* for the *Allgemeine Litteratur Zeitung* in 1794 and he accepted both Schulze's critique of Reinhold and his claim that Kant's view was "contradictory" because it employed the thing in itself as the cause of our sensations; see the "Review of *Aenesidemus*," in *Fichte: Early Philosophical Writings*, ed. and trans. Daniel Breazeale (Ithaca, NY: Cornell University Press, 1988), esp. pp. 69–70.

[26] See Schopenhauer, *The World as Will and Representation*, Vol. 1, p. 436/*Sämtliche Werke*, Vol. 2, p. 516 and *Parerga and Paralipomena*, Vol. 1, pp. 89, 90, and 94/*Sämtliche Werke*, Vol. 5, pp. 95, 96, and 101.

references within his philosophical writings, and then reference was only to Schulze's *Principles of General Logic* [*Grundsätze der allgemeinen Logik*, Helmstädt: Fleckeisen, 1810] and *Critique of the Theoretical Philosophy*, 2 vols. [*Kritik der theoretischen Philosophie*, Hamburg: Carl Ernst Bohn, 1801], but not to the section that duplicated Schulze's earlier charge against Kant's illicit use of things in themselves. Schulze's neo-Humean skepticism also had no appeal for Schopenhauer, who never took any form of skepticism seriously. Although he had great fondness for David Hume, this was limited to his popular essays and his writings on religion. The skeptical results of Hume's work in *A Treatise of Human Nature* (2 vols., London: 1793) and *Enquiry Concerning Human Understanding* (1748) left him cool. Even Hume's skepticism concerning causality, which Kant said had awakened him from his dogmatic slumbers, Schopenhauer referred to as Hume's "palpably false skepticism with regard to his law of causality."[27]

Still, Schopenhauer's auditing of Schulze's lectures in the summer of 1810 marked a turning point in his life. These lectures were sufficient to reawaken his slumbering philosophical interests and to move him finally to overcome his parents' plans for his future career. His mother aided him in abandoning his father's design for his career as a merchant. Schulze helped him in renouncing his mother's desire that he pursue a *Brotstudium*, some bread-providing career. During the Easter holidays in April 1811, Schopenhauer returned home to Weimar. He engaged in a conversation with the seventy-eight-year-old Wieland, who tried to dissuade the young man from philosophy. Schopenhauer did not record whether he mentioned to the old poet that he knew of his confession to Johanna about his regret over abandoning philosophy for a *Brotstudium* in law. In reply to the old man's remark that philosophy was not a solid field of study, Schopenhauer said that life is a troublesome affair and he had resolved to spend his own life reflecting on it. This remark won Wieland to his side: "Young man, I now understand your nature. Stick to philosophy."[28] Later, during a visit with Johanna, Wieland told her, "Madame Schopenhauer, I have recently made a very interesting acquaintance." Johanna asked, "With whom?" To which Wieland replied, "With

---

[27] Schopenhauer, *The World as Will and Representation*, Vol. 2, p. 338/*Sämtliche Werke*, Vol. 2, p. 386.
[28] Schopenhauer, *Gespräche*, p. 22.

your son. Ah, it was a great pleasure to come to know this young man, something great will one day come of him."[29]

Switching his allegiance from medicine to philosophy forced Schopenhauer to leave Göttingen. Its strengths resided in the sciences, so it was attractive to a student of medicine, but not to a student of philosophy. Other than Schulze, it had only one other professor of philosophy, Friedrich Bouterwek, who came to Göttingen in 1797, after the retirement of Schulze's father-in-law, Johann Georg Heinrich Feder, who edited one of the first reviews of Kant's *Critique of Pure Reason* for the *Göttingische gelehrte Anzeigen* (19 January 1782) and who added passages in the review comparing Kant to Berkeley and Hume.[30] Bouterwek, who taught philosophy at Göttingen for thirty years, prided himself on being the first to disseminate Kant's philosophy at the university. But by the time Schopenhauer arrived on campus, Bouterwek was taken by Jacobi, an infatuation that would not have appealed to the young philosopher. Later, Schopenhauer's remarks about Bouterwek were always derisive.[31]

Even if Schopenhauer had had a vibrant social life in Göttingen, its dearth of philosophy courses would have been sufficient for his departure. But he did not have a robust social life. In his *curriculum vitae*, he reported that he continued to maintain an intense focus on his studies, a habit he had developed in Weimar, and that other students could not lure him away from his books, because he was more mature (by at least five years), had richer experiences, and had a fundamentally different nature than other students. Consequently, he said that he spent most of his time in seclusion and solitude, reading many books, studying Plato and Kant on his own, and regularly attending lectures.[32] In his room there were a bust of Socrates, a portrait of Goethe, and his poodle Atma. His days assumed the cadence and general form that he would follow the rest of his life. The morning was for the heavy lifting of intellectual work, after which he

---

[29] Ibid.
[30] See Manfred Kuehn, *Kant: A Biography* (Cambridge: Cambridge University Press, 2001), pp. 251–2.
[31] Schopenhauer cites Bouterwek as a philosopher who could not see connections between Plato and Kant, due to their using different terms for the same ideas, and he chided his vacuous concept of "good;" see Schopenhauer, *The World as Will and Representation*, Vol. 1, p. 174/*Sämtliche Werke*, Vol. 2, p. 205, and *On the Basis of Morality*, p. 204/*Sämtliche Werke*, Vol. 4, "Die beiden Groundprobleme der Ethik," p. 265.
[32] See Schopenhauer, *Gesammelte Briefe*, pp. 52/653.

played his flute. In the afternoon he took long walks with his dog, and at night he went to the theater or parties.

Schopenhauer's description of his life in Göttingen was somewhat of an exaggeration. After all, he was petitioning for the right to lecture at the University of Berlin, and it would have been unwise to mention his fondness for Rhine wine or the details of the parties, and given his earlier behavior in Hamburg, it is not a stretch to imagine that he did not neglect his sex life.[33] He also had his share of friends: Ernst Arnold Lewald, whom he knew from his Gotha days, and who would become a professor of philology at the University of Heidelberg; Friedrich Gotthilf Osann, whom Schopenhauer knew from Weimar, and who would play a fairly continuous role in Schopenhauer's life; and Karl Witte, the prodigy who matriculated at Göttingen at the age of ten, received his doctorate at the age of sixteen, and became a well-known Dante scholar. Then there were his messmates: Christian Karl Josias Bunsen, who described Schopenhauer in terms with which Johanna would have sympathized – "His debating is rough and spiky, his tone is as sulky as his brow, his disputation is heated and his paradoxical argument terrible"; and William Backhouse Astor, the son of the German-born American multimillionaire capitalist John Jacob Astor, the founder of the American Fur Company.[34] Schopenhauer was inclined in his later years to reflect on Bunsen's, Astor's, and his own life: "One reached status, the other wealth, the third – wisdom"; and "the first . . . is now a diplomat, the other a millionaire, and the third a philosopher."[35] Bunsen had become a Prussian diplomat and a baron. Schopenhauer followed his career and often read about him in the London *Times*.[36] Astor would eventually head his father's various business ventures.

[33] Ibid., p. 157, Schopenhauer to Anthime Grégoire de Blésimaire, 10 December 1836.

[34] Quoted in Safranski, *Schopenhauer and the Wild Years of Philosophy*, p. 102.

[35] Schopenhauer, *Gespräche*, p. 318 (reported by Gwinner) and p. 131 (reported by Frauenstädt).

[36] Schopenhauer, *Gesammelte Briefe*, p. 414, Schopenhauer to Bunsen, 28 March 1857. Schopenhauer also wrote, in English, that he read in the *Times* about "Dukes & bishops, & a brilliant entertainment of Chevalier Bunsen." He also teases the religious Bunsen, who wrote a work in theology; "You still are a man of God, but that's gone badly for me. . . . since in the corner of my room, on the console, sits a beautifully gilded – idol – from Tibet, oh woe!" Bunsen may have been the closest of his associates at Göttingen. He accompanied Schopenhauer to his mother's house in Weimar for the Easter holidays of 1811, where he also introduced Bunsen to Goethe.

Fichte and Berlin

The son of a Saxon ribbon weaver, Johann Gottlieb Fichte was born in 1762 into very modest conditions. It was, however, his good fortune to possess an almost photographic memory. One Sunday, Baron von Miltitz arrived too late for the morning church service, and he was directed to the young Fichte, who provided him with a verbatim recitation. This impressed the Baron so greatly that he financed Fichte's education, beginning with private instruction at the home of a local pastor, then at the gymnasium at Pforta, and last at the universities of Jena, Wittenberg, and Leipzig from 1780 to 1784. Then Fichte's benefactor died, failing to leave adequate resources for continuing his education. To support himself, he was forced to become a private tutor. He returned to Leipzig in 1790 to tutor a student in Kant's philosophy. Moved by his reconsideration of Kant's first *Critique* and overwhelmed by the second, the *Critique of Practical Reason*, he moved in 1791 to Königsberg to attend Kant's lectures and to meet his philosophical hero. He found the sixty-seven-year-old philosopher's lectures dry and weakly delivered. Nevertheless, he met Kant, and like others drawn to the great man, he did so only once, which was sufficient for Kant. So to gain Kant's attention, and to establish his philosophical spurs, he wrote in six weeks the *Attempt of a Critique of All Revelation* (*Versuch einer Kritik aller Offenbarung*, 1792). Seeking the master's blessings and aid in securing a publisher, he sent the manuscript to Kant. It is not surprising that he satisfied both of his desires, because his work mirrored in broad terms Kant's own work is the second *Critique*, where he made his ethics the support for his moral theology. Fichte addressed the status of revelations in his manuscript, and made a broadly sketched Kantian ethics the basis for religious revelations. Our autonomy, he argued, our ability to act from our conception of moral laws, without the promise of reward or the threat of punishment, is of such sublimity and nobility that it is as if religious revelations exist. Fichte kept ethics distinct from theology, just as Kant would have it, and the credence he attributed to theological claims was parasitic on morality. It was as if Fichte had added religious revelations to Kant's three postulates of practical reason.

Although Kant received Fichte's *Critique* in the fall of 1791, it appeared in 1792, due to some hesitancy by the censor. When it appeared, however, it did so anonymously. But what appeared first as bad luck for its author, later proved to be a good marketing ploy. From the fact that it appeared through Kant's publisher Hartung and due to its title, many assumed that this was Kant's fourth *Critique*, an assumption that drew a large audience and a number of favorable reviews. Kant, of course, denied authorship and praised its true author. Fichte's star started to ascend in the heavens, where Fichte hoped that it would fill others with the same awe that they felt about the moral law within them.

When Reinhold abandoned his low-paying position in Jena for better remuneration at the University of Kiel, he did so feeling a sting from Aenesidemus Schulze's assault. His departure created a messy void in Jena's philosophy faculty, and Goethe decided to spruce it up by filling it with Fichte, who had further distinguished himself with his review of *Aenesidemus* in the *Allgemeine Littaratur Zeitung* in 1794, the same year as Reinhold's departure. In his review, Fichte deftly dealt blows to both Reinhold and Schulze. He agreed with Schulze that his predecessor at Jena had failed to provide a secure foundation for Kant's philosophy, but he disagreed with Schulze's skepticism and his contentment with leaving things in themselves unknown. For Fichte, this would render them nonsense, a "non-thought."[37] But Reinhold's failure to establish a single first principle to ground the critical philosophy did not render Reinhold's quest meaningless, he argued. Naturally, he would make this his own project. And, as could be expected, this review increased Fichte's reputation, and only diminished his standing with Reinhold, Schulze, and, surprisingly, Kant.

Students flocked to Fichte's lectures, welcoming his insistence that they accept the moral responsibility attached to their status as free beings. It was as if Fichte provided a substitute for their sense of loss of religious certainty, which was shaken by the German philosophical scene and Napoleon's mischief. The still sane poet Hölderlin attended Fichte's lectures and raved about them to his Tübingen seminary buddy Hegel. His other dear friend, Schelling, would later join Jena's faculty, appearing to be a dyed-in-the-wool Fichtean. The ironical and self-absorbed Friedrich Schlegel would claim that "The French Revolution, Fichte's philosophy,

---

[37] "Review of *Aenesidemus*," in *Fichte: Early Philosophical Writings*, ed. and trans. Daniel Breazeale, (Ithaca, NY: Cornell University Press, 1988), p. 71. For a fine discussion of German Idealism, see Terry Pinkard, *German Philosophy 1760–1860: The Legacy of Idealism*, especially pp. 87–130, for Jacobi, Reinhold, Schulze, and Fichte. Also see Rolf-Peter Hostmann, "The Early Philosophy of Fichte and Schelling," in *The Cambridge Companion to German Idealism*, pp. 117–40.

and Goethe's *Meister* [*Wilhelm Meister's Years of Apprenticeship, Wilhelm Meisters Lehrjahre*, 1795–6], are the greatest tendencies of the age."[38] It was as if Fichte made him completely forget Kant.

Although Fichte inspired, charmed, and moved some students to denounce secret fraternities, dueling, and excessive drinking, this also made him unpopular with others. Still, students flocked to his lectures, a state of affairs that created some ill will among some of the old guard faculty, who lost money. He was also viewed as a radical Jacobin by others, due to some of his publications written prior to his time at Jena.[39] Then there were suspicions about his religious faith, occasioned by both his philosophy and his behavior. The so-called "atheism controversy" led to his dismissal from Jena in the summer of 1798. Things started to fall apart for this son of a Saxon ribbon weaver. Schelling arrived in Jena in 1799, and instead of remaining a loyal Fichtean, began to pursue his own agenda, the philosophy of nature. Kant denounced Fichte and his system, and it was said that "it was impossible to mention Fichte and his school without making Kant angry."[40] Jacobi, who delighted in causing controversy (the earlier pantheism controversy) and in throwing gas on other fires, wrote "An Open Letter to Fichte" ["*Sendschreiben an Fichte*," 1799], arguing that Fichte's philosophy, the so-called *Wissenschaftslehre* (science of knowledge), led to nihilism, the belief in nothing at all.[41]

Licking his wounds, Fichte fled to Berlin. He had only been a shooting star in Jena. As Goethe observed laconically, "One star sets, another rises," and he remained content to let life flow as it would.[42] When Fichte arrived at Berlin, there was no university there. He had to make his living through his writings, as a private tutor, and through public lectures. He also labored on his *Wissenschaftslehre*, but he was never able to reach an

---

[38] "Athenäum-Fragment," 216, in Friedrich Schlegel, *Philosophical Fragments*, trans. Peter Firchow (Minneapolis: University of Minnesota Press, 1991), p. 52.

[39] These books were *A Discourse on the Reclamation of the Freedom of Thought from the Princes of Europe, Who Have Hitherto Suppressed It* (1793) and *A Contribution toward Correcting the Public's Judgment of the French Revolution* (1793). Although both were published anonymously, it was common knowledge that Fichte was their author; see Daniel Breazeale, "Fichte and Schelling: The Jena Period," in *The Age of Idealism*, p. 143. Breazeale provides a rich summary of Fichte's and Schelling's philosophical work during their Jena period.

[40] Manfred Kuehn, *Kant: A Biography*, p. 390.

[41] See Friedrich Heinrich Jacobi, *The Main Philosophical Writings and the Novel Allwill*, trans. and ed. George di Giovanni (Montreal: McGill–Queens University Press, 1994), p. 519.

[42] Quoted in Breazeale, "Fichte and Schelling: The Jena Period," p. 45.

exposition that he found worthy of publication – he feared that publishing his developing thought would continue to provoke misunderstandings of his philosophy.[43] Therefore, he pledged "to confine himself to oral communication, so that misunderstanding can be detected and eliminated on the spot."[44] In the summer semester of 1805, the spot to deliver his oral communications was the University of Erlangen, and he returned to Berlin in 1806. But Napoleon's crushing defeat of Prussia and the occupation of Berlin moved him to return to Königsberg, where the great Kant had died two years earlier. He once more delivered yet another form of his *Wissenschaftslehre*. After the battle of Friedland, in east Prussia, Tsar Alexander of Russia decided that it was best to come to terms with Napoleon and, after the Treaty of Tilsit on 1 June 1807, Fichte returned to Berlin. He delivered his *Addresses to the German Nation* shortly after his return, pitching education as the means for developing an explicit sense of German nationalism, and defining having character as being German, a stance that made him an immediately attractive candidate to head the philosophy faculty at the newly founded University of Berlin (1810), which was founded to offset the temporary loss of the University of Halle and to develop a new form of intellectual strength parallel to that which Prussia hoped to develop by reforming its military. The same year in which the university was founded in Berlin, Johanna's official debut as a writer occurred, with the publication of *Carl Ludwig Fernow's Life* [*Carl Ludwig Fernow's Leben*]. Her dear old Weimar confidant provided her with a life, the story of which launched her successful literary career.

The lure of Fichte moved Schopenhauer to travel toward Berlin from Göttingen via the Harz mountains, avoiding a detour to Weimar. On 8 September 1811, near Ellrich, he opined,

Philosophy is a high mountain road which is reached only by a steep path covered with sharp stones and prickly thorns. It is an isolated road and becomes ever more desolate the higher we ascend. Whoever pursues this path must show no fear, but must leave everything behind and confidently make his own way in the wintry snow. Often he suddenly comes to a precipice and looks down upon the verdant valley. A violent

---

[43] Terry Pinkard claims that there were sixteen different versions of the *Wissenschaftslehre* in Fichte's collected writings; see his *German Philosophy 1760–1860: The Legacy of Idealism*, p. 108.

[44] Johann Gottlieb Fichte, *Gesamtausgabe der Bayerischen Akademie der Wissenschaften*, 24 vols, ed. Lauth et al. (Stuggart–Bad Cannstatt: Frommann, 1964–), Vol. 3, Part 5, p. 223. Cited in Breazeale, "Fichte and Schelling: The Jena Period," p. 146.

attack of dizziness draws him over the edge, but he must control himself and cling to the rocks with might and main. In return to this, he soon sees the world beneath him; its sandy deserts and morasses vanish from his view, its uneven spots are leveled out, its jarring sounds no longer reach his ear, and its roundness is revealed to him. He himself is always in the pure cool mountain air and now beholds the sun when all below is still engulfed in dead of night.[45]

Schopenhauer had been to Berlin at least twice before. On a trip with his parents in 1800, he spent ten days in the city. He was impressed with the beauty of Berlin's architecture and the presence of many single-family homes.[46] The second visit to Berlin was depressing – not that he found any particular problem with Berlin – but because it was the endpoint of the European tour in 1804. His father left for Hamburg, and Schopenhauer for Danzig and the beginning of his merchant training. Three times is the charm, and Schopenhauer's descent into Berlin, through its sandy deserts, represented a reversal of the descent of Nietzsche's Zarathustra, who went down to humans to share his wisdom. Schopenhauer went down driven by his love of wisdom. Like Zarathustra, Schopenhauer would also be disappointed.

Schopenhauer arrived in Berlin with his cigars, pistols, flute, and growing library and his "very intelligent poodle."[47] He longed to cultivate both his mind and heart. Well, at least he said that in his *curriculum vitae*, and he thought he would do so in the University of Berlin, because of its many famous instructors. In the same document, he rattled off the names of his professors: Wolf, Schleiermacher, Erman, Lichtenstein, Klaproth, Fischer, Bode, Weiss, Horkel, and Rosenthat. Then, as if it were an afterthought, he included, "Also Fichte, who lectured on his philosophy. I followed it, in order to be able to subsequently correctly assess it."[48] This remark from his *curriculum vitae* (1819) made it appear as if Fichte had just happened to be in Berlin when he transferred schools. By then Fichte's philosophy was almost as dead as its author, who died unexpectedly at the

---

[45] Schopenhauer, *Manuscript Remains*, Vol. 1, #20.

[46] See Schopenhauer, "Journal einer Reise aus dem Jahre 1800," in Wilhelm Gwinner, *Arthur Schopenhauer aus persönlichem Umgange dargestellt*, pp. 245–49.

[47] Schopenhauer, *On the Fourfold Root of the Principle of Sufficient Reason*, trans. E. F. J. Payne, with an introduction by Richard Taylor (La Salle, IL: Open Court Press, 1974), p. 110/*Sämtliche Werke*, Vol. 1, p. 76. The remark about his intelligent poodle occurs within an argument for the claim that nonhuman animals possess the faculty of understanding.

[48] Schopenhauer, *Gesammelte Briefe*, p. 53/p. 654.

age of fifty-one in 1814, struck down by typhus. He had caught it from his wife, who had contracted it while nursing wounded soldiers. Hegel now ruled the roost at Berlin and *The World as Will and Representation* had appeared. Some had scented the spurs of Fichte in the work, which displeased Schopenhauer. Thus it was best to downplay his exposure to Fichte and to emphasize that he attended Fichte's lectures simply to correctly evaluate his philosophy and not to follow it. Thirty-two years later, he was more forthright about his relocation: "In 1811, I moved to Berlin with the expectation that in Fichte I would become acquainted with a genuine philosopher and a great mind; this *a priori* veneration, however, soon changed to disdain and scorn."[49]

Fichte would deliver an introductory set of lectures prior to the start of a new semester, in order to drum up students and to articulate the themes of the upcoming lecture cycle. Schopenhauer attended Fichte's introductory lectures for his course on the "Facts of Consciousness and on the Doctrine of Science [*Wissenschaftslehre*]" in the fall of 1811. In many ways, Fichte was an unconventional lecturer. Most instructors would dictate their lectures, reading from lecture books that remained relatively unchanged for years. Their students would become virtual stenographers, madly writing to capture the profundities pronounced by the star on the stage. Fichte was of a different ilk. Still the star on stage, he did not read from a fixed lecture book when presenting his philosophy. With each new semester, he refreshed, revised, and reorganized his thought. This was one of the reasons that he left so many versions of his *Wissenschaftslehre* behind. He was also eager to cultivate his students' own understanding of his thought. He forbade them to try to capture each and everything he said. Doing so, he believed, was a distraction. They needed to concentrate, to focus on the development of his ideas. They could, he said, jot short sentences to aid their memory. After the lecture, he recommended that they reflect on what he had said, and then they should "compile into an organic whole what he understood in a way suitable to his individual nature; this should be put down in writing.[50]

Schopenhauer was all ears during Fichte's introductory lectures. Afterward, when it came to compiling the lectures into an organic whole, he interjected his own reflections. At first, if he failed to grasp some idea

[49] Ibid., p. 261, Schopenhauer to Johann Eduard Erdmann, 9 April 1851.
[50] Schopenhauer, *Manuscript Remains*, Vol. 2, p. 30/*Der handschriftliche Nachlaß*, Vol. 2, p. 28.

or thought, he blamed himself. This attitude would change as Fichte's lectures unfolded. Nevertheless, when he failed to understand a point, he frequently attributed this to his failure to capture something Fichte said: "This is obscure and not adequately explained, yet it may be that I failed to catch a few remarks, for Fichte's delivery is indeed clear and he speaks slowly."[51] Soon, he found that Fichte was repetitive, dressing the same ideas in different words, which he found distracting. Although Fichte encouraged his students to come to their own ideas, he may have been surprised to discover that Schopenhauer did this immediately with ideas that were typically contrary to his teacher's. Thus when Fichte opined that genius is divine and madness animal, with healthy understanding standing between the two extremes, Schopenhauer took issue; genius is closer to madness than it is to healthy understanding and madness is closer to genius than it is to the animal.[52] He also invoked Kant against Fichte. Still, in his notes to Kant's *Prolegomena to Any Future Metaphysics* (*Prolegomena zu einer jeden künftigen Metaphysik*, 1783), where the sage of Königsberg attempted to concisely and straightforwardly articulate the findings of his difficult first *Critique*, Schopenhauer still shares Fichte's attitude toward the thing in itself: "... the *thing in itself*, the weak side of Kant's teaching. It is difficult to understand why Kant did not consider this concept in greater detail and reflect that *being*, used in the second and third persons, means nothing but *being sensuously cognized*, and hence that, after deducting *being sensuously cognized*, the remainder, – or thing in itself – is equal to nothing."[53]

There will be other points of contact between Schopenhauer's nascent philosophy and Fichte's thought. Already with his first marginal notes to Kant, stemming from early 1811, he was attempting to assimilate the two philosophers whom Schulze recommended he read first, "Plato the divine" and the "immortal Kant," as Schopenhauer would designate them, for the first time, in his notes to Fichte's lectures.[54] "The *Critique of Pure Reason*," he wrote, "could be called the suicide of the understanding (that is to say philosophy)." He continues by drawing an analogy. One person lies and another, who knows the truth, says that this is a pack of lies and

---

51 Ibid., p. 18/ibid., p. 17.
52 See ibid./ibid.
53 Ibid., pp. 290–91/ibid., pp. 265–6.
54 Schopenhauer, *Manuscript Remains*, Vol. 2, pp. 90, 109/*Der handschriftliche Nachlaß*, Vol. 2, pp. 84, 101.

speaks the truth. A third person, who is very acute and clever, shows the contradictions and impossible statements in that lie and exposes it as a fraud and falsehood: "The lie is life, the acute and clever person, however, is Kant; the truth has been brought to us by many a person, by Plato for example."[55] Then, in his second introductory lecture, Fichte speaks of a flash of evidence that moves one beyond the ordinary perception of things to the region of the ground of all experience, to that which is supersensible and intelligible. Schopenhauer, intrigued, concurs:

Within the limits of experience we cannot go farther than becoming aware that the most solid, ultimate and fundamental truth, the basic pillar of all experience, is simply error. This is what Kant achieved when he demonstrated the emptiness and unreality of space and time and reduced the understanding to suicide. There is that flash of evidence, but only where the domain of true knowledge rises above all experience. There comes a moment when the entire world of appearance fades, outshone and eclipsed by the I that cognizes its reality and that of the supersensible world; like a shadow-show it vanishes when a light is kindled. The moment may come to a few, to genuine philosophers. Therefore Plato says: "Many carry the staff of consecration, but only a few are truly and divinely inspired."[56]

Despite his minor qualms about Fichte, he enrolled in Fichte's lectures on the facts of consciousness and on the *Wissenschaftslehre* in the winter semester of 1811–12. It is odd, however, that when Fichte proclaimed in the introductory lectures, "I have been credited with the merit of expressing myself clearly in writing as well as word of mouth," that Schopenhauer did not make some derisive remark.[57] Perhaps Fichte said this in an ironic tone, and so Schopenhauer let it go. Fichte was far from being clear in his writings, and Schopenhauer would increasingly find the same concerning his word of mouth. Still, Schopenhauer hesitates to voice his criticism of Fichte's mouthing of his thoughts. Just as he had

55 Ibid., Vol. 1, pp. 12–13/ibid., Vol. 1, pp. 12–13.
56 Ibid., Vol. 2, pp. 24–5/ibid., Vol. 2, p. 23.
57 Ibid., p. 30/ibid., p. 28. Recent translators of Fichte's *Wissenschaftslehre* provide this description of his writing: " . . . Fichte labors under a number of severe handicaps, not the least of which is his cumbersome, unnecessarily complex style. His thought, which may be difficult enough to follow on the clearest exposition, is obscured by the vagueness and the ambiguities of his writing. Bad punctuation, idiosyncratic sentence structure, and a dismaying overabundance of nonfunctional expletives interfere with a task of understanding, and it is ironic that a thinker in whose philosophy the requirement of unity plays such an exalted role, could have endowed this work with no more readily discernible structure than it displays." *The Science of Knowledge*, trans. Peter Heath and John Lachs (Cambridge: Cambridge University Press, 1982), p. vii.

done in Fichte's introductory lectures, when he fails to follow a point, he is generous. Perhaps he was not paying due attention to the lecture; perhaps he was not in a receptive frame of mind. Worse, perhaps he did not have the intellect to follow this powerful positer of the I or Ego. But, in the eleventh lecture, he had enough of Fichte's torturous ill-locutions. He suspected that Ficthe's science of knowledge was empty of knowledge; that the *Wissenschaftslehre* was the *Wissenschaftsleere*: "In this lecture [the 11th], in addition to what is written down, he has said things which have wrung from me the wish to be allowed to put a pistol to his chest and then say: Now you must die without mercy, but for the sake of your poor soul say whether with the jumble of words you have a clear conception of anything or have merely made fools of us."[58] Fortunately for Fichte, Schopenhauer left his pistol back in his rooms and bravely soldiered through the semester, only taking verbal potshots at his teacher's ideas. His *a priori* veneration for Fichte, which drew him to Berlin, "soon turned to scorn and derision."[59] Nevertheless, he left behind a voluminous set of notes to these lectures, amounting to more than two hundred pages in his *Nachlaß*. Still, one semester's worth of lectures were sufficient for Schopenhauer. He was sick of hearing Fichte's voice. However, in the spring–summer semester of 1812, he embarked on a wide reading of his ex-professor, and he made an extract from Johann Baptist Reinert's notes from Fichte's lectures on jurisprudence and moral philosophy from the 1812–13 winter semester.

"Philosophy," Schopenhauer recorded Fichte as asserting, "is *Wissenschaftslehre*, the science that states the ground of all knowing.... The word philosophy is of no use, because it does not imply a knowledge, but a liking, a striving for knowledge, an attempt to see whether it is obtainable."[60] Then, in the next lecture, he recorded a claim that would be echoed in his own philosophy. The *Wissenschaftslehre* is articulated through a series of thoughts, Fichte continued, "although it is in fact only one thought" [*ein Gedanke*].[61] In the introduction to the first edition of *The*

---

[58] Ibid., p. 43/ibid., p. 41. In an email to me, Christopher Janaway deftly captured Schopenhauer's pun on Fichte's *Wissenschaftlehre* (*Science of Knowledge*) as *Science of Nulledge* (*Wissenschaftleere*).

[59] Schopenhauer, *Gesammelte Briefe*, p. 261, Schopenhauer to Johann Eduard Erdmann, 9 April 1851.

[60] Schopenhauer, *Manuscript Remains*, Vol. 2, p. 28/*Der handschriftliche Nachlaß*, Vol. 2, p. 26.

[61] Ibid., p. 28/ibid., p. 27.

World as Will and Representation, Schopenhauer claimed that his book was the expression of "a single thought [*ein einziger Gedanke*]... I consider this thought to be that which has been sought for a very long time under the name of philosophy."[62] Yet, like a number of points of contact alleged to hold between these philosophers, this is a mere tangent. Schopenhauer read Fichte as presenting a system of thoughts based on a foundational, unconditional first principle. Everything was deduced from this principle, which carried the weight for the whole system. Such a system is sound if and only if each supporting thought bears the one following and the foundational thought supports them all. Schopenhauer's single thought, however, had to be split into parts, in order to be communicated, and "the connection of these parts must once more be organic, i.e., of such a kind that every part supports the whole just as much as it is supported by the whole; a connection in which no part is first and no part is last, in which the whole gains in clearness from every part, and even the smallest part cannot be fully understood until the whole has been first understood."[63] There is, then, no foundational, unconditional first principle.

Fichte's *Wissenschaftslehre* was a philosophy in constant change and revision throughout his life, and the lectures Schopenhauer attended presented it in a different style and in different terms than its expression during Fichte's years at Jena. Still, Schopenhauer's private study of Fichte during the spring–summer of 1812 included his Jena works, *Foundations of the Entire Wissenschaftslehre* [*Grundlage der gesammten Wissenschaftslehre*, 1794], and *Outline of the Distinctive Character of the Wissenschaftslehre with Respect to the Theoretical Faculty* [*Grundriß des Eigenthümlichen der Wissenschaftslehre in Rüchsicht auf das theoretische Vermögen*, 1795]. It is curious that the few times Schopenhauer referred to Fichte's philosophy, it was to these Jena works and not to Fichte's lectures. To be sure, there were good reasons for this. These books were public documents and the lectures, because they were not published, constituted hearsay. Moreover, Fichte's Jena writings were his best-known and most influential writings. Schopenhauer, however, may have also gained a clearer understanding of the *Wissenschaftslehre* by reading these books after attending Fichte's lectures, which had often left him confused.

[62] Schopenhauer, *The World as Will and Representation*, Vol. 1, p. xii/ *Sämtliche Werke*, Vol. 2, p. vii.
[63] Ibid./ibid., p. viii.

Schopenhauer would refer frequently to his old professor in his published works, but the vast majority of his remarks were in the form of
ad hominem attacks. There were only two brief and somewhat thoughtful
considerations of Fichte's philosophy within Schopenhauer's *oeuvre* and
a very late attempt to explain why his critics sensed Fichte's stamp in
his philosophy. Yet he never discussed Fichte to indicate some intrinsic merit of his philosophy or to take some insight to enlarge within his
own theorizing. So when he discussed Fichte in his principal work, he
did so simply because Fichte represented the only philosopher foolish
enough to attempt to derive the object from the subject of experience,
the known from the knower, the object from the subject. And when he
considered Fichte's moral philosophy, he used Fichte's ethics simply to
illustrate problems with Kant's moral philosophy. Still, even in these cases
he spent as much time abusing Fichte as he did carefully evaluating his
philosophy, if not more.

To understand Schopenhauer's objections to Fichte's philosophy, it
is necessary to offer a bare sketch of Fichte's difficult, obscure, but rich
thought. It is also necessary to point to a fixed locus for his evolving
Wissenschaftslehre. Given the nature of Schopenhauer's critique of Fichte,
the *Foundations of the Entire Wissenschaftslehre* provide this fixed point.
Fichte, like Kant, attempted to articulate the necessary conditions for all
possible experiences, and in agreement with Reinhold, he believed that
he had to secure a certain and firm foundation for the critical philosophy.
Thus in the *Foundations of the Entire Wissenschaftslehre*, he sought "to
discover the primordial, absolutely unconditional first principle of all
human knowledge."[64] In addition to this "absolutely unconditional first
principle," whose form and content are not derivable from anything else,
he advanced two additional principles: the second is unconditional only
with respect to its form and not its content, and the third is unconditional
only with respect to its content and not its form.

Fichte's first principle, his absolutely unconditional principle, states
that "the self [*Ich*] begins by an absolute positing of its own existence."[65]

---

[64] Fichte, *The Science of Knowledge*, trans. Peter Heath and John Lachs (Cambridge: Cambridge
University Press, 1982), p. 93.

[65] Ibid., p. 99. The German verb *"setzen"* is translated here as "posits." It can also mean
"to assert," "to put," "to set," "bring forth," and as a reflective verb, *"setzen sich,"* can
mean "to sit down," or "to take a seat." In his marginal notes to his copy of Fichte's *The
System of Moral Philosophy According to the Principles of the* Wissenschaftslehre [*Das System
der Sittenlehre nach den Principien der* Wissenschaftslehre (Jena and Leipzig: Gabler, 1798)],

That is, the self or I constitutes itself as self-consciousness in an act in which it becomes conscious of itself. This positing of itself is a fact/act [*Tathandlung*], and because this is what constitutes self-consciousness, Fichte's first principle is at once practical and theoretical. Moreover, because it is the subject's own act that constitutes itself, autonomy or self-determination is at the foundation of his system. The second principle is that the I posits a Not-I, an act that sets a field for the I's activity, but one that also limits the I. This principle establishes the necessary conditions for knowledge by affecting a split between Knower (I) and Known (Not-I), between the subject and the object. It also intends to account for a commonsense realism, which holds that there are objects that exist externally and independent from perceivers. Naturally, because these "objects" are the work of the I, Fichte retains idealism. His third principle, perhaps the most obscure and problematic one, states that "in the self I oppose a divisible not-self to the divisible self."[66] That is, the I posits a limited I in opposition to a limited Not-I, because it requires something other than itself as a given, something that is not posited by itself. The I, therefore, finds itself in a contradiction, an intolerable state that prompts it to strive to overcome this contradiction by showing how the Not-I is not a mere given, but is something constituted out of the necessity of self-consciousness. This third principle helped to motivate a distinction between the Absolute I and Finite I's or persons.

Schopenhauer briefly addressed the theoretical side of the *Wissenschaftslehre* in the first edition of *The World as Will and Representation*. Already he had established in his dissertation the correlativity of the subject and object as the most basic epistemic distinction. For any experience, he held, there must be the experienced (the object) and the experiencer (the subject): "Now with the subject an object is at once posited [*gesetzt*] (for even the word would otherwise be without meaning), and in the same way the subject is at once posited with the object. Hence being subject means exactly the same as having an object, and being object means just the same as being cognized by the subject."[67] This commitment led

---

p. 70, Schopenhauer drew a chair in reference to Fichte's assertion "*Das Vernunftwesen setzt sich absolute selbständig* . . . [The rational being posits itself absolutely independent . . .]"; see *Der handschriftliche Nachlaß*, Vol. 5, p. 54.

[66] Fichte, *The Science of Knowledge*, p. 110.

[67] Schopenhauer, *On the Fourfold Root of the Principle of Sufficient Reason*, p. 209/*Sämtliche Werke*, Vol. 7, p. 70. In this first edition (1813), Schopenhauer was still disenchanted with the Kantian notion of the thing in itself as something outside cognition: "This much becomes

Schopenhauer to consider two views contrary to his own. The first was a materialist and realist position; a view that attempted to account for everything, including the subject, based on an appeal to material objects that exist externally and independent from the subject. The second, set in polar opposition to materialism, was a view that attempted to derive everything for the subject, including the object. This led him, begrudgingly, to Fichte, because this second view had "only a single example, and a very recent one, namely, that fictitious philosophy of J. G. Fichte. In this respect, therefore, he must be considered, however little genuine worth and substance his teaching had in itself."[68]

Instead of challenging Fichte's "primordial, absolutely unconditional first principle," which he was willing to let sit alone, he challenged the second principle, the idea that the I, or subject, posits the Not-I, or object. Here he found Fichte making the same mistake as the realist, but from the opposite direction. The realist attempts to think an object without the subject, and Fichte's idealism attempts to think the subject without the object. Equally problematic, according to Schopenhauer, was the realist's claim that the object stood in a causal relationship to the subject and the idealist's claim that the subject caused the object. Following what he took to be the lead of Kant, Schopenhauer argued that there could be no causal relationship between the subject and the object, because causality was an *a priori* category of the understanding and was therefore valid only within the realm of experiences and was a relationship only between objects. Fichte, he wrote, "makes the Not-I result from the I as

apparent, however, that our investigation does not become paralyzed with a thing in itself," ibid., p. 71. It is also curious that Schopenhauer used the Fichtean verb "*setzen*" in describing the correlation between subject and object: "Now with the subject the object is at once posited" [*Wie mit dem Subjekt sofort auch das Objekt gesetzt ist*], ibid., 70. Even though he employed Fichte's language here, unlike the latter, who, in one of the lectures attended by Schopenhauer, said that the identity of the intuiter (subject) and the intuited (object) rested on an "absolutely immediate intuition [*absolute unmittelbare Anschauung*]," Schopenhauer rejected this form of privileged access to Fichte's ultimate: "There is only one intuiter, namely the I; and for this very reason this I is never intuited," *Manuscript Remains*, Vol. 2, p. 72/*Der handschriftliche Nachlaß*, Vol. 2, p. 68. As in Kant, the subject or I is elusive and never an object of cognition. Rather subject and object are necessarily correlative and separated only in reflection by determining the conditions necessary for having an experience or representation.

[68] Schopenhauer, *The World as Will and Representation*, Vol. 1, p. 32/*Sämtliche Werke*, Vol. 3, p. 38. In this passage, the only compliment Schopenhauer paid Fichte was that "he possessed considerable rhetorical talent."

the web from the spider. It is the principle of sufficient reason for being in space. For it is only in reference to this that those tortuous deductions of the way in which the I produces and fabricates out of itself the Not-I, forming the most senseless and consequently the most tedious book ever written, acquired a kind of sense and meaning."[69] By beginning his philosophy with experiences or representations, Schopenhauer believed that he avoided the difficulties of realism and Fichte's subjective idealism. Thus his philosophy, contrary to Fichte's and the realist's, begins with a "fact of consciousness": "Now our method of procedure is *toto genere* different from these two misconceptions, because we start neither from the object nor from the subject, but from the *representation*, as the first fact of consciousness."[70] In the second edition of his main work, he would claim that by beginning with the representation, a fact of consciousness, he retained an idealistic standpoint: ". . . the basis of philosophy is limited to the facts of consciousness; in other words, philosophy is essentially *idealistic*."[71]

It took Schopenhauer six years after his exposure to Fichte's lectures to publish his critical remarks attacking both the man and the theoretical dimensions of the *Wissenschaftslehre*. And although he studied the moral dimensions of Fichte's philosophy shortly after he attended the lectures, it would take him twenty-nine years to put into print his negative evaluation of the practical side of the *Wissenschaftslehre*. Once more, however, it was as if Fichte was an afterthought. He had discussed Fichte for the first time simply because his philosophy was the only instance of one sufficiently perverse to attempt to derive everything from the subject. Had he been able to think of another example, one suspects that he would have been happy to have not mentioned Fichte at all. He could not, however, and so Fichte became a primary target.

When it came to his consideration of Fichte's ethical theory, things were different. He was happy to bash Fichte's ethics, but his primary target was his philosophical hero Kant. Whereas Schopenhauer accused Fichte's theoretical philosophy of ignoring Kant's epistemological and metaphysical insights, especially his distinction between appearances and

---

[69] Schopenhauer, *The World as Will and Representation*, Vol. 1, p. 33/*Sämtliche Werke*, Vol. 2, p. 40.
[70] Ibid., p. 34/ibid., p. 40.
[71] Ibid., Vol. 2, p. 5/ibid., Vol. 3, p. 5.

things in themselves, he found Fichte's practical philosophy a caricature of Kant's: one that distorted the original view in troublesome ways, but which also magnified its flawed features. Yet in this case, it was not as if Fichte had managed to ruin something of exquisite value. Instead, Fichte helped to clearly show "the worthlessness of the Kantian basis of morality. Fichte's work is a means to the elucidation of this knowledge."[72] Thus in his essay "On the Basis of Morality" (1841), in which he spent more than one-third of his time attempting to demolish the Kantian foundation for morality, he used "Fichte's Ethics as a Mirror for Magnifying the Errors of the Kantian."[73] Fichte, whom he called Kant's "buffoon" in this section, let his readers see more clearly the fundamental flaws in Kant's moral philosophy.

The practical philosophy of the *Wissenschaftslehre* posited the I under the guise of a freely acting, empirical self-consciousness: a person, striving to realize its goal of framing the world as it ought to be. Fichte's ethics displayed a greater commitment to Kant's practical than his theoretical philosophy, because it was geared to demonstrate the validity of Kant's supreme principle of morality, the categorical imperative, and the material results of his ethical theory are parallel to those of Kant.[74] Schopenhauer, remaining true to his earlier treatment of Fichte, spent more effort attacking the philosopher than his moral philosophy. His broad references to Fichte's *The System of Ethical Theory According to the Principles of the Wissenschaftslehre* and *The Wissenschaftslehre Presented in Its General Outline [Die Wissenschaftslehre in ihrem allgemeinem Umrisse dargestellt*, Berlin: J. E. Hitzig, 1810] are typically to passages that highlighted Fichte's thick and tortuous language or that contained some counterintuitive claim. For example, from the latter work, he cites a statement about "an *ought* of the *ought's* visibility," and from the former, the argument "Every human body is the instrument for furthering the purpose of reason; hence the great possible fitness of every instrument must be for me an end; consequently, I must be careful and heedful of everyone."[75]

---

[72] Schopenhauer, *On the Basis of Morality*, p. 115/ *Sämtliche Werke*, Vol. 4, "Die beiden Grundprobleme der Ethik," p. 180.

[73] This is the title of Sect. 11; see ibid., p. 115/ibid., p. 179.

[74] I owe this point to Rolf-Peter Horstmann; see his "The Early Philosophy of Fichte and Schelling," in *The Cambridge Companion to German Idealism*, p. 127.

[75] *On the Basis of Morality*, pp. 118, 117/ *Sämtliche Werke*, Vol. 4, "Die beiden Grundprobleme der Ethik," pp. 182, 181. Schopenhauer recommended *The Wissenschaftslehre Presented in Its*

The context of Schopenhauer's treatment of Fichte's ethics made it clear that he was not interested in seriously evaluating Fichte's justification for any of his claims, nor was he interested in elucidating the meaning of any of his obscurely stated thoughts. He wrote as if Fichte had unintentionally taken key elements of Kant's moral philosophy and produced a *reductio ad absurdum*. Thus he claimed that Fichte turned the categorical imperative into "a despotic imperative; the absolute ought, legislative reason, and moral obligation," and developed it into "a moral destiny, an unfathomable necessity, that the human race should act strictly in accordance with certain motives."[76] The result of this, he continued, is that Fichte produced a *"System of Moral Fatalism,"* which lapsed into the comic. To illustrate his point, he then cited ten passages from *The System of Ethical Theory*, a couple of which are sufficient for the flavor of those passages: "I am only an instrument, a mere tool, of the moral law, certainly not a purpose or end;" and "The end or purpose of everyone is as means to realize reason: this is the ultimate purpose of his existence: for this alone he exists, and if this should not occur, he need not exist at all."[77]

Schopenhauer had also condemned Kant's moral pedantry earlier in the essay. Again, he found Fichte following suit: "To act in accordance with the impulse of sympathy, compassion and *philanthropy* is not moral at all, but is to that extent contrary to morals."[78] Naturally, for a philosopher who will proceed in the same essay to argue that compassion is the basis of morality, Fichte, like Kant, has a non-moral theory. Moral rules serve

General Outline to readers who considered their time too precious to be wasted on Fichte's lengthier works, because at forty-six pages, it presented the *Wissenschaftslehre* in a nutshell.

[76] Ibid., p. 116/ibid., p. 180.

[77] Ibid., p. 116, fn./ibid., p. 181, fn. Schopenhauer had already written "System of Moral Fatalism" under the title in his own copy of *The System of Ethical Theory*. The two quotations are from *Das System der Sittenlehre nach den Principien der Wissenschaftslehre* (Jena/Leipzig: Gabler, 1798), pp. 342, 343. He also quotes from pages 196, 232, 347, 360, 376, 377, 388, 420 to illustrate how people are treated as tools or instruments for the moral law. Schopenhauer's copy of this book was thoroughly annotated with derisive and negative remarks; see Schopenhauer, *Der handschriftliche Nachlaß*, Vol. 5, pp. 53–8. Most of these notes date to his Berlin private study of Fichte in the spring and summer of 1812.

[78] *On the Basis of Morality*, p. 117/*Sämtliche Werke*, Vol. 4, "Die beiden Grundprobleme der Ethik," p. 181. Earlier, he had cited Schiller's *Scruples of Conscience and Decision [Gewissensskrupel und Entscheidung]* as an appropriate description of Kant's moral pedantry, and Schopenhauer cites a passage from Kant's *Critique of Practical Reason*, AK. 84 as demonstrating it: "The feeling that it is incumbent on man to obey the moral law is that this is to be obeyed from a sense of *duty*, not from *voluntary inclination* or any endeavor, gladly undertaken of itself, perhaps also *without any order being given*"; ibid., p. 66/ibid., p. 134.

to specify lines of conduct possessing moral worth, Schopenhauer would argue, and agents could only be motivated to follow moral prescriptions by some promise of reward or some threat of punishment. That Fichte would condemn kindhearted fellow feelings showed, Schopenhauer continued, that Fichte's teaching never left him any time for learning. Moreover, he also demonstrated that he really lacked a philosophical mind, because he advanced the notion of the *liberum arbitrium indifferentiae*, the free choice of indifference, as the basis of human actions, whereas "Insight into the strict necessity of human actions is the line of demarcation that separates philosophical minds from the rest."[79] Later, Nietzsche would take this observation and, although agreeing with it, turn it against Schopenhauer himself.[80]

Hearing Fichte's lectures for one term was sufficient for Schopenhauer. Better, he thought, to study the books that made his name. Perhaps there were some ideas there. But by the end of the summer of 1812, he arrived at the same conclusion that he had reached at the end of the lectures. Kant's alleged successor was a clown: "Has ever an imitator made a greater parody of his model by failing to recognize what is essential and by exaggerating what is not essential."[81] In the same general observation "On Fichte as a Whole," he praised Fichte: "The crown of Fichte's teaching is that he renders *intelligible* the categorical imperative (moral philosophy) and deduced it from necessary laws."[82] Yet we have seen that the mature philosopher would also see this portion of the *Wissenschaftslehre* as making "intelligible" the defects of Kant's ethics. On the title page for his lecture notes, Schopenhauer made his pun that he continued to make throughout his life. The *Wissenschaftslehre* is *Wissenschaftleere*. On the back of this page, he quoted Kant: "The lie ('from the Father of Lies through whom all evil has come into the world') is really the foul spot in human nature, however much the *tone of truthfulness* at the same time (after the manner of

---

[79] Ibid., p. 117f./ibid., p. 181.

[80] See Friedrich Nietzsche, *Human, All Too Human*, trans. R. J. Hollingdale (Cambridge: Cambridge University Press, 1986), Vol. 2, Sect. 33, p. 223, where Nietzsche takes Schopenhauer to task for not drawing the proper conclusion from this claim; namely, to abandon his prejudice for holding that morality was metaphysically grounded: "Philosophical heads will thus distinguish themselves from the others through their unbelief in the metaphysical significance of morality."

[81] Schopenhauer, *Manuscript Remains*, Vol. 2, p. 413/*Der handschriftliche Nachlaß*, Vol. 2, p. 357.

[82] Ibid., p. 413/ibid. p. 413.

many Chinese shopkeepers who put over their shops in letters of gold the inscription: 'In this very place no one cheats') is the usual tone, especially in that which concerns the supernatural."[83] Still, Kant was not enough. He also had to evoke his other intellectual hero, Goethe, to put Fichte into perspective: "Man usually believes, if only words he hears;/That also with them goes material for thinking."[84]

It is odd, however, that Schopenhauer had absolutely no sympathy for Fichte, who was a progressive figure within Germany's tradition-bound universities. Shortly before Schopenhauer arrived at Berlin, Fichte was appointed Rector of the University. Like Schopenhauer himself, Fichte decried the students' propensities for dueling, drinking, secret societies, brawling, and general rowdiness. Yet he was no more effective in instituting change within the campus culture than he was in making his ideas clear to Schopenhauer. In the middle of February 1812, he resigned his office after failing to draw faculty support concerning the unfair disciplining of a student who refused to fight a duel.[85] The conflict between Fichte and the faculty, many of whom had the attitude that "boys will be boys," was occurring when Schopenhauer was attending Fichte's lectures, but he seemed oblivious to this conflict to the same degree that he was oblivious to any of Fichte's merits. The only compliment he paid to Fichte was to call him a "man of talent," but even this kind remark constituted an instance of damning by faint praise.[86] This was said in comparison to Hegel, a man who Schopenhauer believed had no talent. Indeed, he even took it to Locke's credit that Fichte had referred to him as the worst of all possible philosophers.[87]

Given Schopenhauer's extremely negative assessments of Fichte as both a man and a philosopher, it is not surprising that he mentioned

[83] Ibid., p. 31/ibid., p. 29. The Kant quotation is from *Announcement of Perpetual Peace in Philosophy*, 1798.

[84] Ibid., p. 31f./ibid., p. 29. The Goethe quotation is from *Faust*, part 1, v. 2565–6.

[85] On two occasions a Jewish student by the name of Brogi was assaulted by other students who hoped to provoke him into a duel. He complained to Fichte, who turned the cases over to the Court of Honor. In each instance, both the aggressor and victim received punishment. Fichte viewed Brogi's punishment as resulting from his failure to fight a duel. After the second case, Fichte resigned as Rector; see Rüdiger Safranski, *Schopenhauer and the Wild Years of Philosophy*, pp. 122–3 for a summary of the Brogi incident.

[86] Schopenhauer, *On the Basis of Morality*, p. 14/*Sämtliche Werke*, Vol. 4, "Die beiden Grundprobleme der Ethik," p. xviii.

[87] Ibid., p. 22/ibid., p. xxvii.

him last in his discussion of his Berlin professors in his *curriculum vitae*. In the same document, he also wrote that he did not regret his enrollment in medicine at Göttingen, because his study of science was such that he "had heard lectures that were useful, indeed, necessary for the philosopher."[88] Schopenhauer displayed a voracious appetite for science throughout his life. At Berlin, he attended more lectures in the sciences than he did in any other field, including philosophy. His study of philosophy was largely self-directed, and on his own he studied Kant, Schelling, Fichte, Fries, Jacobi, Plato, Bacon, and Locke. At his death, his personal library contained almost 200 books in the sciences, and Schopenhauer's philosophical *oeuvre* referred to scientific titles not found in his library.[89] Both his formal coursework in the sciences and his continued reading in the sciences made Schopenhauer more scientifically literate than most of his philosophical contemporaries, and he maintained throughout his philosophical career the idea that the philosopher must be cognizant of the best findings of science. In this fourth book, *On the Will in Nature* [*Über den Willen in der Natur*, 1836], he would use the empirical sciences to corroborate his philosophy, and like his beloved Kant, he would claim that the sciences required a metaphysical grounding.[90] It is as if his private life, his own study of philosophy, ultimately overcame his public life, his participation in science lectures, even though he had more science than philosophy in his public life. And, of course, he identified himself first and foremost as a philosopher, as soon as he arrived at Berlin.[91]

---

[88] Schopenhauer, *Gesammelte Briefe*, pp. 52, 653.

[89] Schopenhauer's readings in philosophy, however, tended to reverse the situation concerning his academic study of the sciences. A simple perusal of the listing of books from his posthumous library shows 612 philosophical titles, compared to 196 scientific titles and 10 in mathematics; see *Der handschriftliche Nachlaß*, Vol. 5, pp. 3–190, 236–84, 284–6.

[90] The lumbering subtitle of *On the Will in Nature* tells part of the story: *A Discussion of the Corroborations from the Empirical Sciences That the Author's Philosophy Has Received since Its First Appearance.*

[91] In seven semesters of university education, four at Göttingen and three at Berlin, Schopenhauer is known to have attended five lecture courses on philosophical topics broadly conceived. In his third semester at Göttingen (winter 1810–11), he enrolled in two of Schulze's lectures, "Metaphysics" and "Psychology," and in summer 1811, "Logic." In addition to Fichte's lecture cycle "On the Facts of Consciousness and on the *Wissenschaftlehre*," which he attended during his first semester in Berlin (winter 1811–12), Schopenhauer enrolled in two additional philosophy courses: the philologist Boeckh's lectures "On the Life and Writings of Plato" (which he attended infrequently in either winter 1811–12 or in the summer semester 1812) and the theologian Schleiermacher's "History of Philosophy during the Period of Christianity," which he attended in the summer semester 1812. In contrast, he is know to have

Still, Schopenhauer attended three courses offered by the explorer, naturalist, and professor of zoology Martin Heinrich Lichtenstein. In his first semester, he enrolled in Lichtenstein's lectures on ornithology, amphibiology, ichthyology, and cold-blooded animals. Then, in the summer of 1812, he attended two of Lichtenstein's courses, zoology and entomology. Of all of his teachers, he was probably on the best terms with Lichtenstein, whom Schopenhauer likely met as early as the spring of 1808, at his mother's tea parties in Weimar. Lichtenstein was also the recipient of a dedicated copy of Schopenhauer's dissertation, and he was the only person at Berlin whose advice he sought concerning the possibility of an academic career at Berlin. Lichtenstein, in fact, encouraged him to pursue that possibility and, during a minor argument with Hegel in his qualifying lecture, Lichtenstein supported Schopenhauer's position. And if Lichtenstein's encouragement helped Schopenhauer decide to teach at Berlin, he also helped when the unsuccessful lecturer departed from the university. Schopenhauer entrusted him with lists of his assets, requesting him to "kindly take care of them and in the event of my death to open them at once."[92] Lichtenstein never had to open Schopenhauer's lists, because he died in 1857, three years before his one-time student. His widow, in an untimely fashion, sent the lists to Frankfurt am Main, two years after Schopenhauer's death, and after his estate had been settled.

As Schopenhauer was attending Fichte's lectures in the winter semester 1811–12, he also enrolled in two courses of lectures on scientific subjects. He heard the well-known Martin Heinrich Klaproth's lectures on experimental chemistry. Klaproth helped found the field of inorganic chemistry, and he was credited with the discovery of the elements zirconium, uranium, titanium, and cerium. It is likely, however, that Schopenhauer

attended seventeen lectures in the sciences, seven at Göttingen and ten at Berlin. In his first semester (winter 1809–10) at Göttingen, Schopenhauer heard Blumenbach's "Natural History" and "Mineralogy"; in his second semester (summer 1810), he experienced Strohmeyer's "Chemistry," Mayer's "Physics," and Schrader's "Botany"; in his third semester (winter 1810–11), Mayer's "Physical Astronomy and Meteorology," and Blumenbach's "Comparative Anatomy and Physiology"; and in his last semester (summer 1811), Blumenbach's "Physiology." At Berlin, Schopenhauer enrolled in Klaproth's "Experimental Chemistry," Erman's "Magnetism and Electricity," and Lichtenstein's "Ornithology, Amphibiology, Ichthyology, and Cold-Blooded Animals" in his first semester (winter 1811–12); "Geognosy" by Weiß, and "Zoology" and "Entomology" by Lichtenstein (summer semester 1812); and Fischer's "Physics," Bode's "Astronomy," Horkel's "General Physiology," and Rosenthal's course of lectures on the anatomy of the human brain (winter semester 1812–13).

[92] Cited in Schopenhauer, *Manuscript Remains*, Vol. 2, p. xxi / *Der handschriftliche Nachlaß*, Vol. 2, p. xxi.

personally assigned Klaproth more credit for performing the simple bio-
logical act of fathering his son Julius, who became an orientalist of some
note and to whom Schopenhauer would later refer in his writings – something that was not true of his father.[93] He also experienced that same
semester, "with great pleasure," Paul Erman's lectures on magnetism
and electricity.[94] Later, when he became a *Privatdozent* at Berlin, he
attended Erman's lectures on electromagnetism and folded observations
from these lectures into his earlier lecture notes. The man who performed
groundbreaking work in crystallography, Christian Samuel Weiß, gave
Schopenhauer the opportunity to study geognosy in the summer semester
of 1812.

Schopenhauer could not remain earthbound in his studies. In his last
semester, winter 1812–13, he attended Johann Ehlert Bode's astronomy lectures, and to put things into a greater theoretical perspective,
he enrolled in the physics lectures delivered by Ernst Gottfried Fischer,
who, like Erman, was a follower of Kant. He augmented his study of
the sciences by attending Johann Horkel's course on general physiology, which gave him the story of the metamorphosis of the stag-beetle,
a story he would use as an example of how instinctive behavior illustrated the activity of the will unguided by knowledge.[95] Last, Schopenhauer heard Friedrich Christian Rosenthal's lectures on the anatomy of
the human brain, which were delivered in the anatomy theater. Schopenhauer, always eager to draw connections and to unify phenomenon, sensed
an analogy here: Philosophy bears a great resemblance to the anatomy of
the brain; false philosophy (i.e., a wrong view of the world) and incorrect
anatomy of the brain dissect and separate that which belongs together as
a whole and as one, but then they unite heterogeneous parts from those

---

[93] H. Julius Klaproth was the editor of the *Asiatisches Magazin*. Already in a footnote to the
first edition of *The World as Will and Representation*, Schopenhauer referred to two articles by Klaproth from the first volume of the *Asiatisches Magazin*: "On the Fo Religion"
("Ueber die Fo-Religion") and "Bhagavad Gita or Conversations between Krishna and
Arjuna" ("Bhagvat-Geeta oder Gespräch Zwischen Kreeshna und Arjoon"). This footnote
is significant, because Schopenhauer herein listed many of the writings on Eastern thought
with which he had been acquainted as he wrote his principal work; see *The World as Will
and Representation*, Vol. 1, p. 388fn/*Sämtliche Werke*, Vol. 2, p. 459fn. Schopenhauer also
referred to Klaproth in *On the Will in Nature*, p. 130–31/*Sämtliche Werke*, Vol. 4, "Über den
Willen in der Natur," p. 131.

[94] Schopenhauer, *Gesammelte Briefe*, pp. 52, 653, Schopenhauer's *curriculum vitae*.

[95] See *The World as Will and Representation*, Vol. 1, p. 114/*Sämtliche Werke*, Vol. 2, p. 136.

separated parts. True ph[ilosophy] and true anatomy of the brain dissect and analyze everything correctly, discover and leave as one what is one, and separate and expose parts that are heterogeneous.[96] For Schopenhauer, philosophy was the product of the brain, and like the brain, it should provide a uniform explanation of the totality of all experiences. As he sat through Fichte's lectures with an increasing impatience that transformed into scornfulness, he attended lectures on Norse poetry by the historian and later official historiographer for Prussia Christian Friedrich Rühs. His lecture notes totaled a scant four pages for Rühs's lectures, which may have been due to his purchase of his instructor's recent book on the same topic and not because of his lack of interest.[97] In his second semester, summer 1812, he participated in the classical philologist August Boeckh's course on the life and writings of Plato. Seven years later, as he sought to do his habilitation at Berlin, he wrote to Boeckh, who was then the dean of the faculty: "Seven years ago I attended your lectures on the content of Plato's dialogues. Your presentation of them pleased me the more, as I was already acquainted with the material."[98] Yet, in his *curriculum vitae*, which was attached to his request to habilitate at Berlin, he did not mention Boeckh as one of his Berlin professors. It is probably the case that Schopenhauer's failure to mention Boeckh, who received his *curriculum vitae*, was an example of unconscious honesty. He infrequently attended these lectures and found it sufficient to take his pleasure in Boeckh's presentation from a distance. He used the notes of another student, Carl Iken.

It is curious that Schopenhauer took more coursework from the philologist Friedrich August Wolf than he did from any other professor. Wolf was an acquaintance of Goethe, who wrote for Schopenhauer a letter of introduction to Wolf. Goethe's connection to Wolf, as well as his lively and informative lectures, appears to have made the future philosopher eager to attend Wolf's lectures.[99] Indeed, the summer semester of 1812 was the

---

[96] Schopenhauer, *Manuscript Remains*, Vol. 1, p. 45/ *Der handschriftliche Nachlaß*, Vol. 1, p. 43.

[97] Schopenhauer had purchased Rühs' *The Edda, Together with an Introduction on Nordic Poetry and Mythology* [*Die Edda, Nebst einer Einlietung über nordische Poesie und Mythologie*, 1812], which served as the basis of Rühs' lectures; see *Der handschriftliche Nachlaß*, Vol. 5, p. 404.

[98] Schopenhauer, *Gesammelte Briefe*, p. 56, Schopenhauer to Boeckh 31 December 1819.

[99] Gwinner reported that Schopenhauer attended almost all of Wolf's lectures and esteemed him both "as a human being and as an academic"; *Arthur Schopenhauer aus persönlichem Umgange dargestellt*, p. 47.

summer of Wolf. Schopenhauer sat for three of his lecture courses: "History of Greek Literature" – Wolf borrowed Schopenhauer's notes and corrected them – "On the *Clouds* of Aristophanes," and "On the Satires of Horace." In his final semester, he took his last course from Wolf, "Greek Antiquities." It is even more curious, however, that Schopenhauer, who esteemed Wolf, almost never mentioned him in his published works.[100] Still, in his private diary "About Myself," Wolf received a backhanded compliment. After mentioning his terrible loneliness and his failure to meet a "human being," he wrote in 1831, "I have remained in solitude; but I can honestly and sincerely say that it has not been my fault, for I have not turned away, have not shunned, anyone who in his heart and mind was a human being. I have found none but miserable wretches of limited intelligence, bad heart, and mean disposition. Goethe, Fernow, possibly F. A. Wolf, and a few others were exceptions, all of whom were twenty-five to forty years older than I."[101] It is not clear why Schopenhauer failed to unequivocally afford Wolf full human status.

Besides Fichte, whose star was dimming, the other celebrity at Berlin was the great Protestant theologian of the Early Romantic movement, Friedrich Daniel Ernst Schleiermacher, the one-time confidant of Friedrich Schlegel and translator of Plato, of whom Werner Jaeger said he was "the founder of modern Platonic scholarship."[102] Schopenhauer attended his lectures on the "History of Philosophy during the Period of Christianity," and it is apparent from his notes from these lectures that, unlike his originally open attitude toward Fichte, he approached Schleiermacher in a combative spirit. To be sure, his openness with Fichte was motivated by his desire to hear a great philosopher, and Fichte

---

[100] Schopenhauer only referred to Wolf twice in his philosophical publications, both times in critical ways. He disputed Wolf's claim that Epictetus' *Encheiridon* was written by Arrian, and he mentions Wolf's dispute about the personality and identity of Homer as an example, along with the Ptolemaic system, Newton's theory of color, and Niebuhr's destructive criticism of the Roman Emperors, of views that the "tribunal of posterity" overturned; see, respectively, *Parerga and Paralipomena*, Vol. 1, p. 55; Vol. 2, p. 477/*Sämtliche Werke*, Vol. 5, p. 60; Vol. 6, p. 507.

[101] Schopenhauer, *Manuscript Remains*, Vol. 4, p. 501/*Der handschriftliche Nachlaß*, Vol. 4, pt. 2, p. 112.

[102] Werner Jaeger, *Paideia: The Ideals of Greek Culture* (Oxford: Oxford University Press, 1933–44), Vol. 2, p. 383, n. 8; cited in Friedrich Schleiermacher, *On Religion: Speeches to Its Cultured Despisers*, trans. Richard Crouter (Cambridge: Cambridge University Press, 1988), p. 3, n. 5.

was not lecturing on a subject Schopenhauer prided himself as knowing well. However, he had been studying Plato since Göttingen, so there were no external circumstances that would inhibit his innately cantankerous disposition from manifesting itself. Wolf, moreover, may have already poisoned the well concerning Schleiermacher, because he told Schopenhauer that although Schleiermacher spoke about the scholastics, he never read them.[103] In any case, Schopenhauer came out swinging in his class notes, often diminishing Schleiermacher's originality by sensing Schelling's spurs in his thought. For example, after remarking about the difference between Plato and Plotinus, and claiming that Plotinus fused thinking and being, Schopenhauer wrote, "Fusion of thinking and being; an expression of Schelling's; shows through association how Schleiermacher uses it here, that for him matter and being are identical."[104]

Still, it was Schleiermacher's remarks concerning the relationship between religion and philosophy that Schopenhauer found problematic. Although he had not become at this point in his life the honest atheist Nietzsche so admired, he was moving toward this stance. Thus when his teacher asserted that both religion and philosophy have a knowledge of God in common, Schopenhauer remarked: "Then, of course, ph[ilosophy] would have to assume the concept of a God which, after it progresses far enough, it ought to accept or reject, equally ready to do both."[105] Then when Schleiermacher averred that the principles of the natural sciences and ethics culminated in the particular and that transcendental philosophy ended in the knowledge of God, his student found this idea "a shameless obtrusion of the concept of God," and "he appears to confuse transcendental philosophy with metaphysics, which are the greatest enemies."[106] When Schleiermacher proposed that ancient religion was always at war with ancient philosophy, but that the opposite is the case with the moderns, Schopenhauer immediately thought of two counterexamples: "Kant had to promise the King not to write anything that would have any reference to religion. Fichte has been expelled [from Jena] as an atheist."[107] Worse, when the theologian claimed that one cannot be

---

[103] See Gwinner, *Arthur Schopenhauer aus persönichem Umgange dargestellt*, p. 47.
[104] Schopenhauer, *Manuscript Remains*, Vol. 2, p. 242/*Der handschriftliche Nachlaß*, Vol. 2, p. 225.
[105] Ibid., Vol. 2, p. 240/ibid., Vol. 2, p. 224.
[106] Ibid., Vol. 2, p. 241/ibid., Vol. 2, p. 225.
[107] Ibid., Vol. 2, p. 242/ibid., Vol. 2, p. 225.

a philosopher without being religious, the future philosopher would not have it: "No one who is religious attains to ph[ilosophy]; he does not need it. No one who really philosophizes is religious; he walks without guide wires, dangerously but free."[108] And when Schleiermacher analyzed St. Augustine's argument that evil is a negation and cannot be attributed to God as its cause, Schopenhauer recalls his private study of Schulze's *Principles of General Logic* [*Grundsätze der allgemeinen Logik*, 2nd ed., 1810]: "The error lies in an incorrect conversion; thus he concludes as follows: (1) The essence of things entails negation. All evil is negation (true); (2) All negation is evil (false); (3) Therefore the essence of things entails evil. The extension of *negation* is greater than the extension of *evil*."[109] Schopenhauer knew that a valid conversion of a universal affirmative proposition results in a particular affirmative proposition with reversed subject and predicate terms: From "All evil is negation" it follows that "Some negation is evil," just as from "All cats are mammals" it follows that "Some mammals are cats."[110] According to Schopenhauer, Schleiermacher would draw the inference that "All mammals are cats."

Schopenhauer would publically make a veil and cover his critical opposition to Schleiermacher, until after the latter's death in 1834. He made no references to the theologian in his dissertation, a copy of which he sent to his ex-professor. In the first edition of his principal work, he cited him to support his thesis that prior to our knowledge of mathematical and logical truths, we are non-conceptually, at the level of feeling, "conscious only first intuitively" of these truths. This was something of which "F. Schleiermacher speaks in his *Critique of the Theory of Ethics*. . . of logical and mathematical feeling . . . of the feeling of the sameness or difference of two formulas."[111] Two years after Schleiermacher's death, he once more credits him for the recognition of a feeling, but faults his inference from

---

[108] Ibid., Vol. 2, p. 243/ibid., Vol. 2, p. 226.

[109] Ibid., Vol. 2, p. 244/ibid., Vol. 2, p. 227.

[110] In his copy of Schulze's *Principles of General Logic*, p. 160, Schopenhauer summarized the valid immediate inferences for the four classical categorical propositions. Under the universal affirmative proposition, "All a is b," he listed conversation by limitation as a valid inference:
"Universal affirmative judgments are *converted* only *per accidens*: All a is b; thus some b is a,"
Die handschriftliche Nachlaß, Vol. 5, p. 160. From 'All cats are mammals,' 'Some mammals are cats' logically follows, not as Schleiermacher would have had it 'All mammals are cats.'

[111] Schopenhauer, *The World as Will and Representation*, Vol. 1, p. 52/*Sämtliche Werke*, Vol. 2, p. 62.

this feeling. Thus in the context of a discussion of failed attempts to prove God's existence, and citing Hume, he mentioned Schleiermacher in a footnote: "... even the attempted proof of Schleiermacher the theologian might obtain its truth from the feeling of dependence, though not exactly the truth expected by the man who furnished the proof."[112] With the second edition of *The World as Will and Representation* in 1844, Schopenhauer once more credits his former teacher with an insight, but now it is the only one in his ethics, but he smears the quality of Schleiermacher's delivery of this insight: "... in *practical* philosophy no wisdom is brought to light from mere abstract concepts is the one thing to be learnt from the moral discourses of the theologian Schleiermacher. With the delivery of these he had bored the Berlin Academy for a number of years."[113] Still, he became even more harsh: "There is more to be learnt from every page of David Hume than from the collected philosophical works of Hegel, Herbert, and Schleiermacher taken together."[114] Although he never become the ultimate object of Schopenhauer's hatred, in due course, the unveiled Schleiermacher became like Hegel – falsely perceived as great by fawning contemporaries.[115]

If Schopenhauer perceived madness in Fichte's and Schleiermacher's lectures – "manure," he frequently wrote in his borrowed lecture extract from Fichte's lectures on jurisprudence and moral philosophy – his intellectual curiosity moved him to observe the real thing first-hand.[116] He

---

[112] Schopenhauer, *On the Will in Nature*, p. 50n./*Sämtliche Werke*, Vol. 4, "Über den Willen der Natur," p. 38n, for his reference to Hume's *Natural History of Religion* and his critique of a proof for the existence of God, which Schopenhauer called "the proof *a terrore* [from terror]"; that is, that fear is the basis for belief in gods. Schopenhauer credited Petronius with this argument. Schleiermacher had made "the feeling of utter dependence [Abhängigkeit]" virtually identical with his definition of religion; see his *The Christian Faith* [*Der christliche Glaube nach den Gründsatzen der evangelischen Kirche im Zusammenhangen dargestellt*, 1821–2], Proposition 4.

[113] Schopenhauer, *The World as Will and Representation*, Vol. 2, p. 84/*Sämtliche Werke*, Vol. 3, p. 92.

[114] Ibid., Vol. 2, p. 582/ibid., Vol. 3, p. 668.

[115] See Schopenhauer, *Parerga and Paralipomena*, Vol. 2, p. 279/*Sämtliche Werke*, Vol. 6. p. 296, where the "great Schleiermacher" and "Hegel's gigantic mind" are viewed as sources of "German philosophical humbug."

[116] Hübscher attributes the transcript of Fichte's lectures on jurisprudence and moral philosophy, which Schopenhauer borrowed and copied, to Johann Baptist Reinert, the creator of the Solothurn Civil Code (*code* Reinert). Reinert probably met Schopenhauer in Fichte's lectures on the facts of consciousness and the doctrine of science; see *Manuscript Remains*, Vol. 2, p. xxvii/*Der handschriftliche Nachlaß*, Vol. 2, p. xxvii. Schopenhauer emphatically

frequently visited the "melancholy ward" of the Berlin Charité to observe its inmates. Two of them made an impression. To one he would later send a Bible and to the other, he sent a poem.[117] Earlier, in Fichte's introductory lectures, he had immediately challenged his teacher's contention that the madman is like an animal and the genius like the divine. He wrote, "I believe that genius and madness, although widely different, are yet closer to each other than is genius to common sense and madness to the animal.[118] He would later parlay these early observations on the genial and the insane into his philosophy proper.

But there was another form of insanity intruding on Schopenhauer's studies. As he prepared to write his dissertation, Napoleon's *Grand Armée* passed through Berlin in the spring of 1812, hell-bent on compelling Alexander I of Russia to remain in the Continental System and to forestall his invasion of Poland. The results of Napoleon's campaign against Russia were disastrous. The *Grand Armée* was forced to make a grand retreat. What once had been an army of more than 600,000 souls was reduced to approximately 30,000 men, after the devastation of battles, the disastrous, hard freeze of the Russian winter, starvation, and capture. Emboldened by Bonaparte's enfeebled condition, Prussia joined England, Russia, Sweden, Austria, and a number of other German states and declared war on France. After the Battle of Lützen in May 1813, it appeared as if Berlin would be attacked. Many of Schopenhauer's professors and fellow students took up arms. Wolf and Fichte armed themselves to the teeth, and Schleiermacher preached to the choir, turning inchoate feeling into patriotic charge. But just as Johanna's description of the French sacking of Weimar had failed to stir patriotic passions in her son, Schopenhauer was moved simply to pay

---

wrote "manure (*Mist*)!" after each of Fichte's claims that the world has as its plan the moral education of humans and that the world exists only for this purpose; see ibid., Vol. 2, p. 260/ibid., Vol. 2, p. 243.

[117] Schopenhauer sent the *Bible* to Ernst Hoeffner, a former member of the Prussian Brigade, who hailed from Coeslin in Pomerania and who suffered "*mania partialis.*" Hoeffner gave Schopenhauer a rambling writing concerning the cause of his mental disturbances. Traugott Schultze, a one-time student of theology, who came from Großenhain in Saxony, was the poet. In *Die Flucht ins Vergessen: Die Anfänge der Psycholanalyse Freuds bei Schopenhauer* (Darmstadt: Wissenschaftliche Buchgesellschaft, 1995), Marcel Zentner provides selections from Hoeffner's curious essay in an appendix, pp. 199–208, and Schulze's poem, pp. 23–24. Zentner discusses Schopenhauer's visits to the Berlin Charité in pp. 1–30.

[118] Schopenhauer, *Manuscript Remains*, Vol. 2, p. 118/*Der handschriftliche Nachlaß*, Vol. 2, p. 18.

for the uniform and gear for one of his friends, Ferdinand Helmholtz, the father of the great physicist, Hermann Ludwig Ferdinand. Schopenhauer fled Berlin in such a rush that he failed to bid farewell to Wolf.[119] He had causes other than nationalistic ones in mind. As he wrote in his private diary, he fled Berlin because "I was haunted by the fear of being pressed into military service."[120] Besides, he also had in mind his dissertation.

[119] In the same letter that accompanied a copy of his dissertation, Schopenhauer apologized to Wolf for fleeing Berlin without bidding him farewell; see *Gesammelte Briefe*, Schopenhauer to Wolf, 24 November 1813, p. 7.

[120] *Manuscript Remains*, Vol. 4, 2, p. 507/*Der handschriftliche Nachlaß*, Vol. 4 II, p. 121.

5

The Better Consciousness, Causes, Grounds, and Confrontations

S CHOPENHAUER BECAME A master of the art of distancing, both physically and psychologically. His first flight from Berlin – he would flee
once again in 1831 – was to escape the effects of the unconscious ends
expressed through the troops of Hegel's horse-riding world spirit. But
history's goals lay elsewhere, and Napoleon did not attack Berlin. Thus,
Schopenhauer's flight was not necessary. But he also practiced this art on
himself, at an early age, if one trusts the reflections of the fifty-six-year-old
philosopher: "There was a period in the years of my youth when I was
constantly at pains to see myself from outside, and to picture them to
myself; probably in order to make them enjoyable to me."[1] It was never
enjoyable to be something, he would come to philosophize, but it was
enjoyable to view things as they were, provided that one was uninvolved.
To gaze down at the chaos below from a mountain top and to become a
clear eye on the world below, forgetting oneself by no longer perceiving
things as possible means to sate or frustrate desire, was to escape the
dreamlike, or rather nightmare-like, world of coming-to-be and perishing. It was to become, as he later theorized, a timeless, will-less, painless
subject of cognition, without a sense of either oneself or mundane things.
To obtain this standpoint required a completely objective stance: one that
apprehended things correctly, which "is possible only when we consider
them without any personal participation in them, and thus are under the
complete silence of the will."[2] Unlike his flight from Berlin, this sort of
flight was necessary.

---

[1] Schopenhauer, *The World as Will and Representation*, Vol. 2, p. 372/*Sämtliche Werke*, Vol. 3,
p. 425.
[2] Ibid., Vol. 2, p. 373/ibid., Vol. 3, p. 426.

As Schopenhauer sat through his Berlin lectures and intensely studied Kant, Schelling, Plato, Fichte, Jakob Friedrich Fries,[3] Jacobi, Francis Bacon, and Locke outside the lecture halls, he struggled to articulate his own philosophical insights.[4] He had found that there were moments during which the miserable, transitory world of destruction and death was transcended. Art, especially music, and virtue expressed something immune to the ravaging grind of the wheel of time. These were matters that could be taken seriously, unlike everything else in this wretched world, which were not worth the effort, as he had written to his mother, when he confused Tieck for Wackenroder. Art, virtuous behavior, and saintly withdrawal from life signified something purer, higher, and more enduring than fleeting pleasure, sensuality, and the comfortable bourgeois life enjoyed by those such as the "Gotha Philistines."

Better Consciousness

In 1812, he alights on an idea. For the first time he uses the phrase "the better consciousness," a "consciousness [that] lies beyond all experience and thus all reason, both theoretical and practical (instinct)."[5] It was as

---

[3] Fries was born in Barby, Saxony and studied at the Moravian Academy in Niesky and the universities at Leipzig and Jena, where he attended Fichte's lectures, for which he had little sympathy. He later taught philosophy and mathematics at the Universities of Heidelberg and Jena. Fries viewed himself as a Kantian and he wrote the polemical book *Reinhold, Fichte, and Schelling* [*Reinhold, Fichte und Schelling*, 1803] against the aforementioned. Schopenhauer studied his Kantian work, titled *New Critique of Reason* [*Neue Kritik der Vernunft*, 1807] in 1812–13, finding most of Fries' views to be "babble" or "insipid babble" [*seichtes Geschwätz*]; see *Manuscript Remains*, Vol. 2, pp. 417–25/*Der handschriftliche Nachlaß*, Vol. 2, pp. 358–66 for Schopenhauer's student notes to Fries.

[4] Hübscher dates Schopenhauer's notes for his self-study of these philosophers as follows: Kant, fall 1811–12; Schelling, 1811 to the first half of 1812; Plato, 1812; Fichte, spring and summer 1812; Fries, 1812–13; Jacobi, 1812–13; Bacon, 1812; and Locke, summer 1812. See ibid., Vol. 2, p. xxix/ibid., Vol. 2, p. xxix.

[5] Schopenhauer, *Manuscript Remains*, Vol. 1, p. 23/*Der handschriftliche Nachlaß*, Vol.1, p. 23. Yasuo Kamata finds the likely origin of Schopenhauer's idea of the "better consciousness" in Fichte's idea of the "higher consciousness" [*höhere Bewußtsein*] and he notes that Schopenhauer's idea also bears resemblance to Schelling's notion of "intellectual intuition"; see *Der junge Schopenhauer: Genese des Grundgedankens der Welt als Wille und Vorstellung* (Munich: Alber, 1988) pp. 120–21. For Schopenhauer's endorsement of Schelling's claim in "Philosophische Briefe über Dogmatismus und Kriticismus in philosophische Schriften," in *Philosophische Schriften* (Landshut: Philipp Krüll, 1809) Vol. 1, p. 165–6, that "This intellectual intuition is

if Schopenhauer was attempting to articulate a notion of Fichte's transcendental I, conceived prior to its positing a Not-I or, perhaps, an idea
of a return to some state of being after overcoming the Not-I, the world.
The better consciousness "shows itself to the understanding through its
effects. Yet the understanding never sees more than the outside."[6] "The
better consciousness in me," he wrote, "lifts me into a world where there
is no longer personality and causality or subject or object. My hope and
belief is that this better (supersensible and extra-temporal) consciousness
will become my only one, and for that reason I hope that it is not God.
But if anyone wants to use the expression *God* symbolically for the better
consciousness itself or for much that we are able to separate or name, so
let it be, yet not among philosophers I would have thought."[7] This hope
for the better consciousness becoming his only one entailed allowing it
to "navigate the ship of life even in the dark, until after death only the
better consciousness is left."[8] The eternal better consciousness signified
the ultimate distance from the world.

Schopenhauer's Berlin ruminations developed his general view of
death, of art, of virtue, and of asceticism in nascent form. Behind each,
he found the better consciousness: a transcendence of the temporal world

---

our very own innermost experience, and on this alone depends all that we know and believe
about a supersensible world"; see *Manuscript Remains*, Vol. 2, p. 347 and p. 347n./*Der handschriftliche Nachlaß*, Vol. 2, p. 309 and p. 468. However, by mid-1812, Schopenhauer wrote,
"Schelling's intellectual intuition is yet something different from the *better consciousness* that I
attribute to humans. The reader should always bear that in mind;" ibid., Vol. 2, p. 373/ibid.,
Vol. 2, 369f. Schopenhauer understood Schelling's notion of intellectual intuition as requiring
intellectual development of the understanding, whereas his idea of the better consciousness is
automatic, like a flash of insight, with no connection to the understanding; see ibid., Vol. 2,
p. 351/ibid., Vol. 2, p. 312. For additional studies of the better consciousness in Schopenhauer's early philosophy, see, among others, Hans Zint, "Schopenhauer's Philosophie des
doppelten Bewußtsein," *Schopenhauer-Jahrbuch*, Vol. 10 (1921), pp. 3–45; Rudolf Malter, *Der
Eine Gedanke: Hinführung Philosophie Arthur Schopenhauers* (Darmstadt: Wissenschaftliche
Buchgesellschaft, 1988), pp. 5–12; Rüdiger Safranski, "Hoch auf dem Berge und – entronnen! Schopenhauers bessere Bewußtsein: Ekstase des Sehers," *Lutherische Monatshefte*, Vol. 28
(1989), pp. 267–71; Friedhelm Decher, "Das bessere Bewussein: Zur Funktion eines Begriff in
Genese der Schopenhauerschen Philosophie," *Schopenhauer-Jahrbuch*, Vol. 77 (1996), pp. 65–
83; and Nicoletta De Cian and Marco Segala, "What Is Will?" *Schopenhauer-Jahrbuch*, Vol. 83
(2002), pp. 13–42.

[6] Ibid., Vol. 2, p. 431/ibid., Vol. 2, p. 370, Schopenhauer's note to Jacobi's *On Divine Things*
[*Von den gottlichen Dinge*, Leipzig: Fleischer d. Jung, 1811].

[7] Ibid., Vol. 1, p. 44/ibid., Vol. 1, p. 42.

[8] Ibid., Vol. 1, p. 48/ibid., Vol. 1, p. 45.

of the empirical consciousness and its cognition of the sensory world. The essence of the beautiful, he reflected, "is the theoretical negation of the temporal world and the affirmation of eternity."[9] Artistic beauty, in contrast to natural beauty, was the product of genius: "Faithfulness and objectivity . . . the condition of artistic beauty, and the poet and painter who have best attained the object of art, [make] known that which is outside time and above nature, are simultaneously always the most objective and the most faithful to nature."[10] The contemplation of great works of art also stirred the better consciousness of its consumer: "We are no longer involved in considering the nexus of space, time, and causality (useful for our individuality), but see the Platonic Idea of the object."[11] The intuition of Platonic Ideas connoted for the student Schopenhauer a cognition of a perfect, timeless, and pure object. Later, his very un-Platonic conception of Platonic Ideas would play a key role in his metaphysics and aesthetics, except in his philosophy of music. Already, in these early reflections, music is singled out: "It [music] is not like the other arts, a presentation of the effects of the better consciousness in the material world of the senses, but is itself one of the effects."[12]

Following the spurs of the Early Romantics and sharing the sentiments of challengers to the Enlightenment's deification of reason, Schopenhauer longed for something deeper than the everyday world and for something about humans that was greater than reason and rationality. He demoted theoretical reason on Kantian grounds, but not in Kant's spirit. Theoretical reason shipwrecks itself on the Kantian antinomies, on its capacity to generate equally compelling but contradictory answers to cosmological questions.[13] Reason's own intrinsic yearning to reach the

---

[9] Ibid./ibid.

[10] Ibid., Vol. 1, p. 49/ibid., Vol. 1, p. 46.

[11] Ibid., Vol. 1, p. 50/ibid., Vol. 1, p. 47.

[12] Ibid., Vol. 1, p. 52/ibid., Vol. 1, p. 49.

[13] In the *Critique of Pure Reason*, A426/B454–A460/B488, Kant detailed four antinomies. The first two he called mathematical and the second two dynamic. The antimonies are as follows: (1) Thesis: "The world has a beginning in time, and in space it is also enclosed in boundaries." Antithesis: "The world has no beginning and bounds in space, but is infinite with regard to both time and space." (2) Thesis: "Every composite substance in the world consists of simple parts, and nothing exists anywhere except in the simple or what is composed of simples." Antithesis: "No composite thing in the world consists of simple parts, and nowhere in it does there exist anything simple." (3) Thesis: "Causality in accordance with laws of nature is not the only one from which all the appearances of the world can be derived. It is also necessary to assume another causality through freedom in order to explain them." Antithesis: "There

absolutely unconditioned, against which Kant had warned, leads us into error.[14] Thus Schopenhauer wrote that reason in its speculative use "is the source of all error," and when "theoretical reason [is] used *speculatively* [it] produces the dogmatist, used *empirically* the regular scholar . . . Wagner in *Faust*."[15] And although Kant's critique of speculative reason was to clear the grounds for faith, practical reason stood on its own two feet. But for the Berlin student, practical reason is problematic. Reason does not discover moral laws nor is moral conduct rational: "To deduce from reason the moral element in conduct is blasphemy. In the moral element is manifest *the better consciousness*, which lies *far above all reason*, expressing itself in conduct as holiness, and is the true salvation of the world. This same consciousness expresses itself in art as genius, as a consolation for the earthly life."[16] Reason is instrumental and at the service of the agent's goals. If ones aims are evil, reason serves to calculate the means for realizing these ends. Thus, "so remote is reason from being the source of morality, that it alone makes us capable of being scoundrels. . . . "[17] Conversely, "it is also possible to think of a very virtuous man in whom the better consciousness is always so animated that it speaks at all times and never allows the emotions to become so strong that he is wholly filled with them. Thus he is always guided directly by the better consciousness and not through the *medium* of reason by means of maxims and moral principles. Therefore lofty morality and kindness are possible in spite of feeble reason and feeble understanding. . . . "[18]

is no freedom, but everything in the world happens solely in accordance with laws of nature." (4) Thesis: "To the world there belongs something that, either as a part of it or as its cause, is an absolutely necessary being." Antithesis: "There is no absolutely necessary being existing anywhere, either in the world or outside the world as its cause." Schopenhauer held that the proofs for the theses in all of the antinomies were sophisms, and that only the antitheses were inevitable inferences from the laws of the world as representation, in each case known *a priori*; see *The World as Will and Representation*, Vol. 1, p. 493f./*Sämtliche Werke*, Vol. 2, p. 586.

[14] Kant discussed reason's search for the unconditioned concerning objects given in experience in the first book of the "Transcendental Dialectic," *Critique of Pure Reason*, A310/B366–A338/B396. Schopenhauer found reason's demand for the unconditioned unreasonable, because "The validity of the principle of sufficient reason is so much involved in the form of consciousness that we simply cannot imagine anything objectively of which no why could be further demanded; hence we cannot imagine an absolute Absolute like a blank wall in front of us." Ibid., Vol. 1, p. 483/ibid., Vol. 2, p. 573f.

[15] Schopenhauer, *Manuscript Remains*, Vol. 1, pp. 46, 47/*Der handschriftliche Nachlaß*, Vol. 1, pp. 43, 44.

[16] Ibid., Vol. 1, p. 47/ibid., Vol. 1, p. 44.

[17] Ibid., Vol. 1, p. 54/ibid., Vol. 1, p. 51.

[18] Ibid., Vol. 1, p. 55/ibid., Vol. 1, p. 51f.

Schopenhauer's reflections on the empirical and the better consciousness moved him to consider that which binds a person to the ephemeral
world of misery and despair and that which liberates one from this vale
of tears. He quotes his beloved Sterne: "There is no passion so serious
as lust."[19] The seriousness of lust is the seriousness of animality, and
animals do not laugh. Copulating couples express this seriousness, and
the act perpetuates and thereby affirms this world. Indeed, "the focal
point of this affirmation [of this temporal consciousness] is the satisfaction of the sex drive."[20] Yet, in distinguished and brilliant people, there
are moments during which their sexual and mental activities reach their
peak at the same time, and in such times reason can once more only play
an instrumental role: "Yet, as the faculty for perceiving the totality of
life in its oneness, as the bond between temporal and better consciousness . . . reason is historically acquainted with both principles. . . . It can,
at the moment when consciousness is absorbed in cupidity, vividly picture
itself the maxim 'to take the other direction' – a maxim that has sprung
from the better consciousness. However, the faculty of reason holds up
such a maxim only as a *lifeless concept* against the *living desire*, but it represents it as such and makes choice *possible*, that is to say *freedom*, whose
condition it is."[21] The choice, he continues, is between the kingdom of
darkness, of need, desire, and illusion, and the kingdom of light, of repose,
joy, amiability, harmony, and peace. This choice is, paradoxically, both
infinitely difficult and infinitely easy. To illustrate this, Schopenhauer
mentions a poem about a knight. His task is to enter a castle, which is
surrounded by a rapidly spinning wall with a single, narrow portal. The
knight closes his eyes, gives spur to his horse, and gallops full tilt through
the gate. The poem symbolizes virtue, he continued, the path to light:
"To achieve the immensely difficult, the impossible, we need only *will*,
but *will* we must."[22] Not quite a Kierkegaardian leap of faith, but a gallop
to virtue by the knight of the better consciousness. It is a willed act that
quiets will.

In 1812, almost a year before Schopenhauer's realization of the significance of the poem of the knight, he had used the idea of will. In
a fragment entitled "A Little System," he attributed, *à la* Fichte and

---

[19] Ibid., Vol. 1, p. 45/ibid., Vol. 1, p. 42.
[20] Ibid., Vol. 1, p. 74/ibid., Vol. 1, p. 69.
[21] Ibid., Vol. 1, p. 58/ibid., Vol. 1, p. 54.
[22] Ibid./ibid.

Schelling, a will and a purpose to nature. Nature wills life and well-being as completely and as long as possible for all of its creatures.[23] Evil is that which is contrary to nature's ends. We ought to promote life and well-being, he wrote, we "ought to will what nature wills."[24] This is something, he claimed, we ought to do, "since out innermost being is concerned only with serving and fulfilling the purpose of nature, our pure will is merely her will. . . ."[25] This fragment does not make it clear whether this "little system" is anything more than a thought experiment or whether it reveals Schopenhauer's own philosophical convictions. Soon, however, he reversed the thinking found in this note. Virtue does not spring from following nature's will, and salvation is found in escaping the world. Given the nature of the world itself, it is something that ought not to be:

How can it really surprise us that this world is the realm of chance, error, and folly that cripples wisdom, that wickedness acts therein with unrestrained violence, and every reflected splendor of the eternal finds a place only by accident and is, on the other hand, suppressed a thousand times? How, I say, can this surprise us, for indeed this very world (i.e., our empirical, sensuous, and rational consciousness in space and time) has its origin only through that which, according to the utterance of our better consciousness, ought not to be, but is the wrong direction from which virtue and asceticism are the return journey and, in consequence of this, a peaceful death is the release, like that of ripe fruit from the tree, and Plato (*Phaedo*), therefore, calls the entire life of the "sage a long time dying," i.e., a breaking away from such a world?[26]

Later, he would use the claim that "the world ought not to be" as the hallmark of "pessimistic" religions, and he would argue that the recognition of the pervasiveness of death, as well as suffering, is that which prompts philosophical and religious speculation about the world.[27]

---

[23] Ibid., Vol. 1, p. 21/ibid., Vol. 1, p. 21.

[24] Ibid., Vol. 1, p. 22/ibid., Vol. 1, p. 22.

[25] Ibid./ibid.

[26] Ibid., Vol. 1, p. 43/ibid., Vol. 1, p. 41. The reference is to Plato's *Phaedo*, 64a: ". . . those who really apply themselves in the right way to philosophy are directly and of their own accord preparing themselves for death and dying"; *Plato: The Collected Dialogues*, eds. Edith Hamilton and Huntington Cairns (Princeton, NJ: Princeton University Press, 1973), p. 46 (Hugh Tredennick's translation.)

[27] See Schopenhauer, *The World as Will and Representation*, Vol. 2, p. 170/*Sämtliche Werke*, Vol. 3, p. 188, where he claims that the fundamental difference between religions is whether they are pessimistic and claim that the world ought not to be, or optimistic and claim that the world is justified by itself, and ibid., Vol. 2, p. 161/ibid., Vol. 3, p. 176f., where Schopenhauer claims that knowledge of death and the suffering and misery of life provide the strongest impulse for philosophical reflection and metaphysical explanations of the world.

Yet the poem about the knight also moved Schopenhauer to attribute importance to the words "to will": "To will [Wollen]! Great words! pointer on the scales of the Last Judgment, the bridge between heaven and hell! Reason is not the light shining from heaven, but only a sign post set up by ourselves and directed to the chosen goal, that it may show us the direction when the goal itself is concealed. But one can direct it to hell just as well to heaven."[28] Still, at this point in Schopenhauer's philosophical development, he recognizes neither the metaphysical nor the soteriological significance of the concept of will, which will emerge in the next two years. Nevertheless, as Schopenhauer abandons Berlin, he does so with a sense of philosophical fecundity and a fear of not living long enough to bring his thought to final form; attitudes, one can well imagine, not uncommon to someone planning a dissertation under conditions of war:

In my hands and much more in my mind grows a work, a philosophy, that should be ethics and metaphysics in *one*, since they were just as falsely separated as was the human into soul and body. The work grows, expanding gradually and slowly like the child in the womb. I do not know what was first and what was last, just as with the child in the womb. I who sit here and whom my friends know, do not understand the origin of the work just as the mother does not understand that of the child in her womb. I see it and speak like the mother; "I am blessed with fruit." Chance, ruler of the material world! let me have peace a few more years! since I love my work like a mother her child. When it is mature and has been born, then exercise your right and take your tribute for the reprieve. – But if in this stern time were I to die before my time, oh may these immature beginnings, these studies of mine, be given to the world and for what they are. Some time in the future, perhaps a kindred spirit will appear who understands how to put the parts together and restore the antique.[29]

As Schopenhauer fled Berlin with an uncertain sense of destiny, he found the trip to Dresden slow going. Ironically, he encountered those he dearly wished to avoid. He was compelled to serve as an interpreter between the French and the mayor of a small Saxon town. After twelve days, he reached Dresden, only to be seized once more by the fear that the French would attack. This anxiety drove him to seek shelter at his mother's home in Weimar. But conditions were no better at the home front, but not due to the French: "Certain domestic arrangements displeased me so much that, seeking another place of refuge, I retreated to

---

[28] Schopenhauer, *Manuscript Remains*, Vol. 1, p. 59/ *Der handschriftliche Nachlaß*, Vol. 1, p. 55.
[29] Ibid./ibid.

Rudolstadt."[30] The source of Schopenhauer's displeasure was the Privy Archival Councilor, one Georg Friedrich Conrad Ludwig Müller, who would, around 1815, add "von Gerstenbergk" to his already bloated name by adopting the name of an ennobled uncle from his mother's side of the family. "Müller von Gerstenbergk" met Johanna Schopenhauer in 1810 in Ronneburg, where he was the city syndic and Johanna's landlord during her vacation to that town. Although he was fourteen years younger than the Hofrätin Schopenhauer, Johanna was drawn to the socially ambitious civil servant, who shared her passion for art, literature, and poetry. Gerstenbergk joined Johanna for a four-month tour to Dresden, where Johanna copied paintings of the Old Masters. The couple was so inseparable that Goethe's wife Christiane reported that they probably would marry and that Gerstenbergk's first lover had been so deeply affected that "she had become insane."[31] When Schopenhauer arrived at his mother's apartment in May 1813, the Secret Archival Councilor occupied the upper rooms of the house and regularly took his meals with Johanna and Adele. Schopenhauer shared Christiane von Goethe's suspicions about the couple and was repulsed by his mother's lack of fidelity to his father's name.

Schopenhauer tried to resign himself to the "domestic arrangements" that he found so displeasing. But the sight of Gerstenbergk giving orders to the family servants, collaborating with Johanna on writing projects, escorting her to various social functions, and eating at the same table, destroyed the equanimity the young man required to philosophize. After less than a month in Weimar, he decided once more to leave his troubles behind, and he fled south to the small village of Rudolstadt, where he sought shelter and solitude. He took a room in a small inn, which was called "For the Knight" ["*Zum Ritter*"], suggesting that it was a destination for just those he tried to avoid, when he left Berlin. But not all knights were soldiers, and the potential irony suggested by the name of the inn was undermined by the poem of the knight, which had represented to Schopenhauer a full-tilt gallop to virtue and to the light. In any case, Schopenhauer found nothing ironic about the name of his refuge. He labored there from mid-June to late September on his dissertation.

[30] Schopenhauer, *Gesammelte Briefe*, pp. 53, 654.

[31] Hans Gerhard Gräf, *Goethes Ehe in Briefen* (Leipzig, 1972), p. 346, quoted in Bergmann's *Johanna Schopenhauer*, p. 170.

Schopenhauer's description of his time in Rudolstadt is curious. In his *curriculum vitae*, he expressed self-doubt and wrote that he became "depressed."[32] He felt alienated from his age, because it seemed to require gifts other than those he possessed. He could have passed himself as any "homeless person during a troubled time." Yet those bleak descriptions were balanced by compensating factors. Rudolstadt was surrounded by well-forested mountains, and he enjoyed "the inexpressible charms of the region," and he took solace, as was his custom since youth, of hiking in the mountains and the Thuringian forest. There were other enjoyable factors: "As my entire nature was adverse to military affairs, I was happy that in that valley, surrounded by forested mountains, not a soldier was to be seen and not a drum to be heard during that entire war-like summer, and within the deepest solitude, distracted and diverted by nothing, uninterrupted, I applied myself to the most recondite problems and investigations."[33] Rudolstadt's location physically distanced Schopenhauer from the warring world, and working on his philosophy psychologically distanced him from his woes.

The topic of Schopenhauer's dissertation was not, however, his envisioned philosophy that would be metaphysics and ethics in one. Nor was he inspired to make literal that which was symbolically expressed by the poem of the knight, despite the fact that he was sequestered in a place "for the knight." Instead, he chose an epistemological topic, the principle of sufficient reason, whose general statement he took from Christian Wolff: "Nothing is without a reason for why it is rather than is not" [*Nihil est sine ratione cur potius sit quam non sit*].[34] At this stage of his philosophical career, Schopenhauer did not indicate why he wrote on this topic. Much later, however, the mature philosopher seemed to supply a reason for this decision – one that is, however, not sufficient for explaining this youthful choice, although it serves to cast light on it. In his reflections on the various areas of philosophy and the significance of its method of exposition, he argued that the object of philosophy is experience in general, its possibility, essential content, and inner and outer elements, and its form

[32] Schopenhauer, *Gesammelte Briefe*, pp. 53, 654.
[33] Ibid., pp. 53, 654.
[34] Schopenhauer, *On the Fourfold Root of the Principle of Sufficient Reason*, p. 6 / *Sämtliche Werke*, Vol. 1, p. 5.

and matter. This entailed, he continued, that philosophy must have an empirical foundation; it cannot be spun out of mere concepts in the manner of Spinoza, or in the style of Fichte, Schelling, and Hegel. Because experience itself is the object of philosophy, *Philosophia prima* must "begin with an investigation of the faculty of cognition, its forms and laws, and also the validity and limits thereof."[35] This "first philosophy," he divided into two further divisions. The empirical bases of philosophy called for a dianoiology, or a theory of the understanding, the faculty of sensible intuitions, and a logic, or a theory of reason, the faculty of concepts. The result of this philosophy would be metaphysics in the "narrower sense," because it would make us acquainted with nature, but not with that which is expressed in nature. We would remain on the level of appearances and not on that of the essence of such appearance, that which appears. It is the latter basis, he held, that is the subject of metaphysics, which is divided into the metaphysics of nature, the metaphysics of the beautiful, and the metaphysics of morals. This division of philosophy also describes the philosophical structure of *The World as Will and Representation*, which is divided into four books: *philosophia prima*, metaphysics of nature, of the beautiful, and of morals. Common to the last three books is metaphysics, "Which shows the thing in itself, the inner and ultimate essence and appearance, to be in our *will*."[36]

These reflections on the divisions of philosophy, however, were recorded by a mature thinker who had spent thirty-three years correcting, refining, and extending the fundamental ideas that he had first published in late 1818. In that publication, *The World as Will and Representation*, Schopenhauer had called his dissertation an introduction to that book, and he asserted that "without an acquaintance with this introduction and propaedeutic, it is quite impossible to understand the present work properly. . . . "[37] Nevertheless, it would take the young dissertator the next five years to develop the ideas expressed in *The World as Will and*

---

35 Schopenhauer, *Parerga and Paralipomena*, Vol. 2, p. 18/*Sämtliche Werke*, Vol. 6, p. 18. Schopenhauer called *On the Fourfold Root of the Principle of Sufficient Reason* an "essay in elementary philosophy" [*elementarphilosophische Abhandlung*] in the preface to the second edition; see p. xxvi/*Sämtliche Werke*, Vol. 1, p. v.

36 Ibid., Vol. 2, p. 19/ibid., Vol. 6, p. 20.

37 Schopenhauer, *The World as Will and Representation*, Vol. 1, p. xiv/*Sämtliche Werke*, Vol. 2, p. x.

Representation, where he made the bold claim that the will was the thing in itself. At this stage in his philosophical development, Schopenhauer still agreed with Fichte. The thing in itself was a nonthought. He even bragged in his dissertation that his "investigation does not become paralyzed by a thing in itself," a remark he struck from the massive revision that his dissertation received in 1847.[38]

It is unlikely that the young Schopenhauer possessed a conscious and deliberate plan for the structure of his philosophy, and it is likely that his later analysis of the divisions of philosophy represents a somewhat idealized report of how his philosophy developed. A more likely explanation of the topic of his dissertation is found in the fact that he did not work directly on his envisioned synthesis of metaphysics and ethics because his philosophy of the better consciousness was stalled by his inability to answer an obvious question: "What is the relationship between the empirical and better consciousness?" Schopenhauer directly confronted this question in a note composed in the small village of Hoyerswerda, as he fled from Berlin to Dresden. The question itself was a "transcendent illusion," another term he also borrowed from Kant's philosophical vocabulary. To think that the empirical consciousness followed from the better consciousness assumed succession and, consequently, time, an *a priori* form of the empirical consciousness, which had validity only within the empirical world. The same, he held, was true of the idea that the better consciousness was the cause of the empirical. Causality, like time, was an *a priori* form of human cognition. Thus Schopenhauer held that any question of the relationship between the better and empirical consciousness was meaningless; it raised a question that could never be answered. At best, "If we want to speak at all about this relation, we can say that it is positively unknowable to all eternity. For the better consciousness does not think and know because it lies beyond subject and object. But the empirical consciousness cannot know a relationship where one link is itself. The relation therefore lies beyond the sphere of this consciousness and includes this sphere itself."[39] Although he would continue to use the term "better consciousness" in his early, unpublished notes,

---

[38] *Sämtliche Werke*, Vol. 7, p. 71.

[39] Schopenhauer, *Manuscript Remains*, Vol. 1, pp. 72–3/*Der handschriftliche Nachlaß*, Vol. 1, p. 67.

he would never use the term in any of his books. Later, this concept would transform itself into various states in which a person is set free of will.[40]

Introductory Matters

As Schopenhauer struggled with his philosophy of the better consciousness, trying to ascertain whether the relationship between the better and the empirical consciousness could be explained, he turned his attention to the principle of sufficient reason itself, the basis of all explanation. He reviewed the relevant writings of Wolff, Lambert, Reimarus, Baumgarten, Descartes, Leibniz, Schulze, Hoffbauer, Maass, Platner, Maimon, Jakob, Kieswetter, and Kant.[41] In his so-called "Early Manuscripts," he called his reflections on these earlier philosophers "hardly anything but studies and extracts for the purpose of a dissertation on the principle of

[40] Perhaps the only allusion to the better consciousness in his dissertation is found in the oblique criticism of " blind synchronism" for subsuming under the concept of feeling the best in us "to which indeed the rest of the world bears a relation as does a shadow in a dream to real, solid bodies"; Schopenhauer, *Sämtliche Werke*, Vol. 7, p. 84.

[41] Schopenhauer's preparatory logic studies for his dissertation included Christian Wolff's *Philosophia prima, sive Ontologia methodo scientifica pertractata, qua omnis cognitionis humanae principia continentur* (Francof. Et Lips, 1736), from which he took the term "first philosophy" [*philosophia prima*] to refer to the preliminary philosophical study of the forms, laws, validity, and limits of human cognition; Johann Heinrich Lambert's *Neues Organon, oder Gedanken über die Erforschung und Bezeichnung des Wahren und dessen Untersheidung vom Irrthum und Schein* (Leipzig: Wendler, 1764); Hermann Samuel Reimarus' *Die Vernunftlehre, als eine Anweisung zum richtigen Gebrauch der Vernunft in der Erkenntniß der Wahrheit, aus zwoen ganz natürlichen Regeln der Einstimmung und des Widerspruch hergeleitet*, 5th ed. (Hamburg: Bohn, 1790); Alexander Gottlieb Baumgarten's *Metaphysica* (Magdeburg: Hemmerde, 1757); René Descartes' *Principia philosophiae* (1644); Gottlob Ernst Schulze's *Grundsätze der allgemeinen Logik* (Helmstädt: Fleckeisen, 1810); Johann Christoph Hoffbauer's *Analytik der Urtheile und Schlüsse* (Halle: Schwetschke, 1792); Johann Gebhard Ehrenreich Maass' *Grundriß der Logik zum, Gebrauche bei Vorlesungen* (Halle: Ruff, 1793); Ernst Platner's *Philosophische Aphorismus, nebst einigen Anleitungen zur philosophischen Geschichte* (Leipzig: Schwickert, 1782–4); Salomon Maimon's *Versuch einer neuen Logik oder Theorie des Denkens* (Berlin: Felisch, 1794); Ludwig Heinrich Jakob's *Grundriß der allgemeinen Logik* (Halle: Francke and Bispisch, 1788); Johann Gottfried Carl Christian Kiesewetter's *Grundriß einer reinen allgemeinen Logik nach Kantischen Grundsätzen, zum Gebrauch für Vorlesungen* (Berlin: F. T. Lagarde, 1802/1806); and Immanuel Kant's *Logik* (Königsberg: Jäsche, 1800). Schopenhauer also referred to Kant's *Critique of Pure Reason*, *Prolegomena to Any Future Metaphysics*, and *Critique of the Power of Judgment* in these preliminary studies; see Schopenhauer, *Manuscript Remains*, Vol. 1, pp. 59–72/*Der handschriftliche Nachlaß*, Vol. 1, pp. 55–67, for his notes on the works given above, most of which he incorporated into his dissertation.

sufficient reason."[42] He would incorporate most of these extracts into the second chapter of his dissertation, "Summary of the Main Points Previously Taught about the Principle of Sufficient Reason," including his conclusion that these philosophers had neglected to distinguish clearly between the warrant or ground for the truth of a proposal, the cause of an event, and the motive of an action. In the course of his consideration of these notes for the previous treatment of the principle of sufficient reason, Schopenhauer also referred to his copy book from his private study of Kant, with which he had been engaged since 1811.[43] Kant too, he claimed, had not been clear on the principle of sufficient reason. In neither the *Critique of Pure Reason* nor the *Critique of the Power of Judgment* had the sage of Königsberg distinguished precisely between the principle of sufficient reason itself and the law of causality: "The result is that nowhere are *cause*, *reason*, and *motive*, three very different things defined and separated; they are confused because they all answer the question: Why?"[44] Schopenhauer set about to make clear distinctions between these concepts, moving back to repair Kant instead of springing forth from an inadequate epistemological basis, as did Fichte and Schelling, who, in his mind, only made things worse. Only when he revised his dissertation would Schopenhauer let his true feelings about these men known. Then he included Schelling in the section on "Kant and His School," quoting from his "Aphorisms to the Introduction to Natural Philosophy" ["Aphorismen zur Einleitung in der Naturphilosophie"], where Schelling called gravity a reason and light the cause of things, a remark that Schopenhauer judged to be "frivolous and reckless talk . . . not fit to be numbered among the opinions of serious and honest inquirers."[45] Fichte, curiously enough, is not included within Kant's school. The reason soon becomes apparent. Later, he wrote that "Hegelians and like ignoramuses may continue to talk of a Kant–Fichtean philosophy; there is Kantian philosophy, and there is Fichtean humbug. . . . "[46]

Schopenhauer, however, was more reserved and circumspect in the original edition of *On the Fourfold Root of the Principle of Sufficient Reason.*

---

[42] Ibid., Vol. 1, p. 72/ibid., Vol. 1, p. 67.

[43] See ibid., Vol. 2, pp. 300, 305, 328/ibid., Vol. 2, pp. 272f., 277, 293.

[44] Ibid., Vol. 2, p. 300/ibid., Vol. 2, p. 273.

[45] Schopenhauer, *On the Fourfold Root of the Principle of Sufficient Reason*, p. 31/*Sämtliche Werke*, Vol. 1, p. 27.

[46] Ibid., p. 120/ibid., Vol. 1, p. 83.

After all, he was writing for the Academy, and he realized that he might offend his judges by bashing philosophers who still had their adherents and sympathizers. Consequently, there was no mention of Fichte, for whom it would have been difficult for Schopenhauer not to show contempt, and his few references to Schelling tended to gently minimize their differences. For example, after arguing that the subject of experience and the object of experience are necessary correlates, the most basic feature of cognition, which cannot be reduced to one another or judged to be identical, he wrote, "Should the identity of the subjective and objective, asserted by the philosophy of nature, mean nothing more than being of the same kind, then I entirely agree with it. I doubt, however, that it means simply this, because to arrive at this requires no intellectual intuition, but only reflection. Thus, if one wants to call two things one, because one cannot even be thought without the other, I will not dispute that . . ."[47] Of course, Schelling meant more by that, as did Schopenhauer, who continues his argument by enumerating examples of concepts that require thinking of another; namely, cause and effect, father and son, brother and sister, each of which has significance only through the other. No one, he continued, would claim that each of these two were one. He would drop this passage in the second edition.

In addition to not freely abusing his philosophical contemporaries, something Schopenhauer enjoyed doing in his notes from that period, his dissertation was composed in a somewhat formal, pedantic form – one appropriate for a scholarly work that was geared to reward him with a doctorate. Instead of writing in what would become his overly self-confident voice and indulging in various digressions that featured somewhat idiosyncratic personal observations, Schopenhauer stuck firmly on topic and qualified his assertions. For example, in 1813 he wrote that "The importance of the principle of sufficient reason is so great, I presume to assert that it is the basis of all science."[48] He would simply assert this proposition in 1847. He quoted but once from Goethe's poetry, and he did not refer to works of literature in his first work. But in 1847 he referred to literary works, indulged in digressions, and generally abused his contemporaries. Kant, whom he had mildly attacked in the original iteration of *On the Fourfold Root of the Principle of Sufficient Reason*, was

---

[47] *Sämtliche Werke*, Vol. 7, p. 70.
[48] Ibid., Vol. 7, p. 92.

still attacked in the second edition, but he also received more praise, perhaps as a strategy to further illustrate the folly of those he saw forgetting
their Kant: namely, Fichte, Schelling, and Hegel.

In the Preface to the second edition of *On the Fourfold Root of the Principle of Sufficient Reason*, which first appeared in the massively revised
second edition, Schopenhauer explained the differences between the voice
of the twenty-five-year-old student, found in its first statement, and the
additions by the fifty-nine-year-old philosopher. The differences in style
and method of expression were due to the fact that the young man was
naïve, whereas the old man had been stripped of his youthful delusions.
The former wrote with the faith that anyone seriously engaged in philosophy was concerned only with the truth. The latter knew that he had
fallen in with a company of philosophical tradesmen and submissive adu-
lators whose only concern was with maintaining a career. They lived by
philosophy and not, as he did, for philosophy. Moreover, the old man had
witnessed the prominence a charlatan such as Hegel had achieved, and he
had observed how Hegelian nonsense had rendered incapable of thought
and stupefied the present generation of German scholars. This ruinous
effect of Hegel had made it the case that "German philosophy stands
before us loaded with contempt, ridiculed by other nations, expelled for
all honest science, – like a prostitute who for shameful remuneration sold
herself yesterday to one man, today to another."[49] This bitter discovery
is why, he said, the old man often boils with indignation, something that
a fair and sympathetic reader should forgive.

Schopenhauer's explanation of the differences between the voices in the
second edition of his dissertation shows little sympathy with his younger
self. This may be, however, for good reason. The older philosopher had no
professors of philosophy to please. The younger man sought his doctorate.
He had his spurs to earn, as it were. Although Schopenhauer was far from

---

[49] Schopenhauer, *On the Fourfold Root of the Principle of Sufficient Reason*, p. xxviii/ *Sämtliche
Werke*, Vol. 1, p. vii. In 1813, Hegel was outside of Schopenhauer's philosophical orbit,
although he was not completely unknown to Schopenhauer. The Jena publisher and family
friend Carl Friedrich Ernst Frommann had lent Hegel's *Science of Logic* [*Wissenschaft der
Logik*, 1812] to Schopenhauer sometime in the early summer of 1813. Schopenhauer returned
it, along with a copy of his dissertation, on 4 November 1813. He wrote to Frommann that he
would not have kept the book for so long "had I not known that you were as little inclined as
I to read it;" see Schopenhauer's letter to Frommann, 4 November 1813, *Gesammelte Briefe*,
p. 6.

being diffident – perhaps he was, to a degree, this way with Goethe – his desire for his credentials led him to at least feign this attitude. When he sent his dissertation to the University of Jena and not to Berlin, an alteration born out of the fear that the war would make a casualty of his philosophic first-born, his letter, composed in Latin and addressed to the dean of the philosophical faculty, Heinrich Karl Abraham Eichstädt, expressed diffidence. He had no philosophically educated friends in Rudolstadt to review the text, and due to human weakness, he wrote, it is not wise to simply "rely on his own judgment in matters of philosophy."[50] Consequently, he requested that Eichstädt have his "sagacious" faculty let him know whether they found anything unclear, rambling, not true, and whether he advanced some uncredited claim expressed elsewhere by another. He was particularly keen, he stated, to learn whether his critique of Kant's proof of the law of causality had a predecessor. Personally, he asked Eichstädt to let him know whether he found anything "odious" in his manuscript.

Schopenhauer wrote his dissertation in German, a requirement he learned, among others, from his family's friend the Berlin professor of zoology Martin Lichtenberg.[51] He must have been ambivalent about not composing it in Latin. Almost in an apologetic tone, he wrote to Eichstädt that he had written his dissertation in German rather than Latin, because this was required by the Berlin faculty. Schopenhauer appeared to side with Berlin in this matter. He told Eichstädt that he also found it appropriate to use his native tongue, "because the Latin language is little suited for philosophical-critical investigations."[52] Elsewhere, he directly credited Kant's critical philosophy for forging German into a philosophical language, one that was necessary for the subject matter of his dissertation.[53] He also recognized another benefit of using German: he would gain a wider audience for his work, provided that "there will be a philosophical audience again."[54] Schopenhauer would repeat this claim, as well as explaining why he wrote it in German, to most recipients of

---

[50] Ibid., pp. 6–7, Schopenhauer to the *Dekan der Philosophischen Fakultät in Jena*, 24 September 1813; German translation, pp. 643–5.
[51] Schopenhauer reported his discussion with Lichtenberg concerning the requirements of a Berlin dissertation in his *curriculum vitae*; see ibid., p. 53, German translation, p. 654.
[52] Ibid., p. 6, German translation, p. 643.
[53] Ibid., p. 7, Schopenhauer's letter to Friedrich August Wolf, 24 November 1813.
[54] Ibid.

dedicated copies of his philosophical first-born.[55] He felt it necessary to explain his "choice" of language.

Despite Schopenhauer's ambivalence about not writing his dissertation in Latin, he wrote all of his works in German, with the exception of a Latin recasting of his essay on color theory, which he viewed as more a scientific than a philosophical treatise.[56] As he aged, however, he increasingly lamented the loss of Latin as the *lingua franca* of scholarship. He could tolerate the decline of the use of Greek, something found in his much later willingness to translate Greek passages in his books. But unlike Spanish and English, which he translated into German, he would only provide Latin translation of the Greek. He would always, moreover, let his quotations from works published in Latin speak for themselves. With the second edition of *The World as Will and Representation* (1844), he made public his disdain for the displacement of Latin by European national languages. This robbed scholars of a common scientific literature for all of Europe, creating a new Tower of Babel. By writing in their native tongues, moreover, he said, scholars might have gained an initial, larger audience, but they would be received by a less educated one, and one inclined to tolerate national prejudices in a scholar's work or allow their prejudices to censor the scholar. In German-speaking lands, he argued, things were even worse. Gripped by nationalism, the Germans' "teutomania" led them to translate the *termini technici* of the natural sciences into their native tongue, something other nationalities were sufficiently wise to avoid. This left German scientists at a disadvantage. They had to learn terms twice, once in Latin and once in German, if they wished

---

55 Schopenhauer repeated both claims in letters to Wolf, Schleiermacher, Reinhold, and Böttiger. It is odd, however, that he felt compelled to explain to Wolf and Schleiermacher the Berlin requirement of German, because both were professors at Berlin. He did not, however, make either of these claims in his letters to Frommann and Goethe. (We do not have his letters to Kabrun and Schulze.) For Schopenhauer's letters to recipients of his dissertation, see ibid., p. 6 (Frommann, 4 November 1813); p. 7 (Wolf, 24 November 1813); pp. 7–8 (Schleiermacher, 24 November 1813); pp. 8–9 (Reinhold, 24 November 1813); p. 9 (Böttiger, 6 December 1813); and p. 9 Goethe (13 January 1814).

56 Schopenhauer's "*Commentatio undecima exponens Theoriam Colorum Physiologicam, eandemque primariam*" appeared in the third volume of *Scriptores Ophthalmologici minores*, Vol. 3 (1830) edited by Justus Radius. In its Introduction, Schopenhauer explained that he reworked his *On Vision and Colors: An Essay* [*Ueber das Sehn und die Farben, eine Abhandlung* (Leipzig: Hartknoch, 1816)] into Latin because the German essay had been virtually ignored and a Latin version would make his color theory available to foreign readers, among whom he could find "attentive and just judges;" see *Sämtliche Werke*, Vol. 7, p. 184.

to be participating members of the scientific community. The mania for Germanization of technical terms led to crude, if not barbarous results: " '*Fruchthälter*,' '*Fruchtgang*,' '*Fruchtleiter*' for *uterus, vagina*, and *tuba falloppii*, which every doctor must know, and which can be managed in all European languages, are utterly bewildering."[57] To refer to the *pleura* as the "*Lugensack*" and the *pericardium* as the "*Herzbeutel*" made it appear as if these terms "originated with butchers rather than anatomists."[58]

The decline of Latin as the language of scholars also excommunicated modern scholars from the benefits of belonging to a universal community of scholars that was not restricted by the contingencies of time and place of birth. By reading Latin, not only was it possible to enjoy the thoughts and insights of Roman antiquity, but one could become acquainted with "Scotus Erigena of the ninth century, John of Salisbury of the twelfth, and Raymond Lull of the thirteenth, and hundreds of others,"[59] something that could not be the case, had they written in their native languages. Without preserving Latin, moreover, and by not writing in Latin, one's own works could not speak to future scholars. Bacon realized this, Schopenhauer noted, and he had Thomas Hobbes assist him in translating his *Essays* into the *Sermones Fideles*.[60] There was also the loss of the humanizing effects of Latin authors, which followed from the decline in the knowledge of Latin. The humane and honest ways in which classical writers considered the individual, the community, and nature were natural tonics for the pernicious and stupefying effects of the Middle Ages, with its priestcraft and "half brutal, half idiotic chivalry," from which modern society still suffered.[61]

Yet there were deeper and more personal reasons for Schopenhauer's lamenting the loss of Latin. After philosophizing for more than thirty years without drawing what he regarded as his due, he managed to convince a

[57] Schopenhauer, *The World as Will and Representation*, Vol. 2, p. 123/*Sämtliche Werke*, Vol. 3, p. 135. "*Fruchthälter*" literally means "fruit-holder," "*Fruchtgang*" means "fruit-passage," and "*Fruchtleiter*" means "fruit-producer."

[58] Ibid., Vol. 2, p. 124/ibid., Vol. 3, p. 135. "*Lungensack*" literally means "lungs-sack" and "*Herzbeutel*" "heart-bag."

[59] Schopenhauer, *Parerga and Paralipomena*, Vol. 2, p. 488/*Sämtliche Werke*, Vol. 6, p. 518.

[60] Ibid., Vol. 2, p. 188/ibid., Vol. 6, p. 518.

[61] Schopenhauer, *The World as Will and Representation*, Vol. 2, p. 124/*Sämtliche Werke*, Vol. 3, p. 136.

publisher to issue his massive two-volume work *Parerga and Paralipomena*. He did not, however, appreciate the irony between the pedantic title of this work and its goal. He composed a "philosophy for the world" in order to seek a learned audience, a strategy to bypass "professors of philosophy," whose conspiracy of silence he viewed as responsible for his lack of recognition.[62] This book had to have a Latin title, Schopenhauer insisted, because it was a scholarly work. But the Latin title was for a work written in German, and it was designed for nonscholars. Nevertheless, it also contained additional complaints about the supersession of Latin by national languages. There were very few Europeans, he argued, capable of really thinking and of rendering meaningful judgments. The use of national languages drew linguistic boundaries that diluted further the population of serious readers. This also made it possible, he claimed, for narrow-minded publishers and literary hacks to control the intellectual marketplace. To substantiate this claim, Schopenhauer noted that after a moment of glory, Kant faded from the scene, lost in the quagmire of German critical judgment, whose sham erudition enabled the philosophies of Fichte, Schelling, and Hegel to enjoy flickers of fame. This was also the reason, he thought, that Goethe's theory of color failed to receive a fair hearing. One senses, however, what really served as the basis for Schopenhauer's thinking: "*That* is why I have remained unnoticed." Had scholars demanded Latin, and had he written in that language, he seems to suggest, he would have been noticed.[63]

Yet these reflections on the decline of Latin were not even on the periphery of Schopenhauer's ambivalence about writing his dissertation in German. He still had faith that anyone interested in philosophy was interested simply and solely in the truth, and he thought that he had articulated it in his dissertation. His disillusionment would come later, as would his attempt to account for his failure to create even a ripple in the philosophical world. It is likely that Schopenhauer's ambivalence followed from being deprived of displaying his erudition. Had he written in Latin, he would have dramatically proven wrong the person who

---

[62] See *Gesammelte Briefe*, p. 244, Schopenhauer's letter to F. A. Brockhaus, 3 September 1850, where he wrote that *Parerga and Paralipomena* presented "my philosophy for the world," which, he claimed, would break the passive opposition to his thought by philosophy professors.

[63] *Parerga and Paralipomena*, Vol. 2, p. 486/*Sämtliche Werke*, Vol. 6, p. 517.

mattered the most to him. Johanna had repeatedly raised her concern
about Schopenhauer's ability to learn Latin so late in his life. A successful Latin dissertation would have dramatically demonstrated her inability
to assess her son's skills accurately. It would have shown, beyond the
glowing reports of her son's language tutors, which she tended to treat
skeptically, that Schopenhauer's choice of the life of a scholar was a
wise one.

Still, it was not the language of his dissertation that mattered the most
for Schopenhauer. Words stood for ideas, and he was confident that his
ideas were sound. Not only were they worthy of earning him a degree, they
were worthy of serious philosophical reflections. Even prior to submitting
his work to Jena, he had arranged to have five hundred copies published at
his own expense.[64] He was also certain that Jena would accept a dissertation
originally written for Berlin. Two days prior to sending his dissertation,
he sent to Eichstädt his ten *Friedrich'dor* graduation fee, as well as the
promise to include with his dissertation "a letter fully in Latin" explaining his educational background.[65] Then, according to schedule, the letter
and dissertation were sent on 24 September. Eichstädt acted quickly.
He had Schopenhauer's fee in hand, and like other German universities,
Jena was suffering financially due to the war. He also knew that Arthur
was the son of Johanna Schopenhauer, a close personal friend of Goethe,
who was still overseeing the university. He circulated a letter announcing Schopenhauer's bid for a degree on 26 September, and on 2 October
Schopenhauer was granted his degree *in absentia*, with the distinction of
magna cum laude. Three days later, Schopenhauer had his degree in hand.
He then managed to employ his Latin, scratching in Latin on the window
sash of his room in Rudolstadt, "Arth. Schopenhauer passed the greater
part of the year 1813 in his room. The house deserves praise on account
of the extensive landscape it surveys."[66] Many years later, Schopenhauer's enthusiasts would travel to Rudolstadt to gaze upon their hero's
graffito.

---

[64] See *Gesammelte Briefe*, p. 3, Schopenhauer's letter to Friedrich Justin Bertuch, 15 September
1813. He also assured Bertuch that he should have no concerns about the censor, because his
dissertation made no direct references to religion or politics.

[65] Ibid., p. 3, Schopenhauer's letter to Heinrich Karl Abraham Eichstädt, 22 September 1813.

[66] Cited in Gwinner, *Arthur Schopenhauer aus persönlichem Umgange dargestellt*, p. 50. The Latin
reads "Arth. Schopenhauer *majorem anni* 1813 *partem in hoc conclave degit. Laudaturque domus,
longos quae prospicet agros.*" The last line is from Horace's *Epistles*, I. 10.

On the Fourfold Root of the Principle of Sufficient Reason
(1813)

Schopenhauer opened his dissertation with a statement of method in which he evoked his two philosophical heroes, the "divine Plato" and the "marvelous Kant." These mighty thinkers, he said, recommended two laws for the method of all philosophizing: the law of homogeneity and the law of specification. The former states, "Entities are not to be multiplied unnecessarily" [*entia praeter necessistatem non esse multiplicanda*], and the latter asserts, "Varieties of entities are not to be diminished rashly" [*entium varietates non temere esse minuendas*].[67] The law of homogeneity enjoins philosophical investigators to unite individuals into species, species into genera, genera into families, until they arrive at the highest concept, which embraces everything. The law of specification prescribes the reverse method of consideration. Philosophical investigators should consider differences between genera united under a family, species united under genera, and individuals subsumed under a species. Following Kant, Schopenhauer claimed that both of these laws were transcendental and inherent in our faculty of reason, and as such, owe their origins to the human mind, which guarantees that reality as it appears to us will conform to these laws.

To set the stage for his own work, Schopenhauer surveyed the history of Western philosophy and found that earlier philosophers had ignored the law of specification. Philosophers through Kant and up the present, he argued, had managed to recognize only two forms of the principle; the principle of sufficient reason of cognition (*principium rationis sufficientis cognoscendi*) and the principle of sufficient reason of becoming (*principium rationis sufficientis fiendi*). The former connoted that the truth of a judgment or proposition requires a separate ground or reason for its truth, whereas the latter held that every event in the natural world follows from a cause. Still, despite the recognition of these two forms of the principle, there was still a tendency to conflate the two. Even the great Kant, whom Schopenhauer viewed as ushering in a new stage in world philosophy, was

[67] *Sämtliche Werke*, Vol. 7, p. 3 / *On the Fourfold Root of the Principle of Sufficient Reason*, p. 1. Kant discussed the laws of homogeneity and specification as transcendental principles in *Critique of Pure Reason*, A651/B679–A660/B688. For Plato's reference to these principles, Schopenhauer cites only Plato's *Philebus*, 26e in the first edition, adding the references to the *Politicus* and *Phaedrus* in the second.

susceptible to this confusion. In his great work, the *Critique of Pure Reason*, one found Kant speaking "of the thing in itself as the *ground* of appearances . . . , of a ground of the possibility of all appearances; of an *intelligible cause*, an *unknown ground* of the sensible series in general . . . ."[68] This conflation led only in darkness and delusion, Schopenhauer thought, and moved his contemporaries to employ the concepts of ground and consequent in totally transcendent ways.

Not only had previous thinkers conflated the ideas of reason or ground with that of a cause, Schopenhauer held, but also they had failed to distinguish two additional forms of the principle of sufficient reason; namely, the principle of sufficient reason of being (*principium rationis sufficientis essendi*) and the principle of sufficient reason of acting (*principium rationis sufficientis agendi*). The former governs the domains of geometry and arithmetic, and the latter the domain of human actions, stating that all human actions follow from motives. By clearly distinguishing between the four forms of the principle of sufficient reason, whose common expression he found in Wolff's dictum, "nothing is without a reason why it is rather than is not," he hoped that he would provide greater precision and lucidity to philosophizing. Serious philosophy required such, he argued, in order to guard against error as well as deception. "The real philosopher," he wrote, "always looks for clearness and distinctness; he will invariably try to resemble not a turbid, impetuous torrent, but instead a Swiss lake which by its calmness combines greater depth with greater clearness, the depth revealing itself precisely through its clearness."[69]

Yet Schopenhauer thought that his dissertation offered more than precise intellectual tools for future philosophers. It would serve as the

---

[68] *Sämtliche Werke*, Vol. 7, pp. 92–3. Schopenhauer is quoting here from Kant's *Critique of Pure Reason*, A562/B591 and A564/B592. Schopenhauer, however, was drawing from the fifth edition of Kant's masterpiece, which was based on the second edition. In this quotation, he continued to cite other examples of Kant's confusion. After doing so, and after criticizing unnamed contemporaries, he attempted to mitigate what could have appeared as a mean-spirited attack on Kant by mentioning that his purpose was not to criticize Kant, "but only to illustrate his view by means of examples" (ibid., Vol. 7, p. 93). In the second edition, he eliminated this line, because there was no longer a need to correct his readers' possible response to his treatment of Kant. He also named his contemporaries and subjected them to a harsh critique and vicious ad hominems, and compared to his treatment of Fichte, Schelling, Jacobi, – and especially Hegel – he knew that his readers would not accuse him of attacking Kant.

[69] Ibid., Vol. 7, p. 6/ *On the Fourfold Root of the Principle of Sufficient Reason*, p. 4. When a passage from Schopenhauer's dissertation remains unchanged in the second edition, I will include a citation to this English translation.

means by which philosophy could be set on the right path to knowledge. The principle of sufficient reason was the main principle for all thought and knowledge. It was this which made any science, that is, any body of knowledge, possible, because it was the very principle that united propositions into a system and that made a body of knowledge something greater than an aggregate of disjointed and unconnected ideas. It also justified our asking *why* of any particular claim. For that reason he called it "the mother of all sciences."[70] It served, moreover, as the basis of all proof and demonstration, and as such, he argued, the principle itself could not be proven. To prove a doubtful proposition, one had to base it on a known one, which in turn was grounded on another. Ultimately, he continued, you had to reach propositions that expressed the forms and laws, the very conditions of all thinking and knowing. "Consequently, all thinking and knowing consists of the application of these; so that certainty is nothing but an agreement with those conditions, forms, and laws, and therefore their own certainty cannot again become evident from other propositions."[71] In the second edition of his dissertation, he would supplement this claim by contending that it was absurd to demand a proof for this principle, because this "involved [one] in that circle of demanding a proof for the right to demand a proof."[72] It is in this new edition of his dissertation that Schopenhauer made the well-known claim that the principle of sufficient reason was the "*principle of all explanation*," and that the connection expressed by it in any of its four forms cannot be explained further, "since there is no principle for explaining the principle of all explanation, just as the eye sees everything but itself."[73] In the original, he simply said that to ask for a "why" of the principle of sufficient reason posed a question without an answer.[74]

---

[70] Ibid., Vol. 7, p. 7/ibid., p. 6.

[71] Ibid., Vol. 7, p. 15/ibid., p. 32.

[72] *On the Fourfold Root of the Principle of Sufficient Reason*, p. 33/*Sämtliche Werke*, Vol. 1, p. 24. It is difficult to see how the demand for a proof of the principle of sufficient reason is circular as Schopenhauer charges. He seems to suggest that to demand a proof for the principle is already to assume it to be true. A demand for a proof is not a proof itself, and the failure to have one may very well may serve to maintain the type of skepticism involved in posing the demand for the proof itself; see Dale Jacquette's "Schopenhauer's Circle and the Principle of Sufficient Reason," *Metaphilosophy*, Vol. 23 (1992), pp. 279–87.

[73] *On the Fourfold Root of the Principle of Sufficient Reason*, p. 229/*Sämtliche Werke*, Vol. 1, p. 156.

[74] See *Sämtliche Werke*, Vol. 7, pp. 14, 89f.

A central thesis of Schopenhauer's dissertation was the correlativity of the subject and object, which was the first, universal, and essential form of all cognition. Any experience, any cognition, and any awareness entailed a cognizer and a cognized, an experiencer and an experienced, a subject of awareness and an object of awareness. Later, he would praise George Berkeley and would call him the "father of idealism" for the insight that there could be no object without a subject, and he would take Kant to task for neglecting this profound observation.[75] He would also claim that his philosophy differed from all others by beginning with – and here he used Reinhold's term – a fact of consciousness, a representation, as the starting point of his philosophy, which presupposed the subject/object division.[76] Consequently, he averred that he avoided the pitfalls of both Fichte's idealism and his materialism. The former could not derive the object, and the latter, the subject. For Schopenhauer, the subject and object division was epistemological bedrock. The subject could never be object, or the object the subject. Because, moreover, the principle of sufficient reason applied only to objects of cognition, it could never be applied to the relationship between the subject and the object.

The subject and object correlation assumed a crucial function in Schopenhauer's dissertation, providing him with the means for identifying representations with objects of consciousness, and by delineating different kinds of representations, he articulated classes of objects, which served as bases for the different "roots" of the principle of sufficient reason and for different human cognitive capacities or "faculties":

Our consciousness, in so far as it appears as sensibility, understanding, [and] reason, is divisible into subject and object, and contains, until then, nothing else. To be object for the

---

[75] See *Parerga and Paralipomena*, Vol. 1, p. 77/*Sämtliche Werke*, Vol. 5, p. 82 for the reference to Berkeley and *The World as Will and Representation*, Vol. 1, p. 434/*Sämtliche Werke*, Vol. 2, p. 514, for the remark on Kant.

[76] *The World as Will and Representation*, Vol. 2, p. 5/*Sämtliche Werke*, Vol. 3, p. 5. Schopenhauer wrote in this passage that "*consciousness* alone is immediately given, hence the basis of philosophy is limited to the facts of consciousness; in other words, philosophy is essentially *idealistic*." The correlation of the subject and object also echoes Reinhold, who held that "For each representation a representing subject and a represented object belong . . ."; see C. L. Reinhold, *Ueber das Fundament des philosophischen Wissens* (Jena: Mauke, 1791), p. 200. Schopenhauer borrowed this book from the ducal library in Weimar from 29 July to 20 September 1813. Later, he purchased his own copy. In *Der junge Schopenhauer*, Kamata claims that Schopenhauer identified Reinhold's "Elementary Philosophy" with Kant, due to Schulze's influence.

subject and to be our representation are the same. All of our representations are objects for the subject. But nothing existing by itself and independently, also nothing single and detached, can become an object for us; rather, all of our representations stand in a lawful connection that according to form is determinable a priori. This connection is that kind of relation that the principle of sufficient reason expresses, taken universally. That law ruling over all of our representations is the root of the principle of sufficient reason. It is fact and the principle of sufficient reason is its expression. Yet, we can only acquire through abstraction its general form, as it is put forward here. In every case, it is given to us *in concreto.*[77]

The principle of sufficient reason, as articulated by Wolff's "nothing is without a ground why it is rather than is not," is the general statement under which all other specific instances of ground/consequent relationships were subsumed. As such, it signified the "higher concept that embraced everything," and it satisfied the demand of the law of homogeneity.[78] It was an abstraction from the kinds of ground/consequent relations found in the four classes of objects, which, as he said, were given to us *in concreto.* In a section that he would strike from the second edition, "Its Fourfoldness," Schopenhauer anticipated that the readers of his dissertation would expect that he would supply a deduction like Kant's deduction of the pure categories of the understanding to justify his claim that all objects for a subject, that is, all of our representations, fell into four classes of objects in which different iterations of the principle of sufficient reason were expressed. This section is noteworthy, because it begins to reflect a major difference between the methodologies of Schopenhauer and Kant. Schopenhauer would pride himself as starting with that which is given to consciousness, instead of working from judgments about things like Kant. In the first edition of *The World of Will and Representation*, he put the difference in blunt terms: "But again and again in the *Critique of Pure Reason* we come across the principal and fundamental error of Kant's which I have previously censured in detail, namely, the complete absence of any distinction between abstract, discursive knowledge from the intuitive."[79]

---

[77] *On the Fourfold Root of the Principle of Sufficient Reason*, pp. 41–2/ *Sämtliche Werke*, Vol. 7, p. 18. Schopenhauer modified his style, but not the substance of this passage in the second edition.

[78] See ibid., p. 1/ibid., Vol. 7, p. 3.

[79] *The World as Will and Representation*, Vol. 1, p. 473/ *Sämtliche Werke*, Vol. 2, p. 562. This remark dates from the first edition.

Yet the aspiring doctor of philosophy was not prepared to make a sharp break from Kant. Still, in light of this perceived expectation that he should provide a Kantian-style deduction of the "fourfoldness" of the principle of sufficient reason, Schopenhauer exploited this expectation to have some fun with his contemporaries. It was one of the few times he did so in his dissertation. Ever since Kant's deduction of the twelve categories of the understanding, he joked, there has not been anything so basic and immediate that it had not been deduced *a priori*, even things that no earlier generation would have dared to hope. He evoked Goethe: "The philosopher who steps in/Proves to us, it could not otherwise been."[80] Instead of an *a priori* deduction, Schopenhauer's division of all of our representations into four classes was based on induction, on generalizations grounded on a survey of representations. This, he argued, is not unlike Kant, who founded his division of the categories of the understanding on an induction from the logical table of judgments.[81] He never demonstrated, Schopenhauer continued, that the four titles under which the categories were subsumed could only be four or that the twelve categories themselves had to be twelve. The same was true of Kant's twelve

---

[80] *Sämtliche Werke*, Vol. 7, p. 19. The quotation is from Goethe's *Faust*, part 1, line 1928. After Schopenhauer cut this section in the second edition of his dissertation, he used these same lines specifically against Schelling for trying to deduce *a priori* that which could only be known *a posteriori*. As examples, Schopenhauer cited Schelling's deductions of inorganic nature and gravity found in his *First Sketch of a Philosophy of Nature* (*Erster Entwurf einer Naturphilosophie*, 1799).

[81] Schopenhauer is referring to Kant's *Critique of Pure Reason*, where he provided a "metaphysical deduction" of the twelve pure concepts or categories of the understanding from the twelve forms of judgments. The categories functioned as the necessary conditions for the possibility of experience and for that of the concept of an object in general. The forms of judgment signified the logically meaningful forms of all judgments. Kant held that just as there are necessary features of all judgments, there also must be corresponding ways in which we develop the concepts of objects to permit our judgments to be about objects. Schopenhauer's reference to the "logical table of judgments" refers to a table in which Kant classified the forms of judgments in groups of three, under four "titles," which were quantity, the extension of the subject term; quality, the inclusion or exclusion of the predicate term in the class of the subject term; relation, whether a judgment asserts a relation only between a subject or predicate term, or between two or more judgments; and modality, whether a judgment asserts a possible, actual, or a necessary truth. Under these "titles," Kant arranged the twelve forms of judgment:

Quantity	Quality	Relation	Modality
Universal	Affirmative	Categorical	Problematic
Particular	Negative	Hypothetical	Assertoric
Singular	Infinite	Disjunctive	Apodictic

functions of judgments. He quoted from the *Critique of Pure Reason* to make his point: "For the peculiarity of our understanding, that it is able to produce the unity of apperception *a priori* only by means of the categories and only through this kind and number of them, a further ground may be given just as little as one can be given for why we have exactly these and no other functions for judgment."[82] If his classification of representations were wrong, Schopenhauer bid his critics to provide an example that escaped his four classes or to reduce two of his classes into one.

Schopenhauer, however, did not provide a separate section in which he inductively established his four classes of objects. Instead, he devoted separate chapters for each of these classes, which were (1) intuitive or perceptual representations, or what he called, in shorthand, "real objects," the sum total of which constituted "the objective, real world";[83] (2) abstract representations, or representations of representations, that is, "concepts," which when united, formulate judgments;[84] (3) *a priori* or pure intuitions of space and time, mathematical objects as it were;[85] and (4) a class for each subject having but one object, one's own will.[86] Just as Descartes developed his account of the faculties of the human mind by a survey of different types of ideas, Schopenhauer used the presence of different types of representations to develop his description of the various powers of

---

Kant's table of the categories paralleled his division of the judgments:

Of Quantity	Of Quality	Of Relation	Of Modality
Unity	Reality	Of Inherence and Subsistence	Possibility – Impossibility
Plurality	Negation	Of Causality and Dependence	Existence – Nonexistence
Totality	Limitation	Of Community	Necessity – Contingency

Contrary to Schopenhauer, Kant criticized Aristotle for developing his categories through induction and for lacking a "principle" that would guarantee completeness. Kant's principle, Schopenhauer held, was the ability or faculty that allowed him to systematically generate his division of the categories; see Kant's *Critique of Pure Reason*, A70/B95 for his table of judgments, A80/B106 for the table of categories, and A81/B107 for his remarks about Aristotle.

[82] *Sämtliche Werke*, Vol. 7, p. 19f. He is quoting from Kant's *Critique of Pure Reason*, B145.

[83] Ibid., Vol. 7, p. 25n./*On the Fourfold Root of the Principle of Sufficient Reason*, p. 52n. He used the expression "real objects" to refer to the representations of intuitive perception, the sum total of which "form the complex of empirical reality, such reality in itself always remains ideal."

[84] See ibid., Vol. 7, p. 49/ibid., p. 146. Ultimately, Schopenhauer would argue that all meaningful concepts must be derived from intuitions.

[85] See ibid., Vol. 7, p. 59/ibid., p. 193.

[86] See ibid., Vol. 7, p. 68/ibid., p. 207.

human cognition[87] : "But with regard to the necessary correlative of those representations as their condition, namely to the subject, those powers are abstracted from the representations. Consequently, they are related to the classes of representations precisely as the subject in general is to the object in general. . . . It is immaterial whether I say that objects are divisible into such and such classes, or that such and such different powers are peculiar to the subject."[88] On this basis, Schopenhauer identified sensibility (*Sinnlichkeit*) or receptiveness to data of the outer world and the understanding (*Verstand*) with intuitive representations; reason (*Vernunft*) with abstract representations; the forms of outer and inner sense with pure intuitions; and self-consciousness with awareness of one's own will. For each of the classes of objects, he then articulated the following roots of the principle of sufficient reason: (1) the principle of sufficient reason of becoming; (2) the principle of sufficient reason of knowing; (3) the principle of sufficient reason of being; (4) the principle of sufficient reason of acting.

Becoming

The fourth chapter of Schopenhauer's dissertation, his analysis of the principle of sufficient reason of becoming, which he also referred to as the law of causality, received the most extensive revision of any of its chapters in the 1847 edition, where he more than doubled its length.[89] Although some of this was due to his adding pages chock-filled with direct abuse piled on the heads of the German Idealists, especially Hegel, there were philosophically noteworthy changes. It was not the case, however, that he introduced new ideas; rather, by 1847 he had published two versions of his essay on color theory (1816, 1830), his statement on the relationship of his philosophy and the natural sciences, *On the Will in Nature* (1836), and

---

[87] Descartes takes this tactic in *Meditations on First Philosophy*, "Meditation III," where he divided his ideas into three kinds, but unlike Schopenhauer, Descartes is concerned with determining whether one of these ideas could provide conclusive grounds for establishing some truth beyond that of his own existence. Fortunately, he found the innate idea of God, which enabled him to move beyond the solipsism of his first truth, the *cogito*, that is: I think, therefore I am.

[88] Ibid., Vol. 7, pp. 69–70/ibid., p. 207.

[89] In the 1813 dissertation, the fourth chapter ran about 28 pages, and in the second edition, it was about 68 pages.

the collection of his two prize essays, *The Two Fundamental Problems of Ethics* (1841), and he had revised and greatly expanded the second edition of *The World as Will and Representation* (1844). Consequently, he had been laboring on his philosophy for thirty-four years between editions of his principal work, and his thought had matured in ways antithetical to some of the views advanced in his first book. Quite naturally, he also added numerous references to supporting materials in his other books, which also required bringing his dissertation into conformity with his later views. Schopenhauer also had obtained confidence in the truth of his views, a self-confidence that bordered on arrogance, and so he removed some of the natural qualifications in which he had couched his assertions. The older philosopher, moreover, did not write to please readers who had the power to grant him an academic degree.

The young philosopher was also somewhat coy about the degree to which he had distanced himself from Kant's philosophy. He accepted Kant's claim that spatio-temporal forms in which objects present themselves and causality are impositions of our own cognition on experience. So instead of being features of a world of objects that are passively imprinted on our minds, these features are *a priori* structures of our own cognitions. Although he was willing to claim that this entails that such a world is "repeatedly degraded by Plato to the 'always only arising and passing away, but never really and truly existing,'" he was not prepared to draw Kant's distinction between appearances and things in themselves.[90] At this point in his intellectual development, he eschewed claiming that things in themselves exist beyond our experience. Equally, he was disinclined to posit the existence of Plato's Forms. And although he would reject in the most emphatic terms Kant's claim that our cognition of any natural object involves a synthesis of sensory inputs or intuitions according to the categories of the understanding, he did little in his dissertation to draw attention to his view that intuition itself, the perception of natural objects, immediately involves the nonconceptual and nondiscursive cognition of spatio-temporal objects standing in causal relationships. In 1813 he was prepared to show some respect for Kant's "Transcendental

---

[90] Ibid., Vol. 7, p. 92/ *On the Fourfold Root of the Principle of Sufficient Reason*, p. 232. Schopenhauer quoted Plato's *Timaeus*, 28a in Greek. In the second edition, Schopenhauer argued from the claim that the principle of sufficient reason is *a priori* in all its forms, with its source in our intellect, to the claim that it does not apply to the totality of all existing things, but only to mere appearances and not to the "thing in itself that manifests itself in the world."

Analytic," where Kant painstakingly developed the view that he rejected. It was, he wrote, "an important preliminary" for his own work, and his new explanation of the understanding is something that readers can see for themselves through attentive observation.[91] Still, he also wrote that "I concur, moreover, with Kant that the law of causality, in connection with the other categories, thus with the understanding in general, makes possible the whole of objective knowledge that we call experience."[92] In 1847, Schopenhauer was blunt concerning his claim that the sole function of the understanding is an immediate apprehension of causal relationships and it does not employ "the complicated clockwork of the twelve Kantian categories...."[93]

Schopenhauer, however, was not shy about his rejection of Kant's demonstration of the *a priori* nature of the law of causality. In his letter to the Dean of the Philosophy Faculty at Jena, he requested a judgment about the originality of his criticism. If his letter failed to call his readers' attention to this element of his dissertation, then the title of Sect. 24 should have done so. It read, in part, "Disputation of Kant's Proof of This Principle."[94] He did not dispute, however, the *a priori* nature of the law of causality. This was a basic principle of his own view. Instead, he would one-up Kant both by demolishing Kant's demonstration and by offering his own "proof." In the Second Analogy, Kant had argued that any objective succession of events had to be deduced from causal laws requiring that one event could only occur after

[91] Ibid., Vol. 7, p. 23. There are two main parts in Kant's *Critique of Pure Reason*, the "Transcendental Doctrine of Elements," and the "Transcendental Doctrine of Method." The first part of the former is the "Transcendental Aesthetic," and the second is the "Transcendental Logic." The "Transcendental Analytic" is the first division of the latter, and the "Transcendental Dialectic" is the second division. Although Schopenhauer always held to the "Transcendental Aesthetic" (where Kant argued that space and time are *a priori* forms of all intuition and the contribution of our faculty of sensibility), he rejected the "Transcendental Analytic" (where Kant argued that the understanding is the source of *a priori* concepts). For Schopenhauer's critique of the "Transcendental Analytic," see *The World as Will and Representation*, Vol. 1, pp. 452–80/*Sämtliche Werke*, Vol. 2, pp. 536–70.

[92] Ibid., Vol. 7, p. 32.

[93] *On the Fourfold Root of the Principle of Sufficient Reason*, p. 111/*Sämtliche Werke*, Vol. 1, p. 77.

[94] *Sämtliche Werke*, Vol. 7, p. 31. The full title was "Disputation of Kant's Proof of This Law and Statement of a New One Composed Similarly." This became Sect. 23 in the 1847 edition, with the more direct title "Arguments against Kant's Proof of the A Priori Nature of the Concept of Causality;" see ibid., p. 122/ibid., Vol. 1, p. 122.

another.[95] To show the difference between objective and subjective succession of perceptions, Kant provided an example of a ship moving downstream and the perception of a house. In the first example, we could only perceive the ship moving downstream after having first perceived it upstream. In the second example, the perception of the house is "arbitrary"; that is, we could have perceived it from top to bottom or from bottom to top. In the case of the ship, an objective succession, the succession of perceptions is irreversible, and in the case of the house, a subjective succession, the succession of perceptions is reversible. Yet we cannot deduce the irreversibility of our perceptions of the ship directly from their succession, because our perceptions of the house are also successive. Nor can the irreversibility of the position of the ship be inferred immediately from our perceptions, because they are simply successive. To do this, we must deduce the successive positions of the ship from causal laws implying that in specific circumstances, it is sailing downstream. Then, we can infer the irreversibility of succession of our perceptions from that. The upshot for Kant is that the objective succession of our perceptions is justified only by the faculty of the understanding with its concepts of cause and effect.

Schopenhauer was unmoved by Kant's argument and irreversibly so. Events can succeed one another in an objective sequence without the former event being the cause of the latter, he argued. Imagine that upon your exiting Kant's house, a roof tile falls, knocking you on the head. There is no causal relationship between these events, but this succession is objective. Or consider the succession of the notes in a piece of music, which is not subjectively determined by the listener, but is an objective sequence that is not causal. Last, consider the rotation of the earth. It is known objectively, but not by means of causal laws, "since its cause is completely unknown to us."[96] Indeed, Schopenhauer even thought that Kant's examples of the ship and the house were radically flawed. In both of his examples, Kant had failed to notice that we are dealing with a change in the situation of two objects, between the body of the perceiver

---

[95] See Kant, *Critique of Pure Reason*, "Second Analogy," A190/B235–A198/B244 for his examples of the ship and house. For a critical review of Schopenhauer's disputation of Kant, see Paul Guyer's "Schopenhauer, Kant, and Philosophy," in *The Cambridge Companion to Schopenhauer*, ed. Christopher Janaway (Cambridge: Cambridge University Press, 1999), pp. 120–33.

[96] *Sämtliche Werke*, Vol. 7, p. 35.

and the house in one case, and the ship and the stream in the other. If we were able to pull the ship upstream as we had the power of moving our eyes in opposite directions, the ship's direction would be reversible. But, in the case of the house, there really is no difference from that of the moving ship. Moving one's eyes from top to bottom is one event and the opposite movement from bottom to top is another. Both of these sequences are objective and nonarbitrary. Kant, he claimed, would have found no differences in these examples, had he borne in mind that his own body was an object among objects, and that the succession of his immediately present representations, in so far as they were not phantasms, depended on the actions of other objects upon it.

Schopenhauer's proof of the *a priori* nature of the law of causality was straightforward: its proof "appears to me to already lie in the unshakable certainty with which everyone expects that experience will in all cases turn out in accordance with this law; i.e., the *a priori* nature is confirmed by the apodictic certainty which we attribute to this law and which differs from every other that is based on induction; e.g., from the certainty of empirically known natural laws, by the fact that we cannot even conceive anywhere in the world of experience an exception to this law. We could *think*, e.g., the law of gravitation ceasing to act at some time, but we could never think of this as happening without a cause."[97] However, in 1847, he modified this passage by claiming that he had provided the only correct proof for the *a priori* nature of the law of causality in the newly added, lengthy Sect. 21, "Aprioricity of the Concept of Causality. – Intellectual Nature of Empirical Intuition. – The Understanding." With the inclusion of this new demonstration, his first one is now said to simply confirm the second.

Schopenhauer's "new" proof of the *a priori* status of causality was, however, far from new in 1847. It was an elaboration of a line of thought that he had already published three years after his dissertation. In the Goethe-inspired *On Vision and Colors*, he had already jettisoned the remnants of Kant's view of the understanding as a faculty of concepts and the view that the perception of real objects required the application of concepts to sensuously given percepts. In that essay, he had argued that "all intuition is intellectual," by which he meant that all of our experiences of empirical

---

[97] Ibid., Vol. 7, p. 36. Schopenhauer retained this passage, with minor modification, in the second edition of his dissertation; see *On the Fourfold Root of the Principle of Sufficient Reason*, p. 129/*Sämtliche Werke*, Vol. 1, pp. 89–90.

objects are a function of the understanding, which automatically, that is, nonconceptually, nondiscursively, nonlinguistically, and immediately, referred bodily sensations to spatio-temporal causes.[98] All that remained of Kant's twelve categories was causality, which did not function as a concept at all. To this new account of empirical cognition, Schopenhauer, the erstwhile student of medicine, incorporated an empirical standpoint, or "objective," to his transcendent, or "subjective," account, thereby naturalizing in reserved terms his account of cognition:

> It is only when the *understanding* begins to act – a function not of single delicate nerve extremities but of that complex and mysterious structure of the brain . . . – only when the understanding applies its sole form, *the law of causality*, that a powerful transformation takes place whereby subjective sensation becomes objective intuition. Thus by virtue of its own peculiar form and so *a priori*, in other words, *prior* to all experience (since until then experience was not yet possible), the understanding grasps the given sensation of the body as an *effect* (a word comprehended only by the understanding), and this effect must necessarily have a *cause*. Simultaneously the understanding summons to its assistance *space*, the form of the *outer* sense also lying predisposed in the intellect, i.e., the brain. This it does in order to place that cause *outside* the organism; for only in this way does there arise an outside whose possibility is simply space, so that pure intuition *a priori* must supply the foundation for empirical intuition.[99]

---

[98] *On Vision and Color*, p. 10/*Sämtliche Werke*, Vol. 1, p. 7. In the second edition of his dissertation, Schopenhauer warned that his thesis that all intuition is intellectual should not be confused with the German Idealists' notion of "intellectual intuition." Intellectual should only be predicated to empirical intuition, he wrote, and not to that "which the philosophical windbags of Germany have attributed to a pretended intuition of an imaginary world where their beloved Absolute is supposed to perform its evolutions;" *On the Fourfold Root of the Principle of Sufficient Reason*, p. 79/*Sämtliche Werke*, Vol. 1, p. 53.

[99] *On the Fourfold Root of the Principle of Sufficient Reason*, p. 77–8/*Sämtliche Werke*, Vol. 1, pp. 52–53. Schopenhauer's tendency to combine a transcendental and an empirical, materialistic account of empirical cognition is, perhaps, most dramatically stated in the second volume of his main work: "It is true that space is only in my head; but empirically my head is in space" (*The World as Will and Representation*, Vol. 1, p. 19/*Sämtliche Werke*, Vol. 3, p. 31). This remark, as could be anticipated, has become a headache for his philosophy, beginning with early commentators and continuing today, from Rudolf Seydel in his *Schopenhauers philosophisches System, dargestellt und beurteilt* (Leipzig: Breitkopt and Härtel, 1857), p. 69, through Paul F. H. Lautermann's *Schopenhauer's Broken World-View: Colours and Ethics between Kant and Goethe* (Dordrecht: Kluwer Academic Publishers, 2000), whose fourth chapter is "The Antinomy: Can the World Be in My Head, Yet My Head Be in the World," pp. 83–116. In his dissertation, Petri Räsänen recommended, in a manner that seems right-headed, rewriting this problematic sentence, "It is true that, from a transcendental point of view, space is only a property of my knowing subject . . . empirically (that is, considered from an empirical point of view) my head is in space;" see *Schopenhauer and Kant's Transcendental Idealism* (Tampere: Tampere University Press, 2005), p. 131.

Schopenhauer then employed a number of examples highlighting the
tremendous differences between sensations, which were "beneath the
skin," and the perception of a real object. He thereby continued and augmented the sort of physiological arguments that he had first rehearsed in
his work on color theory. Once more he described the example of new-
borns who experience only impressions of light and color, only apprehending objects when their understanding begins to exercise its function
of attributing a cause for these merely temporal sensations, located in
space. It is then, he claimed, that babies begin to cognize an external
reality. He provides examples of people born blind who have their vision
restored later in life. To a person they testify that they sense a blur,
a general impression of a single piece. They never recognize separate
objects lying behind one another at different distances. It is only when
they learn to apply the causal law to these data, he argued, that they have
an objective perception of things. He mentions the loss of the cognition
of the external world with the destruction of the lobes of the cerebral
hemispheres, and how it has been demonstrated that these subjects still
had sensations. Even later in his life, Schopenhauer quotes the study
by the French physiologist Marie Jean-Pierre Flourens to confirm his
thesis.[100] He describes and charts optical angles and explains how retinal
images are double, upside down, and two-dimensional, yet we perceive
single, upright, and three-dimensional objects. He adds examples of mis-
perceptions: the understanding judging one ball as two when we touch it
with crossed fingers; how we perceive a single coin as two; and the relative
size of the moon. Curiously, Schopenhauer is not troubled by moving
from examples of formless sensory stimuli, items beneath the skin, to
examples in which an empirical object is misperceived, thereby mixing in
a realistic position with his own idealistic one. Nevertheless, his point was
that "the *understanding* is the artist forming the work, whereas the *senses*
are merely the assistants who hand up the material."[101] Yet, other than
lapsing into realism, he ignores the source of sensations, while maintaining that the experience of intuitive representations or "real objects" can
never inform us about a reality beyond consciousness.

[100] *On the Fourfold Root of the Principle of Sufficient Reason*, pp. 108–9/ *Sämtliche Werke*, Vol. 1,
pp. 74–5. Schopenhauer's references are to Flourens' *De la vie et de l'intelligence* (Paris:
Garnier frères, 1858). These references to Flourens were added by Schopenhauer to his own
handwritten manuscript (1847) of *On the Fourfold Root of the Principle of Sufficient Reason*.
[101] Ibid., p. 114/ibid., Vol. 1, p. 79.

Yet what remained consistent through the editions of Schopenhauer's dissertation was his analysis of causality itself. In Sect. 18 of the original edition (or 19 of the second), he provided an outline of an analysis of sensory experience. In the second edition, however, he referred to this as a "transcendental analysis." There was no significant variation in his presentation. It was not as if he presented a Kantian-style deduction of the necessary conditions for the possibility of experience. The addition of the term "transcendental" was probably driven by his attempt, beginning with *The World as Will and Representation* and escalating from 1830 on, to more closely identify his philosophy as the true descendent of Kant's. Certainly, it did not harken to any change in his philosophical methodology. By 1847 he was even more self-consciously employing an inductive methodology that bore a greater kinship to the British empiricists Locke, Berkeley, and Hume than it did to Kant, viewing the latter as correcting the empiricists concerning formal knowledge.[102] Schopenhauer retained his commitment to a more phenomenological analysis of experience, a direct scrutiny of experience itself.[103] In this regard, he identified with Locke. But because he recognized the *a priori* conditions imposed by human cognition, he also identified with Kant. Writing about his own philosophical methodology in 1844, Schopenhauer noted that "we must regard Locke as the originator of this method of consideration; Kant brought it to an incomparably higher perfection. . . . "[104] He always held, as already found in his dissertation, the empiricist-inspired thesis that meaningful concepts must ultimately refer to intuitive representations.

Schopenhauer's statement of the principle of sufficient reason of becoming, that is, of the law of causality, emphasized that causation is a relationship between alterations or states of real objects and not between

---

[102] See ibid., pp. 118–19/ibid., Vol. 1, pp. 117–18. I discuss Schopenhauer's view of his relationship to Locke, via a mediation by Kant, in "Locke as Schopenhauer's (Kantian) Philosophical Ancestor," *Schopenhauer-Jahrbuch*, Vol. 84 (2003), pp. 147–56. In "Induktion oder Expression? Zu Schopenhauers Metaphilosophie," *Schopenhauer-Jahrbuch*, Vol. 69 (1988), pp. 7–40, Dieter Birnbacher considers whether Schopenhauer's metaphilosophy was inductive or expressive in nature. In his magisterial *Arthur Schopenhauer: Transzendentalphilosophie und Metaphysik des Willens*, Rudolf Malter provides a sustained interpretation of Schopenhauer as a transcendental philosopher.

[103] For a thoughtful contrast between Schopenhauer's and Kant's methodologies, see Paul Guyer's "Schopenhauer, Kant, and the Methods of Philosophy," in *The Cambridge Companion to Schopenhauer*, pp. 93–137.

[104] *The World as Will and Representation*, Vol. 2, p. 272/*Sämtliche Werke*, Vol. 3, p. 307.

real objects: "If a new state of one or several real objects appears, another state must have preceded it upon which the new state follows regularly, in other words, as often as the first state exists. Such a following is called *resulting*; the first state is called the *cause*, the second the *effect*."[105] He provided an example. If an object ignites, this ignition must have been preceded by a particular state in which oxygen, fuel, and heat existed, and as soon as that state occurred, the ignition had to follow immediately. This state could not have always existed, he claimed, but only at the moment of ignition. This state is an alteration, and the law of causality is related only to alterations. Thus, when every effect appears, it is an alteration, and because this alteration had not appeared earlier, he deduced that there had to be an even earlier one that preceded that alteration. Because this was true of any alteration, he came to hold that there is a chain of causality without a beginning; that is, for any effect there is a cause, and that cause is the effect of an earlier cause, *ad infinitum*.[106] And as the principle of sufficient reason is the basis of all necessity, he referred to the law of causality as governing "physical necessity."

Reason and Knowing

During his analysis of causality, Schopenhauer alerted his readers that he would propose a new explanation of the faculty of reason – one that would be much different from Kant's. In the *Critique of Pure Reason*, Kant had distinguished between understanding and reason as aspects of human cognitive capacities. Although Schopenhauer gingerly agreed with the Kantian view of understanding as the source of nonempirical or *a priori* concepts whose application to sensory percepts provided empirical knowledge, he firmly accepted Kant's insistence that their only legitimate use was within the bounds of the possibility of experience. Reason, for Kant,

---

[105] *On the Fourfold Root of the Principle of Sufficient Reason*, p. 53/*Sämtliche Werke*, Vol. 1, p. 34. In the first edition, Schopenhauer wrote that a new state or alteration of a real object "follows from a rule" (*Sämtliche Werke*, Vol. 7, p. 29). With his abandonment of Kant's view, he struck this phrase from the second edition.

[106] On this basis, Schopenhauer rejected first-cause forms of the cosmological argument for the existence of God. He quipped derisively that anyone who employed the law of causality to prove that there must be a first cause, God, treated the law of causality as if it were simply a cab that could be dismissed after reaching one's destination; see ibid., p. 58/ibid., Vol. 1, p. 38. These sorts of remarks, like his vitriolic remarks about his contemporaries, stem from the second edition of Schopenhauer's dissertation.

was a philosophically hypocritical faculty. It was this that gave rise to the speculative metaphysics found in rationalists such as Descartes, Spinoza, Leibniz, and Wolff, who claimed *a priori* and substantive knowledge of the world, the soul, and God. Kant had diagnosed that the problem with these metaphysicians was their employment of the concepts of the understanding beyond the bounds of possible experiences. The result simply yielded empty illusions. Yet Kant was sympathetic to the project of these earlier philosophers, even if he could not accept their results. The questions that preoccupied these metaphysicians were inevitable. Reason always sought the ultimate, the absolutely unconditioned, and a totalizing explanation that finally satisfied intellectual curiosity. And if Kant recognized the abuse of reason, he also recognized its legitimate regulative employment in the natural sciences and ethics. The idea of a simple soul could aid our search for a unified psychology, and the idea of God as the author of the universe could help stimulate our search for order in the world. The "postulates of practical reason," God, the freedom of the human will, and the immortality of the soul, followed from morality, even though these postulates could only be thought and could never be known.

Schopenhauer presented his "new" explanation of reason within his analysis of the second class of objects, representations of representations, or concepts. And as he had done during his reflections on the philosophy of the better consciousness, he rejected Kant's ideas of both theoretical and practical reason. Yet he did so in reserved terms and in a nonpolemical manner. The function of reason, he held, is to abstract concepts from intuitive representations, to combine concepts into judgments, and to draw inferences. Although he was willing to attribute the faculty of understanding to nonhuman animals – after all, they too perceived a spatio-temporal world with objects standing in causal relationships – he agreed with Kant that only humans possess reason. But Schopenhauer's calm discussion of the faculty of reason was exploded in the 1847 edition by the inclusion of a new section, "Reason," which tripled the length of the original chapter. Instead of augmenting his original view with fresh insights or teasing out new inferences from elements of his initial discussion, he used it to vent his frustrations about being ignored by the philosophical public for more than thirty years. He lashed out at his contemporaries. Jacobi, Fichte, Schleiermacher, Schelling, and Herbart were all freely abused, and Hegel was abused more than all others. He condemned these men for fighting a rearguard action to reinstate the pretenses of speculative metaphysics, which were crushed by Kant. Moreover, they were keen to protect religion, he charged, for self-serving reasons. These pseudo-philosophers needed family-supporting careers, and the state would only employ professors who would recognize God almighty in some sort of form.

Schopenhauer, however, did not let Kant go unscathed in this new section on reason. He blamed Kant for inspiring the wild flights into the supersensible found in the ersatz philosophies of his contemporaries. Unmindful of how he was undermining the originality of his own "new" view of reason, Schopenhauer claimed that prior to Kant, all philosophers had recognized reason as that uniquely human ability to formulate concepts, make judgments, think discursively, use language, reflect on the past, and plan for the future. Even Kant had recognized reason as the faculty of inferences and principles, but "it is undeniable that he was responsible for the subsequent misinterpretations."[107] To make his point, he then referred his readers to discussions of this point in his other books. Schopenhauer was even more blunt in these analogous discussions. In the first edition of *The World of Will and Representation*, he wrote that Kant had confused and falsified the nature of reason, and whoever would take the trouble to read the "mass" of philosophical writings after him would discover that "just as the mistakes of princes are expiated by whole nations, so do the errors of great minds extend their unwholesome influence over whole generations, centuries even, growing and propagating, and finally degrading into monstrosities."[108] It was like a curse, Schopenhauer wrote, that this sad "rule of bipeds" were attracted to the very worst mistakes of great minds while ignoring what is truly admirable. Nietzsche would later make this observation about Schopenhauer's followers.[109]

Schopenhauer charged that Kant had unwittingly provided the means for subsequent philosophers to transform reason into a mysterious faculty. By setting practical reason as the means for justifying metaphysical beliefs

---

[107] Ibid., p. 164/ibid., Vol. 1, p. 110f.

[108] *The World as Will and Representation*, Vol. 1, p. 38/*Sämtliche Werke*, Vol. 2, p. 45.

[109] See *On the Fourfold Root of the Principle of Sufficient Reason*, p. 176f./*Sämtliche Werke*, Vol. 1, p. 120. Nietzsche praised Schopenhauer's "immortal doctrines of the intellectual nature of intuition, of the *a priori* nature of the causal laws, of the instrumental character of the intellect, and the non-freedom of the will," but he also claimed, in the same passage, that Schopenhauer's followers clung to Schopenhauerian vices and excesses; see *The Gay Science*, Sect. 99.

about freedom, the soul, and God, he emboldened others to transform theoretical reason into the source of knowledge of such things, even though Kant himself had denied it such extraordinary powers. If practical reason could justify such beliefs, if it could become the source of moral laws *a priori*, it was a small step to view theoretical reason as having the capacity to grasp the object for which Kant said it longed, the unconditional. This, he argued, "led crazy philosophers headed by Jacobi to that *reason* which directly *comprehends* the '*supersensible*' and to that absurd statement that reason is a faculty intended essentially for things beyond all experience and so for *metaphysics*, and to the assertion that it recognizes directly and intuitively the ultimate grounds of all things and all existence, the supersensible, the absolute, the divine, and so on."[110] In the second edition of his dissertation, he then traced, from Jacobi's perversion of Kant, the audacious development of Fichte's, Schelling's, and Hegel's philosophies: "And German so-called philosophy has for the last fifty years been based on such a wholly false and fabricated faculty: first as the free construction and projection of the absolute *I* and its emanations into the *Not-I* [Fichte]; then as the intellectual intuition of the absolute identity or indifference, and of its evolutions into nature [early Schelling]; or again as the origin of God from his own dark ground or groundlessness *à la* Jacobi and Boehme [a later Schelling]; finally as the pure self-thinking of the Absolute Idea, the ballet scene of self-moving concepts [Hegel]."[111]

Although the older philosopher could not curb his rage toward his contemporaries and, by blaming the sage of Königsberg for those abusing his thought, this spilled over into an oddly ambivalent treatment of Kant, his treatment of the principle of sufficient reason of knowing remained the same as in the original edition. Reason combined concepts into judgments, and no judgment was intrinsically true; its truth was based on something else. And so he stated this form of the principle of sufficient reason: "If a judgment is to express knowledge, it must have a sufficient ground; because of this quality, it then receives the predicate *true*. Truth is

---

[110] *On the Basis of Morality*, p. 84/*Sämtliche Werke*, Vol. 4, p. 150.

[111] *On the Fourfold Root of the Principle of Sufficient Reason*, p. 181/*Sämtliche Werke*, Vol. 1, p. 123. The two references to Schelling are to a couple of shifts in his philosophy. The first reference, about the "intellectual intuition of the absolute identity and evolution into nature," refers to his *Naturphilosophie*, and the remark about "the dark ground or groundlessness" refers to his *Bruno, or On the Divine and the Natural Principle of Things* [*Bruno oder über das göttliche und natürliche Princip der Dinge*, Berlin: Johann Friedrich Unger, 1802].

therefore the reference of a judgment to something different from it."[112] He then recognized four ways by which a judgment was grounded in something other than itself, and, thus, four kinds of truths: logical, empirical, transcendental, and metalogical.[113] Just as he held that the principle of sufficient reason of becoming articulated physical necessity, which is primarily the inevitability of an effect from a cause, this form of the principle of sufficient reason dealt with "logical necessity," the necessity of a true proposition following from a ground.

Schopenhauer's account of the four types of truths was brief and somewhat perfunctory, tending to be driven by neatly drawn systematic considerations. A judgment or proposition is logically or formally true if it is based simply on conceptual relations with another proposition. Thus the proposition "No P is S" is logically true because it immediately follows from converting the proposition "No S is P." Such a proposition, however, can also be materially true if it is inferred from a proposition with material content – for example, the proposition "No animals are insects." Quite naturally, in his analysis of logical truth, Schopenhauer privileged classical Aristotelian categorical logic, "the whole science of syllogisms," as stating the sum total of rules for applying the principle of sufficient reason to judgments, as formulating the "canon of *logical truth*." Consequently, Schopenhauer recognized that arguing, concluding, and inferring were the proper functions of the faculty of reason and that failure to reason in a way consistent with the rules of syllogistic reasoning

---

[112] Ibid., p. 156/ibid., Vol. 1, p. 105. Curiously, in the first edition Schopenhauer did not state this form of the principle of sufficient reason in the section (31) "Principle of Sufficient Reason of Knowledge," but instead included it in one (30) entitled "Truth," and only in terms of the truth of a proposition and not in terms of expressing knowledge: "A judgment is true, means that it has a sufficient ground. This must be something different from the judgment, to which it is referred. Thus truth is the relation of a judgment to something outside it," ibid., Vol. 7, p. 52.

[113] Originally, Schopenhauer called "transcendental truth" "metaphysical truth." There was, however, no change concerning his analysis of this type of truth. It appears that in 1813 Schopenhauer avoided the word "transcendental," concerning his own views, and this perhaps was in an attempt not to be too closely associated with Kant. In 1847, however, he prided himself for being a Kantian. This may be why he renamed this type of truth and why he changed the title of Sect. 19 in the original from "Outline of an Analysis of Experience: The Understanding" to "Outline of a Transcendental Analysis of Empirical Reality" (Sect. 18 in the second edition); see ibid., Vol. 7, pp. 57, 21/ *On the Fourfold Root of the Principle of Sufficient Reason*, pp. 160, 46.

demonstrates a defect in one's reason, a point he drove home later within a lengthy rant against Hegel.[114]

Schopenhauer's account of empirical truth contained no examples of empirically true propositions. It is likely that he thought no examples were necessary. A proposition, he claimed, is empirically true if it is "brought about by means of the senses, and consequently experience." Because an empirically true proposition is not true by virtue of conceptual relations, it is materially true.[115] The proposition, "The poodle is on the sofa," Schopenhauer might have said, is true only if, in fact, there is a poodle on the sofa. Transcendentally true propositions, conversely, were those propositions that were grounded on the *a priori* forms of intuition – that is, those founded in the faculty of the understanding or pure sensibility. For example, the judgment "two straight lines do not enclose a space" is grounded in the *a priori* form of space; "$3 \times 7 = 21$" is grounded in the *a priori* form of time; "nothing happens without a cause" is based on the *a priori* form of causality.[116] Last, a proposition was metalogically true if it was grounded on the "laws of thought," that is, on the law of identity, the law of contradiction, the law of the excluded middle, or the principle of sufficient reason of knowing itself. These laws were discovered "by making vain attempts to think in opposition to these laws, the faculty of reason recognizes them as the conditions of the possibility of all thought."[117] For

---

[114] In a lengthy rant against Hegel, Schopenhauer cast one of Hegel's arguments into a categorical syllogism: "All things that become heavier on one side dip on that side; this magnetized bar dips on one side; therefore, it has become heavier on that side." Schopenhauer pointed out that this is equivalent to arguing that "All geese have two legs; you have two legs; therefore, you are a goose." One's common sense and inborn logic, he continued, render reasoning of this nature impossible, and the absence of this logic is described as the lack of intelligence. Hegel's argument, he claimed, violated the rule that "from two premises in the affirmative, no conclusion in the second figure can be drawn"; see *On the Basis of Morality*, p. 17/*Sämtliche Werke*, Vol. 4, p. xxi.

[115] *On the Fourfold Root of the Principle of Sufficient Reason*, p. 159/*Sämtliche Werke*, Vol. 1, p. 107. In the dissertation of 1813, Schopenhauer used the section on empirical truth to discuss Kant's derivation of the categories of the understanding from the table of judgments and to develop some criticisms of Kant's conception of practical reason and the idea that moral behavior is rational; see *Sämtliche Werke*, Vol. 7, pp. 55–6.

[116] Ibid., p. 160/ibid., Vol. 1, p. 108. Schopenhauer would classify three of the four forms of the principle of sufficient reason as transcendental truths: those of becoming, of being, and of acting. The principle of sufficient reason of knowing was said to be a metalogical truth; see ibid., p. 162/ibid., Vol. 1, p. 109.

[117] Ibid., p. 162/ibid., Vol. 1, p. 109.

example, the proposition "matter is permanent" is a metalogical truth, Schopenhauer claimed, because we cannot think of matter as "arising or passing away."[118]

Being

The analysis of the third class of objects, pure or nonempirical intuitions of space and time, and the form of the principle of sufficient reason governing these objects underwent the least amount of change in the second edition. Whereas Schopenhauer erased remnants of Kant's categories of the understanding in his treatment of the principle of sufficient reason of becoming and greatly expanded his chapter on the principle of sufficient reason of knowing by including a lengthy section on reason, his account of the principle of sufficient reason of being remained relatively the same between editions. Other than substituting "transcendental" for "metaphysical" in this chapter, a systematic change throughout the second edition, he remained faithful to his original commitment to Kant's intuitionalist philosophy of mathematics by relating mathematical concepts to the pure forms of sensibility, that is, to space and time.[119] Specifically, he held that space and time could be objects of nonempirical intuitions that enable us to know their nature better than considerations provided by either the understanding or reason. Kant, he argued, also held his thesis that the relations of position in space and succession in time are only made intelligible by means of intuition "by saying that the difference between right and left gloves cannot possibly be made intelligible except by means of intuition."[120]

As Schopenhauer had already argued in his earlier analysis of the principle of sufficient reason of becoming, space and time are the *a priori* forms of sensibility. As such, space and time are transcendentally ideal, because they are subjectively imposed frameworks in which we perceive the world. Yet space and time are empirically real, because we intuit

---

[118] Ibid., p. 162/ibid., Vol. 1, p. 109.

[119] See ibid., p. 197/ibid., Vol. 1, p. 133 for his use of "transcendental." Originally he used "metaphysical," ibid., Vol. 7, p. 61.

[120] Schopenhauer did not use the example of the right and left gloves in the original edition of his dissertation. He only cited Kant in the second edition, when he no longer feared being identified with Kant, but desired it instead; see ibid., Vol. 7, p. 60 and *On the Fourfold Root of the Principle of Sufficient Reason*, p. 194/*Sämtliche Werke*, Vol. 1, p. 131.

them as if they were objective structures of experience, existing as it were, independent of our consciousness.[121] Unlike our intuitions of real objects, our experience of spatio-temporal particulars such as tables and chairs, which as intuitive representations are perceived *a posteriori*, Schopenhauer held that intuitions of space and time are pure or nonempirical. Like both Kant and Newton, he held that space and time are particular, and like Kant, he held that space and time are constituted in such a way that every point determines and is determined by every other point. This relationship, he claimed, is called "position" in space and "succession" in time. The principle of sufficient reason of being states, therefore, that "parts of space and time determine one another. . . ."[122]

Following the lead of Kant, Schopenhauer held that arithmetic is associated with the experience of sequential order in time, as when we count a series of numbers in sequence. Each number presupposes the preceding numbers as the ground of its being. Employing Kant's infamous example of "$7 + 5 = 12$," Schopenhauer rejected Herder's view that it is an identity statement. Rather, an identity statement would be "$12 = 12$."[123] It is a synthetic *a priori* judgment, as Kant maintained, because it is nonempirical, necessarily true, and informative: the concepts of seven and five do not contain, as it were, the concept of twelve, like an analytical statement, "All bodies are extended," where the concept "body" contains that of "extension," and which says no more than "All bodies are bodies." Geometry, unlike arithmetic, deals with the nonempirical intuition of space, he argued, and as such, every part of space determines and is determined by every other part. Thus the proposition that "a triangle with two equal angles has equal subtending sides" is something that can be grasped by intuition. Euclid's demonstration of the same, Schopenhauer maintained, simply provides the grounds for the truth of a judgment and fails to provide deep insight into spatial relationships and "the feeling is similar to that which we have when something has been conjured into or out of

---

[121] Schopenhauer borrowed the idea of something being transcendentally ideal and empirically real from Kant. He did not use this idea in the 1813 edition of his dissertation, but added it in 1847; see *On the Fourfold Root of the Principle of Sufficient Reason*, p. 45/*Sämtliche Werke*, Vol. 1, p. 28.

[122] Ibid., p. 194/ibid., Vol. 1, p. 131.

[123] For Kant's account of "$5 + 7 = 12$" as a synthetic *a priori* proposition and his distinction between analytic and synthetic proposition, see, respectively, *Critique of Pure Reason* B15–16 and A7/B11–A13/B26.

our pocket, and we cannot conceive how this may be done."[124] Euclidean geometry, like all products of reason, was less capable than intuition for apprehending the world.

Acting

As an object of the inner sense, the subject of willing was cognized only in time. After reiterating his hallmark claim that the subject of cognition was never an object of cognition, Schopenhauer claimed that the subjects of cognition and willing were identical. This insight, he held, is not gleaned via a Schellingian intellectual intuition. One could arrive at Schelling's standpoint, Schopenhauer argued, simply by analyzing the logic of the terms "subject" and "object," each of which implied its correlate just as the term "father" entailed the term "child" and "child," "father." The identity of the subjects of cognition and willing was, instead, "immediately given," an identity denoted by the word "I." This identity is inexplicable, eluding all forms of the principle of sufficient reason, whose scope of application was confined to objects of cognition. "Whoever really grasps the inexplicable nature of this identity," Schopenhauer wrote, "will with me call it the miracle *kat' exochen* [par excellence]."[125] A short five years later, he would claim that *The World as Will and Representation* was "to a certain extent . . . an explanation of this [miracle]."[126]

Schopenhauer would also recognize another "miracle *par excellence*" in the first edition of his principal work that he did not articulate in his dissertation. The statement of this "miracle" moved the philosopher to acknowledge a new variety of truth that extended his classification of truths into logical, empirical, transcendental, and metalogical varieties. This new truth, that his body and will were identical, he dubbed the *"philosophical truth kat' exochen."*[127] In 1813, however, he was not prepared to acknowledge this truth, just as he was unwilling to give any credence

---

[124] *On the Fourfold Root of the Principle of Sufficient Reason*, p. 200/*Sämtliche Werke*, Vol. 1, p. 135.

[125] Ibid., Vol. 7, p. 73/*On the Fourfold Root of the Principle of Sufficient Reason*, p. 211f. Schopenhauer dropped the reference to Schelling in the 1847 edition and called the identity of the subjects of cognition and will, denoted by the word "I," the "knot of the world."

[126] *The World as Will and Representation*, Vol. 1, p. 102/*Sämtliche Werke*, Vol. 2, p. 121. This remark stems from the first edition of the work.

[127] Ibid., Vol. 1, p. 102/ibid., Vol. 2, p. 121.

to Kant's notion of the thing in itself. This truth would lead him to argue against the traditional thesis that volitions were prior to and causally produced bodily movements. Willing and acting were one and the same, he held, and we only distinguish between the two in reflection: "Every true, genuine, immediate act of will is also at once and directly a movement of the body; one cannot actually will the act without at the same time being aware that it appears as a movement of the body. The act of will and the action of the body are not two different states objectively known, connected by the bond of causality. . . . "[128]

The identity of willing and acting is not something Schopenhauer was willing to recognize in his dissertation. Indeed, it was just the opposite in his original view: "Acting is not willing, but the effect of will as cause."[129] Desires too were not instances of willing for the aspiring doctor of philosophy, that is, unless they caused an action. The cause for an action was a decision, something imparting causality to a particular desire. To explain an action, he provided the following account. If a person P performed action A, then P had a motive M to do A, a desire to do A, which was prompted by decision D to do A. It is thus the decision that made the desire causally effective and a matter of willing. The decision itself becomes a manifestation of P's character in this early theory of action. To provide more content to this account, Schopenhauer evoked Kant's distinction between a person's empirical and intelligible characters, a distinction that he deemed "an incomparable, highly admirable masterpiece of human thoughtfulness."[130] The empirical character is the

---

[128] *Sämtliche Werke*, Vol. 7, p. 73.

[129] Ibid., Vol. 7, p. 73.

[130] Ibid., Vol. 7, p. 77. The dissertator Schopenhauer continued to praise Schelling, in this same passage, for providing an illuminating account of Kant's distinction between the intelligible and empirical character and the relationship between freedom and nature. This compliment seems somewhat disingenuous, because his marginal notes on this very passage from the first volume of Schelling's *Philosophical Writings* (*Philosophische Schriften*, 1809) are bluntly critical. In this passage, Schelling did not refer to Kant, but instead referred to "Idealism." Schopenhauer wrote in the margin, "Kant, you unseemly scoundrel," *Der handschriftliche Nachlaß*, Vol. 5, p. 147. Later, he would suggest that Schelling had tried to pass off Kant's views as his own: "I should commend this work if Schelling had had the honesty to say that he was stating Kant's wisdom and not his own," *On the Basis of Morality*, p. 111/*Sämtliche Werke*, Vol. 4, p. 176. Matthias Koßler and Lore Hühn suggest that Schopenhauer's reception of Kant's distinction between the intelligible and empirical characters was prepared through a mediation by Schelling and Fries; see, respectively, "Empirischer und intelligibler Charackter: Von Kant über Fries und Schelling zu Schopenhauer," *Schopenhauer-Jahrbuch*

general manner of each person's behavior, and it is discovered by reflecting on a person's sum total of actions. It pointed to, he continued, a unity and inalterability of a person's conduct, which suggested that it was the appearance of "something completely unknowable, lying outside of time; to something as if it were a permanent state of the subject of willing."[131] But after making this remark, Schopenhauer was quick to point out that because "state" and "permanent" have application only within the temporal framework, technically there is no means of speaking about anything outside of time. For this reason, he also wrote in a parenthetical remark that Kant's intelligible character "might more properly be called "unintelligible."[132] Nevertheless, he calls it figuratively "a universal act of will outside of time," and as providing the basis for the "liveliest conviction" that our will is not determined by anything else and that our essence is "supremely free in its nature."[133]

Although Schopenhauer would regard Kant's distinction between the empirical and intelligible characters just as significantly and as profoundly as his distinction between appearances and things in themselves, he dropped the section on "Motive, Decision, Empirical and Intelligible Characters" from the second edition of The Fourfold Root, and he carefully removed any passages that cut against his claim that willing and acting were identical. He did the same with his earlier claims that the will caused actions. He changed the title of his earlier section "Causal Influence of the Will on Cognition" to "Influence of the Will on Cognition," in which he claimed that "The influence which the will exercises on knowledge is not based on causality proper, but on identity . . . of the knowing with the willing subject."[134] Whereas in the first edition, he had said that willing itself is given immediately to our inner sense and is impossible to define or describe, in the second he noted that "this immediacy must ultimately throw light on other branches of knowledge which are very

---

Vol. 76 (1995), pp. 195–201; and "Die intelligible Tat, zu einer Gemeinsamkeit Schellings und Schopenhauer," in Selbstbesinnung der philosophischen Moderne, eds. C. Iber and R. Pocai (Dartford: T. Junghans Verlag, 1998), pp. 55–94.

[131] Sämtliche Werke, Vol. 7, p. 76.
[132] Ibid., Vol. 7, p. 76.
[133] Ibid.
[134] On the Fourfold Root of the Principle of Sufficient Reason, p. 214f./Sämtliche Werke, Vol. 1, p. 145.

mediate."[135] By 1847, however, he had long known that this immediate awareness was the key for his viewing the will as the essence of all appearances.

Quite naturally, the older philosopher also revised the theory of action presented by the younger man. To articulate his mature view, he directed his readers to his prize essay, published in 1841, "On the Freedom of the Human Will," where he had directly integrated motives into a general account of the types of causality expressed within the world as appearance. Everything in the world, he argued, follows from a sufficient ground, and among different types of beings, different causal relations prevail. Among lifeless or inorganic beings, the specific causal relationship is between a physical, mechanical, or chemical cause and some effect. Among living beings, in plants stimuli, such as water, heat, and light, lead to a response such as growth, and in animals, both human and nonhuman, the causal relation is motivation, which leads to a willed action, causality functioning through cognition. In any alteration, moreover, there are two necessary factors. There is some original and inherent force attributed to the being upon which some causal influence is exercised, and there is some cause that occasions the manifestation of the force.[136] These forces, he also argued, are outside the scope of the principle of sufficient reason, underlying, as it were, all causal relationships, but not subject to it. Gravity, electricity, and magnetism were the types of forces prevailing in nonliving beings and the types of causes he called "causes in the narrowest sense." Vital force was that which was expressed in plant life, and stimulus was the type of cause prevailing therein. Last, character was the force in animal life, and the types of causes operating therein were motives. Consequently, an action became the manifestation of an animal's character in reaction to a motive.[137] All forces, including the human character, represent the

---

[135] Ibid., p. 212/ibid., Vol. 1, p. 144.

[136] In the second edition of *On the Fourfold Root of the Principle of Sufficient Reason*, pp. 70–1/*Sämtliche Werke*, Vol. 1, pp. 46–8, Schopenhauer included his classification of causal relationships into "cause in its narrowest sense," "stimulus," and "motivation," which he originally detailed in his *Prize Essay on the Freedom of the Will*, pp. 25–9/*Sämtliche Werke*, Vol. 4, pp. 29–33.

[137] In *Schopenhauer: The Human Character* (Philadelphia: Temple University Press, 1990), pp. 58–66, John E. Atwell claims that Schopenhauer employed at least three different theories of the relationship between human agents and their actions. He identifies as the dominant theory, "agent causation," the view that a person's character, given a motive, is the

endpoints of explanation: "Now just as this is the case with causes in the narrowest sense and with stimuli, so too is it equally the case with *motives*; for in essence, motivation is not different from causality, but is only a form of it, namely causality that passes through the medium of cognition. Therefore here too the cause calls forth only the manifestation of a force that cannot be reduced and consequently cannot be explained any further."[138]

Despite the significant alterations found in his second account of the fourth form of the principle of sufficient reason, where he altered his original epistemological work to accommodate his subsequent metaphysics, including his claim that *"motivation is causality seen from within,"* which he called "the cornerstone of my whole metaphysics," Schopenhauer used the same argument for the *a priori* nature of the principle of sufficient reason of acting, the so-called "law of motivation."[139] With each and every decision that we observe in ourselves or others, he argued, we are always justified in asking why. It is appropriate to do this, because we necessarily assume that there is some ground, that is, a motive, from which it ensued.

Conclusions

Schopenhauer concluded his dissertation with a statement of its two main results, ending with an appeal to both of the laws of homogeneity and specification, the beginning points of his reflection. He also referred once more to Plato and Kant, but now the earlier "divine Plato" found in the first section became "the sublime Plato," and the earlier "marvelous Kant" became the guilty Kant, in the second edition of his dissertation, the progenitor of the wild flights of the post-Kantians, none of whom are mentioned by name in the passage in which he leveled this charge.[140] The first

---

ground for the resulting action. Atwell calls the other two accounts "agent-reductionism" and the "imputability thesis," which are, respectively, that an agent's character is the sum total of the agent's actions, and that some actions may not truly reflect an agent's character due to a faulty intellect.

[138] Prize Essay on the Freedom of the Will, p. 41/Sämtliche Werke, Vol. 4, p. 47.

[139] *On the Fourfold Root of the Principle of Sufficient Reason*, p. 214/*Sämtliche Werke*, Vol. 1, p. 145. It is curious to note that Schopenhauer retained in the second edition the language concerning decision that is found in the first edition, even though his later account of the principle of sufficient reason of acting no longer viewed a decision as central to his theory of action.

[140] Ibid., p. 232/ibid., Vol. 7, p. 92.

result, Schopenhauer wrote, was that the principle of sufficient reason was a general expression for four different relationships, each of which rests on different *a priori* principles. The law of homogeneity, he continued, requires the assumption that these four principles, discovered through the law of specification, have a common root and a single common expression; namely, that nothing is without a ground or reason for why it is rather than it is not. This common expression, moreover, signified the unity of the cognitive faculty. The second result, he argued, is closely related to the first. The four specific forms of the principle of sufficient reason, which arise from a single characteristic of consciousness, expressed in faculties of sensibility, understanding, and reason, do not license speaking of a reason *per se*, as something pure and simple.

This first result entails, Schopenhauer continued, that when philosophers base some claim on the principle of sufficient reason, they should specify the type of ground they mean. Not to do so only leads to confusion. Even Kant was not immune to such confusion, and he ignored his own profound insight that "the contingency of things is *itself only phenomenal* and can lead to no other than the empirical regressus that determines phenomena," by referring to the thing in itself variously, as the "ground," "reason," and "intelligible cause" of phenomena."[141] Anyone familiar with more recent philosophy knows, Schopenhauer added, that philosophers after Kant have followed him in these excesses, employing the concepts of the ground and consequent, *principia* and *principata*, in a fully transcendent sense, speaking about something that is beyond the bounds of all possible experience. The principle of sufficient reason only applies within the world, within the whole of all possible experience, and to the world, which Plato recognized as that which is forever coming to be and perishing and never really existing at all and to which Christianity appropriately referred to as the temporal.

Schopenhauer tied the second with the first result. From showing that the four forms of the principle of sufficient reason stem from our cognitive capacity and can be summarized as a single principle, it does not follow that this principle refers to some simple, single, absolute ground. To think that this follows would be like thinking that there is something like a triangle in general, something over and above equilateral, isosceles, or scalene triangles. Although one can formulate the concept of a ground

[141] Ibid., p. 234/ibid., Vol. 7, p. 93.

in general, just as one conceptualizes a triangle in general, there are no possible objects denoted by these concepts, which are simply empty abstractions produced by discursive thought. To think otherwise is to be a realist, falsely believing that concepts denote objects. In this matter, Schopenhauer declared allegiance with the nominalist: these concepts have no objective reference and exist only as names.

Weimar

Rudolstadt lost its charm for the young Dr. Schopenhauer shortly after he had completed his dissertation. Between 16 and 18 October, a coalition of Prussian, Russian, and Austrian forces engaged Napoleon's army. The bloody battle of Leipzig left more than 100,000 dead and injured; Napoleon's army was defeated. Dissipated soldiers began to filter into the vicinity of Rudolstadt, providing Schopenhauer with a sufficient reason to distance himself from his refuge. Once again he returned to Weimar, and on 5 November he took up residence at an inn. According to Johanna, she tearfully begged her son to live with his family. A mother's tears worked their magic, and Schopenhauer took up lodgings with his mother despite the fact that Gerstenbergk continued to reside in the same house as Johanna and Adele. Yet Johanna's motives for her son's return to the family were mixed – part maternal and part defensive in nature. For in the same letter in which she recounted her tearful plea for Schopenhauer's return, she also wrote that "it would be good for you to once again live with your family," adding that by observing her way of life, "you would not entertain false ideas."[142] Johanna did not specify the nature of these "false ideas." She did not have to do so. She knew that Schopenhauer feared that she would remarry and that he harbored this worry despite her many attempts to assure him that she had no desire to shackle herself to a man. Indeed, it is difficult to believe that she would have done so. She valued her independence too greatly to repeat what she had already done.

The son of "the well-known Weimar authoress, Frau Hofrätin Schopenhauer," as Dean Eichstädt described Arthur in his letter that had announced Schopenhauer's dissertation to the philosophy faculty at Jena, found the circumstances surrounding his mother's home no more

---

[142] *Die Schopenhauers*, p. 214, Johanna to Arthur, April 1814.

satisfying than they were prior to his flight to Rudolstadt.[143] Almost immediately upon his arrival, Schopenhauer locked horns with Johanna's friend. Indeed, he also clashed with his mother about Gerstenbergk, and she returned tit for tat. He loathed Gerstenbergk generally as he would have any potential replacement for his father, but he also detested him specifically, classifying him as just another featherless biped, a common product of nature without any special talents that would set him apart from the crowd. Even worse, Gerstenbergk's literary pretensions made him appear pathetic to the young philosopher, who was especially put off by his echoing of popular, nationalistic sentiments, his praise of the bravery of German patriots, and his calling for the invasion of France. These were all worldly distractions, antithetical to any expression of the better consciousness, which Arthur held was the object of a true artist's aspirations. Schopenhauer, moreover, was disinclined to censure his views, and this led to repeated quarrels between the two men.

Adele shared Arthur's dislike of Gerstenbergk's omnipresence in her family life, yet the sixteen-year-old did not share Arthur's suspicion that Johanna was engaged in an intimate, sexual relationship with the younger man. That suspicion would surface many years later.[144] Others, however, shared Arthur's view. Some referred to the couple as "Schoppen-Müller," a moniker that combined a common misspelling of Schopenhauer (Schoppenhauer) with a conscious rejection of the ostentation of Gerstenbergk's adoption of a noble name.[145] Adele's predilection to sympathize with her brother's disdain for her mother's friend was more complex than the grounds of Arthur's contempt for Gerstenbergk. She felt as if she were caught between the warring men, "chained between two boulders that were drawing nearer to one another."[146] But she must have also felt as if

[143] Quoted in Franz Riedinger's "Die Akten über Schopenhauers Doktorpromotion," *Jahrbuch der Schopenhauer-Gesellschaft*, Vol. 11 (1924), p. 98.

[144] Ulrike Bergmann suggests that Adele's later harsh judgment against Gerstenbergk was due, in part, to her coming to view his relationship with Johanna as not being Platonic; see her *Johanna Schopenhauer*, p. 264. There are no smoking guns to be found concerning a sexual relationship between Gerstenbergk and Johanna. Certainly, Johanna would have been sufficiently discrete to hide such a relationship from both her son and daughter, and especially from her daughter.

[145] Otto Fiebiger, "Neues über Friedrich Müller von Gerstenbergk," *Jahrbuch der Schopenhauer-Gesellschaft*, Vol. 12 (1922), p. 68, quoted in Bergmann, *Johanna Schopenhauer*, p. 188.

[146] Quoted in Gabriele Büch's *Alle Leben ist Traum: Adele Schopenhauer, eine Biographie* (Berlin: Aufbau Taschenbuch Verlag, 2002), p. 109.

she were to be torn apart when it came to her situation toward her mother and brother. Her loyalties bound her to both of these individuals, and they were rapidly moving in opposite directions. Adele's sense of being crushed would only last for four months. Unfortunately, her sense of being ripped apart would last for almost twenty-four years, ending only with Johanna's death in 1838.

Gerstenbergk introduced more sorrows into Adele's life than those that simply resulted from his being her brother's nemesis and his precipitating the estrangement between her mother and brother. During the decade he associated with the Schopenhauers, he periodically became the obscure object of Adele's marriage fantasies and her deep longing to be loved passionately by a man. It is likely that Gerstenbergk flirted with Adele, but no more than he did with other young women. Moreover, Gerstenbergk was always around when Adele's other love interests indicated their interests only in being her friend, rather than her husband. In many ways, Adele was a remarkable woman, but in a way that invited friendship and not love. She was intelligent, sensitive, and artistically talented. She knew English, French, and Italian. She sketched, painted, played the piano, and cut filigree silhouettes of great delicacy and grace. She wrote short stories and poems, published her mother's memoirs, wrote several novels, and composed the libretto for Walther von Goethe's opera, *Enzio: or, the Prisoner of Bologna* [*Enzio – Oder: Die Gefangene von Bologna*, 1838].[147] She was also a favorite of Walther's grandfather, whom she referred to as "Father," and Goethe valued highly her acting and reciting skills as well as her judgments regarding literature.

Adele, however, never received a formal education that would have rigorously developed her considerable talents. As a young woman, she was expected to aspire to becoming a wife and mother. Unfortunately, she was not gifted with the physical characteristics that would guarantee success in this quest. She was not a physically attractive woman. She had protruding blue eyes, a broad nose, a thin upper lip, which made her appear toothy, and a large, round head crowned by unruly light-brown hair, all of which rested on a fragile body. In addition to inheriting too many of her

---

[147] Walther Wolfgang von Goethe was Goethe's grandson and the son of August von Goethe and Adele's close friend, Ottilie von Goethe. The libretto was published under the pseudonym Adrian van der Venne, which she had also used in 1835 for her novella, *Die loghringischen Geschwister*.

father's physical characteristics, she also appeared to have shared, albeit to a lesser degree, his inclination toward melancholy and dark moods, which became particularly pronounced, and perhaps sublimated, in her diary. She was the type of woman in whom men, if not repulsed by either her appearance or intellect, found a sympathetic confidante and friend, but never a lover. Her female friends, moreover, were not threatened by her as a rival for a man's affections, and by associating with Adele, by way of contrast, appeared ever more beautiful.

One young woman, whose beauty did not need enhancement by way of contrast with Adele, was Ottilie von Pogwisch, born Freiin von Pogwisch, who would later marry Goethe's son August. She became Adele's lifelong friend and a woman who also introduced many complications into Adele's life. One such complication involved their relationship to one Ferdinand Heinke. Both young women were smitten with the Prussian first lieutenant, who arrived in Weimar in the fall of 1813, on a mission for his commander, Major Anton von Keist, who recently had been named commandant of Weimar. He became a frequent attendee of Johanna's tea parties, after ingratiating himself to Goethe through his earlier acquaintance with the great man's wife Christiane, and his praise for Goethe's *Elective Affinities* (*Wahlverwandtschaften*), which was roundly condemned as immoral. Even more importantly, Heinke spared Goethe the inconvenience of having to billet some Cossacks. Adele introduced Heinke to Ottilie and, as could have been predicted, he was attracted to Ottilie. Ten years after the fact, Adele would still long for Heinke: "I now think of Ferdinand as my destiny, as my hope of the beyond, as I do of God, without wish, without remorse, without tears. That was the call of my fate, I listened to it, and now it is over."[148] In 1815, Heinke returned home to Breslau and married his waiting fiancée, who would bear seven of his children. He named his second daughter Ottilie.

Then there was the case of the British captain, Charles Sterling, who unintentionally aroused Adele's desires, and intentionally those of the already married Ottilie. Adele was dumbfounded that Ottilie could love someone so ardently for a second time in the way that she had loved Heinke, and she imagined that such an overflowing love could perhaps

---

[148] Adele Schopenhauer, *Tagebuch einer Einsamen*, ed. Heinrich Hubert Houben (Munich: Matthes and Seitz, 1985), p. 49, quoted in Safransky, *Schopenhauer and the Wild Years of Philosophy*, p. 175.

seize Heinke as she wrote in her diary, "perhaps, then Ferdinand could love me; probably my ardent reciprocation of this feeling would duly sicken Charlotte [Heinke's wife], and I would be his."[149] But no magical feeling of love moved Heinke to make Adele his and no man was ever seized by a deep passion for making her his wife. The wife of Adele's beloved did not become sick.

Even if Heinke was a distant object of Adele's affections and simply a young girl's unrealizable dream, there would be other men whom Adele thought she might marry. Gottfried Wilhelm Osann, later a professor of chemistry at Dorput and Würzburg, and the brother of Arthur's friend, Friedrich Gotthilf Osann, occupied Adele's thoughts for approximately five years. Yet Osann's mother and older brother Emil were against a union with Adele, and it is doubtful that Osann had seriously contemplated marriage to her. He was content with friendship. In 1827, he would marry a pretty young servant girl, conclusively dashing Adele's marriage dreams. It is probably in reference to Osann that she wrote to Arthur in 1831, "I know only one person whom I could have married without aversion, a[nd] he is *married*. I am strong enough to bear this solitude, but I would be sincerely grateful to the cholera if it would free me of the entire history without violent suffering."[150]

As Adele's moods moved between joy and despair during her ambiguous relationship to Osann, which she must have known at some level would not come to fruition, she met a medical student, who was seven years her junior. During a trip in 1824 to Wiesbaden, she was introduced to Georg Friedrich Ludwig Stromeyer. "Louis," as he was called, was a friend of her cousin, Johann Eduard Gnuscheke. In March 1825, Stromeyer accompanied Gnuscheke on a visit to Weimar. Osann was at Dorput, neglecting to write to Adele. Stromeyer swept Adele off her feet, writing her love poems, pledging his love, and meeting her in secret. Yet Stromeyer was only seriously interested in his studies and not in marriage. He would later become a well-known surgeon, and in 1831 he would marry the daughter of a Hamburg burgomaster. His relationship was simply a young man's fling, and many years later, when he wrote his memoirs, he hardly recalled Adele. Indeed, he had more to say about Ottilie. He did, however, leave behind a curious description of Adele, and perhaps, a hint

[149] *Tagebuch einer Einsamen*, p. 48.
[150] Lütkehaus, *Die Schopenhauers*, p. 319, Adele to Arthur, 27 October 1831.

at the basis of his short-lived feelings for Schopenhauer's sister: "Fräulein Adele was a person of a special kind. Except for a slim figure and delicate hands, she had nothing that could draw the eye; her physiognomy was just as plain. And still she pleased men by her intelligence, culture, and diffuse knowledge. She spoke more than her mother, her conversation was always stimulating and instructive, without reminding one of a bluestocking. She was the fiancée of a splendid man with whom later I became acquainted as a professor of physics at a south German university."[151]

And if the dramas evoked by Adele's relationships with Heinke, Osann, and Stromeyer were capable of driving her from feelings of joy to those of despair, her ambivalent feelings toward Gerstenbergk ultimately moved her to disdain for the ghost of her mother's friend. Johanna, who dimly sensed her daughter's desire for a loving husband, suggested, as Adele reported in her diary, that she marry Gerstenbergk: "Marrying him would be the cleverest thing."[152] Yet Adele also reported that she told Johanna never to say this to Gerstenbergk and never to repeat this idea to her. Nevertheless, Gerstenbergk was charming and flirtatious, and he must have flirted with Adele. "He toys with me and others," Adele noted, and even though she realized that this was Gerstenbergk's typical practice toward young women, it is likely that Adele was attracted to him.[153] She also seemed to believe that Gerstenbergk would ultimately become sexually attracted to her: "From time to time I feared that the emptiness in Gerstenbergk's heart will after *a couple* of years urge him to a passionate feeling for me. It will *never* be love. I am not vain enough to believe that."[154] Nevertheless, when her mother's friend became engaged to the Countess Amelie Häseler in 1824, it was Johanna who graciously moved into the role of a matronly friend to the young couple. Adele became ill instead. Finally, when Gerstenbergk left Weimar and the Schopenhauer

---

[151] Quoted in Büch, *Alles Leben ist Traum*, p. 170. Adele's talkativeness was characterized more harshly by the lawyer Anselm Ritter von Feuerbach, who referred to her as a "silly young girl" [*Gänschen*]; see *Gesammelte Briefe*, p. 687. Adele, contrary to Stromeyer's reflection, was not engaged to Osann. His thinking that this was the case may have made the courtship of the older Adele more exciting for the young twenty year-old student.

[152] Adele Schopenhauer, *Tagebücher*, ed. Kurt Wolff (Leipzig: 1909), Vol. 1, p. 92, quoted in Bergmann, *Johanna Schopenhauer*, p. 262.

[153] Adele Schopenhauer, Ibid., Vol. 1, p. 13, quoted in Bergmann, ibid., p. 264.

[154] Wolfgang von Oettingen, "Aus Ottilie von Goethes Nachlaß. Briefe von ihr und an sie," in *Schriften der Goethe Gesellschaft*, Vol. 28 (1913), p. 282, quoted in Bergmann, *Johanna Schopenhauer*, p. 267.

household, Adele found his absence liberating: "But I was free! Gersten-bergk has left."[155] From that point on, Adele's initial, wavering ambiva-lence toward Gerstenbergk developed into a fixed attitude of repulsion toward her mother's friend, even after he had offered financial aid when Johanna and Adele faced bankruptcy in 1819. But as more years passed, her attitude toward Gerstenbergk became more hostile. She increasingly blamed him for driving a wedge between Johanna and her two children. When Gerstenbergk died in 1838, the same year as her mother, Adele brought a lawsuit against his heirs, seeking to recover money she alleged he had borrowed from her mother. The suit was never settled.[156]

As Adele had still been in the process of beginning to recognize her ambivalent feelings toward Gerstenbergk, Arthur appeared in Weimar in November 1813, hoping for a warm reception of his dissertation. His mood was not enhanced, moreover, when his mother's second book, and the first to bear her name, appeared that winter. Her *Reminiscences of a Journey in the Years 1803, 1804, and 1805* [*Erinnerungen von einer Reise in den Jahren 1803, 1804, und 1805*, 2 vols., 1813/14] was a smashing success.[157] Arthur's teacher in Berlin, a man whose judgment he valued, the philologist Friedrich August Wolf, was enthralled by Johanna's book, as was Johann Gries, the translator of Calderón. It was likely that the success of Johanna's reminiscences of the grand European tour, which included observations drawn from Arthur's travel journal, led to the often repeated, and earlier described, exchange between mother and son, where Johanna derisively described *The Fourfold Root* as something written for pharmacists, and topping her son's retort that his would still be read when scarcely a copy of her writing would be available, by saying that the entire printing of his dissertation would still be in the shops.

This witty but hurtful repartee between mother and son concerning the literary significance of their writings was symptomatic of the deep

---

[155] Adele Schopenhauer, *Tagebuch einer Einsamen*, p. 152, quoted in Bergmann, ibid., p. 267.

[156] See Büch, *Alles Leben ist Traum*, p. 145. Büch also notes that Adele had planned a lawsuit against Gerstenbergk in 1837, but that Ottilie von Goethe talked her out of it.

[157] Johanna's *Reminiscences* appeared through the same publishing house as Arthur's dissertation, the Rudolstadt-based Hof-Buch-und Kunsthandlung, which was owned by the Schopen-hauers' Weimar acquaintance, the entrepreneur Friedrich Johann Bertuch. Curiously, this book, whose two volumes Schopenhauer had bound under a single cover, and Johanna's first book, *Carl Ludwig Fernow's Life*, were the only books of his mother's found in the library Schopenhauer left behind after his death.

tensions running within the household. In January 1814, Arthur invited an impoverished student, Josef Gans, whom Arthur befriended in Berlin, to live with him. Arthur supported Gans, who quite naturally sided with his friend and benefactor during his quarrels with Johanna and Gerstenbergk. Johanna, who sought peace within her household, arranged for Gerstenbergk to take his meals elsewhere. It is likely, moreover, that she also had some success in preventing her friend from reacting violently to the insults of her son. Meanwhile, Gerstenbergk, who befriended Adele's and Ottilie's hero, Heinke, made clear his contempt for Johanna's two lodgers: "I, poor devil, create reports or verses and over me the *philosophus* practices his universal character. He has prescribed for himself a little Jew from Berlin, who is his friend, because he patiently takes his daily dose of the objective laxative, the fourfold root. He hopes that Kleist's corps conquers Paris merely in order to purge the French with it. The Jew's name is Gans, and with this ominous subjective object a veritable Not-I posits itself at the tea-table. . . . "[158]

After four months of heated confrontations, punctuated by periods of icy silence, during which the warring inhabitants of the same household exchanged letters carried by servants, Johanna decided to purge her quarters of her obstinate, moody, and combative son. First, she pleaded economic grounds. She needed income, and she told Arthur that she could rent Gerstenbergk the rooms that were occupied by the *philosophus* and the Not-I. This, of course, did not sit well with Schopenhauer, who all along feared that Gerstenbergk would assume Heinrich Floris' position. Now Johanna wanted to replace him with her friend. Arthur responded somewhat demurely. He offered to pay more for his and Gans' lodging. But he could not completely repress his ill will. He also insinuated that Johanna had spent on herself money he provided to help support his grandmother. It is not clear whether this accusation led to an especially bitter argument between mother and son on May 16, which concluded with a highly agitated Arthur violently slamming the door behind him, as

---

[158] Quoted in Werner Deetjen's "Aus dem Weimarer Schopenhauer-Kreise," in *Jahrbuch der Schopenhauer-Gesellschaft*, Vol. 12 (1925), p. 99. Gerstenbergk's reference to the "fourfold root" as a laxative suggests that he witnessed or heard about Johanna's reference to Schopenhauer's dissertation as a book for pharmacists, and his description of Gans through Fichtean terms as a "Not I" that "posits" itself at the tea-table may also suggest he knew of Schopenhauer's contempt for his old teacher. It is easy to imagine that Schopenhauer would have become enraged by Gerstenbergk's comments.

he stormed out of his mother's room. Johanna took decisive action once more, just as she had after Arthur decided to leave his apprenticeship. The next morning she and Adele fled to Jena, leaving behind a letter, which read, in part:

The door that you slammed so loudly yesterday, after you had conducted yourself extremely improperly toward your mother, closed forever between you and me. I am tired of enduring your behavior any longer. I am going to the country and I will not return home until I know that you are gone. I owe it to my health, since a second scene like that of yesterday would bring on a stroke that might prove fatal. You do not know what a mother's heart is like; the more sincerely it loves, the more painfully it feels every blow from a once beloved hand. Not Müller [Gerstenbergk], this I swear here before God in whom I believe, but you yourself have ripped yourself away from me. Your mistrust, your criticism of my life, my choice of friends, your disdainful conduct toward me, your contempt for my sex, your clearly pronounced reluctance to contribute to my joy, your greed, your moods that you freely vent in my presence without respect for me, this and still much more makes you appear to me thoroughly malicious. This separates us, if not forever, then until your return to me repentant and reformed, only then will I graciously receive you. Remain as you are, I will never see you again. . . . My duty toward you has ended, move on. . . . I write this with profound pain, but it must be so if I am to live and remain healthy. Thus is this the end. I have ordered that you will be served as usual in my house until Thursday morning.[159]

Johanna concluded the letter with the wish that her disowned son should "live and be as happy as you can be." About their flight to Jena, Adele wrote her friend Ottilie, that they did so "in order to flee a person who will still bring endless misery to us."[160] Schopenhauer had managed now to put those close to him at a distance.

---

[159] Lütkehaus, *Die Schopenhauers*, pp. 220–22, Johanna to Arthur, 17 May 1813.
[160] Wolfgang von Oettingen, "Aus Ottilie von Goethes Nachlaß. Briefe von ihr und an sie 1806–1822," p. 71, quoted in Bergmann, *Johanna Schopenhauer*, p. 187.

6

Goethe, Colors, and Eastern Lights

S CHOPENHAUER'S TUMULTUOUS FAMILY life during the six months when he lived in his mother's home in Weimar was counterpoised by two events that would become monumental in the philosopher's life. The first was his breaking into Goethe's orbit, an event for which he had longed and that he had engineered, in part, by sending the poet his dissertation. The second was his introduction to Eastern thought, which was a matter of pure serendipity. In his *curriculum vitae*, Schopenhauer wrote of Goethe's honoring him with his friendship and intimate acquaintance, "which I count as the most delightful and fortunate event in my life."[1] It is curious, however, that he failed to mention the second event in the same document. But thirty-two years later, in another autobiographical reflection, he would mention the second. He encountered the orientalist Friedrich Majer, a friend and disciple of Herder. "At the same time [as his interactions with Goethe], without being asked, Friedrich Majer introduced me to Indian antiquity, which has been an essential influence on me."[2] Whereas Goethe initiated his relationship with the young philosopher at one of Johanna Schopenhauer's parties, exactly when and where in Weimar Majer introduced Schopenhauer to "Indian antiquity" is not clear.

Schopenhauer was awestruck by Goethe. As he suffered through the wretched days of his apprenticeship, he eagerly anticipated Johanna's reports of Goethe's appearances at her parties. During his first visit to Weimar in 1808, he was drawn to these parties simply to quietly observe the great man. Two years later, after he had commenced his study of Kant, he recorded his assessment of the two men who would always remain

---

[1] Schopenhauer, *Gesammelte Briefe*, pp. 53, 654, Schopenhauer to the Philosophy Faculty of the K. Friedrich Wilhelm University at Berlin, 31 December 1819.
[2] Ibid., p. 261, Schopenhauer to Johann Eduard Erdmann, 9 April 1851.

his heroes: "If Goethe had not been sent into the world simultaneously with Kant in order to counterbalance him, so to speak, in the spirit of the age, the latter would have haunted like a nightmare many an aspiring mind and would have oppressed it under great affliction. But now the two have an infinitely wholesome effect from opposite directions and will possibly raise the German spirit to a height surpassing even that of antiquity."[3] Kant's *Critique of Pure Reason*, he reflected in the same note, should be called the suicide of the understanding. Later, he would call Kant the "All-Pulverizer" [*Alleszermalmer*], borrowing from Moses Mendelssohn, because Kant had thoroughly crushed speculative metaphysics, demonstrating that knowledge of God, immortality, and freedom was impossible.[4] Yet Schopenhauer also held that Kant's attempt to "deny *knowledge* in order to make room for *faith*" only succeeded in denying knowledge of anything greater and more profound than the wretched world of appearances.[5] "Kant's regulative use of reason," he wrote, and that which was to provide such faith, "is perhaps the worst miscarriage of the human mind."[6] We would have been in a hopeless situation, Schopenhauer suggested, had not Goethe the artist provided materials that both expressed and invited the better consciousness. Goethe brought forth contemplation.

Goethe, however, paid no attention to the strange young man who attended his mother's parties almost simply as an observer and never as a participant. Goethe's aloofness could have been a function of his character and his sense that there was nothing inviting and interesting about the

---

3   Schopenhauer, *Manuscript Remains*, Vol. 1, p. 13/*Der handschriftliche Nachlaß*, Vol. 1, p. 13. This entry dates to 1810.

4   Moses Mendelssohn referred to the "all-pulverizing Kant" [*alles zermalmenden* Kant] and not the "*Alleszermalmer* Kant," in *Early Morning Hours, or Lectures on the Being of God* [*Morgenstunden, oder Vorlesungen ueber das Dasein Gottes*, 1785]; see *Gesammelte Schriften* (Leipzig:F.A.Brockhaus 1843), Vol.III/2, p. 235. Schopenhauer first cited Mendelssohn's reference to Kant in his reworked "Critique of the Kantian Philosophy" in the second edition of *The World as Will and Representation*, Vol. 1, p. 420/*Sämtliche Werke*, Vol. 2, 497, where he claimed that Mendelssohn was the last sleeper Kant awoke from his dream. Later, he used the term twice: once in reference to Kant's affect on rational psychology, the source for which he found in Plato; and once in his scathing "On Philosophy in the Universities," where, quoting Mendelssohn correctly, he claimed that philosophers such as Herbart, Schleiermacher, and Hegel were glad to see the "'all pulverizing Kant' relegated to oblivion. . . ." See, respectively, *Parerga and Paralipomena*, Vol. 1, pp. 43, 171/*Sämtliche Werke*, Vol. 5, pp. 47, 182.

5   Kant, *Critique of Pure Reason*, Bxxx.

6   Schopenhauer, *Manuscript Remains*, Vol. 1, p. 13/*Der handschriftliche Nachlaß*, Vol. 1, p. 13.

young Schopenhauer. His distance from Schopenhauer might have also been the product of Johanna's descriptions of her moody and combative son. But in November 1813, Schopenhauer received that for which he had longed. As he entered the parlor, Goethe left his seat and greeted him warmly. Shaking his hand, Goethe congratulated Schopenhauer on receiving his doctorate and thanked him for the copy of his dissertation, about which Schopenhauer reported to a friend that Goethe "expressed himself in words of high praise about the essay, which he viewed as highly significant and which had all at once infused in him affection for the young scholar."[7]

But what was it that had really moved Goethe to acknowledge Schopenhauer in such cordial terms, while also including an invitation to visit him the next evening? Although Goethe had long enjoyed celebrity status in Europe, by 1813 he was beginning to live on the credit of his past accomplishments. For some, he was passé and past his prime. For others, his political loyalties were suspicious. He had too much esteem for Napoleon and the French. For still others, his opposition to Romanticism was reactionary. His plays, moreover, were less frequently performed. More personally troubling, however, was the lack of reception of his massive, handsomely produced, two-volume *On the Theory of Colors* [*Zur Farbenlehre*, 1810], which was supplemented by a volume of plates and text, the "Sixteen Tables with Explanation of Goethe's *Theory of Colors.*" This work, the culmination of more than twenty years of reflection on optical color phenomena, was virtually ignored by the public, and his anti-Newtonian stance was viewed by the scientific community as an expression of dilettantism by a scientifically untrained and imaginative thinker. This was a harsh blow to Goethe's ego, one that his customary resignation could not overcome. Three years before his death in 1832, he confided in Johann Peter Eckermann the reason for his grave disappointment. There had been, were, and will be other excellent poets, he told his friend, and it was not his achievements as a writer in which he took pride. Instead, " . . . that in my century I am the only one who knows correctly the difficult science of color theory – that is something I have done well, and from this I have a consciousness of superiority over

---

many."[8] Schopenhauer claimed that his theory of colors ". . occupied its authors [sic] thoughts, during all of his lifetime, far more than all his poetry; as his biography and memoirs amply testify."[9] Ludwig Wittgenstein, who revered Goethe's poetry, and who could sympathize with the nature of Goethe's perplexity about colors, voiced a complaint that the poet's scientific contemporaries could have supported: "Goethe's theory of the constitution of the colors of the spectrum has not proved to be a satisfactory theory, rather it really is not even a theory. Nothing can be predicted with it. It is, rather, a vague schematic outline. . . . Nor is there any *experimentum crucis* that could decide for or against this theory."[10]

Goethe longed for an ally to help promote his color theory. The young doctor of philosophy, who was also well trained in the sciences, appeared to be a likely candidate for this role. Goethe also sensed a kindred spirit in Schopenhauer. Later, Schopenhauer claimed in a conversation with his friend David Asher that Goethe agreed with his views concerning mathematics and Euclidian geometry.[11] In *The Fourfold Root of the Principle of Sufficient Reason*, Schopenhauer had relegated them both to the scope of the principle of sufficient reason of knowing, and as the products of reason; both fell into the province of the abstract and the conceptual. As

---

[8] Johann Peter Eckermann, *Gespräche mit Goethe in den letzten Jahren seines Lebens*, ed. H[einrich] H[ubert] Houben (Leipzig: Klinkhardt & Biermann, 1909), p. 197.

[9] Schopenhauer's English: see *Gesammelte Briefe*, p. 191, Schopenhauer to Charles Lock Eastwood, 1841. (1840).

[10] Ludwig Wittgenstein, *Remarks on Colour*, trans. G. E. M. Anscombe (Berkeley and Los Angeles: University of California Press, 1978), p. 11e. Like Schopenhauer, Wittgenstein did not believe that Goethe had presented a theory of colors. They had, however, different reasons for their shared judgment. Wittgenstein held that Goethe's work failed to provide any predictions and could be either empirically confirmed or empirically refuted. Schopenhauer operated with a different view of the criterion for a theory. Goethe, he claimed, presented systematically a set of facts about color phenomena, but failed to articulate a basic principle that would serve as a grounding explanation of color phenomena. As Schopenhauer wrote in the second edition of his essay on color theory (1854 and after Goethe's death) "to complete Goethe's work . . . to set down *in abstracto* that supreme principle on which all the data in that work rest, and thus to furnish a theory of color in the strictest sense of the word – this indeed is what this present essay will attempt to do," *On Vision and Colors*, p. 7. It is curious to note that Wittgenstein, upon whom Schopenhauer's philosophy made a strong impression, did not mention Schopenhauer in his *Remarks on Colour.*

[11] See Schopenhauer, *Gespräche*, p. 26. In a section that we would later drop from his dissertation, "Motive, Decision, Empirical and Intelligible Character," Schopenhauer compared the law of motivation to the law of optics to describe the difficulty of knowing a person's empirical character; see *Sämtliche Werke*, Vol. 7, p. 79.

such, the best that they could do was to convince us of the truth of various propositions, without providing immediate insight into the *a priori* nature of time and space. "Among others," Schopenhauer wrote, "this may be a reason why many otherwise eminent minds have disinclination towards mathematics."[12] Goethe had just this sort of mind. Moreover, Schopenhauer had also complained about geometrical proofs, viewing them as unsatisfying tricks, because what we desire is to see the relations obtaining between parts of space. Goethe had also aimed at insight rather than lumbering conviction, requiring a visual representation for his optical proofs. And Schopenhauer reiterated throughout his dissertation that intuition was basic, primary, and the ground for any significant insight, whereas the abstract, purely conceptual, was secondary and derivative, and possessed meaning only if it could be tracked back to the intuitive. When it came to colors, Goethe was all eyes.

Goethe, however, failed to perceive Schopenhauer's commitment to idealism, which is something that should have been obvious had he read *The Fourfold Root* with any care. But it was not his style to read philosophy diligently. Instead, he sampled texts, seeking to savor ideas that stirred his own genius. He even told Schopenhauer that when he read a page of Kant, he felt as if he were entering a brightly lit room.[13] But just as Goethe loved light, sometimes the glare caused an after-image that obscured the sight of things that were contrary to his sensibilities. Schopenhauer's epistemology was Kantian in nature and this would become the foundation upon which he would build a color theory contrary to that of its source of inspiration. Once, in a conversation with a friend, Schopenhauer was reported as saying that "Goethe was so completely a realist, he thoroughly refused to consider that objects themselves are there only insofar as they are represented by the cognizing subject. He once said to me, staring at me with his Jupiter eyes, 'Is the light there only when you see it? No, you would not be there, if the light did not see you.'"[14]

---

[12] Schopenhauer, *On the Fourfold Root of the Principle of Sufficient Reason*, p. 205/*Sämtliche Werke*, Vol. 7, p. 67.

[13] See Schopenhauer, *Gesprache*, p. 33. In *Gesammelte Briefe*, pp. 53–4, 654–5, Schopenhauer to the Philosophy Faculty of the K. Friedrich Wilhelm University at Berlin, 31 December 1819, Schopenhauer described his work with Goethe on color theory.

[14] Schopenhauer, *Gespräche*, p. 31. This was originally reported by Ernst Otto Linder and Julius Frauenstädt in *Arthur Schopenhauer. Von ihm. Ueber ihn* (Berlin: A.W. Hayn, 1863), p. 221f.

Nor did Goethe sense that Schopenhauer lacked the type of personality required by a proselyte. He revered Goethe, but it never was in his character to subordinate himself to another, especially when he believed that the other strayed from the truth. Goethe was, at first, blind to this trait of his disciple, just as he was initially blind to Schopenhauer's intellectual potentials. When Schopenhauer transferred to the University of Berlin in 1811, Goethe's letter of introduction of Schopenhauer to Wolf provided only hearsay about the student new to Berlin. Others had told him, Goethe wrote, that he took his work seriously, but he also implied that Schopenhauer might not have settled on a subject: "He seems to have changed his studies more than once."[15] As a favor to him, Goethe then requested that Wolf talk to Schopenhauer and determine whether he truly deserved Wolf's time. But later, during a Jena party, Goethe was said to have interceded obliquely in Schopenhauer's life. As the sullen Schopenhauer stood quietly by a window, simply observing and not participating in the affair, Goethe was reported to have quieted a gaggle of giggling girls by remarking, "Children, leave him in peace; in due time he will soon grow over all of our heads."[16] It is probably safe to say that Goethe was not anticipating that Schopenhauer would experience a literal growth spurt. Goethe had, however, recognized Schopenhauer's intellectual growth via his dissertation, and after their first private meeting at Goethe's home on the Frauenplan, the poet wrote to his good friend Karl Ludwig Knebel: "Young Schopenhauer seemed to me to be a remarkable and interesting young man. You will have few points of contact with him, but you must get to know him too. He plays the card-game of modern philosophy with a certain acute pertinacity, doubling and trebling his stakes. We will wait and see if the masters of the guild of philosophers will admit him as a member. I find him intelligent, and otherwise take him as he is."[17]

---

[15] *Letters from Goethe*, trans. M. von Herzfeld and C. Melvilsym (Edinburgh: Edinburgh University Press, 1957), Goethe to F. A. Wolf, 28 September 1811. Hiding his disappointment concerning the reception of his color theory, Goethe also told Wolf that he was pleased that his *On the Theory of Colors* was "an apple of discord" to its opponents, who nibbled at it like carp at an apple tossed in their pond. It was sufficient, he continued, that his work was now part of the history of physics: "Let it have what influence it can, now or later. . . ."

[16] Hermann Frommann, *Arthur Schopenhauer, Drei Vorlesungen* (Jena: Friedrich Frommann, 1872), Appendix 1, quoted in Gwinner's *Arthur Schopenhauer aus persönlichem Umgange dargestellt*, p. 60.

[17] *Letters from Goethe*, p. 385, Goethe to Karl Ludwig von Knebel, 24 November 1813. Knebel was a lifelong friend of Goethe, who took a lively interest in both his literary and his scientific

Goethe never lived to experience Schopenhauer's acceptance by the masters of the philosophical trade, and Schopenhauer would later use that designation to demean those members of the guild who ignored his work. Goethe, of course, observed his "acute pertinacity" first-hand, immediately detecting it after the first private audience with the young philosopher. This character trait sustained Schopenhauer throughout the decades during which the philosophical masters did not even consider him an apprentice. This doggedness manifested itself in its most acute form, moreover, whenever he thought he had discovered a truth. One of Schopenhauer's central articles of faith undergirded this attitude: namely, that truth would inevitably prevail. Goethe would also benefit from Schopenhauer's tenacity. He would promote Goethe's color theory throughout his life, but in a way that the poet might have predicted, using it to obliquely promote his philosophy. Thus in 1855, Schopenhauer complained, "The fate of my philosophy and that of Goethe's color theory proves what a mean and *worthless spirit* is ruling over *the German republic of scholars.*"[18]

Schopenhauer and Goethe met at least seven times from 29 November 1813 through 3 April 1814.[19] Many years later, Schopenhauer introduced himself, in English, to the British translator of Goethe's *On the Theory of Colours*, Charles Lock Eastlake, as "Goethes [sic.] personal scholar and first publicly avowed proselyte. In the year 1813 and 14 he instructed me personally, and exhibited the more compound and difficult experiments himself to me."[20] In his *curriculum vitae*, Schopenhauer also claimed

work. Knebel, a Prussian officer and later tutor to Prince Constantine of Weimar, seems to have arranged for Goethe to meet Constantine and his older brother, Carl August, in December 1774 in Frankfurt, which helped to prompt Goethe to move in November 1775 to Weimar. On the same day, Schopenhauer wrote to Friedrich August Wolf a glowing account of Wolf's old friend: "Your friend, our great Goethe, is well, cheerful, sociable, gracious, friendly: praised be his name for all eternity!" Immediately after this effusive praise of Goethe, Schopenhauer added, "Weimar has suffered only by forced billeting [of troops], but the countryside has been devastated by Cossacks. Concerning the fortunate liberation of Germany and through that of higher culture from barbarians, it would be superfluous to describe to you my joy"; see *Gesammelte Briefe*, p. 7.

[18] Schopenhauer, *Manuscript Remains*, Vol. 4, p. 374/*Der handschriftliche Nachlaß*, Vol. 4, 2, p. 15.

[19] See Urs App's carefully documented "Schopenhauer's Initial Encounter with Indian Thought," *Schopenhauer-Jahrbuch*, Vol. 87 (2006), pp. 50–51.

[20] Schopenhauer, *Gesammelte Briefe*, p. 191, Schopenhauer to Charles Lock Eastlake, [1841]. Eastlake was a British author and painter. Schopenhauer wrote this letter with no recollection

that their conversations would meander from color theory to long hours considering "all possible philosophical topics."[21] It is likely that Schopenhauer valued these conversations more greatly than those on color theory, because he claimed that he had already had his system of philosophy in mind by the spring of 1814.[22] Goethe valued these philosophical conversations, Schopenhauer reported to a friend, claiming that the poet had said that he passed time with other people, but with Schopenhauer, he philosophized.[23] For his part, Goethe sensed Schopenhauer's character after a few meetings, penning the following lines with Schopenhauer in mind: "I would like to bear the teacher's burden still longer/If only pupils did not at once become teachers."[24] And if this verse shows that Goethe was beginning to find it difficult to take Schopenhauer as he was, he must have found it worth the effort to continue their relationship. Goethe bore the teacher's burden for three more meetings, but not without setting the younger man in his place. During their penultimate visit, Goethe had some fun at Schopenhauer's expense: "How old are you?" Goethe asked, to which Schopenhauer responded, "Twenty-six." Goethe replied: "So young and already so rich in experience. How much would I have been able to create, had I had such rich experiences already at your age."[25] Goethe was twenty-six when he joined the court at Weimar and

that he had met Eastlake twenty years earlier in Berlin. Eastlake recalled the meeting, writing to Schopenhauer that he had met ". . . a gentleman of your name who talked English perfectly: he was also a metaphysician & the author, he told me, of a work called '*Die Welt als Wille und Vorstellung*,'" *Gespräche*, p. 52. Eastlake's translation of Goethe's *Theory of Colours* appeared in London in 1840. Schopenhauer was moved to write Eastlake to induce him to also translate into English his *On Vision in Colors*, as well as to encourage him to fully translate the polemical part of Goethe's work, because "this part is the most essential, as it shews the gross manner in which Newton by his clumsy experiments imposed upon himself and others: for Gods [sic.] sake, if Your [sic.] translation should see a second edition," (p. 192). Eastlake, despite Schopenhauer's desperate pleas, was not moved to translate either Schopenhauer's work or all of Goethe's.

21 Ibid., pp. 54, 655, Schopenhauer to the Philosophy Faculty of the Royal Friedrich-Wilhelm University at Berlin, 31 December 1819.

22 Ibid., pp. 54, 655.

23 See Schopenhauer, *Gespräche*, p. 27, reported by David Asher.

24 "Lähmung," in *Goethes Gedichte*, Part 2 (Stuttgart/Tübingen, 1815), p. 199. Schopenhauer viewed these verses as venting Goethe's ill-humor, which he claimed was provoked by the poet's recognition that Schopenhauer's color theory was an advance over his own; see Schopenhauer, *On Vision and Colors*, p. 8/*Sämtliche Werke*, Vol. 1, p. 5. Out of respect for Goethe, Schopenhauer added this remark in the second edition of *On Vision and Colors* (1854), well after Goethe's death.

25 Schopenhauer, *Gespräche*, p. 34, reported by Carl G. Bähr.

had already become famous, due to the success of *The Sufferings of Young Werther*. He had achieved far more at the same age as the brash young Schopenhauer.

Schopenhauer relocated to Dresden in late May 1814. Prior to this event, Goethe wrote the following verse in his album: "If you wish to enjoy your own value,/You must give value to the world." He signed it, "In consequence and remembrance of many intimate conversations, Weimar 8 May 1814."[26] If Goethe meant this verse to encourage Schopenhauer's continued labor on color theory, it had its desired effect. But if he hoped that Schopenhauer would simply write to promote Goethe's theory of colors, the verse backfired. One year later, through the auspices of one Dr. Schlosser, Goethe received Schopenhauer's manuscript, *On Vision and Colors*.[27] Naturally, its author was eager to receive Goethe's responses, but more importantly, his endorsement and aid in having it published. Goethe did not even acknowledge its receipt. After eight weeks of agonizing silence from his hero, Schopenhauer could no longer endure the situation, and on 3 September 1815, he wrote a letter to call Goethe's hand. This letter commenced a year-long, sporadic exchange of letters between the two men. Schopenhauer's letters were bold, self-confident about his views, manipulative, but always in awe of Goethe. He addressed the poet as "Your Excellency," and he always used a formal tone, never using the familiar "you [*du*]," but always the formal form "you [*Sie*]." Goethe's responses are noteworthy for their restraint, good nature, and ultimate mastery of the situation. He also addressed Schopenhauer formally as *Sie*, but also in a way that reinforced the difference of status between the correspondents: "Your Excellency" wrote to "my most worthy one."

Schopenhauer's 3 September letter to Goethe seems curious. He was polite and willing to recognize that the great man had an obligation neither to read the manuscript nor to send comments if he did read it. He recognized that Goethe was busy, meeting with governmental officials, diplomats, and military people, and he recalled that Goethe himself had told him that literary affairs were a secondary thing compared to real life. But Schopenhauer's tone in the letter became desperate. It was just the reverse with him, he wrote. "What I think, what I write, that holds value

---

[26] Arthur Hübscher's "Lebensbild" in *Sämtliche Werke*, Vol. 1, p. 67.

[27] Hübscher suggests that it was Friedrich Johann Heinrich Schlosser, a public prosecutor from Frankfurt and the executor of Goethe's mother's estate, who brought the manuscript to Goethe; see *Gesammelte Briefe*, p. 493.

to me and is important to me. What I personally experience and what happens to me is secondary to me. Indeed, I scorn it."[28] Consequently, he continued, it pained and distressed him not to be certain that Goethe received the manuscript, although he thought that this was highly likely. Still, not to know whether Goethe had read the manuscript was so unpleasant and agonizing that it provoked his hypochondria, as did the torment of suffering dashed expectations, as he each day waited to hear something. To put an end to his misery, he pleaded for Goethe to return the manuscript, with or without comments. But then, Schopenhauer backed down. He told Goethe that he could keep the manuscript longer, if he wished. Fearing, perhaps, that he had said something to which Goethe might take umbrage, he closed by writing that Goethe should never doubt that his respect for him was unalterable and would remain unchanged throughout his entire life, a pledge that Schopenhauer did make good.

Schopenhauer's desperate letter had its desired effect. It provoked a reply four days later. Goethe wrote that he had read, reflected upon, and enjoyed the manuscript. Had he had a scribe, he continued, he would have sent more detailed remarks, but he had so many duties to discharge that he did not have the time to respond.[29] When he returned to Weimar, he assured Schopenhauer, he would have more time to reply. It is doubtful, however, that Goethe paid more than a few moments with the manuscript, because he did not recognize the many ways his student's views disharmonized with his own. But Schopenhauer's next letter to Goethe mentioned a "disharmony," one that could not have endeared him to his teacher. Goethe had disputed Newton's claim that white light contained the spectrum and he labeled it an absurdity that seven colors mixed together produced white. Now, however, Schopenhauer claimed that he had an experiment that established the production of white light out of colored lights, but not with seven lights. Rather, he said he could produce white light by using two. Violet and yellow; blue and orange; and green and red, each yielded white.[30]

Goethe's response was odd. He told Schopenhauer that when he returned to Weimar, he took the first opportunity to go through Schopenhauer's essay and letters. This gave him great pleasure, he said, as he placed

[28] Schopenhauer, *Gesammelte Briefe*, p. 16, Schopenhauer to Goethe, 3 September 1815.

[29] See Schopenhauer, ibid., p. 483, Goethe to Schopenhauer, 3 September 1815.

[30] See Schopenhauer, ibid., p. 17, Schopenhauer to Goethe, 16 September 1815.

himself within Schopenhauer's standpoint. He could only, he continued, praise and admire the means by which such an independently thinking person faithfully and honestly engaged in his work, keeping purely in mind everything that is objective. Yet, when he abstracted himself from this standpoint to return to his own, he found it difficult to deal with their differences and almost impossible to resolve anything that contradicted his view. He had recently met Dr. Thomas Seebeck, a physicist, and Goethe asked if he could send Schopenhauer's work to Seebeck for an expert's judgment.[31]

Goethe's letter prompted Schopenhauer to write a lengthy reply on 11 November. His reply was a heady mixture of esteem for Goethe and confidence concerning the truth of his own views. He told Goethe that everything he received from him was of "inestimable value" and was "sacred to me."[32] He was thrilled that Goethe praised the faithfulness and honesty of his thinking and pledged that these characteristics would drive everything he would do. Yet sensing that "your Excellency" was displeased by his work, Schopenhauer exploited Goethe's remarks to explain how the very thing about him that the great man praised was that which led to differences in their views. "I cannot rest, cannot take

---

[31] See Schopenhauer, ibid., p. 494, Goethe to Schopenhauer, 23 October 1815. Seebeck was the discoverer of entoptic colors, color phenomena generated by polarized light cast through dual refracting crystals, and thermoelectricity. He was a physicist in Jena, and then in Bayreuth and Nuremberg, and he became a member of the Academy of Science in Berlin in 1818. Seebeck advised Goethe on optics and supported his anti-Newtonian stance. Schopenhauer met with Seebeck in 1830, as he worked on the Latin treatment of his color theory. Schopenhauer did not have a high regard for Seebeck, as evidenced in his letter to Eastlake. After reporting that Seebeck confided to him that Goethe was correct and Newton wrong, he wrote that ". . . [Seebeck said that] he had no business to tell the world so. – He died since, the Old Coward," Schopenhauer, ibid., p. 192, Schopenhauer to Eastlake, 1841 (Schopenhauer's English). Schopenhauer might have had an even lower opinion of Seebeck, had he known that he was once on friendly terms with Hegel, even standing as one of the godfathers for Hegel's son Immanuel. Hegel did some work with Seebeck on entoptic colors, but by the time Schopenhauer met with Seebeck, he was estranged from Hegel, after learning about some desultory remarks he made about Seebeck's intellectual abilities in response to an evaluation request made by Heinrich Paulus, when Seebeck sought an appointment at Heidelberg. It is also curious that Schopenhauer was silent about Hegel's promotion of Goethe's color theory, despite the fact that Schopenhauer kept track of both Goethe's opponents and his supporters; see, respectively, Terry Pinkard, *Hegel: A Biography* (Cambridge: Cambridge University Press, 2000), p. 409, and P. F. H. Lauxtermann, "Hegel and Schopenhauer as Partisans of Goethe's Theory of Color," *Journal of the History of Ideas*, Vol. 50 (1990), pp. 588–624.

[32] Schopenhauer, *Gesammelte Briefe*, p. 18, Schopenhauer to Goethe, 11 November 1815.

satisfaction," he averred, "as long as some part of an object observed by me still does not quite show a clear contour."[33] It was as if, when he engaged in his work, he stood before his own spirit as a prisoner before a judge who questions the prisoner until there are no further questions to be asked. His honesty, moreover, drove him to question even things that lay close to his heart and led him to overturn his pet ideas. Like Oedipus, he opined, who sought enlightenment about his own terrible fate, disregarding Jocasta's and the gods' warning not to pursue the matter any further, he too sought the truth despite its personal costs. "The courage to hold no question close to one's heart is that which makes one a philosopher," he continued, and this philosophical courage is one with the faithfulness and honesty of the investigation that Goethe had recognized in him, and both were a function of the innate tendency of his spirit.[34] His faithfulness and honesty are the characteristics, he continued, that gave him the confidence to speak as openly and freely as he did in this letter.

The subtext of Schopenhauer's letter could not have been lost on Goethe. The poet's disinclination to react to his student's manuscript signified that his personal interests and investments in his own color theory kept him from considering well-supported ideas that threatened his own, whereas his student doggedly pursued the truth, even when it overturned his cherished ideas. The young philosopher, however, yearned for a response from his hero, one that affirmed the truth of his views, despite the personal costs borne by their source of inspiration. This is what faithfulness and honesty demanded. Perhaps to address what Schopenhauer feared was the basis of Goethe's hesitancy to engage his work, Schopenhauer tried to make it clear that his views only challenged some of the poet's secondary propositions and not his main ideas. So Schopenhauer moved to a more direct strategy to provoke Goethe's response than that of his oblique appeal to intellectual integrity. Because some of his ideas

<hr/>

[33] Ibid., p. 18. Some thirty-six years later, Schopenhauer would use the idea of having the courage to question everything, including one's own favored ideas, as one of two primary requirements for philosophizing. The second was to become completely aware of everything that is "self-evident" in order to view it as a problem. He could not help, however, adding a third requirement to "really philosophize," namely, that the mind must be at leisure and not guided by personal interests, so that one can pay undivided attention to the world. Naturally, the older Schopenhauer had to remark that professors of philosophy were incapable of doing this, because they were moved by their personal interests; see Schopenhauer, *Parerga and Paralipomena*, Vol. 2, p. 4/*Sämtliche Werke*, Vol. 6, p. 4.

[34] Schopenhauer, *Gesammelte Briefe*, p. 18, Schopenhauer to Goethe, 11 November 1815.

contradicted Goethe's, Schopenhauer pointed out the obvious – one of them had to be wrong. If he were wrong, Schopenhauer wrote, "why should your Excellency deny yourself the satisfaction and me the instruction by drawing with a few words the line which divides the true from the false?"[35]

But immediately after inviting Goethe to separate the true from the false in his color theory, Schopenhauer doubled the stakes, playing the game of color theory in the same manner that Goethe had noted he played the game of philosophy. He would not keep it a secret, he told Goethe, that he did not believe that Goethe could draw such a line because "My theory is the unfolding of a single, indivisible thought that must be completely false or completely true: it is analogous therefore to an arch from which one could not remove a single stone without the entire structure collapsing."[36] Goethe, he claimed, did not face this risk. His color theory was a systematic collection of numerous facts and given its robust range of date, it would be easy for some trivial errors to slip in under one's guard. These mistakes could be "erased without detriment to the whole."[37] Unless these mistakes were eliminated, Schopenhauer warned, your opponents will seize them and use them as the means to ignore the many truths articulated in his color theory. Moreover, it is better to have these trivial flaws corrected in the "writing of your first proselyte," whose work you would edit, Schopenhauer wrote.[38] Sometimes, he continued, you must surrender to a surgeon's knife a member of your body to save life and limb, and you are lost if you instead cry out "do as you will, only do not touch this spot."[39] Naturally, Schopenhauer implied that he had performed the necessary, life-saving surgery on Goethe's "non-theoretical" color theory.

Schopenhauer's letter advanced additional claims that demonstrate how oblivious he was to the ways in which his behavior alienated other people. After mentioning three ways in which his views "disharmonized" with Goethe's, he bragged to his hero, "I know with complete certainty

---

[35] Ibid., p. 19.

[36] Ibid., p. 19. Four years later Schopenhauer would also claim that his *The World as Will and Representation* was the expression of "*a single thought*"; see Vol. 1, p. xii/*Sämtliche Werke*, Vol. 2, p. viii.

[37] Ibid.

[38] Ibid.

[39] Ibid.

that I have produced the first theory of color, the first in the entire history of science."[40] He could not have accomplished this feat, he continued, without Goethe's earlier work: "My theory has a relationship to your work fully like fruit to the tree."[41] And if these remarks were not sufficient to let Goethe know that his student believed that he had trumped his teacher, Schopenhauer drew another analogy to make his point clear. "If I were to compare your color theory to a pyramid, then my theory is its apex, the indivisible mathematical point from which the entire great structure spreads out, and which is so essential that without it the shape is no longer a pyramid. . . . "[42] Goethe had done the foundational work and Schopenhauer provided the acme. And if this were not bad enough, to encourage the poet to comment on his work, trying to convince him that it would take him little effort, because the manuscript was short, Schopenhauer related that, except for a couple of weeks, he actually "treated it [color theory] as a matter of secondary importance and constantly carried with me in mind far different theories than those of color."[43] This could not have endeared Schopenhauer to a man who had studied and written on color theory for twenty years.

Schopenhauer also made it clear that he was not pleased by Goethe's recommendation that Seebeck review his manuscript. Goethe was the only person whose judgment he sought and the only person whose judgment he valued. Seebeck lacked Goethe's authority and therefore could not help him. Indeed, Goethe's suggestion that he work with Seebeck reminded him of Jean Jacques Rousseau being invited by a noblewoman for dinner, only to learn that he would be eating with her servants. But Schopenhauer was worried by more than his suspicion that Goethe wanted to pass him off to another; he feared that Seebeck might steal his work. Earlier in the letter, Schopenhauer had mentioned that the only way he would not be recognized as the author of the first true theory of color would be if another discovered the same theory or someone robbed him of his theory. He closed his letter by demanding to know exactly what Goethe had told Seebeck about his work or whether Goethe let him read the manuscript.

[40] Ibid., p. 20.
[41] Ibid., p. 21.
[42] Ibid.
[43] Ibid., p. 20. Schopenhauer's reference to the far different theories that he had in mind concerns his work on the ideas that would appear three years later in *The World as Will and Representation*.

He needed to know this because "your Excellency yourself knows how greatly one has to fear plagiarism...."[44]

Goethe replied to Schopenhauer's massive letter five days later. Although there was much that could have provoked Goethe's wrath, his reply was surprisingly good-natured and generous. He referred to Schopenhauer's "friendly letter" and characterized it as an expression of Schopenhauer's wish to put an end to the differences between their views. Toward that end, Goethe provided an accompanying justification for his treatment of the color violet and promised to do so for Schopenhauer's analysis of the production of white. He was silent about the third way in which Schopenhauer's views "disharmonized" with his own: namely, Schopenhauer's claim that polarity applied only to the physiological colors and not to the physical. He also ignored Schopenhauer's grandiose pronouncements concerning his production of the first, correct theory of color in the history of science and his reduction of Goethe's color theory to an unshaped collection of facts that he had raised to the august height of theory. He also sensed the depth of Schopenhauer's distress about Seebeck's knowledge of his work. Goethe immediately set out to calm Schopenhauer's fears. No one had seen Schopenhauer's manuscript, Goethe wrote, and he did not even have it when Seebeck visited him in the country. When he expressed his wish that Schopenhauer meet with Seebeck, Goethe wrote, he did so only because he had hoped to interest Seebeck in physiological colors. Because Schopenhauer declined to meet Seebeck, Goethe said that he would drop the issue. But, before he closed the letter, Goethe slyly offered his verdict concerning their disagreements concerning color theory in a way that gave a Fichtean reading of Schopenhauer's work in his dissertation: "He who is inclined to construct the world from the subject will not decline the observation that the subject is always only an individual in the appearance and therefore requires a certain measure of truth and error in order to obtain individuality. But nothing separates humans more than that the amounts of these two ingredients are mixed in different proportions."[45]

Schopenhauer responded to Goethe's last letter on 3 December. This letter, which has been lost, was lengthy, including his remarks on Goethe's

---

[44] Ibid., p. 23.

[45] Ibid., p. 495, Goethe to Schopenhauer, 16 November 1815.

analysis of the color violet and new observations on color theory.[46] Goethe did not answer this letter. He was in Jena during this time, engaged in some of his official duties – he met with Chancellor Prince von Hardenberg – and he was deeply engaged in his study of clouds – he was reading the British chemist and meteorologist Luke Howard's *Attempt at a Natural History and Physics of Clouds*. After waiting ten weeks, Schopenhauer had had enough. On 23 January 1816, Schopenhauer wrote to Goethe that "Your Excellency has totally forgotten me and my color theory once again."[47] He complained, moreover, that he had waited almost seven months for Goethe to provide substantive remarks about his work and for him to help publicize it. He had now given up his hopes for either. As a final request, he asked Goethe to return the manuscript. This would put an end to the matter. Schopenhauer, however, could not help himself. He had to voice his disappointment in a way that reiterated the overwhelming confidence he had in this and his future work: "Said frankly, it is not even possible for me to imagine that your Excellency would not recognize the correctness of my theory: for I know that through me the truth has spoken – in this small matter, as sometime in the future it will in a greater one – and your mind is too proper and too accurately tuned so as not to resonate at every tone."[48] Schopenhauer continued by diagnosing the cause behind Goethe's failure to endorse or reject his views. Because some of Schopenhauer's propositions clashed with his beliefs, Goethe developed a subjective antipathy toward his student's theory and this was why he hedged and stalled, neither providing nor withholding his consent. Thus he was silent. Quite naturally and sincerely, Schopenhauer closed his communication by assuring Goethe that no one had a deeper reverence for him than he."[49]

Goethe responded promptly to Schopenhauer's request. He returned the manuscript five days later. In a letter accompanying the manuscript,

---

[46] Ibid., p. 23, Schopenhauer to Goethe, 23 January 1816, where Schopenhauer made these claims about the content of his "lengthy" letter of 3 December 1815.

[47] Ibid.

[48] Ibid.

[49] Schopenhauer included a postscript to this letter, in which he confessed to an error in his account of single vision, that is, the explanation of seeing a single object based on the fact that we receive double impressions due to perception with two eyes. Perhaps Schopenhauer mentioned this error to encourage Goethe to provide comments to his work by showing him that he was willing to admit and take responsibility for mistakes in his theory. If this were the case, it did not move Goethe to provide comments; see ibid., p. 24.

Goethe put an end to the matter in a way that gently reestablished his superiority. Frequently during these winter nights, he wrote, he wished that Schopenhauer were with him in Weimar. Had he been there, he continued, he would have set between them his *On the Theory of Colors* and would have engaged in a discussion that would not require agreement. In the absence of this, and not wanting to leave Schopenhauer without encouragement, he told him that he had spent two days in Jena researching what had been published on color theory during the last eight years. His hope was that this research would become the basis of their future discussions. But as quickly as Goethe offered the hope for their future interaction, he withdrew it. His research convinced him that despite the fact that they could agree about how certain phenomena appear as well as on various principles, when it came to applying these principles, they would quickly arrive at different and irreconcilable conclusions. For this reason, Goethe continued, "I saw then that it would be wasted labor for us to want to reconcile our views."[50] As to Schopenhauer's color theory, Goethe then made a request. Could Schopenhauer make an extract of it to include in his *On the Theory of Colors?* Last, he asked Schopenhauer to let him know every now and then with what he was busy; not that he would be able to take up these ideas – he was too old to do so – but simply as something that interested him from an historical point of view.

Schopenhauer fired back at Goethe's letter, feeding the poet his own words from his autobiography. "'So in the end, man is always driven back to himself,'" he wrote, and "I must also now sigh out in pain, 'I work the wine press alone.'"[51] Schopenhauer's meaning had to be clear to his hero. Goethe had used these remarks in his autobiography to describe a crisis faced by those who had reached a state in which one had to proceed alone, without the support of parents, relatives, siblings, friends, or even God. In times of the most urgent crises, one had to go it alone, Goethe observed,

[50] See ibid., p. 496, Goethe to Schopenhauer, 28 January 1816.
[51] See ibid., p. 24, Schopenhauer to Goethe, 7 February 1816. Schopenhauer is quoting from Goethe's *From My Life: Poetry and Truth [Aus meinem Leben: Dichtung und Wahrheit*, 1811–32]. When Schopenhauer wrote this letter, Books 11–15 had recently appeared. Part IV, Books 16–20, appeared in 1832, the year of Goethe's death. Schopenhauer's quotations are from Part III, Chap. 15; see *The Autobiography of Johann Wolfgang von Goethe*, trans. John Oxenford, Vol. 2, p. 276. It is a matter of curiosity that Oxenford's "Iconoclasm in German Philosophy," *The Westminster Review*, New Series VI (April 1, 1853, pp. 380–407, helped usher in Schopenhauer's period of fame in the mid-1850s.

and to face life's vicissitudes, he had decided to ground his independence on his creative talents. Schopenhauer was telling Goethe the same. He too sighed out in pain. Goethe's failure to actively participate in his color theory had injured him: "I cannot conceal that I have been greatly hurt."[52] In developing his color theory and through the seven months of correspondence, Schopenhauer told Goethe, his eagerly optimistic hopes concerning Goethe's involvement were cruelly dashed. He could only have tolerated this state of affairs and let himself be treated thusly by a Goethe or a Kant and by "no other of those who have seen the light of day at the same time as me."[53]

It was odd, Schopenhauer continued to reflect, that Goethe's lack of involvement with his color theory enhanced, instead of diminished, his high opinion of his work. Indeed, he said that it had convinced him that his theory was original and completely true. It also encouraged him to face the world alone. After not receiving the blessings of the man whose judgment mattered the most, he was prepared to send his work into a world that would war against it, but he was now prepared, in thought and deed, to respect nothing about the opinions of cynics and of the human hoards, he said. Despite this pronouncement of his independence from Goethe, Schopenhauer could not let go. Goethe had told him that Seebeck had exact knowledge of Goethe's opponents. He wanted to know exactly who they were. He also wanted to learn from Goethe what he had read about color theory when he researched those publications on color theory in Jena. This all would be very useful to him, he wrote, because the Leipzig publishing house of Johann Friedrich Hartknoch would be publishing his treatise, and he had promised the manuscript in three to four weeks. Naturally, he closed the letter by articulating his deep respect for Goethe, remarking that he hoped that his essay would do much to honor and justify Goethe's work. Goethe promptly replied to this letter four days later. Apologizing for not having Seebeck's bibliography at hand, Goethe mentioned three works on color theory of which Schopenhauer may not have been familiar and wrote that he anticipated the pleasure of working through Schopenhauer's essay when it was in print.[54]

---

[52] Schopenhauer, *Gesammelte Briefe*, p. 24.

[53] Ibid., p. 25.

[54] Perhaps to raise Seebeck's stock in Schopenhauer's eyes, Goethe also mentioned that Seebeck received one-half of the 3,000-franc prize, offered by the Paris Academy, for his discovery of

On Vision and Colors appeared in May 1816. Immediately after its publication, he sent a copy to Goethe. In the letter accompanying the book, he again told Goethe that he had to work the wine press alone. But unlike in his earlier letter, he repressed his distress over being abandoned by the inspiring source of his color theory and he adopted a new attitude: "But I also stand on my own two feet in regard to this and every other matter."[55] Nevertheless, he tried to entice Goethe's response to his work by claiming that his work had been changed considerably and improved by significant additions to his early manuscript. He reiterated his desire to receive Goethe's judgment, but he also wrote that he had given up hope to receive it. According to his diary entries for 9 and 10 May, Goethe busied himself with Schopenhauer's book.[56] Instead of providing Schopenhauer with his assessment – and not because his student did not expect one – he contacted Seebeck on 11 May: "Read as soon as possible a small book, *On Vision and Colors* by A. Schopenhauer and tell me what you think about it. I have already read it in manuscript, but I could not finish it. It has become increasingly difficult for me to clearly understand differences of opinions. One must imagine oneself in the head of another and for that I lost the flexibility."[57]

It is not known what Seebeck told Goethe about Schopenhauer's "small book." Goethe finally wrote to Schopenhauer a friendly letter on 16 June in which he severed the few remaining threads that held any prospects for his substantive responses to Schopenhauer's work. The letter bore a black seal that Goethe used to express his regrets for his tardy reply. He had just commenced the study of Schopenhauer's "well-considered essay," when his beloved wife took ill, he wrote, and her subsequent death had torn him away from all of his scientific studies, including that on color theory.[58] He mentioned that although they had begun their collaboration from the same standpoint, they had vigorously proceeded in

---

entoptic colors, that is, color phenomena produced by polarized light in refracting crystals; see Schopenhauer, ibid., p. 498, Goethe to Schopenhauer, 11 February 1816.

[55] Ibid., p. 28. Schopenhauer to Goethe, 4 May 1816.

[56] See Johann Wolfgang Goethe, *Sämtliche Werke*, ed. Peter Boerner (Munich: Deutscher Taschenbuck Verlag, 1963) Vol. 44, "Tagebücher 1810–1832," p. 43.

[57] Schopenhauer, *Gesammelte Briefe*, p. 499, Goethe to Seebeck 11 May 1816, a citation from Max Hecker, "Dreißig unbekannte Briefe Goethes," *Jahrbuch der Goethe-Gesellschaft*, Vol. 10 (1924), p. 163f.

[58] Schopenhauer, *Gesammelte Briefe*, p. 499, Goethe to Schopenhauer, 16 June 1816.

different directions. If Schopenhauer would not become too tired with the subject and would continue to cultivate his own views, he wrote, perhaps in a few years they could joyfully reach a central point at which they would once again meet. Goethe, however, was somewhat disingenuous. Not even a month after this letter, in response to a query from Christoph Schultz concerning Schopenhauer's work, he responded in a way that expressed his displeasure: "Dr. Schopenhauer is a significant thinker whom I induced to take up my theory of colors.... This young man, proceeding from my perspective, has become my opponent."[59]

What was it about Schopenhauer's theory of colors that drew Goethe's displeasure and let him to view his erstwhile proselyte as ultimately an apostate? By the second edition of *On Vision and Colors*, 1854, Schopenhauer knew of Goethe's remark to Schultz that he had become Goethe's opponent. He was somewhat dumbfounded by the master's judgment, because it was made ". . . on the occasion of the present essay, in which I appear as his most determined champion."[60] He attributed this remark to Goethe's demand of the most unqualified agreement by his followers, and he claimed that his ill humor toward him was provoked by Goethe's realization that the student's work advanced beyond that of his teacher. Schopenhauer's analysis of Goethe's response to his work, however, shows again how oblivious he could be concerning the effects of his behavior on others. Calling, as he did, his work on color theory a sideline compared to other, more important theories he had in mind, saying that Goethe had simply provided data that he himself raised to the exalted heights of theory – the first true theory of colors in the history of science – and his constant badgering of Goethe to bless and help promote his work, had to alienate his hero, who prided himself on his color theory and whose interest in color phenomena spanned more than twenty years, compared

---

[59] Ibid., Goethe to Christoph Friedrich Ludwig Schultz, 6 July 1816. Schopenhauer became aware of this remark and was taken back at Goethe's judgment: ". . . he [Goethe] called me an opponent of his color theory, while I, 40 years ago and 22 years after his death, stood there completely all alone and held up high the standard of his color theory, shouting 'you ass, he is correct,'" *Gesammelte Briefe*, p. 330, Schopenhauer to Julius Frauenstädt, 28 January 1854. Lauxtermann reports an incident between Goethe and Eckermann, when, after the biographer criticized his color theory, the poet accused him of being a "heretic" like others, including Schopenhauer; see his *Schopenhauer's Broken World-View: Colours and Ethics between Kant and Goethe*, p. 79fn.

[60] Schopenhauer, *On Vision and Colors*, p. 7/*Sämtliche Werke*, Vol. 1, p. 5. It is here that Schopenhauer quotes the earlier cited verses from Goethe's *Lähmung*.

to Schopenhauer's intermittent study, which culminated with the publication of his book, some eighteen months after Goethe first approached him at Johanna Schopenhauer's party.

Schopenhauer's analysis of Goethe's response to his color theory turned a blind eye toward his own behavior and placed the blame on Goethe. As he had claimed in his letter of 23 January 1816, it was his philosophical courage that led him to challenge ideas that lay close to his heart and drove him to follow the spurs of truth even if this required him to reject what he had once loved. Naturally, this suggested that Goethe's failure to respond to his student's work was a sign that he lacked such courage. Had he possessed this courage, he would have recognized the truth of Schopenhauer's views. He was, however, as Schopenhauer written, too subjective and too invested to his own ideas to remain faithful to the pursuit of truth. Not only was Goethe both personally and intellectually too timid to face what would have led him to abandon some of his ideas, but also Schopenhauer would later exploit Goethe's remarks about the difficulty he experienced in engaging with ideas contrary to his own, calling this difficulty a debilitating effect of old age.[61] Had he been a younger, more philosophically inclined thinker with the courage to rigorously criticize beloved views, he would have had to accept those of Schopenhauer. Yet if this was what Schopenhauer meant to imply when he mentioned how painful it was to question cherished ideas, he also ignored that the cherished ideas he struggled to question and support were those of Goethe – they were not his own. And although Schopenhauer cherished his relationship to his hero, and he valued Goethe's ideas because they were Goethe's, it was not his own ideas that he had the courage to examine and reject. Certainly, he risked his relationship with Goethe by engaging in this project and thereby risked alienating one of the few men whom he thought his intellectual equals. He may have thought, however, that his constant flattery, his praise of Goethe's work, and his passionate denunciation of Goethe's

---

[61] Later, in the second edition of *On Vision and Colors*, and long after Goethe's death, Schopenhauer mentioned that Goethe failed to respond to French accounts of the polarization of light because "Goethe was too old when these phenomena were discovered – he was beginning to talk foolishly," p. 82/*Sämtliche Werke*, Vol. 1, p. 90. As we will see, Schopenhauer's attitudes toward his other hero, Kant, mirrored those he had toward Goethe. Although he never could have interacted with Kant, who died when Schopenhauer was sixteen, he also described some of Kant's views, which he rejected, as weak offspring of old age; see, for example, *On the Basis of Morality*, p. 51/*Sämtliche Werke*, Vol. 4, p. 119.

detractors would have been sufficient to win back a potentially lost hero. Even long after Goethe's death, he continued to promote his work in color theory and condemn its opponents in loyalty to the memory of his hero.

When it came to recognizing the ways in which his color theory deviated from Goethe's, Schopenhauer demonstrated a modicum of insight, but not a robust sense of his oppositions to his teacher's view. Much later, in 1830, when he published a Latin version of his color theory, *Theoria colorum physiologica, eudemque primaria*, he claimed that his physiological color theory would still be true, even if the physical color theories of both Newton and Goethe were wrong.[62] He would be even blunter in his 1841 letter to Eastlake. His theory of physiological colors " . . . would be true even if Goethe was wrong: it does not depend on his position."[63] So much for his earlier claim that Goethe's work provided the basis on which his theory set the peak! Yet in his correspondence with Goethe from that time, we have seen that he acknowledged three ways in which his theory "disharmonized" with the poet's theory; namely, the production of white light through colored lights; the restriction of Goethe's concept of polarity to physiological colors; and production of the color violet.[64] Yet Schopenhauer overlooked what moved Goethe to view him as his opponent – Schopenhauer's reduction of Goethe's "primary phenomena," which were alleged phenomena incapable of further explanation, to a secondary status.

Goethe had not always been an opponent of Newton's view that white light was a mixture of rays of different refrangibility. By his own account, it was a matter of pure serendipity that he came to reject Newton's view. One day as he was packing to return some books and scientific equipment to a professor at Jena, he looked through a prism at his white wall. To his astonishment, no color spectrum appeared. This experience

---

[62] See *Sämtliche Werke*, Vol. 1, p. 3, where Schopenhauer claimed that his physiological theory was such that both Goethe's and Newton's physical theories could be based on it and that it would still be true if both were mistaken. Schopenhauer recast his color theory in Latin, hoping that scholars outside Germany would recognize the truth of his views. His hope, however, was not realized.

[63] Schopenhauer, *Gesammelte Briefe*, p. 192, Schopenhauer to Eastlake, 1841 (Schopenhauer's English).

[64] See ibid., pp. 19–20, Schopenhauer to Goethe, 11 November 1815. Schopenhauer later agreed with Goethe on violet, and in the second edition of *On Vision and Colors* he listed his limitation of polarity and the production of white from colors as his differences from Goethe; see p. 75/*Sämtliche Werke*, Vol. 1, p. 73.

led him, as if by instinct, to cry out loud that "the Newtonian theory is false."[65] Intrigued, Goethe continued to play with the prism. He observed that the color fringes only appeared at the boundaries of white and black. Goethe would come to view white or light and black or darkness as primary phenomena, the bedrock of his color theory, and colors themselves as something shadowlike or cloudy, as σκιερόν (*skieron*). Aware that a mixture of black and white produced gray, Goethe argued that with the aid of a turbid medium, such as fog, smoke, clouds, or flint glass, the interplay of polarities of light and darkness produced color phenomena. Gazing at darkness through a turbid medium with a light source before it produced blue, whereas looking at a turbid medium with a light source behind it yielded yellow. From the intensification of these opposites, blue and yellow, all other colors are derived, Goethe held, through their union. From these grounds, Goethe's theory recognized six primary colors, compared to Newton's seven, with the intensification of blue yielding reddish blue and its intensification yielding purple, and the intensification of yellow yielding yellowish red, whereas the union of yellow and blue produced green.[66]

Goethe had considered color phenomena produced by the seeing eye, "physiological colors," colored shades, and after-images, but he regarded these color phenomena as merely subjective. Yet this became the peg on which Schopenhauer would hang his hat.[67] The philosopher himself tells us that it took a year after his withdrawing from Goethe's magnetic personality before his work on color theory could turn back to the native grounds of his thought, to a firmer commitment to Kant's transcendental idealism, which was only half-heartedly expressed in his dissertation. But Kant's idealism assumed a greater significance by 1815, as he was working

---

[65] Goethe, *dtv-Gesamtausgabe*, Vol. 42, p. 169. Poor Professor Büttner had to wait for the return of his prisms, because this experience inclined Goethe to keep them for conducting experiments.

[66] Lauxtermann provides a fine overview of Goethe's color theory as compared to those of Newton and Schopenhauer in *Schopenhauer's Broken World-View: Colours and Ethics between Kant and Goethe*, pp. 53–82.

[67] Goethe had discussed "physiological colors" in the first chapter of the "Didactic Section" of his *On the Theory of Colors*; see Goethe, *dtv-Gesamtausgabe*, Vol. 40, pp. 20–57. As Lauxtermann has pointed out, Goethe viewed this consideration of physiological colors as a "propaedeutic" for a serious study of colors and not, as Schopenhauer did, as the essential half of an entire theory of colors, whose other half concerned "physical" and "chemical" colors; see Lauxtermann, ibid., pp. 73–4.

on his philosophy proper.[68] The problem with Goethe, he held, was that he was too much of a realist and too concerned with the objective course of events in the world, forgetting, as it were, that there are no objects without a subject. From Schopenhauer's perspective this meant that Goethe's work simply described states of affairs and that his explanations could only say what was the case instead of showing what must be the case. To make his point, he turned Goethe against himself, quoting the same lines from *Faust* that he had used to mock post-Kantian philosophers in his dissertation: "The philosopher who steps in/proves to us, it could have not otherwise been."[69] Goethe's failure to capture "what could have not been otherwise" now becomes the mark that shows that Goethe was just a poet and not a philosopher. He lacked the ambition to find the ultimate grounds for colors, stopping short at light and darkness as primary phenomena, not realizing that by turning to the seeing eye and physiological colors, his light and dark received a grounding explanation. Lightness or white, darkness or black, and colors are modifications of the eye. Lightness or white is the full activity of the retina. Darkness or black is the inactivity of the retina, whereas color is the qualitatively divided activity of the retina. Consequently, "primary phenomenon properly speaking is only the organic capacity of retina to cause its nervous activity to separate and successively appear in two qualitatively opposite halves, sometimes equal, sometimes unequal."[70] Goethe's primary phenomena were merely that which stimulated the division of the retina's activity!

Thus Schopenhauer's theory expressed a double heresy from his Master's doctrines. Light and darkness lost their status as primary phenomena. Goethe, he also said, was guilty of the same failing as Newton. Both concentrated on the cause of the sensation of color without examining its effect; that is, color as a physiological phenomenon. Newton did so by viewing colors as epiphenomena, subjective correlates of the mechanical properties of light rays, and Goethe did so by focusing on the role of

---

[68] See Schopenhauer, *Parerga and Paralipomena*, Vol. 2, p. 180/*Sämtliche Werke*, Vol. 6, p. 192.

[69] Ibid., Vol. 2, p. 180/ibid., Vol. 6, p. 192. The quotation is from the first part of *Faust*, line 1928.

[70] Schopenhauer, *On Vision and Colors*, p. 67/*Sämtliche Werke*, Vol. 1, p. 73. As Arthur Hübscher has noted, it was Schopenhauer's interpretation of primary phenomenon that led Goethe to view Schopenhauer as his opponent; see his *The Philosophy of Schopenhauer in Its Intellectual Context*, p. 96.

physical media as light moved from its source to the seeing eye. Although Schopenhauer embraced the poet's claims that white light was homogenous, that there were six and not seven primary colors, and that color necessarily included darkness, he also agreed with Newton's claim that color was a divisional process.[71] To be sure, he denied that color was a divisional process of light rays, as Newton held, by claiming that it was a divisional process of the retina, but this concession did little to brighten Goethe's attitude to his student's theory. This was especially the case given Schopenhauer's claim that white could be produced by colors, and his subsequent claim that Goethe's unconditional denial of the production of white from colors was due to the fact that "... he had constantly in mind Newton's erroneous teaching, and quite rightly contended that the aggregation of colors does not lead to light, for each color is related to darkness as well as to light."[72]

Schopenhauer took considerable pride in showing that colors could be described in terms of definite numerical fractions and that this innovation allowed him to demonstrate the production of white from colors.[73] This must have struck the mathematically skeptical Goethe as an incredible betrayal, because his pupil was employing one of the means by which scientists like Newton could ignore the sound findings of intuition. By viewing color as the qualitatively divided activity of the retina, with black or the inactivity of the retina equaling zero, and white or the full activity of the retina equaling one, Schopenhauer claimed that one of the primary colors and its complementary color equaled one or white. In his letter to Eastlake, Schopenhauer emphasized the significance of this, contrary

---

[71] Technically, Schopenhauer recognized that colors shaded imperceptibly into one another, as seen in a color sphere, and that this entailed an infinite number of colors. This provided no difficulty for his theory, he thought, because the activity of the retina was likewise infinitely divisible. The six primary colors, yellow, violet, orange, blue, green, and red, took pride of place in his theory, because these "three pairs of colors are specially distinguished simply by the rational proportion, easily understood and expressed in simple numbers in which the retina's activity is divided. For this reason, these pairs are everywhere and always expressed by names of their own, but, except for this, there is no other reason, because, after all, they have no advantage over the others." Schopenhauer, *On Vision and Colors*, p. 63/*Sämtliche Werke*, Vol. 1, p. 69.

[72] Ibid., p. 49/ibid., Vol. 1, p. 52.

[73] Schopenhauer recognized these fractions as "hypothetical." See Schopenhauer, ibid., p. 30/ibid., p. 34.

to Goethe's claim, immediately after he had mentioned that his theory would still be true even if Goethe's was wrong:

> ... bearing in mind the numerical fractions, (of the activity of the Retina) by which I express the 6 chief colours, you contemplate these colours singly, then you will find that only by this, and by no other theory upon earth, You come to understand the peculiar sensation, which every colour produces in your eye and thereby get an insight into the very essence of every colour, and of colour in general. Likewise my theory alone gives the true sense in which the notion of *complementary* colours is to be take, viz: as having no reference to light, but to the Retina, and not being a redintegration [sic.] of white light, but of the full activity of the Retina, by which every colour undergoes a bipartition
>
>
>
> either in yellow and violet
>
> $\frac{3}{4}$ $\frac{1}{4}$
>
> or in orange and blue
>
> $\frac{2}{3}$ $\frac{1}{3}$
>
> or in red and green
>
> $\frac{1}{2}$ $\frac{1}{2}$
>
>

This is in short the great mystery.[74]

It is easy to understand why Goethe was displeased by the product of his student. There were significant elements of his color theory that were at odds with those of his teacher. Then there were those letters, dripping with arrogance. Still, Schopenhauer's letters also expressed genuine veneration for Goethe and *On Vision and Colors* strongly condemned Goethe's opponents, decried the reception of Goethe's *On the Theory of Colors*, and praised the poet and condemned Newton. Thus there was an amicable parting between the teacher and the student, as one of Goethe's diary entries from 1815 reports: "Dr. Schopenhauer came to me as a benevolent friend. There are many things which we discussed and about which we agreed. Yet, in the end a separation was unavoidable just as two friends who have walked together for a while part with a handshake, one going north, the other south, quickly losing each other from sight."[75]

---

[74] Schopenhauer, *Gesammelte Briefe*, p. 192. P. F. H. Lauxtermann has noted that Schopenhauer's physiological interpretation of Goethe's theory could have suggested to the poet that Schopenhauer's subjective standpoint could be reconciled in principle with Newton, thereby leaving the objective realm to Newton's physical theory. This was later suggested by Werner Heisenberg about Goethe's view in his "Die Goethesche und die Newtonsche Farbenlehre im Lichte der modernen Physik," in *Wandlungen in der Grundlagen der Naturwissenschaft* (Leipzig, 1943), pp. 58–76; see *Schopenhauer's Broken World-View*, p. 68.

[75] Quoted in Hübscher, *The Philosophy of Schopenhauer in Its Intellectual Context*, p. 97.

And if Schopenhauer's tenacious pursuit of his own truths, even when they challenged those of his hero, led to a parting of the ways with Goethe, Schopenhauer's tenacity also served his hero. He promoted Goethe's color theory throughout his entire life, despite his disappointment in not receiving the blessings of the "godfather" of his "small child."[76] When Frankfurt am Main celebrated the centenary of Goethe's birth in 1849, Schopenhauer filled two sides of a page in an album published by the city. In this entry he decried the fate of Goethe's color theory, arguing that monuments, banquets, speeches, firing of salutes, and ringing of bells were insufficient to atone for the grievous wrong Goethe suffered in connection with his *On the Theory of Colors*. To duly honor the great man, ministers of public instruction should charge academies of learning to conduct a detailed examination and evaluation of Goethe's color theory as well as his oppositions to Newton. "This is," Schopenhauer wrote, "the surest way to remove from Goethe that unmerited ignoring."[77]

Indian Antiquity

When Schopenhauer wrote to Goethe that his work on color theory was a secondary matter compared to other, more important theories that he had in mind, he made this remark from Dresden, where he had retreated after the rancorous riff with his mother. He was attracted to Dresden, a city he had visited on several occasions, due to its beautiful scenery, architecture, and climate, its fine library, the Royal Museum of Antiquities, which contained an extensive collection of sculptures, its picture gallery, and its ready access to scientific equipment. That it lacked a university was of no concern for the young philosopher, who went there to work out his system of philosophy, "which at that time already laid in my head."[78] After being assured by a friend of his mother's, Karl August Böttiger, the chief inspector at the Royal Museum, that the war had not devastated those features of the city that he valued, Schopenhauer arrived on 24 May 1814 at what would be his new home for the next four and

---

[76] Schopenhauer, *Gesammelte Briefe*, p. 192, Schopenhauer to Goethe, 11 November 1815.

[77] Schopenhauer's contribution to the Frankfurt Goethe-Album can be found in *Parerga and Paralipomena*, Vol. 2, pp. 198–200/ *Sämtliche Werke*, Vol. 6, pp. 211–13. The quotation is from ibid., Vol. 2, p. 198/ibid., Vol. 6, p. 212.

[78] Schopenhauer, *Gesammelte Briefe*, pp. 59/655, Schopenhauer to the Philosophy Faculty of the K. Friedrich-Wilhelm University at Berlin, 31 December 1819.

one-half years. He was, however, disappointed that Josef Gans, "a young friend whom I love extraordinarily," decided at the last moment to return to Berlin.[79] *The World as Will and Representation* would be the fruit of Schopenhauer's beloved Dresden years, and he would view this time as the most philosophically productive years of his life.

Yet before he retreated to Dresden, according to Schopenhauer's own report, Friedrich Majer introduced him to "Indian antiquity," during his Goethe winter of 1813–14. Schopenhauer's remark, made some thirty-seven years after the fact, provides no specific reference to either the manner or content of this introduction. All that he wrote was that this "introduction" was unsolicited on his part and that "Indian antiquity" exercised an essential influence on him. It is significant, however, that Schopenhauer mentioned that it was Majer who performed this function, because he never mentioned Majer in any of his books and his name is not found in his literary remains.[80] Majer was a member of Herder's circle of friends, and Herder wrote the complimentary preface to Majer's *On the Cultural History of Peoples, Historical Investigations* [*Zur Kulturgeschichte der Völker, historische Untersuchungen*, Leipzig: J. F. Hartknoch, 1798]. Like Herder, Majer was keen to discover the source of all religions as well as the original text for religions. In this regard he was like many of the Romantics, expressing a mania for what was original, primary, and primeval: the "*Ur*" that prefixed and prefigured some subject – *Urpflanze, Urphänomen, Urreligion, Urstuff, Urtext*. Majer located the original religion in India and the original text in the *Upanishads*, a genre of texts that in Hinduism complete the Vedic corpus.[81] It is likely that Majer induced Schopenhauer to read Abraham Hyacinthe Anquetil-Duperron's *Oup-nek'hat (id est, secretum tegendum)* (2 vols. Argentorati: Levrault, 1801). In any case, Schopenhauer borrowed this book on 26 March 1814 from the local library in Weimar, along with Polier's *Mythology of the Hindus*

---

[79] Ibid., p. 10, Schopenhauer to Karl August Böttiger, 24 April 1814.

[80] Even when Schopenhauer referred to Majer's translation of the *Bhagavad-gītā* in the first edition of *The World as Will and Representation*, he did not mention its translator, but only that it was found in the *Asiatic Magazine*; see Vol. 1, p. 388/*Sämtliche Werke*, Vol. 2, p. 459.

[81] See App, "Schopenhauer's Initial Encounter with Indian Thought," pp. 52–6. Schopenhauer owned Majer's *Brahma or the Religion of the Indians as Brahmanism* [*Brahma oder die Religion der Indier als Brahmaismus*, 1818], but as far as I can tell, Schopenhauer never referred to it in any of his works. In addition to owning this book, Schopenhauer also owned his *On the Cultural History of the Peoples*; see *Der handschriftliche Nachlaß*, Vol. 5, p. 336.

[*Mythologie des Indous*, Rudolstadt and Paris: 1809]. He returned the former on 5 May 1814 and the latter on 3 June 1814.[82]

Prior to Schopenhauer's borrowing of Duperron's and Polier's texts, however, he had checked out two volumes of the *Asiatic Magazine* [*Asiatisches Magazin*, 1802], which was edited by Julius Klaproth, the son of Martin Heinrich Klaproth, Schopenhauer's chemistry professor at Berlin. Schopenhauer held these volumes from 4 December 1813 through 30 March 1814. Both Klaproth and Majer were frequent contributors to the *Asiatic Magazine*, but in ways that employed highly questionable tactics, "... which included passing off other people's work as their own, either by leaving articles by others unsigned (editor Klaproth) or by stating in big letters 'by Friedrich Majer' even when his was only translation from English."[83] Majer's translation from the English refers to his German translation of *The Bhagvat-Geeta, or Dialogues of Kreeshna and Arjoon; in Eighteen Lectures* (1785), which was translated from the Sanskrit by Charles Wilkins. Majer's translation "Der Bhagvat-Geeta, oder Gespräche zwischen Kreeshna und Arjoon," appeared as five separate entries in the *Asiatic Magazine* (Vol. 1, 1802), and Schopenhauer made excerpts from this translation that reinforced his earlier distinctions between the better and empirical consciousness, as well as his innovative claim that it is from one's own body that enlightenment can be derived.[84]

---

[82] See App, ibid., p. 51. As App makes clear, Madame Marie-Elisabeth de Polier was the editor of her cousin Colonel de Polier's *Mythology of the Hindus*; see p. 57.

[83] Ibid., p. 51. Also see App, "Schopenhauers Begegnung mit Buddhismus," *Schopenhauer-Jahrbuch*, Vol. 79 (1998), pp. 42–3, for an account of Klaproth's plagiarism of Joseph de Guignes' *Histoire génerale des Huns, des Tures, des Mogols* (1756) in his "Ueber die Fo-Religion in China," *Asiatisches Magazin*, Vol. 1 (1802), pp. 144–69. App views Klaproth's article as Schopenhauer's first reading of Buddhist theories from China.

[84] See App, "Schopenhauer's Encounter with Indian Thought," p. 62. App suggests that the earliest sign of Schopenhauer's "Indian-related" reading may be found in Schopenhauer's use of the metaphor of Atlas carrying the earth, an elephant carrying Atlas, a tortoise carrying the elephant, and nothing carrying the tortoise, at *Manuscript Remains*, Vol. 1, p., 104/*Der handschriftliche Nachlaß*, Vol. 1, p. 96. App cites Majer's "Die Verkörperungen des Wischnu" [The Incarnations of Vishnu], *Asiatisches Magazin*, Vol. 1, pp. 235–6; Vol. 2, p. 250, as a possible source of this metaphor. App, however, notes that the tortoise metaphor was also used by Locke (see *An Essay Concerning Human Understanding*, Bk. II, Chap. xxiii, para. 2). Schopenhauer first read Locke's *Essay* in the summer of 1812, at Berlin. Schopenhauer's few notes from this initial reading of Locke do not mention Locke's use of this metaphor. App also reproduces and analyzes Schopenhauer's two excerpts from Majer's translation of the *Bhagavad-gītā*, pp. 68–75.

It could be said that Majer introduced Schopenhauer to "Indian antiquity" by telling him about his work in the *Asiatic Magazine*. Then again,
Klaproth could have directed him to the *Asiatic Magazine* and by hap-
penstance he may have discovered Majer's translation of the *Bhagavad-
gītā*. Thus this could have been the unsolicited introduction to "Indian
antiquity." Goethe, however, who met with both Majer and Klaproth,
during this time, could have directed Schopenhauer to this "discovery."
Yet if Schopenhauer's reference to "Indian antiquity" was to a single
source, and Majer directed him to a source that had an essential influence
on him, then Schopenhauer was likely referring to the *Upanishads*, which
he borrowed from the ducal library on 26 March 1814. Indeed, Schopenhauer deeply valued the insights found in these works and attributed to
them a significant role in the genesis of his philosophy. Already by 1816,
he set them at par with Plato and Kant: "I confess, by the way, that I do
not believe that my theory could have come about before the *Upanishads*,
Plato, and Kant could cast their rays simultaneously into the mind of
one man."[85] Two years later, in the introduction to *The World as Will
and Representation*, he would articulate the grounds for understanding his
philosophy in a way that suggested the comparative significance of these
light rays. A thorough acquaintance with Kant's philosophy, he said, was
required; a knowledge of Plato would make one more susceptible to his
views; and one who shared the benefits of the Vedas, whose access had
been made possible by the *Upanishads*, would be best prepared to hear
what he had to say, because it would not appear to that reader, as it would
to many others, that he spoke in a foreign and hostile tongue. But, immediately after making this assertion, he wrote, " . . . if it did not sound too
arrogant, I might assert that each of the disconnected utterances that make
up the *Upanishads* could be derived as a consequence from the thought I
am to impart, although conversely my thought is by no means to be found
in the *Upanishads*."[86] Nevertheless, he also recognized the "superhuman

[85] Schopenhauer, *Manuscript Remains*, Vol. 1, p. 467/*Der handschriftliche Nachlaß*, Vol. 1,
   p. 422.
[86] Schopenhauer, *The World as Will and Representation*, Vol. 1, pp. xv–xvi/*Sämtliche Werke*,
   Vol. 2, pp. xii–xiii. Schopenhauer dated the first preface "Dresden, August 1818." His reference to "the thought I am to impart" is a reference to his earlier claim that his philosophy was
   the expression of a "single thought"; ibid., p. xii/ibid., p. viii. Schopenhauer's stance toward
   the *Upanishads* here prefigures his stance toward Eastern thought in general: namely, that the
   core of his philosophical thought was independent from these sources. Here Schopenhauer
   seems to suggest that a reader familiar with the *Upanishads* would find similar ideas in his

conceptions recorded in the *Upanishads*."[87] Later he wrote to a friend that the *Upanishads* "is the primeval thought-base of wisdom and truth."[88] In the first edition to *The World as Will and Representation*, Schopenhauer would preface the "fourth book," the "ethical book," with an epigram from the *Oupnek'hat*: "The moment knowledge appeared on the scene thence abated desire."[89]

Some thirty-seven years after his introduction to the Upanishads, and after reading extensively in philosophy, science, religion, and literature, he judged that work to be "the most profitable and sublime reading that is possible in the world; it has been the consolation of my life and will be of my death."[90] The translation that he borrowed from the ducal library, which he later purchased, would be annotated throughout his life, and he remained faithful to it even when new translations appeared. This translation was even linguistically more distant from its original than Majer's translation of the *Bhagavad-gītā*. Whereas Majer's German translation was of an English translation from the Sanskrit, Schopenhauer's beloved book was a Latin translation from a Persian translation from the Sanskrit. It also contained commentary by Śankara (c. 780–c. 820), the foremost exponent of Advaita Vedānta, the non-dualist form

---

philosophy and so his philosophy would not appear strange, but his single thought was independent from this source and it systematically grounds all of his ideas in a way that cannot be found in the *Upanishads*.

[87] Schopenhauer, *The World as Will and Representation*, Vol. 2, p. 162/*Sämtliche Werke*, Vol. 3, p. 178.

[88] Schopenhauer, *Gesammelte Briefe*, p. 384, Schopenhauer to Adam von Doß, 27 February 1856.

[89] Schopenhauer, *The World as Will and Representation*, Vol. 1 p. 269/*Sämtliche Werke*, Vol. 2, p. 317. The quotation is from Duperron's *Oupnek'hat*, Vol. 2, p. 216. This quotation can also be fond in a note from 1814 (Dresden); see *Manuscript Remains*, Vol. 1, p. 130/*Der handschriftliche Nachlaß*, Vol. 1, p. 120. *The World as Will and Representation* was divided into four "books": the first presented Schopenhauer's epistemology, the second his metaphysics of nature, the third his aesthetics, and the fourth his ethics. He originally prefaced the three earlier books with epigrams by Rousseau, Goethe, and Plato, respectively. With the second edition of this work, he replaced the Goethe quotation, "*Daß ich erkenne, was die Welt/Im Innersten zusammenhält/Schau' alle Wirkenskraft und Samen/Und thu' nicht mehr in Worten Kramen*" [That I learn what holds the world together, view all of its working force and seeds, and no longer be brought to words], *Faust*, Part 1, lines 382–5, with one from Agrippa von Nettesheim: "He dwells in us, not in the nether world, not in the starry heavens. The spirit living within us fashions all this," *Epistles, Opera Omnia*, Vol. 14.

[90] Schopenhauer, *Parerga and Paralipomena*, Vol. 2, p. 397/*Sämtliche Werke*, Vol. 6, p. 427. Gwinner, who called the *Oupnek'hat* Schopenhauer's bible, also claimed that Schopenhauer frequently would look at a passage to perform his devotions before he went to bed; see *Arthur Schopenhauer aus persönlichen Umgange dargestellt*, p. 192.

of Vedānta philosophy, which has been said to bear traces of the idealistic metaphysics of Buddhism.[91] The Persian translation was executed in the mid-seventeenth century by the Sultan Mohammed Dara Shikoh and a group of Persian scholars, an act, Schopenhauer claimed, that resulted in the execution of Sultan Dara by his brother, during a Persian return to Islamic orthodoxy.[92] The author of the Latin translation was the Frenchman Abraham Hyacinthe Anquetil-Duperron, who had also translated into Latin the *Zend-Avesta* (1791), a work that combines the holy book of Zoroastrianism, the *Avesta*, and commentary on that text. Duperron's two-volume *Oupnek'hat*, whose title is a corruption of the word "Upanishad," appeared in 1801, and it included numerous annotations and explanations by its translator, including in its first volume "Parergon De Kantismo," where Duperron attempted to link elements of the Upanishads to Kant's metaphysics, a connection Schopenhauer would also maintain.[93] Schopenhauer valued Duperron's literal translations of the Persian, his faithfulness to its syntax, and his retention of the Persian convention of leaving important Sanskrit terms untranslated in the text. Later, when he encountered translations of Eastern works that employed terms drawn from Western theology to translate Eastern terms, especially using "God" for "Brahma" or "soul" for "ātman," he became beside himself with an anger almost comparable to what he displayed toward European attempts to convert Eastern peoples to Christianity.[94] It would be in Weimar, after his exposure to the *Asiatic Magazine* and the *Oupnek'hat*, as

---

[91] The philosophy of Vedānta, recognized as the end or culmination of the Vedas, is based on the *Bhagavad-gītā*, the *Brahma Sūtra* or *Vedānta Sūtra*, and the *Upanishads*. The sūtra or manual is employed to provide order and connections between the unsystematic and scattered reflections of the *Upanishads*.

[92] See Schopenhauer, *Parerga and Parlipomena*, Vol. 2, p. 398/ *Sämtliche Werke*, Vol. 3, p. 423, where he refers to the beheading of Sultan Daras by his brother Aurengzeb "for the greater glory of God."

[93] App notes that Madame de Polier also "wanted the *Oupenek'hat* to be compared with the metaphysical ideas of Kant," in "Schopenhauer's Initial Encounter with Indian Thought," p. 57.

[94] A good example of Schopenhauer's outrage at the translation of Eastern terms by those drawn from the Western religious tradition can be found in his annotations to Rām Mohan Roy's *Translation of Several Principal Books, Passages, and Texts of the Vedas* (London: Parbury, Allen & Co., 1832). To a passage in which Roy rendered "Brahmā" as "God," he wrote, "by comparison Anquetil [Duperron], that our miserable Apostate [Roy was a Hindu] has corrupted the text, his mind being taken in by those absurd & revolting Jewish superstitions" (Schopenhauer's English), *Der handschriftliche Nachlaß*, Vol. 5, p. 341. For an example of his condemnation of the missionary zeal of Europeans to convert Eastern peoples to Christianity, see *Parerga and Parlipomena*, Vol. 2, pp. 222–26/ *Sämtliche Werke*, Vol. 6, pp. 236–41. He did,

he was developing the basic "dogmas" of his emerging metaphysics, which he had already envisioned in 1813 in Berlin as a metaphysics and ethics in one, where he would begin to formulate and give greater expression to his thought by integrating terms drawn from Indian sources. In what is perhaps his first use of a significant term drawn from "Indian antiquity," Schopenhauer wrote:

> For sharing in the *Peace of God* (in other words for the appearance of the *better consciousness*) it is necessary that man, this frail, finite, and transitory being, be something different; that he become aware of himself no longer as a human being at all, but as something quite different. For insofar as he is alive and is a human being, he is doomed but not merely to *sin* and *death*, but also to *illusion* [*Wahn*] and this *illusion* is as real as life, as real as the world of the senses itself, indeed it is identical with these (māyā of the Indians). On it are based all our desires and cravings, which are again only the expression of life, just as life is only the expression of illusion. To the extent that we live, will to live, and are human beings, the illusion is truth; only in reference to the better consciousness is it illusion.[95]

Here Schopenhauer identifies *māyā* with the world of the senses, which is an "illusion," the ground or field for the expression of our longings and desires, the world of sin and death. It is also that which is transcended by the better consciousness. He will develop further the idea of *māyā* within the context of his epistemology and ethics. *Māyā*, Kant's phenomenal world, and Plato's world of things coming to be and perishing would assume the same status, and the morally good person and the saint would be those who saw through this world of illusion.[96]

Schopenhauer continued to study the *Oupnek'hat*. Shortly after his arrival in Dresden, he borrowed it from the library from 8 June through 16 July 1814. As he labored on the manuscript for *On Vision and Colors*, his notes from that period contain few attempts to integrate Eastern ideas into his metamorphosing philosophy of the better consciousness beyond the notion of *māyā*, but this is done as he also struggles to find stimulating ideas from Kant, Plato, Jacob Böhme, Giordano Bruno, Jacobi, Schelling,

---

however, praise "Christian evangelists" when they provided "faithful" translations of Eastern sacred books; see ibid., Vol. 2, p. 226/ibid., Vol. 6, p. 241.

[95] Schopenhauer, *Manuscript Remains*, Vol. 1, pp. 114–15/*Der handschriftliche Nachlaß*, Vol. 1, p. 104.

[96] For a thoughtful and careful study of Indian influences on the genesis and development of Schopenhauer's philosophy, see Douglas L. Berger's *"The Veil of Māyā": Schopenhauer's System and Early Indian Thought* (Binghamton, NY: Global Academic Publishing, 2004). Berger carefully elucidates, both sympathetically and critically, how Schopenhauer used the notion of *māyā* as a falsification thesis in his epistemology, metaphysics, ethics, and soteriology.

Fichte, and various dicta from the *Bible* and Christian theology and as he is formulating the basic "dogmas" of his philosophy proper. There is no hard evidence that he read any fresh Eastern texts during this time, besides the *Oupnek'hat*, which he likely purchased that summer. But on 7 November he began to borrow various volumes of the *Asiatick Researches*, a journal he had first heard about in Heeren's Göttingen lectures in the summer of 1811.[97] Through May of 1816, he borrowed at least nine volumes of this English journal. Schopenhauer carefully made extracts from this journal, copying passages in which he underlined various interesting words and phrases, made marginal notes that indicated topics, and referred to essays in other articles in the journal and to the *Oupnek'hat*, and he drew connections to various concepts expressed in his emerging philosophy. For example, he copied a passage from the *Taittirīya Upanishad*; "That whence all beings are produced: that, by which they live, when born: that, towards which they tend; & that into which they pass; do thou seek, for that is <u>Brahme</u>. He thought deeply, & having thus meditated, he knew <u>Ananda</u> (or Felicity) to be <u>Brahme</u>: for all beings are indeed produced for pleasure; when born they live by joy; they tend towards happiness; they pass into felicity." Next to this passage he wrote "The will to life is the source and the essence of things."[98]

The articles in *Asiatick Researches* supplemented Schopenhauer's original exposure to Hinduism and Buddhism. In particular, the Buddhist concepts of transmigration of the soul, *nirvāna*, and *karma*, the claim that life was suffering and that enlightenment overcame this suffering, and the statement that followers of Buddha rejected the metaphysics of Vedānta drew his attention. He also copied passages that stated that Buddhism was an atheistic religion and that it explicitly rejected the idea of a creator God. He discovered that the Chinese referred to Buddha as "Fo" and "Shaka" and that the Burmese used "Gotama" for the same person. He noted that there was a Dalai Lama, and he copied the phrase "Buddha was Avatar," without questioning how a godless religion could view Buddha as an earthly manifestation or incarnation of a deity.[99] He also found that

---

[97] The inestimable Urs App provides Schopenhauer's copy-notes, emphases, and marginal notes to *Asiatick Researches* in "Notes and Excerpts by Schopenhauer Related to Volumes 1–9 of the *Asiatick Researches*," *Schopenhauer-Jahrbuch*, Vol. 79 (1998), pp. 15–33.

[98] Ibid., p. 31.

[99] See App, "Schopenhauers Begegnung mit dem Buddhismus," p. 39. App mentions here that he is working on a book tentatively titled *Schopenhauers Entdeckung des Buddhismus*. Given

the Burmese, although ignorant of a supreme being, had a "system of *morals*. . . as good as that held forth by any of the religious doctrines prevailing among mankind."[100] The great number of followers of Buddhism impressed him greatly.

Schopenhauer devoured the ever-increasing Indological and Sinological literature throughout his life.[101] He would favor Hinduism and Buddhism. But although he esteemed Hinduism, particularly Advaita Vedānta, and he never revered a Buddhist text as he did the *Upanishads*, he regarded Buddhism as the most distinguished religion on earth, because of "its intrinsic excellence and truth . . . because of the overwhelming number of its followers."[102] In the same book in which he made this claim, *On the Will in Nature* (1836), he included a chapter on "Sinology," but not one on "Indology," and he included it despite the fact that the main thrust of the book was to demonstrate how the empirical sciences corroborated his philosophy. In the second edition of *The World as Will and Representation*, he held that if the results of his philosophy served as the standard of truth, Buddhism would rank the highest of all religions for articulating the truth.[103] In the last decade in his life, he would refer to himself as a "Buddhist," and he told Frédéric Morin that Buddha, Plato, and Kant were the three immortals of philosophy.[104] He also purchased a

---

the high quality of App's careful work concerning Schopenhauer and Eastern thought, this should be a significant contribution to Schopenhauer studies.

[100] App, "Notes and Excerpts by Schopenhauer Related to Volumes 1–9 of the *Asiatick Researches*," p. 20.

[101] App, "Schopenhauers Begegnung mit dem Buddhismus," pp. 55–6, provides a chronological table on themes concerning Schopenhauer and Buddhism. App also summarized in this article three phases of Schopenhauer's encounter with Buddhism: (1) 1811–17 includes materials from Heeren's Summer 1811 ethnography lectures at Göttingen, his reading of the *Asiatic Magazine*, the *Oupnek'hat*, and the *Asiatick Researches*, with the last containing most of the themes to which Schopenhauer would devote himself, such as *nirvāna* and the "excellent ethics" of this atheistic religion, as well as the idea of transmigration of the soul; (2) 1825–44, his familiarity with Mahāyāna Buddhism, Chinese Chan Buddhism, and additional sources concerning Vedānta; and (3) 1845–60, his more intensive study of works that included more fundamental information about the Sanskrit source texts and on the Indian origin of Buddhism, and his more intensive reading about Mahāyāna Buddhism; see pp. 53–4.

[102] Schopenhauer, *On the Will in Nature*, pp. 130–31/*Sämtliche Werke*, Vol. 4, pp. 130–31.

[103] See Schopenhauer, *The World as Will and Representation*, Vol. 2, p. 169/*Sämtliche Werke*, Vol. 3, p. 186.

[104] More specifically, Schopenhauer referred to "We Buddhists," in a letter to Adam von Doß (10 May 1852), and Carl Georg Bähr reported that Schopenhauer used this phrase in conversations about Buddhism (1 May 1858); see, respectively, Schopenhauer, *Gesammelte*

black-lacquered bronze Buddha, which he gilded and placed on a console
in the corner of his Frankfurt apartment, so that every visitor had to
observe it. He told a friend that it was positioned so that the morning sun
would illuminate it and reflect its light into the apartment of a pastor who
lived across the street from him, and to another acquaintance, Schopenhauer said that the Buddha statue was his counterpart to the crucifix.[105]

Yet in the same passage in which Schopenhauer described his delight
with the close agreement between his philosophy and Buddhism, he also
claimed that his pleasure was enhanced by the fact that he developed
his philosophy without its influence: "For up to 1818, when my work
appeared, there were to be found in Europe only a few accounts of Buddhism, and those extremely incomplete and inadequate, confined almost
exclusively to a few essays in the earlier volumes of the *Asiatick Researches*,
and principally concerned with the Buddhism of the Burmese."[106] This
striking remark is reminiscent of his earlier assertion that each of the
disconnected passages found in the *Upanishads* could be derived from his
philosophy and that the single thought articulated in *The World as Will and
Representation* could not be found in that work. Certainly, his assessment
of the state of European knowledge of Buddhism at the time of the publication of his main work is correct. It does not follow, however, that the

---

Briefe, p. 281 and *Gespräche*, p. 244. Morin reported that Schopenhauer made the remark
about Buddha, Plato, and Kant in a conversation with him that took place in the beginning
of March 1858; see *Gespräche*, p. 324.

[105] Eduard Crüger's conversation with Schopenhauer (1856) is the source for the illuminated
Buddha story; see ibid., p. 198.

[106] Schopenhauer, *The World as Will and Representation*, Vol. 2, p. 169/ *Sämtliche Werke*, Vol. 3,
p. 186. Schopenhauer, who acknowledges reading *Asiatick Researches* prior to his publishing
his principal work, was straightforward concerning his sources. Even in the first edition of
The World as Will and Representation, he carefully mentions the sources of his claims about
Eastern thought. In a footnote, he mentions Duperron's *Oupnek'hat*, Polier's *Mythologie des
Indous*, Klaproths's translation of the *Bhadavad-gītā*, "On the Fo-Religion," from the first
volume of the *Asiatic Magazine*, and Sir William Jones' "Moha-Mudgava," and "Institutes of
Hindu Law, or the Ordinances of Manu," from the second volume of the *Asiatic Magazine*.
Last, he mentions *Asiatick Researches*; see Schopenhauer, ibid., Vol. 1, p. 388 [p. 557 first
edition]/ibid., Vol. 2, p. 459 (Schopenhauer's only addition to his original note, made in
the third edition [1859], was "In the last forty years Indian literature has grown so much in
Europe, that if I now wished to complete this note from the first edition, it would fill several
pages"). He also included a list of recommended books on Buddhism in *On the Will in Nature*,
pp. 130–31/ *Sämtliche Werke*, Vol. 4, pp. 130–31, where he credited Spence Hardy's *Eastern
Monachism: An Account of the Origin, Laws, Discipline . . . of the Order of Mendicants Founded
by Gôtama Buddha* (London, 1850) and *A Manual of Buddhism, in Its Modern Development*
(London, 1853) as providing him with "more insight into the true nature of the Buddhist
dogma than have any others."

little he knew about Buddhism had no formative role in the development of his thought. To be sure, Schopenhauer never used the language of influence to describe the agreements between his philosophy and those of Plato and Kant, but neither did he deny that their philosophies played a role in the genesis of his own. Why would he say this about Buddhism?

The context of Schopenhauer's remark about Buddhism may answer the last question. It was made within an extended discussion of the relationship between philosophy and religion. He considered both philosophical and religious systems of thought as attempting to address a profound human need for metaphysics, a need prompted by wonder or astonishment about the world. But unlike the wonder that Plato and Aristotle claimed gave rise to philosophy, the astonishment Schopenhauer found as giving birth to metaphysics was more visceral. It was grounded and intensified by the recognition of the ubiquity of suffering and death. Both philosophy and religion attempted to provide metaphysical explanations of the world to account for these troubling features of existence, ones that also tried to provide consolation for these woes by articulating the significance of living in a world seeped in misery and death. But although Schopenhauer recognized a common source and common goal for philosophy and religion, he also found them employing radically different means. Religion produced a metaphysics for the masses, one suitable for the level of intelligence possessed by the common person. The truth cannot appear naked for such folk, Schopenhauer thought, and it had to be veiled by myths, mysteries, and allegories to console the common person. Whatever truth was presented by religion was truth *sensu allegorico*. Conversely, the philosopher wrote for those of a higher intellect and for those to whom the truth must appear raw. Consequently, the philosopher must present the truth *per se* and demonstrate each and every one of its claims. The more valuable a religion, Schopenhauer argued, the greater truth it has under the veil of allegory and the more transparent its veil.[107]

Schopenhauer assessed Buddhism as the religion having the greatest value, because it expressed truth beneath the lightest of veils.[108] Still, its

---

[107] See Chap. 17, "On the Human Need for Metaphysics," *The World as Will and Representation*, Vol. 2, pp. 160–87/*Sämtliche Werke*, Vol. 3, pp. 175–209, for Schopenhauer's discussion of the relationships between philosophy, religion, and the natural sciences. This chapter also includes the best description of his non-Kantian conception of metaphysics as providing the correct explanation of experience as a whole.

[108] Douglas L. Berger has noted that Schopenhauer's knowledge of Indian philosophy was almost restricted to its presystematic period and that "Schopenhauer had no real knowledge

truth was veiled. Although Schopenhauer became familiar with the topic and themes of Buddhism as he was laboring on his philosophy, it was only later in his philosophical career that he was able to see through its veil and to discover some of the same truths nakedly expressed by his philosophy. And as his knowledge of Buddhism increased, he also began to understand some of the most significant experiences parallel to those of Buddha. For example, he copied a passage from *Asiatick Researches* in which it was said that *nirvāna* ended transmigration and that obtaining *nirvāna* allowed a person to no longer be subject to weight, old age, disease and death. In 1817, almost a year afterward, he rejected transmigration as a "dogma," but commended it as a myth, a copy or image of the truth, and found this myth negatively suggesting a reward to virtue, *nirvāna*, "a state in which there are not four things, namely pain, old age, sickness, and death." Then, in 1832, he would come to view the misery that he encountered closing his grand tour of Europe in 1803–4 as parallel to the Buddha's youthful confrontation with sickness, old age, pain, and death.[109] It still waits for us to see what Schopenhauer would make of Buddhism and what Buddhism would make of him.[110]

---

or appreciation of classical or new *Nyāya* logic, Vaiśesika ontology, the Grammarian's philosophy of language, the Buddhist phenomenalist, logical or epistemological systems, not even the sophisticated formulations on consciousness developed by the sects of Vedānta's great commentarial traditions." Berger also correctly indicates that Schopenhauer's claim that Hindu and Buddhist traditions were largely "mythological," which was a view that he shared with the Schlegels, Schelling, and Hegel, was widely adopted in Europe for almost a century and was a perspective promoted by twentieth century neo-Vedāntins; see '*The Veil of Māyā*': *Schopenhauer's System and Early Indian Thought*, pp. 241–2. It should be mentioned, however, that Hegel and Schopenhauer viewed all religious traditions as mythological.

[109] For the passage from *Asiatick Researches*, see App, "Notes and Excerpts by Schopenhauer Related to Volumes 1–9 of the *Asiatick Researches*," p. 21, where Schopenhauer quotes pp. 180, 266 of Vol. 6. The 1817 note can be found in Schopenhauer, *Manuscript Remains*, Vol. 1, pp. 487–8. Schopenhauer would use most of this note in the first edition of *The World as Will and Representation*, pp. 512–13 (Vol. 1, 355–6), but expanded it to include remarks about the *Upanishads*. For the parallel Schopenhauer drew between his youthful experiences and Buddha's, see *Manuscript Remains*, Vol. 4, p. 119/*Der handschriftliche Nachlaß*, Vol. 4, p. 96.

[110] Moira Nicholls provides a comprehensive listing of Schopenhauer's "oriental sources," listed under specific titles in his *oeuvre*, in "The Influence of Eastern Thought on Schopenhauer's Doctrine of the Thing-in-Itself," in *The Cambridge Companion to Schopenhauer* (Cambridge: Cambridge University Press, 2000), pp. 197–204. In this worthwhile essay, Nicholl builds a plausible case that the shifts in Schopenhauer's view of the thing in itself were, in part, responses to his increased knowledge of Buddhism and Hinduism.

7

The Single Thought
of Dresden

D RESDEN PROVIDED A safe haven for Schopenhauer's conflicted life. He abandoned Weimar, deeply wounded by his mother's rejection, and he sought refuge in this Saxon city of around fifty thousand souls, a city with which he was familiar even before his family reposed there for ten days at the close of the European tour. At that earlier time, he found the city "beautiful and interesting," and he savored its picture gallery and robust natural beauty. It is likely that upon his return he revisited the "magnificent Catholic church" to re-experience its "glorious church music," which moved the young man to attend High Mass twice in 1804.[1] Much later, he would recommend the use of a large organ, reduced to the very limits of audibility, to constantly lay down the ground-bass and thereby to enhance the effect of the orchestra, "as is done in the Catholic church in Dresden."[2] Yet if his heart hurt from his experience with his mother, his head was alive, focused on color, the sunrise of the East, and the foundational ideas for his system of philosophy. In Dresden he would practice what he would soon preach; the head as the cure for the pangs of the heart and the intellect's triumph over the will. And although Dresden was his home for only fifty-two months, from the end of May 1814 to the end of September 1818, it became the permanent home ground for his philosophical thought. It was the hometown of *On Vision and Colors*, and in Dresden his "whole philosophy emerged, rising like a beautiful landscape from the morning mist".[3] It was the birthplace of *The World as*

---

[1] Schopenhauer, *Reise-Tagebücher aus den Jahren 1803–1804*, pp. 308–9. The Schopenhauers spent from 12 to 22 August 1804 in Dresden. In his journal entry, Schopenhauer remarked that they had been in Dresden "many times."

[2] Schopenhauer, *Parerga and Paralipomena*, Vol. 2, p. 433/*Sämtliche Werke*, Vol. 6, p. 461.

[3] Schopenhauer, *Manuscript Remains*, Vol. 1, p. 122fn/*Die handschriftliche Nachlaß*, Vol. 1, p 113.

Will and Representation, whose ideas he would spend the remainder of his life seeking to clarify, to correct, and to extend into ever new domains of thought. Intellectually he was always connected to Dresden.

Schopenhauer attracted some associates in Dresden who were later transformed into "youthful friends" by the grinding wheel of time, which smoothed over some of the rough edges of their relationships. In Dresden, however, he had no comrades with whom he forged a deep, lifelong, and strong bond or a sense of common cause and purpose. He did not find someone whom he judged his equal, nor did he share a sense of brother-hood as he had earlier with his "French brother," Anthime Grégoire de Blésimaire. Still, he was well received in Dresden, perhaps because his mother was not there to caution others away from her moody, morose, and loudly opinionated son. He even told Goethe that he was generally well received by others, even though his innate disposition to truth and honesty –which moved him to question ideas such as Goethe's that lay close to his heart – also extended into his practical and personal lives. He felt, he wrote, a sense of well-being in Dresden, because "almost no person nurses any suspicions about me, rather almost everyone trusts me without any closer personal acquaintance."[4] Despite his tendency to bois-terous sarcasm, his delight in bashing the literary dilettanti, with whom the city was thick, and his inclination to demonstrate his erudition to friend and foe alike, Schopenhauer managed friendly relationships with the landowner and art critic Johann Gottlob (later von) Quandt, the writer Friedrich August Schulze, who wrote under the pseudonym "Friedrich Laun," and the artist Ludwig Sigismund Ruhl.

Quandt, who was a year older than Schopenhauer, maintained a loose contact with Schopenhauer throughout the philosopher's life. The philosopher had a lasting affection for the art critic. The former thought little about the latter's intellectual abilities, and Quandt was unimpressed by Schopenhauer's philosophical accomplishments. It annoyed Quandt that whenever he made some insightful remark, Schopenhauer would ask him where he had read it.[5] Yet he trusted Quandt to receive and hold the author's copies of *The World as Will and Representation* while Schopenhauer toured Italy. Quandt, however, did not read the pub-lished work until thirty years later, and then he read the first and not the

4 Schopenhauer, *Gesammelte Briefe*, p. 16, Schopenhauer to Goethe, 3 September 1815.
5 Gwinner mentions this in *Arthur Schopenhauer aus persönlichem Umgange dargestellt*, p. 64.

second volume of its second edition. Afterward, he sent to Schopenhauer a twelve-page "polemic," which included the barb, "The route that you found from realism to idealism is a discovery greater than that made by the Portuguese, which required crossing the ocean to go from Europe to India."[6] Instead of being offended by this polemic, which he was inclined to do even when one of his philosophical allies crossed him, Schopenhauer was simply amused that this "arch-Hegelian" had criticized him from the standpoints of realism, pantheism, and optimism, a trio of "isms" that he loathed. Moreover, for the older Schopenhauer to call someone an "arch-Hegelian" was usually the same as calling another the chief agent of the devil. Nevertheless, he forgave Quandt his vices, suggesting that he thought that his old acquaintance knew not what he did. Instead of replying to Quandt's criticisms he simply told him to read the second volume of his principal work. He wrote to Frauenstädt that the only part of *The World as Will and Representation* that Quandt approved was its aesthetics, because that was the only part he understood. It would be a wasted effort to respond to Quandt's criticism, he continued, because ". . . he is not a man like Becker with whom I engaged in controversy."[7] Becker had the type of intellect that made it worthwhile to challenge; Quandt was not worth the trouble. Schopenhauer believed that he was simply a harmless philosophical dabbler.

But what accounted for Schopenhauer's affection for a man whose philosophical allegiances should have drawn his contempt? Quandt had met Johanna and Adele Schopenhauer in the summer of 1815 in Karlsbad. He became a confidant and friend of the philosopher's sister, who even vaguely contemplated marrying the rich aesthete, a union Schopenhauer would have endorsed.[8] Quandt never seriously entertained the notion of marrying the desperate young woman, but he was particularly sensitive

---

[6] Schopenhauer, *Gesammelte Briefe*, p. 234, Schopenhauer to Frauenstädt, 2 March 1849. The letter contains Schopenhauer's remarks about the realism, optimism, and pantheism behind Quandt's polemic, as well as his claim that he was an "arch-Hegelian."

[7] Ibid., p. 234, Schopenhauer to Frauenstädt, 2 March 1849. After paging through Quandt's *Knowledge and Being [Wissen und Seyn*, 1859], Schopenhauer told David Asher that "my good old friend attempts things that are beyond his sphere," ibid., p. 460, 10 November 1859.

[8] As late as 1836, Schopenhauer mentioned Quandt as a husband for his sister. Adele told him sharply to not speak to her of this, because ". . . regret does not lie in my nature, I have reasons *that still stand*, and I regret nothing of this sort. Respect that, dear Arthur!" Lütkehaus, *Die Schopenhauers*, p. 380f., Adele to Arthur, 23 January 1836. Quandt's affection for the brother, however, was deeper than that for the sister. He wrote to Adele that "I am so very fond of

to the desultory effects of the Schopenhauers' fragmented family life. It
appears that it was Adele who encouraged Quandt to contact her brother
in Dresden, and due to his relationship to Adele and his knowledge of
his family's history, Schopenhauer spoke more candidly with Quandt
about his break with his mother than he did with others.[9] It was not,
however, that the philosopher opened his heart to the art critic – he was
too reserved and suspicious to do so with any person. Yet he said enough
for Quandt to sense his despair. He reported to Adele that he had observed
" . . . in his [Schopenhauer's] heart the throbbing of a monstrous pain that
appeared to accompany the memory of a terrible epoch in his life."[10] He
attributed this pain to Schopenhauer's break with his mother and sensed
that it resulted from an enduring affection for his mother. Believing that
Schopenhauer longed for reconciliation, Quandt encouraged Adele to take
action. Had Fernow been alive, he told her in the same letter, he could have
served as an intermediary between mother and son, given Schopenhauer's
great respect for the man. Absent Fernow, Quandt encouraged Adele to
try to convince Johanna to take the first step in reconciliation, which,
he assured Adele, Schopenhauer would welcome, but would not make
himself. "After all," he wrote, "should it not be your mother's desires to
win back and to save such an excellent son?" Quandt was as correct about
Schopenhauer's unwillingness to make the first move as he was incorrect
about Adele's willingness to try to persuade her mother to reconcile. She
knew her mother all too well. Nevertheless, the deep concern Quandt
demonstrated about the philosopher's well-being and his friendship with
Adele endeared him to Schopenhauer.[11]

    Schopenhauer also associated with "my good, dear, loyal, old *Schulz[e]
Friedr: Laun.*"[12] Schulze was a highly prolific and popular author, known
for the humor and simplicity of his writings. With August Apel he edited

him [Schopenhauer] that I feel that I will be fond of him forever," quoted in Paul Deussen's
"Schopenhauers Leben," *Sechstes Jahrbuch der Schopenhauer-Gesellschaft* (1917), p. 21.

[9] See Gabriele Büch, *Alles Leben ist Traum: Adele Schopenhauer*, p. 109. In *Johanna Schopenhauer*, Ulrike Bergmann reports that Quandt had already told Adele in Karlsbad that he
"never wanted to marry"; see p. 215.

[10] Quoted in Han Zint's "Schopenhauer und seine Schwester, Ein Beitrag zur Lebensgeschichte
des Philosophen," *Sechstes Jahrbuch der Schopenhauer-Gesellschaft* (1917), p. 210.

[11] Quandt also reported to Adele that "I believe that he [Schopenhauer] is as fond of me as much
as it is possible for him"; ibid., p. 209.

[12] Schopenhauer made this remark in a letter to Quandt, in which he asked him to extend his
heartfelt greetings to Schulze. Schopenhauer's request was triggered by Schulze's friendly

the well-known five-volume *Ghost Book* [*Gespensterbuch*, Leipzig, 1811–15]; selections from its first volume appeared in French translation as *Fantasmagoriana*, a work that has been said to have helped inspire Mary Shelley's *Frankenstein*. Schulze/Laun has been credited with aiding the young philosopher's escape from an "amorous affair" and with dubbing the boisterous and quarrelsome much younger man "Jupiter tonans," a designation that endeared Schulze to Schopenhauer, instead of alienating him.[13] Indeed, is his *Memoirs* [*Memoiren*, Bunzlau, 1837], Schulze considered "my acquaintance with Dr. Schopenhauer among the most joyful experiences of my life."[14]

It is difficult to explain Schulze's fondness for Schopenhauer, who enjoyed bashing Dresden's various literati, including a flock of writers and intellectuals who hovered around Schulze's *Dresden Evening News* [*Dresdener Abendzeitung*], a publication that distributed politics, poetry, philosophy, and literature in the solid, commonsensical, and moderate doses demanded by a readership with Biedermeierian sensibilities. Both its writers generally and its readers particularly connoted the smug conventionalism Schopenhauer associated with philistines. Baron Ferdinand K. K. von Biedenfeld, an acquaintance of Johanna Schopenhauer, who would also aid Arthur in securing a publisher for his main work, left behind a memorable sketch of Schulze's "thundering Jupiter":

As the son of the respected Johanna Schopenhauer, [he was] fully independent through a considerable fortune and was already early absorbed in philosophical studies. Previously, before his arrival in Dresden, he had made a very rich circle of acquaintances within the social life in different regions in Germany, neither without relinquishing in the least his own personal peculiarities nor by accommodating patiently the weaknesses of others. In this regard he was obviously a bit like a *l'enfant gâté*, with the most candid honesty; direct, outspoken, superior, rough and firm, extremely resolute in all scientific and literary questions. On all matters, saying what he thought to friends and foes alike, being much given to jokes, often a genuinely humorous ruffian, . . . [whose] fair head with its sparkling blue-gray eyes, the long folds of his cheeks to both sides of his nose, his somewhat strident voice with the short, forcible gesticulations of his hands, presented a quite grim appearance. . . . Although a decided opponent of any

---

remarks about his philosophy in Brockhaus's *Konversations-Blättern*; see *Gesammelte Briefe*, p. 233, 28 January 1849.

[13] Gwinner reports the "amorous affair" and the designation as "Jupiter tonans" in *Arthur Schopenhauer aus persönlichem Umgange dargestellt*, p. 65. He provides, however, no specific description of the nature of this "amorous affair."

[14] Quoted in *Gesammelte Briefe*, p. 547.

Abendzeitung, almanac, and *Liederkranz* fuss, whose collected participants he referred to only as the literary clique, but he especially mocked Böttiger, whom he loudly called the puss-in-boots. Still he frequently found himself in public places where these men usually took their pleasure. As a rule a quarrel would ensue, in which he, with his blunt outspokenness, acted very much the unpleasant fellow, frequently salting their coffee with the most caustic sarcasm, allowing, without hindrance, his critical humor to throw the angriest fragments of Shakespeare and Goethe into people's faces. . . . He appeared to them always as a barking dog; all feared him, but no one of them would ever have dared to return like with like. . . . Journalistic gossip was not his concern; it appeared to him as trivial and contemptible.[15]

The painter, novelist, and later Director of the Electorate of Hesse collection of paintings, Ludwig Sigismud Ruhl, who was six years Schopenhauer's junior, obliquely became familiar with the philosopher in Göttingen. Both attended Blumenbach's lectures on physiology, but Ruhl did so after Schopenhauer was drawn to Berlin by Fichte. The painter recorded his unanticipated encounter with Schopenhauer in Dresden "behind the Church of the Cross," and claimed that "we were inseparable companions from then on in spite of our daily quarrels."[16] In the same reflection, he emphasized Schopenhauer's competitive nature, much like Biedenfeld, but without a sense of some of the foibles of the philosopher's nature:

I see you still in spirit among all the figures on the Bruhl'chen Terrase, every trace of whose previous existence time and forgetfulness has scattered. You stand before me again with that blond aspiring Phoebus lock upon your brow, with your Socratic nose, with your piercing, dilating pupils directing shattering lightning bolts against Kuhn and Kind, against Theodor Hell, Langbein, Streckfuss *e tutti quanti*, on all the great poets of that time in Dresden *le haut du pavé*. I was all ears at your disputes which both delighted and instructed me. . . . You aided in my brooding over three questions: Who am I? Why am I? And would it not have better if I were not at all?

Blond aspiring Phoebus locks, Socratic nose, piercing, clear blue eyes, sans lightning bolts, were features Ruhl had captured in his well-known,

---

[15] *Gespräche*, pp. 39–40. Unlike Quandt, with whom Schopenhauer was less guarded concerning his family life, Biedenfeld reported that Schopenhauer called his mother and sister "silly geese," ibid., p. 40.

[16] Ibid., p. 36. This reflection was recorded in Ruhl's novel *Grotesque* [*Eine Groteske*, Cassel, 1882], where he imagines addressing Schopenhauer's spirit. His references to the contemporary poets of Dresden include members of the *Liederkreis*, a circle of writers that included Schulze, Theodor Hell, and Friedrich Kind, each of whom was involved in the *Dresden Evening News*. Karl Heuw (pseudonym H. Clauren), August Friedrich Langbein, and Karl Streckfuß were writers. Also see Gwinner, *Arthur Schopenhauer aus persönlichem Umgange dargestellt*, pp. 64–5.

electric oil painting of the twenty-seven-year-old Schopenhauer. In Ruhl's romanticized portrait, about which Kuno Fischer quipped that the artist's subject must not have been before him during its creation, Ruhl lengthened Schopenhauer's front-illuminated face, triangulated his jaw, and accented his cheekbones, while remaining faithful to his beautiful eyes, the space between which he shortened, and reproducing the small, full-lipped sensuous mouth, which only lengthened years later, when the philosopher lost his teeth.[17] If there is a hint of lightening, the portrait suggests it in the blue-gray background and the vague mountainous landscape behind its subject's left shoulder. Cosima Wagner thought that Ruhl had transformed Schopenhauer into an English poet and delighted in the lively light-brown curls that graced the subject's high forehead.[18] Adele, whose attention was drawn to Ruhl by the power of his painting, thought this painting "too wild."[19] Ruhl, who seemed to have tumbled out of Schopenhauer's life after his Italian tour, left behind, as one of his last paintings, The Ascetic, a depiction of a wan woman, gazing toward the heavens, surrounded by figures representing all of life's temptations, beneath which a Schopenhauerian quotation states, "Resignation in this world, the turning of all hopes to a better one, is the essence of Christianity."[20]

From 1814 to 1816, Schopenhauer lodged at Große Meißensche Gasse 35, in which the philosopher Karl Christian Friedrich Krause (1781–1832) took rooms from Michaelmas 1815 to Easter 1817 and to which he returned after a nine-month study of Sanskrit in Paris. On Michaelmas 1818, Krause left to seek his fortunes in Berlin. Schopenhauer was naturally drawn to the obscure, struggling philosopher, who was then making his living by teaching music, due to their mutual passion for mysticism and Eastern thought. Even after Schopenhauer moved to Ostra-Alle 897, he remained in contact with Krause, meeting him frequently at the library and through their exchange of books. Unlike Schopenhauer, who experienced the success of his philosophy after decades of neglect, the

---

[17] Fischer, Kuno, Schopenhauers Leben, Werke und Lehre, p. 91f, quoted in Arthur Hübscher's Schopenhauer-Bildnisse: Eine Ikonographie, p. 100. I am following Hübscher's dating of the Ruhl portrait to the first half of 1815, as well as his report of Wilhelm Gwinner's remarks about the accuracy of the depiction of Schopenhauer's eyes and mouth.

[18] Hübscher, ibid., p. 99; also see Cosima Wagner: Briefe an Ludwig Schemann, ed. Bertha Schemann (Regensburg, 1937), p. 50f.

[19] Lütkehaus, Die Schopenhauers: Der Familien-Briefwechsel, p. 273, Adele to Arthur, 5 February 1819.

[20] McGill, V.J., Schopenhauer: Pessimist and Pagan (New York: Haskell House, 1971) p. 130f. McGill does not provide the source of the Schopenhauer quotation.

intellectually bold Krause never lived to enjoy the effects of "Krausism" in Spain and Portugal during the years 1854–74 and then in the early twentieth century in various Latin American countries.²¹ Krause promoted "panentheism" [*Panentheismus*], a hybrid between theism and pantheism. Unlike pantheism, which viewed everything as God, he maintained that everything that we comprehend in the universe was in God, but God exceeded the universe as we conceive it.²² Although Krause's thought embraced ethics and social rights, his philosophy embraced theism as it connected obliquely to Catholic concerns, and by promoting respect for freedom, equality, and the individual, it also connected to classical liberalism. It thusly presented a meditating view between Catholic orthodoxy and liberalism, which made his philosophy attractive to many Spanish and Latin American political thinkers. Krause's philosophy itself probably was outside of Schopenhauer's philosophical concerns, and Krause himself noted that his emphasis on the significance of the reunification of European with Indian thought and art found resonance in Schopenhauer's main work.²³

Entering into boisterous literary quarrels, engaging in love affairs, and collecting a loose group of acquaintances and friends were, however, the outer wrappings masking Schopenhauer's rich inner philosophical life. Immediately on his arrival in Dresden, he worked through Kant's *Metaphysical Rudiments of Natural Science* (*Metaphysische Anfangsgründe der Naturwissenschaft*, 1786), and the first *Critique* was always lying ready to hand, but at this point Schopenhauer knew only its fifth edition. He sketched a brief essay "Against Kant" between 1816 and 1818, and this would become the basis of the appendix of his main work, the "Critique of Kantian Philosophy." In 1816, he turned to reconsider Locke's *An Essay Concerning Human Understanding*, already drawing connections between Locke and Kant, which, he would later claim, provided the line of thought

---

²¹ See O. Carlos Stoetzer's *Karl Christian Friedrich Krause and His Influence in the Hispanic World* (Cologne: Böhlau, 1998) for a thoughtful study of Krause's influence in Spain, Portugal, and various Latin American nations.

²² In *Schopenhauer* (Malden, MA: Blackwell, 2008), pp. 6–7, Robert Wicks sees Krause's panentheism echoed in an "Upanishadic-mystical" interpretation of Schopenhauer's philosophy and suggests that Krause and Schopenhauer may have crossed paths as students in Berlin.

²³ See Schopenhauer, *Gespräche*, p. 38 for Krause's remark about the significance of Indian knowledge and art. Safranski claims that Krause taught Schopenhauer meditation techniques, see *Schopenhauer and the Wild Years of Philosophy*, p. 202.

that his philosophy completed.[24] He read Aristotle and returned to Plato, struggling through the *Timaeus, Phaedrus, Gorgias, Cratylus, Meno*, and other dialogues. He worked through the New Testament and maintained his reading of *Asiatick Researches*. His last year in Dresden was spent composing *The World as Will and Representation*. He must have discussed his work with Biedenfeld and his desire to find a publisher. On 25 March 1818, the Baron wrote to Friedrich Arnold Brockhaus (1772–1823), seeking to solicit his interest in the project. This work, Biedenfeld wrote Brockhaus, has as its author an "extremely interesting thinker who in mental power, earnest determination and depth of study is not surpassed by any living man."[25] Brockhaus, who had heard about the philosophical talents of Schopenhauer from friends, and who was preparing to publish Johanna Schopenhauer's *Travels through England and Scotland* (1818), was willing to double up on Schopenhauers. Biedenfeld also told Schopenhauer's future publisher that the philosopher desired a large firm as his publisher and would not require much in the way of royalties, because he was a man of independent means.

Once Schopenhauer discovered that Brockhaus was willing to accept his manuscript, he sent a bold letter to his future publisher. "My work," he wrote, "is a new philosophical system; new, however, in the full sense of the term and not a new presentation of the already at hand, but a series of thoughts cohering together in the highest degree that up to now had never come into any human head."[26] It would become, he correctly predicted, the basis of a hundred other books. The basic ideas articulated in this work, he said, he had had in mind from years earlier, and he had spent the intervening time in intensive study and reflection, striving to make them perfectly clear. The last year, he continued, he had spent composing his work and it was almost done. Unlike his post-Kantian contemporaries, he assured Brockhaus, his writing is concise and clear to the highest degree and not full of meaningless, empty, and bombastic-sounding words. His writing, he permitted himself to say, is not without

---

[24] In *Parerga and Paralipomena*, Vol. 1, p. 87f/ *Sämtliche Werke*, Vol. 5, p. 93f, Schopenhauer wrote that "Accordingly, it will be seen that Locke, Kant, and I are closely connected, since in the interval of almost two hundred years we present the development of a coherently consistent train of thought." Also see my "Locke as Schopenhauer's (Kantian) Philosophical Ancestor," pp. 147–56.

[25] Quoted in McGill, *Schopenhauer*, p. 157.

[26] Schopenhauer, *Gesammelte Briefe*, p. 29, Schopenhauer to Brockhaus, 28 March 1818.

beauty, and he claimed that his work was of great value to him, because it represented the complete fruit of his being. By thirty, the thirty-year-old Schopenhauer explained, the impressions of the world made on any mind, and the thoughts so stimulated, are set and these ideas are only developed into variations of the same throughout the duration of one's life. He knew, he told Brockhaus, that the publisher was a man of honor and that he would not tell anyone about his work, not even its title, until it was published in his catalog.

Schopenhauer also had the audacity to lay down the terms for publication. The book should appear next Michaelmas (29 September 1818) in a run no greater than 800 copies. It should be in a single volume, produced on high-quality paper. It should appear in octavo, with each page having wide margins and no more than thirty lines of sharp type on each page. The work must be proofread three times, the last by a scholar who would read the proofs against the manuscript. He would deliver the first two-thirds of the manuscript by the middle of July and the remainder no later than early September. Brockhaus would have the rights for a second edition. In return, Schopenhauer requested "the hardly worth mentioning honorarium of one ducat per printed sheet" and ten author's copies.[27] Brockhaus accepted the author's terms and promised him the honorarium upon receipt of the manuscript. He also inquired whether Schopenhauer desired a contract. Both to put his mind at ease and to sate the desires associated with his training in business, Schopenhauer requested a formal contract. He also assured the publisher that his work would not face any obstacles with the censor. He had not uttered a syllable against the government; had said nothing that would offend common decency; and had not launched a direct attack against the church. In fact, he wrote, "in the final book [of *The World as Will and Representation*] a moral philosophy is presented that agrees exactly with genuine Christianity."[28] Nevertheless, in case of difficulties, because his work did clash with some Judeo-Christian "dogma," Schopenhauer recommended that Brockhaus could have the book published in the more liberal cities of Jena or Merseberg. Besides, he added, being banned is not a misfortune for a book. Brockhaus accepted Schopenhauer's request and sent him a contract in which he articulated all of Schopenhauer's initial terms,

---

[27] Ibid., p. 30.
[28] Ibid., p. 31, Schopenhauer to Brockhaus, 3 April 1818.

adding that he would have it printed in Altenberg, where it would pass the censor.[29]

Brockhaus probably knew from the onset that he was dealing with a nervous and difficult personality. Schopenhauer delivered his manuscript as specified in the contract and naively anticipated that he would receive galley proofs promptly. On 11 July he sent the first three of the four divisions or "books" that composed *The World as Will and Representation* and promised that the last book and the appendix would be sent by early September. Brockhaus received this first part of Schopenhauer's manuscript on 17 July and he immediately informed the high-strung author that he had forwarded the work to the printer. By 8 August, Schopenhauer could no longer restrain himself and wrote to the publisher about his failure to receive proofs. He feared that the book would not appear at Michaelmas, in time for the book fair, and he mentioned his planned trip to Italy. He reminded Brockhaus that he was abiding with the terms of their contract, suggesting that Brockhaus was not. Schopenhauer then complained again, less than a week later, about his failure to receive the proofs. He reminded Brockhaus that he was dealing with the very product of his last four years, "indeed, actually of my entire life," and although he said that he had not mentioned previously the insignificant honorarium attached to his labor, he did so now.[30] He would not tolerate being treated as if he were one of the authors of Brockhaus' most lucrative publication, the *Konversations-Lexikon*, he continued; the only thing he had in common with that pack of scribblers was the use of pen and ink. He did, however, apologize in a backhanded fashion, by claiming that he was sorry about being so harsh, but he also excused himself by holding that "as I have fulfilled each agreed upon obligation, so I demand the same of others; otherwise there is no certitude in life."[31] It was as if the ghost of Heinrich Floris was channeled through his son. Brockhaus responded to Schopenhauer's insulting letter by simply sending the proofs.

Brockhaus had exercised restraint with the philosopher, but his patience would last only so long. Schopenhauer became increasingly worried about the "insignificant" honorarium. He complained that the proofs had

[29] Brockhaus signed the contract on 8 April 1818 in Leipzig and Schopenhauer on 11 April 1818 in Dresden. The contract can be found in Schopenhauer, ibid., pp. 32–3.
[30] Ibid., p. 38, Schopenhauer to Brockhaus, 14 August 1818.
[31] Ibid., p. 39.

thirty-five lines per page and not the agreed upon thirty. This would lower his payment by forty printed sheets. He expected payment for forty sheets as stated by the contract. As a proof of Brockhaus' seriousness, he demanded full payment immediately. Then he hurled an insult that his publisher could not ignore. "I hear from various parties," Schopenhauer wrote, "that you are frequently slow with the payment of honoraria or even totally hesitate."[32] The publisher, who had called Schopenhauer a "chained dog," was compelled to fire back: "If you allege that it is 'commonly' said there that I am slow in the payment of honoraria, then as long as you do not provide me with the name of *a* single author, whom I can call into account, you will allow me to hold that you are *not* a man of honor."[33] Schopenhauer tacitly allowed Brockhaus his inference, because he said nothing to substantiate his charge. Brockhaus essentially washed his hands of the philosopher. His main work would not appear by Michaelmas, but in December 1818 and bearing a publication date of 1819. (Michaelmas, Brockhaus said, meant nothing to book dealers.[34]) By this time, however, Schopenhauer was in Italy enjoying a vacation, which he informed Brockhaus on numerous occasions he would not postpone. Schopenhauer did receive his forty-ducat honorarium, but strictly according to the terms of the contract.

On 12 December, Brockhaus sent Quandt the ten author's copies, and through Quandt Schopenhauer communicated his joy at the publication of his life's "fruit." He did not complain, however, that there were thirty-five lines per page in his book of 742 pages. And he also missed Brockhaus's last letter of 24 September, because he had left a day earlier for Italy. In this letter, Brockhaus articulated his disdain for his dealings with Schopenhauer. He closed by saying, "I only hope that my fears that by publishing your work I am only printing waste paper will not be realized."[35] Brockhaus died in 1823 with the belief that he had printed waste paper. Indeed, in 1828, when Schopenhauer approached Brockhaus's sons, Friedrich and

---

[32] Ibid., p. 41, Schopenhauer to Brockhaus, 31 August 1818.

[33] For the "chained dog" remark, see Schopenhauer, ibid., p. 502; the Brockhaus quotation is taken from Rudolf Malter's monograph, "Ein neues philosophisches System – neu im ganzen Sinn des Worts" which accompanies the facsimile printing of the first edition of Schopenhauer's *The World as Will and Representation* (Frankfurt am Main: Insel Verlag, 1987), p. 45, Brockhaus to Schopenhauer, 1 September 1818.

[34] See Malter, ibid., p. 42, undated letter from Brockhaus to Schopenhauer.

[35] Malter, ibid., p. 47.

Heinrich, about a second edition, he was told that they still possessed 150 copies of the original edition of 750, and that this was after many of the copies were sold as scrap.[36]

The World as Will and Representation

The "fruit" of Schopenhauer's life, his *magnum opus*, the expression of the thoughts raised in his mind by his impression of the world during his first thirty years of life, would constitute the basis for his next forty-two years of philosophy. Thus what he told Brockhaus was true in his case: "All later thoughts are only developments and variations [of those gained by the age of thirty]."[37] In 1844, the second edition of *The World as Will and Representation* received a massive revision. He added a second volume of essays designed to supplement, extend, and clarify his original thought. The original book became the first volume. Schopenhauer was, however, a different sort of philosopher in 1844 than he was in 1818. Around 1826 he discovered the first edition of Kant's *Critique of Pure Reason* – up until that point he had only studied its significantly revised second edition – and he came to recognize a more robust commitment to idealism in its first edition. This led him to an even greater identification with Kant and moved him to make significant changes to the appendix of his main work, his "Critique of the Kantian Philosophy." To the first volume, he now added section numbers, so that he could more precisely refer to his original work, both in the supplementary essays of the second volume and in his other books. His *On the Will in Nature* (1836) was recognized in the supplementary essays of the second volume of his main work as "the really essential supplement to this book" [the second "book" of the first volume of *The World as Will and Representation*].[38] In 1841, he published *The Two Fundamental Problems of Ethics*, and in the second volume of his principal work he said

---

[36] See Schopenhauer, *Gesammelte Briefe*, p. 517, for Brockhaus's response to Schopenhauer's letter of 24 November 1828, in which the philosopher inquired about the sales of his main work.

[37] Ibid., p. 30, Schopenhauer to Brockhaus, 28 March 1818.

[38] See Schopenhauer, ibid., p. 260, letter to Johann Eduard Erdmann, 9 April 1851, where Schopenhauer blames the prevailing "Hegel*gloria*" of the times for his seventeen-year "silence of indignation." For the reference to *On the Will in Nature* as the essential supplement to his philosophy of nature, see *The World as Will and Representation*, Vol. 2, p. 191/*Sämtliche Werke*, Vol. 3, p. 213.

that this book supplements the fourth book of its first volume, adding the characteristic remark, "In general, I make the demand that whoever wishes to make himself acquainted with my philosophy shall read every line of me."[39] Even in his last book, *Parerga and Paralipomena* (1851), which was his attempt to write a philosophy for the world, with the hope of drawing an audience, he viewed its second volume as supplementing his "systematic philosophy," and the first volume helped illuminate his work, he claimed, because everything that emanated from his mind served to do so.[40]

Preface and Reading Instructions

But let us return to the first edition of Schopenhauer's masterpiece and its basic ideas. The book begins with a preface that is pure Schopenhauer – bold, demanding, ironic, sarcastic, witty, and instructive. Its purpose is to explain how to read the book to obtain a thorough comprehension of its content. He calls the work an expression of a single thought, a thought that delivers everything that has been sought under the name of philosophy. It is not, he claims, a system of thought, which must possess an architectonic connection between its "parts," such that a later part is supported by an earlier, but this earlier part is not supported by the later. Ultimately, a system of thought has both a "foundation stone" that carries the entire structure but that is not carried by any other, and a pinnacle that is upheld by all the parts but that upholds nothing. Conversely, a single thought constitutes a unity. If it is split into parts to be communicated, the connection between parts is organic; that is, every part supports the whole just as the whole supports every part. Thus to clearly understand the whole, he continues, one must understand each part, and each part is not fully understood until the whole has been understood. Moreover, he observes that his book, by its very form, contradicts the matter of his single thought. A book must have a first and last line and for this reason is not an organic whole, which has no beginning and no end.

To deal with the contradiction between the form of his book and the matter of his single thought, Schopenhauer makes the first of three demands on his readers: "In order that the thought expounded may be

---

[39] Ibid., Vol. 2, p. 461/ibid., Vol. 3, p. 527.
[40] See Schopenhauer, *Parerga and Paralipomena*, Vol. 1, p. xv/*Sämtliche Werke*, Vol. 5, p. vii.

fathomed, no advice can be given other than *to read the book twice. . . .*"[41] This requires great patience, he advises, because one has to bear in mind that its beginning presupposes its end almost as much as its end does its beginning. Patience is also required, moreover, because the book will contradict many current opinions, including those of his readers, and readers should bear in mind that the second reading will cast everything in a different light. Because of the organic structure of the work, readers will also have to realize that he will need to repeat himself to show the close interconnections between his ideas. For this reason, he writes, he will not divide his work into chapters and sections, as much as he values these divisions, but only into four aspects or main divisions of the one thought, which he technically calls "books [Bücher]." Then Schopenhauer digs at his readers: "And thus is expressed the first, and like those that follow, absolutely necessary, demand on the reader, who is unfriendly toward the philosopher just because he himself is one."[42]

Schopenhauer's second demand relates his earlier publications to the present one. His dissertation is the "introduction" to this work, and it would have been included word for word, had he not been loath to repeat himself. Thus his readers must read this book first. Still, the philosopher of 1818 is different from the dissertator of 1813, when he came out of the gates with an attitude common to many post-Kantian philosophers and bragged that his thought did not lock itself into the rigidity of Kant's thing in itself. The philosopher now proclaims that "*Kant's greatest merit is the distinction of the appearance from the thing in itself,*" and he now holds Fichte and Schelling in contempt for denying this distinction, as he would later hold Hegel, who is still not on Schopenhauer's philosophic radar screen.[43] During the intervening years between his dissertation and his main work, he credited Kant with arriving at the same truth as Plato. Indeed, he finds Kant's distinction to parallel Plato's distinction between the sensory world and Ideas and the Upanishadic doctrine of *māyā* and Brahman. Each viewpoint recognized that the world as given

---

[41] Schopenhauer, *The World as Will and Representation*, Vol. 1, p. xiii/*Sämtliche Werke*, Vol. 2, p. viii. Schopenhauer also claimed that a thorough comprehension of his dissertation required his readers to read it twice. In the case of his dissertation, this was necessary, he said, because his analysis of the forms of the principle of sufficient reason was not arranged systematically, but was arranged for clarity; see *Sämtliche Werke*, Vol. 7, p. 86.
[42] Ibid., Vol. 1, p. xiii/ibid., Vol. 2, p. ix.
[43] Ibid., Vol. 1, p. 417/ibid., Vol. 2, p. 494.

to the senses is a world of constant change and becoming, an illusion compared to an underlying, unchanging being. Plato and the Indians, he asserts, expressed this truth mythically and poetically, whereas Kant did so philosophically.[44]

Yet if this recognition of the significance of Kant's distinction between appearances and things in themselves represents a return to Kant, his principal work also distances Schopenhauer from the Kantian features of his dissertation. In his dissertation he was still willing to recognize the validity of several of Kant's pure concepts of the understanding and to uncritically accept his views of the inner and outer sense. In his principal work he argued that intuitive perception of the world is a function of the *a priori* forms of sensibility, space and time, and the understanding's non-conceptual application of causality. He recognized this difference in his views, but then enunciated an attitude that has caused much misunderstanding of his thoughts by claiming that his readers would be able to note the changes in perspective, saying that "the correction of such passages in that essay [*The Fourfold Root*] will come about quite automatically in the reader's thoughts through acquaintance with the present work."[45] He also mentions *On Vision and Colors*, at least the first chapter, "On Vision," as required reading for his principal work. He does not, however, say why. But it is that chapter in which he presented his physiological arguments for the intellectual nature of perception.

Schopenhauer's third requirement is that the reader possess "an acquaintance with the most important phenomenon which has appeared in philosophy for two thousand years . . . the principal works of Kant."[46] Even though he claims to have discovered grave problems with the work of his philosophical hero, Kant is his starting point. To understand how he separated the wheat from the chaff in Kant's philosophy, Schopenhauer directs his reader to study the appendix, the "Critique of the Kantian Philosophy," before reading the first book of *The World as Will and Representation*. Although Kant's philosophy is the only one with which his book requires a thorough acquaintance, he also says that knowledge of Plato would also better prepare his reader to hear what he had to say and that a knowledge of the *Upanishads* would lead to an even better comprehension

---

44 See ibid., Vol. 1, p. 419/ibid., Vol. 2, 496f.
45 Ibid., Vol. 1, p. xiv/ibid., Vol. 2, p. x.
46 Ibid., Vol. 1, p. xv/ibid., Vol. 2, p. xi.

of his thought, which would not seem to be articulated by a strange and foreign tongue. He then makes a remark that Krause claimed that he gave Schopenhauer: namely, that the greatest advantage enjoyed in this still young century over previous ones is that "the influence of Sanskrit literature will penetrate no less deeply than did the revival of Greek literature in the fifteenth century."[47]

But after so much seriousness, Schopenhauer decides to have some fun with his readers and to mock the German philosophical scene. By now, he writes, the reader has grown impatient and angry. How could he make such presumptuous and immodest demands of his reader? In Germany alone there are more living philosophers than could be found in several successive centuries and their unique thoughts and profound ideas have become common property, distributed through numerous periodicals and newspapers. Yet he demands so much that one could never reach the end of his book. Schopenhauer confesses that he has nothing to say in reply to the reproaches of this indignant reader, but he hopes that his reader would show him some gratitude for sparing the reader the trouble of trying to understand his work without the requisite background. Still, he knows that the reader bought the book and so he feels compelled to suggest uses other than that of reading it. Bind it handsomely and use it to fill a gap in your library; set it on the table of a learned lady friend or – and here he may have been thinking of his mother – her tea table; best yet, and this is what he recommends, review it. But after he allows himself this joke, he closes the preface on a serious note. Sooner or later his book will reach those to whom it alone is addressed, and he is resigned in patience, realizing that for truth, as well as for its author, there is only a brief celebration of victory between the lengthy periods in which truth is first condemned as paradoxical and last disparaged as trivial: "But life is short, and truth works far and lives long: let us speak the truth."[48]

The four books of *The World as Will and Representation* move in an alternating pattern, between the world as representation and the world as will. The first considers the world as representation, viewing the world of experience subject to the principle of sufficient reason. The second shifts

---

[47] Ibid., Vol. 1 p. xv/ibid., Vol. 2, p. xii. Krause reports this in his *Nachlaß*; see Schopenhauer, *Gespräche*, p. 38. He claimed to have told this to Schopenhauer in 1817.

[48] Schopenhauer, *The World as Will and Representation*, Vol. 1, p. xvii/*Sämtliche Werke*, Vol. 2, p. xv.

to the consideration of the world as will, whereas the third returns to the world as representation, but this time to representations not subject to the principle of sufficient reason, but with Platonic Ideas, which are the objects of art (except music). The last book, which is the lengthiest, "proclaims itself as the most serious, for it concerns the actions of humans . . . " and it returns to the world as will.[49] Thus Schopenhauer's master work moves dynamically from epistemology, to metaphysics, to aesthetics, and finally to ethics. This movement, Schopenhauer reminds his readers in the fourth book, does not proceed like the progress of history, in a straight line, so that repeated study of his work is required to understand the multiple connections between all the parts of his thought.

First Book: Epistemology

The first book, "The Representation Subject to the Principle of Sufficient Reason: The Object of Experience and of Science," begins with the extraordinary and bold pronouncement "The world is my representation" [*Vorstellung*], a truth whose realization, Schopenhauer asserts, marks the dawn of philosophical discernment.[50] This statement is the beginning of his philosophy in a twofold sense. It is the first proposition in the book and it delineates the start of the range of phenomena his philosophy set out both to explain and to determine the meaning of. This first proposition is balanced by the very last line of the work: "To those in whom the will

---

[49] Ibid., Vol. 1, p. 27/ibid., Vol. 2, p. 319.

[50] Ibid., Vol. 1, p. 3/ibid., Vol. 2, p. 3. The term "*Vorstellung*" is a major term of craft, occurring both in the title of Schopenhauer's principal work and within the first proposition of this work, "*Die Welt ist meine Vorstellung.*" Literally, a *Vorstellung* is something "put or placed before [someone]," and it is notoriously difficult to translate with a single English equivalent. Schopenhauer's English translators have used "idea," "representation," and most recently, "presentation" (*World as Will and Presentation*, Vol. 1, trans. Richard E. Aquila with David Carus [New York: Pearson/Longman, 2008]), which had been proposed by Schopenhauer's first English biographer, Helen Zimmern, who suggested that the best title for Schopenhauer's principal work was *The Universe as Impulse and Presentation*; see *Arthur Schopenhauer, His Life and His Philosophy* (London: Longmans, Green and Co., 1876), p. 147. It is not clear from whom Schopenhauer appropriated this term. Kant equated *Vorstellung* with the Latin "*repraesentatio,*" but Schopenhauer translated Kant's use of the term as "idea;" see Schopenhauer, *Gesammelte Briefe*, pp. 122–3. Personally, I prefer "idea," given Schopenhauer's translation of Kant, and because of his reference to the British idealist Berkeley as the first philosopher to positively state the opening proposition. (Later, in the second edition, he credited Descartes with stating it negatively, through his skeptical considerations.) I will, however, defer to tradition and use "representation" for "*Vorstellung.*"

has turned and denied itself, this very real world of ours with all its suns and galaxies, is – nothing."[51] This statement is the end of his philosophy in a twofold sense. It is the last proposition in the book and it states the end of the phenomena he set out to explain, along with determining their significance. As he said elsewhere, the range of his philosophy is from the affirmation to the denial of the will. To say anything about the will prior to its affirmation, its expression as the world, or after its denial, would lead to empty speculation and transcendent nonsense.[52]

If any truth can be said to be *a priori*, Schopenhauer continues, it is that the world is my representation, and no truth is more certain, more independent of any other truth, and less in need of a proof than this proposition. There is no perception of the sun and the earth, he claims, but only an eye that sees the sun or a hand that feels the earth. Schopenhauer here is reiterating a claim already advanced in his dissertation – that there is no experience without an experiencer, no object for experience without a subject of experience. The converse is also true, as he makes clear in the second section – there is no subject of experience without an object of experience. Thus Schopenhauer is reiterating a major point from his dissertation, one that, if his reader followed his instructions concerning how to read this book, he or she would already know, because it reemphasizes the correlativity of the subject and object, highlighting the subject/object distinction as the most basic and universal epistemic distinction. Everything of which we are aware is an object for a subject, and the entire world itself is an object for a subject, a representation, and everything is conditioned by the subject, by one of the four forms of the principle of sufficient reason. With intuitive or perceptual representations, this conditioning is by the principle of sufficient reason of becoming. Items in the world are in space and time, standing in causal relationships with other things. To say that the world is my representation, Schopenhauer writes, is to say that "Everything that in any way belongs and can belong to the world is inevitably associated with being conditioned by the subject and it exists only for the subject."[53]

---

[51] Ibid., Vol. 1, p. 412/ibid., Vol. 2, p. 487.

[52] See Schopenhauer, *Gesammelte Briefe*, pp. 288, 291, Schopenhauer to Frauenstädt, 6 August 1852 and 24 August 1852.

[53] Schopenhauer, *The World as Will and Representation*, Vol. 1, p. 3/*Sämtliche Werke*, Vol. 2, p. 3.

Schopenhauer does not claim originality concerning this truth. In fact, he credits the British "immaterialist" philosopher, George Berkeley, as the first to elucidate this idea and as, thereby, rendering an immortal service to philosophy, and he faults Kant for neglecting the principle "no object without a subject." In the second edition, he would first mention Descartes's skeptical considerations as articulating this truth negatively, and in the third, he would claim that this fundamental truth had long been recognized by the sages of India and that it was a basic principle of "Vedanta Philosophy," and he quotes Sir William Jones's observation, in English, that "The fundamental tenet of the Vedanta school consisted not in denying the existence of matter, that is, of solidity, impenetrability, and extended figure (to deny that would be lunacy), but in correcting the popular notion of it, and in contending that it has no essence independent of mental perception; that existence and perceptibility are convertible terms."[54] (As was his wont, Schopenhauer was always alert to "great thinkers" who shared his insights, and it would become his continuous practice on his part to find ancestors for his views – although his stance would also be that he alone provided the philosophical justification for these shared insights.)

This first book treads familiar ground for Schopenhauer. In conjunction with emphasizing the significance of the subject and object correlativity, he considers the various forms of the principle of sufficient reason; the distinctions between the faculties of sensibility, understanding, and reason; the differences between intuitive and abstract representations, that is between perceptions and concepts. He points to the way in which his philosophical starting point is *"toto genere"* different for all others, because he begins with the first fact of consciousness, the representation, whose first, essential, and most basic form is the division into subject and object. He chides, as discussed earlier, the one-sided approaches of Fichte, who starts from the subject, and the materialist, who starts from the object. He rejects Kant's account of perception of an object, which requires the application of concepts to intuitions, by holding that the perception of an object does not involve any element of judgment or the application of a concept to some sensible given. Animals perceive objects and, lacking reason, lack the capacity to develop concepts, and all concepts are formed, he argued, through abstraction from intuitions of objects. He states the

[54] Ibid., Vol. 1, p. 4/ibid., Vol. 2, p. 4.

position he arrived at in *On Vision and Colors*; namely, perception is intellectual – the understanding creates objects by referring to those objects felt changes in the body, sensations, which it automatically takes as the effect of some cause located in space and time.

Schopenhauer, who never was shy about engaging in Shandean digressions in his philosophical thought, also provided a theory of humor, which, like most theories, is humorless. It is even odd that he provided no examples of jokes, leaving his readers to think of their own. One would have thought that he would have referred his readers to the joke that closed his preface, to his recommendation that instead of reading his book, the reader should review it. Laughing, as he would later claim about weeping, is a uniquely human trait, because it requires the possession of faculty of reason. Laughter, he theorizes, is the expression of a "suddenly perceived incongruence between a concept and the real objects that have been thought through it in some relation."[55] But the much older philosopher would come to the aid of "mentally inert" readers by providing examples in the third and final edition of his main work. He mentions an incident at the National Theater in Berlin involving the comic actor Karl Wilhelm Ferdinand Unzelmann and a horse. No sooner had the comic appeared on horseback on the stage, than the horse defecated, an act that led him to say to his mount, "What are you doing? Don't you know that you are forbidden to improvise?"[56]

Schopenhauer's theory of humor occurs in a wide-ranging discussion of the faculty of reason. He agrees with a tradition central to Western philosophical and religious thought by viewing the possession of reason as the distinguishing characteristic between humans and nonhuman animals, but he dissents from this tradition in two significant ways. He does not identify rationality as the essence of humans. Just as in animals, he claims that the will is our essence. He also rejects the idea that because humans alone possess reason, humans alone are morally considerable. If a being can suffer, it is morally considerable, because preventing and relieving suffering is the hallmark of moral behavior.

Indeed, he found the possession of reason a mixed blessing. Although the ability to think conceptually and discursively is the basis for everything that distinguishes us from other animals, reason also opens us to torments,

[55] Ibid., Vol. 1, p. 59/ibid., Vol. 2, p. 70.
[56] Ibid., Vol. 2, p. 93/ibid., Vol. 3, p. 102.

forms of suffering, and follies to which animals are immune. Reason is the source of knowledge *(Wissen)*, of certainty and truth, but it is also the source of error, doubt, and confusion. Due to reason, we possess language and speech, and so we can communicate in more complex and sophisticated ways than animals, but we also are able to mislead, dissemble, and deceive as animals cannot. By denoting concepts by words, we have language, but language misleads more than it enlightens, and language is too blunt an instrument to do justice fully to the richness and detail of intuition, of direct and immediate experience. Although thought enables us to escape the narrow confines of the immediately present, the world of intuitive representations that animals inhabit, having a sense of the past and the future comes at a great cost. We can be haunted by the past and suffer feelings of sorrow, remorse, and regret for what has been. We can suffer anxiety and concern about the future. We know, unlike animals, that death lies in our future. Reason also enables us to deliberate and plan our future actions, having a greater choice than is possible for animals, who are motivated by immediately present circumstances, but this freedom of choice is only apparent, because human behavior, even motivated by abstract thought, is equally as caused and necessary as that of other animals.

Reason, of course, is the faculty of philosophy, and Schopenhauer declares that " . . . [P]hilosophy will be a sum of very universal judgments, whose ground is immediately the world itself in its entirety, without excluding anything, and everything to be found in human consciousness. It will be *a complete recapitulation, so to speak, a reflection of the world in abstract concepts*, and this is possible only by uniting the essentially identical into one concept, and by relating the different and dissimilar to another."[57] Philosophy, Schopenhauer argues, strives to say what the world is and to reproduce it conceptually. The world is a unity, a whole in which there is an agreement between all its parts and aspects. Philosophy must also mirror this unity in abstract thought, and all the propositions expressed in philosophy must harmonize with one another, because they

---

[57] Ibid., Vol. 1, p. 83/ibid., Vol. 2, p. 98f. Here Schopenhauer credits Francis Bacon with setting the task of philosophy: "That philosophy only is the true one which reproduces most faithfully the statements of nature, and is written down, as it were, from nature's dictation, so that it is nothing but a *copy and a reflection* of nature, and adds nothing of its own, but is merely a repetition and echo." *On the Dignity and Advancement of Learning* [*De dignitate et augmentis scientiarum*, 1623], Bk. 2, Chap. 13.

aim to express the harmony and unity of the world. Just as the world is a unity, ultimately, he claims, the propositions expressed by true philosophy must "flow together even in the unity of one thought."[58] As he reflected very early in the development of his philosophy, upon his arrival in Dresden, "My philosophy will never in the least go beyond the realm of experience, that is to say the perceptible in the fullest range of the concept. For, like any art, it will merely repeat the world."[59] Schopenhauer, however, will be tempted frequently by the transcendent.

In the second edition of *The World as Will and Representation*, Schopenhauer added a note to the statement concerning the task of philosophy, referring his reader to his most robust reflection on philosophy, the supplementary essay, "On the Human Need for Metaphysics," found in its second volume. Reason is what makes humans the *animal metaphysicum*. Like Plato and Aristotle before him, he argued that philosophy is born from wonder, but unlike these more Apollonian Greeks, he held that philosophical astonishment arises not from a simple confrontation with an unknown world, but from a deeply existential recognition of the vanity and ephemeral nature of existence. Out of astonishment at the ubiquity of suffering and death, philosophers experience a hurtful ignorance, he averred, and they need to know why conflict and strife, pain and suffering, destruction and death are omnipresent features of existence. The philosopher desires to also know the meaning of living in a world permeated by these twin "evils." For the philosopher, existence itself becomes an "ever-disquieting riddle," the very riddle that began to vaguely haunt the young Schopenhauer during his European tour.[60] The nitty-gritty, deeply existential drive behind Schopenhauer's philosophy, his confrontation with the problems of suffering and death, will assume full force in the last book, where he turns his attention to the most serious subject, human conduct.

Second Book: Metaphysics of Nature

Schopenhauer had declared the first book one-sided, an exploration of the world as representation, as object for a subject. It ignored the grave and

---

[58] Ibid., Vol. 1, p. 83/ibid., Vol. 2, p. 99.
[59] Schopenhauer, *Manuscript Remains*, Vol. 1, 281/*Der handschriftliche Nachlaß*, Vol. 1, p. 256. The note is from 1815.
[60] Schopenhauer, *The World as Will and Representation*, Vol. 2, p. 171/*Sämtliche Werke*, Vol. 3, p. 189.

terrible truth that "The world is my will."[61] It is in the second book, "The Objectification of the Will," that this serious and horrifying truth received its first articulation, motivated by the question of whether the world is simply and only the representations of the subject and is, therefore, like a dream. Schopenhauer worried about this question because our normal perceptions of all objects in the world are intuitive representations dependent upon the subject, so he wanted to know whether the external world is simply and only his representation, something dreamlike, or whether what we perceive as the external world has a reality other than simply being perceived by the subject.

Schopenhauer first turned to the natural sciences, to see if they offered an answer. The natural sciences, he argued, deal with our ordinary perceptions of the world, operating within the scope of the principle of sufficient reason, but with one important exception. Our ordinary perception of everyday things is "interested"; that is, things are viewed as potential means for sating or frustrating our desires. Thus, our ordinary cognitions of the world focus on particular things at specific times and places and within definite causal relationships, and are cognized in terms of their particular effects on our own well-being and misfortune. Although concerned with such objects, the sciences assume a more objective stance toward representations, because they seek to understand the world as representation by subsuming numerous particular things within organizing and classifying schemes or by formulating casual or universal laws describing changes in matter. Thus, Schopenhauer classified the natural sciences into two branches. The morphological sciences, which included "natural history," botany, and zoology, develop classificatory schemes by uniting particular things under recurring natural kinds. The etiological sciences, such as physiology, chemistry, and physics, extrapolate causal laws governing representations by articulating observed regularities within the changing natural world.

Still, Schopenhauer viewed the natural sciences as expressing an interested stance toward the world, even if it is less interested than ordinary, everyday perception. Ultimately, scientific knowledge is practical. It produces more efficient means for reshaping, responding, and manipulating the world to serve human needs. As he argued then, and as he would always maintain, any form of interested cognition could never clearly

---

[61] Ibid., Vol. 1, p. 4 / ibid., Vol. 2, p. 5.

reach that which is. Later, in the second edition of his principal work, he would try to make his original view concerning knowledge of the thing in itself clear by recognizing that all cognition distorts being: "... where the being in itself begins, cognition ceases, and all cognition primarily and essentially concerns solely appearances."[62] Art, he will soon argue, has a higher cognitive value than science, because it affords an experience that escapes the interested tone of both ordinary and scientific cognition by transcending the principle of sufficient reason.

Like Kant, Schopenhauer also held that science itself requires a metaphysical grounding. The morphological sciences had to account for recurring natural kinds, such as granite and lion; and the etiological sciences recognized natural forces, such as gravity and electricity. To account for natural kinds and for natural forces, which are used by science as "occult qualities," his metaphysics of nature sought to provide an explanation of necessary and scientifically unexplainable elements of the scientific world view. It is within this context that he would introduce his doctrine of Platonic Ideas as the metaphysical analogs to natural kinds and natural forces.

The orientation of the sciences, Schopenhauer argued, points in a direction that cannot ascertain whether the world is something more than representation and something more than a dream or an illusion produced by the subject. If the world is conditioned by the subject through the principle of sufficient reason, and if the world is dependent on the subject, perhaps it is as if it were a dream, the product of a dreaming subject. Science then would be doing nothing more than classifying and noting lawlike regularities in what, for Schopenhauer, is a nightmare. In the second edition, he mentioned that his bold, opening statement, that "the world is my representation," was already "found in the skeptical reflections from which Descartes started."[63] He had in mind Descartes' *Meditations on First Philosophy* (1641), where the skeptical Descartes worried that everything that he had experienced was no more than the product of a dream.[64] Of course, Descartes mentions this possibility only to have God guarantee later that there is an external world to which some of our ideas

---

[62] Ibid., Vol. 2, p. 275/ibid., Vol. 3, p. 311.
[63] Ibid., Vol. 1, p. 3/ibid., Vol. 2, p. 4.
[64] See René Descartes, "Meditations on First Philosophy," in *The Philosophical Works of Descartes*, trans. E. S. Haldane and G. R. T. Ross (Cambridge: Cambridge University Press, 1972), Vol. 1, pp. 145–8.

correspond. Schopenhauer regarded this as a cheap trick, and he loathed
even thinking of an imaginary God as being responsible for this wretched
world, even if such a God provided science with a real world as its object.
Descartes and science, resorting to the objective path, the world as object
for a subject, could never posit a real world without some sort of dodge,
or, as materialists, just assume that there is no problem all along.

To discover whether the world is something more than mere representation, Schopenhauer trod a path in a different direction than that of
science, one prefigured by his "revolutionary principle," a variation of the
Greek dictum "know yourself," namely, the dictum "From yourself you
will understand nature, not yourself from nature."[65] Thus he shifted his
gaze away from the consciousness of intuitive representations, away from
outer experience, to inner experience or self-consciousness. Each of us,
he argued, is aware of our body in a twofold fashion. We perceive our
body as an object of outer experience, viewing it as a thing in space and
time, and as standing in causal relationships with other like objects. Thus
like our cognitions of intuitive perceptions, we are aware of our bodies
as we are of all other objects in the natural world. I see my hand holding
a pen just as I observe its movements and the letters appearing on the
page. My hand is a representation just like everything in my visual field.
But unlike other representations, which appear as surface phenomena, I
have a unique experience of my hand, because I experience it from the
inside, as it were. I experience my hand, my body, unlike other representations. The pressure I feel of the pen in my hand, the resistance I
sense as the pen touches and moves on the page, the meaning I strive to
express through the series of words appearing on the page, and the pain I
feel as my hand clumsily slides across the edge of the paper, resulting in a
paper cut on my hand and small drops of blood on the page, are *toto genere*
different from my experience of any other representation. And if I lacked
these experiences of the interior of my hand, Schopenhauer would say, it
would appear simply like the pen, letters, blood and paper. It would not
be *my* hand, but simply another item in my visual field. It would be all
surface, floating before me, with which I would have no connection. And
although the words appearing on the page might have a meaning, I would
be struggling to discover it, rather than trying to have the words say what

---

[65] Schopenhauer, *Manuscript Remains*, Vol. 1 p. 466/*Der handschriftliche Nachlaß*, Vol. 1,
p. 421.

I mean. The experience of the interior of the representation of our body, an experience we have only of our bodies, " . . . is denoted by the word will."[66]

The twofold experience of one's body as will and representation became the key to Schopenhauer's metaphysics. The immediate experience of the interior of one's body as will grounds one in the world, and the world is the objectification or visualization of the will. The identification of one's body and will establishes a new form of truth for Schopenhauer, one that falls outside the four types of truths that he had articulated in his dissertation under the principle of sufficient reason of cognition: namely, logical, transcendental, empirical, and metalogical truths. "I would therefore like to distinguish this truth from every other, and call it *philosophical truth* κατ᾽ ἐξοχήν [*par excellence*]. We can turn the expression of this truth in a different way and say: My body and my will are one; or what as representation of intuition I call my body, I call will insofar as I am conscious of it in an entirely different way comparable with no other: or my body is the *objectivity* of my will; or apart from the fact that my body is my representation, it is still my will, and so on."[67] The identity of the will and the body entailed for Schopenhauer that each part of the body objectified the primary desires and demands of the will. Teeth, gullet, and the intestinal canal are objectified hunger, the brain the intellect, and the genitals the sexual impulse. Even more specifically, each human's body made visible a person's will. In this way, the older philosopher provided a philosophical justification for the curiosity of the younger man. His striving to get a clean look at Napoleon was not driven simply to view a celebrity; rather, his physiognomy would reveal his character, his will.

Schopenhauer's identification of the body with the will led him to identify actions of the body with acts of the will. This was a rejection of a long-standing philosophical tradition that viewed acts of the will or volitions as causes of actions. Instead, Schopenhauer viewed an action as a volition, but viewed from the standpoint of self-consciousness or the inner sense, and a volition as an action, but viewed from the standpoint of the consciousness of other things or the outer sense. This stance concerning the identity of bodily actions and volitions became his stance toward the

---

[66] Schopenhauer, *The World as Will and Representation*, Vol. 1, p. 103/ *Sämtliche Werke*, Vol. 2, p. 123.

[67] Ibid., Vol. 1, p. 102f/ibid., Vol. 2, p. 122f.

world as will and the world as representation. The world viewed one way is the will; viewed from another way, it is representation. There is no causal relationship between the two, because they are identical. By adopting this perspective, Schopenhauer prided himself with avoiding the Achilles' heel of Kant's philosophy, having the thing in itself function as the cause or ground of appearances. He had learned well his lesson from Aenesidemus Schulze.

Schopenhauer motivated his metaphysics by noting that this unique experience of one's own body raised the question of whether other representations also have will as a backside like the representation of his body, or if this representation is essentially different from all others. If the latter were the case, Schopenhauer claims that other representations would be *mere* representations, "mere phantoms," and one "must assume that his body is the only real individual in the world, i.e., the only appearance of the will, and the only immediate object of the subject."[68] He referred to this solipsistic view as "theoretical egoism," and he viewed it as entailing the denial of the reality of the external world. Schopenhauer, however, never took any form of skepticism seriously, and he did not attempt a refutation of theoretical egoism. He simply conceded that it could never be conclusively refuted by philosophical proof. Instead, he called it a "skeptical sophism" that was incapable of becoming a serious conviction, except for someone in a madhouse where its advocate needed not a refutation but a cure.

After categorically rejecting theoretical egoism, Schopenhauer used an argument by analogy to conclude that the will is also the interior or backside for all other representations: "We will judge all objects which are not our own body, and therefore are given to consciousness not in a double way, but only as representations, according to the analogy of this body."[69] Other representations are just like the representation of our bodies, and if we abstract from their existence as our representation, what remains over, their inner essence, must be what we refer to as "will." Schopenhauer adds the modal "must" to his argument by claiming that besides will and representation absolutely nothing else is known or conceivable to us, and if we want to attribute the greatest known reality to the external world, then we must assign it the same reality our body

[68] Ibid., Vol. 1, p. 104/ibid., Vol. 2, p. 124.
[69] Ibid., Vol. 1, p. 105/ibid., Vol. 2, p. 125.

has for us. By doing this, he was making that which is most immediately and intimately known, the will, the mouthpiece for everything else. Later, in the second edition of his principal work, he would claim that unlike the ancients, who viewed humans as the microcosm, he had reversed this view by showing that the world was the *"macranthropos,"* the great human being.[70] Schopenhauer became the philosopher of the body by making the human body the key for understanding the world.

It is here in the second book that Schopenhauer made a claim designed to set the philosophical world on fire. He pronounced that the will is the thing in itself, the great unknown in Kant's philosophy and that which was abandoned by Fichte, Schelling, and Hegel, the last of whom mocked it by claiming it was the best thing known, the concept of negation.[71] And so Schopenhauer reasoned, "Appearance means representation and nothing more. All representation, be it of whatever kind it may, every *object* is *appearance*. But only the will is *thing in itself*; as such it is not representation at all, but *toto genere* different therefrom. It is that of which all representation, every object, is the appearance, the visibility, the *objectivity*. It is the innermost essence, the kernel of every particular thing and also the whole. It appears in every blindly acting force of nature, and in the deliberate conduct of humans, and the great difference between the two concerns only the degree of the manifestation, not the essence of what is manifested."[72]

It was as if by magic that nature revealed itself in self-consciousness, and Schopenhauer needed a word to refer to that which magically appeared. "But the word *will*, which, like a magic word, is to reveal to us the innermost essence of everything in nature, by no means expresses an unknown quantity, something reached by inferences and syllogisms, but something known absolutely and immediately, and that so well that we know and understand what will is better than anything else be what it may."[73] The world as representation is simply the mirror of will, and will is his *ens realissimum*, the most real being. This magical word, used

---

[70] Ibid., Vol. 2, p. 642/ibid., Vol. 3, p. 736.

[71] Contrary to Kant, who claimed that the thing in itself is unknowable, Hegel claims that "there is nothing we can know so easily," because it is simply the concept of negation; see *Hegel's Logic*, trans. William Wallace (Oxford: Clarendon Press, 1975), Sect. 44, p. 72.

[72] Schopenhauer, *The World as Will and Representation*, Vol. 1, p. 110/*Sämtliche Werke*, Vol. 2, p. 131.

[73] Ibid., Vol. 1, p. 111/ibid., Vol. 2, p. 133.

in its most expanded, cosmological sense, referred to a goalless striving to be that exemplifies itself in the world as representation, from the most universally expressed phenomena, forces of nature, such as gravity, through the deliberate conduct of humans. The only difference between the kinds of things was the degree to which will was objectified. There was no difference in the inner nature of that which is manifest. Yet he held that will exists whole and undivided in each of its manifestations, and a careful analysis of any appearance or representation would ultimately end with reference to will. The objectification of will, he argued, has endless graduations analogous to that found from the feeblest to the brightest sun ray or as that between the loudest tone and its softest echo. The world as representation, moreover, revealed a hierarchical ontology that ranged from forces of nature, the least expressive representations of the will, through the human being, the most expressive representation of the will.

Still as will, each element in the world as representation strives to be: "Every grade of the will's objectification fights for the matter, space, and the time of another."[74] The world, therefore, displays a super form of animism that exhibits constant conflict and strife. But a world of struggling and conflicting physical and chemical forces is merely a world of coming into and going out of existence. Existence becomes problematic when the inevitable conflicts involve cognizant beings: "Pain concerns *will* alone and consists in checking, hindering, or thwarting this; yet an additional requirement is that this checking be accompanied by cognition."[75] In other words, it is not until the evolution of human and nonhuman animals that existence becomes problematic. All of these creatures suffer, from their essence, and humans suffer the most, being aware of their deaths. Schopenhauer's metaphysics of the will sets the ground for his pessimism and answers one of the questions that drive philosophical astonishment. Suffering and death are ubiquitous features of the world because the world is will.

Will is one, Schopenhauer theorized, but not one as an object or a concept can be said to be one. An object is one, because it occupies a specific place at a particular time, and a concept is one, because it is abstracted from a plurality of particulars, which are then members of its extension. Will is one, because it is outside of the scope of the principle of sufficient reason,

---

[74] Ibid., Vol. 1, p. 147/ibid., Vol. 2, p. 174.
[75] Schopenhauer, *Parerga and Paralipomena*, Vol. 2, p. 297/*Sämtliche Werke*, Vol. 6, p. 316.

and therefore it is beyond the possibility of plurality and individuation. It is as if the oneness of will is simply a form of nonplurality. Because will is not subordinated to the principle of sufficient reason, it eludes all forms of necessity. Consequently, he argued that will is free. He would claim in the second edition of this work that the freedom of will is transcendent and this freedom of will is just as compatible with the necessity governing the world as representation as the transcendental ideality of appearance is with its empirical reality.[76] Borrowing a term from theology used to describe God, Schopenhauer attributed "aseity" to the will, independence from everything else, with everything else having dependent existence. For this reason, he would later claim he had a greater right than Spinoza to call his metaphysics "ethics," because his *ens realissimum* satisfies the two conditions for morality – it was both free and responsible for the world. Even later in his career, he would assert that his philosophy avoids the claim "that the world has only a physical and not a moral significance . . . a fundamental error, one that is the greatest and most pernicious, the real perversity of mind . . . that faith had personified as antichrist."[77] The ever-ironic one-time fan of Schopenhauer, Nietzsche, would proudly dub his amoral, Dionysian worldview "antichrist."[78]

By the end of the second book, Schopenhauer had delivered what his title had promised, an account of the world as representation and as will. He concluded this book by observing that "The sole self-knowledge of will as a whole is the representation as a whole, the whole world of perception."[79] This claim echoed what he had designated in his Dresden notes as his single thought: "My entire philosophy can be summarized in one expression: The world is the self-knowledge of the will."[80] That *The*

---

[76] Schopenhauer, *The World as Will and Representation*, Vol. 2, p. 320/*Sämtliche Werke*, Vol. 3, p. 364. It is curious that in a note written in Dresden (1814), as Schopenhauer stated writing his principal work, he equated Plato's Ideas with Kant's thing in itself, simply because both were beyond space and time, making them beyond plurality, change, and beginning and end; see, *Manuscript Remains*, Vol. 1, p. 250/*Der handschriftliche Nachlaß*, Vol. 1, p. 150.

[77] Schopenhauer, *Parerga and Paralipomena*, Vol. 2, p. 201/*Sämtliche Werke*, Vol. 6, p. 214.

[78] See Nietzsche's *The Birth of Tragedy*, Preface, Sect. 5, for his use of the term "antichrist" in opposition to Schopenhauer, and for a careful analysis of the same, see Jörg Salaquarda's "Der Antichrist," *Nietzsche Studien*, Vol. 2 (1973), pp. 90–136.

[79] Schopenhauer, *The World as Will and Representation*, Vol. 1, p. 165./*Sämtliche Werke*, Vol. 2, p. 196.

[80] Schopenhauer, *Manuscript Remains*, Vol. 1, p. 512/*Der handschriftliche Nachlaß*, Vol. 1, p. 462.

World as Will and Representation did not end with the second book is not surprising. Had it ended, Schopenhauer would not have considered the topics that drove his philosophy of the better consciousness, namely, art, ethics, and salvation. Moreover, at the conclusion of his main work, he asserts again, "for the world is the self-knowledge of will," but what this "self-knowledge" entails required two more books.[81]

Third Book: Metaphysics of Art

In the third book Schopenhauer returns to considering the world as representation from a fresh perspective, one that transcends observation of the world through the lens of the principle of sufficient reason. The rather clunky title of this book obliquely announces that it presents his aesthetics; "The Representation Independent of the Principle of Sufficient Reason: The Platonic Idea: The Object of Art."[82] Schopenhauer's aesthetics could have followed only after his first consideration of the world as will, where he argued that will was the essence of all representations, his thing in itself, and the basis for the omnipresence of strife, conflict, pain, suffering, destruction, and death. Art provided release, repose, and a cool spot within the burning coals that were life. Art presented the innocent side of life; it was the "flower of life."[83] But more importantly, it was also within the context of the metaphysics of will that he would introduce his very unPlatonic conception of Platonic Ideas, which would play the leading role in his analysis of aesthetic contemplation and his description of artistic genius, and which would serve as his standard for his classification of the arts.

Schopenhauer's analysis of the natural sciences sought to establish that the classificatory schemes of the morphological sciences culminated in the recognition of natural kinds and that the etiological sciences ultimately employed the notion of natural forces within their formulations of causal laws describing the regularity of changes in the natural world. There are numerous particular examples of granite, shark, rose, tigers, and humans, and Platonic Ideas serve as philosophical counterparts of these natural types of things, just as they do for forces of nature, such as gravity, fluidity,

---

[81] Schopenhauer, *The World as Will and Representation*, Vol. 1, p. 410/*Sämtliche Werke*, Vol. 2, p. 485.

[82] Ibid., Vol. 1, p. 167/ibid., Vol. 2, p. 197.

[83] Ibid., Vol. 1, p. 266/ibid., Vol. 2, p. 315.

elasticity, and electricity. Schopenhauer had also posited a hierarchical ontology of the world as representation, based on the degree to which the will was manifest. This hierarchy ranged from the most universal and least expressive to the most individualistic and most highly expressive level of the will's objectification. Thus he held that "there is a higher degree of objectification in the plant than in the stone, a higher degree in the animal than in the plant."[84] Within this context, Schopenhauer remarks, "Now I say that these *grades of the objectification of the will* are nothing but Plato's Ideas."[85] More specifically, a Platonic Idea, be it of gravity, granite, shark, rose, tiger, or human, is a fixed grade of the objectification of the will.

Grades of the objectification of the will are expressed in numerous individuals, but Platonic Ideas exist as the eternal forms of things, which are never perfectly exemplified in any particular thing. These particulars are always coming to be and perishing. Schopenhauer contended that these fixed grades of the will's objectification are related to particular things as eternal forms or archetypes, and they are themselves definite, unchanging, nonspatial, nontemporal, and outside of the scope of the principle of sufficient reason. This, he claimed, was Plato's original and genuine meaning of the term, and he warned his readers that he did not use the concept illegitimately, like Kant, who bastardized Plato's great insight by making Ideas the necessary products of pure reason, empty concepts that could never find an object of experience. For Schopenhauer, Ideas are not bastard products of reason's drive to know the unconditional, as Kant would have it, nor the product of any human cognitive faculty, but are, instead, objects for a subject, reached by pure and disinterested contemplation. More specifically, Kant's Ideas of pure reason, the soul, the world (as a closed totality), and God are empty phantoms, concepts without percepts and mere empty thoughts, which have not even a regulative use for a rational being.

Schopenhauer, however, found an intimate point of contact between the philosophies of his heroes: "We find Kant's thing in itself and Plato's Ideas... those two great and obscure paradoxes of the two greatest philosophers of the West... not exactly identical, but yet very closely related, and distinguished by only a single modification."[86] Both Plato's

[84] Ibid., Vol. 1, p. 128/ibid., Vol. 2, p. 153.
[85] Ibid., Vol. 1, p. 129/ibid., Vol. 2, p. 154.
[86] Ibid., Vol. 1, p. 170/ibid., Vol. 2, p. 200.

Ideas and Kant's thing in itself connote that the world revealed by the senses is merely a world of appearances and not true reality. Thus Schopenhauer claims that the inner meanings of Plato's and Kant's philosophies were the same. Both declare the sensory world to be mere appearance and its "borrowed" reality to come from that which is expressed in it, Ideas for Plato and the thing in itself for Kant. Naturally, Schopenhauer claimed that he demonstrated the true relationship between Ideas and things in themselves by claiming that "the Idea is only the immediate, and therefore adequate, objectivity of the thing in itself, which is *will* – will insofar as it is not yet objectified, has not yet become representation."[87] Platonic Ideas, however, differ from will, he continued, because they are necessarily an object, something cognized by a subject, and thereby reside under the most general form of any representation, that of being an object for a subject. Ideas subordinate to the principle of sufficient reason are multiplied, Schopenhauer reasoned, into the particular, individually cognized things of mundane experience, which are indirect objectifications of the will. Ideas stand between the will and particular things.

Schopenhauer's aesthetics was less in debt to Kant's than it was to his theoretical philosophy, but the centerpiece of his aesthetics, his analysis of the aesthetic experience, followed the general contours of that of his hero. He found the same problem in Kant's aesthetics that he found in his epistemology. Thus he complained that Kant operated from judgments about things rather than experience itself, and he chided Kant for operating from judgments about the beautiful itself. He also opined that Kant had very little receptivity for beauty and that he had few opportunities to experience great works of art, because he never left Königsberg during his entire life. Thus he compared Kant to a very intelligent blind person who had to rely on the precise statements of others to develop a theory of color: "And actually we can regard Kant's philosophemes on the beautiful as being in much the same position."[88] Yet, although he thought that Kant's analysis of the beautiful was deeply flawed, he credited Kant for blazing a new path in aesthetics. Schopenhauer had observed previously that Aristotle, Edmund Burke, Johann Joachim Winckelmann, Lessing, Herder, and others had focused on objects referred to as "beautiful" and sought

---

[87] Ibid., Vol. 1, p. 174/ibid., Vol. 2, p. 205f.
[88] Ibid., Vol. 1, p. 531/ibid., Vol. 2, p. 629.

for the characteristics or properties of these objects. By starting from judgments, however, Kant directs aesthetic inquiry back to the subject. Schopenhauer followed Kant back to the subject, but he went one step further by skipping over the judgment to go on to the subject's experience of the beautiful.

Aesthetic experience, the experience of the beautiful or sublime, involves the contemplation of either a natural object or a great work of art, and it is a unique and extraordinary experience. In the ordinary course of our lives we perceive many individual things standing in relationships of various kinds with other like things. More fundamentally, he claimed that our mundane experiences of things are always interested; that is, we perceive things under the scope of the principle of sufficient reason and as possible means for either sating or frustrating our desires. In an aesthetic experience, we are suddenly torn away from our commonplace view of things. It is as if we lose ourselves and become lost in our cognition. Woes and worries disappear, time seems to stand still, and calm and tranquility prevail. It is as if we become one with the object of cognition and our eyes seem to become a pure mirror reflecting the object of our awareness, which is no longer a mundane thing.

Aesthetic experience involves a radical transformation of both the subject and the object of cognition, Schopenhauer argued. The subject, the aesthetic contemplator, morphed into a "*pure*, will-less, painless, timeless *subject of cognition*" and the object of cognition was a Platonic Idea.[89] This extraordinary experience abandons the principle of sufficient reason and everything falling under its scope. The world of spatio-temporal objects standing in the causal nexus with others of their kind disappears. No longer is there a world populated by things to quell or aggravate desire, and by overcoming desire, aesthetic experience entails liberation from the will, an escape from suffering, and a foretaste of what Schopenhauer would call the denial of will. Because Platonic Ideas are direct expressions of the will, aesthetic experience is more metaphysically revealing than science. The will as thing in itself is not a representation; when it becomes an object, it is the Idea, and when the will is objectified in time, space, and causality, it is multiplied into the fleeting and changing mundane things in the world. Science only concerns itself with the last. Art, with

---

[89] Ibid., Vol. 1, p. 179/ibid., Vol. 2, p. 210f.

the exception of music, presents Platonic Ideas, and so art presents a more adequate expression of the will.

A great work of art is the product of genius, and Schopenhauer used the term "genius" almost exclusively to refer to either a great artist or a great philosopher. He viewed artists as possessing an overabundance of intellect, compared to the ordinary person, and as having an ability to see what other people cannot. This wealth of intellect enables artists to view things more objectively, without reference to their wills, and thereby to cognize Platonic Ideas. The artistic genius, therefore, can view a stone, plant, animal, or human not as a particular, but as the universal instantiated in the particular, the Platonic Idea of a stone, plant, animal, or human. Not only does the artist possess a predilection for objective contemplation, he – Schopenhauer denies genius to women – also possesses a robust imagination, because no individual item perfectly expresses a Platonic Idea. Consequently, the artist has to creatively remove unnecessary and inessential features of a thing to cognize its Idea. Naturally, the artist also has to possess the technical skills to convey the Idea in a work of art.

Schopenhauer's reflections on genius also moved him to consider madness. Already in the fall of 1811, during his attendance at Fichte's very first lecture, he disputed his professor's positing of genius and madness as opposite poles of humankind. Fichte claimed that both deviated from ordinary people, but genius inclined upward to the divine and the mad downward to the animal. The student objected: "On the contrary, I believe that genius and madness, although widely different, are closer to each other than is the former to a person with common sense and the latter to the animal."[90] By the time of this note, the aspiring philosopher had visited the Berlin Charity, where he observed " . . . in frequent visits to lunatic asylums, individual subjects endowed with unmistakably great gifts. Their genius appeared distinctly from their madness which had completely gained the upper hand."[91] Genius itself inclined to madness, Schopenhauer observed, something that can be gleaned by reading the biographies of men such as Rousseau and Byron, and the connection between genius and madness had been noted by Plato in the *Phaedrus* and in his infamous allegory of the cave. Those who left the darkness to enter

---

[90] Schopenhauer, *Manuscript Remains*, Vol. 2, p. 18/ *Der handschriftliche Nachlaß*, Vol. 2, p. 18.
[91] Schopenhauer, *The World as Will and Representation*, Vol. 1, p. 191/ *Sämtliche Werke*, Vol. 2, p. 225.

into light, who experience things as they actually are, the Ideas, can no longer perceive in the dark and thus appear mad to the cave dwellers.[92]

Like the genius, whose life expresses moments that transcend the principle of sufficient reason, the insane suffer an interruption in memory, being unable to connect the present with the past. Like the animal, demented people are restricted to the present, but unlike animals, which lack all notions of a past, insane people possess the faculty of reason, and they have a past, but one that is fictitious. Anticipating Freud, Schopenhauer observed that the loss of a correct memory of the past and the substitution of a fictitious one is often the product of trauma: "The fact that violent mental suffering or unexpected and terrible events are frequently the cause of madness."[93] Suffering as an actual event is limited to the present and it is transitory. Yet it can become a lasting pain as a *memory*. To preserve itself, the mind destroys the painful memory and fills up the gap with fictions, and the result is madness. The point of contact between genius and madness is a loss of connection to the present. The genius, cognizing Platonic Ideas, is removed from the recognition of particular things, according to the principle of sufficient reason. By cognizing the Idea, the genius is aware of the universal and not the particulars and individual things of everyday experience. The mad person also lacks a connection to everyday reality due to a fictitious memory that prohibits the true relationships to the things and events of everyday life. It is as if the metaphysically penetrating vision of the genius is as abnormal as that of the insane, when measured by the standards of the average person who experiences only appearances, but according to their proper connections under the principle of sufficient reason. The difference is that the genius experiences a reality that is greater than the mundane one of ordinary people, whereas the insane experience one that is less.

Schopenhauer's account of artistic genius entails that everything in nature is beautiful because the genius potentially could cognize a Platonic Idea for any natural object. Indeed, any person could enjoy the feeling of the beautiful, provided that a natural object was viewed disinterestedly and objectively. Any object of aesthetic contemplation, a natural object or a work of art, elicits the feeling of the beautiful when its cognition

---

[92] See Plato's *Republic*, Bk. VII, 514–17b, for the allegory of the cave.

[93] Schopenhauer, *The World as Will and Representation*, Vol. 1, p. 193/*Sämtliche Werke*, Vol. 2, p. 227.

transforms the spectator into a pure, will-less, painless, timeless subject. The transition into this peaceful, tranquil state is smooth and automatic. This state is "the painless state, prized by Epicurus as the highest good and as the state of the gods; for that moment, we are delivered from the miserable pressure of the will, and we celebrate the Sabbath of the denial of the servitude of willing; the wheel of Ixion stands still."[94] Natural beauty, he argued, facilitates the feeling of the beautiful to such an extent that even those who are the most insensitive enjoy, however fleetingly, some aesthetic satisfaction in its presence. This is especially true, he observed, with the plant world, and he conjectured that perhaps this was the case because plants need cognitive beings to provide for them that which is denied to them, an entrance into the world of representation.[95]

Schopenhauer viewed the sublime as closely related to the beautiful. Both entail the cognition of a Platonic Idea by a pure will-less, timeless, painless subject of knowledge. Common to both is the escape from cognition in the service of will. Indeed, he held that the difference between the beautiful and the sublime is a matter of degree rather than kind. To show this, he provided an example concerning the experience of the beauty of architecture, describing how it is enhanced by the play of light against a building's mass. In the depth of winter, as we observe the play of light cast by the setting sun on the mass of the structure, we are moved into contemplation of the beautiful effect of light and into a state of pure cognition. Yet there is also a recognition, he continued, that the light produces no warmth, something that is required to sustain life. Consequently, there is a slight challenge to our turning away from the will, a turning that is totally smooth and automatic in other instances of the experience of the beautiful. Due to the feeble challenge to the transition into a pure subject of cognition, we experience "the faintest trace of the sublime in the beautiful and beauty itself appears here only in a slight degree."[96]

Schopenhauer distinguished between the beautiful and the sublime by focusing on the object of cognition and its interplay with the subject. In the experience of the sublime, the object of cognition is, to some degree, threatening to the agent, because it connotes something hostile to the will

---

[94] Schopenhauer, *The World as Will and Representation*, Vol. 1, p. 196/*Sämtliche Werke*, Vol. 2, p. 231.

[95] Ibid., Vol. 1, p. 201/ibid., Vol. 2, p. 237.

[96] Ibid., Vol. 1, p. 203/ibid., Vol. 2, p. 240.

to life. Because of the threat to one's well-being or one's very life, the transition into a pure subject of cognition involves a struggle through which the contemplator is elevated above the threat suggested by the object. With the experience of the beautiful, its objects suggest no such threat to life and limb, and the transition from ordinary cognition to that of pure cognition is automatic and without any resistance or struggle. Because objects that affect the feeling of the sublime are hostile to a person's will, however, the transformation from ordinary, willful cognition to pure cognition involves some violent turning away from these objects, which also involves an exaltation of the subject beyond the hostile relations of the object to the will. Like the experience of the beautiful, Schopenhauer also recognized various degrees to the experience of the sublime. He argued that the more threatening the object, the greater the struggle to overcome such threats, and the greater the experience of the sublime. The recognition of the potential threat to one's well-being had to be such that the contemplator did not actually feel fear, distress, or panic. These emotions are willful responses toward and object and they inhibit any aesthetic experience.

Schopenhauer held that the most excellent thing in Kant's *Critique of the Power of Judgment* was his analysis of the sublime, although he rejected the moral implications that he thought Kant had attached to this feeling, as well as his description of "the inner nature of the impression [of the sublime]."[97] But he followed Kant in distinguishing between the dynamically and the mathematically sublime. Once more Schopenhauer based this distinction on the nature of the objects that occasion the feeling of the sublime. The dynamically sublime involves natural objects or events that threaten to annihilate the spectator, such as a howling storm in a raging sea, with lightning flashing from thick, ominous, black clouds, resounding with booming thunder-claps that momentarily drown out the crashing of the waves. The monstrous and unfettered powers of nature lead the observer to feel helpless and feeble, and as nothing compared to

---

[97] Schopenhauer., ibid., Vol. 1, p. 205/ibid., Vol. 2, p. 242. Kant discusses the dynamically and mathematically sublime in the *Critique of the Power of Judgment*, AK. 247f., and in the conclusion of the *Critique of Practical Reason*, AK. 161, he claimed that two things filled his mind with awe: the starry sky above him and the moral law within him. Although Schopenhauer saw the starry sky as occasioning the feeling of the sublime, he rejected the idea that one could find some moral law within oneself. It is likely that Schopenhauer read this passage as suggesting that Kant attributed a moral basis to the feeling of the sublime.

these raging forces. Unshaken spectators, however, may sense that this terrible spectacle is only their representation and, as such, is dependent on them. This recognition lifts a spectator into a pure subject of cognition.

In contrast to the prompts for the dynamically sublime, the objects of the mathematically sublime involve the contemplation of the infinite greatness of the universe in space and time and the subsequent recognition that we are less than a drop of water in a vast ocean. The starry sky at night, bringing countless worlds before our eyes, solicits a double consciousness. On the one hand, we feel reduced to nothing, given this infinite magnitude of the universe. On the other hand, we are subjects of cognition, and the supporters of all worlds and of all times. What once caused unrest now is viewed as resting on us, and any sense of one's dependence upon the world is obliterated by the world's dependence on one.

Platonic Ideas also function centrally in Schopenhauer's analysis of the arts. His hierarchical classification of the arts is based on the degree to which a particular art expresses metaphysical truth. With the exception of music, this classification concerns the types of Platonic ideas conveyed by a particular art and the grade of the objectification of the will represented by the idea. Architecture as a fine art ranks at the low endpoint of Schopenhauer's hierarchy, because it presents occasions for the expression of ideas at the lowest levels of the will's objectification: namely, of gravity, cohesion, rigidity, and hardness, the Ideas of forces of nature. The artistic arrangement of water, hydraulics, is next in the hierarchy. Tumbling waterfalls, springs gushing upward as columns of water, and reflecting ponds reveal the Idea of fluidity and its resolution with gravity. Because artistic horticulture concerns plant life, which is a higher objectification of the will, it is more expressive of the nature of the will than architecture and hydraulics. Yet, because the plant world naturally and more readily offers itself for aesthetic enjoyment than artistic gardening, Schopenhauer holds that landscape painting is more suitable for the artistic presentation of plants than gardening, whose artificial arrangements are always subject to the whims of nature. In painting and sculpture of animal life, however, Schopenhauer claimed that still higher grades of the will are expressed, and one can begin to sense the restlessness, striving, and conflict that are found in more vehemently expressed human life. The highest visual arts, however, are concerned with the human form, but are limited in their ability to depict the complexity of human life because of the static nature of their media – paint, marble, and the like.

The verbal arts, all of which Schopenhauer referred to as "poetry," are the most expressive of human life and the Idea of humanity. He divided the verbal arts into three kinds, lyrical, epic, and dramatic poetry. At the pinnacle of the verbal arts stood tragedy or tragic drama, because it not only presents human life, which is the highest expression of the nature of the will, but also depicts the deep, terrible side of human existence, which is subject to the scornful play of chance and in which the innocent, just, and good often fall. Tragedy shows the antagonism of the will itself. The fall of the tragic hero illustrates the dreadful nature of the will, and Schopenhauer held that the hero's atonement for "sin" represented atonement for the guilt of existence. The tragic effect urges the turning away from life, and the ultimate significance of tragedy is that it counsels resignation and the denial of the will. Thus he saw Gretchen in Goethe's *Faust* and the Prince in Calderón's *The Constant Prince* as heroes found in the very best tragedies because they ultimately resign from life. It was largely for this reason that the dramas of the ancient Greeks were inferior to those of the modern.[98] Yet, even if a tragedy failed to show resignation, Schopenhauer believed that a good tragedy could still teach resignation. Greek tragedies displayed little of the spirit of withdrawal from life, but still they presented life's horrors on stage, allowing the spectators to recognize that life is not something to love and that it is better to turn away from life and the world. Great tragedy provokes the highest degree of the feeling of the sublime, because it lifts spectators above the will and desire, occasioning a pleasure at the sight of that which directly opposes the will and that leads to the recognition that there is something in them that does *not* will life.

Music was a great solace in Schopenhauer's life, and he valued the discovery of the truth about this miserable world unconditionally. Because music conveyed truth to a higher degree than any other art, he placed it at the very summit of his hierarchy of the arts, and he attributed to it a truth-conveying ability identical to philosophy itself. The reason for this, Schopenhauer philosophized, was that music passes over Ideas and as such, completely ignores the world of appearances. It is an "*immediate*

[98] See ibid., Vol. 2, p. 585/ibid., Vol. 3, p. 672f. Schopenhauer recognized Greek tragedy as demonstrating both the Greeks' keen awareness of the wretchedness of life and their maintaining a standpoint that affirmed the will – a standpoint that, unlike Schopenhauer, Nietzsche saw as the genius of the Greeks; also see my "Reversing Silenus' Wisdom," *Nietzsche-Studien* 20 (1991), pp. 309–13.

objectification and copy [*Abbild*] of the whole *will* as the world itself is, indeed as the Ideas are, the multiplied appearance of which constitutes the world of individual things. Therefore music is by no means like the other arts, namely a copy [*Abbild*] of the Ideas but a *copy of the will itself*, the objectivity of which are the Ideas."[99] Playing on Leibniz's observation that music was an unconscious exercise in arithmetic, he called music an unconscious exercise in metaphysics.[100] Just as philosophy properly carried out reproduces the world conceptually, music does the same in tones. In this regard, "We could just as well call the world embodied music as embodied will."[101] He would not, however, call the world embodied concepts. Concepts are simply the tools of philosophy. They are abstracted from the world as representation and are incapable of expressing with the same precision and grandeur what could be expressed by music. Schopenhauer's philosophy of music would appeal to composers with deep philosophical aspirations and provide them the means to think they could express the same thing as the philosopher, but more immediately and effectively and with a greater clarity. Philosophy provides the husk, music the meat.

Schopenhauer's account of music ended, however, with a dissonance. Music was said to be the copy of something that cannot be copied – a mirroring of an original that cannot be reflected, a representation in tunes of that which cannot be represented. He, therefore, left it to his readers to accept or reject his view of music, but, he continued, they should do so after they had grasped his single thought and experienced the effect produced by great music. But he also closed the third book by noting that the artist, the genius, despite the ability to purely contemplate the world, does not overcome the world. At best, the artistic genius has moments of consolation, but like anyone, but more astutely, "he himself bears the cost of producing the play; in other words, he himself is the will objectifying itself and remains in constant suffering. That pure, true, and profound knowledge of the inner nature of the world now becomes for him an end

---

[99] Ibid., Vol. 1, p. 257/ibid., Vol. 2, p. 303.
[100] See Schopenhauer, ibid., Vol. 1, p. 264/ibid., Vol. 2, p. 313. Schopenhauer is paraphrasing Leibniz, "Musica est exercitium arithmeticae occultum nescientis se numerare animi," from *Epistolae ad Diversos, Theologici, Juridici, Medici, Philosophici, Mathematici, Historici et Philologici Argumenti*, ed. Christian Kortholtus (Bern: Christoph Breitkopf, 1734), Vol. 1, p. 154.
[101] Ibid., Vol. 1, p. 263/ibid., Vol. 2, p. 310.

in itself; at it he stops. Therefore it does not become a quieter of the will. . . ."[102] Still, if the artist were to become tired of the brief moments of peace afforded by contemplation, such an artist would turn to the more serious side of things, which is the topic of Schopenhauer's fourth book.

Fourth Book: Metaphysics of Morals

To turn to the serious side of things is to return to the world as will. Whereas the second book focused on Schopenhauer's metaphysics of nature, even though its beginning point was the human body, in this book he focuses on that which most graphically expresses the nature of the will, human conduct. The title of the fourth book also deftly captures its broad, teleological range: "With the Attainment of Self-Knowledge, Affirmation and Denial of the Will to Life." This is his "ethical book," and he warned his readers that it is not "practical philosophy" as normally understood. All philosophy is theoretical and it proceeds in a purely contemplative manner no matter what its subject matter. He eschewed calling his ethics "practical philosophy," moreover, because that typically suggests the development of a set of rules for conduct aimed to alter human behavior and ultimately transform a person's character. The dead concepts of philosophy cannot affect this sort of transformation. What decides the worthlessness or worth of existence, damnation or salvation, is the innermost essence of a person; what Plato called a person's guiding voice or *daemon* and Kant called the intelligible character. Virtue, Schopenhauer argued, is just as little taught as genius, and it is foolishness to expect that a moral system could produce a good person or saint just as it is to think that aesthetics could make the unpoetic poetical. Nor will he tell people what they ought to do. One talks that way to children and not to people whose natures are will through and through. He will provide no doctrines of duties, no prescriptions, especially nonsensical ones such as those of Kant, who spoke of an "unconditioned *ought*," not realizing that he could just as well been speaking of a square circle. Later, in 1839, in his unsuccessful prize essay *On the Basis of Morality*, he would harshly analyze Kant's ethics, the area of his hero's philosophy for which he had the least sympathy and toward which he had no compassion.

[102] Ibid., Vol. 1, p. 267/ibid., Vol. 2, p. 316.

The range of topics in Schopenhauer's "ethical book" is broad: life and death, freedom and determinism, the goalless nature of the will, suffering and boredom, the negative nature of happiness, religious superstition, the sex drive as the strongest expression of the will to life, eternal and temporal justice, philosophy of right, compassion as the basis of righteousness and moral goodness, asceticism, suicide, and salvation as overcoming the world and denying the will. Then there is his closing proposition that neatly counterbalances the opening proposition, which had affirmed that the world is one's representation: "To those in whom the will has turned and denied itself, this very real world of ours with all its suns and galaxies, is – nothing."[103] Given this breathtaking array of topics, the fourth book is the longest book, running 206 pages in the first edition. Book one ran 135 pages, two was 103, and three was 143. His appendix, "Critique of the Kantian Philosophy," displayed his understanding of all the major areas of Kant's philosophy and his critical remarks muscle in at 134 pages.

Teleological language permeates *The World as Will and Representation*, and nowhere is it more apparent than in the fourth book. In the first three books, he tried to show "That in the world as representation the will has risen a mirror in which it recognizes itself with increasing degrees of distinctness and completeness, the highest of which is the human being."[104] He contended that will, considered purely in itself, is devoid of consciousness and cognition, and it is a blind, ceaseless urge as it appears in inorganic nature and the plant kingdom and its laws, as well as in the vegetative part of our own life. It obtains cognition of its willing and what it wills dimly in animal life and most clearly in human life, through the world as representation, which, he wrote, it developed for its service. The will wills only life, he continued, so it is a mere pleonasm, a redundancy, "if instead of simply saying 'will,' we say will to life."[105] Because will is the thing in itself, the inner content, essence of the world and life, he continued, if will exists, life and the world exist.

Schopenhauer employed this last observation to confront the issues of death and suffering. Few philosophers before him, and not many after him, have made death and suffering such an intimate aspect of their philosophical reflections. In the second edition of his principal work, he

---

[103] Ibid., Vol. 1, p. 412/ibid., Vol. 2, p. 487.
[104] Ibid., Vol. 1, p. 274f/ibid., Vol. 2, p. 323. I have significantly altered Payne's translation.
[105] Ibid., Vol. 1, p. 274/ibid., Vol. 2, p. 324.

would refer to humans as the *animal metaphysicum*, and he would agree with Plato's and Aristotle's contention that wonder or astonishment about the world prompts philosophical speculation about the world. He would, however, hold that the disposition to philosophize is intensified by the recognition of the wretchedness of life, the omnipresence of death and suffering. Without these twin evils, humans would be much like other animals and take life just simply as it came, he hypothesized, and "if our life were without end and free from pain, it would not possibly occur to anyone to ask why the world exists, and why it does so in precisely this way, but everything would be taken purely as a matter of course."[106] A continuous theme in Schopenhauer's work, initiated here in the first edition, will be to prove a metaphysical explanation for death and suffering, one that honestly examines these issues with an unrelenting commitment to the truth and with an eye to providing consolation for suffering and ephemeral humankind – as if there were no tensions to these commitments.[107] Indeed, the longest chapter in *The World as Will and Representation* would appear in its second edition as "On Death and Its Relation to the Indestructibility of Our Inner Nature." It was written when Schopenhauer sensed his own mortality.

What we fear in death, Schopenhauer diagnosed, is our extinction and end. Our greatest anxiety is our anxiety about our own death. Because death is inevitable, and because there is nothing that we can do to forestall death, we feel helpless and hopeless in regard to our demise. Nevertheless, we are so full of the will to life that we constantly struggle against this "evil," a struggle in which we know that we cannot prevail. This natural stance toward our ephemeral existence is philosophically naive, according to Schopenhauer. Although we perceive individuals coming into and passing out of existence, individuals are only on the one side of the world, appearances, representations, and on the other side, they are will, our essence, which as thing in itself, the inner content and essence of things, is beyond the *principium individuationis*, space and time, and all forms of the principle of sufficient reason. Our essence never comes to be nor perishes. To consider life and death philosophically, Schopenhauer argued, is to

---

[106] Ibid., Vol. 2, p. 161/ibid., Vol. 3, p. 177.

[107] I discuss the tensions between these two commitments in "Schopenhauer on Suffering, Death, Guilt, and the Consolation of Metaphysics," in *Schopenhauer: New Essays in Honor of His 200th Birthday*, ed. Eric von Luft (Lewiston, NY: Edwin Mellen Press, 1988), pp. 51–66.

realize that "Neither will, the thing in itself in all appearances, nor the subject of the cognition, the spectator of all appearances, is in any way affected by birth and death. Birth and death belong only to the appearance of the will and hence to life; and it is essential to this that it manifest itself in individuals that come to be and pass away, as fleeting appearances, appearing in the form of time, of which it knows no time, but must be manifest precisely in the way aforesaid in order to objectify its true nature."[108]

Our essence, the will, is nontemporal and never comes to be or perishes. By this observation, however, Schopenhauer also rejected the idea that anything that delineates us as an individual, including our consciousness, survives death. Consequently, there is no personal immortality, no afterlife, no soul that escapes death and enjoys eternity. Yet because our essence is the will to life, which always wills life, our essence always lives, and it always lives in the present: "Past and future contain mere concepts and phantasms, hence the present is the essential form of the appearance of the will, and is inseparable from the form."[109] It is as if, he continued, there is an "eternal noon": the will to live and life is manifest always in the endless present. The sun burns without intermission, and daybreak and twilight mask this truth and make it appear that a new sun appears each day and that it is lost forever at night. But this is a delusion and to fear the loss of the sun is ignorance. The fear of death is likewise a function of ignorance, taking this dreamlike world of coming to be and perishing as ultimate reality is a delusion: "If a person fears death as his annihilation, it is just as if he were to think that the sun can lament in the evening and say: 'woe is me' I am going down into eternal night."[110]

From the standpoint reached by his reflections on the nature of the essence of the world, Schopenhauer continued, one could overcome the fear of death to the degree that reason has power over feeling:

A man who had assimilated firmly into this way of thinking the truths so far advanced, but at the same time had not come to know, through his own experience or through a deeper insight, that constant suffering is essential to life; who found satisfaction in life and too perfect delight in it; who desired, in spite of calm deliberation, that the

---

[108] Schopenhauer, *The World as Will and Representation*, Vol. 1, p. 275/*Sämtliche Werke*, Vol. 2, p. 324.
[109] Ibid., Vol. 1, p. 279/ibid., Vol. 2, p. 329.
[110] Ibid., Vol. 1, p. 280/ibid., Vol. 2, p. 331.

course of his life as he had hitherto experienced it should be of endless duration or of constant recurrence; and whose courage to face life was so great that, in return for life's pleasures, he would willingly and gladly put up with all the hardships and miseries to which it is subject; such a man would stand "with firm, strong bones on the well-grounded, enduring earth," and would have nothing to fear.[111]

But, of course, one could only will eternal recurrence if one were ignorant that suffering was essential to life.[112] The will to life is the essence of the world. Everything, therefore, manifests a constant striving, and "all striving springs from want or deficiency, from dissatisfaction with one's own state or condition, and is therefore, suffering so long as it is not satisfied. No satisfaction, however, is lasting; on the contrary, it is always merely the starting point of a flesh striving, we see striving everywhere impounded in many ways, everywhere struggling and fighting, and hence always suffering. Thus there is no ultimate aim of striving means that there is no measure or end of suffering."[113]

To be is to be will, and to be will is to constantly strive and desire. To strive and to desire is to suffer. Therefore, to be is to suffer. The wretchedness of existence, Schopenhauer reasons, is not due to the accidental, the coincidental, or bad luck. The basis for the misery of existence lies within the very heart of being, within the essence of all. Death is inevitable for any living being. It is the price paid for being an appearance or representation of will. Suffering is inevitable, moreover, because the world is the objectification of will. At this point in his philosophical reflections, Schopenhauer had answered one of the gut-wrenching prompts for philosophical and theological speculations about the world. Suffering and death, the twin evils of existence, are necessary features of the world, because these evils of existence are necessary features of a world, because that is the objectification of a blind, ceaseless, ever-striving impulse to be. Nothing can meliorate the melancholy nature of existence, for the world is thoroughly will.

[111] Ibid., Vol. 1, p. 283/ibid., Vol. 2, p. 334.

[112] Nietzsche, who agreed with Schopenhauer that suffering was essential to life, affirmed eternal recurrence in light of this knowledge; see Richard Schacht's *Nietzsche* (London: Routledge and Kegan Paul, 1983), p. 260; Laurence Lampert's *Nietzsche's Teaching: An Interpretation of* "Thus Spoke Zarathustra" (New Haven, CT: Yale University Press, 1986), p. 164; and my "The Last Temptation of Zarathustra," *Journal of the History of Philosophy*, Vol. 31 (1993), pp. 54–6.

[113] Schopenhauer, *The World as Will and Representation*, Vol. 1, p. 309/*Sämtliche Werke*, Vol. 2, p. 365.

By demonstrating that suffering and death are necessary features of existence, Schopenhauer also thought that he presented a worldview that brought consolation to his readers. "Nothing is more effective for our consolation," he wrote, "than a consideration of what has happened from the point of view of necessity, from which all accidents appear as the tools of governing fate."[114] It is not the case that had we some good luck, discovered the means to please the gods, been born at a different time, in a different place, to different parents, that we would have had a happy life. What was, what is, and what will be the case is always the same, because the world is the objectification of the will. Schopenhauer, however, went even deeper. Not only are our miseries, our woes, and death a matter of necessity for beings who are essentially will, but also we deserve what we get; eternal justice prevails. Schopenhauer quotes from his beloved Calderón's *Life Is a Dream* [*La Vida es Sueño*, 1635]: "For man's greatest offense/Is that he has been born."[115]

Schopenhauer saw Calderón's observation as expressing the Christian dogma of original sin and as indicating the very guilt of being itself. Myths such as this made the ethical significance of life intelligible to crude human minds by clothing such truths in mythical garments. But for those of keener intellect, for those of a philosophical mind, these garments must be torn away to expose the naked truth. The world is the mirror of will, and "all finiteness, all suffering, all miseries that it contains, belongs to the expression of what will wills, are as they are because will so wills."[116] Will, which is beyond the principle of sufficient reason and, therefore, is beyond all forms of necessity, is free; and because will is self-determining and independent from everything else, will is also responsible for all the evils in the world. But insofar as everything is will, the will suffers all the evils in the world. If, Schopenhauer argued, we want to know what humans are, morally considered, their fate demonstrates their

---

[114] Ibid., Vol. 1, p. 306/ibid., Vol. 2, p. 361.

[115] Ibid., Vol. 1, p. 355/ibid., Vol. 2, p. 419. In the first edition, he quoted Calderón in German, and in the second edition, he cited the Spanish and translated it into German. It was also in the second edition that he once again used the same quotation in his supplementary essays, Vol. 2, p. 603/Vol. 3, p. 692. In the third edition, he cited these lines in his discussion of tragedy; see Vol. 1, p. 254/Vol. 2, p. 300. In Sect. 141 of *Human, All Too Human* [*Menschliches, Allzumenschliches*, 1878] Nietzsche called Calderón's remark "the craziest paradox there can be."

[116] Ibid., Vol. 1, p. 351/ibid., Vol. 2, p. 415.

worth. "Their fate is want, wretchedness, misery, lamentation, and death. Eternal justice prevails; if they were not as a whole contemptible, their fate as a whole would not be so melancholy."[117] As objectifications of will, we deserve what we get, because it follows from what we are. Not only does everything follow from necessity, but also this necessity yields what is deserved. Our sufferings and death, Schopenhauer suggests, are fair through the perfectly retributive nature of existence. If we could put all the misery of the world in one pan of the scales of justice and all the guilt in the other, the scales would balance.

The idea of eternal justice is beyond any perspective following the principle of sufficient reason, Schopenhauer argued, and it is only apprehended by peeking behind the veil of *māyā*. For those incapable of stealing a glance behind the veil, it appears that some flourish and others wither, that there are tormentors on the one hand, and the tormented on the other. Yet "tormentor and tormented are one. The former is mistaken in thinking he does not share the torment, the latter in thinking he does not share the guilt. If the eyes of both were opened, the inflictor of suffering would recognize that he lives in everything that suffers pain in the whole wide world. . . . The tormented person would see that all wickedness that is or ever was perpetrated in the world proceeds from the will which constitutes also *his* inner being, and appears also in him."[118] And if one realizes that truth, then one realizes that when one individual seeks to enhance his or her well-being by engaging in conduct that leads others to suffer, this is also that person's suffering. It is as if cannibals buried their teeth in their own flesh.

Everyone, Schopenhauer continued, is aware of eternal justice and the unity and identity of the will "at least as an obscure feeling."[119] This observation moved him to directly turn to the ethical significance of human conduct and the dim sense each possesses of these metaphysical truths. The victim of a wicked deed, as well as an uninvolved witness, longs to see the evildoer suffer the same measure of pain as he or she inflicted on the victim. This is a twisted sense of eternal justice due to – and here Schopenhauer uses a Kantian phrase – "an amphiboly of concepts," demanding on the level of appearances that which belongs properly to

[117] Ibid., Vol. 1, p. 352/ibid., Vol. 2, p. 416.
[118] Ibid., Vol. 1, p. 354/ibid., Vol. 2, p. 419.
[119] Ibid., Vol. 1, p. 357/ibid., Vol. 2, p. 422.

the level of the thing in itself, the will.[120] The mania of the spirit for
retaliation can rise to such an extent, he continued, that it transcends the
common drive for revenge, which simply attempts to mitigate suffering
endured by causing the wrongdoer to suffer. In rare cases, individuals are
driven by a wrath so extreme that they will sacrifice their own lives to
punish others, who have escaped punishment by the state. Schopenhauer
mentions a case in which a man becomes so indignant at a great outrage
that he spends years seeking out the perpetrator of the wrong, murders
him, and dies on the scaffold as he had foreseen. This, he wrote, "springs
from the deepest consciousness that he himself is the whole will to life
that appears in all creatures through all periods of time, and that therefore
the most distant future, like the present, belong to him in the same way
and cannot be a matter of indifference."[121] This person became the arm
of eternal justice, Schopenhauer theorized, but at the confused level of
affirming the will, because he had no clear recognition that this was the
purpose.

The stirring of conscience also signifies a dim sense of the underlying
unity of being. The sting of conscience, the feeling of disapprobation
after the performance of a bad deed, and a good conscience, the feeling of approbation following a good deed, express an obscure sense of
the delusive nature of individuality. The wrongdoer suffers a haunting,
obscure negative feeling following a wicked deed, an echo of the pain that
he or she inflicted on another. Conversely, the feeling of approbation and
satisfaction found in good conscience is a presentment arising "from the
direct realization of our own inner being in itself in the appearance of
another . . . of the knowledge that our true self exists not only in our own
person in that particular appearance, but in everything that lives."[122] It
is as if conscience itself hints at the metaphysical unity of being and the
illusion of individuality.

The underlying unity of will in all representations, which is dimly
sensed by the feelings of conscience, becomes the key to both Schopenhauer's analysis of moral virtue and his account of redemption as the
denial of the will. As objectifications of will, egoism, the desire for continued existence, for freedom from pain, and for enhancement of personal

---

[120] Ibid., Vol. 1, p. 357/ibid., Vol. 2, p. 422, see Kant's *Critique of Pure Reason*, A260/B316f.
[121] Ibid., Vol. 1, p. 359/ibid., Vol. 2, p. 424.
[122] Ibid., Vol. 1, p. 373/ibid., Vol. 2, p. 441.

well-being, represent the natural standpoint of humans. Living in a world peopled with such beings, each living to affirm its will, leads to inevitable conflicts among people, conflicts that display what Schopenhauer interpreted as the conflict of will with itself. Wrong is also inevitable, because in affirming their wills individuals intrude upon the lives of others. Such an intrusion Schopenhauer referred to as a "wrong," and as was his custom, he considered the negative, the wrong, as the original and primary concept, and "right" as derivative and secondary – that which is not wrong.

Extremely egoistic and malicious individuals, he contended, are inclined to do wrong, and are evil characters: "If a person is always inclined to act unjustly the moment the inducement is there and no external power restrains him, we call him evil."[123] Evil characters act as if there is an absolute distinction between individuals. Extremely egoistic people will inflict all sorts of harm on others, living as if they were the only real beings. Malicious characters, however, represent the most evil sort of person. Where an egoistic person may inflict incredible misery on others and sacrifice others' vital interests to satisfy a trivial interest – later Schopenhauer would dramatically express this by claiming that an egomaniacal man "... would be capable of slaying another, merely to smear his boots with the victim's fat" – malicious people intentionally inflict harm on others, simply to enjoy their suffering.[124] Unlike egoists, for a malicious man "the suffering of another becomes for him an end in itself; it is a spectacle over which he gloats; and so arises the phenomenon of cruelty proper, of bloodthirstiness, so often revealed by history in the Neros and Domitians, in the African Deys, in Robespierre and others."[125]

Evil characters act as if they are absolutely distinct and separate from everyone else, and they live their lives enveloped by the veil of *māyā*. They act as if space and time, the *principium individuationis*, are real, truly separating their essential being from that of others. Schopenhauer argued that the opposite was the case with good characters. They live as if others were an "I once more." As was the case with evil characters, Schopenhauer also claimed that moral goodness admitted of degrees.

---

[123] Ibid., Vol. 1, p. 362/ibid., Vol. 2, p. 428.

[124] Schopenhauer, *On the Basis of Morality*, p. 134/*Sämtliche Werke*, Vol. 4, p. 198.

[125] Schopenhauer, *The World as Will and Representation*, Vol. 1, p. 364/*Sämtliche Werke*, Vol. 2, p. 430.

Some good people were better than others. He explained this phenomenon once more by understanding the behavior of good people following from the degree to which they recognized their own inner being in others; the degree to which they saw through the *principium individuationis* and were able to peek behind the veil of *māyā*. A righteous person does not affirm his or her will at the expense of others and does not injure others to gain self-serving ends. Not harming or wronging others, however, the dispositional hallmark of a person possessing the virtue of justice, represents for Schopenhauer a less penetrating glance through the veil of *māyā* than that exemplified in the behavior of those possessing the virtue of loving kindness and a true goodness of disposition. These individuals show a pure, unselfish love toward others, regarding the plight of others as equivalent to their own. They penetrate the *principium individuationis* "in the higher degree that urges a person to positive benevolence and beneficence, to love."[126] Lovingly kind or philanthropic individuals do not simply refrain from harming others in pursuit of their own interests, but they are moved to treat the actual sufferings of others as if they were their own – they act to relieve the other's misery. "The character that has reached the highest goodness and perfect magnanimity," Schopenhauer wrote, "will sacrifice its well-being and life completely for the well-being of many others."[127] Thus died, he continued, Codrus, Decius Mus, and Arnold von Winkelried; Socrates and Jesus of Nazareth died for the welfare of humankind by opposing pernicious errors and by standing for significant truths.[128] Extreme egoism and malice drive the behavior of

---

[126] Ibid., Vol. 1, p. 371/ibid., Vol. 2, p. 439. In the second edition, Schopenhauer substituted loving kindness or philanthropy (*Menschenliebe*) for love (*Liebe*) in this passage, a substitution that made his treatment of morals in his principal work more consistent with his "Prize Essay on the Basis of Morality" (1841). Unfortunately, he did not make this change in his bold claim, "All love (ἀγάπη [*agape*], *caritas*) is compassion," because there is a clearer connection between *Menschenliebe* and the Greek and Latin notions of love than there is with *Liebe*, which is not directly connected with relieving suffering; see ibid., Vol. 1, p. 374/ibid., Vol. 2, p. 443.

[127] Ibid., Vol. 1, p. 375/ibid., Vol. 2, p. 433.

[128] Given his attitudes toward his own countryman's opposition to Napoleon, it is ironic that Schopenhauer tended to view figures such as Codrus, Decius Mus, and Arnold von Winkelried – in the second edition he would add Leonidas and Regulus – as reaching the highest goodness and magnanimity by sacrificing themselves for their native countries. In the first edition, he also recognized, along with Socrates, Jesus of Nazareth as dying for important truths and the welfare of humankind. In the second edition, he removed the reference to Jesus and substituted the Italian philosopher-scientist, Giordano Bruno, as a hero of truth.

evil characters. Extreme egoists ignore the misery that their unchecked self-interest produces, and malicious persons delight in the wretchedness of others. Conversely, good people seek to prevent causing others pain and are moved to relieve the distress of others. Compassion, Schopenhauer argued, leads good characters to treat the suffering of others as if it were their own. Consequently, they act toward others as if they were an "I once more." Using one of the *mahāvākyas* of the *Chandogya Upanishad*, "*tat tvam asi*" [this art thou], Schopenhauer claimed that compassion signifies this standpoint, holding that whoever could declare this with firm conviction and clear knowledge "about every creature is certain of all virtue and bliss, and is on the direct path to salvation."[129] By including animals as members of the moral community, by viewing compassion as *the* moral response to other sentient beings, he prided his ethics for avoiding a pernicious failing of Judeo-Christian morality, one that even intruded in secular form into Kant's philosophy. The same will is manifest in all living things, and to exclude animals from the moral community signifies ignorance and a cold, indifferent hardness of heart. Hindus and Buddhists realized this solidarity with all sentient beings, he observed, and did not separate humankind from all of suffering nature. They were not deluded by the pretentiousness of believing that they were separated from all by being created in the image of God.

The identification with others, Schopenhauer explained, is less for righteous individuals than it is for those who express the virtue of loving kindness. The former less clearly recognize themselves in others, and, unlike the latter, they are simply moved not to act in way that would harm others. Lovingly kind people, however, express this identity with others to the extent that they are moved to relieve the suffering of others. This remark moved Schopenhauer to advance a provisionally "paradoxical" claim that "All love ἀγάπη [agape], caritas is compassion."[130] Works of love only still suffering and silence the burning of the will. In Schopenhauer's worldview, there is no positive state or condition of pleasure or well-being; rather pleasure is the absence of displeasure, well-being the absence of woe. Therefore, to do anything to advance another's well-being is always tied to either the prevention or relief of another's woe, and this is always tied to compassion. In Schopenhauer's world, there is no

---

[129] Ibid., Vol. 1, p. 374/ibid., Vol. 2, p. 444.
[130] Ibid.

unconditional valuing of another person and no love in this sense of the term at all. Thus he held that whatever goodness, affection, and magnanimity do for others is always only a preventing or alleviation of their sufferings. There is no sense of making someone better off who is faring well or of treating another well, simply because of valuing another unconditionally.

By claiming that all true and pure affection for others is compassion, and by holding that all virtue is based on compassion, Schopenhauer self-consciously and directly opposed Kant's ethics. In fact, he claimed to have directly contradicted his hero's moral philosophy by denying that morally good actions are the result of acting from universal moral laws, which are discovered by the categorical imperative, and by the agent, then, acting out of a sense of duty.[131] Moral rules, laws, and prescriptions are effective only if the source is an agent who could promise reward or threaten punishment to motivate compliance. Consequently, Schopenhauer held, actions following from these sources were self-interested and lacked moral worth. The moral quality of a person's conduct is ultimately a function of one's character, of one's individual will, and the only means to motivate most people to act justly or benevolently is to appeal to their self-interests, their innate egoistic tendencies, by threatening punishment or promising reward. Here he would agree with Kant. Actions so motivated lack moral worth. Later in his career, he would argue that Kant's ethics was ultimately egoistic.

Schopenhauer's analysis of compassion and its connection to morally good conduct was relatively thin in each of the three editions of his principal work. He had little to say about the nature of compassion itself, and he said almost as much about the phenomenon of weeping, which he attributed to "compassion for ourselves," as he did about compassion per se. It would not be until his "Prize Essay on the Basis of Morality" that

---

[131] See ibid., Vol. 1, p. 376/ibid., Vol. 2, p. 444. Schopenhauer is referring to Kant's *Critique of Practical Reason*, AK. 118, where he claims that the feeling of compassion [*Gefühl des Mitleids*] and of warmhearted fellow feeling [*weichherzigen Teilnehmung*], preceding the consideration of duty and serving as a determining ground for action, is burdensome to right-thinking people, confusing their carefully considered maxims, and creating a wish in them to be free from such feeling and to be subject only to law-giving reason. Later, in his "Prize Essay on the Basis of Morality," from *The Two Fundamental Problems of Ethics* (1841), Schopenhauer would spend more than a third of the essay on a wide-ranging and harsh critique of Kant's moral philosophy.

he would provide a detailed analysis of compassion as the source of all virtue and morally good behavior. Yet his neglect of compassion is easy to understand. It resulted from the "soteriological grand narrative" of his philosophy, which made "the denial of the will as the central theme" of the final book of *The World as Will and Representation*.[132] Consequently, Schopenhauer had bigger fish to fry, and he treated moral virtue merely as a step along the path to the denial of the will: "From the same source from which all goodness, affection, virtue and nobility of character spring, there ultimately arises what I call denial of the will to live."[133]

Schopenhauer locates the common source of both virtue and denial of the will in a cognition that sees through the *principium individuationis*, one that lifts the veil of *māyā* to reveal the naked truth. For the denier of the will, for the ascetic, for the mystic, and for the saint, this cognition of the unity of the will behind all representations is more complete and more penetrating than that of the virtuous person. They know the whole and recognize the inner nature and essence of the world. They find the world in a constant state of passing away, involved in futile strivings, inner conflict, and continued suffering. They recognize that the wretched state of the world is due to the will, the essence of all. Life, the chasing after desires whose satisfaction always promises more than they deliver, becomes repugnant to those who clearly cognize the unity of the will. This shocking insight into the core of the world leads the world denier to "attain to the state of voluntary renunciation, resignation, true composure, and complete will-lessness."[134] This state of being, he argued, is achieved neither forcibly nor by intention or design. It comes suddenly, as if it flowed from without. In Christian theology, he claimed, it is metaphorically referred to as "*rebirth*" and the cognition from which it springs "the *effect of divine grace*."[135] Denial of the will signifies for Schopenhauer the ultimate triumph of the intellect over the will, a silencing of the will that "appears only when the will, having arrived at the cognition of its essence in itself obtains from this a *quieter*, and is just removed from the effect of

---

[132] See, respectively, Gerard Mannion's *Schopenhauer, Religion, and Morality: The Humble Path to Ethics* (Burlington, VT: Ashgate, 2003), p. 284 and Rudolf Malter's *Die eine Gedanke. Hinführung zur Philosophie Arthur Schopenhauers*, p. 63.

[133] Schopenhauer, *The World as Will and Representation*, Vol. 1, p. 378/*Sämtliche Werke*, Vol. 2, p. 447.

[134] Ibid., Vol. 1, p. 379/ibid., Vol. 2, p. 448.

[135] Ibid., Vol. 1, p. 403/ibid., Vol. 2, p. 477.

motives, which lies in the province of a different manner of cognition where objects are only appearances."[136] Denial of the will is the only expression of freedom in the world, he claimed, and it makes an end of that which appears. This freedom is transcendental, he will later argue in his "Prize Essay on the Freedom of the Will," claiming that it is a mystery.

Schopenhauer's earlier account of aesthetic contemplation provided a hint into the ultimate state and stance of those who have denied the will, overcome the world, and obtained resignation. In the pure contemplation of the beautiful, one is transformed into a pure subject of cognition, whose object is a Platonic Idea. This is a deliverance from the fierce demands of willing and a liberation from the heavy atmosphere of the earth. Individual things, cognized for the sake of willing, vanish, and one is at peace, serene and calm. But the enjoyment of the beautiful, Schopenhauer held, is relatively brief. For those who have taken the "transcendental turn," it is as if this state of peace and tranquility endures. Nothing makes these individuals anxious; nothing moves them. The thousands of threads of willing that bind people to the world and that are the source of constant craving, along with fear, envy, anger, and despair, are severed. Resigned individuals look calmly and with a smile at the phantasmagoria of this world. Life floats by as a light morning dream to one half awake, but through which reality shines through and no longer deceives. Like this morning dream, these people finally vanish as their bodies wither away and without any violent transition, and with no fear of death. From these considerations, Schopenhauer noted, we should be able to understand the words of the great French quietist and mystic, Madame Guyon: "Everything is indifferent to me; I *cannot* will anything more; often I do not know whether I exist or not. . . . The noonday of glory; a day no longer followed by night; a life that no longer fears death, even in death itself, because death has overcome death, and because whoever has suffered the first death will no longer feel the second."[137] By overcoming the will, the

[136] Ibid., Vol. 1, p. 404/ibid., Vol. 2, p. 478.
[137] Ibid., Vol. 1, p. 391/ibid., Vol. 2, p. 462. Schopenhauer is quoting from *La vie de Madame de la Motte Guyon* (Cologne: J. de la Pierre, 1720), Vol. 2, p. 13. He had borrowed Guyon's autobiography from the library in Dresden from 7 May 1817 to 2 January 1818. He used this quotation to illustrate the standpoint toward death expressed by someone who had quieted the will. Schopenhauer also remarked that although Madame de Guyon's memory filled him with awe and her disposition was superb, he "indulged" the superstition of her reason; see

will is silenced and suffering ceases. By transcending the will, the fear of death is vanquished. The twin evils that prompt both philosophical and religious speculation about the world are no longer. It is not, however, as if this denial is the annihilation of being, the obliteration of some entity; rather, it is an annulment of willing, a not willing.

Schopenhauer closed his work by acknowledging an objection to his discussion of resignation and denial of the will – one that, he said, lay in the very nature of the case and was impossible to remedy. If the world is only the appearance of the will, and if one denies the will and thereby shakes off everything in this vain and miserable world, then it seems that what we see in that perfect saintliness of those who have been delivered from this wretched existence is a leap into the deep oblivion of empty nothingness. There is "no will: no representations, no world."[138] Yet the philosopher wanted to console, and even if a positive knowledge of the accomplished state of the overcomer of the world is not possible, he also said that it has been referred to as ecstasy, rapture, union with God, and the like. The cool, calm, tranquility, and serenity of those who had attained this standpoint, he also claimed, has been depicted by Raphael and Correggio in their paintings. Yet this dark impression of nothingness is something that he will not evade by myths and meaningless words like the Hindus, by talking about reabsorption into Brahman, or like Buddhists, with their idea of *nirvana*. Still, he reminds his readers that the concept of nothingness is relative, a *nihil privativum* or "primitive nothing," a concept parasitic on something that it denies. A *nihli negativum*, "a negative nothing," is something totally inconceivable, and even a logical contradiction, "A and not A," is simply a *nihil privativum*, whose signs can always be reversed while retaining logical equivalence; namely, "A and not A" entails "not A and A." In this sense, the positive becomes the negative and the negative positive. Likewise, he continues, what is, being, has generally been assumed as the positive, and the negation of being as nothing. The world as representation has been assumed to be being and its denial to be nothing. But this is just the standpoint of those who affirm the will. The standpoint of those who deny the will, to switch signs,

---

ibid., Vol. 1, p. 385/ibid., Vol. 2, 454. Guyon represented for him the obvious fact that saints are not required to be philosophers and, of course, philosophers are not required to be saints.
[138] Ibid., Vol. 1, p. 411/ibid., Vol. 2, p. 486.

finds – and now he closes his book – that "this very real world of ours with all its suns and galaxies, is – nothing."[139]

Schopenhauer never articulated his single thought as a single proposition, which was said to be expressed in *The World as Will and Representation*. As he labored on this work, he wrote, "The whole of my philosophy can be summarized into one expression, namely: the world is the self-knowledge of the will," but when he repeated this claim in the last section of his masterwork, he gave no indication that this expression summarized his single thought.[140] In a broad sense it did, but only if one understands that Schopenhauer attempted not simply to demonstrate that the world is the mirror or the objectivity of will. Had this been the sum and substance of his single thought, he could have concluded his work with the second book. Yet the third and fourth books, his aesthetics and, more importantly, his ethics, provide the deeper meaning of what it is to realize the implications of will coming to self-knowledge. Schopenhauer wrote as if the metaphysical will unfolds itself through each grade of its objectification until it reaches the human intellect, which provides it with self-knowledge of its own nature. He argued, moreover, that once will expressed itself in the world, its development in nature was absolutely necessary, until it obtained cognition of itself and willed no more. In the second edition, Schopenhauer would write as if his philosophy articulated this to the will itself: "With me . . . will arrives at self-knowledge through its objectification, however this may come about, whereby its abolition, conversion, and salvation became possible."[141] Salvation, the denial of the

---

[139] Ibid., Vol. 1, p. 412/ibid., Vol. 2, p. 487.

[140] Schopenhauer, *Manuscript Remains*, Vol. 1, p. 512/*Der handschriftliche Nachlaß*, Vol. 1, p. 462. He repeated this claim, "the world is the self-knowledge of the will," in op. cit., Vol. 1, p. 410/ibid., Vol. 2, p. 485, but without attributing any special status to the phrase.

[141] Ibid., Vol. 2, p. 643/ibid., Vol. 3, p. 739f. The idea of the progressive development of the will through nature, leading to its self-knowledge of its horrid nature, is a main theme in ibid., Vol. 1, Sect. 70 and Vol. 2, Chap. 50; also see my "Schopenhauer on Suffering, Death, Guilt, and the Consolation of Metaphysics," p. 65. John E. Atwell proposed that the following captures Schopenhauer's single thought in a single proposition: "The double-sided world [as both will and representation] is the striving of the will to become conscious of itself so that, recoiling in horror of its inner, self-divisive nature, it may annul itself and thereby its self-affirmation, and then reach salvation," *Schopenhauer on the Character of the World: The Metaphysics of the Will* (Berkeley: University of California Press, 1995), p. 31. Atwell's formulation has the virtue of capturing the teleological and soteriological dimension of Schopenhauer's thought, as well as including the claim that the world is the self-knowledge of the will.

will, not-willing, this is the state that quiets "the ever-disquieting riddle of existence."

With the riddle of existence solved, Schopenhauer tossed the philosopher's stone to what he had hoped would be an appreciative philosophic public and made his way to Italy.

8

Failure in Berlin

O N 23 SEPTEMBER 1818 Schopenhauer struck out, as planned, for
Italy. He was excited to leave Dresden and the serious business of
excavating for the philosopher's stone. He wrote to Goethe that he longed
for the gentle clime of Italy and to enjoy the country that Dante described
as "where yes resounds," and where, he added, "the no, no of all literary
journals would not reach me."[1] He had already heard a singular "no" in
the only review of his *On Vision and Colors*. An anonymous reviewer had
published a negative review in the *Leipziger Litteratur-Zeitung*, a journal
that had already bashed Goethe's *On the Theory of Colors* a few years
earlier.[2] The sensation caused by his color theory, he told Goethe, was
like throwing a stone into a bog – no ripples. Little did he realize that
he would be tossing the philosopher's stone into the same bog. Just as he
had told Brockhaus, he also told Goethe that his philosophy, which he
still thought would appear at Michaelmas, was not simply the fruit of his
time at Dresden, but to a certain measure, the fruit of his life. Again, he
evoked Helvetius's observation that between the thirtieth and thirty-fifth
years, all meaningful impressions about the world are fixed in one's mind,
with everything that follows being simply the further development of
those ideas. He reminded Goethe that he was now in his thirty-first year.
Schopenhauer also revealed the title of his book to the poet, claiming
that until then it had only been known to himself and Brockhaus. A
handsomely bound copy, he continued, would be sent to Goethe through
Brockhaus. Although Schopenhauer doubted that Goethe would read it,

---

[1] Schopenhauer, *Gesammelte Briefe*, p. 34, Schopenhauer to Goethe, 23 June 1818.
[2] The anonymous review appeared in the *Leipziger Litteratur-Zeitung*, 14 July 1817 (179),
pp. 1425–8. It is reprinted in the *Fünftes Jahrbuch der Schopenhauer-Gesellschaft*, Vol.5 (1916),
pp. 187–92.

he told him that a copy would be sent to him, "just in case you still have the patience to look into a foreign train of ideas."[3] It was not clear whether the poet realized that his one-time student was repeating Goethe's excuse for not reading the manuscript for his color theory. Goethe, however, replied that he would read Schopenhauer's book with sympathy.[4]

Brockhaus did send Goethe a copy of *The World as Will and Representation*, but not directly. He entrusted its delivery to Adele, who gave it to the poet on 18 January 1819.[5] Goethe, she reported to her brother, was delighted to receive it. He quickly cut up the whole thing (it was printed in octavo), divided it into two parts, and immediately began to read it in his typical way by opening the book randomly – a method, he held, that always served him well, allowing him to discover the most significant passages. An hour after Goethe sampled the work, he sent Adele a snip of paper on which he expressed his thanks to Arthur and in which he prophesized that the entire work would be good. He also promised to convey to its author the "opinions of his heart," a promise he never kept. Adele reported Goethe's daughter-in-law's observation: "A few days later Ottilie told me that her father sits down with the book and reads it with an eagerness as she had *never* before seen in him. He said to her that he now had an entire year's pleasure, since he was going to read it from beginning to end."[6] Goethe also told Adele that he was happy that Schopenhauer was still attracted to him, despite their disagreements about color theory. He praised, moreover, the clarity of Schopenhauer's presentation and vivacious writing style – although it took the poet some effort to become accustomed to some of Schopenhauer's language. He told Adele that in

---

[3] Schopenhauer, *Gesammelte Briefe*, p. 35, Schopenhauer to Goethe, 23 June 1818.

[4] Ibid., p. 501, Goethe to Schopenhauer, 9 August 1818.

[5] According to his diary, Goethe read *The World as Will and Representation* on January 18, 19, 21, and 24. Contrary to his remarks to Ottilie, it is unlikely that he read the entire book; see Goethe, *Tagebücher 1810–1832*, ed. Peter Boerner (Munich: Deutscher Taschenbuch Verlag, 1963), pp. 64–5.

[6] Lütkehaus, *Die Schopenhauers*, p. 273, Adele to Arthur Schopenhauer. Lütkehaus records 5 February 1819 as the probable date of the letter. In the final edition of *The World as Will and Representation* (1859), Schopenhauer added a note in which he claimed that a letter from his sister in March 1819 communicated Goethe's approval of the book. Yet he also claimed in this note that Goethe had received the book in December 1818, whereas he received it from Adele on 18 January 1819. The older Schopenhauer's memory may have failed him here. It may be the case that he received Adele's letter in Naples in March. It is also curious that Schopenhauer used a remark by Goethe to Eckermann as evidence that the great man had read his book; see ibid, Vol. 1, p 281n./*Sämtliche Werke*, Vol. 2, p. 331n.

order to deal with the book's great length, he had to feign that it consisted of two volumes, a remark that should have displeased Schopenhauer, who had objected to Brockhaus's intent to publish it in two volumes.

The way in which Schopenhauer launched his book seemed designed to draw the poet into his train of ideas. The motto on the title page was one of Goethe's verses: "Might not nature yet finally phantom itself."[7] Perhaps Goethe had read the work more carefully than is usually imagined, or maybe his random sampling was serendipitous, for the first passage Goethe noted as giving "great pleasure" followed a quotation from his *Elective Affinities [Die Wahlverwandtschaften,* 1809]: "Whoever beholds human beauty cannot be infected with evil; he feels in harmony with himself and the world."[8] But shortly thereafter, Schopenhauer attributed to the artist the ability to anticipate the beautiful, to presage it prior to experience. Nature merely stammers beauty in half-spoken words, which precludes any simple *a posteriori* discovery of the beautiful. This entails that the artist cannot simply imitate nature, and the artist must sort through nature's many failures, operating with a preexisting sense of the beautiful analogous to a Platonic reminiscence. The same is the case, Schopenhauer argued, with the critic's appreciation of the artist's expression of beauty. The anticipation of the beautiful, operating in the artist and connoisseur, is possible – and now Schopenhauer answers the question posed by his Goethean motto – "For, as Empedocles said, like can be recognized only by like: only nature can understand itself; only nature will fathom itself. . . . "[9] Both the artist and connoisseur, of course, are themselves the "in itself" of nature, the will. The idea of anticipation, moreover, seems to have found resonance in Goethe's understanding of his own creative power. In his *Annals or Day and Year Books [Annalen oder Tag- und Jahreshefte],* on 14 February 1819, Goethe reflects "since the poet through anticipation presages the world, this real world, which

---

7 The verse is from a poem Goethe wrote for the fiftieth year celebration held for his colleague, State Minister Klaus von Voigt, 27 September 1816, and published in the *Jenaische Litteratur-Zeitung*; see Schopenhauer, *Sämtliche Werke,* Vol. 7, p. 216.

8 Schopenhauer, *The World as Will and Representation,* Vol. 1, p. 22/*Sämtliche Werke,* Vol. 2, p 261. The four passages that Goethe highlighted were on pp. 320, 321, 440, and 441 of the first edition, pp. 221, 222, and 304–6 in Payne's translation, and pp. 261–3 and 359–60, in the second volume of the *Sämtliche Werke.*

9 Schopenhauer, *The World as Will and Representation,* Vol. 1, p. 222f./*Sämtliche Werke,* Vol. 2, p. 262f.

pushes on him from all sides, bothers and distracts him. It wasn't to give him what he already has."[10] Later, in reply to Eckermann's claim that *Faust* must have been carefully constructed from a deep observation of the world and life, the poet once more said that had he not carried the world within, through anticipation, neither research nor observation would have opened his eyes.[11]

Pure serendipity may not explain Goethe's lighting upon Schopenhauer's discussions of the artist's anticipation of the beautiful, nor does it show an assiduous reading of the entire work. One could imagine that the artist was eager to discover references to him, and the discussion of anticipation followed a quotation from Goethe. The book abounded with such quotations, but the second set of passages favorably mentioned by Goethe did not cite the philosopher's hero. These passages concerned the idea and significance of the "acquired character," which involved, Schopenhauer claimed, "nothing but the most complete possible knowledge of our own individuality."[12] This knowledge is gained from a diligent and honest reflection on one's previous behavior, the sum total of which – and here he evoked Kant – is the empirical character, which is the temporal unfolding of the extratemporal intelligible character, the innermost essence from which all of a person's actions invariably follow. Schopenhauer analogized that just as a fish is only happy in water, a bird in air, a mole under the ground, "every man is happy only in an atmosphere suitable to him."[13] Knowledge of one's character allows one to determine the type of atmosphere where one can breathe in a way attuned to one's fundamental dispositions, a requirement for doing anything solid. Instead of crashing through life in a hurdy-gurdy, haphazard manner, one can discover the home grounds to carry out deliberately and methodically the unalterable rule of one's character without being tempted to perform deeds too noble or base and without suffering the agony and distress of being something one is not. Knowing one's character, he claimed, prevents one from trying to imitate others, an act as outrageous as wearing another's clothing. Acquiring character, moreover, consoles. By discovering what one

---

[10] Quoted in Arthur Hübscher's *The Philosophy of Schopenhauer in Its Intellectual Context*, p. 108.

[11] See Hübscher, ibid., p. 109.

[12] Schopenhauer, *The World as Will and Representation*, Vol. 1, p. 305/*Sämtliche Werke*, Vol. 2, p. 359.

[13] Ibid., Vol. 1, p. 304/ibid., Vol. 2, p. 359.

necessarily is, one realizes that things could not have been otherwise; "we are like entrapped elephants, which rage and struggle fearfully for many days, until they see that it is fruitless, and then suddenly offer their necks calmly to the yoke, tamed forever."[14]

Acquiring character, Schopenhauer held, is not as significant for ethics proper as it is for life in this world. Later, his reflections on the acquired character would become the basis for the observations in the famous and widely read essay "Aphorisms on the Wisdom of Life," from the first volume of *Parerga and Paralipomena*. Nietzsche, who seems always to take overbidding for outstripping – to use one of Schopenhauer's phrases – appears to reaffirm Schopenhauer's view of the acquired character in his injunction to become who you are and in the consoling dimensions of his one-time educator's account of character in his doctrine of *amor fati*. Schopenhauer himself seemed to have tried to live as if he had acquired character, but in a way that perhaps displayed the self-undermining nature of his own doctrine. If one's life is the inevitable unfolding of an extratemporal, intelligible character, then whether one acquires character or not is equally a matter of necessity. And if this is the case, one can rest content whether one acquires character or not – because this would also follow necessarily. One should not lament the hand one was dealt, unless one of the cards is to lament one's hand. But then, it is not a matter of "should" at all. Willing cannot be taught.

But how did Goethe react to Schopenhauer's notion of the acquired character? If Schopenhauer's discussion of anticipation enabled Goethe to better understand himself – perhaps he had anticipated Schopenhauer's anticipation – what he favored and what he took from the discussion of the acquired character is oblique. In *Art and Antiquity* [*Kunst and Altertum*, 1820] Goethe provided commentary to his *Orphic Primary Words* [*Urworte Ophisch*, 1820] in which he wrote of the necessity, the irrevocability of the individual character, which develops against those forces incidental and accidental to its expressions, leading to a state of coercion, until everything is restored as the stars had willed it.[15] Later, Schopenhauer would highlight *Orphic Primary Words* as containing one of Goethe's

[14] Ibid., Vol. 1, p. 306/ibid., Vol. 2, p. 362.
[15] See Arthur Hübscher's *The Philosophy of Schopenhauer in its Intellectual Context*, pp. 109–10, for a discussion of Goethe's *Orphic Primary Words* and Schopenhauer's concept of the acquired character.

finest stanzas and as articulating his view that the ends to which a human aspires are invariably determined by a person's unchangeable and innate character:

> As on the day that lent you to the world
> The sun received the planets' greetings,
> At once and eternally you have thrived
> According to the law whereby you stepped forth.
> So must you be, from yourself you cannot flee,
> So have the Sibyls and the prophets said;
> No time, no power breaks into little pieces
> The form here stamped and in life developed.[16]

When Schopenhauer worked his way home to Dresden, he lay over for two days in Weimar. Buoyed, perhaps, by Adele's glowing report of Goethe's reception of his freshly published philosophy, he called on the poet on 19 August 1819, without an appointment. Instead of a warm greeting, Goethe, who was busy with a visitor in his garden, turned an icy shoulder to the young philosopher, asking him "how he, whom he still supposed to be in Italy, could so suddenly appear here?"[17] He was asked to return later. Schopenhauer was deeply affected by Goethe's cool and formal attitude, something he could not hide when he returned later that day. He also returned the next morning for a short meeting. Goethe noted in his diary that they discussed Schopenhauer's studies and travels and that they discussed entoptic phenomena the following day. Later, in 1830, Goethe published his diary entry for 19 and 20 August, recording the visit by "Dr. Schopenhauer," whom he called "usually misjudged, but also a difficult to know, meritorious young man," whose visit "stimulated" him and was "mutually instructive."[18]

Although Adele had dutifully delivered her brother's book to Goethe, she must have done so with some apprehension. She dreaded its publication. As she confided to Ottilie, she feared its appearance as "I fear death."[19] She worried that her brother's unconventional views on religion and morality, as well as his polemical and brooding nature, would discredit

[16] Schopenhauer, *Prize Essay on the Freedom of the Will*, p. 50/*Sämtliche Werke*, Vol. 4, p. 57.
[17] Schopenhauer, *Gespräche*, p. 35, reported by C.G. Bähr.
[18] Ibid., p. 35.
[19] Quoted in Arthur Hübscher's "Adele an Arthur Schopenhauer. Unbekannte Briefe 1," *Schopenhauer-Jahrbuch*, Vol. 58 (1977), p. 137.

his reputation and that of his family. It is not clear whether Schopenhauer
would have been affected by his sister's concerns. Certainly, the breach
with his mother had drawn him closer to his sister, who would serve
periodically as his confidante. Had it not been for his horrid relationship
with his mother, he would have visited his sister before his journey to
Italy, he wrote Goethe. In the same letter, he said that during his time
in Dresden, Adele "must have become an extraordinary young woman,"
as he could judge by her letters and by her poetry-accompanied silhouettes, which an acquaintance had displayed to him with great feeling and
appreciation.[20] Yet even if Adele had become an "extraordinary young
woman," what she told her brother about his book simply served as further
evidence for his views concerning the intellectual inferiority of women.
Both Adele and Ottilie tried to read it. The preface alarmed Adele, and
the book itself contained too many unfamiliar terms whose significance
she could not understand. Had she someone who could explain the book
to her, Adele told her brother, she would read it, but she was surrounded
by fools.[21] Adele became *de facto*, after Goethe, the second critic of her
brother's principal work.

If Schopenhauer longed for Italy as a reward for completing his life's
work and to escape the "nos" of reviewers, he was also fleeing an awkward
situation. One of his sexual escapades bore unexpected fruit. A maid to
one of Dresden's families gave birth to his daughter in the spring of 1819.
He must have written to Adele about the situation, confiding that it was
not due to an affair of the heart, but to one of the loins. He must have also
told his sister that she was the only woman he could love in a nonsexual
way. Adele's response challenged her brother's claim and encouraged him
to do the right thing:

You write, you foolish man, that I am the only women you could love without
sensuality. I laughed very much over this but might I ask, whether you could have
loved me if I had not been your sister? For, after all, there are many women who have a
status higher than mine. If therefore your love is given to my being and not to my name
as your sister, you could almost love another in the same way – notice, I say *almost*. I
feel sorry for the girl you mentioned; I hope to God that you have not betrayed her,

---

[20] Schopenhauer, *Gesammelte Briefe*, p. 34, Schopenhauer to Goethe, 23 June 1818. The man
who so proudly displayed Adele's silhouettes was the author and officer Hermann Ludwig
Heinrich Fürst von Pückler-Muskau (1775–1871).
[21] See Lütkehaus, *Die Schopenhauers*, p. 274, letter from Adele to Schopenhauer, 5 February
1819.

since you are *true* to everyone, why not to a poor, weak thing like her? . . . Domestic happiness is the most beautiful thing that life gives us, yet most people pass by silently and uncomplaining and do not have it and *dare* not seek it. I do not have it.[22]

Schopenhauer admitted paternity and was willing to provide support for his child. Adele must have sensed that her brother wanted her to play some role in this affair, and she must have also been suspicious about the financial support her tight-fisted brother would provide the young woman and his daughter. Consequently, she wrote her vacationing brother, "Can I do something for the girl? Say so frankly, take your duty not in the usual narrow sense to which the baseness of men like you reduces it. I wished that the child would not have been born, but it's here, so care for it according to the degree of the needs that will develop later in its life."[23] Adele was willing to see how things were going in Dresden, she told her brother. She would be there at the end of June. Yet she was undecided whether she would visit the young woman because she was living with another man. Adele's remarks do not make it clear whether she was worried about disrupting the unfortunate women's domestic situation – perhaps this man may have thought himself to be the father – or whether she found this state of affairs below her station.

By the end of the summer, Schopenhauer's daughter was dead. The cause of her death is as unknown as is the philosopher's reaction to her demise. Yet, less than a year afterward, he recorded in his travel book an observation that may have revealed his philosophical attitude toward the unfortunate young woman and his child. The affection and longing glances between two persons of the opposite sex connotes the will to life of a new individual whom their union could produce. But "antipathy between them indicates that which they would inevitably produce, if it materialized, would be a badly formed, sorrowful and luckless being not in harmony with itself."[24] Perhaps Schopenhauer had an aversion to the mother of his child, except for the times she was simply an object for his sexual desires. In any case, he never praised his daughter as he did Lessing's son, who was dragged into this world by forceps, but had the

---

[22] Ibid. *Die Schopenhauers*, p. 277, Adele to Arthur Schopenhauer, 5 February 1819. I am once more following Lütkehaus's dating of the letter, instead of Gwinner's dating of March 1819. I am also following Lütkehaus's reading of Adele's reference to "the girl you mention" as referring to Schopenhauer's Dresden affair.

[23] Ibid., p. 279, Adele to Arthur Schopenhauer, 12 May 1819.

[24] Schopenhauer, *Manuscript Remains*, Vol. 4, p. 17f./ *Der handschriftlich Nachlaß*, Vol. 3, p. 14.

wisdom to soon leave it.[25] Adele, who had wished that the child would
have never been born, seemed to have become upset by its death. And
even though the death of the child allowed her to escape the unpleasant
role of serving as an intermediary between her brother and the mother of
his child, she felt sorrow for her brother's loss. "That your daughter is
dead," she wrote, "I am sorry; since if the child had lived, it would have
given you *joy*. You would not be so alone. You would have had someone
for whom to care."[26]

Adele was writing from experience. Her relationships with her mother
and Gerstenbergk had deteriorated and her concern for her brother served
to draw her out of her own loneliness. She also envied her brother's
independence, one not afforded a young woman of her times. She longed
to travel to Italy – she had been studying Italian for years – so she lived
vicariously through her brother's letters.[27] Arthur must have written
her that Byron was in Venice, but that he had not seen the poet. This
both puzzled and amazed Adele. Both brother and sister esteemed Lord
Byron's poetry, and the young English nobleman enjoyed rock-star-like
celebrity. "You have not seen Byron," the young women wrote; "that is
highly disagreeable and inexplicable to me, since few poets have touched
me so; fewer have created in me a desire to see them."[28] She naturally
assumed that her brother would have possessed a like desire and would
have sated it.

Schopenhauer had been less than forthright with his sister. He had
seen Byron in Italy and could have met him, but he did not. Prior to
his trip, he requested Goethe to write some letters of introduction, so
that he could establish some "interesting or important" acquaintances.
Goethe had supplied him with one for Byron, one that he never used
due to his own "stupidity." One morning as he and his current beloved
were strolling along the Lido, "my *dulcinea* cried out in great excitement,
'behold the English poet.' Byron swept by me on horseback and the donna

[25] See Schopenhauer's reference to Lessing's son, *The World as Will and Representation*, Vol. 2,
p. 579/*Sämtliche Werke*, Vol. 3, p. 665.
[26] Lütkehaus, *Die Schopenhauers*, pp. 294–5, Adele to Arthur Schopenhauer, 8 September 1819.
At this time, Arthur had returned to Dresden and Johanna and Adele were in Danzig, trying
to receive some recompense from the financial crisis of Abraham Ludwig Muhl's trading firm.
[27] Adele Schopenhauer would live at various locations in Italy from September 1844 through
May 1848; see Gabriele Büch's *Alles Leben ist Traum*, pp. 301–25.
[28] Ibid., p. 278, Adele to Arthur Schopenhauer, 5 February 1819.

could not let loose of this impression for the entire day. I decided then not to send Goethe's letter. I was afraid of being cuckolded. I still regret this."[29]

It is not surprising that Schopenhauer did not tell Adele about the Byron incident. It would have knifed against the image he crafted in his letters to his sister –that of a lady's man. He wrote to Adele of a rich sweetheart, but his sister worried about the woman's social standing and whether she would be willing to follow him to Germany. Adele recommended that if he had really found love, he should do whatever it took to keep his beloved. She also expressed her dismay concerning her brother's account of two loveless love affairs, relationships she did not wish for her sibling. She also reminded him of the unhappy girl he left behind in Dresden and the sad turn of events that resulted from his sensuous inclinations. "May you not lose the ability to value a woman," she chided her brother, "by continuing to waste your time with the vulgar and common ones of our sex. May heaven lead you one day to a woman for whom you could feel something deeper than that agitation *that I never once understood.*"[30]

If Adele was upset by her brother's behavior, she was disturbed also by his philosophy. Although she kept her eyes and ears open for any mention of his book, she did this with some dread. She also continued carefully reading it. Although she had not found his philosophical views totally strange, and although she never identified herself as a strongly devout Christian, she found that her brother's views on religion contradicted her own, and she felt pained by the difference. She feared that his religious views could get him into trouble if he were to seek a university or state appointment. She worried that Arthur's contempt for humankind and the arrogance expressed in his book, as well as by his conduct, would rob him of ever having any meaningful friendships. Nevertheless, Adele's

[29] Schopenhauer, *Gespräche*, p. 220, a conversation reported between Schopenhauer and Robert von Hornstein. Hübscher, in a footnote to this passage, reports that Gwinner was skeptical about Goethe's providing Schopenhauer with a letter of introduction to Byron, because Schopenhauer took great effort to preserve everything from Goethe's hand and no such letter was found in the philosopher's estate. Hornstein also reported that Schopenhauer attributed his failure to meet Byron to his "stupidity." In the same conversation, Schopenhauer told that Hornstein: "Did you know that the three great pessimists were in Italy during a single year? Doß counted Byron, [Giacomo] Leopardi, and me. Yet none of us became acquainted with the other." He told Hornstein that he also regretted a lost opportunity to meet Byron's widow at the Englischer Hof; see ibid.
[30] Lütkehaus, *Die Schopenhauers*, p. 285, Adele to Arthur Schopenhauer, 22 May 1819.

temperament resonated at a deeper level, and Arthur's book forced her to recognize that she too shared her brother's dark view of human existence. She even had more despair at this time than her brother. As he toured Italy, indulging in affairs of the loins, if not the heart, she told her brother that she was encircled by sickness and death, the very recognition of which, Schopenhauer would later claim, constitutes the type of astonishment that drove both religious and philosophical speculations about the world. Arthur would witness the success of his philosophy later in his life, but Adele would continue to experience despair. She wrote to Ottilie von Goethe, "You were able to be a sister, friend, daughter, woman, mother, housewife, and everything good and satisfying – and I was ___?"[31] She left the end blank. She was also a sister, daughter, woman, and friend, but never a mother or housewife.

Schopenhauer spent approximately eleven months in Italy, which was long enough to enable him to perfect his rudimentary grasp of Italian. Yet when he arrived in Venice in October 1818, he felt, at first, as if he had been thrown into cold water. The language and mode of life he encountered made a powerful impression on him, but one that made him feel anxious, self-conscious, and conspicuous. Instead of his delighting in making discoveries, such surprises frightened him. But once he adjusted to his new surroundings, he began to feel extraordinarily well, like a man who becomes refreshed by a cold bath after the initial shock of the cold water. After he lost his feeling of strangeness and became assimilated to his new environment, he also lost his concern with himself, and he was able to turn his attention – and now he strikes a familiar stance – "purely to his surroundings and precisely through an objective and disinterested contemplation of them he now feels superior to them instead of being depressed by them as previously."[32] How long Schopenhauer engaged in this disinterested contemplation is questionable. Venice was the site of the Byron incident and where he had a dalliance with Teresa Fuga, a young woman of a generous disposition toward wealthy foreign tourists. It is unlikely, however, that she was the "*dulcinea*" upon whom the British poet made such a strong impression. If Fuga was the woman to whom Schopenhauer referred to his sister as his "rich beloved," he was

---

[31] Letter from Adele to Ottilie von Goethe, 2 January 1828, quoted in Bergmann, *Johanna Schopenhauer*, p. 277.

[32] Schopenhauer, *Manuscript Remains*, Vol. 3, p. 4/*Der handschriftliche Nachlaß*, Vol. 3, p. 2. Schopenhauer dated this entry to his travel book 1 November [1818].

exaggerating both her station and their relationship. And if Schopenhauer personally made an impression on the young woman, his name did not. Later, she referred to him as "Dr. Arthur Scharrenhans."[33]

In mid-November, Schopenhauer left Venice for Bologna, where he noted that all happiness was negative, unnoticed when possessed, and only positively felt after it is gone – as a lack for which one had remorse due to one's inability to maintain it. He also observed that "Demaria, Prof. in Bologna, is a sculptor of genius," but unlike happiness, Professor Demaria's genius is never again mentioned, a lack that brought the philosopher no remorse.[34] From Bologna he traveled to Florence, to observe that "Christianity says: 'love your neighbor as yourself,' but I have said: recognize in your neighbor actually and indeed yourself, and in the one at a distance again recognize the same."[35] As he drew this connection between Christian *agape* and his metaphysics, his elastic and far-ranging thoughts drew connections between physiological color after-images and male masturbation. Both connote the natural need for the real thing, eyes and genitals, vision and the sexual impulse, intellect and sexuality, the opposite poles of a person, the intellect and the will – salvation and damnation.

In December, Schopenhauer was in Rome, where he overwintered for three months. Following the pattern that was indelibly imprinted in him from his youth, he attended plays and operas. His lifelong love of Rossini's music can be traced to this period. He also sought to enjoy all the great works of art found within the ancient state, but he found himself indifferent to the Gothic and Renaissance architecture of Rome, preferring, like Goethe, the simpler and cleaner lines employed by the Greeks and Romans. But the massive dome of St. Peter reminded him of the dome of St. Paul's in London, and its grand expanse prompted the feeling of the mathematically sublime, as he became aware of the vanishing nothingness of his own body in the presence its greatest, but also knowing that as perceiver, he was the subject that supported the object. It was his representation.[36] At the Sciarra Gallery, Raphael's painting of a violinist showed him how painting could capture an action that reflected a person's

---

[33] See Hübscher's "Lebensbild," in *Sämtliche Werke*, Vol. 1, p. 80.

[34] Schopenhauer, *Manuscript Remains*, Vol. 3, p. 6/*Der handschriftliche Nachlaß*, Vol. 3, p. 4.

[35] Ibid., Vol. 3, p. 6/ibid., Vol. 3, p. 4.

[36] See Schopenhauer, *The World as Will and Representation*, Vol. 1, p. 206/*Sämtliche Werke*, Vol. 2, p. 243, for his references to the domes of St. Peter and St. Paul as prompts for the feeling of the mathematically sublime.

character. He toured the vast art collection at the Vatican and complained that his companion finished the entire collection in one half hour, whereas he had hardly started.[37]

The quick aesthete at the Vatican was none other than the *Wunderkind* Karl Witte, whom Schopenhauer had met eight years earlier at Göttingen, and whose presence in Rome was due to his good fortune for some bad fortune. At the tender age of sixteen, Witte received his doctorate, and in 1817, he attempted his habilitation at Berlin. Students stormed out from his lecture, refusing to be instructed by a youth. As compensation, the Prussian King, Friedrich Wilhelm III, provided him with a travel stipend of 600 *Taler* a year for three years. Schopenhauer thought highly of Witte, a judgment not shared by Adele. Indeed, she was puzzled by her brother's willingness to befriend the *ingenia praecocia*, whom she regarded as "fundamentally a miserable fellow," who supported himself by hook and by crook and who had never displayed the power of intellect or genius, but only of learned arrogance.[38] Curiously, Witte's family was also concerned about his Roman association with Schopenhauer, whose break with his mother was even known by Witte's parents in Berlin. In a letter to his mother, Witte defended his philosophical friend: "I associated frequently with Schopenhauer. During the entire time, I observed nothing bad about him. . . . On the contrary, I found many virtues in him, not the least of which was his unconditional love of truth."[39]

Witte, who confessed to not having a head for philosophy, certainly did have one for the philosopher's personality. If one of Schopenhauer's virtues was his unconditional love for the truth, a second was his willingness to express it, regardless of the consequences. Later, he would attribute his unswerving commitment to express his truths as one of the grounds for the lack of reception of his philosophy by his contemporaries: "Philosophers want to please the world and hence to please it, I will not move one step from the path of truth."[40] The *Wunderkind* also experienced this feature of Schopenhauer's character. "By his paradoxes," Witte

---

37 See Schopenhauer, *Gespräche*, p. 241. This was reported by Carl Georg Bähr, from a conversation with Schopenhauer on 1 May 1858.

38 Lütkehaus, *Die Schopenhauers*, p. 283, Adele to Arthur Schopenhauer, 22 May 1819. In his 1 May 1858 conversation with Bähr, the latter reported that Schopenhauer spoke about people being prejudiced against Witte.

39 Schopenhauer, Gespräche, p. 44, Witte's letter to his mother, 19 February 1819.

40 Schopenhauer, *On the Will in Nature*, p. 142/*Sämtliche Werke*, Vol. 4, p. 143.

observed, "he had made almost everyone an enemy."[41] Many of Schopenhauer's enemies were made at the Café Greco, where a number of German artists, scholars, and art lovers formed a clique. One day, Witte reported, Schopenhauer held forth, praising Greek polytheism for providing artists with a rich palette of different individual personalities. One of the Germans observed that Christians had the twelve apostles. Schopenhauer sneered – "leave me alone with your twelve philistines from Jerusalem."[42]

The historian Johann Friedrich Böhmer also reported that the philosopher behaved badly at the Café Greco, where he said that Schopenhauer's "Mephistophelian wit" had been a long disturbing element. He drew the wrath of its patrons one day, Böhmer noted, by claiming that Germany was the dumbest of all nations, but had achieved an advantage over all others by having no religion. This remark was met by a chorus of "let's toss the fellow out."[43] Afterward, according to Böhmer, Schopenhauer avoided the cafe. Böhmer was not a fan of Schopenhauer, and whether the philosopher made this disparaging remark about Germany at the Café Greco is open to question. Böhmer also attributed this remark to Schopenhauer through a conversation he had with a Frenchman and an Englishman who had traveled with the philosopher. According to this story, these men asked Böhmer whether he knew Schopenhauer. Böhmer said he did, adding that Schopenhauer was a "fool." Both men were reported to have said that they found the philosopher unpleasant, and the Frenchman then related Schopenhauer's remark about Germany. He added that had he thought this about his own country, he would have kept it to himself.[44]

In any case, Böhmer was repulsed by Schopenhauer's behavior. Elsewhere, he called Schopenhauer not simply a "fool," but a "complete fool," adding that for the well-being of the people, "the entire tribe of un-German and non-religious philosophers must be imprisoned."[45] Certainly, Schopenhauer did decry the "dumbness" of Germans, despite the fact that Germany produced Kant and Goethe. He was also inclined to say uncensored what he thought – and to anyone. In his "Travel Book," he recorded the following observation during his stay in Rome: "To me close acquaintances often become and are strangers and strangers are often

---

[41] Schopenhauer, *Gespräche*, p. 44.
[42] Ibid., p. 44.
[43] Ibid., p. 46.
[44] Ibid., p. 45.
[45] Ibid., p. 46.

familiar, and to them all I speak the same language, whereas others make a great difference in this respect. This is really because I stand so far from them that for me the difference between what happens to be near and what happens to be remote vanishes. . . . "[46] If he said what Böhmer claimed, his acquaintances at the Café Greco became hostile strangers.

Schopenhauer traveled from Rome to Naples in March. He preferred to travel with English tourists whom he called "the best and most trustworthy companions."[47] In Naples, he observed a painting by a young Venetian artist named Francesco Ajes S. Hayez depicting Ulysses at the court of King Alcinous, weeping upon hearing others speak of his heroic actions and life. Schopenhauer would use the subject of this painting as one of the data supporting his analysis of weeping as compassion for oneself.[48] Fourteen miles south of Naples was the ancient and tragic city of Pompeii. The philosopher was deeply moved by his experience of this scene of suffering and despair, which signified for him the terrible free play of natural forces and their indifference to human well-being. The destruction of Pompeii became one of many examples he fired against the "pernicious" Leibnizean claim that this is the best of all possible worlds. This is the *worst* of all possible worlds, Schopenhauer argued; but not in the sense that one could not imagine a more horrid world, but in the sense of a world that could actually exist and endure. Pompeii, however, also prompted the young antioptimist to recognize an equally powerful force, one that he gave free play in Italy. On the door of the *fornix*, adorned with a phallus, was the inscription *Heic habitat felicitas* [Here happiness dwells].[49] Schopenhauer found the inscription humorous – naïve for those entering the brothel and ironic for those leaving it. At Paestum, the ancient Temple of Poseidon, still standing proud after twenty-five centuries, filled him with awe, as he thought that "I stood on the ground upon which the soles of Plato's feet perhaps trod."[50]

---

[46] Ibid., *Manuscript Remains*, Vol. 3, p. 7 / *Der handschriftliche Nachlaß*, Vol. 3, p. 5.

[47] Schopenhauer, *Gesammelte Briefe*, p. 434, Schopenhauer to David Asher, 31 August 1858.

[48] See Schopenhauer, *Manuscript Remains*, Vol. 3, p. 11 / *Der handschriftliche Nachlaß*, Vol. 3, p. 8, for his reaction to Ajes' painting, and *The World as Will and Representation*, Vol. 2, p. 592 / *Sämtliche Werke*, Vol. 3, p. 679, for his analysis of the weeping Ulysses.

[49] See Schopenhauer, *The World as Will and Representation*, Vol. 2, pp. 513, 583 / *Sämtliche Werke*, Vol. 3, pp. 587, 670, for his reflections on Pompeii.

[50] Schopenhauer, *Gesammelte Briefe*, pp. 54, 656 – from his *curriculum vitae*.

When he was in Naples, Schopenhauer received Adele's letter describing Goethe's reception of his book. When he returned to Rome a month later, his head was swimming with vainglorious thoughts about his philosophy. He composed a poem celebrating himself, which concluded with the line "Posterity will erect a monument to me."[51] In a cooler moment, he crossed out the word "monument" and substituted "memorial." (Perhaps he was prophetic, as well as hasty in his modesty, because in 1895, a monument was erected to him in the north end of the *Rechneigraben* in Frankfurt.) In May he returned to Naples, and in June he ventured to Milan. There he received a disturbing letter from his sister, informing him that the banking house of A. L. Muhl in Danzig had suspended payments. Johanna and Adele had invested their entire inheritances with Muhl, and Arthur, who wisely ignored his mother's advice that he should do likewise, still had entrusted more than a third of his inheritance to Muhl. Adele was beside herself. Her mother's somewhat lavish lifestyle had consumed most of her money and was beginning to eat away at Adele's. For the time being, Johanna and Adele were out of money. They immediately dismissed their servants, and following the advice of their cousin and Schopenhauer's godfather, Wilhelm Ernst Friedrich Goermann, they borrowed money to travel to Danzig to discuss a settlement with Muhl, who had warned his creditors that this was needed to avoid bankruptcy. Adele was beside herself; "how will we live?" she wrote her brother. "My heart is crushed by mother's condition and by the departure that stands before me."[52] At least, she continued, one of them was not completely out of luck, because Schopenhauer had only 8,000 *Taler* with Muhl. She also conveyed the message from their mother that Johanna would do everything she could to also protect her son's investment. Given Schopenhauer's view of Johanna's business acumen, this remark brought him no consolation.

The Muhl crisis moved Schopenhauer to make a grand gesture. He offered to divide his money with his family. Johanna rebuffed his aid, just as she would do likewise with Gerstenbergk's offer to help. Whereas her refusal of aid by her onetime "house guest" was a matter of pride, her

---

[51] Schopenhauer, *Manuscript Remains*, Vol. III, p. 11/*Der handschriftliche Nachlaß*, Vol. 3, p. 9.

[52] Lütkehaus, *Die Schopenhauers*, p. 288, Adele to Arthur Schopenhauer, 28 May 1819.

rejection of her son's pledge was a matter of wrath. Instead of repairing his damaged relationship with his mother, his offer made their relationship worse, and it further strained the increasingly tenuous relationship between mother and daughter. Irritated by his mother's foolish investment with a single firm – Schopenhauer would always diversify his assets – and still bemoaning what he viewed as his mother's lavish lifestyle – Schopenhauer would always live within his means – he accompanied his pledge of financial support with a remark made for Adele's eyes only. He wrote his sister that he would share his assets, "although she [Johanna] had honored the memory of her husband, of my father, neither in his son nor in his daughter."[53] Adele dismissed this remark, viewing Schopenhauer's offer as an act that spoke louder than his harsh judgment. Johanna found and read her son's letter and flew into a rage in which she said terrible things about her husband and son. Johanna must have also accused Adele of sharing her son's opinion of her, because Adele recorded that she could not convince her mother that she did not share her son's views. Things became so heated between the two women that Adele thought about throwing herself out of the window. Fortunately, she recorded, "but when I felt this horrible urge, God gave me resolve and power."[54] The screaming ended with both women in tears, and with Adele believing that Johanna would never again trust in her love. "I remained for two long days feeling like dying," Adele wrote in her diary, "and mother also suffered physically."[55] Adele would carry the bitter memory of this quarrel for years.

It is likely that Johanna would have rejected Schopenhauer's offer to share his money, even if she had not discovered his cutting remark about her failure to honor the memory of her husband. Almost more than anything else, she valued her independence from men. Thus she rejected Gerstenbergk's assistance. But to accept support from a man who was her son, and a son with a history of trying to direct her life, would have been an act that both contradicted her own sense of propriety concerning a mother's relationship with her child and would have forced her to

---

53 Ibid., p. 289. Like most of his correspondence to Adele at this time, Schopenhauer's letter is lost. Adele quoted from Schopenhauer's letter of July 1819 in her letter to Ottilie von Goethe, 28 July 1819.

54 Schopenhauer, Adele, *Tagebücher*, Vol. 2, p. 32; quoted in Bergmann's *Johanna Schopenhauer*, p. 217.

55 Schopenhauer, Adele, ibid., Vol. 2, p. 32.

recognize her son's superiority. She should not be dependent on her son, she told Adele, but "he should have been dependent on her."[56] During another financial crisis in 1827, Johanna shared her analysis of her son's seemingly kind gesture with a friend: "I believe that if I were to become completely poor, he would share his assets with me. He had himself written in a few harsh words something similar, when Muhl became bankrupt. I know that he would give me bread, tossing it to me as one tosses alms to a beggar."[57] Her son's harsh words had to provoke Johanna's wrath, because she harbored a grudge against her deceased spouse due to the original division of his estate. It made her children financially independent and decreased her inheritance. She had managed to keep Adele close at hand and had made her daughter's inheritance virtually her own. She controlled it, managed it, and would live from it. Arthur was trying to use his inheritance, she thought, to control her life. It was as if Heinrich Floris was exercising his power from the grave through his obstinate son.

To wiggle his way out of a potential bankruptcy, Muhl pressed his creditors for a settlement of thirty percent of their capital. Both Johanna and Adele favored the offer, and Adele begged her brother to also accept Muhl's terms. The banker had convinced the Schopenhauer women that it was either this or bankruptcy, in which case all would be lost. Schopenhauer was unmoved by his sister's pleas, and he recommended that she should not settle and join him to wait for Muhl to become solvent. Muhl himself wrote his resolute creditor that he had debts of 430,000 *Taler* and assets of 130,000, figures that supported his settlement offer. Schopenhauer stood pat, declining his creditor's offer. He was willing to call what he viewed as Muhl's self-serving bluff. The women, however, had 22,000 *Taler* at stake, almost all of which was Adele's. They only had 2,000 *Taler* left in Weimar, and they owed 800 to Quandt. They were unwilling to gamble. They capitulated to Muhl, but only after making a side deal. They would receive a life annuity of 300 *Taler* and four paintings. When Adele told Schopenhauer about this side settlement, it is likely that she

[56] Wolfgang von Oettingen (ed.), *Aus Ottilie von Goethe's Nachlaß. Briefe von ihr und an Sie* (Weimar: Verlag der Goethe-Gesellschaft, 1812), p. 352; quoted in Bergmann's *Johanna Schopenhauer*, p. 218.

[57] Gruber, Robert, "Die Familie Schopenhauer und der Ausgleich Muhls," in *Suddeutsche Monatshefte*, Vol. 30 (May 1933), p. 499; quoted in Bergmann's *Johanna Schopenhauer*, p. 218.

confirmed his suspicions about his family's motives. From his perspective, it seemed as if his mother and sister were only out for themselves.

Schopenhauer's correspondence with his sister became increasingly dark and distressing as the Muhl affair played out. At one point he threatened to withhold the small stipend that he contributed to the support of his Aunt Julie Trosiener, a petty and mean-spirited act that amazed Adele. Johanna, who also helped support her sister, had pledged to continue this support, despite her own precarious conditions. Schopenhauer also gave free expression to his suspicions about Muhl's honesty, and ultimately about the motives of his family. At first, Adele attempted to win back her brother's trust and to retain the cordial relationship that was developed during Schopenhauer's stay in Italy. "Do not harden your heart against me," she pleaded; "no one on earth loves you like me. Think of what that means and hold fast to that heart which had not been easily won."[58] If the philosopher had pondered the meaning of his sister's love, he must have concluded that it did not matter. He let that heart go, but not until after causing it to break. Less than a month later, Adele gave full vent to her frustrations. "You make us miserable," Adele said, speaking also for her mother; "so know also what you do and how the world views our situation. I have not for a single moment been false or untrue or mistrustful of you. Consequently, I have nothing to take back."[59] She concluded the same letter by attempting to make the philosopher feel guilty about his conduct, while she withdrew from his life: "I can hear nothing from you that does not tear my heart apart; that you mistrust your own sister and your mother is an *infamie* capable of inflicting the most severe punishment. I can also do nothing for you that could be useful." By May 1820, Adele and Johanna settled with Muhl. They lost seventy percent of their investment. Schopenhauer did nothing to protest Muhl's settlement with his other investors, because Muhl's solvency would enable him to benefit.

Schopenhauer was always suspicious about the motives of other people toward his money. He suspected that Muhl was trying to swindle his creditors. Nevertheless, Adele's desperate pleas for him to settle for thirty percent and the Danzig businessman's description of his tenuous financial position moved him to make a concession. He would settle, but only if he received seventy percent of his investment no later than 15 April

58 Lütkehaus, *Die Schopenhauer*, p. 313, Adele to Arthur Schopenhauer, 14 January 1820.
59 Ibid., p. 315, Adele to Arthur Schopenhauer, 1 February 1820.

1820. This offer was carved in stone. After that date, which gave Muhl approximately six weeks to comply, he threatened to press the banker for full payment, plus interest, or until Muhl became bankrupt. "I am sorry with all of my heart that I must be such a pain in the neck to you," Schopenhauer wrote his troubled debtor; "I can also imagine from your standpoint that my proceeding may appear hard and unfair. But that is a mere illusion, which disappears, as soon as you realize that what I want is nothing more than that which I cannot allow to be taken from me and is mine by the greatest and most incontrovertible right. It is that, moreover, upon which my entire happiness, my freedom and my scholarly leisure depends; a good that is so seldom granted in this world to those of my kind, and it would be almost as unconscionable as weak, not to defend it to the utmost end and to hold it fast with all one's might."[60]

The philosopher held fast, as promised. While Muhl settled with his other creditors, Schopenhauer demanded full payment, plus interest. Muhl requested more time. He could pay, if he had between three to six years. He told Schopenhauer that he possessed a fine flock of genuine Merino sheep, which should bring 2,400 *Taler* in three or four years. He had security, he told his unrelenting creditor. A substantial life insurance policy would protect Schopenhauer if something were to happen to him. And if he doubted his sincerity and honesty concerning his promise to repay, Schopenhauer could come and live with him in Uhlkau and observe firsthand his business conduct. Schopenhauer rejected Muhl's offers in no uncertain terms. He told the businessman that he was not just another Merino sheep, willing to graze among his flock. He would not be fleeced. As for his life insurance policy, that was no security. Whether he was paid and whether Muhl lived, were two distinct events. "But of course," Schopenhauer sneered, "I will not strike you dead, in order to be paid."[61] As for moving to Uhlkau, Schopenhauer declined the invitation. As long as Muhl was his creditor, Schopenhauer continued, he could not go to Uhlkau, unless he wanted him to press his claims "like the merchant who visited Don Juan in the final act." Muhl, he said, had shown him his weapons, and he had shown him his. He was better armed.

Schopenhauer's hardball strategy would allow him to prevail and profit. Two and a third years after the beginning of the Muhl crisis, he managed

---

[60] Schopenhauer, *Gesammelte Briefe*, p. 60, Schopenhauer to A. L. Muhl, 28 February 1820.
[61] Ibid.., p. 72, Schopenhauer to A. L. Muhl, 22 May 1821.

to recoup his money, with interest. He received 9,400 *Taler* from his reluctant debtor in three payments. When he submitted his first bill, Schopenhauer set aside the question of Muhl's insolvency. He knew Muhl had bought out many of his creditors at thirty percent and when he tried to move the philosopher to return to his earlier offer of seventy percent, Schopenhauer knew he had him. One hundred percent is better than seventy percent and by offering seventy percent, Schopenhauer told Muhl that he knew he could pay this bill. "Therefore should you nevertheless still want to plead insolvency," Schopenhauer wrote in a way to show his philosophical chops, "I will prove the opposite to you through the famous argument that the great Kant introduced into philosophy, in order to prove the moral freedom of humans; namely, the inference from ought to can."[62] Schopenhauer, however, was playing fast and loose with the Danzig merchant. He did not accept Kant's inference, nor did he embrace Kant's account of moral freedom. They only way a person was motivated to comply with a statement of moral obligation, he argued, was if that person already desired to do that which was entailed by the obligation, in which case the statement of obligation was superfluous, or another could promise reward or threaten punishment and thereby make it in a person's self-interest to do what he or she should do.[63] But after dangling Kant, Schopenhauer articulated his true view on the matter: "This means if you do not pay me voluntarily, I will sue you for the bill. Observe that one can be a philosopher, therefore, without being a fool." Of course, Schopenhauer had business in his blood and his training for the life of a merchant had allowed him to observe the machinations employed in the business world. He also knew that Kant's moral philosophy applied only to "dear little angels" and not to flesh and blood people, whose essence was the will.[64] Instead of relying on Muhl to act out of a sense of duty, Schopenhauer threatened punishment.

Berlin

The financial troubles in Germany forced Schopenhauer to cut short his stay in Italy. He also faced an existential crisis. He had given the

---

[62] Ibid., p. 69, Schopenhauer to A. L. Muhl, 1 May 1821.
[63] See Schopenhauer's *On the Basis of Morality*, pp. 88–94/ *Sämtliche Werke*, Vol. 4, pp. 155–60.
[64] Ibid., p. 64/ibid., Vol. 4, p. 132.

world his philosophy, the fruit of his life, and he faced a philosophical form of postpartum depression. The Muhl crisis also made him aware of his financial vulnerability. A few years later, he noted the connection between these crises. He had, he wrote, acted contrary to nature and human rights by deciding to employ his talents and powers not for the egoistic advancement of his well-being, but for the good of humankind. This, his mission, which would assume an almost messianic form later in his life, had been completed. He had used his intellect to serve the world and not to serve himself. Yet in doing this, he felt anxious and uneasy: "But I have carried out my task, have solved this problem and have fulfilled my mission. For this reason I was justified in carefully watching and seeing that the support of my father's inheritance had to continue even into old age, for without such support the world would have had nothing from me. No worldly office, no position as minister or governor, could have compensated me for the loss of my leisure that was granted to me at the very outset."[65]

As Schopenhauer made his nervous way back to Dresden, a stopover in Heidelberg led to a brief reunion with his old schoolmate from Gotha, Ernst Anton Lewald, who was a professor of classical philology at the university. A note from this time is instructive, showing the traveler appreciating the often insurmountable gap between ideas and reality. He had imagined that books facilitated a rapid and smooth communication between minds, and that by publishing his philosophy, he had now given his thoughts to all of Europe. But his travels, plus his sister's reports of his book drawing few responses, led him to realize that the world of humans and the world of books were separate realms. At one place, you observed local customs, prejudices, superstitions, and habits. At another, you would observe a different set: "We became acquainted with the wide *gulf between the populace and books* and with how slowly (though surely) acknowledged truths reached the populace, and *therefore with regard to the velocity of the propagation of the physical light nothing is less like it than the light of the mind.*"[66]

Schopenhauer always believed that the world of books made possible the communication of geniuses of all times and all places, connecting living

---

[65] Schopenhauer, *Manuscript Remains*, Vol. 4, p. 484/ *Der handschriftliche Nachlaß*, Vol. 4, 11, p. 107. Hübscher dates this reflection as "about 1822."

[66] Ibid., Vol. 3, p. 13/ibid., Vol. 3, p. 10.

scholars with a community of thinkers unbounded by space, time, and even death. Every original and profound intellect has the drive to express ideas with the greatest precision and clarity, something that is only done to perfection by writing. A great mind is the educator of the human race, he thought, and "one speaks *to humanity* only in writing."[67] It was also an article of his faith that ultimately the truth is recognized, and he believed that *The World as Will and Representation* contained the truth; that he had discovered the philosopher's stone. But he had given the world the truth, and he still had time on his hands. He needed something to do. He decided that he would cast the light of his mind directly upon his contemporaries. An academic position would enable him to do so. It would enable him to immerse himself in practical life, and if his hardline stance with Muhl would cost him his investment, an academic position would provide some income. He asked Lewald to inquire whether it would be possible for him to obtain the right to teach at Heidelberg.

It is curious that Schopenhauer made his first inquiry about an academic position at Heidelberg. That he did so may have been due simply to the fact that Heidelberg had the first university he encountered on his return to Dresden, and that he had a friend on its faculty. Lewald must have also told him that there was a lacuna in its philosophy faculty, because when Schopenhauer began his tour of Italy, Berlin had managed to lure Hegel away. Hegel had hit Heidelberg just as he hit Jena, a beat behind the leading impulse of the age. When he arrived at Jena, most of its stars had moved to shine elsewhere. After Hegel's horse-riding World Spirit made a shambles of Jena, Hegel fled to Bamberg, spending a year editing the *Bamberg Newspaper* [*Bamberger Zeitung*]. He then became the rector at the Gymnasium at Nurenberg, a position he held for eight years, before he became a professor in Heidelberg in 1816. But by this time the German Romantics had vacated the university, put off by its very practically minded students and its empirically minded science faculty, a body that was also suspicious about any form of idealism. Berlin, however, was at the forefront of German intellectual life when it sought Hegel, and it provided a more effective platform for his modernizing agenda. Moreover, unlike the financially independent Schopenhauer, Hegel had to live by philosophy, because he had a family to support. Berlin offered Hegel

---

[67] Schopenhauer, *Parerga and Paralipomena*, Vol. 1, p. 41 / *Sämtliche Werke*, Vol. 5, p. 45.

Fichte's vacant chair in philosophy and a salary of 2,000 *Taler*, more than double his salary at Heidelberg.

Lewald investigated Schopenhauer's prospects at Heidelberg. He reported to the philosopher that there would be no obstacles to his habitation at Heidelberg, although no one was familiar with his philosophy.[68] Schopenhauer, however, made no further overtures to Heidelberg. It is not clear why he did not do so. Perhaps the air still bore the spurs of the departed Romantics, or perhaps he had thought then what he would publish later, namely that Hegel's two years at the university had "an extremely pernicious, really stupefying, one might say pestilential influence" on any potentially philosophical mind, thereby making it unreceptive to his thought.[69] Heidelberg's students, like all reform-oriented students, celebrated the murder of the reactionary playwright August von Kotzebue on 23 March 1819 by the student Karl Sand in Mannheim, and they were still riding the wave of the nationalistic and reform fever that rocked many of the more progressive locations within Germany. All of this may have disgusted the conservative philosopher. But it is more likely that Schopenhauer made no further advances to Heidelberg because he had better alternatives in mind and that the relocation of his library and other personal possession from Dresden would be too troublesome. It is unlikely that he worried about Hegel's influence on Heidelberg's students. He was confident that he could expose the nonsense that constituted its core, and students at the other two universities he considered, Göttingen and Berlin, were not much less nationalistic than those at Heidelberg. Besides, Hegel was in Berlin. From Schopenhauer's perspective, any lingering scent left by the German Romantics was that of a decomposing corpse.

Schopenhauer did nothing that would have severed his prospects at Heidelberg, but at the beginning of December he contacted his old professor of anatomy and physiology at Göttingen, Friedrich Blumenbach. That he addressed his letter of inquiry about an academic position at Göttingen to Blumenbach and not his first philosophy professor Schulze was not surprising. Aenesidemus Schulze had given a lukewarm review of

---

[68] See Schopenhauer, *Gespräche*, p. 401 for Lewald's letter to Schopenhauer, 10 October 1819. Lewald also mentions that Schopenhauer had known other Heidelbergers, such as the painter Roux, a merchant named Fries, and a fellow named Mohrstadt.

[69] Schopenhauer, *On the Basis of Morality*, p. 14/ *Sämtliche Werke*, Vol. 4, p. xvii.

Schopenhauer's dissertation, and Schopenhauer himself gave scant reference to Schulze in his principal work. He also probably anticipated that
Schulze would have viewed his philosophy as building from a discredited
source, Kant, and that the skeptical Schulze would have been troubled by
his former pupil's return to Kant's distinction between things in themselves and appearances. Moreover, Schopenhauer never took skepticism
as a viable philosophical stance, and in *The World as Will and Representation* he dismissed "theoretical egoism" or solipsism, the view that one's
body is the only appearance of the will – that is, one is the only real
individual in the world – as a skeptical sophism whose serious advocates
could only be found in a madhouse, and needed not so much a refutation
as a cure.[70]

Schopenhauer told Blumenbach that ever since his tour of Italy he
had been planning and preparing to enter into "practical life" and had
decided that the only way this would be possible for a "theoretical person,"
which he was by his very nature, would be to teach and to lecture at a
university. He had served his apprentice's and journeyman's years, and
now his plan was to become a master by qualifying as an academic lecturer
at some university that would be keen to offer speculative philosophy
of his brand. He was considering Göttingen, Berlin, and Heidelberg, he
confided to his old professor, and he favored Göttingen, because it was
the most worthwhile, perhaps the best university in the world, known for
having the most learned men in all fields and for having the best of all
libraries. Schopenhauer was laying it down fast and thick for his former
teacher, who, he said, was the most valuable among all of his teachers. Did
Blumenbach think that he could find audience there, he inquired, and to
whom should he make a formal request to do his habilitation, he asked.
He wished to enter his new career by Easter. When was the latest time
he could apply, he asked, and could Blumenbach scout the faculty on his
behalf?[71]

Schopenhauer did not place his eggs in only two baskets. Shortly after
writing Blumenbach, he contacted Martin Hinrich Carl Lichtenstein at
Berlin. Schopenhauer had met the professor of zoology and director of the

---

[70] See Schopenhauer, *The World as Will and Representation*, Vol. 1, p. 104/ *Sämtliche Werke*,
Vol. 2, p. 124.
[71] Schopenhauer, *Gesammelte Briefe*, p. 43. Schopenhauer to Johann Friedrich Blumenbach,
beginning of December 1819.

zoological museum eleven years earlier at his mother's home in Weimar, and he had attended his lectures during his school years at Berlin. In many regards, his letter to Lichtenstein paralleled his letter to Blumenbach, but diplomatically reversing the order of Göttingen and Berlin in his list of potential universities. He was undecided between Berlin, Göttingen, and Heidelberg, but he anticipated that in Berlin he would attract a larger audience than elsewhere, especially from outside the student body. Berlin was, he said, the center of the highest intellectual culture. He also mentioned that there was a void in its philosophy faculty, because Karl Wilhelm Solger had recently died. Despite his praise of Berlin, however, Schopenhauer confided to Lichtenstein that his choice of a university was still up in the air. Because of its "fatal location in a sand desert" and the ills that beset all large cities, such as high costs of living, he preferred Göttingen and Heidelberg to Berlin. But he noted that a full lecture hall would more than compensate him.[72]

As with his letter to Blumenbach, so it was with his letter to Lichtenstein. Could he determine the sentiment of the faculty about his seeking a position? Had they heard of his work? Exactly to whom should he petition to do his habilitation? He apologized to his old professor and family friend for troubling him by his requests, but there was no one in Berlin whom he trusted more and who had shown him as much friendship, he wrote. As he had done in his letter to Blumenbach, he assured the physiologist that his philosophy did not bear the slightest hint of a political tendency or incli- nation designed to win influence among his contemporaries. Instead of the ephemeral concerns of his contemporaries, his very nature compelled him to occupy himself with that "which concerns humanity in the same way at all times and in all countries, and I would hold it as an abasement of myself, if I were to direct my intellectual powers to a sphere that appears to me so small and narrow as the present conditions of any particular time or country. Indeed, I am even of the opinion that any scholar, in the higher sense of the term, should hold this conviction and should leave the improvement of the machine of the state to statesmen, just as they should leave to the scholar the advancement and perfection of knowledge. But I have a quite extremely low opinion of those *soi-disant* philosophers who have become commentators on politics and public affairs and who, by this, seek an immediate influence in and on their contemporaries, which

---

[72] Ibid., p. 45, Schopenhauer to Lichtenstein. Hübscher dates this letter early December 1819.

is the clearest confession that they are also incapable of writing a single line that a descendant would find worthy to read."[73]

Schopenhauer's articulation of his perennialism was authentic, even though it was also politic. He had no interest in contemporary politics. Indeed, political philosophy itself was the least developed area in his thought. Yet by articulating his contempt for *soi-disant*, "self-described" philosophers, who were bent to influence current political affairs, he was telling his old professor that he was not one of the subversives or "demagogues" whom the ruling powers were purging from the universities. Following Kotzebue's murder, political reactionaries, such as Prince Clemens Wenzel Lother Metternich of Austria, exploited the assassination to transform the nobility's fear of revolution into opposition to any reform that would threaten the status quo. From 6 to 31 August 1814, German rulers, including the Prussian King, Friedrich Wilhelm III, met in Karlsbad and issued the "Karlsbad Decrees," a set of repressive political measures designed to quash reform. The Karlsbad Decrees enabled the dismissal of any member of a German university who presented a threat to the established social order. These so-called "demagogues" were banned from all German universities. The Decrees also established a censorship board with oversight of publications within the German confederation, as well as a commission in Mainz, which was charged with sniffing out any subversive forces.

Both Blumenbach and Lichtenstein reported to Schopenhauer that their respective faculties would not be an obstacle to his securing a position, despite that fact that no one was familiar with his philosophy. Blumenbach, however, was skeptical about his ability to attract an audience. He sensed that Göttingen did not appear to need more lectures in philosophy. Göttingen had suffered a severe enrollment decline due to the student unrest following Kotzebue's murder. Its enrollment dropped from approximately 1,300 students to 658 students. Lichtenstein was more hopeful, writing that Hegel had renewed interest in philosophy in Berlin. Berlin had a much larger student body, with approximately 1,100 students. Schopenhauer decided on Berlin.

Schopenhauer petitioned the philosophy faculty at Berlin for the right to do his habilitation on the last day in 1819. Along with his petition he

[73] Ibid.

included his dissertation, his essay on color theory, and The *World as Will and Representation* as "specimins" of his work. His petition, as well as the accompanying *"Vitae Curriculum Arthurii Schopenhaueri, Phil: Doct,"* was composed in Latin. In an accompanying letter to the Dean of the Berlin faculty, Philipp August Boeckh, whose lectures "On Plato's Life and Writings" Schopenhauer sporadically attended during his Berlin summer semester 1812, Schopenhauer made two requests. First, he asked to have his lectures announced in the very next catalog. To have this done, he would have to pass his test-lecture by mid-January, a time-frame that Schopenhauer knew was impossible. But, without being listed in the next catalog, he feared that he would be unable to attract students. So he asked Boeckh if he would be so kind as to grant his request, something that was done at other universities, he reminded Boeckh. He wanted his lectures described as covering "general philosophy, i.e., the theory of the essence of the world and the human spirit," noting that he would do so six times a week.[74] Second, and now he made the request that would draw that outrage of the faculty, he wanted to teach at the same time that Hegel was delivering his principal lectures.

Despite Schopenhauer's arrogant request, which was soon known by the faculty, his test lecture, covering the four different types of causes, was scheduled for 1:00 p.m., 13 March 1820. The lecture was presented *in consessu facultatis*, and during the *viva voce* afterward, Hegel and Schopenhauer engaged in a minor dispute. The philosopher of the absolute was displeased with the treatment of motives by the philosopher of the will. "When a horse lies down on the street," Hegel inquired, "what then is the motive?" Schopenhauer replied, "The ground, which it finds beneath it, in connection with its fatigue, a disposition of the horse. If it stood next to an abyss, it would not lie down." Hegel sought clarification: "You consider animal functions likewise as motives? Therefore the beating of the heart, the circulation of the blood, etc., follow as the results of motives?" Schopenhauer retorted, "These are not called animal functions. In physiology, one calls such the conscious movements of the animal body." He then referred to Albrecht Haller's *Physiology* to support his claim. Hegel, however, charged, "Oh, but one does not understand that as animal functions." Before Schopenhauer could reply, Schopenhauer's friend, the

[74] Ibid., p. Schopenhauer to Boeckh, 31 December 1819.

physiologist Lichtenstein, stood and interrupted the dispute, claiming that Schopenhauer was using the term animal functions correctly.[75] The examination ended.

Schopenhauer would later tell his friend Carl Bähr that he had exposed Hegel as "monsieur know-nothing" through this dispute.[76] And although he would come to loathe Hegel more than any other person, he was particularly appalled by what he saw as his ignorance of the natural sciences.[77] This small exchange between the fifty-year-old professor and the thirty-two-year-old aspiring *Privatdozent* did not reflect well on either party. Hegel was seeking to have Schopenhauer clarify his use of the term "motive," which the former understood as a reason for an action, whereas the latter understood a motive as a cognition that caused an action. Schopenhauer seized on Hegel's misuse of the term "animal functions," probably to embarrass his interrogator, and he did not clarify his view. Hegel should have brought the younger man back to his original inquiry, but instead he took the bait and the dispute became one about the meaning of "animal functions." Lichtenstein's interruption and his siding with his young friend provided both men with a natural end to the discussion.

Hegel probably did not feel as if he had been shown to be a know-nothing, and he also had other duties and concerns greater than showing a philosophical upstart his place. His *Repetent*, or teaching assistant, Friedrich Wilhelm Carové had been accused of writing a justification of Kotzebue's assassination, and Hegel was worried that he himself would be suspected of being a "demagogue." He also was engaged in a well-known dispute with Schleiermacher, whose dislike for Hegel was reciprocated by Hegel's disdain for him, over the dismissal of Wilhelm Martin Leberecht de Wette from the university for subversion. Hegel supported the dismissal and Schleiermacher, whose own lectures were being observed for

---

[75] Schopenhauer, *Gespräche*, pp. 47–8.

[76] Ibid., p. 47.

[77] In the vitriolic first preface to *The Two Fundamental Problems of Ethics*, Schopenhauer drew from the *Encyclopedia of Philosophical Sciences in Outline, for the Use of His Lectures* [*Encyklopädie der philosophischen Wissenschaft im Grundrisse, zum Gebrauch seiner Vorlesungen*, 2nd ed., 1827] to demonstrate how Hegel lacked common sense and ordinary understanding of science; see *On the Basis of Morality*, pp. 16–20/ *Sämtliche Werke*, Vol. 4, pp. xx–xxv. Hegel's *Encyclopedia of the Philosophical Sciences* had already championed Goethe's theory of colors in its first edition. Hegel had sent the *Encyclopedia of the Philosphical Sciences* to Goethe in 1817, just as he had his *Phenomenology of Spirit* in 1807; see Goethe's letter to Hegel, 8 July 1817 in *Letters from Goethe*, p. 412. Schopenhauer ignored Hegel's support of Goethe's color theory.

demagogic activities, opposed the firing. Hegel was also putting the finishing touches on his *Elements of the Philosophy of Right* [*Grundlinien Philosophie des Rechts*, 1821].[78] Examining aspiring and quarrelsome unsalaried teachers must have appeared to Hegel as a waste of his time. In any case, Hegel voted to pass the "know-everything" younger philosopher, in full knowledge of Schopenhauer's request to schedule his classes in competition with his own.

If the payoff from Schopenhauer's brief exchange with Hegel was a greater confidence in his plan to draw Hegel's students to his lectures, this confidence was purchased with false coin. Boeckh granted Schopenhauer's self-defeating request to hold his lectures at the same time as Hegel's. Students, however, continued to flock to hear the mouthpiece for the absolute idea, even though the idea [*Idee*] was mediated through Hegel's thick Swabian accent as "*Uedäh*."[79] Schopenhauer may have correctly said "i'de," but only a literal handful of students heard it.[80] His class, offered in the summer semester of 1820, drew only five students. No one else had any idea, however one might pronounce it, what the fresh unsalaried lecturer had to say. But even these five students did not hear a full semester's worth of well-pronounced words. Schopenhauer never completed the course. He announced his lectures in the winter semester of 1820/21, the summer of 1822, the winter of 1821/22, and then in all semesters from the winter of 1826/27 through the winter of 1831/32.[81] The lectures on "general philosophy" remained incomplete. He never enrolled and completed a course at Berlin. His challenge to Hegel was a disaster.

---

[78] See Terry Pinkard's *Hegel: A Biography, pp. 435-63* for a thorough discussion of the political tensions Hegel faced during the period of Schopenhauer's test-lecture and pp. 464–5 for his account of Schopenhauer's dispute with Hegel.

[79] Hegel was known for his clumsy, stuttering lecture style, full of coughs, pregnant pauses during which he would search his lecture notes for his next thought, and for beginning almost every sentence with "therefore," see Pinkard ibid., pp. 371, 611-12. Schopenhauer mocked Hegel's pronounciation of *Ideen* in the second edition of *On the Fourfold Root of the Principle of Sufficient* Reason; "When, however, anyone speaks to German's about ideas [*Ideen*], especially when the word is pronounced *Uedähen*, their heads begin to swim, all reflectiveness foreshakes them and they feel as if they were about to go up ina ballon," p.68 / *Sämtliche Werke*, Vol. 1, p. 113. Ina letter to Frauenstädt, 21 August 1852, he refers to Hegel's pronunciation of "*Idee*" as "*Uedähn,*" *Gesammelte Briefe,* p. 290.

[80] It did not matter, however, that this final lecture drew no students. Schopenhauer had fled Berlin prior to the start of the term.

[81] The gap in the listing of Schopenhauer's proposed courses between the winter semester 1821/22 and the winter semester 1826/27 was due to his absence from Berlin.

Schopenhauer blamed his academic failure on Hegel, just as he would blame his "rival" for the failure of his philosophy to draw an audience. Hegel, however, never viewed Schopenhauer as a philosophical threat. He did nothing personally to derail Schopenhauer's academic career. He did not make a fuss about the *Privatdozent's* arrogant request to hold his lectures at the same time as his own principal lectures. Schopenhauer even wrote to Boeckh about Hegel's "kindness" in accepting the subject of his test lecture, because it gave him the opportunity to develop in greater detail the four types of causality that he had only mentioned in his dissertation.[82] Nevertheless, Schopenhauer began to develop a seething hatred for Hegel, a hatred that would endure for the remaining forty years of his life.

But why did Schopenhauer loathe Hegel and all things Hegelian? His attitude toward Hegel, his followers, and what he perceived as the effects of the two was not based on anything approaching a dispassionate and measured assessment of their merits. Indeed, all of his writings subsequent to his principal work are thick with some of the most vicious *ad hominems* ever launched by a philosopher against his perceived opponents. Even the second editions of his dissertation (1847) and his essay on color theory (1854) were expanded by diatribes against Hegel, as were the second and third editions of *The World as Will and Representation* (1844, 1859). In *On the Will in Nature* (1836) he publicly vented his ill will against his *bête noire*, breaking a seventeen-year period of philosophical silence, which he also blamed on the prevailing "Hegelgloria" of the times. He also used the volume's second edition (1854) to continue his rant, a tactic he also employed in the second edition of *The Two Fundamental Problems of Ethics* (1860), whose first preface (1841) contained the most unrestrained condemnations of the philosopher of the absolute within a body of complaints that reflected little restraint. The only exception to this continuous pattern of Hegel abuse was the Latin *aperçu* of his color theory, where Hegel or Hegelianism is not mentioned at all. Although one might think that this was due to Hegel's support of Goethe's theory of color, it is likely due to Schopenhauer's view that the essay was scientific in nature and he could not have drawn on some Hegelian remark to motivate his position. Certainly, he would have been disinclined to mention Hegel's support of Goethe. When an acquaintance told him that Hegel shared his

---

[82] See Schopenhauer's letter to Boeckh, 18 March 1820, *Gesammelte Briefe*, p. 61.

esteem for Mozart's *Magic Flute*, Schopenhauer replied: "Ordinarily, one must be alarmed to hear that one shares with Hegel the same opinion on a topic."[83]

Schopenhauer's first published salvo, launched directly at Hegel, came in *On the Will in Nature*. Instead of a careful critique of Hegel's philosophy of nature, which would have been an appropriate target for a work in which he argued that the best findings of the natural sciences corroborated his metaphysics and that his metaphysics provided a grounding explanation for the work done by honest empiricists, it was as if Hegel's philosophy was beyond serious consideration, and all one needed to do was to berate its author. In the introduction, Schopenhauer took the stance that the German Idealists and post-Kantian thinkers had taken dead-end paths from Kant and that one needed to return to Kant to stake out the proper path to philosophy. All that Fichte, Schelling, and Hegel had done was to obscure Kant's profound insights and throw dust in the eyes of anyone seeking truth. But Hegelian mystification has so enthralled the philosophy of the present time, he argued, that his own work had to be addressed to posterity. For the present time Schopenhauer was unable to repress his sarcasm; "may . . . Hegel's philosophy of absolute nonsense . . . continue, as hitherto, to pass for unfathomably profound wisdom, without anyone proposing as a motto to his works the words of Shakespeare: 'Such stuff as madmen tongue and brain not,' and, as an emblem at the head of these works, a cuttlefish creating a cloud of obscurity around itself so no one sees what it is, with the legend, *mea caligine tutus* [fortified by my own obscurity]."[84] Of course, Schopenhauer was proposing such a motto and emblem for his enemy.

Five years after mocking the "cuttlefish," Schopenhauer penned his most venomous condemnation of Hegel. In 1839, he wrote "On the Foundation of Morality" [*Über das Fundament der Moral*] in response to an essay contest sponsored by the Royal Danish Society of Sciences. Despite its being the only entry, the Society did not award him the prize. The Society mentioned several substantive philosophical reasons for its decision in its

---

[83] Schopenhauer, *Gespräche*, p. 207, reported from a conversation with Carl Hebler, 28 August 1855. Hebler also reported that Schopenhauer referred to Fichte's son, Immanuel Hermann, who was also a *Privatdozent* with Schopenhauer at Berlin, as "Simplicissimus."

[84] Schopenhauer, *On the Will in Nature*, p. 24/*Sämtliche Werke*, Vol. 4, p. 7. Schopenhauer is quoting from Shakespeare, *Cymbeline*, v. 4. Schopenhauer quoted the Bard in English and translated the quotation into German in a footnote.

verdict, which concluded with a remark that incensed the philosopher: "Finally, we cannot pass over in silence the fact that several distinguished philosophers of recent times are mentioned in a manner so unseemly as to cause just and grave offence."[85] Schopenhauer responded to the Society in a lengthy preface to *The Two Fundamental Problems of Ethics* (1841), a work that included his unsuccessful essay and "On the Freedom of the Human Will" (1838), an essay that had been "crowned" as the victor in a contest sponsored by the Royal Norwegian Society of Sciences. He spent as much time berating Hegel as he did criticizing the Society's negative judgment of the essay in the preface.

But why did Schopenhauer seize this moment to rage against Hegel? Schopenhauer had been defeated in Berlin due to the failure of his academic career and to the failure of *The World as Will and Representation*. He waited seventeen years to publish his next philosophical work, already sensing a decline of Hegel's influence, but *On the Will in Nature* failed to draw an audience for his work.[86] But then he won the prize with his essay on the freedom of the will from a Scandinavian society and he was confident that he would also succeed in Denmark, so much so that in the letter accompanying that essay he announced that he would publish *The Two Fundamental Problems of Ethics*, a book consisting of "two award winning prize essays" that together would form a complete outline of ethics and whose publication would be due to two Scandinavian academies.[87] Then he received the Society's negative verdict and its side remark about his offensive treatment of several contemporary philosophers. It was as if his disappointments, frustrations, and failures reached a critical mass, leading him to focus on Hegel's philosophy as the source for all of his failures. Through the Society's negative verdict, it was as if he was being victimized for his willingness to say that the emperor wore no clothes: "If I were to go on and say, this supreme philosopher of the Danish Academy has smeared nonsense like no other mortal before him, so that whoever could read his prize work, the so-called *Phenomenology of Spirit*, without thereby feeling as if he were in a madhouse – he would belong there; in saying so, I would not merely be correct."[88] Schopenhauer felt as if he

---

[85] Schopenhauer, *On the Basis of Morality*, p. 216/ibid, Vol. 4, p. 276.

[86] See Schopenhauer, *On the Will in Nature*, p. 19/*Sämtliche Werke*, Vol. 4, p. 1.

[87] Schopenhauer, *Gesammelte Briefe*, p. 183, Schopenhauer to the Royal Danish Society of Sciences in Copenhagen, 26 July 1839.

[88] Schopenhauer, *On the Basis of Morality*, p. 16/*Sämtliche Werke*, Vol. 4, p. xx.

was "the man who honestly, fearlessly, and forcefully stands up against false, vile, deceitful, purchased and wholly fabricated fame, a man who alone appropriately estimates impertinent praise of the false, the bad, and the mind rotting," and that by being censored by a learned society that praised a philosophaster as a distinguished philosopher, "then the matter becomes serious; for such an authoritative judgment could lead to great and pernicious error."[89]

To demonstrate the justness of his unrestrained slam of the Society's distinguished philosopher, Schopenhauer quotes from Hegel's *Encyclopedia of the Philosophical Sciences in Outline* [*Encyklopädia der philosophischen Wissenschaften im Grundrisse*, 2nd ed., 1827], a student compendium that Schopenhauer acquired in 1827. He selected three *specimina philosophiae Hegelianae* from this work to do double duty.[90] Because this work was a student compendium, he would illustrate Hegel's stupefying effect on young German minds. Because he selected passages that dealt with the natural sciences, he would also demonstrate the distinguished philosopher's want of understanding of the sciences, a failing that he had exposed during his test lecture twenty-one years earlier. Schopenhauer took particularly malicious delight in citing a discussion of specific weight, where Hegel had argued that "if a rod poised at its middle point subsequently becomes heavier at one end, it dips down at that end. Now if an iron rod dips down at one end after it has had been magnetized, it has thus become heavier at that end."[91] In addition to demonstrating Hegel's ignorance of physics, Schopenhauer also exploited this example to show Hegel's lack of a command of elementary logic. Schopenhauer translates the argument of his nemesis into a classical syllogism: All things that become heavier on one side dip on that side. This magnetized bar dips on that side; therefore, this magnetized bar has become heavier on that side. He then constructs a logical analogy to immediately expose the fallacious character of the argument: "All geese have two legs. You have two legs, therefore, you are a goose." That a man would articulate an argument with such a fallacious form, Schopenhauer sneers, shows a lack of common sense and inborn

---

[89] Ibid., p. 15/ibid. Vol. 4, p. xix.
[90] Schopenhauer, *On the Basis of Morality*, p. 19/*Sämtliche Werke*, Vol. 4, p. xxi. Schopenhauer quotes from Sects. 293, 269, and 298 from the second edition of Hegel's *Encyclopedia of the Philosophical Sciences in Outline*.
[91] Ibid., p. 19/ibid., Vol. 4, p. xxi.

logic, not to say, ignorance of the elementary rule that "from two premises in the affirmative no conclusion in the second figure can be drawn."[92]

Schopenhauer's vehement ill-will toward Hegel exemplified in its most extreme fashion a failing that he recognized in himself. Around 1833, Schopenhauer noted that "nature has done more than is necessary to isolate my heart, in that she endowed it with suspicion, irritability, vehemence and pride in a measure that is hardly compatible with the *mens aequa* of a philosopher."[93] His lack of a philosopher's *mens aequa*, equanimity, reached its greatest expression in his irrational condemnation of all things Hegelian. Although he prided himself about his outsider's stance to his age and to what he saw as the particular and ephemeral concerns of his philosophical contemporaries, his pride also motivated his harsh criticisms of philosophers who enjoyed the popularity that he felt should belong to him. The outsider obviously wanted to be an insider, but only on his own terms. He identified Hegel as enjoying what should be his position, and as the worst of a sad lot of philosophers who had despoiled Kant's rare insights and thereby set philosophy, itself, back into the dark ages.

But even before Schopenhauer published his first denunciation of Hegel, he tried to bring Kant to England, a country untainted by the

---

[92] Ibid., p. 19/ibid., Vol. 4, p. xxi. A classical or Aristotelian syllogism contains three terms. The term that occurs as the predicate term of the conclusion is the major term; the subject term of the conclusion is the minor term; and the term that occurs once in each premise is the middle term. The figure of a syllogism concerns the place of the three terms in the premises. There are four possible figures, and in the second figure, the first premise, or the major premise, has the major term as the subject term of the proposition and the middle term as the predicate term. The second premise, the minor premise, has the minor term as the subject term and the middle term as the predicate term. The conclusion in each figure always has the minor term as the subject term and the major term as the predicate term. In both Schopenhauer's translation of Hegel's argument into syllogistic form and his analogous argument, the premises (as well as the conclusion) are affirmative propositions, asserting class inclusion. In contemporary terms, these syllogisms commit the fallacy of undistributed middle term. In a valid categorical syllogism, the middle term must be distributed, that is, reference must be made to all members denoted by the term. In Schopenhauer's analogous syllogism, the middle term is "being with two legs," and to assert that all geese have two legs refers to all geese as being members of the class "beings with two legs," but it does not refer to all members of the class "being with two legs." The minor premise, a singular proposition, also fails to refer to all members of the class referred to by the middle term. It simply asserts that you are a member of this class. For the analogous argument to be valid, the major premise would have to be "All beings with two legs are geese," and for Hegel's argument to be valid, his major premise would have to be, "All things that dip on one side are things that become heavier on that side."

[93] Schopenhauer, *Manuscript Remains*, Vol. 4, p. 506/ *Der handschriftliche Nachlaß*, Vol. 4, part 2, p. 120.

post-Kantian mind-numbing philosophers. He read a review of Philibert Damiron's *Essai sur l'histoire de la philosophie France au XIX siècle* (1828) in the *British Foreign Review and Continental Miscellany* of July 1829. Within the course of the review, the anonymous author expressed the need to have Kant translated into English. Schopenhauer wrote a lengthy letter in his best English, and sent it to the publishers of the journal, Black, Young & Young, with the request for the publisher to forward it to the anonymous reviewer. Before he made his formal proposal to translate Kant's principal works into English, he described the current philosophic scene in Germany. After dismissing Fichte and Schelling as being *passé*, he took aim at Hegel: "I will not mention the numberless monstrous and mad compositions which were call'd forth by Kant's works as 'the sun, being a god, breeds maggots kissing carrion' – but so much did by and by degenerate our German philosophy that we now see a mere swaggerer and charlatan, without a shadow of merit, I mean Hegel, with a compound of bombastical nonsense and positions bordering on madness, humbug about a part of the German public, though but the more silly and untaught part, to be sure, yet by personal means and connexions to get a philosopher's name and fame."[94] It was as if Schopenhauer wanted to make an end around Germany. By translating Kant into English, he hoped to prepare an audience for his own philosophy. As he told the unknown reviewer of Damiron's book, "I sincerely believe the English nation to be the most intelligent in Europe," and despite producing exceptional talents like Kant and Goethe, "the [German] nation is extremely dull."[95] He said that he longed to be Kant's apostle in England, and that he wanted to spread "my great master's doctrines" in England. Then he made a remark that revealed his own philosophical position; he had "grafted on his [Kant's] my own system which appeared in 1819."[96] If the original appeared in English, then the British would be prepared for that which grew from the Kantian understock.

To properly prepare the British for his great master's work, Schopenhauer proposed to first translate Kant's *Prolegomena to Any Future Metaphysics*, a work, he noted, that stated the main tenets of Kant's philosophy in a simpler and more intelligible form than in the *Critique of Pure*

---

[94] Schopenhauer, *Gesammelte Briefe*, p. 117, Schopenhauer to the author of Damiron's Analysis, 21 December 1829. The quotation is from *Hamlet*, II, 2, 181f.

[95] Ibid., p. 118.

[96] Ibid.,

Reason.[97] Mindful that he was making a business proposal, he observed that the *Prolegomena* would be less expensive to publish, because it was a much shorter work than the *Critique of Pure Reason*. He also observed that the success of the *Prolegomena* would cultivate a receptive audience for the more sophisticated work. He estimated that it would take him three months to translate the *Prolegomena* and a year for the *Critique*. These translations were projects on which Schopenhauer would work *con amore*, but he also made it clear that he would not do it *gratis*. Consequently, he required "pecuniary retribution" of £2.3 per sheet, or roughly £30 for the *Prolegemena*.

Schopenhauer's proposal ultimately went for naught. The journal editors sent the proposal to the anonymous reviewer, Francis Haywood, who had his own ideas about translating Kant. He proposed a joint translation of the *Critique of Pure Reason*. Schopenhauer was suspicious of both Haywood's motives and his skills as a translator. He sensed that the reviewer simply wanted him to play second banana in the project by reading Haywood's translation against the original text for suggested improvements. Schopenhauer also suspected that Haywood would

---

[97] Schopenhauer included a sample translation from the *Prolegomena to Any Future Metaphysics*, AK. 288–9. This translation is significant because it contains Schopenhauer's English translations of such terms as *Anschauung*, "perception," *Erscheinungen*, "appearances," and *Vorstellungen*, "ideas," terms that play a central role both in Kant's and in his own philosophy. His selection of this passage was a matter of both politics and philosophy. He was selling this project to a British publisher and in the passage Kant aligned himself with Locke, while defending himself against the charge of advocating idealism, the view that only minds or "thinking beings" exist and that all things given to perception were ideas to which no external, mind-independent objects corresponded (Kant was keen here to distance himself from the charge of being a Berkeleyan idealist). Following Jacobi and Schulze, Schopenhauer also thought that this passage presented the "Achilles' heel" of Kant's philosophy, namely, the transcendent employment of the principle of causality, where things in themselves are said to cause our ideas. In Schopenhauer's translation the passage suggesting this reads, " . . . things subsisting extrinsically of us [*Dinge als außer uns*] are manifest to us as objects of our senses; but nothing do we know [*wissen*] of what they may be in themselves, our knowledge [*Kennen*] of them extending no further than to their appearances [*Erscheinungen*], i.e. to the ideas [*Vorstellungen*], which they produce in us by affecting our senses [*unsere Sinne affizieren*]. Accordingly, I certainly allow bodies extrinsical of us to exist i.e. things which, though entirely unknown to us as to what they may be in themselves, yet come into our notice by means of the ideas, which we acquire from their influence on our sensitive faculty [*ihre einfluß auf unsre Sinnlichkeit*]. . . ." One might wonder whether Schopenhauer wanted to guarantee that the British would be immediately aware of this fatal flaw in Kant's philosophy, a flaw that he corrected in his own philosophy. For Schopenhauer's translation, see ibid., pp. 122–3.

translate a Latin version of Kant's masterpiece and not the original. Even if this would not be the case and Haywood were to translate from the German, Schopenhauer also believed that Haywood would not understand Kant's philosophy and would be incapable of conveying the meaning of Kant's thought. Schopenhauer found Haywood to be the sort of translator from whom Kant should be protected.

After rejecting Haywood's proposal, Schopenhauer approached Black, Young & Young, offering to translate Kant's complete works for them. Despite Schopenhauer's observation that "Now for all I know a century may pass ere there shall again meet in the same head so much Kantian philosophy with so much English as happen to dwell together in mine," the British publisher tried in vain to reconcile the cautious philosopher with Haywood.[98] A year later, Schopenhauer approached the English poet, the author of *The Pleasures of Hope* (1799), Thomas Campbell, with the project. Campbell, who was among the directors of an institute designed to purchase copyrights and to publish meritorious books, gave Schopenhauer neither hope nor pleasure. In 1848, Haywood would publish Kant's *Critick of Pure Reason*, an even less promising title than Schopenhauer's suggested *Critic of Pure Reason*. Haywood opted for the old English for the German *"Kritik"* and Schopenhauer for the contemporary. Both shunned the French-derived "critique," favored by subsequent translators of Kant.

Although Schopenhauer delighted in obtaining any information that he could use to demean the philosopher of the absolute – he even mocked the fact that J. T. Hermes's highly popular sentimental novel, *Sophie's Journey from Memel to Saxony* [*Sophies Reise vom Memel nach Sachsen*] was one of Hegel's favorite novels – his ill will toward Hegel was more than an expression of his envy of his exalted status in the German philosophical world.[99] Although Schopenhauer unfairly blamed Hegel for the failure of both his philosophy and academic career, his animosity was further fueled by his perception that Hegel was a sham philosopher, one who sought personal advancement over the advancement of the truth. This was in direct contradiction to Schopenhauer's belief that truth was the only goal of philosophy. To succeed in life, Schopenhauer held, Hegel

---

[98] Ibid. p. 124, Schopenhauer to Black, Young & Young. Hübscher dates this letter 3 February 1830.

[99] See Schopenhauer, *Gespräche*, p. 254. In *Georg Wilhelm Friedrich Hegel's Life* [*George Wilhelm Friedrich Hegels Leben*, Berlin: Duncker and Humbolt, 1844], p. 446, Karl Rosenkranz reported that the sixteen-year-old Hegel was thoroughly taken by Hermes' *Sophie's Journey*.

had made himself a lackey for the church and state, and because he had nothing to say, he had to hide the paucity of his thought within convoluted sentence structures, thick with obscure jargon, and moved by wild, at times absurd, dialectical word play. Hegel's style mystified and misled the learned world, and Schopenhauer saw that the obscure became identified with the profound. Worse, from his point of view, just as Hegel's stumbling, coughing, and disjointed lecture style was imitated by others, the same was true of his horrid writing style. To write badly was now to write well. Truth, Schopenhauer affirmed, was best observed in the nude, and Hegel's writing had more than seven veils, and the veils covered nothing.

Schopenhauer's hostility toward Hegel evinced the dark side of his passion for philosophy. Hegel was Schopenhauer's philosophical antichrist, and this viewpoint kept Schopenhauer from looking for any points of contact and parallels in their philosophies, which was always part and parcel of Schopenhauer's attempts to confirm his philosophy. He never did this with Hegel, and to do so would have never crossed his mind. Yet both men maintained, to use Hegel's words, that "every genuine philosophy is idealism."[100] Perhaps, as part of the legacy from Schelling, which both philosophers wished to deny, they agreed that the essence of all objectifies itself into a diversity of opposing manifestations, with this singular essence moving to more expressive objectifications as it presents itself within the hierarchy of nature, until it reaches its zenith in human beings.[101] For both

---

[100] *Hegel's Logic*, trans. William Wallace, p. 140. Schopenhauer held that "true philosophy must at all costs be *idealistic* . . . to be honest." Hegel's "absolute idealism," however, asserts that everything is a manifestation of a rational necessity, the Idea, whereas Schopenhauer's idealism is Kantian, that is, transcendental, holding that the world is empirically real, but transcendentally ideal. See *The World as Will and Representation*, Vol. 2, p. 4/*Sämtliche Werke*, Vol. 3, p.

[101] In a passage that Schopenhauer would have found an instance of the pot calling the kettle black, Hegel wrote of the "charlatanism that the philosophy of nature, especially Schelling's, has become discredited," but he should have been amused by Hegel's apparent reference to Schelling's philosophy as an attempt "to palm off its absolute as the night . . . [in which] all cows are black"; see, respectively, *Hegel's Philosophy of Nature*, trans. A. V. Miller (Oxford: Clarendon Press, 1970), p. 1, and Hegel, *Phenomenology of Spirit*, trans. A. V. Miller (Oxford: Oxford University Press, 1981), p. 9. Schopenhauer studied Schelling intensely, and he found some merit in his philosophy of nature. Indeed, just as he called Fichte "Kant's buffoon," he called Hegel "Schelling's buffoon;" see *Parerga and Paralipomena*, Vol. 1, p. 27/*Sämtliche Werke*, Vol. 5, p. 30. Not ironically, Eduard von Hartmann wrote *Schelling's Positive Philosophy as a Unity of Hegel and Schopenhauer* [*Schelling's positive Philosophie als Einheit von Hegel und Schopenhauer*, Berlin: Otto Loewenstein, 1869]. See Robert Wicks's *Schopenhauer*, pp. 161–72, for a discussion of some of the striking structural parallels between

philosophers the Cartesian separation of mind and matter, of intellect and nature, was a fundamental mistake. Nature, itself, is dynamic and eludes the dead mechanical worldview found in Newtonian physics. Like Goethe, these Berlin colleagues downgraded mathematical knowledge, viewing it as purely formal and serviceable only for understanding the lower realms of nature and as incapable of describing living beings. Neither philosopher was ultimately sympathetic to skepticism, and both were deeply sympathetic to religious sentiments, holding that philosophy ultimately articulated profound truths Christianity allegorically expressed.[102] Both could view themselves as proceeding from Kantian insights and as surpassing the sage of Köningsberg.[103] Philosophy, for both, must always deal with the universal, and it must be content with describing why the world must be as it is and not with prescribing how it ought to be.

Had Schopenhauer any sympathy for Hegel, had he sensed some enduring formative influence on his thought, he might have been like Marx, willing to avow himself "the pupil of that mighty thinker," even if he felt compelled to turn him right-side-up "to discover the rational kernel within the mystical shell."[104] After all, he had made his allegiance to Kant well known. Schopenhauer had, however, no sympathy for Hegel and there was no formative influence by the master of the dialectic on his philosophy. Nevertheless, like Marx, he thought that Hegel had things inverted. Hegel, Schopenhauer charged, turned "everything upside-down, namely of making concepts the first and original thing, that which is immediately

Hegel and Schopenhauer as well as for a concise statement of their oppositions. Also see Alfred Schmidt's *Idee und Weltwille. Schopenhauer als Kritiker Hegels* (Munich: Hanser Verlas, 1988), pp. 45–64 for an analysis of Schopenhauer's criticisms of Hegel's logic, his commitment to a superindividuated intelligence, the conceptual foundations of Hegel's philosophy, and the dialectical method.

[102] See Robert Wicks' *Schopenhauer*, pp. 161–72, for a discussion of some of the striking structural parallels between Hegel and Schopenhauer as well as for a concise statement of their oppositions. Also see Alfred Schmidt's *Idee und Weltwille. Schopenhauer als Kritiker Hegels* (Munich: Hanser Verlas, 1988), pp. 45–64 for an analysis of Schopenhauer's criticisms of Hegel's logic, his commitment to a superindividuated intelligence, the conceptual foundations of Hegel's philosophy, and the dialectical method.

[103] In his *Science of Logic*, 2 vols., trans. W. H. Johnson and L. G. Struthers (London: Allen and Unwin, 1929), Vol. 1, p. 44, Hegel wrote "I am calling attention to the fact that I often take the Kantian philosophy into consideration in this work . . . it constitutes the basis and point of departure of modern German philosophy."

[104] Karl Marx, *Capital*, trans. Samuel Moore and Edward Aueling (New York: International Publishers, 1974), Vol. 1, p. 20. Marx, of course, pledges here his commitment to the dialectical method and refers to himself as a pupil of Hegel, this "mighty thinker."

given and from which we have to start."[105] But Marx thought that he had put Hegel back on his feet by returning the dialectical method to its native ground in the material world, removing the dialectic from Hegel's realm of ideas. Ideas, for Marx, were simply reflections of the material world in the human head. Schopenhauer agreed with Marx here. The source of concepts was intuitive representations, and so he echoed part of Kant's deep insight, "thoughts without intuitions are empty."[106] And although Schopenhauer might have credited Marx with sensing that concepts required some external source, grounded in experience, to give them significance, he would have also held that like all materialists, Marx maintained a philosophy that forgot the subject. More, by his substituting a materialist dialectic for an idealist one, Schopenhauer would have also accused Marx of abandoning logic.

If a philosopher's personal animosity for another were a function simply of the oppositions between the fundamental ideas of their philosophical systems, then Schopenhauer's enmity for Hegel would have had a substantial philosophical basis, despite their points of contact. Schopenhauer's philosophy was antithetical to Hegel's in profound ways and perhaps, had Hegel been simply a materialist and a realist, the oppositions would have been so great that there would have been an isomorphic philosophical basis for Schopenhauer's vigorous contempt for his Berlin colleague. Schopenhauer's logic was classically Aristotelian, and truth was simply a property of propositions, a relational property – as he made clear in his dissertation. No proposition is true except in relationship to some external ground. Without attempting to ascertain its meaning, and dismissing it as the view of a "shameless charlatan," who desired no more than to fool simpletons, he quoted from Hegel's *Phenomenology of Spirit:* "But it is not difficult to see the *way* of stating a proposition, of adducing grounds for it, and likewise of refuting its opposite through grounds, is not the form in which truth can appear. Truth is its own self-movement. . . . "[107] According to Schopenhauer, "truth" spun widely in Hegel's thought, and he was

---

[105] Schopenhauer, *Manuscript Remains*, Vol. 4, p. 239/*Der handschriftliche Nachlaß*, Vol. 4.1, p. 208.

[106] Kant, *Critique of Pure Reason*, A51/B75. Schopenhauer, however, would not accept the second part of this Kantian insight; namely, "intuitions without concepts are blind," because he held that concepts were derived from intuitions.

[107] Hegel, *Phenomenology of Spirit*, p. 28. Schopenhauer quotes this in *Parerga and Paralipomena*, Vol. 1, p. 22/*Sämtliche Werke*, Vol. 5, p. 24.

appalled by Hegel's dialectical logic, which was ontology to boot. In the first part of his *Encyclopedia*, the so-called "Logic," Hegel started with the attempt to describe the absolute as "being," and through a dazzling chain of dialectical links, reached the moment in which the idea produces from itself a real world in conformity with itself. Then, in the second part, the "philosophy of Nature," from which Schopenhauer chose his *specimina philosophiae Hegelianae* to denigrate its author, Hegel worked the idea's course through space, time, gravity, physical bodies, plants, and animals, displaying "nature as a free reflex of spirit: to know God, not in contemplation of him as spirit, but in his immediate existence."[108] Then, in its third part, the "philosophy of spirit," in a virtual *tour de force* of dialectical pyrotechnics, Hegel hurled his grand project through subjective spirit and objective spirit to reach absolute spirit, the point at which "the eternal idea, in full fruition of its essence, eternally sets itself to work, engenders and enjoys itself as absolute spirit."[109]

Schopenhauer, however, viewed Hegel's philosophy as tainted fruit. It was nothing and no more than a "monstrous amplification" of the ontological proof for the existence of God, a proof that Kant had discredited long ago.[110] Had Hegel remembered his Kant, and had he carefully read Aristotle, he would have realized that the definition of a thing and the proof of its existence were two separate matters. And although Schopenhauer would agree with Hegel that reason is the philosophical faculty, he viewed Hegel's reason as a faculty gone wild. For Hegel, reason was the capacity to reconcile the limited, finite, and putatively contradictory concepts upon which the subphilosophical faculty of understanding shipwrecked itself. Reason alone was capable of thinking the unlimited, infinite, and absolute objects of genuine philosophical thought. Understanding stumbles and stalls when it discovers that calling the absolute "being" is just the same empty abstraction as saying it is "nothing." But reason reconciles this contradictory puzzle by recognizing both in the notion of "becoming,"

---

[108] *Hegel's Philosophy of Nature*, p. 445.

[109] *Hegel's Philosophy of Mind*, trans. William Wallace (Oxford: Clarendon Press, 1971), p. 315.

[110] Schopenhauer, *On the Fourfold Root of the Principle of Sufficient Reason*, p. 16/*Sämtliche Werke*, Vol. 1, p. 12. This reference to Hegel was added in the second edition. Schopenhauer may have had assertions like the following in mind: "Being itself and the special sub-categories of which follow, as well as those of logic in general, may be looked upon as definitions of the absolute, or metaphysical definitions of God . . . for a metaphysical definition of God is the expression of his nature in thoughts as such . . ."; *Hegel's Logic*, p. 123.

the truth of being and nothing: "In becoming the being which is one with nothing and the nothing which is one with being, are only vanishing factors; they are and they are not."[111] It is only, he continued, from the perspective of the imagination that "the proposition that being and nothing is the same seems so paradoxical," Hegel averred, "that it is perhaps taken for a joke."[112] Schopenhauer understood this as worse than a joke, and imagined a different location than a philosopher's chair for its advocate: "A philosophy whose fundamental theme is 'being is nothing,' really belongs to a lunatic asylum."[113] It is surprising that he did not add, "in the company of the solipsist." From a contradiction you can draw any proposition you pleased, and Schopenhauer thought that Hegel's dialectic operated through mystifying wishes. To think that thought and being were one and the same was to think a circle a square.

The oppositions between Hegel's and Schopenhauer's philosophies ran even deeper than that of method. Hegel's absolute idealism, which posited everything as a manifestation of the idea, and hence of a rational necessity, made "what is rational actual and what is actual rational."[114] Schopenhauer's metaphysics of will constituted an antithesis to Hegel so great that it could not be reconciled within some greater, more encompassing standpoint – not even by the imaginative efforts of such an imaginative philosopher as Eduard von Hartmann. Schopenhauer's essence of all, will, is a thoroughly nonrational, insatiable, goalless striving to be – one that feasts on its own flesh. History has a goal, Hegel held, the actualization of the idea of freedom, spirit becoming conscious of itself; " . . . the idea of freedom [is] the essence of spirit and [the] absolutely final purpose of history."[115] This goal is progressively realized through human activity, and Hegel found that it is actualized in a perfected state, which serves as the home ground for its citizens' civil and moral lives and as what provides the conditions where the realization of spirit is also found in a union of free and equal citizens. In articulating this notion, Hegel would lapse into language that Schopenhauer saw as an obvious pandering to

---

[111] Ibid. p. 133.

[112] Ibid. p. 128.

[113] Schopenhauer, *Manuscript Remains*, Vol. 4, p. 240/*Der handschriftliche Nachlaß*, Vol. 4, 1, p. 208.

[114] Hegel, *Philosophy of Right*, trans. T. M. Knox (Oxford: Oxford University Press, 1967), p. 10. Hegel, *Reason in History*, p. 29.

[115] Hegel, *Reason in History*, p. 29.

both the State and Church. "Only the Germanic peoples came through Christianity," Hegel observed, "to realize that humans as humans are free and that freedom of spirit is the very essence of human nature," and despite the slaughter bench of history, such freedom represented " . . . [The] final aim is God's purpose with the world. But God is the absolutely perfect being and can, therefore, will nothing but himself, his own will. The nature of his own will, his own nature, is what we call the idea of freedom."[116] By calling the nature of God the idea of freedom, Hegel translated the language of religion into that of philosophy.

Schopenhauer rejected Hegel's philosophy of history categorically, and he denounced Hegel's teleological view of history absolutely. Ever the perennialist, as if it were even possible for a perennialist to change, he included the essay "On History" in the second edition of his principal work, and by doing so helped bury the historicism of Hegel, which was already in the mortuary. His Swabian Protestant nemesis, he charged, should be referred to Plato, who clearly acknowledged that the proper object of philosophy is the unchangeable, the permanent, and the universal. History dealt with what had been, the ephemeral, and the particular – mere clouds in the wind. The fundamental truth of all philosophy is that which is real and is at all times the same. To misuse the Platonic concept of "Ideas," the unchanging, permanent objects of philosophical contemplation, by viewing an Idea as a coming to be through time, was a fundamental misuse of Plato's mighty concept. Hegel had also forgotten that both Plato and Kant had established that time itself was ideal, a mere form governing a world of appearance. "The true philosophy of history should recognize the identical in all events," Schopenhauer theorized; "of ancient and of modern times, of the east as of the west, and should see everywhere the same humanity, in spite of all difference in the special circumstances, in costume and customs."[117] Moreover, to think the world

---

[116] Ibid., pp. 24–5.

[117] Schopenhauer, *The World as Will and Representation*, Vol. 2, p 444/ *Sämtliche Werke*, Vol. 3, p. 507f. In this passage, Schopenhauer articulated a remark that the Swiss historian and colleague of Nietzsche's at the University of Basel, Jacob Burkhardt, paraphrased: namely, that the object of history is "the suffering, striving, and actions of man, as he is and ever was and will be," *Weltgeschichtliche Betractungen* [*Reflections on World History*] (Stuttgart, 1955), p. 5f. Burckhardt's book, a compilation of his Basel lectures from 1868 to 1871, has frequently been cited as the first philosophy of history from a Schopenhauerian perspective; see Herbert Schnädelbach's *Philosophy in Germany 1831–1933*, trans. Eric Matthews (Cambridge: Cambridge University Press, 1984), pp. 59–62.

was some rational whole was itself irrational. Worse, to regard appearance as the being-in-itself of the world is a crude form of realism. And the worst, Schopenhauer argued, is to think that things ultimately work out well in the end. This promotes a shallow form of optimism, made worse by claiming that "things ultimately end in a comfortable, substantial, fat state with a well-regulated constitution, good justice and police, and useful industries." Not only does that show a misunderstanding of the function of the state, but also it betrays all of those who were sacrificed on the slaughter bench of history.[118]

Reviews of *The World as Will and Representation*

Hegel was not Schopenhauer's only philosophical problem in Berlin. During its first two years of life, *The World as Will and Representation* drew five reviews and a critical monograph, none of which provided Schopenhauer with the reception he desired. Indeed, he probably thought that the reviewers followed the advice found in its preface: namely, to review the book without reading it. Yet he could not honestly blame Hegel for the reviews. None of his critics were Hegelians. The first, lengthy, and anonymous review appeared in the *Annuals of Literature* [*Jahrbücher der Litteratur*, April–June 1819]. Its author was the Platonist and fan of Schelling's philosophy of identity Friedrich Ast. Although Ast called the book "a work that is excellent in many respects," and he appreciated Schopenhauer's employment of Platonic Ideas in his philosophy of nature and aesthetics, he could not endorse Schopenhauer's claim that the will was the essence of all, preferring instead to conceive of the world of Ideas as true being and the world of the senses as its imperfect copy.[119]

A second, short review followed in October 1819, in the *Weimar Literary Weekly* [*Litterarisches Wochenblatt*], penned by "a friend of literature," who turned out not to be a friend of Schopenhauer's philosophy. Like Ast, this critic praised the book, calling it "quite excellent and very much worth reading," and like Ast, this critic also sensed the spurs of

---

[118] Ibid., Vol. 2, p. 442f./ibid., Vol. 3, p. 506.

[119] *Jahrbücher der Litteratur*, Vol. 6 (April, May, June 1819), pp. 201–29; reprinted in *Sechstes Jahrbuch der Schopenhauer-Gesellschaft* (1917), pp. 47–81; see p. 47. Schopenhauer misidentified the reviewer as a Dr. Bernhard; see *Manuscript Remains*, Vol. 4, p. 133/*Der handschriftliche Nachlaß*, Vol. 4.1, p. 110.

Schelling in Schopenhauer's thought, but far more deeply.[120] The friend of literature charged that Schelling had already said what Schopenhauer claimed to have said for the very first time, because all of his main ideas were simply Schelling's expressed in different terms. He was baffled by Schopenhauer's harsh and unseemly treatment of Schelling. Although this critic praised Schopenhauer's "masterful" treatment of art, he was not satisfied by his treatment of moral and religious themes in the final book of *The World as Will and Representation*. The final book, he claimed, abounded with "contradictions," leveling for the first time what continues to be a standing objection to Schopenhauer's thought. Although this critic praised Schopenhauer for simplifying and naturalizing philosophy, he contended that the latter was undermined, in part, by his supernatural account of asceticism.[121]

A gymnasium teacher from Zittau, one Johann Gottlieb Rätze, penned a polemic in which he defended the theological status quo, "true morality and religion," as he put it, against what he judged as their contradictions in Schopenhauer's philosophy.[122] Rätze found Schopenhauer's doctrine of the mortification of the will to exemplify the tendency of the age to embrace irrational standpoints and to melt into a vainglorious *Schwärmeri*. "The Gospels are for us the only certain source of the divine wisdom, holiness, and salvation," he declared, "which cannot be derived for a philosophy of the mortification of the will."[123] Yet, despite his firm opposition to the philosopher's ethics and asceticism, the teacher was charitable to the target of his criticisms. Schopenhauer was still a young man, he said, whose sagacity, talents, and knowledge would eventually lead him to better views about the world and its creator. Given time, Pastor Rätze prophesied, he

---

[120] *Litterarisches Wochenblatt*, ed. Wilhelm Hoffmann, Vol. 4, no. 30 (October 1819), pp. 234–6; reprinted in *Sechstes Jahrbuch der Schopenhauer-Gesellschaft* (1917), pp. 81–5; see p. 83 for the quotation.

[121] See ibid., p. 85.

[122] The curious title of Rätze's monograph is *What the Human Will Is Able to Do in Moral and Divine Things through Its Own Power and What It Is Not Able to Do, with Reference to Schopenhauer's Book, The World as Will and Representation* [*Was der Wille des Menschen in moralischen und göttlichen Dingen aus eigener Kraft vermag und was er nicht vermag. Mit Rücksicht auf die Schopenhauerische Schrift: Die Welt als Wille und Vorstellung*] (Leipzig: C. H. F. Hartmann, 1820). I will be quoting from the preface of this work, reprinted in the *Sechstes Jahrbuch der Schopenhauer-Gesellschaft* (1917), pp. 86–9.

[123] Ibid., p. 89.

might even withdraw his harsh judgment of Fichte and some of those leveled against Kant. Rätze, however, was not a prophet.

Rätze's monograph should have drawn Schopenhauer's ire. The gymnasium instructor even had the audacity to mount the same charge against Schopenhauer that he had mounted against Fichte: namely, that Schopenhauer had also become a philosopher due to puzzlement about Kant's philosophy and not from astonishment about the world. Schopenhauer ignored this, and he bore no ill will toward this critic. Even Jean Paul, he observed, who was favorably disposed to his thought, had also been troubled by the seemingly paradoxical nature of the ascetic results of his philosophy. He excused Rätze's reproach of his asceticism, as he did Jean Paul's, by viewing it as symptomatic of the cultural limitations of a Protestant thinker. Among Eastern people, he fancied, the ascetic results of his ethics would have been reproached for being commonplace, and his ethics would have been judged as orthodox by Hindus and Buddhists. But unlike Jean Paul, Rätze had written a book against his philosophy. Why did Schopenhauer treat the unknown teacher as he did the well-known author? Rätze had been moved to write a book against Schopenhauer and had, therefore, taken his thought seriously. He also, of course, flattered Schopenhauer, even in a backhanded way, by noting that the philosopher's talents would ultimately lead him to produce something useful and correct. And so he wrote that as with Jean Paul, the paradoxical consequences of his ethics "also induced Herr Rätze (who did not know that against me only the method of secreting is applicable) to write in 1820 a book against me that was well meant. . . ."[124]

The "method of secreting" was not a strategy to which all academic philosophers subscribed. Three of the reviewers of Schopenhauer's principal work were professional philosophers. Johann Friedrich Herbart, since 1809 the occupant of Kant's chair at Königsberg, who returned in 1833 to replace Schulze at Göttingen, where he had been granted his doctorate in 1802, published a lengthy review in *Hermes*, a journal printed by Schopenhauer's publisher Brockhaus. Friedrich Eduard Beneke, like Schopenhauer a novice *Privatdozent* at Berlin, authored a piece that drew a

---

[124] Schopenhauer, *On the Will in Nature*, p. 143/ *Sämtliche Werke*, Vol. 4, p. 144. His remarks about Jean Paul and the orthodoxy of his views for Hindus and Buddhists also occur in this passage.

bitter reproach by the philosopher. Last, Wilhelm Traugott Krug, Kant's successor and Herbart's predecessor at Königsberg, who would also publish a scathing review of the second edition of Hegel's "game of ideas," his *Encyclopedia of the Philosophical Sciences*, published a less harsh review of Hegel's would-be rival in the *Leipzig Literary Journal* [*Leipzig Litteratur-Zeitung*], of which he was the co-publisher.[125]

The form of Herbart's review followed Schopenhauer's instructions concerning how to approach *The World as Will and Representation*. He briefly considered the "introductions" to this work, Schopenhauer's dissertation and the first chapter of his essay on color theory, "On Vision," and he discussed the appendix, "Critique of the Kantian Philosophy," prior to reflecting on the text's four books. If Schopenhauer was pleased that Herbart followed his instructions, he was not pleased with the review. In all likelihood, he thought of Herbart as just that sort of reader he worried about – one whose philosophical commitments would keep the reader from giving his novel philosophy a fair hearing. Worse, Herbart classified Schopenhauer among a group of philosophers whom the reviewer and the reviewed rejected, each of whom proceed from Kant, who endeavored to improve his insights by their own, and who, by doing so, radically distanced themselves from Kant's main ideas. "Reinhold is the first," Herbart insisted, "Fichte the most thoughtful, and Schelling the most comprehensive, but Schopenhauer is the clearest, most adroit, and most convivial."[126] Yet he did more than merely group Schopenhauer with these philosophers. He meant to trace the genealogy of Schopenhauer's philosophy to that of Fichte and Schelling. Moreover, by doing so he had already dismissed this bastard child of dubious parents. As a student of Fichte in Jena, Herbart had rejected this alleged successor to Kant, and he

---

[125] Schopenhauer gave limited praise to Hegel's philosophical rival at Berlin, Jakob Friedrich Fries, and to Krug for opposing Hegel, but he also blamed both for not carrying their criticisms farther and for degrading Kant's "lofty teachings;" see *Parerga and Paralipomena*, Vol. 1, p. 182; Vol. 2, p. 339/ *Sämtliche Werke*, Vol. 5, p. 194; Vol. 6, p. 360. Although Krug's review did not promote Schopenhauer's philosophy, his death in 1842 helped increase Schopenhauer's library, because it appears that he was able to purchase at auction several books from Krug's personal library; see Schopenhauer, *Gesammelte Briefe*, p. 194, Schopenhauer's letter "*An Einen Auktionskommissarius*," 24 November 1842.

[126] Herbart's *Hermes oder kritisches Jahrbuch der Litteratur*, no. 3, 1820. I will quote from the reprint in *Sechstes Jahrbuch der Schopenhauer-Gesellschafte* (1917), pp. 89–115. This quotation is from p. 90.

would reject the entire development of German idealism. In particular, he repudiated the metaphysical primacy Fichte had given the absolute I and its constitutive acts. Herbart, a realist, instead maintained an empiricist epistemology, and he viewed the I or "soul" as a Humean theater in which autonomous representations interacted. Even worse for Schopenhauer, he had identified himself in the review as an optimist, and he took umbrage at Schopenhauer's reference to optimism as an absurd, wicked way of thought, a bitter mockery of the unspeakable suffering of human kind.

Herbart wrote that his first impression of *The World as Will and Representation*, derived from its title, was that he was about to read the work of a Fichtean, and he noted his astonishment at discovering that its author freely denounced Fichte. Nevertheless, he heard echoes of his old teacher in Schopenhauer's words. The very opening paragraph of the first book, which contained the claim that there was no truth more certain than that the world is only an object for the subject, or a representation, struck him as Fichtean. The same was also true, he thought, of Schopenhauer's claims that every act of will was a bodily movement; that the will and body were identical; that we know ourselves only in willing; and that nature was an organic whole, posited by the I. The differences between the two philosophers, he asserted, were primarily a matter of how they arrived at their views. Schopenhauer tended to leap to his conclusions, whereas Fichte sought his with a diligence worthy of respect, although, at times, his plodding course of thought expressed inconceivable ideas. Herbart noted, moreover, that Schopenhauer exhibited an unfortunate custom of the times by simply claiming immediate knowledge of truths that were incapable of proof, which put them conveniently beyond rational debate. Thus, in a mocking reply to Schopenhauer's claim that we have immediate knowledge of the identity of the will and the body and that this cannot be proven, Herbart asserted the same about their nonidentity. Comparing the older philosopher, Fichte, to the younger, Schopenhauer, it was as if the former were an ancient language and the latter its corrupted and abbreviated contemporary descendant, Herbart averred.

Herbart was willing to concede that Schopenhauer may have thought that he alone developed his views, intimating that he may not have read the work that bore the greatest analogy to Schopenhauer's, the so-called *System of Ethics*, but he was also willing to chide Schopenhauer for allowing himself to forget that the entire form of Fichte's project was determined by the claim that he "sought in objects, which are necessarily posited by the subject, the very conditions for self-consciousness."[127] He knew Fichte personally, Herbart mentioned, and he could not allow it to pass that Schopenhauer denied Fichte the philosophical seriousness that he merited.

Like Ast and the "friend of literature," Herbart also detected parallels between Schelling and Schopenhauer. The same heavy mixture of Platonic, Fichtean, and Spinozistic theory, found in Schelling's philosophy of nature and aesthetics, congealed in Schopenhauer's, but Herbart preferred not to thrust his fingers into such a sticky mélange. He was more interested in poking around in what he saw as a polemic directed against Schelling, which was located in Schopenhauer's "practical philosophy," as Herbart called it, knowing full well that his target went to great lengths to emphasize that all philosophy could only be theoretical. To do this, he quoted a lengthy passage in which Schopenhauer pledged his commitment to a philosophy that remained within the limits that Kant had set for philosophy: that is, to remain within the bounds of all possible experience. Consequently, Schopenhauer promised in this passage not to resort to empty, negative concepts such as "the Absolute," "the Infinite," or "the Supersensible." He would not reach for "cloud-cuckoo-land." Nor would he try to pass off history as philosophy, pretending that the essence of the world could be comprehended historically, which is not the case:

As soon as *becoming*, or *having-become*, or *will-become* enters into the view of the inner nature of the world; whenever an earlier or a later has the least significance; and consequently whenever points of the beginning and of the ending in this world, together with a path between the two, are sought and found, and the philosophizing individual recognizes his own position on this path. Such *historical philosophizing* in most cases furnishes a cosmogony admitting of many varieties, or a system of

---

[127] Herbart, ibid., p. 106. During the spring and summer of 1812, as a student in Berlin, Schopenhauer intensely studied Fichte's *System of Ethics Following the Principles of the Science of Knowledge*. Below the title page of his personal copy, Schopenhauer wrote, as a subtitle, "*System of Moral Fatalism*"; see Schopenhauer, *Der handschriftliche Nachlaß*, Vol. 5, pp. 53–8 for his extensive marginal notes, almost all of which are critical of Fichte. His student notes on Fichte's *System of Ethics* can be found in *Manuscript Remains*, Vol. 2, pp. 399–406/ibid., Vol. 2, pp. 347–52. For a careful examination of the development of Schopenhauer's philosophy from his exposure to Fichte, see Günter Zöller's "Kichtenhauer: Der Ursprung von Schopenhauers *Welt als Wille und Vorstellung* in Fichtes *Wissenschsftslehre 1812* und *System der Sittenlehre*," in *Der Ethik Schopenhauer im Ausgang von Deutschen Idealismus*, ed. Lore Hühn with Philipp Schwab. Würzburg: Ergon, 2006: 365–86.

emanations, a doctrine of diminutions or finally, when driven in despair over the fruitless attempts of those paths to the last path, it furnishes, conversely, a doctrine of a constant becoming, springing up, arising, coming to light out of the darkness, out of the obscure ground, primary ground, groundlessness, or some other drivel of this kind.[128]

Although Herbart was also willing to denounce the standpoint articulated in this passage, he also held that Schopenhauer had expressed drivel of the same kind. He quotes Schopenhauer claiming that the will "is devoid of knowledge, a blind, irresistible urge."[129] An urge is a becoming, Herbart notes, and it is an original unity that objectifies itself in appearances, in numerous individuals, which become the means for the will's self-comprehension, and from which this will ultimately denies itself. Thus Schopenhauer's metaphysics travels from an original not-willing to a willing and finally to a willing nothing. There are a beginning, middle, and an end here, and so Herbart contended that Schopenhauer presented a history as philosophy reminiscent of Schelling's natural history of God.

Herbart had remarked earlier in his review that Schopenhauer had overestimated the significance of Plato and Kant for his philosophy and had underestimated the significance of his contemporaries. This last reference to Schelling, in combination with his earlier remarks to Fichte, allowed Herbart to view Schopenhauer as an epigone of Fichte and Schelling. By tracing this philosophy to its roots in Fichte and Schelling, he also found Schopenhauer's philosophy passé. Yet, Herbart still wished to administer a philosophical *coup de grâce* by claiming that this was a philosophy fraught with contradictions. On a single page, he argued, Schopenhauer claimed that the will is the thing in itself, something that can never be an object of experience, but then claimed that all representations, all appearances are the visibility, the objectification of the will; that the thing in itself is most clearly cognized as the human will.[130] Then Herbart referred to the "great contradiction" that concluded the book, the denial of the will, which signified the appearance of the freedom of will in the strictly determined

---

[128] Herbart, ibid., p. 114. Herbart is quoting *The World as Will and Representation*, Vol. 1, p. 273 /*Sämtliche Werke*, Vol. 2, p. 322; pp. 290–91 in the first edition. I have restored Schopenhauer's emphases, which were absent in Herbart's quotation.

[129] Herbart, ibid., 115, quoting from Schopenhauer, ibid., Vol. 1, p. 275/ibid., Vol. 2, p. 323; p. 393 in the first edition.

[130] See Herbart, ibid., p. 109. Herbart is referring to Schopenhauer, ibid., p. 110/ibid., Vol. 2, p. 131f.; p. 162 of the first edition.

world of appearance. In response to Schopenhauer's own recognition of this "contradiction," and instead of trying to determine the success of the author's attempt to resolve it, Herbart simply remarked, "yes indeed! a contradiction!!!"[131] What held all of the discordant intuitions together, Herbart remarked, was Schopenhauer's fierce personality, and he commended Schopenhauer for his clear, vivid, and lively writing style. It was due, moreover, to Schopenhauer's writing style that he would recommend the book, but only to a small group of readers. "The reviewer, in fact, knows of no book more fitting, written in the spirit of modern philosophy, for enthusiasts of this type of study, who are not able to work through Fichte's and Schelling's obscurity." In the clear mirror of Schopenhauer's philosophy, which unified both thinkers, Herbart continued, you would find "that this most recent, idealistic-Spinozistic philosophy still remains equally false in all of its twists and turns."[132]

Schopenhauer made no public response to Herbart's stinging review. Years later, he told his friend Carl Bähr that he had read the review only once in his entire life and that was when it first appeared.[133] Although this remark may be literally true, if he was referring to the entire review, it is of dubious veracity concerning parts of the review. His notes from that time show that Herbart's charge of contradictions within his metaphysics of will drew his reflection. Schopenhauer most likely said this to Bähr to show his contempt for Herbart, suggesting that anything he had to say was not worth a second thought. Indeed, he never even credited Herbart for having the good sense to oppose Hegel, something he would do for Krug, who also wrote an unfavorable review of Schopenhauer's principal work. Krug, however, did not have the audacity to view him as descending from Fichte and Schelling. It was this remark that must have cut Schopenhauer to the bone, and it must have been this remark that moved him not to totally ignore Herbart in his published writings, as he did Beneke, but to only refer to him derisively. Thus, in his caustic essay "On Philosophy at the Universities," next to the "three sophists," Fichte, Schelling, and Hegel, Herbart is the fourth target of his scorn. He becomes an example of philosophers who have "turned their intellects inside out."[134]

---

[131] Herbart, ibid., p. 113. Herbart quotes here Schopenhauer, ibid., Vol. 1, p. 403/ibid., Vol. 2, p. 477; p. 579 of the first edition.
[132] Herbart, ibid., p. 117.
[133] See Schopenhauer, *Gespräche*, p. 206.
[134] Schopenhauer, *Parerga and Paralipomena*, Vol. 1, p. 176/*Sämtliche Werke*, Vol. 5, p. 188.

Signed simply "F.E.B.," a review appeared in the *Jena General Litera-ture Journal* [*Jenaische Allgemeine Litteratur Zeitung*], in December 1820. Schopenhauer had to have read this review more than once. The reviewer was the twenty-two-year-old Beneke, who had sat in some of his fellow *Privatdozent's* lectures earlier that summer. This review, which also con-sidered Rätze's polemic, inflamed Schopenhauer. Beneke continued with themes already established by the "friend of literature" and Herbart. *The World as Will and Representation* was a joy to read; its author's style bold, lively, and clear, even poetic at times. Like Herbart, however, he could not recommend a philosophy abounding with contradictions. Again, like Herbart, he was troubled by Schopenhauer's claim that will was the thing in itself, something alleged to be beyond the subject/object correlation and beyond all cognition. Yet Schopenhauer had also said that we expe-rience acts of will, an experience that made the will an object for a subject and, as successive acts, something within the *a priori* form of time. And although Beneke frequently sided with Rätze's critique of Schopenhauer, he was also sensitive to the various weaknesses of Rätze's naive theological standpoint, also finding it contradictory. In closing his review, he took Schopenhauer to task for his *ad hominems* directed at his contemporaries. Although he had no sympathy for Fichte, he objected to his colleague's calling him a "windbag." After quoting Schopenhauer's claim that for the last twenty years, Germans had been led by their noses by one windbag today and another tomorrow, and that since the turn of the nineteenth century in Germany, it was as if philosophy were playing a philosophical farce on Kant's grave, Beneke announced that "we hold such language extremely unworthy of a philosopher."[135]

Schopenhauer was so incensed by Beneke's review that he felt com-pelled to respond publically to a critic for the first and only time in his life. He fired off a letter to the editor of the journal, Heinrich Karl Eichstädt, the dean of the philosophy faculty at his *alma mater*, the University of Jena. He demanded that the reviewer, whose identity he had discovered, be reprimanded. He enclosed a document titled "Necessary Censure for False Quotations," and he demanded its unedited publication in the next edition of the *Jena General Literature Journal*. Schopenhauer wrote that

---

[135] Beneke's review, from the *Jenaische Allgemeine Litteratur-Zeitung*, Nos. 226–9 (December 1820), is reprinted in the *Sechstes Jahrbuch der Schopenhauer-Gesellschaft* (1917), pp. 118–49; see p. 149 for this quotation.

he fully expected gentlemen of the philosophical trade to criticize and oppose anyone who is different from them. This he would be willing to accept, because it was almost a law of nature that they would do so. He could not, however, stand silent when a reviewer sought to defame a writer through misrepresentations and slanderous lies. Silence on his part would constitute a tacit admission of guilt. He then detailed ten specimens of distorted and inaccurate quotations from his book. Justice required publication of his rebuke, he told Eichstädt, and he assured the editor, in less than an honest manner, "that I generally take a friendly countenance towards reviewers, as is nature for me," but that Beneke's review was beyond the pale.[136]

Eichstädt responded to Schopenhauer in a reasonable way, telling him that he wanted the reviewers' responses to the accusations, before he would make a decision concerning the philosopher's demand. Schopenhauer sensed that the editor was trying to stall. In some tense and accusatory letters Schopenhauer insinuated that Eichstädt's lack of a prompt decision meant that he sided with Beneke's "forgery" and was, thus, an accessory to this injustice. Finally, Schopenhauer's "censure" appeared that February in the "Announcements" of the journal.[137] Schopenhauer was far from pleased. His work was retitled "Reply to Criticisms: Necessary Censure for False Citation." He had objected to this designation. He had not written an "*Anti-Kritiken*," a reply to criticisms of his philosophy, he had told the compositor of the essay. This was something he would never do. His piece was merely to expose a fraud; designed to show the damnable, slanderous lies embedded in the false and inaccurately quoted materials from his book. Schopenhauer was doubly upset, however. Beneke was allowed to publish, immediately following the censure, his "Reviewer's Reply," in which he blamed the typesetter for printer's errors for five of the inaccurate quotations. The other quotations, he argued, represented the spirit of Schopenhauer's views, even if they were not exact. All that he had done was to argue from a higher standpoint, he claimed, seeking to keep philosophy free from fanciful and dangerous errors. He also addressed the harsh tone of Schopenhauer's censure by saying that its tone spoke

---

[136] Schopenhauer, *Gesammelte Briefe*, p. 63, Schopenhauer to Heinrich Karl Abraham Eichstädt, 6 January 1821.

[137] Schopenhauer's censure appeared in the *Intelligenzblatt der Jenaischen Allgemeinen Litteratur-Zeitung*, no. 10 (February 1821). It, along with Beneke's "Reviewer's Reply," is reprinted in the *Seschstes Jahrbuch der Schopenhauer-Gesellschaft* (1917), pp. 149–58.

for itself. Beneke was embarrassed that this spat became public, and he apologized to his readers for their having to witness this exchange. He tried to settle the problem by talking personally to Schopenhauer, but Schopenhauer refused to meet. Years later, Schopenhauer told Frauenstädt that Beneke had tried to visit him twice, and with the second visit, he told his maid to tell the young man that he was at home, but would not speak to him. He enjoyed the fact that his maid told him that upon hearing this, "the poor young man turned completely pale."[138]

Schopenhauer believed that Beneke, who had completed his qualifying exams shortly before the review, wanted to call attention to himself by undermining a rival. Beneke, however, was more successful at drawing students than Schopenhauer, who had sabotaged his own lectures by scheduling them at the same time as Hegel's. Even though Beneke, like Herbart, was an opponent of Hegel, and could have been an ally, Schopenhauer viewed him as a naïve empiricist, someone *a priori* dumb. When Beneke was summarily dismissed from the university, because his *Groundwork for the Physics of Morals* [*Grundlegung zur physik der Sitten*, 1822] attempted to found ethics on science, a move that displeased a number of Hegelians and left him branded an Epicurean, Schopenhauer simply remarked that "Beneke was disqualified because of expressing a de Wettian moral philosophy or some other nonsense; the young man made his career impetuously."[139] Beneke's bad luck continued when he was also kept from lecturing at Jena and at Göttingen until 1827. After Hegel's death, he obtained a professorship in 1832 at Berlin, where he managed to forge a successful academic career. The last few years of his life were difficult due to various illnesses. In 1854, he was found floating in a Berlin canal, most likely a suicide. Schopenhauer had kept a watchful eye on his young critic, and had a friend send him his obituary. Schopenhauer's ability to hold a grudge was elephantine. He told his friend Frauenstädt that he had always been interested in the life of this "sinner," who wished to imitate the Pre-Socratic philosopher Empedocles, who was said to have killed himself by leaping into the crater at Etna. Instead of sympathy for a man who may have died as Schopenhauer's father had died, he simply

---

[138] Schopenhauer, *Gesammelte Briefe*, p. 336, Schopenhauer to Frauenstädt, 26 March 1854. Schopenhauer also mentions Beneke's intent to undermine him.

[139] Ibid., p. 84, Schopenhauer to Karl Friedrich Osann, 20 April 1822. Wilhelm Martin Leberecht de Witte, a professor of theology, was dismissed from Berlin in September 1819 for writing a sympathetic letter to the mother of Kotzebue's assassin.

remarked that he believed that the number of suicides in Berlin was due to its being "physically and morally a cursed hole."[140]

Krug's review appeared on 24 January 1821, in the *Leipzig Literature Journal* [*Leipzig Litteratur-Zeitung*], but Krug's review did not jar Schopenhauer into making some noteworthy response. Of course, the reviewer did not complain about Schopenhauer's philosophy being rifled by contradictions, and he had the good grace not to view the philosopher as a mere epigone of Fichte and Schelling – although he did charge that Kant would have had the same objection to Fichte's doctrine of the "I" and Schopenhauer's doctrine of the "will," because both tried to theorize about an absolute, about the thing in itself. To be sure, Krug attempted to score a number of philosophical points against the philosopher of will. He found his identification of acts of will with bodily actions to be psychologically confused, and he rejected Schopenhauer's reduction of all forces to will, preferring, instead, to view the human will as exhibiting a pure spontaneity, one that supported Kant's nonnatural account of freedom as an alternative type of causality and one subject only to the moral law and exempt from natural necessity. Even more deeply, Krug, like Rätze, was upset by the religious implications of Schopenhauer's worldview. He would have been inclined to accept the mysticism in which the philosopher's work culminated, had it a religious character, and he would have given credence to the philosopher's doctrine of the denial of the will, had this been the denial of the human will to serve God's will. Ultimately, Krug was disappointed by the book. When he read that it was the articulation of a single thought, whose content was what had been sought for a very long time under the name of philosophy, he thought that Schopenhauer would show that "the world is a divine will and divine representation . . . that, therefore, it appears also in the human will and representation, with which it will be practically the same as what it is already ideally."[141] Instead, he discovered that Schopenhauer not only de-deified but demonized reality, finding the world to be the constant striving of an ungodly, demonic will and one that is best denied. At least, Schopenhauer might have thought, Krug's disappointment was not like Herbart's. He did not anticipate that

---

[140] Ibid., p. 338, Schopenhauer to Frauenstädt, 9 April 1854.

[141] Krug's review, which appeared in the *Leipziger Litteratur-Zeitung*, No. 21 (24 January 1821). It is reprinted in the *Sechstes Jahrbuch der Schopenhauer-Gesellschaft* (1917), pp. 158–75. The quotation is from p. 160 from the reprint.

he would be reading a Fichtean. Moreover, unlike Beneke, he did not attribute false quotations to discredit the subject of his review.

Then, almost four years after Krug's review, an ambivalent notice – really no more than a reader's general impression of *The World as Will and Representation* – appeared in 1825. As Schopenhauer wrote in English, its author was "our highly celebrated humoristic writer Jean Paul."[142] The wily Paul had included Schopenhauer's book among a number of works that had failed to garner the general applause that Paul thought they deserved. Schopenhauer cited Paul's note to convince a potential publisher of his translations of Kant that he was the author of a philosophy that would, one day, receive the recognition it merited. He even translated the beginning of the note, in which Paul called his book "a work of philosophical genius, bold, universal, full of penetrating profoundness." But had Schopenhauer continued the quotation, Paul's ambivalence would have appeared. Immediately after Schopenhauer's quotation, the note continues: " . . . but with an often desolate and bottomless depth – comparable to a melancholy lake in Norway, on which, because of its dark, encircling wall of steep cliffs, one never sees the sun, but – in its depth, only the bright, daytime sky, and over which no bird or wave moves. Fortunately, I can only praise the book, not subscribe to it."[143]

Curiously, all of Schopenhauer's reviewers had also mirrored Jean Paul's judgment about his book. They found his thoughts clearly and beautifully expressed, but not worth endorsing. So why did he cherish Paul's remarks? An acquaintance of the philosopher, Robert von Hornstein, observed that "as unjust, hard, indeed almost fierce, could the animosity about his literary fate make him, just as grateful, indeed childishly grateful, could an inoffensive word of recognition from the early years incline him. He was sentimentally devoted to Jean Paul for his entire life, because of a few words he wrote about him."[144] Hornstein, however, ignores two significant differences between the observations of

---

[142] Schopenhauer, *Gesammelte Briefe*, p. 119, Schopenhauer to the author of Damiron's *Analysis*, 21 December 1829.

[143] Jean Paul (Johann Paul Friedrich Richter), "Short Book Reviews, Collected Prefaces and Reviews, Including a Little Secondary School," supplement to *Elementary School for Aesthetics*, Vol. 2 (*Vorschule der Ästhetik*, Breslau: Josef Max und Komp, 1825), pp. 197–204: reprinted in *Sechstes Jahrbuch der Schopenhauer-Gesellschaft* (1917), pp. 175–8. The quotations are from p. 178 of the reprint.

[144] Schopenhauer, *Gespräche*, p. 219.

the "humoristic writer" and those of reviewers. Paul had praised *The World as Will and Representation* as a work of philosophical genius and he did not attempt to articulate reasons for his not subscribing to Schopenhauer's views. The reviewers did not recognize the book as the product of genius, and they attempted to demonstrate why they could not endorse his theories. Besides, the reviewers were also academics, and among the "gentlemen of the trade," as Schopenhauer derisively referred to them, and their comments carried weight with the philosophy community and Jean Paul's did not. Schopenhauer's good will toward Jean Paul even moved him to supply an excusable reason for his failure to endorse his book. He viewed Paul's remark about no bird or wave moving over the melancholy lake of Schopenhauer's philosophy as a metaphorical reference to the culmination of his philosophy into an immovable Fohism and Quietism.[145] With this reference to "Fohism" [*Fohismus*], Schopenhauer took it that Paul was troubled by the ascetic results of his philosophy, and he ascribed it to Paul's limited, European perspective.[146]

Philosophical Reactions

The reviews of and responses to *The World as Will and Representation* prompted Schopenhauer to rethink his metaphysics of will and his philosophical heritage. He never, however, viewed this rethinking as a redoing of his original views. Thus, when he was finally able to convince Brockhaus to publish a second edition of his principal work, he asserted that during the twenty-five years between editions, "I find nothing to retract; my fundamental convictions have been confirmed, at any rate as far as I myself am concerned."[147] This would be his attitude toward his subsequent forty-one years of philosophy. He never changed his mind about his "fundamental convictions." All of his later writings served simply to clarify, augment, confirm, and extend his original insights into new

---

[145] See Jean Paul, reprint *Sechstes Jahrbuch der Schopenhauer-Gesellschaft* (1917), p. 178n. The reference to "Fohism [*Fohismus*]," is a reference to Chinese Buddhism. "Fo" is Chinese for the Buddha.

[146] See Schopenhauer, *On the Will in Nature*, p. 143/*Sämtliche Werke*, Vol. 4, p. 144, where he excuses Jean Paul for his inability to come to terms with the ascetic results of his philosophy.

[147] Schopenhauer, *The World as Will and Representation*, Vol. 1, p. xxi / *Sämtliche Werke*, Vol. 2, p. xxi.

areas of inquiry. Indeed, he took considerable pride in his fidelity to his initial doctrines, viewing it as signifying his genius and philosophical seriousness. This was unlike Schelling, he argued, whose Protean philosophy took on a chameleon-like form through its various phases of development. In the case of Schelling, this lack of a sustained core showed him to be a philosophical dabbler, a sampler of current and changing ideas, a man swept along with changing philosophical fashions. Schopenhauer viewed his philosophy as standing rock-firm. The truth does not change.

Schopenhauer parried Herbart's and Beneke's cries of contradiction not by engaging in some dazzling Hegelian dialectic, hoping to resolve contradictory tensions into some grander synthesis, but by seizing upon elements of his presentation of his metaphysics of will, where he had already tempered the bold claim that will is the thing in itself. Still, it took him more than a year to come to terms with his critics' complaint, and he would only publish his reply in 1844, with the second edition of *The World as Will and Representation*. A remark from 1851, made within the context of a reflection on his philosophy, likely signifies his reaction to the critics' charge of contradiction. After bragging about the simplicity of his philosophical system and the harmony and agreement of its fundamental ideas, he dropped a curious remark. "I was never concerned about the harmony and agreement of my propositions," he reflected, "not even when some of them seemed to me to be inconsistent, as was occasionally the case for a time."[148] This observation, so characteristically Schopenhauerian, evinces the confidence he had in himself and the fate of his philosophy, a confidence that sustained him through the decades during which his work was ignored. It is also characteristically Schopenhauerian in another sense. He did not say when or about which propositions he had such doubts. Publically exposing potential areas of weakness or vulnerability was never Schopenhauer's style. To do so would enable others to exploit them for their own advantage.

Schopenhauer's notebooks, however, show his concern about the charge of inconsistency. Referring to the very same passage cited by Herbart to demonstrate the contradictions found in his metaphysics of will, he asserts that "the *will*, as we cognize it in ourselves, is not the *thing in itself*, because it only becomes apparent in individual and successive acts of will; these have *time* as their form and therefore are already

---

[148] Schopenhauer, *Parerga and Paralipomena*, Vol. 1, p. 130/*Sämtliche Werke*, Vol. 5, p. 140.

appearance."[149] Acts of will constitute an immediate transition of the thing in itself into appearance, he continues: one that emerges from the depths of our inner nature and into cognition. Thus the word "will" is used as a stand-in for the thing in itself, a naming after its most distinct appearance. Repeating almost verbatim what he had stated in his principal work, calling the thing in itself "will" is only "a *denomination a portiori*, i.e., ... we describe the thing in itself according to what it looks like in the lightest of all husks, and with a name it borrows from that which is by far the most distinct of its appearances." "Had we had the same access to other appearances as we have to our will," he hypothesizes, "*they would present themselves just as the will does in ourselves.*" By recognizing that acts of will are objects for a subject and are temporal, and by calling will the thing in itself, he asserts that he had only modified Kant's claim that the thing in itself was unknowable, by holding that it was not absolutely and entirely unknowable. One might ask what the thing in itself is beyond its presenting itself as will, he notes, but this is a question that could never be answered. Still, the existence of the question itself tells us that this thing in itself, which we call will, might possess properties, characteristics, and modes of existence distinct from those found in any and all of its appearances. These would be absolutely unknowable and inconceivable for us, but they would be those that remained after will was nullified. Schopenhauer assured himself of this possibility by reminding himself that he had recognized that the denial of the will did not imply a transition into some total, absolute nothingness; rather, this was a state of relative nothing, a denial of the will, the world, and all representations.[150]

---

[149] Schopenhauer, *Manuscript Remains*, Vol. 3, p. 40/*Der handschriftliche Nachlaß*, Vol. 3, p. 36; also see Vol. 3, pp. 103, 104/Vol. 3, pp. 103, 179. In his Berlin lectures, from the same time, he asserted that "the will, as far as we discover and perceive it in ourselves, is not actually the *thing in itself*. For this will enters consciousness in individual and successive acts of will; thus, these already have the form of time and therefore are already appearance." Schopenhauer, *Metaphysik der Natur: Philosophische Vorlesungen aus dem handschriftlichen Nachlaß, Teil II*, edited with an introduction by Volker Spierling (Munich: Piper, 1984), p. 101f.; also see Chaps. 28 and 41 from the second volume of *The World as Will and Representation*, "On the Possibility of Knowing the Thing-In-Itself," and "On Death and Its Relationship to the Indestructibility of Our Inner Nature," for the distinction between the will as the essence of all appearances and the thing in itself as something other than will.

[150] In response to the claim that Schopenhauer had modified his original equation of the will with the thing in itself, due to objections like Herbart's and Beneke, Arthur Hübscher has noted that "we are not able to adequately perceive the will as the thing in itself, but can do so only in its own acts and hence temporally and phenomenally; but this could be inferred

Schopenhauer also set out to establish his philosophical pedigree by claiming a line of descent that recognized a common ancestor with Fichte and Schelling and one that would account for any vague family resemblances between his and their philosophies. Provoked by the claim that the fundamental idea of his philosophy could already be found in Schelling's claim that "willing is the original and primary being," he noted that his philosophy was rooted in Kant's, and "therefore we need not wonder if the philosophemes of Fichte and Schelling, which also start from Kant, show traces of the same fundamental idea, although they appear there without sequence, continuity, or development, and accordingly may be regarded as a mere foreshadowing of my doctrine."[151] Moreover, he continued, before any great truth had been discovered, there had been vague presentations, a sensing of it as if it were a figure enveloped by fog, but its true discoverer was the person who clearly justified and articulated it, recognizing its true value and significance. We credit Columbus with discovering America and not the first shipwrecked sailor simply cast upon the shore by pounding waves, he analogized, suggesting that he should be recognized as the Columbus of his fundamental idea and that Fichte and

---

already from the first volume [the first edition of *The World as Will and Representation*]," *Manuscript Remains*, Vol. 3, p. xviii/*Der handschriftliche Nachlaß*, Vol. 3, p. xviii. Ruldolf Malter provides a useful gloss of the secondary literature, prior to 1990, concerning the tensions between Schopenhauer's assertions that the will is the thing in itself and that the thing in itself appears veiled in the will; see *Arthur Schopenhauer: Transzendental Philosophie und Metaphysik des Willens*, p. 235n. In "Two Senses of 'Thing-in-Itself' in Schopenhauer's Philosophy," *Idealistic Studies*, Vol. 31 (2001), pp. 31–53, I discuss the standard view of Schopenhauer's metaphysics, as well as the critics of this view. I argue that it is best to view the claim that will is the thing in itself in a relative sense; that is, compared to other appearances, as the least conditioned experience, it is the thing in itself. I also argue that Schopenhauer employed a second sense of "thing in itself," an absolute sense, in which the thing in itself is something beyond the subject and object distinction and all *a priori* forms of cognition, a conception of the thing in itself that allows for the validity of mysticism. Although Schopenhauer's view of the will as the essence of all appearances and as the thing in itself under the "lightest of veils" was already found in the first edition of Schopenhauer's principal work, all of his works contain what appears to be the problematic claims that straightforwardly equated the will and the thing in itself, claims that provoked, and continue to provoke, criticisms like those of Herbart and Beneke; see Hübscher's *The Philosophy of Schopenhauer in Its Intellectual Context*, p. 383. A critical review of Schopenhauer's major Anglophone commentators on this issue is found in Nicoletta De Cian and Marco Segala, "What Is Will?" pp. 13–41. Thomas Dürr's "Schopenhauers Grundlegung der Willensmetaphysik," *Schopenhauer-Jahrbuch*, Vol. 84, (2003), pp. 91–119, contains a discussion and critique of the more recent literature on this issue.

151 Schopenhauer, *Parerga and Paralipomena*, Vol. 1, p. 132/*Sämtliche Werke*, Vol. 5, p. 142.

Schelling were the castaways. As for Schelling's observation prefiguring his own, the same recognition of the primacy of the will could already be found in Clement of Alexandria and Spinoza.[152]

Besides claiming his birthright as Kant's legitimate philosophical heir and distancing himself from those whom he considered mere bastards, Schopenhauer wanted to claim a particular descent from Kant that would show that his Kantian roots were founded on the very distinction rejected by Fichte, Schelling, and Hegel, namely, that between appearances and the thing in itself. Schopenhauer held that the relationship between the ideal and real, that is, between how things appear to us and how they are in themselves, was "the axis on which the whole of modern philosophy turns."[153] He honored Descartes for raising this problem to philosophical consciousness, but by following the lead of Kant, he rejected the speculative metaphysics of the continental rationalists, Descartes, Spinoza, and Leibniz, and their claim that we could have substantive *a priori* knowledge of the world. John Locke, he claimed, had rightly insisted on investigating the origin of concepts and had properly rejected pure reason as the source of knowledge by rejecting the notion of innate ideas. Locke's insistence that experience is the source of all concepts made Locke the progenitor of his own philosophical method: "We must regard Locke as the originator of this method of consideration: Kant brought it to an incomparably higher perfection, and our first book [the first volume of the second edition of

---

[152] See ibid., Vol. 1, p. 133/ibid., Vol. 5, p. 143. He refers to Titus Flavious Clemens Alexandrinus' remark, "therefore willing precedes everything; for the forces of reason are the handmaidens of willing," from *Opera quae exstant* (Würzburg: ex officing off. Staheliana, 1779), Vol. 2, p. 304; and Spinoza's *Ethics*, PT. III, prop. 57, demonstr. and PT. III, prop. 9, schol., which are, respectively, "Cupidity is precisely that which constitutes everyone's nature or true essence," and "This impulse is called will when it is referred to the mind alone; it is called appetite when it is referred simultaneously to mind and body; and it is nothing but man's *real essence*."

[153] Ibid., Vol. 1, p. 133/ibid., Vol. 5, p. 143. Here Schopenhauer credits Descartes not simply with setting reason on its own two feet by rejecting authority as the source of knowledge, but also with introducing the problem of the relationship between the ideal and real into modern philosophy. What Schopenhauer had in mind was Descartes' dreaming argument from the first of his *Meditations on First Philosophy*, in which he argued that all of our experiences of an external world could simply be a dream. In the second edition of his principal work, Schopenhauer added that his own truth, that the world is my representation, could already be found in the skeptical reflections of Descartes (in the first edition he had only credited it to Berkeley); see *The World as Will and Representation*, Vol. 1, p. 3/*Sämtliche Werke*, Vol. 2, p. 4.

The World as Will and Representation] together with its supplements [the second volume], is devoted to this method."[154]

Schopenhauer viewed Kant as producing an incomparably higher perfection of this method by turning Locke's view into a transcendental perspective. It is not surprising that the very passage from Kant's *Prolegomena to Any Future Metaphysics* that he had offered as a sample of his skills in translating Kant into English likely served as the basis for this claim. Within this passage Kant was defending himself against the charge of idealism, which he characterized as "the assertion that there are none but thinking beings, all others that we think are perceived in intuition being nothing but the representations in the thinking being to which no object external to them in fact corresponds."[155] Kant continued to argue that as little as a person who denies that colors are properties of an object, but are only modifications of the sense of sight cannot be called an idealist – and here he references the realist Locke – "so little can my thesis be named idealistic merely because I find that none, nay, *all the properties which constitute the intuition of a body belong merely to its appearance.*" Kant then claimed that all he had done was to make properties such as extension, place, shape, and impenetrability belong to the appearance of things and not the object itself. He concluded that this is not idealism, because he did not deny the existence of objects external to the perceiver; rather, he simply denied that we could perceive these objects. These objects, he also said, produce ideas in us.

Locke had argued in *An Essay Concerning Human Understanding* (1689) a realist view.[156] He held that we only experience ideas. Sensory ideas are those of external things and were caused by material objects, which possessed only primary qualities, properties such as solidity, extension,

---

154 Ibid., Vol. 2, p. 272/ibid., Vol. 3, p. 307.

155 Kant, *Prolegomena to Any Future Metaphysics*, trans. Lewis White Beck (Indianapolis: Bobbs-Merrill, 1950), p. 36, AK 288–9. Schopenhauer's translation of the same passage is, "Idealism consists in maintaining that there exist no other but thinking beings and that all things besides, which we deem to perceive [*Anschauungen*] are merely ideas [*Vorstellungen*] of those thinking beings without any really outward object corresponding to them," *Gesammelte Briefe*, p. 122. It is worth noting that Schopenhauer translated "*Vorstellungen*" as "ideas," and that he was following the tradition, but, of course, in the reverse, of rendering Locke's "ideas" by the German "*Vorstellungen*." Subsequent quotations from the *Prolegomena* follow Beck's translation.

156 Hübscher dates Schopenhauer's studies of Locke's *Essay* to the summer 1812 and January 1816; see Schopenhauer, *Manuscript Remains*, Vol. 2, pp. 244/*Der handschriftliche Nachlaß*, Vol. 2, pp. 381–3. Schopenhauer made no significant references to Locke in the first edition of *The World as Will and Representation*.

figure, and mobility. Our sensory ideas of these qualities resembled these qualities themselves, but our experiences of so-called secondary qualities, color, odor, sound, smell, and temperature, were simply features of our ideas of things, supervening on the primary qualities of objects. Thus, for Locke, ideas of secondary qualities did not resemble properties of objects. Schopenhauer read Kant as if he retained a Lockean framework by reducing Locke's primary qualities to *a priori* forms of cognition and thereby rendering them like secondary qualities, properties that do not resemble features of the external object. In this way, he claimed Locke's distinction between primary and secondary qualities was "the origin of the distinction between thing in itself and appearance, which later on in the Kantian philosophy becomes so very important."[157] Yet this move, Schopenhauer argued, had catastrophic implications. Kant had "deprived the real or thing in itself of materiality, but for him it also remained a wholly unknown X."[158] Although Kant could escape the charge of idealism by holding that objects exist independent from our perceptions and by claiming that nothing in our ideas resembles them, he also committed the blunder alleged by Jacobi and Aenesidemus Schulze; namely, he had illicitly employed the concept of cause by viewing things in themselves as causes of our ideas of external objects. By following Kant and avoiding this "Achilles heel" of his philosophy, by denying any causal relationship between will and representation, and by maintaining the distinction between appearance and the thing in itself, Schopenhauer held that "Locke, Kant, and I are closely connected, since in the interval of almost two hundred years we present the gradual development of a coherently consistent train of thought."[159]

By establishing his philosophical pedigree on a Lockean ancestry as mediated through Kant, and by retaining the distinction between appearances and things in themselves, Schopenhauer saw himself as avoiding the metaphysical fantasies exemplified in Fichte's subjective idealism,

---

[157] Schopenhauer, *Parerga and Paralipomena*, Vol. 1, p. 17/*Sämtliche Werke*, Vol. 5, p. 17; also see *Manuscript Remains*, Vol. 3, p. 186f./*Der handschriftliche Nachlaß*, Vol. 3, p. 75 (Munich, June 1823), where he had first developed his analysis of Kant and Locke. He also chides Schelling's philosophy of identity, which equates the real and the ideal, for mistakenly claiming to follow Kant.

[158] Ibid., Vol. 1, p. 87/ibid., Vol. 5, p. 93.

[159] Ibid. l, Vol. 1, p. 87f./ibid., Vol. 5, p. 93. To help establish that Locke was truly a *summus philosophus*, Schopenhauer remarked that it was to Locke's credit that "Fichte calls him the worst of all philosophers," *On the Basis of Morality*, p. 22/*Sämtliche Werke*, p. xxvii. For a general discussion of Schopenhauer's Lockean reading of Kant, see my "Locke as Schopenhauer's (Kantian) Philosophical Ancestor."

Schelling's philosophy of identity, and Hegel's absolute idealism. By conceiving the will as the essence of all appearances, he thought that he had given content to the Lockean material object that Kant had stripped of all qualities: "Thing in itself expresses that which exists independently of perception through any of our senses, and so that which really and truly is. For Democritus this was formed matter, it was the same for Locke, for Kant it was an X; for me it is *will*."[160] This insight, he had argued in his principal work, can never be gained through our consciousness of external things, because sensation can never reveal more than what Locke attributed to ideas of sensation. And, although Locke had recognized both sensation and reflection as the sources of all our ideas, Schopenhauer exploited reflection as the means for discovering the key to solving the puzzle of the real and the ideal, "by availing ourselves of the *self-consciousness* of the subject of cognition, and by making it the exponent of the *consciousness of other* things, i.e., of the intuitively perceiving intellect. This is the path taken by me as the only correct one, the narrow portal to truth."[161] Through cognition of acts of will, and by his cosmic analogy attributing the will to all other appearances, will becomes the inner content, the essence of all appearances. And whereas metaphysical inquiry in the first edition of Schopenhauer's principal work was driven to find the thing in itself and that which lay behind all appearances; in its second edition, he provided more explicitly the aim of his metaphysics. "Metaphysics," Schopenhauer wrote, "is the correct explanation of experiences as a whole."[162] Experience itself is like a cryptographer, and he saw as the task of philosophy its deciphering, a task completed by providing a comprehensive account of the totality of all experiences. By limiting himself to accounting for experience, Schopenhauer reconfirmed his commitment to a fully immanent philosophy, one he found in Locke and Kant. The three sophists, on the contrary, merely played fast and loose with the absolute,

---

[160] Schopenhauer, *Parerga and Paralipomena*, Vol. 2, p. 90/*Sämtliche Werke*, Vol. 6, p. 96.

[161] Ibid., Vol. 1, p. 94/ibid., Vol. 5, p. 100.

[162] Schopenhauer, *The World as Will and Representation*, Vol. 2, p. 182/*Sämtliche Werke*, Vol. 3, p. 203. D. W. Hamlyn has referred to Schopenhauer's metaphysics as providing an "argument to the best explanation;" that is, Schopenhauer thought that his philosophy presented the best possible explanation of experience as a whole, "Why Are There Phenomena?" In *Zeit der Ernte: Studien zum Stand der Schopenhauer-Forschung, Festschrift für Arthur Hübscher zum 85. Gerburtstag*, ed. Wolfgang Schirmacher (Stuttgart/Bad Cannstadt: Fromann/Holzboog), 1982, p. 343.

inventing new cognitive powers, analogous to the sixth sense of a bat, to mouth nonsense. In this regard, Schopenhauer saw himself remaining faithful to a pledge he made in 1815: "*My philosophy* will never in the least go beyond the realm of experience that is to say of the perceptible in the fullest range of the concept. For, like every art, it will merely repeat the world."[163]

[163] Schopenhauer, *Manuscript Remains*, Vol. 1, p. 281 / *Der handschriftliche Nachlaß*, Vol. 1, p. 256.

9

Ich Bin Kein Berliner

S CHOPENHAUER'S EARLY YEARS in Berlin were punctuated by periods of discontentment and despair, and his unhappiness moved him to struggle with feelings of self-abandonment. In a revealing reflection recorded in his secret diary, the philosopher set out to steel his nerve and to return to himself:

When at times I felt unhappy, this was by virtue of a misunderstanding, of a flaw in my person. I then took myself to be other than I was and then lamented that other person's misery and distress, e.g., for a *Privatdozent* who does not become a professor and has no one to hear his lectures; or for the one of whom the philistines speak ill and the gossips spread stories; or for the defendant in an assault case; or for the lover who will not be heard by the girl with whom he is infatuated; or for the patient who is kept at home by illness; or to be other similar people who are affected by like miseries. I have not been any of these. All of this is strange cloth from which at most the coat had been made that I wore for a while and that I then discarded in exchange for another. But then who am I? The man who has written the *World as Will and Representation* and has provided a solution to the great problem of existence that perhaps will render obsolete all previous solutions, but which in any case will engage thinkers in the centuries to come. I am that man, and what could disturb him in the few years in which he has still to draw breath?[1]

The philosopher, however, would be continuously disturbed, and he would constantly attempt to restore equilibrium by standing on his philosophy, which in later years provided a firm foundation. At this point it appeared to him that he was losing the only thing he had – himself. Sometimes it even seemed to the struggling *Privatdozent* that this would not be a bad thing.

[1] Schopenhauer, *Manuscript Remains, Vol. 4, p. 488/Der handschriftliche Nachlaß* Vol. 4,2 p. 109. Hübscher dates this note from about 1822–3.

Schopenhauer's litany of Berlin despair contained two references to women, one direct and the other oblique. Curiously, both women were named Caroline, and both would continue to disturb the man who thought he had solved the riddle of existence. Indeed, one could conjecture that along with his mother, these women helped lead him to his misogynistic solution to his problem with women. The "girl [Mädchen]" who would not heed her lover was Caroline Richter, later called "Medon." She was between twenty and twenty-one when Schopenhauer recorded his therapeutic note. He would have an intermittent love affair with her for a decade. The second Caroline was Schopenhauer's neighbor, the forty-seven-year-old seamstress Caroline Marquet. Like the first Caroline, she also did not heed the philosopher. But unlike Medon, who might have become Schopenhauer's wife, Marquet did ultimately receive the philosopher's financial support for twenty years – 60 *Taler* per year, 15 *Taler* each quarter. Medon would fare even better. Never having forgotten her, the philosopher left her 5,000 *Taler* in his will. Medon was the object of Schopenhauer's *amor*, which he claimed "is rooted in sexual impulse alone."[2] Marquet was the object of his disdain, which, he also claimed, was rooted in the will alone.

The seventeen-year-old Richter arrived at Berlin in 1819, where she appeared as a dancer and "chorus girl" at the Berlin Opera. In May 1820, she gave birth to her first son, Johann Wilhelm Adolf, the likely offspring of the privy secretary Louis Medon. Later, she would use his name and claim to be his widow. It is not known exactly when Schopenhauer met her, but it was sometime in 1821. "Ida," or "Little Princess," as he affectionately called her, was a lively, dark-haired young woman. Later, Schopenhauer would theorize that light-haired, blue-eyed people were attracted almost instinctively to brunettes, but seldom the latter to the former, and that men were naturally drawn to women between the ages of eighteen and twenty-eight and women to men between the ages of thirty and thirty-five, ages that represented to him the acme of the procreative powers of the sexes. The dark-haired, brown-eyed Medon was nineteen and the light-haired, blue-eyed Schopenhauer was thirty-three when they met.[3] Medon, who practiced the more liberal sexual mores of those of her

---

[2] Schopenhauer, *The World as Will and Representation*, Vol. 2, p. 533/*Sämtliche Werke*, Vol. 3, p. 610.

[3] In *The World as Will and Representation*, Vol. 2, p. 547/*Sämtliche Werke*, Vol. 3, p. 627, Schopenhauer attributed the sexual attraction of blondes to brunettes as representing nature's

craft, driven by both financial necessity and adventure, had more men in her life than the philosopher. Ten months after Schopenhauer embarked on his second trip to Italy, his beloved gave birth to her second son, Carl Ludwig Gustav Medon, whose father was described simply as a "foreign diplomat."[4] Medon's second son would help drive a wedge between the philosopher and the chorus girl. When Schopenhauer fled Berlin's cholera epidemic in 1831, he wanted Medon to flee with him, but without her son Carl. Medon declined to yield to Schopenhauer's will. Later, when Schopenhauer generously remembered Medon in his will, his ill will toward Carl continued. He stipulated that none of the 5,000 *Taler* she received should find its way to Carl.

Schopenhauer was very fond of Medon, as he confided to his "French brother" Anthime, and he contemplated marriage during his Berlin years. As is evident from his notebooks and his private diary entries of that time, he went to Berlin to immerse himself in practical life, part and parcel of which would customarily involve establishing a family, something for which Adele lobbied. Marriage and a family had the potential of expanding her brother's heart and curing his loneliness, which she believed was reaching unhealthy proportions. But as he thought of his relationship to Medon and his own sexual appetites, he contemplated an unconventional form of marriage. Tetragamy, he thought, was naturally superior to monogamy. The latter was an unnatural relationship, given the sexual drives of men and women, drives that followed the genius of the species, which was always aimed at the reproduction of the next generation. Given that women's attractiveness to men was coextensive with their capacity to reproduce, and given that the duration of their capacity to bear children was half that of men, monogamy was an unwholesome relationship for both sexes, especially because women were compensated for their relatively short reproductive life with a greater sexual capacity than men. Monogamy served neither men nor women, he argued. The man is tied to a woman who becomes old and no longer sexually attractive.

---

drive to return to the original human archetype, which was dark skin, hair, and eyes. Blonde hair, blue eyes, and white skin, he thought, were not natural to humans, constituting an abnormality analogous to that of white mice (also see *Parerga and Paralipomena*, Vol. 2, pp. 156–60/*Sämtliche Werke*, Vol. 6, pp. 166–70). For his remarks concerning the ages of procreative power see ibid., Vol. 2, pp. 542–4/ibid., Vol. 3, pp. 166–70.

[4] In 1826 Medon became pregnant for a third time, but this pregnancy did not lead to a live birth; see *Sämtliche Werke*, Vol. 1, p. 96.

He then pursues other women. Early in the marriage the woman seeks other men, because "in monogamy she uses only half her capacity and gratifies only half her desires."[5] Monogamy requires a woman to restrict herself to one man throughout her brief period of bloom and physical fitness, preserving and holding for one man what he cannot use and what others desire from her, and this denial requires the woman to lead a miserable life. But the sex drive is the strongest expression of the will to life, he theorized, and young women are frequently unfaithful to their husbands; thus they are deceivers. But as they age, they are the deceived, for their husbands seek other women. The man is a cuckold for the first part of the marriage, a whoremonger for the second part, Schopenhauer observed.

Tetragamy adjusted marriage into an institution that would make life better for men and women, Schopenhauer theorized, because it accommodated the natural sexual and reproductive capacities of humans in ways in which monogamy did not. It also addressed the material and financial needs of all parties in a more rational way. Two young men should marry a young woman, and when she outgrew her reproductive ability, and thereby lost her attractiveness to her husbands, the two men should marry another young woman who would "last until the two young men were old."The financial advantage of this type of marriage would be considerable, Schopenhauer thought. At first, when the two young men's incomes were low, they would only have to support one woman and her small children. Later, when their wealth increased, they would have the means to support two women and many children.

The philosopher anticipated, however, that there would be various tensions inherent to tetragamy. There were bound to be more quarrels and occasions for jealousy than in monogamy, given the number of people involved. Still, he thought that just as in monogamous marriages, the men and women involved in this quadripartite relationship would have to learn to adapt to it. The men, he reflected, might be troubled by their lack of certainty about which children were their own. They could, Schopenhauer reflected, look for resemblances between themselves and their children, but then he cynically observed that in matters of paternity "even now it is not always certain."[6] He did not worry about the women's

---

[5] Schopenhauer, *Manuscript Remains*, Vol. 3, p. 177/*Der handschriftliche Nachlaß*, Vol. 3, p. 161.
[6] Ibid., Vol. 3, p. 178/ibid., Vol. 3, p. 162.

lack of certainty concerning the fathers of their children. It was likely that, as he would later argue, their goal was simply to have children.

Schopenhauer never published his musings on tetragamy, but in his notorious essay "On Women" he once more critiqued monogamy, and he advocated a one-sided form of polygamy – men should be allowed multiple wives. The philosopher was no longer concerned with a form of marriage that would also be attuned to female sexuality as he understood it. On the contrary, his view was based on male sexuality and the alleged deleterious effects European monogamy thrust on the proper relationships between men and women. The latter, he argued, are clearly the *sexus sequior*, the inferior sex, childlike by nature, incapable of producing works of genius, endowed with a feeble form of reason, whose wills should be subordinate to their husbands'. Monogamy, however, gave women an unnatural status by affording them privileges and rights that tended to make them equal to males. Not unsurprisingly, given his relationship with his mother, he was hypercritical of allowing women the right to inherit property. Men produce property, he argued, so women are not entitled to inherit landed property or capital – unless there are no male descendants. Instead, widows and daughters should receive only life annuities secured by mortgage, because women were inclined to extravagance and whim and were not capable of managing real property. They needed, he wrote, a male guardian to manage their inheritance and "in no case whatsoever should they receive the guardianship of their children."[7] By inheriting property, he continued, a woman is placed in an unnatural state of independence and therefore will "attach herself to some man by whom she allows herself to be guided and ruled, because she needs a master. If she is young, he is a lover and if old, a father confessor."[8] There can be little doubt that Schopenhauer was thinking of his mother and her relationship with Gerstenbergk when he penned these lines.

Monogamy also left a large number of women unfulfilled, not properly supported, and with few choices. The result of this, Schopenhauer reasoned, was that "in the upper classes they vegetate as useless old maids [was he thinking here of Adele?], but in the lower they have to do hard and unsuitable work, or become prostitutes who lead a life as joyless as

---

7 Schopenhauer, *Parerga and Paralipomena*, Vol. 2, p. 626/*Sämtliche Werke*, Vol. 6, p. 663.
8 Ibid.

it is disreputable, but who in such circumstances become necessary for the satisfaction of the male sex. They thus appear as a publicly recognized class or profession whose special purpose is to protect from being seduced those women who are favored by fortune and have found or hope to find husbands. In London alone there are eighty thousand of this class."[9] Polygamy would solve, he claimed, this problem and rid Europe of these unfortunate women, and it would also eliminate that monster of European civilization, he sneered, the European Lady, whom he compared to the sacred apes at Benares and who he called a byproduct of – and here he employed a phrase that Nietzsche would use – "Christian–Germanic Stupidity." Such Ladies would be brought down to the domesticity and submissiveness proper to their sex, he gleefully imagined; they could not demand veneration, and they would not be able to display the arrogance of her class. Their sisters would be happier, he thought, because they could also marry rich husbands.

Last, the legalization of polygamy would automatically improve the sexual morality found in Europe. We all live for a time in polygamy, Schopenhauer observed, and in most cases always. Monogamy, therefore, made this natural behavior immoral. If polygamy were legalized, these natural sexual relationships would not be stigmatized. Besides, he reflected, a man needs many women and "nothing is more just than it should be open to him, indeed incumbent on him, to provide for many women."[10] As it stood, he concluded, no prudent and cautious man would marry in Europe. It halved one's rights and doubled one's duties. Schopenhauer would always be a prudent and cautious man.

Schopenhauer's reflections on tetragamy already demonstrated his willingness to compromise the austere findings of his philosophy, which recognized voluntary chastity as the first step toward asceticism and denial of the will.[11] This compromise prefigured his stance in some of his essays

---

[9] Ibid., Vol. 2, p. 623/ibid., Vol. 6, p. 660.

[10] Ibid., Vol. 2, p. 624/ibid., Vol. 3, p. 661.

[11] The unconscious aim of all love affairs, Schopenhauer argued, is the production of the next generation. Thus, it is not simply that every Jack find a Jill – or an Arthur a Caroline – but that a new being come into existence. He held that the next generation are the *dramatis personae* of all love affairs, but in this regard, "lovers," he wrote, "are the traitors who secretly strive to perpetuate the whole trouble and toil that would otherwise rapidly come to an end," *The World as Will and Representation*, Vol. 2, p. 560/ *Sämtliche Werke*, Vol. 3, p. 643.

from *Parerga* and *Paralipomena*. He did so explicitly in "Aphorisms on
the Wisdom of Life," where he provided a eudemonology, instructions
for the art of living as successfully and pleasantly as possible – and in "On
Women," where he did so implicitly in his attempt to describe how the
sexes could live lives more in tune with their natures. Such compromises,
moreover, were necessary for a man who recognized the omnipresence of
sexuality, which, he held, was the most robust expression of the will to
life, next to the love of life and the pursuit of personal well-being. In his
ground-breaking "The Metaphysics of Sexual Love," from the second
edition of his principal work, he saw sexuality as providing the invisible
goal and central point of all actions and conduct, the dominant theme
of the human drama. The vast majority of people could never escape
its force, he thought, and promoting chastity would only make matters
worse. Consequently, as a practical matter, the point was to discover the
means for ameliorating the often pernicious effects of sexuality, which he
saw as enhanced by monogamy.

An Old Woman and a Burden

In 1821, Schopenhauer's desire to leave Berlin would be helped by an
event that would forever tarnish his reputation.[12] On 21 August, as he
returned to his two-room apartment in Niederlagstrasse 4, he came upon
a scene about which he had complained two weeks earlier to his landlady,
the widow Becker, who promised the philosopher that it would not occur
again. Three unknown women were chatting away in an antechamber
that adjoined the rooms that he shared with another man. He requested
that the gossiping women leave his *entrée* and then entered his apartment.
Shortly thereafter, while he was still wearing his hat and carrying his
cane, he opened his door, only to discover that the women had paid him
no heed. Now, he firmly demanded that they leave his room. The two
younger women started to leave, but the third, the forty-seven-year-old
seamstress and fellow lodger, Caroline Louise Marquet, refused, telling
the increasingly irate Schopenhauer that she was "a respectable person."
Schopenhauer, who claimed to have offered her his arm to escort her

---

[12] In *Schopenhauer: The Human Character*, John Atwell rightly includes the Marquet incident
among the alleged facts most students know about Schopenhauer's life, including the misin-
formation that he pushed her down a flight of stairs; see p. 3.

from the antechamber, demanded more forcefully that she leave his room, calling Marquet an "old wench."[13]

What exactly happened next was a matter of dispute, provoking lawsuits that wound their way through the legal system for almost six years. What was not a matter of dispute, however, was that Schopenhauer called Marquet a name and that he physically removed the seamstress from the *entrée*. But how he did it and its effects on Marquet are not clear. Schopenhauer claimed that after making numerous requests for the women to leave the room, he had to grab Marquet around her torso and drag her out of the room as she struggled with all of her might to stay. When he succeeded in removing the resolute woman, she began, he claimed, to scream for her things that remained in the room. He promptly tossed them out of the room, but under the pretext of retrieving some trinket, the philosopher claimed that she reentered the room, forcing him to seize her once more and to push the struggling woman out of the antechamber. She fell to the ground, the philosopher said, on purpose, threatening to sue him.

Marquet painted a darker and more violent image of the philosopher's conduct. She claimed that he tore the bonnet from her head, seized her by the neck with such force that she was lifted from the ground, called her vile names, beat her with his fists, kicked her, and tossed her out of the room. The ferocity of the attack, she charged, caused her to faint. The next day she filed assault and slander charges against her unneighborly neighbor with the *Hausvogteigericht* at Berlin. Because this was a private complaint and not an official criminal case, the main question entertained by the court was whether the alleged wrongdoer was to be punished. Schopenhauer defended himself against the complaint and on 1 March 1822, that court ruled in his favor, requiring Marquet to pay the court costs. Frau Marquet, whose sense of being wronged equaled her sense of entitlement for using the *entrée*, appealed the decision to the *Kammergericht*. Schopenhauer, however, did not defend himself in that forum, nor would he do so during the next five years, as the suit slowly snaked its way through the court system. He was keen to shake off the dust of Berlin, escape his convoluted love life, and put his academic failure behind him. He left Berlin for Italy

---

[13] Marquet claimed that the philosopher called her both a "wretch" and an "old hussy." In his response to her complaint, Schopenhauer wrote "I have never insulted her by calling her a 'wretch' and 'old hussy,' but only once, in subject and predicate, an 'old wretch'"; Schopenhauer, *Gesammelte Briefe*, p. 76. He also admitted that he was wrong to have done so.

on 27 May 1822, being assured by the head of the *Kammergericht* that the original judgment would be upheld. Indeed, Marquet was but a seamstress and he was a relatively rich *Privatdozent*. Consequently, Schopenhauer thought that justice, at least as he saw it, would prevail.

As Schopenhauer prepared for his travels, the court convened on 25 May and the *Kammergericht* did not uphold the earlier judgment, as he expected. He was fined 20 *Taler* for causing minor injuries to his neighbor. This verdict was made public on 7 June, when Schopenhauer was in Nuremberg, and unknown to him, his banking house, Mendelssohn and Fränckel, paid the fine.[14] He ultimately appealed the verdict to the *Oberappellationssenate* of the *Kammergericht* for a reverse of the judgment, but the appeal was not successful.

Marquet also brought a civil suit against Schopenhauer with the *Instruktionssenat* of the *Kammergericht*. She now claimed that she had become paralyzed on her right side due to the assault, and that she could not move her right arm without great difficulty, a situation that made it impossible for her to continue her trade. She also claimed that Schopenhauer pushed her against a commode, which caused injury to her genitals.[15] She sought the costs of her medical care and treatments, maintenance, and to have her attacker arrested. This new turn of events led Schopenhauer to have Mendelssohn and Fränckel hire a lawyer, Georg Carl Friedrich Kunowski, who, the philosopher would ultimately hold, was too busy with other clients to pay full diligence to his case.[16]

As the proceeding slowly unfolded, Schopenhauer's assets were attached and Marquet was awarded maintenance. This turn of events moved Schopenhauer, who was once more living in Dresden, to return to Berlin. Kunowski managed to free the philosopher's accounts and to have Marquet's award of maintenance reversed. Marquet, of course, appealed. Ultimately she prevailed, winning 60 *Taler* per year in maintenance, and

[14] Mendelssohn and Fränckel, later Mendelssohn and Company, was founded by the second son of Moses Mendelssohn, Joseph.

[15] Schopenhauer believed that Marquet was feigning her injuries and that she would be sly enough to do so for the remainder of her life. The only visible signs of the assault were a few minor bruises. The seamstress was forced to undergo an examination by Dr. Adam Elias von Siebold, a professor of obstetrics at the University of Berlin, concerning her claim of injury to her genitals. Upon close examination, Dr. Siebold found no apparent damage.

[16] Thus alleged Schopenhauer's friend Gwinner; see his *Schopenhauer's Leben* (Leipzig: Brockhaus, 1878), p. 319.

her assailant was assessed five-sixths of the court costs. The judgment was finalized on 4 May 1827, after the philosopher made a futile attempt to have the Minister of Justice, Count Alexander von Danekelmann, intercede on his behalf. Schopenhauer was compelled to provide maintenance until Marquet was able to resume her trade or until she died.[17] The seamstress died in 1842, and Schopenhauer put an end to this notorious affair by scribbling an anagram by Sulzer Tobianus on Marquet's death notice, *"obit anus abit onus"* [the old woman has died; the burden has been lifted].[18]

Hiatus from Berlin

In May of 1822, after Schopenhauer prematurely thought that the Frau Marquet affair was over, he abandoned Berlin. He would remain away for three years, until May of 1825, when his legal troubles compelled him to return. When he left Berlin, he traveled to Leipzig and Nuremberg, and then to Stuttgart, Schaffhausen, Vevey, and Milan, arriving in Florence on 11 September 1822. He would spend eight months in the Tuscan town. He was now living a dream he had ever since his arrival in Berlin. He wrote his friend Osann that for three years he had dreamt that he was in Italy, only to wake up in his apartment in Berlin. Unlike his first sojourn to the country of his dreams, Schopenhauer thoroughly enjoyed the second: "The 2nd entry into Italy is more enjoyable than the first; with what rejoicing I greeted every Italian idiosyncrasy! The strange and unusual does not provoke anxiety the second time as it did the first – even annoying, hostile, and irksome things are greeted as old acquaintances. One knows how to find good things and understands how to enjoy them. I discovered that everything, the sky, earth, plants, trees, and human countenance, arose immediately from the hands of nature just as it ought properly to be."[19]

---

[17] For a careful and thorough description and analysis of the Marquet case, see Karl-Heinz Muscheler's *Die Schopenhauer-Marquet-Prozesse und das Preußische Recht* (Tübingen: J. C. B. Mohr, 1996).

[18] Hübscher credits Johann George Sulzer as Schopenhauer's source for Johann Samuel Tobianus' Latin anagram; see *Sämtliche Werke*, Vol. 1, p. 96.

[19] Schopenhauer, *Gesammelte Briefe*, p. 88, Schopenhauer to Friedrich Gotthilf Osaan, 29 October 1822.

Books were expensive to acquire, and Schopenhauer found the local library inadequate to his intellectual needs. Consequently, he served his philosophical muse by reading from what his father called the "book of the world." Observation and experience were as necessary for the philosopher as reading and study, he told his friend Osann, and the genuine philosopher drew the richest thoughts through reflection on experience. He leisurely savored Florence's works of art, gathering data to enrich his aesthetics. He was moved by the Italians' aesthetic sensibilities and praised them for their keen sense of the beautiful. He particularly commended them for mounting on low pedestals the many statues decorating the streets and square. This type of display made a close examination of the statuary possible, something that Schopenhauer felt the English and French made difficult by perching their statues on high pedestals.[20] Close examination of Donatello's marble figure of an emaciated John the Baptist led Schopenhauer to reflect that it was a masterpiece of execution, but its total effect he found repulsive – an odd remark for the philosopher who had argued that voluntary starvation was the highest degree of asceticism.[21] But if he was put off by the marble skin and bones of John the Baptist, he was provided with more ammunition for his claim about the inadmissibility of allegory in painting. At the library of the Palazzo Riccardi, the former palace of the Medici, he encountered, spread on the ceiling, Luca Giordano's pictorial allegory, representing science's freeing the understanding from ignorance. A strong man bound by cords that are beginning to fall is looking in a mirror held before him by a nymph, as another offers him a large, detached wing. Above this scene, Science sits on a globe, beside her naked truth with a globe in hand. Without first understanding the symbolism, Schopenhauer reflected, it would be impossible to imagine what the elements in the painting represent: "What would such a picture say without the explanation of its hieroglyphs?"[22] The purpose of paintings is to convey Platonic ideas and not to confuse the mind with

---

[20] See Schopenhauer, *Parerga and Paralipomena*, Vol. 2, p. 450/*Sämtliche Werke*, Vol. 6, p. 479.

[21] For Schopenhauer's observation concerning Donatello's *John the Baptist*, see *The World as Will and Representation*, Vol. 2, p. 419/*Sämtliche Werke*, Vol. 3, p. 478, and for his observations on voluntary starvation, see ibid., Vol. 1, p. 401/ibid, Vol. 2, p. 474.

[22] Schopenhauer, *Manuscript Remains*, Vol. 3, p. 177/*Der handschriftliche Nachlaß*, Vol. 3, p. 161. Schopenhauer also refers to Giordano's allegory in *The World as Will and Representation*, Vol. 2, p. 422/*Sämtliche Werke*, Vol. 3, p. 482.

strange symbolism. The Apennine god at nearby Pratolino was more to his liking. Composed of large masses of rocks, it was only noticeable when viewed at a distance, analogous to a mosaic or theater decorations, but such distance was often necessary in life to see the bigger picture.[23]

He was more social in Florence than he had been for many years, and the Italians themselves provided him with interesting subjects of observation. His associations with aristocrats served to confirm his observations concerning the vanity of life. "It has become especially clear to me," he wrote Osann, "how close the wretchedness of life is to the nobles, and how boredom tortures them, despite all preparations against it."[24] Life, he had already theorized, "swings like a pendulum to and fro between pain and boredom, and these two are in fact its ultimate constituents."[25] We suffer, and when we do not, we are bored; satisfied desire leaves us empty, driving us to will once more. Boredom is such a great evil that we are led to gambling, drinking, extravagance, intrigue, and a mania to travel. Boredom even makes porcupines social:

One cold winter's day, a number of porcupines huddled together quite closely in order through their personal warmth to prevent themselves from being frozen. But soon they felt the effect of their quills on one another, which made them again move apart. Now when the need for warmth once more brought them together, the drawback of the quills was repeated so that they were tossed between two evils, until they had discovered the proper distance from which they could best tolerate one another. Thus the need for society which springs from the emptiness and monotony of human's lives, drives them together.... Yet whoever has a great deal of internal warmth of his own will prefer to keep away from society in order to avoid giving and receiving annoyance.[26]

Schopenhauer's bright mood in Florence shielded him from the pricks of Italian quills, not that he had become that close to any Italians, except, perhaps, for the dark Italian women whose warmth a fair-haired, blue-eyed man would seek by his very nature. He did, however, observe the quills, and he was amused. Italy was a country of beautiful faces and bad inclinations, he wrote Osann. Its people were endlessly cheerful and

[23] The *Appenine* god at Pratolino is discussed by Schopenhauer, ibid., Vol. 2, p. 335f./ibid, Vol. 3, p. 383.

[24] Schopenhauer, *Gesammelte Briefe*, p. 92, Schopenhauer to Osann, 21 May 1824.

[25] Schopenhauer, *The World as Will and Representation*, Vol. 1, p. 312/*Sämtliche Werke*, Vol. 2 p. 368.

[26] Schopenhauer, *Parerga and Paralipomena*, Vol. 2, p. 651–2/*Sämtliche Werke*, Vol. 6, p. 690–91.

merry, and healthy, which he attributed to the climate, and they appeared ingenious and as if there was something more to them than met the eye. They were polite and crafty, and they knew when to appear upright and honorable. Yet they were also treacherous, dishonorable, and shameless, but in such a way that "we forget our anger in astonishment."[27] But if he thought that he had understood the Italian character, he could also be beguiled by it. In his private diary he noted, along with other flattering remarks by "foreigners," that of an Italian who said, "Sir, you must have created something great: I do not know which it is, but I see it in your face."[28] Nevertheless, although the philosopher made many acquaintances, he associated primarily with foreign tourists, "mostly English," and in a conversation some thirty-five years after the fact, Carl Bähr reported that "He [Schopenhauer] associated with Lords and did nothing more than read Homer."[29]

"With Italy, one lives as with a beloved," Schopenhauer wrote, "today in violent quarrel, tomorrow in adoration: – with Germany, as with a housewife, without great anger and without great love."[30] After eleven months, the same length of time as his first Italian journey, he abandoned his beloved to return to his housewife. Whereas his first tour was terminated by the financial troubles of Muhl, no crisis compelled the philosopher to return to the German countries. The Marquet lawsuit had not yet reached a critical mass, nor did he plan to resume his teaching career at Berlin. Perhaps the philosopher tired of the endless happiness and good cheer of the Italians, and perhaps their "shamelessness" was no longer amusing. Maybe he was bored; in any case, he never recorded his reasons for leaving Italy, and he would never return.

Schopenhauer left Florence for Trent and then from Trent to Munich, where he would spend a year. Six weeks after his arrival at the Bavarian city, he began suffering a myriad of illnesses – hemorrhoids with fistulas, gout, and nervous disorders. It was as if his German housewife made him

---

[27] Schopenhauer, *Gesammelte Briefe*, p. 87, Schopenhauer to Osann, 29 October 1822; also see a note dating from the second Italian tour, where he also emphasized "Shamelessness as the Italian national character," *Manuscript Remains*, Vol. 3, p. 184/*Der handschriftliche Nachlaß*, Vol. 3, p. 168.

[28] Ibid., Vol. 4, p. 489/ibid., Vol. 4, 2, p. 110.

[29] Schopenhauer's remark about his association with mostly English people is found in a letter to Osann (21 May 1824), *Gesammelte Briefe*, p. 92, and Bähr's report is from a conversation that took place on 9 May 1858, *Gespräche*, p. 254.

[30] Ibid., p. 88, Schopenhauer to Osann, 29 October 1822.

pay for his enjoyment of his Italian beloved. His hands trembled so greatly that he found it almost impossible to write, and he lost hearing in his right ear, the sad culmination of a problem that plagued him from his youth. He traveled to the baths at the small resort town of Gastein, where he had heard of miraculous cures – a report that he did not discount, an attitude that was odd for a student of David Hume. And although it is unlikely that the baths had any profound effect in restoring his health, Gastein gave him time to reflect and to reconfirm what he had already argued. We step into the world seeking happiness and pleasure, but "experience then comes along and teaches us that happiness and pleasure are more chimeras which an illusion shows us at a distance; whereas we are taught that suffering and pain are real and immediately make themselves felt without the need for illusion and expectation." Aristotle was correct, he continued, the prudent man strives for painlessness and not for pleasure.[31]

In Munich, from October through December 1823, Schopenhauer was intensively treated for his ailments in his quarters and in the office of Dr. Ernst von Grossi, late professor of Medicine at Salzburg. The nature of Grossi's treatments suggests that the philosopher had contracted syphilis, a predictable result for a frequenter of whorehouses.[32] Protection from venereal diseases became a key concern for Schopenhauer, who would pride himself with gaining the knowledge of how to avoid infection while remaining sexually active. It also seems that he was more than willing to share such knowledge. One Xaver Schnyder von Wartensee, a music teacher and writer, recorded a curious conversation he had with Schopenhauer at a dinner table in Frankfurt. After praising science for conferring upon the human race the "greatest benefit" by discovering the means whereby one could satisfy the "demands of nature" and escape infection, always a great risk at bordellos, Schopenhauer describe a prophylactic measure: "One dissolves a portion of chloride of lime in water and then, after coitus, bathes one's penis in it, which in any case, will completely destroy any contracted poison."[33]

[31] Schopenhauer, *Manuscript Remains*, Vol. 3, p. 192/*Der handschriftliche Nachlaß*, Vol. 3, p. 176. The entry is dated May 1824, Gastein. In this entry he quotes Aristotle's *Nicomachean Ethics*, VII.

[32] The diagnosis of syphilis was made by Iwan Bloch in "Schopenhauer's Krankheit im Jahre 1823," *Medizinische Welt* (1906).

[33] Schopenhauer, *Gespräche*, p. 63. The conversation took place sometime between the winter of 1831/2 and 1833. After arguing that nature itself will gradually cure an illness, a process

Another acquaintance, the British officer T. Edwards, did not heed Schopenhauer's medical advice and reported suffering from ignoring the philosopher, who had warned Edwards about the dangers that awaited the young man along his trip to India. After bragging that he had made his way through Turkey, Asia Minor, and Persia without encountering any of Schopenhauer's predicted disasters, he confessed, "I was not even furnished with one of the patent pocket cases for *Khlor-Wasser* invented for the benefit of mankind's salvation of pricks by that distinguished learned pundit & Philanthropist the great Schopenhauer. . . . But Alas! Since I have been in India twice have I suffered the last time most severely from neglecting this simple remedy. This dreadful case of Gonorrhoea which confined me for a month and took three months to get rid of, put me in mind of what you used to say. Young man wait till you get a bad clap."[34]

While in Italy, the "learned Pundit & Philanthropist" had not known about the benefits of dipping one's wick in a bath of chloride of lime as a preventative of what was called the "French disease" [*Franzosenkrankheit*]. Nor did he carry a "patent pocket case for *Khlor-Wasser*" on his visits to Italian bordellos. So, as he lay suffering in Munich, he received a curious letter from Osann, who, as a friend to both brother and sister, attempted to mediate a reconciliation between the siblings. To generate some compassion for Johanna, he also informed Schopenhauer that his mother suffered from cramps, joint stiffness, and a free-floating form of anxiety. Four months later he replied to this letter, explaining that the delay in his reply was due to his trembling hands and his depressed spirit. He politely told Osann to mind his own business; "What you wrote in regard to my sister is certainly very well meant. Only Adele and I know best what we have to expect from each other. The recommendation of a third party can help nothing here."[35] Schopenhauer made no response to the report of his mother's physical problems, and requested that Osann immediately inform him whether his mother and sister were going to be in Mannheim that summer, as Osann had mentioned in his letter. He wished to avoid his family.

---

that makes us feel even better than before, he observes, "I admit that there are exceptions, or cases in which only the physician can help; in particular, the cure of syphilis is a triumph of medicine," *Parerga and Paralipomena*, Vol. 2, p. 173/ *Sämtliche Werke*, Vol. 6, p. 184.

34 Schopenhauer, *Gespräche*, p. 64, letter from Edwards to Schopenhauer July 1835.

35 Schopenhauer, *Gesammelte Briefe*, p. 92, Schopenhauer to Osann, 21 May 1824. Osann's letter to Schopenhauer was dated 25 January 1824; see ibid., p. 512.

After a little more than a month at the baths at Gastein, Schopenhauer returned briefly to Munich to gather his gear. Fleeing the bitter scene of his protracted illness and a climate he disliked, he made his way to Dresden via Stuttgart, Heidelberg, Mannheim, Frankfurt, and Leipzig. He overwintered in Dresden, hoping to reexperience the joys surrounding the birthplace of his principal work. Yet with his academic career in shambles and his philosophy drawing a response comparable to the dust collecting on his unsold books, Schopenhauer sought a new avocation. He proposed a series of translations, using his language skills to fill the time until the truth of his views would be recognized and, he hoped, create a demand for his work.

Schopenhauer first attempted to secure a contract for the translations of two of his favorite writings in David Hume's oeuvre, "The Natural History of Religion" (in Four Dissertations. London: 1755) and *Dialogues Concerning Natural Religion* (1779). He made a pitch for these translations to an unnamed publisher, and he argued that these writings should be published jointly as *David Hume's Religionsphilosophie*, because the intention of the first book was to show that faith in the gods or God originates from timidity and fear of unknown forces, and the intention of the second was to demonstrate the inadequacy of all proofs for the existence of God.[36] Although both books had previously been translated into German, Schopenhauer complained that they had been poorly translated, used antiquated language, and were often incorrect.[37] He assured the publisher that his command of English was first rate because he had thoroughly learned it as a youth in England, and he mentioned that he had been told by English people, especially those he met in Italy, that they had never heard a foreigner speak the language as perfectly as he. Quite naturally, the philosopher also pitched his proposal by claiming that Hume would attract many readers from the general public, because he wrote in

---

[36] In the opening paragraph of "Schopenhauer as Educator," Nietzsche added laziness to timidity and fear as qualities of people everywhere; see *Untimely Meditations*, trans. R. J. Hollingdale (Cambridge: Cambridge University Press, 1983), p. 127.

[37] The earlier translations that Schopenhauer had in mind were F.G. Resewitz's translation of *The Natural History of Religion* as "Natürliche Geschichte der Religion," which appeared in *Vier Abhandlungen über die Geschichte der Religion* (1755), and K. G. Schreiter's translation of the *Dialogues*, which appeared as *Gespräche über die natürliche Religion* (1755), and K. G. Schreiter's translation of the *Dialogues*, which appeared as *Gespräche über die natürliche Religion* (Leipzig 1781).

a masterful, sagacious, and clear style, with spirit and wit to be found on each page. And although the general public may have become indifferent to German philosophy, due to its ponderous and obscure language, Hume could be universally understood.

Schopenhauer's pitch for the Hume translation was only part of his desperate search to secure a contract. After he made his case for Hume, he also volunteered to translate English works beyond philosophy, including those in the natural sciences, history, politics, and literature. Almost as if he did not wish to leave any Rosetta stone unturned, he closed his letter with an offer to translate into Latin Giordano Bruno's *Della causa, principio ed uno* (1584), a work that "in recent times, through Schelling and Jacobi, received a great deal of celebrity."[38] A Latin translation was appropriate for this Italian text, he noted, because Latin would make the work available to scholars in all countries. He was also willing to provide a German text to accompany the Latin.

As Schopenhauer waited for a response that never came, he worked on prefaces for *David Hume's Religionsphilosophie*. Whereas he had mildly berated his contemporaries in his preface to *The World as Will and Representation*, these sketches set the tone for every preface he would write for his future books and for the prefaces he would attach to each new edition of his books. The first brief note, written before his translation proposal, is telling: "Later times will see why I try through a new translation to draw the attention of contemporaries to the present work of the admirable and excellent David Hume. If my contemporaries were able to appreciate my efforts, this would be superfluous."[39] The second sketch for a preface, written after his proposal, sarcastically berates his contemporaries to praise Hume and closes with an honest description of his own situation.

Had Hume, he wrote with venom dripping from his quill, the good fortune of sharing the profound discoveries of our days, he would have found that the faculty of reason provided direct access to the supersensible and the divine, and he would not have had to trouble himself with

[38] Ibid., p. 96, Schopenhauer, "An Einen Verlagbuchhändler" [to a publishing house], 25 November 1824.

[39] Schopenhauer, *Manuscript Remains*, Vol. 3, p. 194/*Der handschriftlich Nachlaß*, Vol. 3, p. 177. Later, in a note written during his return to Berlin, he possibly revealed an unstated goal of translating Hume. "Without that which Kant did, Hume's demonstration of the origin of theism was never accepted: Now armed with both, we can overthrow theism," ibid., Vol. 3. p. 237/ibid., Vol. 3, p. 216.

arguments and counterarguments on religious issues. Moreover, had he lived in Germany, he would have abandoned his lucid, precise, vivid, and comprehensible prose and replaced this with strange, homespun terms, wrapped in ponderous and endless sentences in order to appear profound because he was obscure. In this way, his reader could have marveled at how much he could read without getting hold of a single idea, which would allow his readers to think that the less they were able to think with the text, the more the author had thought. As for himself, he continued in the same note, he could do the translation, because "I have quite a lot of spare time because I consider myself exempt from having to elaborate for communication my own ideas. Experience has now confirmed what I previously foresaw and foretold, namely that such ideas find no reading among my contemporaries."[40] Like Hume, it appears that Schopenhauer did not truly know of the marvelous powers of the faculty of reason and did not learn how to spread a thick coat of mysterious obscurity over his writings.

Schopenhauer's Hume proposal went nowhere, so he approached F. A. Brockhaus, the publishing house of his principal work, with another offer. Friedrich Arnold Brockhaus had died in August 1823, taking to the grave the animosity he bore toward that difficult and "dishonorable" Schopenhauer. Standing at the head of the firm were his two oldest sons, Friedrich and Heinrich, with whom, along with their head clerk Karl Ferdinand Bochmann, Schopenhauer briefly visited on 13 September 1824, during a stopover in Leipzig. During his visit, Schopenhauer offered his services as a translator of English and Italian. It is not known whether he offered his condolences regarding the death of his nemesis Friedrich Arnold. Several months later, Schopenhauer heard that Brockhaus was issuing a new series, the "Library of Foreign Classical Novels and Novellas." Immediately, the philosopher offered to provide a new translation of Sterne's *Tristram Shandy*. The earlier translation by Johann Joachim Christoph Bode (Hamburg 1776), he surmised, was likely to be antiquated, he wrote in his prospectus, without ever seeing Bode's work. "In any case," Schopenhauer continued, "I would be completely independent of this translation, and would translate it *con amore*, in order to duplicate the lively impression and spirit of the exquisite original, and since I learned the English language as a youth in England, I almost have as

---

[40] Ibid., Vol. 3, p. 199/ibid., Vol. 3, p. 182.

much mastery of it as I have of my own language."[41] Brockhaus politely declined the offer.

After failing to secure a contract for any type of translation whatsoever, Schopenhauer returned to Berlin to address the attachment of his funds due to the lawsuit, and to revive his dead teaching career. Once in Berlin, he embarked on an intensive study of Spanish, in order to read Calderón, Lope de Vega, Miguel de Cervantes, and Baltazar Gracián in their original language. As much as he loved Calderón, he dubbed Gracián "my favorite Spanish author," and in 1829, he sent Brockhaus a proposal to translate into German the seventeenth-century Spanish Jesuit's *Oraculo manual y arte de prudencia* [*Hand Oracle and Art of Worldly Wisdom*, 1647], a work he admired for its fine, tense, and subtly expressed thoughts and for its directions for navigating through the roughness and vicissitudes of everyday life.[42] He also sympathized with Gracián's cautionary approach to other people, his mistrust of women, and what he saw as the Jesuit's pessimism. He included in his proposal a sample translation of fifty of the three hundred maxims that composed the book, and instead of his own name, he requested that the fancifully named "Felix Treumund" be listed as the translator, a promise to his readers that they would enjoy an accurate translation. Once more Brockhaus refused the offer, fearing that it would not draw an audience, and returned the manuscript.[43] Schopenhauer would later claim that Brockhaus refused his offer because the translation was not as good as it could have been, and that he had requested too high of an honorarium.[44]

When Schopenhauer later fled Berlin in 1831, he left the Gracián manuscript behind, entrusting it to his friend Baron Heinrich von Lowtzow, whom he also asked to keep an eye on Caroline Medon. Once he arrived in Frankfurt, he was seized by the desire to have his translation published, but because the original manuscript remained in Berlin, he had to retranslate the work. He sent the manuscript, with a "Note to the

---

[41] Schopenhauer, p. 97, Schopenhauer to F. A. Brockhaus, 26 January 1825.

[42] Schopenhauer, *On the Basis of Morality*, p. 23/*Sämtliche Werke*, Vol. 4, p. xxix. Elsewhere, Schopenhauer referred to Gracián as simply "my favorite author," *Gesammelte Briefe*, p. 131, Schopenhauer to Johann George Keil, 16 April 1832.

[43] For the manuscript Schopenhauer sent to Brockhaus, the one translated by "Felix Treumond," see *Der handschriftliche Nachlaß*, Vol. 4, 2, pp. 268–84.

[44] See Schopenhauer, *Gesammelte Briefe*, p. 131, Schopenhauer to Johann George Keil, 16 April 1832.

Publisher" in which he harshly evaluated earlier translations of Gracián, to Johann Georg Keil, a noted linguist, translator, and editor of Spanish and Italian literature, whose collection of Calderón's plays Schopenhauer was currently reading. The philosopher knew Keil and his wife, Henriette, from his Weimar days, when Keil was a librarian and friend of his teacher Franz Passow. Schopenhauer was hoping that Keil would help him secure a publisher, and he requested that his old acquaintance read his translation against the original. He did this, he wrote, "since you now probably have the first word in Germany in matters of Spanish literature." Schopenhauer knew that if he impressed Keil, it was more likely that he would find a publisher, given Keil's reputation and connections. And although Schopenhauer was confident that he had captured the sense, style, and spirit of the original, to further flatter Keil, he wrote "I risk appearing before your tribunal."[45]

Keil's tribunal ruled in Schopenhauer's favor, unlike the *Kammergericht*, and he agreed to aid in finding a publisher. Unfortunately, his attempt to mediate a contract between Schopenhauer and the publisher Frederick Fleischer failed. Schopenhauer became suspicious about the publisher and whether he would print a sufficient number of books and pay a sufficient honorarium. Consequently, the philosopher asked Keil to find an "honest" publisher for his "honest" translation. Keil backed off of this task, retaining the manuscript for another seven years, at which time the philosopher asked for its return. It was not that Schopenhauer himself had found a publisher; rather, a translation by Frederick Kölle appeared in 1838. Schopenhauer's Gracián translation would eventually be published, but in 1862, two years after his death. Just as death is a good career move for artists and rock stars, Schopenhauer's death made a popular philosopher even more popular. After his death F. A. Brockhaus found it lucrative to publish anything by Schopenhauer, including the Gracián translation. But if Schopenhauer never enjoyed the publication of this translation, twenty-one years before it appeared he had the pleasure of using his translation of a lengthy passage from Gracián's *El criticón* [*The Critic*, 1640] in the form of a philippic within his fiery and intemperate

---

[45] Ibid., p. 131. To demonstrate his mastery of Spanish, Schopenhauer also told Keil that he was reading, without difficulty, Keil's edition of *Pedro Calderón de la Barca: Las comedias* (Leipzig 1827–30), and that he wished that Keil would have indicated each change of scene and stage setting. He also alerted Keil to several typographical errors.

first preface to *The Two Fundamental Problems of Ethics*, lambasting those who would place fame's sacred garlands on Hegel's common brow.[46]

Shortly after his initial proposal of the Gracián translations, Schopenhauer made his ill-fated attempt to translate Kant into English. By the time he solicited Keil's aid with the Gracián project, however, he had been successful with two other translations, although the second of the two was an abbreviation and reworking of the original, a reworking of which the author approved. The first was a short story by a Lord Norman, "The Prophet of St. Paul," which appeared in the British almanac *The Keepsake* (1830). In his account book from March 1830, the philosopher recorded receiving an honorarium of a little more than 22 *Taler* for "Der Prophet von St. Paul." This work, unfortunately, is lost.[47] In June of 1830, he published the second, a Latin recasting of *On Vision and Colors*. "Theoria colorum physiologic, eademque primaria," appeared in the journal *Scriptores ophthalmologici minors*, edited by Justus Wilhelm Martin Radius, a *Privatdozent* in the medical faculty at the University in Leipzig. Schopenhauer had worked on the Latin recast of his color theory from April to the beginning of June in 1829. When he received the proof sheets from Radius, he was annoyed that the editor had listed the philosopher as a citizen of Berlin. He fired back, in terms just the opposite of those of the United States president John F. Kennedy, "I am no Berliner" [*Ich bin kein Berliner*].[48]

In 1833 Schopenhauer made a final attempt to employ his language skills. When it came to his attention that a French edition of Goethe's collected works was under way in Paris, he wrote its general editor, the French politician, diplomat, author, and translator François Jean Philibert Aubert de Vitry, and offered to correct the final proof sheets. As only natural, he wrote the letter in his very best French, and to demonstrate his mastery of the language, he even critiqued the planned title for the publication: "One must say either *Oeuvres de Göthe* or *Oeuvres de J.W. de Göthe* – but never *Oeuvres de J.W. Göthe* – that would be as if one

---

[46] See Schopenhauer, *On the Basis of Morality*, pp. 25–30/*Sämtliche Werke*, Vol. 4, the "Vorrede zur ersten Auflage," *Die beiden Grundprobleme der Ethik*, pp. xxx–xxxvii.

[47] See Arthur Hübscher's "Eine verschollene Arbeit Schopenhauers," *Schopenhauer-Jahrbuch*, Vol. 22 (1935), pp. 239–441.

[48] Schopenhauer, *Gesammelte Briefe*, p. 125, Schopenhauer to Justus Radius, 9 June 1830. Not only did Schopenhauer say that he was no Berliner, but also he added "and prefer not *to be* one."

would say *Oeuvres d'Arrouet Voltaire.*"[49] He assured the editor that he had learned French as a youth and was as proficient in it as he was in his native language. And he made a claim concerning his mastery of French parallel to those he made about his English; namely, French people often found it hard to believe that he was not French.

Yet Schopenhauer offered more than simply his language skills. He mentioned his friendship with the great man, his work with him on color theory, Goethe's references to him in his published diary, and his collection of Goethe's letters to him, which he carefully bundled to preserve. This intimate knowledge of Goethe the man, as well as his work, furnished the backdrop for one of his typically bold claims: "I can say freely that," he continued in the same letter, "there are very few people in the world who understand Goethe just as well and completely as I." As a warning of the risks of proceeding without a man possessing his skills, he mentioned a Berlin writer who had him proof his English translation of *Faust.* This man possessed a complete command of English, he wrote, but abandoned the project after he had demonstrated, much to the translator's surprise, that he had failed to capture the true meaning of many of the passages. Goethe's prose is straightforward and simple, he continued, as is his autobiographical work. But his poetry and scientific writing require someone possessing a keen knowledge of both the man and his works. He could even provide notes to some of Goethe's poetry, he added, based on the factual events that prompted their genesis, something only personal friends of the author would know.

Nothing ever came from Schopenhauer's Goethe proposal. It is not even known whether Aubert de Vitry responded to the philosopher's offer of assistance. It is unlikely, however, that the Frenchman would have embraced an unsolicited offer from an unknown German philosopher who had the *chutzpah* to lecture him on his business. Finally, three years later, an equally audacious advance to editors of another collected works provided Schopenhauer with his first taste of success, and better yet, it was a project involving his other hero – Kant.

When Schopenhauer wrote his dissertation, his color theory, and his principal work, he had only known the *Critique of Pure Reason* in its fifth edition (1799). It was not until 1826 that he obtained a copy of its rare first

---

[49] Ibid., p. 139, Schopenhauer to Aubert de Vitry, 16 January 1833. Schopenhauer, *Gesammelte Briefe*, p. 125.

edition. He studied Kant's masterpiece then and more intensely around 1835. The first edition changed his view of Kant. To be sure, Kant had already obtained heroic proportions for the young philosopher by the time of *The World as Will and Representation*. Yet often it seemed as if his praise for Kant served as a means for demeaning his philosophical contemporaries and, by his returning to Kant, especially to the distinction between the thing in itself and appearance, it looked as if he decided to embrace that very feature of the critical philosophy that Fichte, Schelling, and Hegel attempted to obviate. After reading the first edition, Schopenhauer believed that Kant's radicalism, his commitment to idealism, and his crushing of rationalist metaphysics obtained their clearest, boldest, and most powerful expressions in it.

Schopenhauer's study of the original edition of Kant's *magnus opus* required him to rework his "Critique of the Kantian Philosophy" in the second edition of his own great work. In the first edition of *The World as Will and Representation*, he reproached Kant for failing to properly appreciate an insight Schopenhauer attributed to Berkeley: namely, there is no object without a subject. Kant failed to do this, Schopenhauer stated, because "he feared the accusation of idealism; indeed, he reproached idealism in his own mind as that which made the world a mere shadowy image and left no thing in itself remaining." He then cited a number of passages from the *Critique of Pure Reason* in which Kant clearly expressed idealism and accused the great philosopher of contradicting himself.[50] In the second edition, Schopenhauer retracted this charge and explained his change of mind:

In my first edition, I had explained Kant's avoidance of this Berkeleyan principle as resulting from an evident aversion to its decided idealism, whereas, on the contrary, I found this distinctly expressed in many passages of the *Critique of Pure Reason*, and accordingly had accused Kant of contradicting himself.... Now when later I read Kant's principal work in its first edition ... all those contradictions disappeared, and although Kant does not use the formula "no object without subject." I found that Kant, with just as much emphasis as Berkeley and I, explains that external world lying before us in space and time to be a mere representation of the cognizing subject.[51]

So, when Schopenhauer heard that two professors at Kant's home university were preparing a collected edition of Kant's works, he carefully

---

[50] Schopenhauer, *Faksimilenachdruck der 1. Auflage der Welt als Wille und Vorstellung*, p. 614.

[51] Schopenhauer, *The World as Will and Representation*, Vol. 1, p. 435/*Sämtliche Werke*, Vol. 2, p. 514f. Shortly after this passage, he mentions his letter to Rosenkranz.

prepared a letter offering advice concerning the form in which they should publish the *Critique of Pure Reason* to the Königsberg professors; Johann Karl Friedrich Rosenkranz, a philosopher, and Friedrich Wilhelm Schubert, a historian, geographer, and political scientist. To gain some credibility for his recommendations, he presented his credentials, claiming that Kant's philosophy had been the primary subject of his study and reflection for twenty-seven years. "I would like to know," he asked rhetorically, "who among the living would be as competent in Kant's philosophy as I?"[52] The *Critique of Pure Reason* was the most important book ever written in Europe, he continued, and it should be published in its first edition (1781) and not in its second (1787) or any of its subsequent editions, each of which was a virtual reprint of the second edition. In the harshest of terms, he condemned the second edition as mutilating, disfiguring, and spoiling Kant's original insights, and as producing a contradictory text. "In truth," he asserted, "the second edition is like a person whose leg was amputated and replaced by the wooden one."[53] By publishing the first edition, Schopenhauer implied, Kant's great work would not be hobbled by its author's act of self-mutilation.

Schopenhauer also diagnosed the causes for Kant's mutilation of his great work. His reviewers had accused him of offering a renewed form of idealism akin to Berkeley's, and many of his critics were upset by his crushing the sacred doctrines of rationalistic metaphysics, along with its safe religious implications. Moreover, Friedrich II, "the great King, the friend of light and defender of truth had just died [1786] and to his successor [Friedrich Wilhelm II] he [Kant] had to promise to write no more on religion. . . . "[54] This intimidated Kant, who was already suffering the effects of old age and infirmity, and so he was too weak to refrain for acting beneath himself. Consequently, he eliminated "offensive" material from his original work, added material that was contrary to his original and profound insights, and toned down other passages to appeal to public opinion. This was especially true concerning his original commitment to idealism, but due to carelessness he was not able to eliminate many passages that expressed his idealism, and this made his work fraught

---

[52] Schopenhauer *Gesammelte Briefe*, p. 166, Schopenhauer to Rosenkranz and Schubert, 24 August 1837.

[53] Ibid., p. 166; see *Critique of Pure Reason*, trans. Paul Guyer and Allen W. Wood (Cambridge: Cambridge University Press, 1998) pp. 66–72, for a discussion of the differences between the two editions.

[54] Ibid., p. 166.

with contradictions, many of which Schopenhauer had discussed in the appendix to *The World as Will and Representation*.

After Schopenhauer documented some of the "disfigurement" inflicted on the *First Critique*, he plead for the publication of the first edition and for relegating to an appendix changes and variants found in the second. "My good Sirs, fate has placed in your hands the return to the world of the most important book ever written in Europe, the *Critique of Pure Reason*, in its pure, non-falsified, and genuine form." He further intoned, "by your venture of a just *Restitutio in integrum* [restatement to previous condition], you will gain approval from all judicious people, win the gratitude of future generations and true honor, just at the point in time when real European life already begins to demand the book, which was written for all times.... Meanwhile, England and France are asking for that source of wisdom."[55] He then offered to accept all responsibility for their decision to follow his advice, promised to send them a collation of variants in the two editions, and gave them permission to publish the portion of his letter that specifically addressed the difference between the two editions.

Rosenkranz accepted Schopenhauer's advice and published the first critique in its first edition, relegating to an appendix the additions and variants of the second – a form in which the book would endure for years.[56] He also published extracts from the philosopher's letter almost exactly as Schopenhauer recommended, dropping, according to Schopenhauer's direction, a reference to Jacobi, who shared his assessment of the two editions.[57] Rosenkranz also dropped the passage in which Schopenhauer suggested that Kant had been intimidated by Friedrich Wilhelm II. The editor correctly pointed out that Kant had prepared the second edition of his masterpiece prior to the King's coronation. Schopenhauer, of course, countered Rosenkranz's claim by stating that this intimidation was not simply from this source, but also from the charge of offering a

---

55 Ibid., p. 167.
56 This is true of earlier English translations of the *Critique of Pure Reason*, such as those by J. M. D. Meiklejohn (1854) and Max Müller (1881).
57 See Schopenhauer, ibid., p. 167. Jacobi had claimed in his *David Hume on Belief* that he could understand many points from the first edition of the *Critique of Pure Reason* but that Kant's theory appeared as a complete impossibility in the second; see Jacobi's *Gesammelte Werke* (Leipzig, 1812–5), Vol. 2, p. 291fn. It is likely that Schopenhauer requested the removal of his reference to Jacobi to avoid association with the philosopher and, perhaps, to take full credit for the discovery of the radical differences between editions.

renewed Berkeleyanism. Kant, he also pointed out, served at the pleasure of the King and always had anxiety about losing his position. Rosenkranz was not persuaded by Schopenhauer's reply. Besides, he was correct. Schopenhauer had implied that Friedrich Wilhelm II had intimidated Kant to make changes in his manuscript. The Prussian King did demand that Kant not write on religious matters and on matters that could disparage the King's standing, but this was in 1794. At that time the practically minded Kant promised the King that he would not write or lecture on religion.

Given Schopenhauer's past history with such projects, one might imagine that he was astonished by Rosenkranz's acceptance of his advice. He was always confident that he only gave sound advice, grounded in good reasons. But the problem was, from his perspective, that the world was full of self-serving people, incapable of discerning between the good and bad. He must have been astonished that Rosenkranz had the good sense to follow good advice. After all, he knew that Rosenkranz was a Hegelian. Once he received Rosenkranz's letter announcing his decision, Schopenhauer praised the editor for putting aside his own personal commitments in order to serve humanity. Indeed, he praised the editor for ignoring all those things that might have kept him from doing the right thing, for ignoring worldly demands, and for distinguishing between a man and his office, station, nation, faith, and philosophical system or sect. In other words, he praised Rosenkranz for his nonpartisanship and for not holding Schopenhauer's philosophy against him. Even officers from warring armies, Schopenhauer wrote, can associate in a friendly way on neutral ground – implying that Kant's philosophy provided neutral ground.

But Schopenhauer could not maintain a nonpartisan attitude for long, and he felt compelled to say something about Rosenkranz's allegiance to Hegel – perhaps he did this because, as he said in the same letter, unlike the cautious Kant, he called everything by its name – he called a spade a "spade." "I hope that you vacate the shaky building of Hegelry," he teased, "before its collapse buries you and many others. And we who know the material from which it is constructed need no great sagacity to say this with certainty in advance of its collapse."[58] He then invited Rosenkanz to take

---

[58] Ibid., p. 169, Schopenhauer to Rosenkranz, 25 September 1837. He now charged that instead of omitting 32 pages from the first edition, Kant actually omitted 57. He also mentioned in this letter Kant's inclusion of "Refutation of Idealism" in the second edition – an odd omission from Schopenhauer's first letter, where he emphasized Kant's fear of idealism.

refuge in the old, but solid, structure of Kant's philosophy, where he need not fear "falling into the old abandoned rat nest of Leibnizianism, haunted by monads, pre-established harmony, optimism, and other grotesqueries and absurdities of the highest order." Never shy about making recommendations, he also suggested that Rosenkranz use an engraving of Kant by Johann Heinrich Lips to grace the edition. Of the four engravings of Kant that Schopenhauer owned, which all hung near one of Hume, this one best captured the great man's true appearance – as he was told by the painter Moses Siegfried Löwe (later Johann Michael Löwe), for whom Kant had sat. Rosenkranz, however, had taken as much advice as he would from Schopenhauer, and used an engraving by Johann Karl Barth, one that Schopenhauer had not mentioned. Schopenhauer closed this letter by including a lengthy collation of the two editions, as well as a list of printer's errors in the *Prolegomena to Any Future Metaphysics*, the *Critique of Practical Reason*, the *Critique of the Power of Judgment*, and an essay to which Schopenhauer attributed an especial significance, "What is the real progress that German metaphysics has made since the times of Leibniz and Wolff?" This essay, he held, was the most concise depiction of Kant's system and deserved to be published with his principal writings.[59]

Rosenkranz sent Schopenhauer a copy of *Kants Sämmtliche Werke* as a token of appreciation for his participation in the project.[60] The editor also praised the fourth book of *The World as Will in Representation* for its "magnificent, genuine mysticism," referring to it as a "sublime, deeply affecting poem."[61] Thus, the Königsberg philosopher set aside Schopenhauer's snide remark about the collapse of Hegel's philosophy and his

---

59 Kant drafted this essay in response to a question that its title restates. This question was posed by the Berlin Academy in 1793; see Kuehn, *Kant: A Biography*, pp. 376–7.

60 Rosenkranz and Schubert's edition appeared as *Kant's Sämtliche Werke* (Leipzig: Leopold Voss, 1838–42), 12 vols. Extracts from Schopenhauer's letter appear in the second volume, pp. xi–xiv. In his letter thanking Rosenkranz for this gift, Schopenhauer solicited his aid in obtaining Kant's autograph, and he also told Rosenkranz about a failed attempt to do so, when he traded one of Goethe's letters for what turned out to be a fake Kant autograph. Schopenhauer never recovered the Goethe letter. Later, the philosopher received, from Eduard Crüger, a copy of the *Critique of Practical Reason* with Kant's handwritten marginal notes; see, respectively, *Gespräche*, p. 198, and *Gesammelte Briefe* letter to Rosenkranz, 12 July 1838, p. 178 and the letter to Crüger, who also gave him the Buddha statue that he had gilded and displayed proudly in his apartment, p. 406.

61 Rosenkranz's words of praise are found in "History of the Kantian Philosophy," ("Geschichte der Kantischen Philosophie," 1842), *Kant's Werke*, Vol. 12, quoted in *Gesammelte Briefe*, p. 529.

warning about the rats' nest of Leibniz's philosophy. Rosenkranz, however, retained his loose allegiance to the philosopher of spirit, and although Hegel's philosophy did collapse, Rosenkranz was not completely buried by it, and he emerged from it with sufficient strength to attack his one-time collaborator for the very feature of his philosophy that he had at one time praised. In "To the Characterization of Schopenhauer" ["Zur charakteristik Schopenhauers," 1854], he tossed a stone from the old and solid foundation of Kant's philosophy, managing, at the same time, to take a swing also at the flute-playing of the man he dubbed "the Kaiser of German philosophy, crowned in Frankfurt":

Instead of the philosophy of death, let us hold on to Kant's philosophy of life, and let us wish that in place of the former, we firmly hold on to the so customary German optimism, which results from the faith in the inevitable victory of truly good things and also from the desire for actions leading to great deeds. A philosophy like the Schopenhauerian would completely lull us by its plaintive flute-tones into the region of death, of earthy passivity, while we need to be inspired by the trumpet charge of Kant's categorical imperative for the struggle with the misery and troubles of life.[62]

Schopenhauer dismissed Rosenkranz's essay as a rant full of hate and lies, fed by the Hegelian's envy and rage toward his success. Instead of replying to this assault, Schopenhauer used a common ploy – he had his followers do so for him.[63] It is almost needless to say that Rosenkranz became a member of Schopenhauer's enemies list.

Back in Berlin

Schopenhauer's return to Berlin naturally led him to attempt to jump-start his stalled teaching career. Obstinate as ever, and failing to learn from past experiences, he tried once more to steal Hegel's thunder by scheduling his lectures at the same time as those of his nemesis – three times a week,

---

[62] Rosenkranz, "Zur Charakteristik Schopenhauer," *Deutsche Wochenschrift*, ed. Karl Gödeke (Hannover: Rümpler, 1854), no. 22, p. 684, quoted in *Gesammelte Briefe*, p. 595; see p. 673 for his remarks about Schopenhauer as the "Kaiser of German Philosophy." Rosenkranz also insinuated that the essay that helped make Schopenhauer famous, John Oxenford's "Iconoclasm in German Philosophy," was probably written in Germany, by one of Schopenhauer's admirers; see p. 675.

[63] See Schopenhauer's letter to Julius Frauenstädt, 22 June 1854, for his claim that Rosenkranz's essay was motivated by envy and rage, and in which he sneered, "What a pitiful scoundrel this Rosenkranz is still"; see Schopenhauer, *Gesammelte Briefe*, p.

between noon and one o'clock. From 1826–7 through 1831–2, for eleven semesters during that period, his courses were listed in the Catalog of Lectures. He was not allowed to teach his moral philosophy, which was too unorthodox, so his lectures were on "The Foundations of Philosophy or Theory of the Whole of Cognition." Once he added "Comprising Dianoiology and Logic" to the title, supposing that future students would realize that unlike Hegel's tumbling dialectic of concepts, Schopenhauer viewed philosophy as the science of experiences as a whole and that experience itself devolved into representations, such that *philosophia prima* had to develop a theory of representations, which were of two kinds: intuitive or sensory representations, whose theory was a dianoiology, and abstract representations, whose theory constituted logic.[64] Four times he modified the title by adding "Including the Quintessence of Logic." But no matter what lure he used to hook students, they were not biting. He never attracted any dedicated philosophy students. One semester he drew three medical students (Winter 1826–7); another he drew a privy councilor, a dentist, a captain, and a riding master (Winter 1828–9) – dilettantes upon whose attendance one could not count. Once more, Schopenhauer failed to deliver a complete cycle of lectures. Again, his teaching career was a disaster.

Schopenhauer did not abandon hope for an academic position elsewhere, despite this second round of failure. He could blame the failure on the pestilential and mind-numbing effects of Hegel, who, while Schopenhauer was out of town, had had three more years to ruin Berlin's students. During his early Berlin years, he was considered for a faculty position at Giessen, with his despised reviewer Herbart as one of his rivals. But neither author nor reviewer received the appointment, which went to Joseph Hillebrand, whose son Karl and his wife, Jessie Taylor, would play a vital role in promoting Schopenhauer's philosophy. Mme. Karl Hillebrand would translate two of the philosopher's books into English.[65] Two years

---

[64] By 1826 Schopenhauer had developed his account of the subdivisions of philosophy, which would appear in the second edition of his principal work and then more clearly in *Parerga and Paralipomena*; see, respectively, *Manuscript Remains*, Vol. 3, p. 274f./*Der handschriftliche Nachlaß*, Vol. 3, p. 251f.; *The World as Will and Representation*, Vol. 2, pp. 179–83/*Sämtliche Werke*, Vol. 3, pp. 180–85; and *Parerga and Paralipomena*, Vol. 2, pp. 17–19/ibid., Vol. 6, pp. 18–21.

[65] Karl Hillebrand would favorably review Nietzsche's "Schopenhauer as Educator" in the *Allgemeine Zeitung Augsburg*, 18 December 1874. Hillebrand especially appreciated the essay

later, in 1823, Fries's old position at Jena was put up for grabs. Hegel's old nemesis was suspended by Duke Karl August, due to pressure exerted by the conservative Austrian and Prussian governments. Fries's liberalism, his call for representative government, and his advocacy of German unification could not be tolerated. Although Goethe supported Schopenhauer's candidacy for the Jena position, it was won by Johann Christian Schaumann.[66]

Tasting the failure of his teaching career for a second time, and sensing that a faculty position was not yet out of reach, Schopenhauer sought to become a *Privatdozent* elsewhere. In the fall of 1827, he contacted an acquaintance from Munich, Friedrich Wilhelm Thiersch, inquiring about the possibility of joining some university in southern Germany. He had in mind the University at Würzburg, because "no place appears to me so thoroughly suited to my inclination."[67] Würzburg had an inviting climate and it offered a slower, less hectic, and less expensive way of life than Berlin, "the large, crowded, restless city in the middle of a terrible sand desert, under a northern sky." He estimated that the cost of living was half that of Berlin. His interest, he told Thiersch, was to join bourgeois society and to go to a place where students were as eager to learn as he was eager to teach. His interest was not to make money, he continued; he had all he needed. He just desired to have *Jus legendi* at the University. Schopenhauer asked Thiersch to be discrete. He was already listed in the winter catalog of lectures at Berlin.

Thiersch was discrete, but also too slow in response to Schopenhauer's inquiry. After waiting two months for Thiersch's reply, the philosopher wrote another letter, reminding him of his request. Eventually, in the spring of 1828, Schopenhauer made a bid to join the University at Würzburg. This triggered the standard type of investigation. The Royal State Minister of the Interior contacted the Bavarian Envoy in Berlin,

---

for its idolization of Schopenhauer. The Jesse Taylor (Mme. Karle Hillebrand) translation appeared as *Two Essays. I. On the Fourfold Root of the Principle of Sufficient Reason. II. On the Will in Nature* (London: G. Bell, 1889). It has been recently reprinted by Cosimo Classics, New York, 2007. Taylor met Schopenhauer around 1859 in Frankfurt and was reported to have told the philosopher that she found his principal work too wordy, to which he replied, "Not one word too many!" See Schopenhauer, *Gespräche*, p. 368. Madame Hillebrand was the first to translate Schopenhauer's "*Vorstellung*" as "representation."

[66] See Hermann Kantorowiez's "Schopenhauer's akademische Erfahrungen," *Frankfurter Zeitung*, 28 May 1929, excerpted in *Kantstudien*, Vol. 34, pp. 516–17.

[67] Schopenhauer, *Gesammelte Briefe*, p. 105, Schopenhauer to Thiersch, 4 September 1827.

the Count of Luxburg, for a report on the philosopher. The Envoy reported that Schopenhauer's father had been a successful banker in Danzig and that his mother was a well-known author. He also explained Schopenhauer's desire to relocate as a function of the Marquet lawsuit. Of the candidate himself, he continued, "he has no reputation whatsoever as a writer or teacher . . . Schoppenhauer [sic], whose unattractive exterior is well-known to me, would not be a great gain for the University of Würzburg."[68] The minister of culture, Edward von Schenk, also asked a former instructor at Berlin, Friedrich Karl von Savigny, to assess Schopenhauer's fitness for Würzburg. Once more, the reply was negative. "You ask about *Privatdozent* Dr. Schopenhauer," Savigny reported, spelling the applicant's name correctly. "I cannot judge his writings, since I am not acquainted with them at all. But concerning his person, he has always appeared to me to be very arrogant, and I have heard more against than for him."[69] Although Schopenhauer was inclined to Würzburg, it was not inclined to him.

But even before the fatal negative reports drizzled down to Würzburg, Schopenhauer contracted Georg Friedrich Creuzer about his prospects at Heidelberg.[70] As was his wont, and just as he did when he first sought an academic position, he gave the Heidelberg philologist the same set of reasons for his desire to "transplant" himself that he had used elsewhere. But Heidelberg had as little interest in a failed academic as it had earlier, in 1819, in an unknown philosopher. Thus the second Heidelberg attempt also came to naught. With no prospects at Würzburg or Heidelberg, Schopenhauer had to remain in Berlin, where his desire to teach was not matched by students' desires to learn – from him.

Schopenhauer's remark to Thiersch regarding his desire to enter *"bürgerlich"* society was sincere. A note from his private diary from that time is revealing. "I associate with the desire to possess a wife who will wholly belong to me," he recorded, "the plan to move to a country town where I have no opportunity to buy books – a need whose satisfaction is threatened by my financial position in Berlin in the event of my getting married."[71] Schopenhauer's economic worries were a function of his

---

[68] Quoted in Schopenhauer, ibid., p. 516.

[69] Quoted in Ibid., p. 516.

[70] See Schopenhauer, ibid., p. 106, his letter to Creuzer, 2 February 1828. He reminded Creuzer that they had met in the summer of 1819 in Heidelberg.

[71] Schopenhauer, *Manuscript Remains*, Vol. 4, p. 493/ *Der handschriftliche Nachlaß*, Vol. 4, 2, p. 112.

losses through his investment is Mexican bonds in 1826, following the bad advice of his friend Heinrich von Lowtzow – whom, oddly, Schopenhauer did not blame – and Alexander von Humboldt.[72]

Caroline Medon was probably not part of his game plan "to possess a wife." And, if his desire was to possess a new love interest, Flora Weiß, then it was an ill-conceived plan, because it was carried out in a manner that made Schopenhauer appear as a pathetic, perhaps even lecherous, older man.

Weiß was just seventeen when she caught the philosopher's eye. But as much as he was attracted to her, she was repelled by the thirty-nine year-old *Privatdozent*. During a boating party on one of Berlin's lakes, according to one of the Weiß family's stories, Schopenhauer brought along some grapes that he shared with Flora and one of her girlfriends. Weiß quietly slipped the grapes over the side of the boat, "because the old Schopenhauer had handled them."[73] It was also part of the family lore that when Schopenhauer asked Johann Weiß for leave to court his daughter, he was taken aback, exclaiming that she was still a child, to which the philosopher replied that that was what pleased him. But after he mentioned that he had sufficient income to care well for Flora's future, the Berlin art dealer left the decision to the young girl, believing that the relationship would go nowhere – which it did: "She felt such a lively aversion towards [Schopenhauer], which would only be proven and intensified by his small gifts, that the failure of the courtship could not be doubted."[74] Curiously, Schopenhauer's father was twenty years older than his mother – but not twenty-two.

As early as 1821, Schopenhauer had anticipated that a second edition of *The World as Will and Representation* would be demanded by the public ten years after its publication, and in 1825, he drafted a brief sketch for a preface for a second edition: "The first edition appeared at the end of 1818. As the public began to read the book eight years after, a second edition became necessary in the tenth year. For me it was very desirable to live to see this edition which was so unexpected; for I myself was then able to prepare this with all the additions which I had made to my work in those years, as I was its only reader (for the little professional men at the

---

[72] For Schopenhauer's reference to Alexander von Humboldt and the Mexican bonds, see his letter to Anthime Grégoire Blésimaire 10 December 1836, *Gesammelte Brief,* p. 158.

[73] Schopenhauer, *Gespräche,* p. 58.

[74] Schopenhauer, *Gespräche,* p. 59.

universities are not to be reckoned as readers)."[75] Schopenhauer never said why he expected any such readership; perhaps he overestimated the effect of Jean Paul's ambivalent book note about his principal work. The year 1826 came and went, without any significant notice of his work.

Almost ten years to the date from the appearance of *The World as Will and Representation*, Schopenhauer contacted his publisher discreetly as to whether a second edition was needed. He did so under the guise of asking for an accounting of the book's sales. Schopenhauer wanted to know exactly how many books sold and whether the later demand was greater than its earlier demand. He made this query "not from a pecuniary interest," he wrote, but from a literary one.[76] Brockhaus's response dashed the philosopher's plan for a second edition, despite the fact that he had been assiduously developing material to clarify, augment, and extend his ideas into new areas of inquiry. Of the original run of 750 books, 150 remained on the shelves. Exactly how many were sold could not be determined, because a significant number had been converted into wastepaper. This disturbing bit of news provided Schopenhauer with a greater incentive to become a translator: if not of Hume and Sterne, then of Gracián and Kant. What else could a teacher without students and a philosopher without readers do? Translate his color theory into Latin and hope that foreign scholars would recognize the errors of Newton and laud the author of the first, true, and genuine theory of color? And in that work, one could chide the British and the French for being under the realist sway of Locke and the French sensualist Étienne Bonnot de Condillac, who naively championed both Newton and Locke. Perhaps by emphasizing how Kant had demonstrated that space, time, and causality are *a priori* forms of human cognition and that we experience the appearances of things and not things in themselves, perhaps he would then interest the British and French in Kant, and in Kant's one true heir. Schopenhauer attempted all of this and none of it worked.[77]

---

[75] Schopenhauer, *Manuscript Remains*, Vol. 3, pp. 219–20/ *Der handschriftliche Nachlaß*, Vol. 3, p. 199.

[76] Schopenhauer, *Gesammelte Briefe*, p. 108, Schopenhauer to F. A. Brockhaus, 24 November 1828.

[77] Schopenhauer criticized the British for being unduly influenced by the realist Locke, and he criticized the French for likewise being influenced by Locke through his French popularizer, Condillac. People in both countries, he lamented, were ignorant of Kant; see, for example,

As Schopenhauer continued to struggle in Berlin, and as he increasingly tried to console himself with the belief that the time for his philosophy lay in the future, the plague from the East, the so-called "Asiatic cholera" or "Asiatic hyena," erupted in Russia in the fall of 1830. Commencing in Odessa, it killed its way to the Crimea, reaching Moscow early in 1831. Unwittingly, Russian soldiers carried the deadly *Vibrio comma* into Poland, infecting Danzig, then under Prussian control, in the late spring 1831. The King of Prussia ordered the eastern boarders of Prussia sealed, requiring all travelers to be put under quarantine. Despite these efforts, by the late summer of 1831, the epidemic spread to Berlin. Those who could flee the city fled. Hegel moved his family to the nearby town of Kreuzberg to wait out the deadly disease. Lured to return to Berlin for the new semester of 1831, and believing that the worse of the plague was over, the dialectician returned to assume his teaching duties. It was too soon, and he died during the late afternoon on 14 November.[78]

Fleeing Berlin Again and the Metaphysics of Ghosts

Schopenhauer did not witness the lengthy funeral procession that followed two days after the spirit left Hegel. Nor did he attend the benediction that was delivered at the Great Hall of the University. Moreover, he did not hear the graveside eulogy. Had he been in Berlin, it is not clear whether he would have attended any or all of these ceremonies. If he had been in Berlin and had attended any part of the funeral spectacle, he would not have done so to pay his respects to his fallen colleague. Instead, it is easy to imagine that Schopenhauer would only have attended in the hope that the physical absence of the dead philosopher would break his spell and the crowd would have come to its senses exclaiming, "What simpletons we have been! That was no giant, but a pygmy in whom there was nothing and came to nought."[79] If Schopenhauer experienced any sadness about

---

the second chapter of his "Theoria colorum physiologica," *Sämtliche Werke*, Vol. 1, pp. 6–13, and his letter of 14 March 1829 to Justus Radius, *Gesammelte Briefe*, p. 109.

[78] The standard view is that Hegel was a victim of cholera. Terry Pinkard makes a convincing case that he died from a chronic upper gastrointestinal disease; see *Hegel: A Biography*, p. 659.

[79] Schopenhauer, "On the Basis of Morality," p. 30/*Sämtliche Werke*, First Preface to *Die beiden Grundprobleme der Ethik*, p. xxxvi, which is a lengthy quotation from Gracián's *The Critic* [*El criticón*, 1657]. Schopenhauer translated this quotation into German, using it to blast Hegel's followers.

Hegel's death, it would only be because Hegel was not alive to witness his brilliant success.[80]

Schopenhauer was in the cholera-free city of Frankfurt when his *bête noire* perished. He had abandoned Berlin on 25 August with even greater haste than he had in 1813, when he feared being conscripted to defend the city against a possible assault by Napoleon. His books remained behind, a significant loss for a bibliophile, as well as his Gracián manuscript. Caroline Medon, though, remained in Berlin. She had promised to go with the philosopher, but balked at his demand that she not bring her second son. Cholera was a greater threat to Schopenhauer than the Grand Army, however. Napoleon never attacked Berlin, but the cholera did. And Schopenhauer believed that he was forewarned about the danger of the disease more than a year earlier. On New Year's Eve in 1830, he had a dream that he analyzed as foreseeing his death in the next year. The dream was so vivid and thick with meaning that the philosopher recorded it for posterity: "From my sixth to tenth year I had a bosom friend and constant playmate of exactly the same age who was called Gottfried Jänish and who died when I in my tenth year was in France. In the last thirty years I had rarely thought about him. – But on that night in question, I arrived at a country unknown to me: a group of men was standing in a field and among them was a tall, slim, grown-up man who had been introduced to me, I do not know in what way, as that very Gottfried Jänish, and who greeted me."[81]

The dream induced the philosopher to flee the great city, and he believed that it articulated a hypothetical truth, that is, "If he left Berlin, then he would not die." Schopenhauer knew how to draw the proper inference from this hypothetical. He left Berlin. Consequently, he did not die. The power of *modus ponens* led him to construct a valid argument to conclude his Berlin Period. Of course, the argument was not sound. He could have fled and then died. Nevertheless, he bid farewell to Berlin.

Immediately upon his arrival in Frankfurt on 28 August, the philosopher had another extraordinary experience. This time it was not a dream, but a "perfectly clear apparition" of his parents. "In it," he hedged,

---

[80] This was Schopenhauer's analysis of why we would mourn the loss of an enemy almost as much of that of a friend; see *Parerga and Paralipomena*, Vol. 2, p. 586/*Sämtliche Werke*, Vol. 6, p. 620.

[81] Schopenhauer, *Manuscript Remains*, Vol. 4, p. 61/*Der handschriftliche Nachlaß*, Vol. 4, 1, p. 46.

"(I think) were my parents and it indicated that I would now outlive my mother who at that time was still alive; my father who was already dead was carrying a light in his hand."[82] It appeared that his father was lighting the way to the land of the dead, and because he witnessed this ghostly procession, he believed that this was a sign that he would live after his mother's death. Of course, this was an ambiguous scene. He could just have well concluded that his mother had died, which would also have implied that he already outlived her. When Schopenhauer told his mother about this vision, she viewed it "as proof that you [Schopenhauer] still think of the old times."[83] In any case, the philosopher understood this "waking dream" as also signifying that his "transplantation" to Frankfurt was well-conceived. He was wrong – for the time being.

During the time of Schopenhauer's dream about Jänish and his waking dream about his parents, animal magnetism, ghosts, spirit phenomena, mind reading, prophetic dreams, clairvoyance, telekinesis, and communication with the dead had been very much on his mind. He was reading *The Seeress of Prevost. Discourses on the Inner Life of the Human and on the Arising of a Spiritual World in Ours* [*Die Sehern von Prevost. Eröffnungen über das Innere Leben des Menschen und über einer Geisterwelt in die unsere*, Stuttgart: J. G. Cotta, 1838]. Its author was the physician and poet Justinus Kerner, the tireless interviewer of mediums and advocate for the spiritual world. *The Seeress of Prevost* was a massive tome featuring a lengthy account and analysis of the behavior of a young country girl, a "clairvoyant somnambulist," who, while in a trance, communicated with the spiritual world. This young woman, Friederike Hauffe, was also credited with possessing healing powers.

Schopenhauer considered Kerner to be gullible. Nevertheless, he credited him with compiling "the most detailed and authentic reports on spirit seeing that have appeared in print."[84] The scientifically trained philosopher also endorsed the physician's attempt to provide a physiological

[82] Ibid., Vol. 4, p. 62/ibid., Vol. 4, 1, p. 47.

[83] Lütkehaus, *Die Schopenhauers*, p. 335, Johanna to Schopenhauer, 24 February 1832. Although Johanna referred to his New Year's Eve dream in her letter, he must have also told her about his waking dream of his parents. Given Johanna's warm tone in her letter, it is doubtful that Schopenhauer shared his analysis of the vision.

[84] Schopenhauer, *Parerga and Paralipomena*, Vol. 1, p. 308/*Sämtliche Werke*, Vol. 5, p. 328; See ibid., Vol. 1, p. 264/ibid., Vol. 5, p. 286; and *Gespräche*, p. 91, for his claim about Kerner's credulity.

explanation of this phenomenon. Schopenhauer was willing to accept the claim that there was a "dream organ," the "ganglionic sensorium," which also functioned during typical sorts of dreams. When this organ was stimulated, allegedly by spirits, it produced a dreamlike state in the waking brain, which also tired the waking brain and produced the trance, which was a light slumber. Only the clairvoyant could experience the visions so produced, given their source – although Schopenhauer also believed, as did Keiner, that such vision could be transferred sympathetically from the seer to other sensitive parties. He also endorsed Kerner's insistence that spirit seeing was an "objective" phenomenon and not simply a "subjective" one, akin to the dreams of a sick mind. Likewise, he found apt the ghost hunter's claim that spirits "are seen not by the somatic eye, but with the spiritual."[85]

Schopenhauer, however, would not accept Kerner's claim that just as the somatic eye revealed the physical world, the spiritual eye revealed the spiritual world. With this bit of nonsense he considered Kerner to be like many scientists who attempted to explain phenomena that transcended the realm of natural science. If these scientists do not dismiss these phenomena as superstitious nonsense, because they hold some crude form of materialism, then they become like Kerner – that is, "proclaim themselves as enlighteners of the world who have learned their chemistry, physics, mineralogy, zoology, or physiology, but nothing else on earth; to this they add their only other knowledge, namely what sticks to them from the catechism they learned in their school years."[86] This leads such thinkers, he continued, to dogmatize randomly on these phenomena, ignorant of philosophy and as if the *Critique of Pure Reason* had been written and remained on the moon.

Kerner's credulity and his philosophical ignorance could be found in both his willingness to accept almost all reports and demonstrations of spiritual phenomena as authentic, and in his willingness to understand these phenomena in the same terms as the somnambulists, which Schopenhauer attributed to the fact that Kerner shared the same

---

[85] Ibid., Vol. 1, p. 306/ibid., Vol. 5, p. 325f. Schopenhauer provided no citation for this quotation from Kerner.

[86] Schopenhauer, *On the Will in Nature*, p. 4/*Sämtliche Werke*, Vol. 4, "Ueber den Willen in der Natur," p. x.

"catechism" as his subjects. The featured medium in *The Seeress of Prevost* was once described as kneeling, singing, and praying with a group of spirits, who were condemned to haunt the scenes of their crimes. She was described as guiding them through the Ten Commandments and as providing the condemned with religious instruction as "the clergy does to children." Kerner reported that in these instances, sinners and murderers were blessed, or would have a change of heart, which moved them to reveal the burial place of their victims so that they could be brought to the churchyard for proper burial. Schopenhauer thought that Kerner's acceptance of the superstitions and simple-minded religious beliefs of the prophetess, whom the philosopher viewed as a naïve, unsophisticated young girl from the hills, demonstrated his own lack of sophistication. Schopenhauer derided, "In such a stupid world-order I would certainly not like to become so blessed, but would sooner saunter around in order to be able to sneer at it undisturbed."[87]

Schopenhauer recognized fraud and deception by alleged clairvoyants. There was good money and fame to be had by such practices, as well as by promoting and publicizing such miracles. Yet he believed that there were authentic instances of paranormal phenomena, just as there were inauthentic cases. His attitude toward spirit seeing and related phenomena was similar to his attitude toward mysticism. There were fake mystics and there were financial and other self-serving interests in being or reporting about one. But there were authentic mystics and genuine mystical experiences. Schopenhauer accepted the authenticity of these extraordinary experiences because, as he was fond of reiterating, they have been reported in all countries, at all times, and by all people. The same was true of magic, spirit seeing, clairvoyance, and related phenomena. For that reason, he concluded that there must be something to them and something worthy of philosophical explanation by someone who knew that the First Critique had not been written on the moon.

The philosopher was also sensitive to the difficulty of describing uncommon experiences. One of his most cherished mystics, the seventeenth-century French quietist Jeanne-Marie Bouvier de la Guyon, was a case in point. He recommended her autobiography and *Les Torrens*

---

[87] Schopenhauer, *Manuscript Remains*, Vol. 4, p. 55/*Der handschriftliche Nachlaß*, Vol. 4, 1, p. 41.

to his readers for the accounts of her mystical states. But he also warned that this great and beautiful soul should be read with "allowances for the superstitions of her faculty of reason."[88] This remark was made not simply because he believed that women possessed a feebler faculty of reason than men, but from what he saw as a failing common to all mystics. As they attempted to "eff" the ineffable, they drew on their own superstitions and religious beliefs. Although paranormal experiences did not have the same profound status as mystical states, their uncommon and at times ambiguous presentations invited the same misinterpretations and explanations as those of mystics. These simple souls only had religion, the metaphysics of the people, to attempt to explain these extraordinary experiences.

Besides the aspiration to provide a comprehensive explanation of the totality of all experiences, as Schopenhauer would later describe the goal of his philosophy, he possessed a ravenous curiosity that made him open to all types of subjects.[89] Moreover, he took considerable pride in exploring topics that other philosophers neglected, even if by his doing so, others would cast aspersions on his character and his philosophy, a risk he knew he had taken by writing on sexual love, pederasty, and spirit seeing.[90] But even at a more personal level, Schopenhauer had experienced some of the things for which he attempted to provide a philosophical explanation. In addition to his own prophetic Berlin dream, and his waking dream of his parents, he reported other like episodes in his life. Once when he had finished composing a lengthy and important business letter, he mistakenly poured ink over the letter instead of writing sand. The ink poured onto the floor, and he summoned his maid to take care of the

---

[88] Schopenhauer, *The World as Will and Representation*, Vol. 1, p. 385/*Sämtliche Werke*, Vol. 2, p. 455.

[89] See Schopenhauer, *The World as Will and Representation*, Vol. 2, p. 181/*Sämtliche Werke*, Vol. 3, p. 201, where he claims that "metaphysics is the correct explanation of experience as a whole." This chapter of his principal work, "On the Human Need for Metaphysics," is his most elaborate and detailed discussion of the aims of his philosophy.

[90] See Schopenhauer, *Gespräche*, p. 127. Frauenstädt reports Schopenhauer saying that the subjects of sexual love and spirit seeing, phenomena to which philosophers had paid little heed, were granted their rights by his metaphysics; also see p. 91, where Frauenstädt describes the philosopher's irritation at his suggestion that the essay on spirit seeing would lead his readers to have scruples and doubt about his principal work. But when Schopenhauer added the appendix on pederasty to his chapter on the metaphysics of sexual love in the last edition of his principal work (1859), he closed it by remarking that he had to do so to give his critics "the opportunity of slandering me by saying that I defend and commend pederasty," *The World as Will and Representation*, Vol. 2, p. 567/*Sämtliche Werke*, Vol. 3, 651.

mess. As she scrubbed the ink off of the floor, she said that she had dreamt last night that she would be doing so. The skeptical philosopher asked her for proof, and she told him that she had told another maid about her dream. The second maid verified the story. Another time, during a lively dinner party in Milan, his "beautiful hostess" asked whether he knew the three numbers she had chosen for the lottery. Almost in a trance, her guest "correctly mentioned the first and the second, but gave the third incorrectly, because her merriment confused me; I woke up, as it were, and now reflected."[91] Schopenhauer took this experience as evidence that he was mildly clairvoyant.

Schopenhauer's interest in paranormal experiences has been described as expressing his "queer weakness for occultism."[92] And although he did possess an abiding curiosity about what might be called borderline or fringe phenomena, as well as an edacious appetite for the abnormal and unusual, there was nothing "queer" or "weak" about these interests. Even if the accounts of these experiences were, from his point of view, absurd, these phenomena were universally reported. He also considered his own philosophical stance as abnormal and unusual and, for that reason, "queer." Indeed, as he was reading *The Seeress of Prevost* and other such books – at his death, his library contained more than 100 books dealing with the paranormal – he noted that his idealism articulated miracles surpassing in all incredibility all fairy-tales and fables ever invented, and whose articulation risked his losing all credence among the vast majority of Europeans, whom he viewed as materialists and realists. To claim that one carried the whole world around in one's head, and to view it as the objectification of will, was as wild as a central event in the *Bhagavad-Gītā*, "when Krishna appeared to Arjuna in his true divine form with his hundred thousand arms, eyes, mouths, and so on."[93]

Schopenhauer was silent about animal magnetism, magic, clairvoyance, extra-sensory perception, spirits, and the like in the first edition of his principal work. Although he had already exhibited an interest in

---

[91] Schopenhauer, *Parerga and Paralipomena*, Vol. 1, p. 305 / *Sämtliche Werke*, Vol. 5, p. 324; see ibid., Vol. 1, p. 254 / ibid., Vol. 5, p. 270, for the story of the maid.

[92] Arthur O. Lovejoy, "Schopenhauer as an Evolutionist," *Mind*, Vol. 21 (1911), p. 116. Lovejoy also makes a convincing case that Schopenhauer was an evolutionist and mutationist of a strange sort. This article still repays the costs of its reading.

[93] Schopenhauer, *Manuscript Remains*, Vol. 4, p. 45 / *Der handschriftliche Nachlaß*, Vol. 4, 1, p. 32.

these phenomena, no ghosts haunted his work. He had not arrived at a proper explanation of such, so the caution of silence was the most prudent stance. After all, he knew that he had already provided sufficient grist for his critics' mills, and it made no sense to attempt to treat these topics sympathetically – it would have merely provided them with further means to discredit his views. Moreover, the camps were radically split on animal magnetism between hard-headed scientists, who rejected it almost out of hand, and those who were inclined to some form of spiritualistic or super-natural explanation to support its validity. It is likely that Schopenhauer first became interested in both animal magnetism and its controversial nature as a student at Berlin. His physics professor, Paul Erman, viewed it as superstitious nonsense, and he convinced the Prussian government to form a commission to explore the existence of an alleged new force, animal magnetism, which was analogous to magnetism. The Wars of Liberation, however, disrupted the commission's work and they came to no certain conclusions. In 1817, the government sponsored a prize-essay contest on animal magnetism, but by 1822, none of the twenty-two replies were judged worthy of being awarded a prize.

Meanwhile, two proponents of magnetism were appointed to the medical faculty, much to the chagrin of Erman and many of the faculty. Schopenhauer became acquainted with one of the two, Karl Christian Wolfart, who had met earlier with the agent provocateur for the controversial phenomenon, Franz Anton Mesmer, an Austrian physician, who, with bar magnets in hand, introduced magnetism into hospital treatment. Later, Mesmer would drop the magnets, using other and various means to affect, in various ways, the all-penetrating cosmic ether to hypnotize his patients. As a *Privatdozent* in Berlin, Schopenhauer became acquainted with Wolfart and thought of him as a "good fellow," despite the fact that he had completely ruined his reputation and wrecked his career due to his sexual antics with one of his married somnambulists.[94] Schopenhauer, of course, was not beyond sexual indiscretions himself, and he recognized the almost omnipotent power of sexuality even over those of a noble nature. It was easy for him not to hold this against someone who, with the addition of a couple of well-placed h's, would have a last name that

---

[94] Schopenhauer, *Gespräche*, p. 262. Schopenhauer's remark about Wolfart was reported by Carl George Bähr, from a conversation on 14 May 1858.

literally meant "welfare [*Wohlfahrt*]," the very condition he consciously hoped to promote among his patients.

Schopenhauer may have been well disposed to Wolfart because the magnetizing physician gave the ever-curious lecturer a tour of the sleeping quarters of his somnambulists and others of his patients, allowing the philosopher to observe magnetism first hand. Wolfart even allowed him to interview a forty-year-old female somnambulist, whom Schopenhauer magnetized simply by looking at her. He was impressed by what he observed. "When one of the somnambulists falls into a trance and becomes clairvoyant," he reported to a friend, "her facial features reach a state of sublimity, her speech becomes more refined than it is otherwise. One stands before her as before nature itself.... "[95] His own reaction to the clairvoyant somnambulist was so great that he forgot a number of questions he meant to ask her.

Schopenhauer's reaction to Wolfart's somnambulists was reminiscent of his response to the "invisible girl" almost twenty years earlier when, in London, he heard a girl's voice, speaking in French, German, and English, through different trumpets projecting from a hollow metal ball suspended by a wire from the ceiling. He was thoroughly amazed by that phenomenon just as he was by the somnambulists. The young Schopenhauer, however, recognized the invisible girl's ability as a "strange, clever trick," even though he could not explain it.[96] The older Schopenhauer did not likewise recognize clairvoyance as a trick, and he sought to ultimately explain it. He tended to accept magnetism and other paranormal phenomena at face value and with the same nonskeptical attitude he expressed in his philosophy. Although he was generally suspicious about the motivations of people he encountered in his everyday life – especially those who dealt with his finances – his attitude was much different toward anything that he thought could help corroborate his philosophy. And just as many people eagerly embraced animal magnetism because they saw it as evidence of a spiritual world, which helped validate their belief in an afterlife, Schopenhauer saw in paranormal phenomena evidence to help corroborate his metaphysics. Indeed, he did so in ways that demonstrated

[95] Ibid., p. 262.
[96] Schopenhauer, *Reise-Tagbücher aus den Jahren 1803–1804*, p. 65, footnote, for the entry dated 6 October 1803.

his own credulity. After witnessing the performance of the magnetizer "Signor Regazzoni of Bergamo," he became as hypnotized as one of the entertaining Italian's subjects. "No one," he wrote, "could be left in any doubt about their genuineness [of Regazzoni's feats] except perhaps those to whom nature had completely denied all capacity for a comprehension of pathological conditions." There are such persons, he continued, but "they should become lawyers, parsons, merchants, or soldiers, but not in heaven's name doctors . . . since in medicine diagnosis is the principal thing."[97]

Dr. Schopenhauer, though, had the skills to diagnose the metaphysics whose symptoms were expressed in animal magnetism. With no prospect looming on the horizon for a second edition of his principal work, and as a strategy to cultivate an audience sufficiently large to demand a new edition, Schopenhauer published *On the Will in Nature*, which bore the stumbling subtitle, *A Discussion of the Corroborations from the Empirical Sciences That the Authors Philosophy Has Received since Its First Appearance*. Although Schopenhauer's private and professional lives had been a shambles during his Berlin years and the four years thereafter, his intellectual life was inversely rich. He rethought his philosophy through the hundreds of pages he wrote for unheard lectures. His manuscript books for that period continue the process of reviewing, correcting, enhancing, and extending his basic ideas to new domains of inquiry. As Arthur Hübscher has noted, this period in Schopenhauer's life is "in a remarkable way [one] . . . of an enhanced productivity."[98] Many of Schopenhauer's reflections from these notebooks would later find their way into his future books and into new editions of his earlier ones. So would his reflections on animal magnetism and magic.

Schopenhauer had continued to study the natural sciences during this period – indeed, this was a lifelong practice – and he agreed with Kant that the natural sciences required a metaphysical support. *On the Will in Nature* was written to supply that and to demonstrate that the best findings of the natural sciences required exactly the metaphysical grounding provided by

---

[97] Schopenhauer, *On the Will in Nature*, p. 105n./*Sämtliche Werke*, Vol. 4, p. 102n. In the same footnote, Schopenhauer recommended L. A. V. Dubourg's *Antoine Regazzoni de Bergame à Francfort sur Mein* (Frankfurt am Main, 1854) for an accurate account of Regazzoni's feats. Schopenhauer claimed that these feats were genuine, "which is unmistakable to anyone who is not devoid of all sense for a comprehension of organic nature."

[98] Schopenhauer, *Manuscript Remains*, Vol. 3, p. x/*Der handschriftliche Nachlaß*, Vol. 3, p. xi.

his metaphysics. By 1835, he had come to accept animal magnetism as a settled fact, and because he thought that magnetism produced phenomena analogous to those that had been referred to as "magical," the philosopher drew connections between the two subjects. He would also provide a metaphysical ground for these phenomena in the lengthiest chapter of that book, "Animal Magnetism and Magic."

It was in the second edition of *On the Will in Nature* that he would later introduce the amazing Signor Regazzoni, the great magnetizer, who hypnotized members of his audience through the mere force of his will – well, according to the awestruck philosopher. For example, a woman was invited on stage to play the piano. Standing fifteen paces away, Regazzoni paralyzed the woman, making her unable to play. Another woman was summoned on stage and as the magical Italian walked behind her, he made her fall backward, without any physical contact. To explain this event from a physical standpoint, Schopenhauer hypothesized that the Signor had isolated her brain from her spinal cord, and thereby her sensible and motor nerves, which produced a cataleptic state. Like the tumbling woman, Schopenhauer fell for Regazzoni's act – it never occurred to him that the woman was a plant.[99]

Ragazzoni accomplished his effects not through the magical influence of his will, Schopenhauer believed, but simply through will. Theorizing from his transcendental standpoint, which recognized the *principium individuationis*, space and time, as ideal, Schopenhauer viewed Ragazzoni's feats and magnetic phenomena in general as expressing "pure will itself, separated as much as possible from all representations."[100] Such occurrences cannot be explained through appeal to the *nexus physicus*, he realized. By violating natural laws, these events could only be pronounced frauds. They could be explained, Schopenhauer argued, by positing a *nexus metaphysicus*, something provided by his metaphysics of will, which obviated individuality by

[99] See William von Schröder's "Der Frankfurter Skandal um den Magnetiseur Ragazzoni," *Frankfurter Allgemeine Zeitung*, 31 December 1957, for scandals associated with Ragazzoni's Frankfurt act. Two Frankfurt physicians investigated Ragazzoni, interviewing him in his apartment, and found him incapable of reproducing the feats of his stage act; see Schopenhauer, *Gesammelte Briefe*, p. 593. The star-struck Schopenhauer reported to the skeptical Frauenstädt that he had signed Regazzoni's scrapbook as a witness to his feats; see ibid., p. 356, letter to Frauenstädt, 30 November 1854.
[100] Schopenhauer, *On the Will in Nature*, p. 104/*Sämtliche Werke*, Vol. 4, p. 102.

viewing magnetizer and somnambulist ultimately as one.[101] Thus it was not the bar magnets Mesmer first held in his hands that he postulated as activating a magnetic force that affected animal bodies, nor was it a stimulation of some all-pervading ether that produced some event at a distance. Such physicalistic explanations could not survive scientific investigation, and so to cling to these would discredit the very real phenomena that led to such failed attempts. Thus by providing a metaphysical grounding for magnetic phenomena, Schopenhauer viewed himself as doing what he had thought he had done for the natural sciences; that is, as having completed the scientific image of the world by providing an metaphysical explanation of what is presupposed and unexplainable by science. This metaphysics, moreover, would also serve to explain observable phenomena that eluded scientific explanation. And, if hard-nosed empiricists discredited his views, it was simply, he thought, that for them the *Critique of Pure Reason* was written and remained on the moon.

If communication between magnetizers and somnambulists were possible through a *nexus metaphysicus*, Schopenhauer reasoned, then clairvoyance, mind-reading, telekinesis, projecting one's thought into those of others, sharing the same dream with another, and other spirit phenomena were also possible due to this *nexus*. Thus foreknowledge of future events and the presence of those who are absent, of the dying, and of the dead, which all seem impossible, given the laws of space, time, and causality, become possible due to the metaphysical unity of will. Schopenhauer's waking dream of his absent mother and dead father and the warning of a future death in Berlin rested on the unity of will. One could only deny these paranormal experiences, Schopenhauer argued, if one were a realist, like the English and French, naively believing that we experience

---

[101] In the second edition of his principal work, Schopenhauer classified compassion, sexual love, which asserts the life of the species over the individual, and magic, including such phenomena as animal magnetism, sympathetic cures, and action at a distance, as forms of sympathy (*Sympathie*), which he defined "as the empirical emerging of the will's metaphysical identity, through the physical multiplicity of its appearance," *The World as Will and Representation*, Vol. 2, p. 601/*Sämtliche Werke*, Vol. 3, p. 691f. Schopenhauer was sometimes insensitive to the fact that he was trespassing on the transcendent with such claims, although he did recognize this at other times. For example, he said that his readers would find his metaphysics of sexual love too transcendent, and he would term his essay, "Transcendent Speculation on the Apparent Deliberateness in the Fate of the Individual," a "mere metaphysical fantasy;" see Schopenhauer, ibid., Vol. 2, p. 533/ibid., Vol. 3, p. 610 and *Parerga and Paralipomena*, Vol. 1, p. 201/*Sämtliche Werke*, Vol. 5, p. 213.

things in themselves and that we are furnished directly with absolutely true relations and connections between things. One would have to be like a physicist who believed that the laws of the material world were unconditioned. But then, like the English, the French, and this physicist, one would be only under the sway of Locke and ignorant of Kant.

By regarding animal magnetism as an established fact and opposing opinions as mere prejudice, Schopenhauer had reason to accept magic. Animal magnetism produced results analogous to those of "white magic," and so he held that magnetism itself produced evidence for this "ill-famed occult art."[102] Using spells, charms, symbolic acts, rituals, incantations, totems, and strange potions, white magic produced the same mysterious salutary effects as magnetism and sympathetic cures. But magic itself was a broader phenomenon than animal magnetism, Schopenhauer averred, because "black magic," sorcery and witchcraft, were notorious for conjuring pernicious and destructive results by the same mysterious means. And if magnetism supported a belief in white magic, it did so for black magic as well, because the force that immediately operated in magnetism appeared capable of also occasioning destructive and harmful results. Schopenhauer also appealed to the historic record to justify the reality of magic. The belief in some nonnatural force used to produce astonishing and mysterious results could be found among all cultures and at all times and, given the universality of this belief, he opined, there must be something deep within human nature, or in the nature of things, that would account for the seemingly ineradicable nature of this belief.[103] To be sure, Schopenhauer realized that one had to carefully sort through fraud, deception, superstition, and plain nonsense to discover genuine expressions of magic, but he also believed that such a sorting would be insufficient to dismiss all magical acts as spurious.

Schopenhauer's analysis of magic continued on the path he had established for his explanation of magnetism. Both white and black magic transcend the normal means for producing changes in the world and their

---

[102] Schopenhauer, *On the Will in Nature*, p. 107/*Sämtliche Werke*, Vol. 4, p. 105.

[103] In the second edition to *The World as Will and Representation*, Schopenhauer replaced the original quotation from Goethe's *Faust* Part 1, lines 382–5 as the motto for the second book, his metaphysics of nature, with one from Agrippa von Nettesheim's *Opera Omnia*, "He dwells in us, not in the nether world, not in the starry heavens. The spirit living within fashions all this." Both quotations concern the magical revelation of that which underlies nature.

effects violate causal laws. It is one thing to make a man lame by pounding a nail through his heel; it is another to affect the same result by pounding a nail though the drawn figure of that man.[104] The first case falls completely within the causal nexus and is fully explainable by causal laws – although the reason one would pound a nail through another's heel would require for Schopenhauer a metaphysical explanation, just as would the various natural forces presupposed by causal laws. The second case, however, is immune to this form of explanation, and instead of evoking physics to ultimately ground the physical account, one had to immediately appeal to the metaphysical. It is not that driving the nail into the image of the man's heel caused the lameness in the real man's foot, as if we now had to discover some unrecognized causal law expressed by this phenomenon. The image of the victim and the act of driving the nail do not cause the lameness; rather, they are merely vehicles used to fix and direct the emergence of the will into the material world. Magical power lies in the will itself, and operates magically as the individual will of the magician asserts itself as the metaphysical will.

Thus, the fundamental idea behind magic, Schopenhauer argued, is found once more in our self-consciousness of will. Through self-consciousness, "one becomes aware every moment of a wholly inexplicable and hence evidently metaphysical influence of the will. Ought it not be possible... for such an influence to be extended to all bodies as well?"[105] Just as in his principal work, where self-consciousness revealed the will to be that which is the interior of the representation of our bodies, in *On the Will in Nature* he once more exploited self-consciousness as the means to recognize the magical way that will exerts "metaphysical influence" over other bodies. The trick of the magician was to discover the means for extending the sphere of the will beyond its expression in his or her body. Spells, charms, waxen images, and drawings served merely as vehicles to direct and fix the metaphysical will. As long as people looked at these vehicles as the agents of magical effects, or as long as people appealed to gods, spirits, or demons to explain magic, magic did not understand itself, Schopenhauer argued. It was as if the magician found the means

---

[104] This example, which one could also say hits the nail on the head as an example of magic, is given by Schopenhauer in *On the Will in Nature*, p. 119/*Sämtliche Werke*, Vol. 4, p. 119. He took it from Theophrastus Paracelsus' *Archidoxorum* (Strassburg, 1603), Vol. 2, p. 298.

[105] Schopenhauer, *On the Will in Nature*, p. 113/*Sämtliche Werke*, Vol. 4, p. 112.

to summon the metaphysical will to do his or her own biding. He conveniently overlooked, however, how his metaphysical account of magic itself became transcendent. After all, how can the magician influence or direct the will, when the will is beyond all causality?

Schopenhauer anticipated that his explanation of magic would strike his readers as fantastic. To disembroil his audience from this impression, he employed a tactic that he would use in his later works with a frequency greater than in his earlier ones.[106] To show that his view was neither idiosyncratic nor without precedent, he cited analyses of magic that anticipated, in a prescient manner, his view that will was the force expressed by the power of magic. Thus, he amassed lengthy and labored quotations from the writings of the sixteenth-century Swiss physician and natural philosopher Theophrastus Paracelsus; the sixteenth- and early seventeenth-century Italian poet and philosopher Tommaso Campanella; his near contemporary and countryman, the natural philosopher Giolio (Julius Caesar) Vanini; the eighteenth-century Flemish physician and natural scientist Johann Baptist van Helmont; the fifteenth-century Renaissance philosopher and neo-Aristotelian, Petrus Pomponatius (Pietro Pomponazzi); the sixteenth-century German theologian and occultist Heinrich Cornelius Agrippa von Nettlesheim; and the seventeenth-century English mystic and founder of the Philadelphian Society for the Advancement of Divine Philosophy Jane Leade. To sense his metaphysics lingering behind their somewhat inchoate views, one only had to disenchant them from their allegiance to their superstitions and religious confessions, replacing their gods, God, demons, and devil – elements of the metaphysics of the people – with the true metaphysics. Schopenhauer would tolerate neither a god-enchanted nor a demon-haunted world.

Schopenhauer's "Animal Magnetism and Magic" was not his final word on occult phenomena. Still haunted by ghosts, he sought not to exorcise them from his ontology, but to explain why they were possible and to provide them with a metaphysical home. This was his task in the "Essay on Spirit-Seeing and Everything Connected Therewith," which ran for more than eighty pages in the first volume of *Parerga and Paralipomena*. Some

---

[106] An especially striking example of this tactic is found in his "Prize Essay on the Freedom of the Will," pp. 56–80/*Sämtliche Werke*, Vol. 4, "Die beiden Grundprobleme der Ethik," pp. 63–89, where, in the chapter "Predecessors," Schopenhauer referred to or quoted from numerous figures who also denied the freedom of the human will.

eighty-five years earlier, his hero Kant had also considered the subject of spirits. Prompted by curiosity from reports about the incredible prophetic and visionary powers of his contemporary, the Swedish biblical scholar, theosophist, and mystic Emmanuel Swedenborg, Kant took a precritical glance at the spiritual world in *Dreams of a Spirit-Seer, Illustrated by Dreams of Metaphysics* [*Träume eines Geisterseher, erlautert durch Träume der Metaphysik*, 1766]. Kant was not afraid of ghosts, and in this spirited, sometimes satirical, and sometimes scatological essay, he dismissed the spirit world as the product of bad digestion, of winds raging in one's guts, which, when drifting downward, produce flatulence, but which, when drifting upward, produce sprits. Kant washed his hands after dealing with such gaseous phenomena, recommending that we focus our attention on this world.

Before composing his own ghostly essay, Schopenhauer carefully studied Kant's. He accepted his mentor's dismissal of Swedenborg's spiritualistic account, rejecting the view that there were two substances, one material and the other immaterial, soul and body, and that ghosts were the appearances of the souls of dead folks. But for Schopenhauer, to reject spiritualism did not entail that ghosts were either the product of poor digestion or simply the dreams of the sick. Kant had not yet taken the transcendental turn when he wrote his essay, Schopenhauer noted, and therefore he lacked the means for a deeper investigation of such phenomena. Instead of a spiritualistic explanation, Schopenhauer strove to provide an idealistic one, employing what he regarded as the most significant distinction found in Kant's critical philosophy, the distinction between appearances and things in themselves, transformed, of course, into his distinction between representations and will. Just as in his analysis of magic and animal magnetism, spirit-seeing was possible due to the *nexus metaphysics* provided by the will.

Schopenhauer's explanation of spirit-seeing has a tentative and hesitant quality, unlike his earlier and bolder account of animal magnetism and magic. He accepted the experience of ghosts as a fact, and he assumed that his readers were familiar enough with reports of such phenomena so that he did not feel the need to extensively quote from the literature to describe ghosts and the like. He did, however, mention his own experience with spirits, although he did not provide any concrete case. His task, he claimed, was not to establish the spirit-phenomenon as a fact – he took this to be the case – but to theorize about it. When all was said and done, with an uncharacteristic modesty, he claimed that his theorizing only cast "a feeble light" on spirit-seeing, one not sufficient to illuminate the phenomenon in a way that would resolve the millennia-long debate between those who accepted and those who rejected the appearance of the dead. He made this judgment for a good reason, as we will see.

Ghostly apparitions were not public phenomena such as ordinary objects of normal sensory perception, nor were they intersubjective phenomena, experienced invariably and generally the same by anyone of sound mind and body. The experience of his father's ghost sitting next to his poodle on the sofa might look as if his living father were sitting by his dog. However, everyone with good vision would only see Atma, and only those very rare people capable of spirit-seeing might see Heinrich Floris. In this sense, Atma is a public object and intersubjective, whereas Heinrich Floris is a private object and rarely an intersubjective one. Yet Schopenhauer held that ghosts were not simply and fully subjective phenomena, akin to a normal dream, hallucination, illusion, or dream of the sick, an *aegri somnia*, the product of winds raging in the guts, drifting upward – as a mocking Kant exorcised all spirits. Ghosts were objective phenomena, Schopenhauer held, and not subjective ones, which would be attributed fully and only to the cognizing subject.

Schopenhauer argued that one could not rule out *a priori* the possibility of spirit-seeing, because the essence of a person's will is not destroyed or annihilated by death. But unlike his explanation of clairvoyance, which appealed to a *nexus metaphysicus* provided by the will, which united all existence and was present in everything that was, is, or will be, Schopenhauer was at a loss to use the same explanation. Clairvoyants thought through another's brain as their own brain "slept," but the rub was that the dead had no intellect, and thus no brain – indeed, nothing "physical" to direct the will.[107] More deeply, death annihilated anything that would

---

[107] In *On the Basis of Morality*, Schopenhauer claimed that compassion involves the immediate participation in another's suffering, which prompts the agent to treat another's suffering as the agent's own; that is, to act to eliminate it. He explained this participation as involving the experience of another's suffering in another's body. Due to this extraordinary experience, he claimed that compassion could not be explained psychologically, calling compassion the great mystery of ethics and a phenomenon that required a metaphysical explanation. Once again, he appealed to Kant's distinction between things in themselves and appearances to argue that good characters' view of others as an "I once more" is metaphysically justified because individuality is only apparent, an illusion. Curiously, he never returned to provide a metaphysical explanation of how one person could literally feel another's pain in the other's body. It is also interesting to note that he could have used the same metaphysical explanation that he used for his claim that a clairvoyant could literally think through another's brain.

individualize one dead person from another – each and everything at the level of will is just will. Later, he would pronounce the question concerning how deeply the roots of the individual go into the being in itself of all things as one of many questions that required a transcendent answer, an impossible one.[108] Even if it made sense to ascribe individuality to the essence of a dead person, all Schopenhauer could say was that there must be some magical power whereby Heinrich Floris's ghost was experienced just like Atma the poodle, but the ghost of dear old dad was just in his head, private and therefore not intersubjective; that is, it was unavailable to perception by other people, but it was objective and not simply a creation of his own brain: "A perception which is only apparently external and has arisen as a result of an internal impression, but which is to be distinguished from mere fantasy, does not happen to everyone."[109] But this "must be" is only if there were, in fact, ghosts. Consequently, the light he threw on spirit-phenomena was simply feeble. But let us go back in time, but not by bending time back on itself, and return to Frankfurt at the time after Schopenhauer encountered the ghost of his father.

Frankfurt

Schopenhauer arrived in the city of Goethe's birth on 28 August 1831. His flight from Berlin was hasty, and he left behind no recorded reason for

Schopenhauer may have hesitated to use his explanation of clairvoyance to explain the extraordinary experience of feeling another's pain in another's body (after all, if one can think with another brain, why not feel the pain of another in the other's body?) because the judges of this prize-essay, members of the Royal Danish Society of Scientific Studies, would have not understood his view. In any case, this was his explanation of his failure to discuss one of his ultimate incentives for human action, the desire for one's own misfortune, in that very same essay; see *The World as Will and Representation*, Vol. 2, p. 607fn./*Sämtliche Werke*, Vol. 3, p. 697fn. and see my "Compassion and Solidarity with Sufferers: The Metaphysics of *Mitleid*," *European Journal of Philosophy*, Vol. 16: 2 (2008), pp. 292–310, for Schopenhauer's attempts to ground compassion metaphysically.

108 In a note from 1834, Schopenhauer recorded a tension between his claims that the ethical diversity of character was a function of the will and that the will was not individualized. He scratched his head over the tension and wished "perhaps someone after me will shed light on this abyss," *Manuscript Remains*, Vol. 4, p. 222/*Der handschriftliche Nachlaß*, Vol. 4, p. 193f. No one, however, kindled a torch that illuminated his way out of this abyss., fo

109 I Schopenhauer, *Parerga and Paralipomena*, Vol. 1, p. 306/*Sämtliche Werke*, Vol. 6, p. 326. For a thorough account of Schopenhauer's work on occult phenomena in the context of the second half of the nineteenth century, see Marco Segala, *I fantasmi, il cervello, l'anima Schopenhauer, l'occulto e la scienza* (Florence: Leo S. Olschki, 1998).

choosing Frankfurt, although it was rumored to be a cholera-proof city. He had entertained the idea of moving to Sweden or England, but his desire to go to Frankfurt may have been tied to Hegel's death, which created a vacancy in Berlin's philosophy faculty. Only after Beneke received the position – an appointment that would have upset Hegel as much it did Schopenhauer – did he have his friend Lowtzow arrange to have his books and other furnishing shipped to Frankfurt.

Frankfurt's population hovered around 50,000 souls when the philosopher hurried into town. After the Congress of Vienna, Frankfurt received autonomous status, and it impaneled a quasi-republican constitution in which the patricians-loaded senate was balanced by a citizens' committee and a legislative body, some of whose members were even elected. It also served as the home of the parliament for the German League and, as such, drew a diverse set of politicians, royal envoys, nobles, and dignitaries from throughout Germany and other European countries. Mixing with these figures were those who were drawn to its trade fair, which contributed greatly to the diversity of people the philosopher could observe – a most fortunate situation for Schopenhauer, because he found Frankfurt's solid citizens to be – and here he drew from Wieland – a "farmer-proud nation of Abderites, whom I prefer not to approach."[110]

This remark on the people of Frankfurt was made in 1838, after his decision to make Frankfurt his permanent home. Earlier, in 1832, he had distanced himself from everyone in Frankfurt, not only those whom he would later call narrow-minded fools or "Abderites," but even from those diverse figures he had became drawn to by 1838. Sick and depressed in early 1832, Schopenhauer holed up in his rooms. We only learn of his condition through a letter exchange with his mother, but only from one point of view, because only one of Schopenhauer's letters to his mother is extant. Just as she had done earlier, Johanna destroyed her son's letters, as well as those he wrote to Adele. Not surprisingly, the resumption of

---

[110] Schopenhauer, *Gesammelte Briefe*, p. 175, Schopenhauer to Carl Labes, 23 January 1838. Labes, whom Schopenhauer had briefly met through his brother, Eduard, was hired as Schopenhauer's lawyer in 1833 to handle his affairs in Ohra. Schopenhauer's reference to "Abderites" is an allusion to Wieland's satirical and comic novel *History of the Abderites* [*Geschichte der Abderiten*, 2 vols. Carlsruhe: Schmieder, 1774–81] set in the fifth century B.C.E., in the ancient Greek city of Abdera. Wieland depicted Abderites as smug, narrow-minded, dull, and self-satisfied rubes. The novel was read as a critique of small-town German life.

communication between the two was due to mutual financial interests in their property in Ohra. Schopenhauer had not communicated with his mother for twelve years, preferring to do so indirectly through Adele, and doubly indirectly through Osann's letters to his sister.

From the information in Johanna's letters, it can be inferred that after a discussion of the various strategies and demands for resolving their financial problems, Schopenhauer gradually and vividly described his depressive moods and bad health. It was almost like their correspondence when Schopenhauer bemoaned his unhappy fate as a merchant apprentice in Danzig, but it was also different. At that time, he wanted his mother to free him from his bondage – to tell him what to do. This time, he wanted to tell his mother how to handle their financial affairs, but he also sought his mother's love, or at the least, her compassion for his distress. Moreover, Schopenhauer was psychologically vulnerable, not simply from his depression, mixed at times with feelings of paranoia, but also from feelings of failure concerning his philosophical career, the possibility of which was due, in part, to Johanna's advice and actions and his father's death. During the letter exchange neither Johanna nor Arthur mentioned her literary success – the 24-volume collected edition of her works had just appeared – and that Schopenhauer's own works went unread.

Johanna's letters to her son contain no salutatory greetings, no familiar "Dear Arthur." She did write as a mother to a son, using the familiar second person form of you, *du*, and not the formal *Sie*. The polite form would have shown great distance from her son. Schopenhauer's one extant letter contains both the proper salutary greeting and pronouns used in a letter from a son to a mother. And Johanna's letters, when they address the misery of her son, adopt a tone of closeness and concern. At first, however, Johanna responded to Schopenhauer's report of illness with reserve: "That you have been sick and for so long, I would have not imagined. I hope you have had a good doctor and regular care."[111] In that first letter, she did not write about her own poor health, and her letter was somewhat curt. She excused the briefness of her letter by mentioning that it had taken a long time to write, as she was distracted by noise in the street (Schopenhauer, who hated noise, should have understood this

---

[111] Lütkehaus, *Die Schopenhauers*, p. 335, Johanna to Arthur, 24 February.

problem). She also told him that she did not expect him to answer her letter.

Schopenhauer did reply, though, with more financial advice, and he must have revealed more about his health, drawing the following response from Johanna: "Your illness worries me. I beg you to take care of yourself. What exactly is the nature of your sickness? Grey hair! A long beard! I cannot imagine you so. The first is not so terrible and the second is easily remedied. Two months in your room without seeing a single person, that is not good my son and troubles me. A person dares not and should not live in such isolation. . . ."[112]

Upsetting descriptions of his plight continued in Schopenhauer's letters. Ten days later, with obvious concern about her son's woeful condition, Johanna expressed a fear that her son was on the verge of suicide: "What you wrote me concerning your health, your unsociability, your dark disposition, saddens me more than I can and dare say; you know why. God help you and send you light, courage, and confidence into your gloomy mood; that is my most sincere wish."[113] What she could and dare not say – what she need not say, because Arthur knew it – was her worry that her son would follow his father's path and kill himself. Johanna had witnessed her husband's psychological decline, and she may have sensed that the same symptoms were occurring in her son. Heinrich Floris killed himself when he was fifty-eight, and her son had just turned fifty.

Adele shared her mother's fears about her brother. She, too, had observed her father's behavior toward the end of his life, and, during the financial crisis with Muhl, she had learned that her mother and brother viewed her father's death as a suicide. But, unlike Johanna and like Arthur, she knew from experience that darkness within, as she, too, was Heinrich Floris's child. Although she would articulate her unhappiness in letters to her intimates, she did so more poignantly and profoundly in her letters to her brother – especially in reply to those that articulated Schopenhauer's despair. When her brother first resumed correspondence, she was reserved in reply, but as their letter exchange unfolded, she revealed her own inner struggles and miseries.

In a lengthy letter to her brother, Adele unburdened her woes, reaching out to Schopenhauer not only to identify with him, but also to save her and

---

[112] Lütkehaus, *Die Schopenhauers*, p. 335, Johanna to Arthur, 24 February 1832.
[113] Ibid., p. 339f, Johanna to Arthur, 20 March 1832.

him. She wrote of having no joy, no hopes, and no plans. Like her brother, she had been sick and suffered terribly the previous winter, believing she would die. In her desperation she had even considered a marriage of convenience, but fate had intervened, she said, and it became clear as day to her that she could only marry someone whose spirit would harmonize with her own. Such a man, however, was nowhere to be found. Worse, it would be almost impossible for such a man to find her. Almost no one knew her, she continued, because her soul was hidden by social attire that was like Venetian veils and masks, cloaking her true self. She feared old age, and she feared living a lonely life. Then she revealed her own death wish: "I am strong enough to bear the solitude but I would be sincerely grateful to cholera if it freed me from the whole of history without violent pain."[114]

But Adele recognized something in her brother's death wish that he did not see himself. For someone so wretched, his flight from cholera was odd: "Thus your *anxiety* is to me – strange, since you feel miserable and often want to spring out of life with a violent step."[115] Adele needed to have her brother realize that his own behavior showed that he really did not want to die. Moreover, despite her own tale of woe, she also told him that she could live quite well and often was cheerful. These remarks did not leap out of thin air. She made it very clear at the beginning of her letter that she found it very difficult to satisfy her brother's request for the details of her life during their period of silence. That period was bleak, she wrote, until she met "Madam Mertens," whose love saved her from her entrapment between madness and death. Through her relationship with this woman, "few have, no doubt, been as fortunate in life as I."[116]

Adele tried to reach out to her brother, tacitly suggesting that she might be his "Madame Mertens." For better or worse, she wrote, their characters had much in common and she knew that both wanted to see one another. She suggested that they should meet to see if they could get along together. She would not pry into his affairs, she promised. Perhaps next spring, if he were to travel south, they could rendezvous in some small town to which she could easily travel. And, almost as a task to keep

---

[114] Ibid., p. 319, Adele to Schopenhauer, 27 October 1831. Ibid., p. 337 Johanna to Arthur, 10 March 1832.
[115] Ibid.
[116] Ibid., p. 318.

him busy, she asked Schopenhauer to write to her about himself, others, books, cities, music – whatever he wished.

Schopenhauer did not travel south that spring. He did not meet his sister. Sensing desperation in Adele, instead of coming to her aid and accepting her invitation to have her save him, he moved to Mannheim. He had his own demons and Adele had hers. They may have just fed on each other's despair, doing no good for either. Just as his mission in life, to solve the puzzle of existence, represented an act of love for human kind, his love for Adele was analogous. His love of human kind was abstract, universal, and not directed to the particular. Particular people, flesh and blood living people, human bipeds, or factory products, as he called them, were best loved at a distance. His love of Adele had that distance. He loved her abstractly, as a sister, and not personally, as an individual. He could not have her play a role in his everyday life, because then he would have had to recognize her as a person. He would continue to correspond with her until her death, drawn to her because of their dark blood ties and mutual financial interests.

Bickering about property caused Johanna to cease corresponding with her son. Once more Adele was caught in the middle. Schopenhauer was directed to write only to his sister. Johanna's last letter to her son was a letter jointly signed by the Schopenhauer women in which they acceded to the philosopher's financial plans. That was in August 1837. Johanna and Adele were living in Bonn and were preparing to move to Jena.

The End of the Family

Johanna's and Adele's move from Bonn to Jena could have provided both women the opportunity to visit Schopenhauer. Their final letter to Arthur prior to the move carried a postscript that immediately eliminated this possibility. They would not travel via Frankfurt because another route enabled them to stay with friends and avoid spending nights in inns. Johanna, of course, wished to avoid her son; Adele wanted to see her brother; and Schopenhauer preferred to see neither.

The Schopenhauer women left Weimar in 1829 due to economics. They could no longer afford to live there. The Muhl settlement cost them most of their inheritance and Johanna's writings brought in little money. They traveled to the Rhine, spending the summer months in a country house in the small village of Unkel and their winters in Bonn.

Schopenhauer: A Biography

They lived frugally, but by 1837, they were impoverished, despite the fact that Johanna's collected works received a second edition in 1834. But her popularity as a writer had waned, drying up even that meager source of income. Johanna's health had greatly declined, exacerbated by the stroke suffered in 1823, and Adele increasingly became her nurse. Out of desperation, Johanna described her plight to the Grand Duke of Saxony-Weimar, Karl Friedrich, the son of Carl August. The Grand Duke awarded her a pension. The pension allowed the women to live modestly in Jena, with sufficient funds to hire two young girls to care for the ailing Johanna and to assist Adele with housework.

The Schopenhauers did not return to Weimar. It appears that the Duke's pension included a stipulation that they live in Jena. It is not clear why he attached this stipulation to his act of kindness. It may have involved Johanna's continuing relationship with Gerstenbergk, who, for some unknown reason, had fallen into disgrace. As Adele told her brother, Gerstenbergk was living in Dresden, separated from his wife and "was implicated in some sordid affairs."[117] She did not describe, however, the nature of these "sordid affairs" or her mother's friend's involvement in them. Had Johanna moved to Weimar, Gerstenbergk's visits might have upset the Grand Duke and his associates.

When she was able, Johanna worked on her memoirs during her time in Jena. She died before completing the project, and Adele edited what Johanna left behind and secured its publication. Even after death, Adele served her mother.[118] It is not known whether Schopenhauer read the memoirs. At his death, Schopenhauer's library contained two of his mother's books; her travel book covering the family's grand European tour and her *Carl Fernow's Life*, both of which appeared before the falling out between mother and son. Had the alienated son read his mother's *Youthful Life and Travel Portraits* (1839), he would have sensed something of himself in his mother. The first chapter, "Truth without Poetry," a play on Goethe's autobiography *Truth and Poetry*, contains some observations

---

[117] Ibid., p. 388, Adele to Schopenhauer, 2 December 1836, quoted in Bergmann, *Johanna Schopenhauer*, p. 301; also see Bergmann's discussion of the move to Jena and Gerstenbergk, pp. 300–06.

[118] Johanna's memoirs appeared as *Jugendleben und Wanderbilder*, edited by her daughter, 2 vols. (Braunschweig: Westermann, 1839). She was the first Schopenhauer to be translated into English, when her *Jugendleben* appeared as *Mme Schopenhauer, Youthful Life and Pictures of Travel: Being the Autobiography of the Authoress* (1847).

the philosopher could have made himself. "I will provide pure, unadulterated truth," she wrote, "without an admixture of poetry." Had she said "naked truth," it would have been pure Arthur Schopenhauer. And when Johanna explained what her readers might detect about her through these sketchy descriptions of events in her life, her son would have endorsed, maybe with delight, her claim that her readers would find "What I am and am not, or rather who I believe I am and am not, since who could ever attain the complete knowledge of his own enigmatical self."[119] Johanna's "enigmatical" or "puzzling" self, her "*rätselhaften*" self – and here she used a term her son used to refer to the puzzling or enigmatical problem of existence – points to the same deep unknown that serves as the basis of her son's philosophy. But Johanna continued her last observation by making it clear that she did not look "with a philosophical glance and male courage at all of the circumstances of life."[120] Schopenhauer's assessment of Johanna as a bad mother and good writer barely scratched the surface of a remarkable woman.

Johanna died peacefully, in her sleep, on the night of 16 April 1838. Although it was clear that she was losing her battle with disease, her death was unexpected. Early in the evening, Johanna had difficulty breathing and retired to her room. Adele was in nearby Weimar, visiting Ottilie von Goethe, and was summoned when it became obvious that Johanna's end was near. "Dear Arthur," she wrote, informing her brother of their mother's death, "our mother passed away very gently this night around 11:00! – It came suddenly. – I was in Weimar and returned two hours late! . . . I know that she was cared for perfectly – but I will never forget it and never overcome it that they had come to fetch me too late!"[121]

Adele and her friends made Johanna's funeral arrangements, and when Johanna was laid to rest in the *Johannisfriedhof* in Jena, Arthur did not attend. He did not want to see his mother in life, and he had no desire to see her in death. Adele inherited what remained of Johanna's estate, both debts and assets, and she provided her brother with a careful accounting of both. Adele closed this accounting, in anticipation of her brother's

[119] Schopenhauer, Johanna, "Jugenderinnerungen" in *Johanna Schopenhauer: Im Wechsel der Zeiten, im Gedränge der Welt*, ed. Rolf Weber (Munich: Winkler, 1986), p. 32.. See, for example, Schopenhauer, *The World as Will and Representation*, Vol. 2, p. 171/*Sämtliche Werke*, Vol. 3, p. 189, where Schopenhauer wrote of the "ever-disquieting puzzle of existence."
[120] Schopenhauer, Johanna, "Jugenderinnerungen," p. 33.
[121] Lütkenhaus, *Die Schopenhauers*, p. 392, Adele to Schopenhauer, 17 April 1838.

objection, but requesting that he "let mother rest; what she may have done to us both be forgotten."[122] Surprisingly, Arthur did not contest the will. As he told an acquaintance, "I could have contested the will, but I did not wish to do so."[123] He did not mention the grounds for such a challenge, nor did he say why he did not want to mount an objection. The net value of Johanna's estate was not insignificant, approximately 2,000 *Taler* and land in Ohra. Schopenhauer certainly did not need the money, and he knew that his sister was on her own and that Johanna had gone through almost all of Adele's inheritance.

Johanna's death did not appear to have had a significant effect on the philosopher. Almost as an aside, he mentions his mother's passing to his French brother Anthime: "My mother died in April. My sister appears to regret this no more than me. Look, I will say nothing more about this. She rests in peace."[124] Schopenhauer's assessment of the impact of his mother's demise on Adele was one-sided – his side. Adele's life had been dominated by Johanna's, but this dominance also provided stability. Although her mother's death had a liberating effect on Adele, it also removed that stability. Moreover, Johanna's cheerfulness, optimism, and disciplined life as an author helped counterbalance Adele's own darker moods. In addition, she was fortunate to have developed a strong network of friends, particularly through her mother's tea parties and her renown as an author. These friends would encourage Adele and support her in her quest to live a life more in tune with her nature, one that did not require her to become dependent on her brother.

Adele found her own literary voice after Johanna's death, although it never enjoyed the popular resonance achieved by her mother's. She was also able to live for a time in Italy, a desire dating back to her familiarity with Fernow. She collaborated with two of Goethe's grandsons: Walter, for whose opera *Enzio* (1838) she wrote the *libretto*, and Wolfgang, with whom she wrote the short story "Erlinde" (1842). Her novella "Theolinde" appeared in 1841, and in the same year as the second edition of *The World as Will and Representation* appeared, her *Home- Forest- and Field-Fairy-Tales* [*Haus-, Wald- und Feldmärchen*, Leipzig: F.A. Brockhaus, 1844] was

[122] Ibid., p. 396 Adele to Schopenhauer, 23 April 1838.
[123] Schopenhauer, *Gesammelte Briefe*, p. 179, Schopenhauer to Carl W. Labes, 12 July 1838. I.
[124] Ibid., p. 176, Schopenhauer to Grégoire de Blésimaire, 17 June 1838.

also published by her mother's and brother's publisher, Brockhaus. Her novel *Anna* was published by Brockhaus in 1845 and *A Danish Story* [*Eine dänische Geschichte*], written in 1847, was published by Georg Westermann in 1848. From 1844 to 1849, Adele lived in Genoa, Rome, Naples, and Florence, returning periodically to Germany.

After Johanna's death, the relationship between brother and sister improved. They continued to correspond and in 1842, after twenty-two years without face-to-face contact, the siblings met in Frankfurt. Adele was surprised to discover that the philosopher had a portrait of his mother. He offered it to his sister, but she declined because she found it disgusting and inaccurate. Even in Schopenhauer's final year of life, the same painting hung on the wall, along with a daguerreotype of the philosopher, across from the sofa in his last apartment, Schöne Aussicht 16.

Adele knew her brother better than any other person, and during her remaining days they entered into a friendly relationship, but at a distance. Schopenhauer sent her the second edition of his principal work, just as he did with his *The Two Fundamental Problems of Ethics*, and Adele managed to see through what a recent scholar called his "misanthropic façade," recognizing his incredible sensitivity to suffering as a sign of his character that signified an almost holy concern for all living beings.[125] This was radically unlike Johanna, who viewed his brooding about human misery as a sign of mental illness. Adele came to understand her brother even more after her 1842 visit, and that he required a mode of life that would not disturb his "Brahman soul," and that would allow him his quest for an enlightenment he would share with others. "I regard you as a profound, I prefer to say holy thinker," she wrote her brother, "[I] respect and always honor your opinion, admire your mind, even more your penetrating understanding, even the marvelous poetry that often steps forth from your adorable way of looking at things."[126] Although she valued his opinion, she also told her brother that she did not follow him unconditionally when it came to business of a ordinary sort – she would listen to professional men, a direct reminder that she would manage her own money as well as her declining health.

---

[125] Lütkehaus, *Die Schopenhauers*, p. 39. I found Lütkehaus' analysis of Adele's and Schopenhauer's complex relationship extremely helpful. Ibid., p. 459, Adele to Schopenhauer, 20 January 1844.

[126] Lütkehaus, Die *Schopenhauers*, p. 448f.

Adele began suffering from lower abdominal distress nine years before her death, and as the years progressed so did the cancer. Finally, in 1848, an extremely ill Adele made her way from Florence to Bonn. She met with her brother in Frankfurt for the last time in March 1849. Virtually nothing is known about what transpired during this brief visit. Schopenhauer's knowledge about his sister's health and her physical condition should have told him that Adele's death was imminent. Adele was accompanied by her loyal and loving friend Sibylle Mertens-Schaaffhausen. Schopenhauer also knew that the art collector and archaeologist had played a significant role in his sister's life, especially after their mother's death, and that she would also take good care of his dying sister. After meeting with her brother, Adele and Mertens took, as it were, a farewell tour to visit friends and acquaintances in Berlin, Jena, and Weimar, to return ultimately to Mertens's home in Bonn, where Adele would die.

Sensing death closing in, Adele dictated to Mertens a final letter to her brother. In it she requested that he not object to the disposal of her property; Mertens would make it according to her wishes. Said property, she added, was not worth much, so it would not be worth his effort to try to sell it. She closed the letter by giving the philosopher her heartfelt thanks for all of his friendliness during the past few months. Adele could only muster the strength to sign the letter "your loyal sister Adele."[127]

Schopenhauer responded immediately to his sister's request for a quick reply to her letter:

Dear Adele,

I received the letter signed by you and see with great sorrow that you occupy yourself in your sick bed with all sorts of trivial, worldly, and hopefully completely superfluous concerns. Meanwhile, if it brings you peace of mind, then I assure you that I will follow your desired instructions as stated by you in your letter, in case that you should, as we Buddhists call it, exchange life. Hopefully this will still not happen this time and that heaven strengthens and preserves you, that is my truthful and sincere wish.

Your Brother, Arthur Schopenhauer[128]

Adele received the letter the day before she died. She was too weak to read it, so Mertens read it to her. Louise Adelaide Lavinia Schopenhauer

---

[127] Ibid., p. 491, Adele to Schopenhauer, 20 August 1849.
[128] Schopenhauer, *Gesammelte Briefe,p. 236*, Schopenhauer to Adele; Hübscher dates this letter as around 23 August 1849.

died at 3:15 P.M., 25 August 1849. Arthur learned of her death from
Mertens's letter of the same day. As an act of kindness, Mertens told
the philosopher that she had read his last letter to his sister and that "she
indicated by a nod and wink to say thanks for your friendship."[129] Mertens
did not report whether Adele responded at all to her brother's Buddhist
reference, which the philosopher knew would not be lost on his sister. She
had a long association with August Schlegel and through this association,
as well as through reading English books on the subject, she had become
acquainted with the various types of Indian religions. And, although
Adele was skeptical about the theory of transmigration of souls, she would
have recognized that her brother was offering her comfort by saying that
something about her would not perish, and he was kind enough not to say
that this was her will.

Like her mother, Adele was buried in Bonn, but on the 100th anniver-
sary of Goethe's birth. Her friends made all of the arrangements. The
deeply grieving Mertens arranged for a monument to mark her friend's
grave and composed a lengthy epitaph in Italian that praised Adele's excellent heart, intellect, and talents, referring to her as the "best daughter"
and describing her as "tender and loyal to her friends."[130] No mention
was made of Adele as a patient, long-suffering, loyal sister. Schopenhauer
did not attend the funeral, but there can be little doubt that he was saddened by his sister's death. There was now no one to whom he could so
freely unburden his soul, and nowhere would he find another who could
understand him as he was understood by Adele. There is even less doubt
that no one was moved as deeply by Adele's death as Mertens. She had
carved near the bottom of her friend's gravestone that it was erected by
her "inconsolable friend, Sibylle Mertens-Schaaffhausen."

Schopenhauer appreciated Mertens' loving care of his dying sister. He
recognized that Adele's demise affected a deep melancholy in her friend,
and he tried to console the grieving woman: "Time will overcome this
[melancholy] and in such cases, we are completely right not to oppose but
to aid time. Before everything else, we must make it clear to ourselves that

---

[129] Ibid., p. 491, Mertens-Schaaffhausen to Schopenhauer, 25 August 1849.Ibid., p. 491,
Schopenhauer to Adele, undated [August 1849].

[130] See Büch, *Alles Leben ist Traum*, p. 356, for a German translation of the Italian epitaph.
Büch also provides a quotation from a letter by Ottilie von Goethe to a friend, in which
Ottilie expressed her displeasure with the use of an Italian epitaph for a German author, see
ibid.

in no conceivable case can our grief and lamentations somehow serve or help the dead just as little as it does ourselves." He continued his quest to help ease Mertens's despair by quoting from Shakespeare's seventy-first sonnet, taking some liberties: "no longer mourn for me when I am dead/as the sullen bell sounds, announcing my going home."[131] It must have also relieved some of Mertens's anxiety that Schopenhauer honored his promise not to interfere with her administration of Adele's will. In this regard, he was civil with Sibylle. Adele, unlike their mother, did not disinherit Schopenhauer, who received various items from Adele's estate; 2,000 *Taler*, the 150 *Taler* per annum rent for Ohra, a couple of Schopenhauer signets, the family silver, and a portrait of his grandmother, Elizabeth Trosiener. He was especially pleased to receive a miniature painting of himself as a twenty-one-year-old and his father's notebooks from the family's grand European tour. Mertens was gracious toward the philosopher and they remained on relatively good terms until Mertens died in Rome in 1857.

The Stationary Philosopher

Schopenhauer had been living for more than sixteen years as a noncitizen resident in Frankfurt am Main at the time of his sister's death. And although he fled from Berlin to Frankfurt, where his father's ghost appeared, the shade of Heinrich Floris only appeared to suggest that Schopenhauer would outlive his mother – he did not specify where his son would do this outliving. Driven by his illness and depression, Schopenhauer retreated to Mannheim in July 1832. Ten hellish months in Frankfurt gave him a sufficient reason to relocate to the city at the juncture of the Rhine and Neckar rivers.[132]

---

[131] Schopenhauer, *Gesammelte Briefe*, p. 237, Schopenhauer to Sibylle Mertens-Schaaffhausen, 9 September 1849. The Shakespeare quotation should have read "No longer mourn for me when I am dead/Than you shall hear the surly sullen bell/Give warning to the world that I am fled." It is likely that Schopenhauer quoted these verses from memory, adapting them for the situation at hand. Perhaps, as an act of kindness, he did not provide the very next line, "From this vile world, with vilest worms to dwell."

[132] Prior to leaving Frankfurt, Schopenhauer attempted to visit Sir Water Scott, who stopped in the city during a tour of Germany. He sent Scott a card requesting a visit, but the ill author sent the philosopher a brief, signed note excusing himself from a meeting. Schopenhauer, who regarded Scott as the greatest British novelist, cherished possessing Scott's autograph; see ibid., pp. 135 and 136, Schopenhauer's letters to Johann Keil, 12 June 1832 and 24 June 1832.

Schopenhauer was more social in Mannheim, joining the Harmony Society, an association of local dignitaries and those aspiring to become such. For a man who seldom had harmonious relationships with "human bipeds," he found both the Society and its library to his liking. Mannheim, with its slow-paced life, had its charms, but Frankfurt still lay on his mind. Where should he make his permanent home? To answer this question, he did a cost/benefit analysis, comparing the two cities. He counted in Mannheim's favor the Harmony Society and its library, its lower danger of thieves – an important perception by a somewhat paranoid philosopher – its better foreign bookseller, its better baths in the summer, the Heidelberg library, and an excellent restaurant.[133] But it also had its negatives: crowded plays and dining establishments, and intolerable heat in the summer. Frankfurt had a healthy climate, all the comforts and anonymity afforded by a large city, more Englishmen, better plays, concerts, and operas, the natural history museum, the Senckenberg library, better table fare and coffeehouses, and, perhaps most importantly, an able dentist and fewer bad physicians.[134]

Frankfurt won out, and Schopenhauer resigned from the Harmony Society, packed his bag, books, flute, and poodle. But before he embarked to the great commercial city, he was gripped by a Kierkegaardian sense of dread: "As I was about to leave Mannheim in July 1833, I was overcome by an indescribable feeling of fear without any external cause."[135] His *Angst*, however, did not freeze the philosopher in Mannheim. He arrived in Frankfurt on 6 July. During the next twenty-eight years of his life, he was anchored in Frankfurt, only venturing forth for a four-day tour of the Rhine in 1835 and for short day trips to Mainz and Aschaffenburg. Schopenhauer would continue to experience loneliness in Frankfurt, but not during the last seven years of his life, when he would ironically savor his success. He would die there and be buried there.

---

[133] Schopenhauer recorded in his private diary his fear of thieves: "If there was a noise in the night, I jumped out of bed and seized sword and pistols that I always had ready loaded," *Manuscript Remains*, Vol. 4, p. 507/*Der handschriftliche Nachlaß*, Vol. 4, 2, p. 121.

[134] Schopenhauer's cost/benefit analysis, which was recorded in his account book, is given in Gwinner's *Schopenhauers Leben*, third ed. (Leipzig: Brockhaus, 1910), pp. 242–3.

[135] Schopenhauer, *Manuscript Remains*, Vol. 4, p. 507/*Der handschriftliche Nachlaß*, Vol. 4, 2, p. 121.

10

The Frankfurt Philosopher

A SEVENTEEN-YEAR period of self-imposed philosophical silence was broken in March 1836, when the Frankfurt publisher Siegmund Schmerber printed a run of 500 copies of Schopenhauer's *On the Will in Nature*. Its author was so eager to have his voice appear once again in print that he waived the author's honorarium. But without a sense that he would need to cultivate an audience for his philosophy if ever he were to have a second edition of *The World as Will and Representation*, it is unlikely that he would have published *On the Will in Nature*. Almost as an act of desperation, he collected his observations on the natural sciences, which he would have nonetheless used to supplement his philosophy of nature, the topic of the second book of his principal work, to try to make himself heard. All he needed to do was to flesh out that notes that he had assiduously developed since the appearance of his principal work, something he accomplished, in part, by making good use of the Senckenberg Library, which figured positively in his decision to locate in Frankfurt. *On the Will in Nature* was a lure cast to hook readers for his earlier work.[1]

---

[1] The Senckenberg Library was a large, private library specializing in the natural sciences. It was owned by the Senckenbergische Naturforschende Gesellschaft [Senckenberg Nature Research Society], of which Schopenhauer was a member. Schopenhauer himself assembled a good collection of books in the natural sciences, and when he died, he had almost 200 separate titles; see *Der handschriftliche Nachlaß*, Vol. 5, pp. 236–83, for a catalogue of his books concerning the natural sciences. It is curious to note that Schopenhauer had more than 100 titles dealing with paranormal and occult themes; see ibid., Vol. 5, pp. 287–318. Schopenhauer, who had more formal university training in the sciences than in philosophy, always kept abreast with developments in the natural sciences. A few months before his death, he read a detailed account of Charles Darwin's *On the Origin of Species by Means of Natural Selection, or the Preservation of Favored Races in the Struggle of Life* (London: John Murray, 1859). The philosopher told his friend Frauenstädt that Darwin's thoughts were "shallow empiricism" and simply a variation

Schopenhauer attempted to demonstrate in *On the Will in Nature* that "unprejudiced empiricists," who were unaware of his philosophy, had articulated from *a posteriori* sources theories that corroborated his fundamental idea: namely, that which we recognize in ourselves as will is that which is expressed in all natural phenomena.[2] Not only did Schopenhauer hold that his metaphysics was compatible with the best findings of science, but also he argued that his philosophy provided a grounding explanation for the scientific worldview. This was a natural stance for Schopenhauer, because he held that both philosophy and science ultimately had to appeal to experience to justify and meaningfully express their claims. But, as he had argued in *The World as Will and Representation*, science remained on the surface of things. Its domain was particular spatio-temporal objects standing in causal relationships, which it either classified under larger genera (morphology) or understood the changes of by discovering causal laws that ultimately described necessary changes in matter (etiology). He believed that whereas science is confined to the experience of the external world, philosophy is concerned not with individual and specific phenomena, but with providing an explanation for and the meaning of the totality of experience. Because science ultimately employed explanations of natural phenomena that involved necessary and scientifically unexplainable elements, by explaining these elements, Schopenhauer viewed his philosophy as completing the scientific image of the world. Unlike Schelling, who he argued took what was discovered *a posteriori*, and by twisting and turning it inside out forced it into his *a priori* philosophy of nature, he would show how the sciences naturally led to a point of contact in the philosophy that would ground them. Yet he would not confine his

of Lamarck's, and they were "in no way related to my theory"; Schopenhauer, *Gesammelte Briefe*, p. 472, 1 March 1860. Curiously, Darwin would quote a passage from Schopenhauer's essay from the second volume of his principal book " The Metaphysics of Sexual Love," in Chap. 20 of his *The Descent of Man* (second ed., 2 vols. London, 1874) to help justify his account of sexual attraction. He found the quotation in David Asher's "Schopenhauer and Darwinism," *Journal of Anthropology*, Vol. 1 (1866).

[2] Schopenhauer, *On the Will in Nature*, p. 19/*Sämtliche Werke*, Vol. 4, p. 1. Much to Schopenhauer's chagrin, he would discover that the Danish physician and professor of physiology Joachim Dietrich Brandis, from whose works he had quoted extensively in the first chapter to verify the claim that an unconscious will was the source of all vital functions, had known his philosophy all along and utilized it without mentioning its source. In the second edition of *On the Will in Nature* (1854), instead of striking references to Brandis, he lambasted the Danish physiologist for his dishonest borrowing and used the case of Brandis to discuss other examples of such behavior.

work simply to the natural sciences. Indeed, his first four chapters covered the natural sciences, as Schopenhauer moved through "physiology and pathology," "comparative anatomy," and "physiology of plants" and finally to "physical astronomy." By the fourth chapter he had shown how the natural sciences were completed by his metaphysics of will.[3] But to truly understand the world, one needed more than a metaphysically grounded science. One needed to know how language, animal magnetism and magic, and Eastern wisdom helped motivate the understanding of the ultimate ethical meaning of existence. There had to be four more chapters.

On the Will in Nature

In the first chapter, "Physiology and Pathology," Schopenhauer argued that the will is the agent in both voluntary and involuntary bodily functions, and in the second, "Comparative Anatomy," he attempted to show that the physical structures of animals, including humans, were spatio-temporal objectifications of their wills. By drawing from teleologically suggestive features of animal life and its adaptation to its environment, he concluded that this was due to a will, unguided by intellect. The philosopher continued this theme in "Physiology of Plants," arguing that what sprouts forth in vegetative life is will. In this chapter he provided the clearest discussion of the varieties of causality prevailing in animal life, plant life, and inorganic nature; namely, motivation, stimulation, and causality in the narrow sense. He would later fold this rich treatment of the varieties of causality into the second edition of *The Fourfold Root*.

Schopenhauer attributed great significance to "Physical Astronomy," the fourth chapter, where he would later claim, "I have there discussed that fundamental truth of my teaching with greater distinctness than anywhere else, and brought it down to the empirical knowledge of nature ... whoever wishes to know my philosophy thoroughly and investigate it seriously must take that chapter into consideration."[4] Schopenhauer's aim in this chapter was to show that will is the agent in all fundamental forces of nature. Curiously, besides a footnote in which he refers

---

3 See Marco Segala's *Schopenhauer, la philosophy, le scienze* (Pisa: Scuola Normale Superiore, 2009), for a comprehensive treatment of Schopenhauer's views concerning the relations between science and philosophy.

4 Schopenhauer, *The World as Will and Representation*, Vol. 2, p. 191 / *Sämtliche Werke*, Vol. 3, p. 213.

to Copernicus, the only "unprejudiced empiricist" he used to corroborate his view was the British physicist, Sir John Herschel, the son of
Sir William Herschel, whose telescopes, mounted on house-sized platforms, earned simply a mention in the philosopher's European tour diary
entry for 26 June 1803. Schopenhauer believed that gravity was the most
basic, universally expressed force of nature. He cited Herschel as holding that gravity was an expression of will. But Schopenhauer also noted
that Herschel was not without his prejudices, because he labored under
the misconception, like many empiricists, that "will is inseparable from
consciousness."[5] Nevertheless, he was delighted and surprised that Herschel would find will expressed in inorganic nature, an insight that he
exploited to show "the fundamental truth that Kant's thing in itself is
will, and that what is active in all the fundamental forces of nature shows
itself to be simply identical with what we know in ourselves as will."[6]

Schopenhauer's remark that "Physical Astronomy" contained that
most distinct presentation of the fundamental truth of his philosophy
is significant. In his principal work, he employed a grand cosmic analogy
to claim that will was expressed in all representations. But by 1835, he
more self-consciously understood that his metaphysics aimed at the correct explanation of the totality of experience and that his philosophy had
to remain within the bounds of all possible experience. So he more closely
adhered to the view that the source of metaphysical knowledge is confided to sensory perception, our consciousness of other things, and inner
experience, introspection or self-consciousness. Explaining the totality
of experience, he held, "consists in combining at the right place outer
experience, with inner, and making the latter the key to the former."[7] In
On the Will in Nature he would use our intimate cognition of will as that

---

[5] Schopenhauer, *On the Will in Nature*, p. 57/*Sämtliche Werke*, Vol. 4, p. 83. Schopenhauer
refers to Herschel's *A Treatise on Astronomy*, new ed.

[6] Ibid., p. 85/ibid., p. 80.

[7] Schopenhauer, *The World as Will and Representation*, Vol. 2, p. 181/*Sämtliche Werke*, Vol. 3,
p. 201. This remark is from the second edition of his principal work, where he clearly articulates
his un-Kantian conception of metaphysics as the correct explanation of experience as a whole
and where he claims that the foundation of metaphysics is empirical. He also claims here that to
solve the riddle of existence, one has to provide an account of experience that combines outer
with inner experiences. After Schopenhauer presented his view of metaphysics, he referred
his readers to "Physical Astronomy," where "I have explained [this combination] thoroughly
and fully." Scholars have tended to ignore Schopenhauer's attempt in *On the Will in Nature* to
combine the self-conscious experience of the will with objects of outer experience.

key for understanding an unknown x, which is discovered in our attempt to know nature.

Schopenhauer drew the connection between outer and inner experience by first exploring causality as it runs through the hierarchy of nature, from the most universally and commonly expressed elements, the forces of nature, to the most individualistic and uniquely expressed elements, human characters. Our understanding of nature is the clearest and most certain with the *a priori* sciences, arithmetic, geometry, and logic, he thought, because these sciences dealt with the *a priori* forms of cognition. Once, however, we attend to something with a modicum of empirical content, which increases as we move upward in the scale of nature, our understanding of phenomena decreases and our explanations became less complete, leaving us with an increasing sense of an unknown x in nature. For example, when one billiard ball strikes another, we have the most adequate understanding of a causal relationship: namely, that the struck ball receives as much motion as the striking ball loses. Yet there is a mysterious, unknown element – the very possibility of something incorporeal, motion, being transmitted from one corporal object to another. In the inorganic realm, he held, more complex causal relationships show a greater heterogeneity between cause and effect: the same increase of heat softens wax and hardens clay. Turning to the organic realm and considering living beings, plants and animals, the scheme of cause and effect still applies; however, there is neither a qualitative nor a quantitative relationship between cause and effect, especially with humans who, possessing reason, act from abstract motives. If you throw water on a plant, this may stimulate growth; if you throw water on a dog, it may flee; and if you throw it on a human, who knows what will happen. The separation between cause and effect has become so great, Schopenhauer held, it appears as if there is no cause for the once-wet person to yell at us two weeks later: "To the crude intelligence it now seems as if there no longer exists any cause at all, and the act of will depends on nothing and is groundless, viz., free."[8] Thus he concludes that we become aware of some mysterious, unknown x in nature that eludes our understanding.

To comprehend this unknown x operating in nature in general, Schopenhauer turns to the experience of our body as both representation and will as the key to understanding nature. This shift from perception,

---

[8] Schopenhauer, *On the Will in Nature*, p. 93/*Sämtliche Werke*, Vol. 4, p. 90.

which is directed outward toward other representations, to introspection, which is directed inward, makes the judge and the judged the same and recognizes the will as the agent expressed in bodily movements. From this recognition we discover the same force as the unknown x in nature. "The two primarily different sources of our knowledge," he averred, "the outer and inner, must at this point be connected by reflection. The comprehension of nature and our own self springs solely from that connection. But then the inner phase of nature is disclosed to our intellect, to which by itself alone only the external is accessible, and the secret for which philosophy has searched so long lies before us."[9] From this, he argued, one becomes clear about what is ideal and what is real; what is the appearance and what is the thing in itself. Causality reigns in appearance, identical through mechanical, physical, and chemical causes, and then as stimulus and motive. Through these expressions of causality, there runs that unknown x, which we discover in ourselves as will. These are not two distinct things, but are identical, although known in two different ways. "Causality and will are known in two fundamentally different ways: causality entirely from without, entirely mediate, entirely through the understanding; will entirely from within, entirely immediate, and that therefore, in any given case, the clearer the knowledge of one, the more obscure is that of the other."[10] Schopenhauer concluded that because causality is the essence of representations and it is an *a priori* form of the intellect, this is only one side of the world, and the other side is will. There are not, as the old philosophical prejudice would hold, two sources of motion for a body, will that proceeds from within, and causality that proceeds from without, but only one; the internal condition of movement is will and its external occasion cause, which can appear as stimulus or motive.[11]

The chapter "Physical Astronomy" concluded Schopenhauer's account of the corroboration of his philosophy by the natural sciences. The next three chapters drew on other "empirical" sources that supported his metaphysics. "Linguistics," the briefest chapter of the book, contains his observation that various languages recognize a will operating in natural

[9] Ibid., p. 94f./ibid., 91.
[10] Ibid., p. 96/ibid., p. 93.
[11] See Schopenhauer, ibid., p. 88f./ibid., p. 84f, where the philosopher tracked the standard view of nature, which assumes two different principles of motion, from Plato, to Cicero, then to Aristotle, to Rousseau, up through the physiologist Carl Friedrich Burdach.

objects, including inorganic ones. Thus he quotes from Seneca, Pliny, Aristotle, and French and German sayings to support his claim. He even quotes from the *I-Ching*: "the yang or celestial substance *wants* to return to heaven, or (to use the words of Ching-tse) wants to occupy a superior place, for its nature necessarily entails this or a law inherent in it."[12] Although Schopenhauer saw embedded wisdom in language, he never considered whether apparent attributions of will to noncognizant beings represented a deep human tendency to anthropomorphize nature, a charge that could be leveled against his own thought. By attributing what we discover deep in ourselves to everything in nature, are we, perhaps, anthropomorphizing nature?

"Animal Magnetism and Magic," as discussed earlier, is the lengthiest chapter in the book. Accepting as matters of fact phenomena such as magnetism, sympathetic cures, telekinesis, telepathy, clairvoyance, and magic, he argued that by the positing of a *nexus metaphysicus*, due to will, such extraordinary experiences receive a grounding explanation. The next chapter, "Sinology," details various affinities between his philosophy and Taoism, Confucianism, Buddhism, and Hinduism, and it includes references to many of the sources through which Schopenhauer gained his familiarity with Eastern thought. It also contains a curious feature. The philosopher always quoted extensively from world literature, religion, philosophy, and science in all of his books. In many cases, his aim was to show that other important thinkers expressed insights that receive a more thorough explanation in his philosophy. But although Schopenhauer did this to help substantiate his views, he also suggested that he came to ideas independently and from his own puzzlements about the world. The great exception to this was Kant, and throughout his philosophical career he increasingly identified himself as a Kantian, going so far as to claim that his philosophy "is merely the perfection of Kantian transcendental idealism."[13] "Sinology," however, contains a rare instance in which he attempted to show that his fundamental idea, that our introspective experience of will is the key for understanding the world, is found in the writings of a twelfth-century Chinese scholar, Chu-fu-tse, who said "*the mind of Heaven is deducible from what is the will of humankind.*"[14]

[12] Ibid., p. 100/ibid., p. 97.
[13] Schopenhauer, *Gesammelte Briefe*, p. 284, Schopenhauer to Julius Frauenstädt, 22 July 1852.
[14] Schopenhauer, *On the Will in Nature*, p. 136/*Sämliche Werke*, Vol. 4, p. 137.

Schopenhauer was quick to point out that this statement was first published in the *Asiatic Journal*, 1826, eight years after the appearance of his
principal work.

At first blush, the final chapter, "Reference to Ethics," appears tacked
onto a work seeking to ground the natural sciences metaphysically. Yet it
clearly expresses the type of philosophy Schopenhauer envisioned in 1813,
one that was ethics and metaphysics in one.[15] "From time immemorial,"
he claimed, "all people have recognized that the world besides its physical
significance has a moral one as well."[16] Well indeed, that is, he noted,
as long as one is not a crude materialist. He claimed, moreover, that he
had a greater right than Spinoza to call his metaphysics "ethics," because
he had demonstrated that the will expressed in nature satisfies the two
requirements for any moral attribution: that is, it is free and responsible.
Borrowing a term from theology, Schopenhauer claimed that the will
alone has aseity; it is self-derived, self-determining, and independent
from everything else. Everything in the world is as it is because it is
will. Consequently, all the guilt or merit found in the world accrues
to the will. Indeed, unlike other philosophies, which have nothing but
empty sonorous words to account for the monstrous, unspeakable evils
expressed in the heart-rending misery of the world, Schopenhauer prided
himself in honestly confronting the problem of evil, by recognizing that
evil is woven within the very fabric of being. Death and destruction are
necessary features of the world that is the objectification of will. Due to
this, as he would later claim, "nothing else can be stated as the aim of our
existence except the knowledge that it would be better for us not to exist.
This, however, is the most important of all truths, and must therefore be
stated however much it stands in contrast with the present-day mode of
European thought."[17]

Standing in contrast to European thought was something Schopenhauer knew he had been doing throughout his philosophical career. He
mentioned in "Reference to Ethics" how the paradoxical nature of the
ascetic results of his philosophy offended Jean Paul, who was favorably
disposed to him, and made Rätze write a well-meant book against him.

---

[15] See Schopenhauer, *Manuscript Remains*, Vol. 1, p. 59/*Der handschriftliche Nachlaß*, Vol. 1,
p. 55.

[16] Schopenhauer, *On the Will in Nature*, p. 139/*Sämtliche Werke*, Vol. 4, p. 140.

[17] Schopenhauer, *The World as Will and Representation*, Vol. 2, p. 605/*Sämtliche Werke*, Vol. 3,
p. 695.

He gave voice, moreover, to the type of statement that Nietzsche saw as his heroic stance against his age and as connoting the deep honesty running through his philosophy. He knew that by finding the essence of existence evil, his anti-optimistic stance would knife deeply against the *Zeitgeist* of his time – to use a word he loathed. "[T]he optimism of all philosophical systems is a point closely related to ethics, and as being obligatory," he admonished, "it must not be wanting in any of them; for the world wishes to hear that it is praiseworthy and excellent, and philosophers want to please the world. With me it is different; I have seen what pleases the world, and hence to please it I will not move one step from the truth."[18] In this way, he claimed that his philosophy differed from all others and stood alone. This, of course, was written by a man who ardently desired readers. The short, two-page "conclusion" ends the book with a rant against "philosophers by profession," members of the "philosophical trade," who have ignored his writings and whose aim is to please self, family, church, and state, and who, he writes, would not become aroused if stark naked truth came down from Olympus – rather, they would bow her back to her Olympus, putting three fingers over their mouths, and return to their studies.

Freedom Is a Mystery

On the Will in Nature broke Schopenhauer's period of philosophical silence only in the sense that he had published another book. It did not break the silence of the philosophical world about his work. The book was received in a more dismal fashion than his dissertation and his principal work. At least *The Fourfold Rout* received three initial lukewarm reviews and *The World as Will and Representation* drew a half-dozen reviews, including Rätze's well-intended book and the Beneke controversy. Moreover, his principal work would continue to earn him references in German compendia on philosophy during the 1820s and early 1830s. His attempt to use science to corroborate his philosophy drew a single, negative review, which appeared anonymously, signed simply "H," in the *Repertory of*

---

[18] Schopenhauer, *On the Will in Nature*, p. 142/*Sämtliche Werke*, Vol. 4, p. 143. Nietzsche, who prided himself as giving Schopenhauer's pessimism greater depth in his Dionysian pessimism of strength and in his tragic world view, seems to be a philosopher who fits Schopenhauer's criterion for the typical philosopher; namely, one who wants to please the world; see my "Nietzsche's Use and Abuse of Schopenhauer's Moral Philosophy," p. 150.

the Entire German Literature [*Repertorium der gesammten deutschen Litteratur*, 1836]. The reviewer, a professor of philosophy in Leipzig, one Gustav Hartenstein, a former student of Herbart, shared his teacher's assessment of Schopenhauer's philosophy – that his fundamental ideas could be found in Fichte and Schelling. Hartenstein also proved himself prophetic, correctly predicting that this small work on the philosophy of nature would fail to draw an audience to Schopenhauer's principal work. Hartenstein, however, did not say whether this foresight was an expression of the *nexus metaphysicus*. The prophetic critic would also provide negative reviews of *The Two Fundamental Problems of Ethics* and the second edition of Schopenhauer's principal work. After a year in print, *On the Will in Nature* sold 125 copies.

While *On the Will in Nature* was gathering dust on the publisher's shelves, the Trondheim-based Royal Norwegian Society of Sciences puzzled about the freedom of the human will, and to overcome its perplexity, the Society decided to sponsor a prize-essay contest. In April 1837, Schopenhauer came across an announcement for the contest in the *Halle Literary Journal* [*Hallische Litteratur-Zeitung*]. The philosopher was immediately intrigued by the question for the contest, "Can the freedom of the human will be demonstrated from self-consciousness," and he felt compelled to answer it.[19] After all, he had obliquely addressed the issue in his dissertation, his principal work, and his treatise on the will in nature, but not in a concentrated, sustained, and single-minded fashion. Consequently, he already knew that the answer to the question was "no!" and because he had recently found his philosophical voice, he was determined to speak again, knowing that at least some members of a society would hear him.

Schopenhauer worked conscientiously on his essay from the fall of 1837 through the spring of 1838, through his correspondence with Rosenkranz concerning the proper form of Kant's collective works, through his attempt to convince Frankfurt to honor Goethe properly, and through his mother's last days. The Royal Norwegian Society received his answer

---

[19] The original question was in Latin: "*Nun liberum hominum arbitrium e sui ipsius conscientia demonstrari potest.*" Schopenhauer noted the ambiguity of the word "*conscientia*," which can mean both "consciousness" and "conscience." He correctly rejected the idea that the Royal Norwegian Society wanted some discussion of "*conscience*," because the phrase "*ipsius conscientia*," "consciousness of oneself," immediately ruled out "conscience." See Schopenhauer, *Prize Essay on the Freedom of the Will*, p. 9/ *Sämtliche Werke*, Vol. 4, p. 10.

to their question on 19 June 1838, and on 26 January 1839 it crowned Schopenhauer's essay. In addition to a gold medal, which the philosopher valued highly, he was also named a member of the Society. The Society published the essay in 1840, but without providing Schopenhauer with the opportunity to correct the proof-sheets, an act that angered its author.[20] The Society itself owned the publication rights to the essay, but after some negotiations, Schopenhauer was given the rights for its publication in Germany.

Schopenhauer had to submit the essay anonymously. Consequently, he could not write it in a manner that presupposed his own philosophy. And unlike his treatment of freedom in *The World as Will and Representation*, written with the assumption of his metaphysics of will, he had to develop his view within the framework of the question; that is, whether the freedom of the human will could be derived from self-consciousness. For these reasons, "On the Freedom of the Human Will" is a self-contained treatise on the issue of freedom and determinism. It is also the clearest of all his writings, which are generally known for their clarity.

On the Freedom of the Human Will

The essay is divided into five sections and an appendix. The first section, "Definitions," reads almost as if it were written by a twentieth-century Anglo-American philosopher, instead of a nineteenth-century German philosopher. By carefully observing ordinary language and by keying on the central concepts employed in the Society's question, Schopenhauer sharply delineates the meanings of key terms and frames the question with precision. In "Definitions," he distinguished between three ideas of freedom. "Physical freedom" connotes the expression of some force, absent material hindrances or barriers. Thus a stream is "free" when it flows unimpeded by mountains or sluices, and an animal is free when it can roam unrestricted by a cage, and a human is free when his or her road home is not blocked by an accident. "Intellectual freedom" concerns a human's ability to do as he or she will, absent some cognitive defect or error that would lead him or her to act contrary to his or her desires.

---

[20] The essay appeared as "Kan Menneskets frie Villie bevises af dets Selvbevidshed? En med det Kongelige Norske Videnskaber-Selskabs større Guldmedaille belonnet Priis Afhandling," *Det Kgl. Norske Vidselsk Skr. i det 19deAarh., 3.B. 2.H* [1840].

Schopenhauer would expand on the significance of intellectual freedom is an appendix.

Using "moral" in its older and broader sense as having to do with the psychological or mental sphere rather than the physical, Schopenhauer defined "moral freedom" as the freedom of the will absent motivational constraints. He claimed that "moral freedom" is the species of freedom designated historically by the very Latin phrase, used in the essay question, *liberum arbitrium*, "free choice of will."

Schopenhauer's essay properly focused on the idea of moral freedom. He accepted any claim that merely ascribed physical freedom to human conduct, because any being or thing can be said to be "physically free," even though everything about it is causally determined. The vital question for Schopenhauer was not whether humans can do what they want (physical freedom), or even whether they could want what they want, but whether will itself is free; that is whether "the particular manifestations of such will (acts of will) would . . . proceed absolutely and quite originally from itself, without being brought about necessarily by antecedent conditions, and thus without being determined by anything according to a rule."[21] Schopenhauer observes that with this concept clear thinking is at an end, because it requires abandoning the principle of sufficient reason, the essential form of our cognitive faculty, but he notes that scholars have employed a technical term to denote this concept, "*liberum arbitrium indifferentiae*," free choice of indifference.

To consider whether freedom can be grounded in self-consciousness, Schopenhauer first defined it. Self-consciousness is the immediate awareness of one's own will, he asserted, and concerns the entire sphere of a person's introspective experiences. It includes not simply consciousness of definite acts of will that express themselves as specific actions and the decisions that lead to such behavior, but also a person's affective life in all of its different modifications in degree and kind. Thus, self-consciousness is the awareness of "all desiring, striving, wishing, longing, rejoicing, exulting, and the like, as well as the feelings of unwillingness or repugnance, in short, all affections and passions . . . , including feelings of pleasure and pain and the countless sensations lying between these two extremes."[22] The realm of self-consciousness, of the inner sense, extends,

---

[21] Schopenhauer, *Prize Essay on the Freedom of the Will*, p. 8/*Sämtliche Werke*, Vol. 4, p. 8f.
[22] Ibid., p. 10/ibid., Vol. 4, p. 11.

he asserts, to a thoroughgoing and universally recognized relationship to what is perceived and recognized in the external world, awareness of which is the consciousness of other things, the domain of outer sense, and whose objects denote the end of self-consciousness. Objects perceived in the external world, he claims, are the material and occasion for all acts of will, which are always concerned with these objects, and which are occasioned by them insofar as they are cognized as ends of action and function as motives. To think otherwise, he held, would leave the will completely separated from the external world, "imprisoned in the dark inside of self-consciousness."[23]

Schopenhauer makes relatively short work of the Society's question in the second section, "The Will before Self-Consciousness." Employing his broad conception of self-consciousness and his distinction between physical and moral freedom, he argues that the data of self-consciousness cannot establish moral freedom. At best, self-consciousness can reveal physical freedom, such as, after work I could go to the library, go home, go to the coffee house, or decide to flee my miserable life and roam the great wide world. I could do any of these if I wanted, and unless I am physically hindered, I am free to do so, provided I want to do so. Schopenhauer is willing to concede that all of this is true, but it has absolutely nothing to do with the freedom of will. The germane question here is whether in this case I can will one thing as well as its opposite, and all self-consciousness can reveal is that I can do as I will. Here, however, are the limits of self-consciousness. Merely being able to imagine that I could do any of a number of things in a given set of circumstances, provided that I wanted to do so, says nothing about whether I could have wanted to do so; it says nothing about whether I could have wanted to do anything other than what I had in fact wanted to do. Consequently, Schopenhauer concludes that self-consciousness cannot establish a *liberum arbitrium*.

Schopenhauer then explores our consciousness of other things, where he sets out to demonstrate the impossibility of the freedom of the will. Instead of exploring the question subjectively through the limited lens of a person's self-conscious experiences of will, in the third section, "The Will before the Consciousness of Other Things," he shifts to an "objective standpoint" by examining the will as possessed by a being embedded in

---

[23] Ibid., p. 11/ibid., Vol. 4, p. 12.

the world and as an object of the faculty of cognition. Remaining faithful to his Kantian roots and, consequently, to his work in his dissertation and principal book, Schopenhauer argues that all objects of the outer sense are subject to the law of causality, and in this section, he traces the varieties of causes operating within the inorganic and organic realms of nature.

Central to Schopenhauer's argument is his discussion of the variety of causality that is unique to animal life: that is, motivation. Nonhuman animals are confined to intuitive perceptions of the world, which serve as motives for their actions, whereas humans or rational animals are also receptive to a different type of motivation that frees them from the influence of the immediate present. By having the ability to formulate abstract representations or concepts, which are then denoted by words and are used in all manners of combination to form judgments, humans have the capacity to think. Although Schopenhauer held that this provides humans with a much higher degree of choice than nonhuman animals, this freedom is only relative and only frees them from the immediate present, but not from the law of causality. Just as with nonhumans, the efficacy of a motive is absolute; motivation is causality operating by means of cognition that produces an action. Each and every action follows from a sufficient motive, and what determines a sufficient motive is a function of the character of an actor. A person's character, he argued, is individual, constant, empirical, and innate; it is his or her essence. Using the Latin phrase "*operari sequitur esse*," acting follows being, he claimed that each and every human action follows necessarily from a person's character and motives. Although it may appear that after work, I could go home, to the library, or to the coffee shop, or flee my miserable life and wander the world, if I went home, I could not have done differently, given my character and that set of motives. To think that I could have fled my miserable life to roam the world when, in fact, I went home after work would be like a stone flying through the air, thinking that it was free to continue to move or to drop to the ground.[24]

After Schopenhauer made his case for the strict necessitation of all human actions, he referred to numerous forerunners of his view in the fourth section, "Predecessors." He cites religious figures, such as Clement

[24] See ibid., p. 69/ibid., 76, where Schopenhauer quotes from Spinoza's *Ethics*, prop. 2, Schol., which is the source for the stone example.

of Alexander, Saint Augustine, and Martin Luther; philosophical figures, such as Thomas Hobbes, Spinoza, Hume, Joseph Priestly, and Kant; and literary figures, such as Shakespeare, Sir Walter Scott, Goethe, and Schiller as recognizing the strict determinism of human behavior. He mentions Schelling and Fichte, making it clear that they are not among his forebears. He even chides Schelling for trying to pass off Kant's view as his own. Yet, despite acknowledging that others have shared in his insights, he reminds the Society that he did not mention these men to make an illicit appeal to authority to justify his view, but that he had already demonstrated his position.[25] His main interest, he said, was to show how his position differed from earlier, analogous views. He noted two differences. First, by carefully distinguishing between inner and outer experiences, he had shown, unlike all others, why the deception of free will is irresistible. Second, he treated the subject systematically and completely by considering the will in its connection to all of nature.[26]

"True moral freedom" is the topic of the fifth and final section, "Conclusion and Higher View," and in it Schopenhauer presented his Kant-inspired view that freedom is compatible with the necessitation of human actions. Building from Kant's distinction between the intelligible and empirical characters, to which he had first paid an odd sort of homage in his dissertation, he argues that our intelligible character is outside the scope of the principle of sufficient reason, the basis of all necessity. Because the intelligible character constitutes human essence – and here he adopts the opposite position of Jean Paul Sartre – our essence is free; that is, it is not necessitated, although all of our actions follow inevitably from this character and motives.[27] But unlike his mentor Kant, Schopenhauer rejected the claim that freedom is some type of causality different than the type of causality exhibited in the natural world. For Schopenhauer, our essence or intelligible character is expressed in all of our actions, our acting follows our being, but our essence itself is neither caused nor

---

[25] Ibid., p. 81/ibid., p. 90.
[26] See Schopenhauer, ibid., p. 73/ibid., p. 82.
[27] Sartre argued in the well-known essay "Existentialism" that human existence precedes essence and that we create our essence through our actions. Schopenhauer holds that our essence logically precedes our existence and what we do follows necessarily from what we are (our essence). See Jean-Paul Sartre, *Existentialism and Human Emotions* (New York: Citadel Press, 2000), pp. 13–15, and Schopenhauer, *On the Will in Nature*, pp. 51 and 87/*Sämtliche Werke*, Vol. 4, pp. 57 and 97.

causing, and like all forces of nature it is expressed in all causality. Freedom is transcendental and applies to our essence and not to the world.

To account for the transcendental nature of freedom, Schopenhauer argued in a way reminiscent of that which the novice philosopher used to sense the better consciousness in the world. Various "facts of consciousness" point to our nontemporal, nonspatial, and noncausal intelligible character, our will and essence, as that which is expressed in our actions, each of which are products of necessity. We have a deep feeling of responsibility and accountability for what we do, he noted, and we are conscious of the spontaneity and originality of our actions, which makes them feel as if they are *our* actions. We have a sense that we are the doers of our deeds. Just as Kant had argued that an "I think" attaches to all of our representations, Schopenhauer claimed that an "I will" attaches to all of our actions.[28] These feelings point to our intelligible character, which is, along with motives, the second necessary factor for any action. Our character underlies the efficacy of motives, and it is that which makes a particular motive the sufficient motive for a specific action. This character, however, is neither motivating nor motivated, but it is that which is expressed in all of our actions. Our actions, moreover, exhibit the moral quality of our character. Others, he argued, use our actions as evidence for the moral quality of our character, and our conscience makes us aware of the same. By assessing the moral value of our character through our deeds, and by realizing that our deeds follow from our character, Schopenhauer ultimately attached our feelings of responsibility and accountability to our character. Had we a different character, our actions could have been different, but given who we are, they follow necessarily. But we are who we are and our actions follow from who we are. Because the intelligible character is outside the scope of the principle of sufficient reason, which is the source of all necessity and the principle of all explanation, this character is not necessitated and cannot be explained. Thus freedom is transcendental. It attaches not to our deeds, but to our character, and not to the world as representation, but to the very core of that world. Paraphrasing Nicolas Malebranche, Schopenhauer wrote, "freedom is a mystery," something beyond explanation.[29]

[28] See Kant, *Critique of Pure Reason*, B131f.

[29] Schopenhauer, *Prize Essay on the Freedom of the Will*, p. 88/*Sämtliche Werke*, Vol. 4, p. 98. Hübscher attributes this remark to Claude-Adrien Helvétius, *De Lésprit* and not Malebranche; see *Der handschriftliche Nachlaß*, Vol. 5, p. 66.

The Philosopher of Compassion

In 1837, another northern learned society found itself puzzled: not about the freedom of the human will, but about the foundations for morality. Its perplexity spawned yet another prize essay contest and so it posed the question, "Is the source and foundation of morals to be looked for in an idea of morality lying immediately in consciousness [*conscientia*] and in the analysis of the other fundamental concepts springing from that idea, or are they to be looked for in a different ground of knowledge?"[30] Schopenhauer ran across the announcement of the contest again in the *Halle Literary Journal*, May 1838. Still feeling in a competitive mood, and still seeking to gain an audience for his philosophy, the philosopher decided to resolve the perplexity of the Royal Danish Society for Scientific Studies. Just as he had with his Norwegian essay, he already knew the answer to the question. It was given in the fourth book of *The World as Will and Representation*. Once again all that he had to do was to develop his perspective from an *a posteriori* path, without the assumption of his metaphysics.

Schopenhauer sent his entry, "On the Foundation of Morality," to the Royal Danish Society on 26 July 1839.[31] Mustering his very best Latin, the philosopher composed a letter to accompany his essay. It was a letter that had to strike the Society as highly presumptuous and arrogant. In its very first line, Schopenhauer requested to be notified by post of his victory. He then bragged about his recent victory in the Royal Norwegian Society's contest, and he told the Royal Danish Society of how honored he felt by also being named a member of the other society. Within the next year, he continued, he would publish his two "crowned" essays together as *The Two Fundamental Problems of Ethics*, a work that would form a complete outline of a system of ethics, and a book for which "one would have to thank Scandinavian academies for their munificence."[32] Schopenhauer might have just as well told the Royal Danish Society that they need not read the essay, but should simply send him the gold medal.

---

[30] Schopenhauer, *On the Basis of Morality*, p. 215f/ *Sämtliche Werke*, Vol. 4, p. 105.
[31] With the publication of *The Two Fundamental Problems of Ethics*, Schopenhauer changed the title of the essay from "Über das Fundament der Moral" to "Preisschrift über die Grundlage der Moral [Prize Essay on the Basis of Morality]," although on the title page of that book, he referred to the essay by its first title.
[32] Schopenhauer, *Gesammelte Briefe*, p. 183.

Schopenhauer never received via mail the announcement of his victory, nor was the prize delivered to him through the Danish envoy in Frankfurt, as he also requested in his letter to the Danish society. It was not that the Society decided not to honor Schopenhauer's requests. Had he won the contest, the Society might have done so. But he did not win, despite the fact that his was the only entry to the contest. The essay was deemed not worthy of wearing the crown. In its verdict, the Society declared that the essay did not deserve the prize because its author misunderstood the question. He had thought that the principal task was to lay down some principle of ethics, whereas the first and foremost task was to show the connection between ethics and metaphysics, a task that the author relegated to an appendix. Moreover, the Society also found the author's argument that compassion was the foundation of morality to be inadequate. Last, the Society could not "pass over in silence the fact that several distinguished philosophers of recent times are mentioned in a manner so unseemly as to cause just and grave offence."[33]

The Royal Danish Society made its negative finding on 17 January 1840 and delayed its publication until the summer, in a journal that circulated primarily in Copenhagen. Schopenhauer learned of the verdict later that summer, through the auspices of his friend and lawyer Martin Emden. To say that Schopenhauer read the Society's judgment without a philosopher's equanimity would be an understatement of the first order. He was enraged. He published 500 copies of *The Two Fundamental Problems of Ethics*, as planned, through the Frankfurt publishing house of Johann Christian Hermann, F. E. Suchsland. He noted on the title page that his essay on the freedom of the will was "crowned" by the Royal Norwegian Society and that his essay on the foundations of morality was "not crowned" by the Royal Danish Society.

Schopenhauer vented his rage in a lengthy and vitriolic preface where he systematically analyzed the Royal Danish Society's question, demonstrating that the Society had asked precisely what he supplied; namely an account of the ultimate basis of morality and not an essay focusing on the connection between metaphysics and morals. He had, moreover, provided the latter, not in an "appendix," as the Society charged, but in the concluding chapter. And in reply to the Danish Society's claim

[33] Schopenhauer, *On the Basis of Morality*, p. 216/ *Sämtliche Werke*, Vol. 4, p. 276.

that he failed to adequately establish his foundation of ethics, the philosopher replied: "On the contrary, I refer to the fact that I have actually and seriously *proved* my foundation of morals with an almost mathematical precision. In *morals* this is without precedent and was possible only because I had penetrated more deeply than had been done before into the nature of the human will."[34] Schopenhauer, who could hold a grudge like an elephant that is said to never forget, was still spitting fire at the Royal Danish Society when he wrote the preface to the second edition of *The Two Fundamental Problems of Ethics* in 1860, a few weeks before his death.

On the Basis of Morality

What roused Schopenhauer's ire more than the Society's criticisms of his essay was its remark that "several distinguished philosophers of recent times are mentioned in a manner so unseemly as to cause just and grave offence."[35] Indeed, he spent more time in his preface lambasting those he took to be these "distinguished philosophers," namely Fichte and Hegel, and the Society for honoring these men, than he did replying to the Danish Society's critical remarks. It is in this preface that Schopenhauer launched his most unrestrained attack on his one-time colleague at Berlin. In the course of his rant, to further demean Hegel, he called Fichte "a man of talent" compared to Hegel, and he also made it clear that Fichte had very little talent. To castigate the Society, he also translated a lengthy passage from Gracián's satirical *The Critic*, implying that the Danes were complete fools for thinking that a philosophical hack such as Hegel deserved respect.

It is curious that Schopenhauer identified only Fichte and Hegel as the Society's "several distinguished philosophers of recent times," and this is the case for reasons beyond the fact that "several" implies more than two. He did freely abuse Fichte in the essay, especially in Sect. 11, "Fichte's Ethics as a Mirror for Magnifying the Errors of the Kantian." Yet he made more snide and scurrilous remarks about Schelling and Jacobi than he did about Hegel, whom he mentioned only once in the essay. To be sure, he slammed Hegel mightily by calling him a "clumsy and senseless charlatan" and by claiming that he possessed even less talent than the

---

34 Ibid., p. 13/ibid., Vol. 4, p. xvi.
35 Ibid., p. 216/ibid., Vol. 4, p. 276.

"philosophasters" Fichte and Schelling.[36] Nevertheless, it should have occurred to him that the Society might have had his treatment of Kant also in mind. Schopenhauer devoted more than one-third of the essay to a harsh and wide-ranging critique of Kant's ethics, one that, as a recent commentator has noted, "enumerates most of the criticisms urged against [the ethics of] Kant over the past two centuries."[37] Because Kant's moral philosophy constituted for Schopenhauer the last and most significant work in that field, he felt compelled to demolish its very foundations before constructing his own groundwork for morals. Schopenhauer also viewed Kant's practical philosophy as an absolute catastrophe, especially when compared to the brilliance of his theoretical philosophy, and he would propose an ethics that was diametrically opposed to Kant's. Within his critique of his hero's ethics, moreover, Schopenhauer made a number of derisive remarks about Kant himself, diagnosing Kant's love for architectonic symmetry, a rashness emboldened by his increasing fame, and the garrulity of old age as responsible for his ultimately vacuous moral philosophy. He even claimed that Kant's *Metaphysical Principles of the Doctrine of Virtue* [*Metaphysische Anfangsgründe der Tugendlehre*, 1797] was the product "of the feebleness of old age."[38]

Schopenhauer may have been oblivious to the possibility that the Royal Danish Society was offended by his treatment of Kant. Certainly, Schopenhauer considered Kant the greatest philosopher, and he had

---

[36] Ibid., p. 80/ibid., Vol. 4, p. 147.Paul Deussen notes that Schopenhauer wrote on the title page of the first edition of *The Two Fundamental Problems of Ethics* that a Dr. Nordwall from Upsalla (Sweden) reported that the actual judge of the Copenhagen essay was a fellow named Martensen, a Hegelian academic, author of a Hegelian ethics, and later Bishop; see, his edition of *Sämtliche Werke*, (Munich: Piper, 1911-1942), Vol. 3, p. 793.There can be little doubt that Schopenhauer was referring to Kierkegaard's nemesis Hans Lassen Martensen, who is frequently credited with introducing Hegel to Copenhagen's intellectual world and whom Kierkegaard criticized mightily in a series of writings now published as *Attach upon "Christendom"*; see Curtis L.Thompson's introduction to *Between Hegel and Kierkegaard: Hans L. Martensen's Philosophy of Religion*, trans. Curtis Thompson (Atlanta: Scholars Press, 1997), which includes a translation of Martensen's "Hegelian ethics," "Outline of a System of Moral Philosophy" (1841). Because Martensen's ethics did not appear until 1841, and because he did not become Bishop of Sjaelland until 1854, it is most likely that Schopenhauer did not know that Martensen was the "actual judge" of the Copenhagen essay, when he wrote the first preface for *The Two Fundamental Problems of Ethics*.

[37] Atwell, John, *Schopenhauer: The Human Character*, p. 91. Also see my "Schopenhauer's Narrower Sense of Morality," in *The Cambridge Companion to Schopenhauer*, ed. Christopher Janaway (Cambridge: Cambridge University Press, 1999), pp. 254–69.

[38] Schopenhauer, *On the Basis of Morality*, p. 51/*Sämtliche Werke*, Vol. 4, p. 119.

personally identified himself as a Kantian long before the time of this essay. But there was little in his Danish essay that expressed these beliefs. It is true that he praised Kant for purging eudaemonism from ethics, for denying that self-interested actions possessed moral worth, for separating ethics from theology, and for recognizing that human conduct is metaphysically significant. He even called Kant's doctrine of the coexistence of freedom and necessity "the greatest of all achievements of the human mind," just as he referred to the same doctrine in his successful prize essay.[39] Yet, except for this doctrine, Schopenhauer took back his praise for Kant. He argued that Kant's conception of the highest good, the union of happiness and virtue, made his rejection of eudaemonism only apparent and not real, because Kant made it seem that the virtuous will be happy. Moreover, he also argued that only self-interest could move a person to follow Kant's moral laws and that his moral philosophy was a continuation of theological ethics, a form of ethics that always relied on God's promised rewards or threatened punishments to move one to obedience. Indeed, Kant's moral theology, which he held was based on his ethics, was just the reverse, according to Schopenhauer. The very logic of Kant's moral concepts, such as the absolute ought, categorical imperatives, unconditional moral laws, and the like, presupposed a commander who issues such unconditional laws and who backs these statements of unconditional obligations with threats of punishment or promises of rewards.[40] Thus Schopenhauer argued that Kant's ethics presupposed theology and his alleged moral theology simply smuggled through the back door what was there all along: God, immortality, and freedom. Naturally, Schopenhauer also found this to be an inadequate account of the metaphysical significance of human conduct. He blamed Kant's ethics for providing the springboard for the wide flights of fantasy found in Reinhold, Fichte,

---

39 Ibid., p. 111/ibid., Vol. 4, p. 175; also see Schopenhauer, *Prize Essay on the Freedom of the Will*, p. 86/ibid., Vol. 4, p. 95.

40 John Atwell has noted that Schopenhauer's critique of Kant's ethics anticipated a number of claims against a Kantian-style ethics of duty such as those found in G. E. M. Anscombe's "Modern Moral Philosophy," *Philosophy*, Vol. 33 (1958), pp. 1–19 and Phillippa Foot's "Morality as a System of Hypothetical Imperatives," *Philosophical Review*, Vol. 8 (1972), pp. 305–16; see his *Ends and Principles in Kant's Moral Thought* (Dordrecht: Martinus Nijhoff, 1986), pp. 218–20. Richard Taylor's critique of an ethics of duty in *Virtue Ethics: An Introduction* (Interlaken, NY: Linden Books, 1991) is greatly indebted to Schopenhauer's Kant critique; see my "Schopenhauer's Narrower Sense of Morality," *The Cambridge Companion to Schopenhauer*, pp. 254–63.

Schelling, and Jacobi: "Thus in the Kantian school practical reason with its categorical imperative appears more and more as a hyperphysical fact, as a Delphic temple in the human soul. From its dark sanctuary oracular sentences infallibly proclaim, alas! Not what *will*, but what *ought* to happen."[41]

Schopenhauer rejected Kant's claim that we have duties to ourselves, his views on lying and suicide, his theory of conscience, his view of moral motivation, Kant's view of the function of kind-hearted emotions, such as love, sympathy, and compassion in our moral lives, and his unenlightened view of the moral status of animals, which, simply because they lacked reason, also lacked, for Kant, moral considerability.[42] Not only did Schopenhauer object to Kant's making pure reason the means for discovering synthetic *a priori* moral laws, he also objected to his developing an ethics "for all possible rational beings and 'solely on this account,' and hence incidentally and *per accidens*, for human beings as well."[43] This is like developing an ethics for dear little angels, Schopenhauer charges, and is meaningless for flesh and blood human beings who are will through and through. Like Hume, Schopenhauer held that reason is that slave of the passions, and he claimed that reason only functions instrumentally in human life. The will is metaphysically and ethically primary, and the essence of humans is not rational nor is reason the bearer of moral personality. An ill will uses the cunning of reason to realize its evil ends just as a good will does so to bring about its kindly ends. According to Schopenhauer, "it never occurred to anyone *prior* to Kant to identify just,

---

[41] Ibid., p. 79/ibid., Vol. 4, p. 146. Schopenhauer is referring to Kant's *Critique of Practical Reason*, where Kant postulated both the moral law and practical reason as a "fact of reason," a move that Schopenhauer read as a reversal of Kant's stance in the *Groundwork of the Metaphysics of Morals* and as signifying a return to a precritical stance. Like Schopenhauer, Henry Allison sees Kant's treatment of the moral law as a "fact of reason" as a confession that his deduction in the *Groundwork* failed. But unlike Schopenhauer, Allison finds this move an advancement of Kant's thought; see his *Kant's Theory of Freedom* (Cambridge: Cambridge University Press, 1993), p. 201.

[42] G. E. Varner has argued that Schopenhauer developed a metaethics sufficient for generating an environmental ethics that synthesizes holism and individualism while granting moral patience to natural objects. He also claimed that Schopenhauer anticipated Lynn White's famous thesis, articulated in "The Historical Roots of our Ecological Crisis," *Science*, Vol. 155 (1967) that our Christian heritage is responsible for our regarding animals as things; see "The Schopenhauer Challenge in Environmental Ethics," *Environmental Ethics*, Vol. 7 (1985), pp. 209-29.

[43] Schopenhauer, *On the Basis of Morality*, p. 63/*Sämtliche Werke*, Vol. 4, p. 131.

virtuous, and noble conduct with *reasonable* or *rational*. There is nothing contradictory in saying that a person is both rational and vicious or that a person is virtuous and unreasonable.[44]

To locate Kant's first false step in ethics, Schopenhauer quoted the master himself: "In practical philosophy we are not concerned with what happens, but with giving laws as regards what *ought to happen, even though it may never happen*."[45] This assumption, Schopenhauer argued, needs a justification, and it allowed Kant to develop an ethics in the legislative, imperative form, by divorcing moral laws from experience and all empirical content. Yet by divorcing ethics from all experience, he contended, Kant's ethics hovers in the heavens, divorced from human reality, suited for angels and not willful creatures. In diametrical opposition to Kant, Schopenhauer developed an ethics that shuns the issuing of categorical moral laws that are said to be binding on people, regardless of their interests, and he eschews an ethics for all rational beings, one that prescribes what they ought to do. Instead, and consistent with his general philosophical methodology, Schopenhauer argued that the moral philosopher is to provide a unified explanation of moral phenomena:

The purpose of ethics is to indicate, explain, and trace to its ultimate ground the extremely varied behavior of humans from a moral point of view. Therefore there is no other way for discovering the foundation of ethics than the empirical, namely, to investigate whether there are generally any actions to which we must attribute *genuine moral worth*. These are then to be regarded as a given phenomenon that we have to explain correctly, that is, trace to its true grounds. Consequently, we have to indicate the particular motive that moves humans to actions of this kind, a kind specifically different from any other. The motive together with the receptivity to it will be the ultimate ground of morality [*Moralität*], and knowledge of it will be the foundation of morals [*Moral*].[46]

The voluntaristic Schopenhauer resolved the moral point of view into the affective responses of agents to their deeds and to those of uninvolved witnesses to the same actions. Actions possessing a positive moral value, those to which Schopenhauer ascribed moral worth, drew the agent's feeling of self-satisfaction and approbation and the approbation of an impartial witness. An example of this would be the act of a poor man returning

---

44 Ibid., p. 83/ibid., Vol. 4, p. 150.
45 Ibid., p. 52/ibid., Vol. 4, p. 120. Schopenhauer is quoting from Kant's *Groundwork for the Metaphysics of Morals*, AK. 427. The emphases are Schopenhauer's.
46 Ibid., p. 130/ibid., Vol. 4, p. 195.

lost property to a rich man or, to use Schopenhauer's paradigm case of an altruistic act, Arnold von Winkelried's heroic sacrifice of his life to save his comrades at the Battle of Sempach (1386). Actions bearing a negative moral value, those that Schopenhauer called morally reprehensible, drew the actor's disapprobation or the "sting of conscience" toward his or her own deed as well as the disapprobation of an uninvolved observer. An example of a morally reprehensible act is that of a winner of a brawl who "tore away the whole lower jawbone of [the loser] and carried it off as a trophy, leaving the other man alive."[47] Actions lacking either positive or negative moral value, morally indifferent actions, those that are neither worthwhile nor reprehensible, elicit no affective responses from either the doer of the deed or its witness. An example of this type of action would be that of a merchant who diligently caters to his or her customer's needs in order to maximize his or her profits.

Having classified human actions into three categories, and after dismissing the challenge mounted by the "moral skeptic," someone who would argue that all human actions are self-interested, Schopenhauer set out to determine what moves people to perform these different types of actions. Drawing both on his dissertation and his successful Norwegian essay, he argued that all human actions are a function of a person's character and a sufficient motive, having as their ends something "in agreement or contrary to a being's will."[48] By identifying things in agreement with a person's will with a person's weal or well-being, and things contrary to a person's will with a person's woe or misfortune, he claimed that all human actions have as their final end someone's weal or woe. After rejecting Kant's duties to ourselves, he held that morality dealt with relationships between individuals and that there are four ultimate ends for human actions; that is, one's own weal, one's own woe, another's weal, and another's woe. The cognition of these ends are motives that could serve to stimulate four basic or primitive incentives for actions; namely, egoism, a desire for one's own weal; an unnamed incentive, which he did not discuss in his essay, a desire for one's own woe; compassion, a desire for another's weal; and malice, a desire for another's woe.[49] Every

---

[47] Ibid., p. 169/ibid., Vol. 4, p. 232f.; see, respectively, ibid. pp. 126 and 139/ibid., Vol. 4, pp. 191 and 203 for the merchant example and the Arnold von Winkelried example.

[48] Ibid., p. 141/ibid., Vol. 4, p. 205.

[49] Schopenhauer did not discuss the unnamed incentive in *On the Basis of Morality*, claiming that he did not do so because he wrote the essay in the spirit of philosophical ethics prevailing in

action, he argued, must be attributed to one of these incentives, although he held that some actions are an expression of some combination of these incentives. He also claimed that each person possesses these incentives to varying degrees and that the human character is an amalgam of these incentives.

Schopenhauer proceeded to argue that egoism is the incentive for morally indifferent actions, malice for morally reprehensible actions, and compassion for actions possessing moral worth. To establish his claim that compassion is the sole incentive for morally worthwhile actions, he mounted first an argument from elimination (Sect. 16) in which he contended that neither egoism nor malice can explain acts of genuine justice and pure loving kindness. This entails that these actions must be due to compassion. Realizing that arguments from elimination are not fully satisfying, he also provided positive proof. Earlier in the essay he had stated his moral principle, *neminem laede, imo omnes, quantum potes, juva* [Injure no one; on the contrary, help everyone as much as you can].[50] Schopenhauer's moral principle did not prescribe conduct, but simply summarizes lines of conduct to which moral worth can be attributed. The first clause captures Schopenhauer's view of justice and the second his view of loving kindness or philanthropy (*Menschenliebe*). Justice and loving kindness constitute the cardinal virtues for Schopenhauer, the twofold source or basis of all virtues. In the seventeenth and eighteenth sections, he argued that the virtues of justice and loving kindness are based on compassion. By doing so, he thought that he demonstrated that compassion is the basic source of all virtues.

As the philosopher of the will, Schopenhauer emphasized the dominance of egoism in animal and human life, something that follows from their very essence as will. He continued to do so in "On the Foundation of

Protestant Europe and because members of the Royal Danish Society would not understand it; see *The World as Will and Representation*,, Vol. 2, p. 607/*Sämtliche Werke*, Vol. 3, p. 697n. Elsewhere, he claimed that this desire for one's own woe possessed "ascetic value"; see *Gesammelte Briefe*, p. 221, Schopenhauer to Johann August Becker, 10 December 1844. It is likely that Schopenhauer suppressed the discussion of this incentive for asceticism, remembering Jean Paul's response to his principal work, and by avoiding discussing it, he thought he would be spared a like puzzlement about the paradoxical "ascetic results of his ethics" by the Royal Danish Society; also see *On the Will in Nature*, p. 143/*Sämtliche Werke*, 146. If this was the case, this is an example of Schopenhauer deliberately trying not to "displease" his readers.

50 Ibid., p. 92/ibid., Vol. 4, p. 158.

Morality," calling egoism the chief and fundamental incentive in human life by recommending that anytime one attempts to explain a given action, one should attempt an egoistic explanation. Naturally, he felt especially compelled to explain both how compassion defeats the natural standpoint of egoism and how compassion is possible. Playing directly on the literal meaning of the German term "*Mitleid*," which like its English counterpart "compassion," means to "suffer with [another]," Schopenhauer wrote "in the case of his *woe*, I suffer directly with him [*ich bei seinem Wehe als solchem geradezu mit leide*], I feel *his* woe just as I ordinarily feel only my own; and likewise, I directly desire his weal in the same way I otherwise desire only my own."[51] By feeling another's woe as one's own, by identifying with the other by directly participating in the other's woe, compassionate agents treat the other's suffering like their own; that is, they are disposed to act to prevent or relieve the other's woe.

Compassion cannot be explained psychologically, according to Schopenhauer, because it involves an extraordinary experience – that of feeling another's pain in the other's body: "... it is precisely in *his* person, not in ours, that we feel the suffering, to our grief and sorrow. We suffer with him and hence *in him*: we feel his pain as *his*, and do not imagine that it is ours."[52] Due to this extraordinary experience, he called compassion the "great mystery of ethics," something that requires a metaphysical explanation. That compassion requires such an explanation, moreover, also follows from – and here he uses a term taken from Goethe –the fact that compassion is the primary phenomenon (*Urphänomen*) for morally worthwhile conduct; that is, compassion explains all human behavior possessing positive moral value, but compassion itself remains unexplained by any other experience. Without a metaphysical explanation, compassion lies before us as a "riddle" and Schopenhauer could never leave such philosophical puzzles unsolved. In the fifth and concluding section of his essay, he provided something he said was not required by the question posed by the Royal Danish Society, a metaphysical explanation of the primary ethical phenomenon. He did this, he said, because he could not shore up his foundation of morals without the deeper footing provided by metaphysics, and because when faced by primary phenomena, "the human mind does not find ultimate satisfaction and peace

---

[51] Ibid., p. 143/ibid., Vol. 4, p. 208.
[52] Ibid., p. 147/ibid., Vol. 4, p. 211.

here."[53] Yet the satisfaction required here is more significant and urgent that that required with primary phenomena in science and aesthetics, Schopenhauer noted, because both philosophical and religious systems agree that the ethical significance of human behavior must be metaphysical and that the supreme point at which the meaning of existence generally arrives is ethical. So by grounding his ethics in metaphysics, Schopenhauer thought that he was delivering a satisfaction for the human mind that was of ultimate importance. Naturally, for a philosopher presenting a philosophy that was ethics and metaphysics in one, he was personally compelled to draw the connection between the two.

Because Schopenhauer thought he was providing more than was required to answer the prize question, and because the strict incognito mandated by the contest precluded the use of his metaphysics, Schopenhauer gave only an outline of a metaphysics of morals, one broadly based on Kant's metaphysics, to whose transcendental standpoint he had referred earlier in his essay. Oddly, he did not offer a metaphysical explanation of that extraordinary experience of another's pain in the other's body, the very experience that made compassion the great mystery of ethics. Instead, he entertained the question whether the apprehension of the relationship between self and others of a morally good character, a compassionate person, is mistaken and due to a delusion, or whether that of a morally bad character, a person strongly disposed to egoism or malice, is a delusion. Perhaps, had he been able to appeal to his body of metaphysical work, he would have drawn from his analysis of magic in *On the Will in Nature*, viewing a compassionate person as an ethical clairvoyant, with the *nexus metaphysicus* making possible this literal sharing of suffering between apparently distinct beings.[54] Schopenhauer was being cautious in this essay, however. He did not discuss the fundamental incentive of a desire for one's own woe, because he feared that the Society would not understand it. The same is likely about his decision not to appeal to magic to explain the mysterious experience behind compassion.

Schopenhauer argued that the behavior of morally good people toward others expresses a standpoint that is metaphysically justified, whereas

---

[53] Ibid., p. 199/ibid., Vol. 4, p. 260.

[54] Three years after "On the Basis of Morality," Schopenhauer classified compassion as a form of "sympathy" [*Sympathie*], along with sexual love and magic, three phenomena by which the will's metaphysical identity shows itself within the physical multiplicity of its phenomena; see *The World as Will and Representation*, Vol. 2, p. 602/*Sämtliche Werke*, Vol. 3, p. 691.

that of bad characters does not. Good characters make less of a distinction than do the rest between themselves and others, treating others as an "I once more," whereas bad characters treat others as an absolute "non-I."[55] From a strictly empirical perspective, he continues, it appears as if the bad person's attitudes and behavior are correct, because each person is spatially distinct, and so it seems as if others are absolute "non-I's." But this empirical standpoint itself is not warranted, Schopenhauer claimed, and he appealed once more to a twofold experience we have of ourselves. Through intuitive perception, our consciousness of other things, we experience our bodies as we cognize other spatio-temporal objects. Through introspection or self-consciousness, we are also aware of ourselves as a continuous series of aspirations or acts of will. But ultimately we discover that we are not transparent, that is, our cognitive faculty itself, that which knows, does not know itself; it is never an object for a subject and "our innermost *essence in itself*, that which wills and knows, is not accessible to us."[56] Because of this unknown dimension of ourselves, we cannot infer that we are absolutely distinct from others, and this leaves open the possibility that our innermost essence may be and is identical in all.

Moving from our phenomenological experiences of ourselves, Schopenhauer turns to the empirical standpoint, our consciousness of other things, a standpoint that appears to warrant the stance of bad characters. Space and time, the *principium individuationis*, make plurality and numerical diversity possible, Schopenhauer observed, but now he appeals to Kant; he had demonstrated in the "Transcendental Aesthetic" in the *Critique of Pure Reason* that space and time are ideal, that they are our own contribution to our experiences. This entails that we experience only appearances of things and not things in themselves. From this insight Schopenhauer concluded that "if plurality and separateness belong only to appearances and if it is one and the same essence that manifests itself in all living things, then that conception that abolishes the difference between I and not-I is not erroneous; but on the contrary, the opposite conception must be [true]."[57]

---

[55] See Schopenhauer, *On the Basis of Morality*, p. 211 / *Sämtliche Werke*, Vol. 4, p. 271.

[56] Ibid., p. 205 / ibid., Vol. 4, p. 266.

[57] Schopenhauer concludes with this complex conditional statement because he could not appeal to his metaphysics, and because he was only offering an outline and sketch for his metaphysics of morals. Naturally, he believed that he had proven in his principal work both of the antecedents of the conditional statement, namely "that plurality and separateness belong

On the basis of his brief sketch of self-consciousness and the consciousness of other things, he concluded that good characters live in tune with the nature of reality and bad characters live a delusion. The former express in their attitude and behavior a form of life that is consonant with the deepest metaphysical knowledge, living as if their true natures, their own selves, reside in others. This form of life is warranted by the metaphysical unity of being, and all gentleness, leniency, loving kindness, and mercy is an appeal and a reminder that we are all one and the same. Anticipating that this metaphysical grounding of the conduct of good people would puzzle Western scholars, he mentioned that the monism upon which he rests his theory had been recognized by the Eleatic philosophers, the Neo-Platonists, Scotus Erigena, Christian mystics, Giordano Bruno, Spinoza, and Schelling's philosophy. Each had recognized the ultimate singularity of being and, he added, his "metaphysics of ethics has been the fundamental view of Indian wisdom for thousands of years." For this reason, Schopenhauer found it particularly apt to claim that good characters apprehend others according to the great word, the *mahavakya*, "*tat tvam asi* (this art thou)*,*" and that bad characters lived, as described by Hinduism, within *māyā*, delusion.[58]

The Two Fundamental Problems of Ethics turned out to be just another stone tossed into a bog, landing with a thud and producing no meaningful ripples. It drew two brief reviews in what were little more than entertainment newspapers, although the one that appeared in *The Pilot [Der Pilot]* referred to Schopenhauer as "the greatest philosopher of the age."[59] Two reviews appeared in scholarly journals, both of which were negative. Once more Gustav Hartenstein struck. This time his review appeared in the Brockhaus-published *Repertory of Collected German Literature [Repertorium der gesammten deutschen Litteratur]*, signed "78" instead of "H," as he signed his review of *On the Will in Nature*.[60] Each number represented his initials, the seventh and eighth letters in the alphabet. Although "78"

---

only to appearances" and that "one and the same essence manifests itself in all things." Consequently, he believed that he had proven the consequent – "the conception that abolishes the difference between ego and non-ego is not erroneous; the opposite one must be true."

[58] Ibid., p. 213/ibid., Vol. 4, p. 274 for his remark about "Indian wisdom" and ibid., p. 211/ibid., Vol. 4, p. 272 for his use of *tat tvam asi.*

[59] Quoted in Hübscher, *The Philosophy of Schopenhauer in Its Intellectual Context*, p. 508, note 17.

[60] See Hübscher, *Schopenhauer-Bibliographie* (Stuttgart–Bad Cannstatt: Frommann-Holzboog, 1981), p. 28, No. 37, for Hartenstein's signature "78" for his review.

praised "119" for the clarity of his writings, he dismissed both essays as derivative and as containing things stated better elsewhere: namely, in Herbart's philosophy. Hartenstein's review with its slight praise and its failure to recognize his ethics as "the most important work on ethics that had been since Kant" led Schopenhauer to tell its publisher, Brockhaus, that he would prefer to be torn apart by "enraged Hegelians" than to receive a review such as Hartenstein's.[61] He would almost receive his preference with the next review.

Professor Hartenstein said nothing against Schopenhauer's scathing treatment of Hegel. As a Herbartian, he may have enjoyed it. The same is not true of the second reviewer, *"Spiritus asper,"* whose twenty-two-page lampoon appeared in the *Halle Yearbooks for German Science and Art* [*Hallische Jahrbücher für deutsche Wissenschaft und Kunst*]. The reviewer was none other than Friedrich Wilhelm Carové, Hegel's *Repetent*, or teaching assistant, at Berlin, who had been banned for life from a university position by the Prussian government, due to his activities in one of the *Burschenschaften*, or student fraternities, which promoted a politically progressive agenda. Carové approached Schopenhauer's book on ethics with an unkind, even cruel spirit, refusing both to crown the work and to find its author a "distinguished philosopher." Such a finding, he snidely remarked, he left for posterity.[62] Schopenhauer quite naturally hated the review, finding it to be just another example of how the Hegel*gloria* of his times, although a dying phenomenon, was still trying to silence his philosophy. Curiously, during the time of the review, Carové was on friendly terms with Schopenhauer, and even discussed that review with the philosopher. For some unknown reason, they had a falling out. Three years after the review, and only after Carové's death, did Schopenhauer discover through his friend Martin Emden that Carové was "Spiritus asper." As Schopenhauer told Frauenstädt, "He [Carové] was a very vile human being and often showed it."[63]

---

[61] Schopenhauer, *Gesammelte Brief*, p. 209, Schopenhauer, to F. A. Brockhaus, 22 March 1844. In this letter he had named Hartenstein as the reviewer of *On the Will in Nature* as well as *The Two Fundamental Problems of Ethics*. He also accused Hartenstein of engaging in the practice of professors of philosophy of keeping his philosophy secret from the public [*sekretiren*], because he had published his own work on ethics that ignored Schopenhauer's *The Two Fundamental Problems of Ethics*. "It is time" Schopenhauer wrote in the same letter, "that I unmask these men [such as Hartenstein]."

[62] Quoted in Hübscher, *The Philosophy of Schopenhauer in Its Intellectual Context*, p. 345.

[63] Schopenhauer, *Gesammelte Brief*, p. 347, Schopenhauer to Julius Frauenstädt, 29 June 1854.

Coloring a Sketch

Failure never deterred Schopenhauer. He learned to take his lack of
reception by the academic world as a badge of honor and as a spur to
soldier on, writing for those he considered exceptions to the ephemeral
tide of popular fads. And despite Carové's derisive remark at the end of
his review about consigning to the future Schopenhauer's designation as
a *summus philosophus*, this had become Schopenhauer's article of faith. In
one of the sketches for a preface to a second edition of his principal work,
the possibility of which seemed doubtful when he wrote it in 1832, the
philosopher had learned through bitter experience that his peers were
not interested in truth, at least not his truths: "It was no surprise to me
that my contemporaries took no interest in me, since like everything of a
similar nature, it is not written for the contemporaries of any period, but
for those who are at all times exceptions."[64]

Despite the fact that Schopenhauer's last two books did not find a
sufficient number of exceptions among his contemporaries to create a
demand for *The World as Will and Representation*, in 1843, after working
on a supplement to his principal work for three years, and driven by a
sense of his own mortality, the fifty-five-year-old philosopher once more
approached Brockhaus with a request to publish a second edition. He did
so boldly, not asking to simply revise and add material to a book that
had few readers, but to more than double its original length by adding a
second volume of fifty essays, arranged to mirror the four books of the
original edition. These essays, the philosopher told his hesitant publisher,
represented twenty-four years of careful study and continued reflection
on the ideas expressed in his principal work, and stood to the 1819 edition
"as a fully painted picture to a mere sketch."[65] The essays were, moreover,
the best he had ever written. He could speak more freely in this work,
he continued, because of his decided and certain independence from
demands placed on those attached to a university, who were, or had to
become, mercenaries for church and state. Schopenhauer also appealed to
what he saw as very different social conditions from those prevailing when
he first spoke, conditions that made it the case that the present time would

---

[64] Schopenhauer, *Manuscript Remains*, Vol. 4, p. 121/*Der handschriftliche Nachlaß*, Vol. 4, 1,
p. 99.
[65] Schopenhauer, *Gesammelte Briefe*, p. 195, Schopenhauer to Brockhaus, 7 May 1843.

be more receptive to his thought. Religious faith had declined, fostering a stronger feeling of need for philosophy and, therefore, a universal interest in philosophy, far greater than ever before. Thus the times were ripe for the appearance of his work in a revived and perfected form. The false and base could only endure for a short time before the true and good was brought to light, he continued, and so "my time will and must come, and the later the more brilliant."[66] It is a fact, he said, that this philosophy is of such value and significance that he dared to offer it to a publisher who he knew would not believe him. And to demonstrate that his interest was simply to have his work appear again, he was willing to leave it to the publisher's discretion to pay royalties for both volumes. This was his life's work and he had not done it for money. He closed his letter by saying that he could have the new volume ready for print in the next month, and that as it was being prepared for publication, he would revise the first edition, with significant changes only to his "Critique of the Kantian Philosophy."

Brockhaus was not impressed by Schopenhauer's proposal. The 1819 work had been a "bad deal," and they still had nine copies of it at hand, after scrapping for paper all but fifty copies of it in 1830. Naturally, the publisher was not keen to reissue the book unless Schopenhauer would assume the printing costs for both volumes. But if the author was willing to pay half of the production costs, Brockhaus was willing to share one-half of the net profits, distributed so that the publisher received the profits for the first and third hundred volumes sold, the author for the second and fourth, and so on.[67] Schopenhauer was surprised by Brockhaus' response. He was, he wrote in reply, willing to make a gift to the public, but he found the publisher's terms unsatisfying – even insulting. He would not pay for this gift. Hegel's nonsense, he complained, had enjoyed a collected edition, and he was being asked to pay the printing costs of the work of his entire life. This was something he could not abide. He would rather that it appear posthumously, when a new generation would joyfully welcome his philosophy, than to pay for its printing costs.

Schopenhauer was desperate to have his new volume of essays published, because he knew that it would be next to impossible to convince a publisher to issue supplementary essays for a work owned by another publisher. He proposed that Brockhaus publish only these new essays. He

---

[66] Ibid., p. 195.
[67] See Schopenhauer, ibid., p. 536, for the description of Brockhaus' offer.

was willing to forgo royalties, he wrote, but he was unwilling to pay the printing costs. These would be recovered, he argued, simply by owners of the 1819 work, who would want to possess its supplements. Moreover, the essays themselves could be read separately from the earlier work, because each essay treated its subject in a self-contained manner. Once again the philosopher attempted to have the reluctant publisher realize the work's significance and why it would be popular. So he reiterated his claim that the essays represented the quintessence of twenty-four years of sustained thought, and he reemphasized that the supplements constituted the very best material that he had ever written. They would prove popular, he said, because they were composed in a clear, lively, and intuitive style; they were free of jargon and a pleasure to read. Had the publisher been in Frankfurt, he would have let Brockhaus read his essay, "Metaphysics of Sexual Love," he wrote, and he predicted that the publisher would have found that "For the very first time, this passion was traced to its ultimate, most deeply lying ground, with the most precise detail."[68] Schopenhauer may have been hoping that sex would sell.

Despite his offer for the separate publication of the supplementary essays, Schopenhauer made a final pitch for publishing the 1819 work. He mentioned Jean Paul's praise of that book, Rosenkranz's assessment of him as a "philosopher of the first rank" in his "History of Kantian Philosophy," found in the twelfth volume of his edition of Kant's works, and the reference to him as the "greatest philosopher of the age," by the anonymous reviewer in *The Pilot*. "Am I then a man," he asked rhetorically, "whose things are not worth the printing costs?"[69] He reminded the publisher that he knew of books that became popular many years after they appeared. He cited David Hume's *History of Great Britain from the Invasion of Julius Caesar to the Revolution of 1688* (6 vols., London: 1754–62), which after the first year sold 45 copies, but after eighty years received either a new edition or translation every couple of years. Last, Schopenhauer wrote that if his modified proposal was not accepted, he would like to secure the rights to his original book, so that he could seek another publisher for both volumes.

---

[68] Ibid., p. 197, Schopenhauer to Brockhaus, 17 May 1843. Schopenhauer told Brockhaus that he would not send a copy of the essays, because their content was so "completely novel" that he would not let it leave his hands. In other words, he feared that someone would steal his ideas.

[69] Ibid., p. 197, Schopenhauer to Brockhaus, 17 May 1843.

Brockhaus's response to Schopenhauer's modified proposal was just as unexpected as was his reaction to the first. He accepted both volumes of Schopenhauer's principal work, much to the philosopher's delight. A thrilled Schopenhauer assured the once reluctant publisher that he had made a "good deal." There was certain to be an audience for this book, he wrote, because "the great, bloated soap-bubble of Fichte–Schelling–Hegelian philosophy is just now finally ready to burst. And, there is a need for a philosophy greater than ever before. One longs for solid nourishment. This can only be found with me, the long unrecognized philosopher, because I have only sought the truth and no other thing, working from an inner calling, throughout a long life."[70] After Schopenhauer dissuaded the publisher from combining the revised 1819 book and its supplementary essays in a single volume, which he argued would either be too large and thick to hold or have print too small to read, publisher and author negotiated a contract. Schopenhauer waived royalties, accepting as an honorarium ten free copies. The first volume of *The World as Will and Representation* would have a run of 500 copies and the second 750. After the second edition sold out, the rights to the book would revert to the author.

Schopenhauer's bold claim that Brockhaus had made a good deal with the second edition of *The World as Will and Representation* proved to be an untruth spoken by a philosopher who only sought the truth. The great soap-bubble of the Fichte–Schelling–Hegelian philosophy had burst, but this had nothing to do with Schopenhauer, and his book lacked the nourishment sought by a philosophically hungry public. To offer nourishment that would sustain both church and state, Friedrich Wilhelm IV brought the old Schelling to Berlin in 1841, much like a declaration of war against the ghost of Hegel, especially as his spirit moved to the left, and the Young Hegelians, men such as Michael Bakunin, Friedrich Engels, Karl Marx, and Arnold Ruge, fought as a Hegel listing to the left. All this happened as the second edition of Schopenhauer's principal work drew even less notice than the first edition. Again, Hartenstein thundered anonymously, in one of Brockhaus's own *repertoria*, once more banging a familiar drum, that the author had ignored Herbart's exact and thorough criticisms.[71]

---

[70] Ibid., p. 198, Schopenhauer to Brockhaus, 14 June 1843.

[71] Hartenstein's unsigned review appeared in *Leipzig Repertory of German and Foreign Literature* [*Leipziger Repertorium der deutschen und ausländischen Litteratur*], Vol. 3, (1844), pp. 91–3.

Schopenhauer suspected that it was Herbart's lackey speaking under-cover once more.

A stilted and lazy review appeared in another of Brockhaus' journals. In *Pages for Literary Diversion* [*Blätter für Litterarische Unterhaltung*, 1845], Friedrich Köppen, friend and devotee of Jacobi, attempted to interject some reason into what he regarded as the excessive oriental mysticism of the philosophy of will. It was as if he never even read the second volume of supplementary essays – he never mentioned it. Schopenhauer would later praise as an unbiased and complete compendium of Buddhism Köppen's *The Religion of Buddha and Its Origin* [*Die Religion des Buddha und ihre Entstehung*, 1857], citing it favorably in the third edition of his principal work. The philosopher did so despite the fact that he detected Hegelian proclivities in its author.[72]

The third review appeared in the *New Jena General Literary Journal* [*Neue Jenaische Allgemeine Litteraturzeitung*, June 1845] by a man Schopenhauer said "chases me like a snapping dog with a muzzle."[73] This dog with the bark that was worse than its bite was Carl Fortlage, who came to Fichte after fleeing and denouncing his allegiance to Hegel; who journeyed to Berlin to witness the old Schelling's philosophical resur-rection; and who befriended, followed, and referred to favorably in his review Schopenhauer's old nemesis Beneke. Fortlage was sympathetic to Schopenhauer's willingness to confront the dark side of existence, and he agreed with his claim that genuine Christianity was pessimistic. He deeply respected Schopenhauer's heartfelt existential commitment to philosophy, viewing it as something authentic and praiseworthy in his character. Still, he trod familiar ground by emphasizing Schopenhauer's position in the philosophical development of Fichte from Kant, just as had the first reviews of Schopenhauer's principal work. Fichte, Fortlage

Schopenhauer correctly concluded that Hartenstein was the reviewer, because he had used some passages, virtually unchanged, from his earlier reviews.

[72] For Schopenhauer's praise of Köppen's book on Buddhism, see his letter to Adam von Doß, 14 March 1858, *Gesammelte Briefe*, p. 425. In a marginal note to Köppen's book, Schopenhauer highlighted the passage "Brahmanism, we would say, comprehended in the concept of becoming only being," by writing "we Hegelians"; see *Der handschriftliche Nachlaß*, Vol. 5, p. 334. It is curious that his sensing the spurs of Hegel in Köppen's work did not keep him from praising it.

[73] Schopenhauer, *Gesammelte Briefe*, p. 335, Schopenhauer to Frauenstädt, 26 March 1854. In this letter, Schopenhauer expressed his disdain for Fortlage's review of Frauenstädt's *Letters on Schopenhauerian Philosophy* [*Briefe über die Schopenhauer'sche Philosophie*, 1854].

argued, had recognized prior to Schopenhauer that the will was the thing in itself, but in a more satisfying way by establishing the I's unity in pure activity and pure willing, the resolution of a dichotomy that Schopenhauer never could reconcile. Fortlage claimed that it was a delusion, based on a deep psychological confusion, that Schopenhauer did not see that his attempt to purge eudaemonism from ethics by his doctrine of the denial of the will had been done by Fichte much earlier, and in a more adequate fashion, through his view of the absolute activity of the pure activity of willing. He closed the review with a semi-kind remark that could have only displeased Schopenhauer by calling his book "Among the few works that gives living testimony of the fact that the full day might yet dawn for the German philosophy of nature, which saw only the beautiful pale dawn under Schelling's auspices."[74] This remark most especially stung Schopenhauer, because he knew that Fortlage had read *On the Will in Nature*.

Schopenhauer had complained about professors of philosophy "ignoring" and "secreting," that is, suppressing his philosophy, in the "Preface to the Second Edition."[75] Fortlage validated the philosopher's charge: "Schopenhauer complains about a certain 'secreting' of his works that had earlier been the agenda. Unfortunately, this is not a vacuous complaint. The author of this [review] has a document in hand of a certain editor's office that secreted against a review, from his own pen, of Schopenhauer's *On the Will in Nature* (Frankfurt, 1836)."[76] Although Schopenhauer thought that Fortlage lacked any insight into his philosophy, and he was especially troubled by the reviewer's sensing parallels between his ethics and Fichte's, which he had thoroughly dismissed as a gross caricature of Kant's already deeply flawed ethics, he was pleased that Fortlage provided evidence for his charge of secreting. Schopenhauer later identified this journal as the *Heidelberg Annuals* [*Die Heidelberger Jahrbücher*]. "He [Fortlage] himself said to me, when he visited me here [in Frankfurt], that he had written a review for this journal. He was a lecturer in Heidelberg."[77]

---

[74] Quoted in Hübscher's *The Philosophy of Schopenhauer in Its Intellectual Context*, p. 347.

[75] Schopenhauer, *The World as Will and Representation*, Vol. 1, p. xxv/ *Sämtliche Werke*, Vol. 2, p. xxvii. Schopenhauer attributed the idea of "secreting" to Goethe.

[76] Schopenhauer, *Gesammelte Briefe*, p. 583.

[77] Ibid., p. 335, Schopenhauer to Frauenstädt, 26 March 1854.

The second edition of *The World as Will and Representation* failed to lift Schopenhauer's philosophy out of limbo. The reviews suggested that he was philosophizing well behind the times; that even the passé Fichte had thought beyond his one-time student and that Herbart and even Beneke had stretched the bounds of philosophical thought beyond Schopenhauer's eloquent musings. None of the critics sensed the significance of the supplementary essays. Köppen may have had the excuse of having not read the second volume, because he never mentioned it in his review, but this excuse also spoke against his quality as a reviewer. Hartenstein's *modus operandi* in each of his reviews was to denigrate Schopenhauer in order to promote Herbart. Hartenstein was just a hard rock, out to smash his victim. Fortlage took a more advanced position by expressing some sympathy for Schopenhauer's pessimism and by admiring his deep and authentic commitment to philosophy. Nevertheless, he viewed Schopenhauer's evolution out of Kant to be a dead end, and he longed for revelations from the old, mystical Schelling.

The critics, each with his own agenda, failed to appreciate the ways in which Schopenhauer clarified his original views and how he boldly extended his earlier insights into new subjects. Although Fortlage appreciated the philosopher's insistence that genuine Christianity, like Hinduism and Buddhism, was pessimistic in the vital seventeenth essay, "On the Human Need for Metaphysics," like other critics, he failed to grasp the significance of Schopenhauer's contrary-to-Kant view of metaphysics as the explanation of the totality of experiences. He also ignored the criterion the philosopher employed to judge the validity of his philosophy; namely, its ability to provide an exhaustive explanation of experience, leaving no remainder behind. Each commentator overlooked Schopenhauer's attempt to clarify his claim that his philosophy recognized the will as the thing in itself.

In the eighteenth essay, "On the Possibility of Knowledge of the Thing in Itself," Schopenhauer argued that knowledge of the thing in itself was impossible; to know something is for it to be an object for a subject, and the thing in itself is never object for a subject. The will is, he claimed, the thing in itself appearing under the lightest of veils: it is an object of self-consciousness, conditioned only by the *a priori* form of time. Beyond our self-conscious experience of the will, we cannot have knowledge. As he put it later in the supplements, "strictly speaking . . . we know our will only as appearance and not according to what it may be absolutely in and by itself."[78] Seven years later, in *Parerga and Paralipomena*, he would leave the possibility of some peeking behind the will's light veils being open to the mystic, although also realizing that whatever is found there is beyond the pale of meaningful discourse. Presaging Wittgenstein's famous final proposition from the *Tractatus Logico-Philosophicus* (1922), Schopenhauer, too, advocated silence about that of which we cannot speak. The truth may appear naked, but truth resides within the principle of sufficient reason, and where this principle ends, so does philosophy.[79]

No one took notice of the thirty-first and thirty-second essays, in which Schopenhauer expanded on his analyses of genius and madness, subjects that had gripped the philosopher from his early university years and that represented what he thought about himself (genius) and what he feared he might become (madness). No critic recognized the ways in which the thirty-eighth essay, "On History," where the philosopher insisted that history was not a science, would serve as water to douse the flickering embers of Hegel's historicism and the historicizing of philosophy, moving others later, such as the Swiss historian Jacob Burckhardt, Professor of History at the University of Basel, to lecture on history from 1868 to 1871 in Schopenhauer's spirit.[80] It is likely that Burckhardt's younger colleague, Nietzsche, attended some of these lectures, but it is sure that their mutual passion for Schopenhauer drew them to each other. The very same essay helped Richard Wagner abandon historical operas in light of Schopenhauer's arguments in the very next essay, "On the Metaphysics of Music," where, once more, Schopenhauer attributed a more effective truth-expressive force to music than to the concept mummies of metaphysics. Naturally, Wagner's enthusiasm for Schopenhauer and

---

[78] Schopenhauer, *The World as Will and Representation*, Vol. 2, p. 494/ *Sämtliche Werke*, Vol. 3, p. 565f.

[79] I discuss Schopenhauer's view of the will as thing in itself in "Two Senses of 'Thing-in-itself' in Schopenhauer's Philosophy." Also see Bryan Magee's *Misunderstanding Schopenhauer* (London: University of London Institute of Germanic Studies, 1990); John E. Atwell's *Schopenhauer: On the Character of the World*, pp. 126–7, 165–72; Rudolf Malter's *Arthur Schopenhauer: Transzendental Philosophie und Metaphysik des Willens*, p. 235; and Nicolletta De Cian and Marco Segela's "What is Will?"

[80] See Herbert Schnädelbach's *Philosophy in Germany 1831–1933*, trans. Eric Matthews (Cambridge: Cambridge University Press, 1982) pp. 40–43, 59–62 for a discussion of Burckhardt's debts to Schopenhauer and for a discussion of Burckhardt and Nietzsche's mutual enthusiasm for Schopenhauer, see Erich Heller's *The Disinherited Mind* (Orlando, FL; Harcourt Brace Javanovich, 1975).

his philosophy of music also helped draw Nietzsche to his one-time idol, and Nietzsche would later demote the composer as he did his one-time philosophical hero as his antipodes.[81]

When Two Are Gathered Together in My Name

Despite the failures of *On the Will in Nature*, *The Two Fundamental Problems of Ethics*, the second edition of his principal work – the three reviews of which were three more than garnered by the second edition of *The Fourfold Root* (1847) – Schopenhauer's philosophy slowly and gradually attracted followers. These men were not professors of philosophy or academics, but practical, solid men, successful in life; men who had pursued *Brotstudium* at the university, law in particular, or were private scholars. With a sense of irony made light by Schopenhauer's secular messianic sense of his philosophical mission, the philosopher referred to these men as either "evangelists" or "apostles," depending on the activities they were willing to take in spreading his word. Those who were willing to write tracts in his favor and publish against his critics were "evangelists," whereas those who would merely keep watch for references to his work, either positive or negative, and who would express their enthusiasm and engagement through their correspondence with him were "apostles."

The first follower to find sustenance in Schopenhauer's philosophy was the aspiring philosopher and provincial court judge in Madeburg, Friedrich Ludwig Andreas Dorguth, who had, himself, attempted to pop the bloated soap-bubble of the Fichte-Schelling-and Hegelian philosophy. Unfortunately, he could not even wield a dull pin. To secure aid in his quixotic challenge, the then sixty-two-year-old judge sent the still Hegelian Ludwig Feuerbach a copy of his vague and unclear *Critique of Idealism and Materialism from the Basis of Apodictic Real-Rationalism* [*Kritik des Idealismus und Materialien zur Grundlage des Apodiktischen Real-rationalismus*, 1837]. Feuerbuch promptly and deftly critiqued Dorguth's critique, putting to an end his flirtation with Feuerbach. The next year, oddly enough, Feuerbach would launch his career with his essay in the

---

[81] See, for example Nietzsche's *Nietzsche Contra Wagner*, "We Antipodes," where he opposes himself to the romantic pessimism of Schopenhauer and Wagner, and the preface to *The Case of Wagner*, where he discusses overcoming his own decadence, that is, his attraction to Wagner and Schopenhauer, his two "antipodes."

Halle Yearbooks, "Toward the Critique of the Hegelian Philosophy" ["Zur Kritik der Hegelischen Philosophie," 1839].

Dorguth wrote to Schopenhauer in 1836, after reading *On the Will in Nature.* Along with an inquiry concerning how to best understand Schopenhauer's system, he included, much to the philosopher's delight, a poem that satirized Hegel's philosophy. Schopenhauer recommended that he read both his dissertation and his principal work. Gradually, Dorguth became fanatical about Schopenhauer's philosophy. "I cannot refrain from acknowledging," Dorguth wrote a still Schopenhauer-friendly Karl Rosenkranz in 1843, that "Schopenhauer is the first real systematic thinker in the entire history of literature."[82] Dorguth would write several tracts promoting and defending his "master's" philosophy, and he would compare the treatment of Schopenhauer's thought by professors of philosophy to that suffered by Caspar Hauser, a German foundling youth who claimed that he had been forced to spend most of his life in solitary confinement. The philosopher would give Dorguth credit when he used this comparison in the preface to the second edition of *On the Will in Nature,* informing professors of philosophy that "their Caspar Hauser, I say, has escaped."[83] Although Schopenhauer appreciated Dorguth's enthusiasm, dubbing him his "original evangelist" [*Urevangelist*], he did not think much of Dorguth's intellect. Nevertheless, he felt compelled to read whatever his fan wrote, out of a sense of duty. He also deeply lamented Dorguth's death from cholera, at the age of 77, in 1854. As he told another of his followers,, Dorguth propagandized for his philosophy right up to the end, "thus faithful unto death."[84]

Another "arch-evangelist," however, would match Dorguth's loyalty and play a central role in popularizing Schopenhauer's philosophy. This man who would write more than one Schopenhauerian Gospel was the Berlin Doctor of Philosophy and private scholar Julius Frauenstädt. Unlike Dorguth, Frauenstädt briefly flirted with Hegel's philosophy, only to become absolutely discouraged by its fleshless spirit. Like Dorguth, he sensed an affinity with Feuerbach's thought, which prompted him to send Feuerbach his *God's Becoming Human, According to Its Possibility,*

---

[82] Quoted in Hübscher's "Lebensbild," *Sämtliche Werke,* Vol. 1, p. 110.

[83] Schopenhauer, *On the Will in Nature,* p. 5/*Sämtliche Werke,* Vol. 4, p. xii. Schopenhauer sent Dorguth a copy of the second edition of *On the Will in Nature* and Dorguth's daughter reported that her father read it two days before he died in 1854; see *Gesammelte Briefe,* p. 359.

[84] Ibid., p. 359, Schopenhauer to Adam von Doss, 10 January 1855.

Reality, and Necessity [*Die Menschwerdung Gottes nach ihrer Möglichkeit, Wirklichkeit und Nothwendigkeit,* 1839]. Feuerbach did not respond. He was too busy considering how humans became God, as he would explain in his revolutionary and celebrated *The Essence of Christianity* [*Das Wesen des Christentums,* 1841]. Feuerbach's lack of response was sufficient to move the Berlin scholar to seek another philosophical ally. It was quite by accident that Frauenstädt found his way to Schopenhauer. He never even heard Schopenhauer's name during his five years at the university, and it was during his research for a paper in reply to an essay contest that he came across a reference to the "ingenious and original *World as Will and Representation* by Arth. Schopenhauer" within an article on "Idealism" in Ersch and Gruber's *Encyklopädie.*[85] Frauenstädt was sufficiently intrigued by this brief reference to seek out Schopenhauer's *geistreich* book. As he later explained, his reading of Schopenhauer was a life-transforming experience, one that drove out all shadows of Hegel's *Geist* from his mind: "*The World as Will and Representation* is yet a higher kind of philosophy than the Hegelian, and one could learn more from ten pages of Schopenhauer than from ten volumes of Hegel."[86]

Frauenstädt propagandized, pamphleteered, and proselytized on Schopenhauer's behalf, the most active and dedicated of the early followers. He visited the philosopher when he could, and when Schopenhauer would allow it. His contacts enabled Schopenhauer to publish *Parerga and Paralipomena,* and he continued to promote Schopenhauer's philosophy long after his hero's death, serving as the editor of the first collected edition of Schopenhauer's works.[87] Between 1847 and 1856, the men carried on a rich correspondence. Frequently the younger man pressed the older man to explain crucial aspects of his philosophy, something Schopenhauer did in a half-hearted way and frequently in an irritated tone. Sometimes one beats the hardest the dog one loves the best, to paraphrase Nietzsche, and Frauenstädt was Schopenhauer's favorite dog. Frauenstädt was an energetic and excitable man, and he always was uncomfortable with both

---

[85] Quoted in Hübscher, "Lebensbild," p. 111. The full title of the encyclopedia was *Allgemeine Encyklopädie der Wissenschaft und Künste* (1838). The article "Idealism" was authored by C. F. Bachmann.

[86] Ernest Otto Linder and Julius Frauenstädt, *Arthur Schopenhauer. Von ihm. Ueber ihn,* p. 134; quoted in Hübscher, "Lebensbild," *Sämtliche Werke,* Vol. 1, p. 111.

[87] *Arthur Schopenhauer's Sämtliche Werke,* 6 vols., edited by Julius Frauenstädt (Leipzig: F. A. Brockhaus, 1873/4).

Schopenhauer's claim that the will was the thing in itself and his doctrine of the denial of the will, something he thought impossible if the will were truly the thing in itself.[88] He also thought that the ascetic results of Schopenhauer's philosophy undermined the significance of his ethics of compassion, which was dedicated to the prevention and relief of others' suffering, whereas the denial of the will appeared only to address that of the overcomer of the will.[89]

It was the subject of ethics that moved Schopenhauer to break off correspondence with his arch-evangelist. In his *Materialism: Its Truth and Its Error* [*Der Materialismus. Seine Wahrheit und sein Irrthum*, 1856], Frauenstädt engaged in polemic against Ludwig Büchner's highly successful *Energy and Matter* [*Kraft und Stoff*, 1855], and he also attempted to promote Schopenhauer's *On the Will in Nature*. In the course of his book, the arch-evangelist quoted from an article by the then student and later Professor of Philosophy at Bonn Jüngen Bona Meyer to show that Schopenhauer was not alone in recognizing the dangerousness of materialism. It just also happened to be the case that Bona Meyer mentioned Frauenstädt favorably in the same passage. Schopenhauer was appalled, because he recognized Bona Meyer as a sensualist and materialist and by Frauenstädt's use of this passage; he saw his arch-evangelist siding with Bona Meyer. "You must be ashamed of yourself," the philosopher fired at his admirer, "to be praised by that student, because you and he have taken the same line with an apology for the morality of materialists."[90] He wanted Frauenstädt to honor him, Schopenhauer continued, and he had done the opposite, and he never wished to say as Voltaire did when the French philosopher quoted Spinoza, "I have dull students and bad critics," but now he felt he had to do so. Implying that his admirer was psychologically ill, he prescribed as "intellectual medicine," a reading of

---

[88] See Schopenhauer, *Gesammelte Briefe*, pp. 287–97, Schopenhauer's letters to Frauenstädt of 6 August 1852, 24 August 1852, 12 September 1852, and 12 October 1852; see ibid., pp. 568, 570 for Frauenstädt's questions and replies to Schopenhauer. I discuss Frauenstädt's letters in "Two Senses of 'Thing-in-Itself' in Schopenhauer's Philosophy," pp. 42–4. Schopenhauer reiterated the position found in the second edition of his principal work; namely, that the will is only the thing in itself in relationship to other appearances, that beyond this, we can know nothing about the thing in itself, and that the denial of the will is not the denial of some being – it is simply not-willing.

[89] Frauenstädt waited until after Schopenhauer's death to articulate his differences in *The Moral Life: Ethical Studies* (*Das Sittliche Leben, Ethische Studien*), Leipzig: Brockhaus, 1866.

[90] Schopenhauer, *Gesammelte Briefe*, p. 403, Schopenhauer to Frauenstädt, 31 October 1856.

his prize-essay on the basis of morality and the fourth book of *The World and Will and Representation*.

Schopenhauer neatly closed his outburst against Frauenstädt by quoting from Shakespeare's *Midsummer Night's Dream*, "Well roared, lion!" Frauenstädt's reply did not please the lion. He would have spared him his "roaring," the disciple replied, if he correctly understood the sense in which he agreed with Bona Meyer. Both recognized, as did Schopenhauer, that virtuous actions are not derived from abstract dogma or maxims produced by reason. He did not, he emphasized, advocate materialism or agree with Bona Meyer. Schopenhauer had misread him.[91] After receiving this less than deferential response, Schopenhauer broke off correspondence with Frauenstädt. The arch-evangelist, though, continued to promote Schopenhauer's philosophy, and Schopenhauer reestablished contact with his faithful advocate in 1859, by sending him a copy of the third edition of *The World as Will and Representation*. Ultimately, the philosopher rewarded Frauenstädt by making him the heir to his literary estate and writings.

The World as Will and Representation brought Schopenhauer another "apostle" with whom he would maintain a friendship and correspondence that would last until the philosopher's death. Schopenhauer would also view their correspondence as containing the very best discussion of his philosophy. After a decade of their letter exchange, Schopenhauer complimented the fifteen–year younger man: "Among all living people, you are the most thorough expert on my philosophy, understanding it as I do myself."[92] In the same letter, the older man tried to induce the younger one to proselytize about his thought because "no human being is as competent [as you] to write about my philosophy." Unfortunately, Schopenhauer never was able to convince this "apostle" to become, as Frauenstädt viewed himself, and as Dorguth was, an "active apostle;" one of the evangelists who testified in the philosopher's name.[93] This refusal did not alienate Schopenhauer, but rather seemed to endear this apostle to him. Unlike the others, whose intellects he did not respect, and whose motives for their involvement in his philosophy did not seem

---

[91] See ibid., p. 613, for Frauenstädt's reply to Schopenhauer's "roaring" at him.

[92] Ibid., p. 341, Schopenhauer to Johann August Becker 20 May 1854.

[93] See Linder and Frauenstädt, *Arthur Schopenhauer, Von ihm Ueber ihn*, p. 475, for this distinction between an "apostle" like Becker and "active apostles" like Frauenstädt and Dorguth.

pure – by promoting Schopenhauer, they were promoting themselves – this apostle's motives appeared pure. Becker seemed to sense the truth in Schopenhauer's thought, and it was the naked truth he alone pursued.

Johann August Becker was a lawyer in Alzey when he read Schopenhauer's masterpiece, and the forty-one-year-old was deeply moved by Schopenhauer's darkly compelling worldview. He was also sincerely and genuinely perplexed by the metaphysics of will, the theory of redemption as denial of the will, and elements of the ethics of compassion. On 31 July 1844, the lawyer wrote to the philosopher in a respectful and careful manner, requesting permission to ask about some of the doubts he had with Schopenhauer's philosophy. The philosopher was willing to entertain Becker's doubts, but before doing so, he requested that Becker carefully read the second volume of essays of his principal work to see whether his "scruples" would disappear. He also sent a copy of *On the Will in Nature*, telling the younger man that it contained the clearest presentation of the essence of his philosophy: specifically, his claim that the will was the inner essence of all things, the only real thing in the world, and therefore, it was the thing in itself. Will is discovered by self-consciousness, he continued, and it is completely different from the intellect. This, he wrote, is shown in the nineteenth essay in the second volume of his principal work.[94] Two claims constituted the bases of his entire philosophy, he told to Becker: first, that the will is the essence of everything in the world; second, that the entire material world exists merely as our representation. "Proceeding from these claims," Schopenhauer closed his letter, "one can easily comprehend the remaining elements [of his teaching] and the power of truth itself will be discovered."[95]

Becker did not possess the second edition of *The World as Will and Representation*, so he lacked the volume of supplementary essays that Schopenhauer said would make his "scruples" vanish. Through a series of letters, each of which drew a careful response by the philosopher, Becker demonstrated a keen understanding of Schopenhauer's views as well as the deft ability to post challenges and questions that did not alienate the philosopher, because they struck him as good-faith efforts to discern the truth. How was it possible for an evil man to become a saint, given the immutability of character? The denial of will appears in the world,

---

[94] The title of this essay is "On the Primacy of the Will in Self-Consciousness."
[95] Schopenhauer, *Gesammelte Briefe*, p. 213, Schopenhauer to Becker, 3 August 1844.

but how could this be something uncaused and unmotivated, because everything in the world is an expression of strict necessity? How can the intelligible character constitute an extratemporal act of will, and how can a person's empirical character be its appearance? If compassion proceeds from a person's recognizing others as an "I once more," is not compassion ultimately egoistic, because the compassionate person is ultimately just helping him- or herself?[96]

Becker's criticisms, questions, and challenges moved Schopenhauer to write a significant set of letters in reply; letters that helped to clarify his metaphysics and ethics. The philosophically skilled lawyer made the philosopher admit that some of his doctrines were meant to be taken figuratively and not literally. "That the intelligible character of a person is an extra-temporal act of will," he replied to Becker, "I present not as an objective truth or as an adequate notion of the relation between the thing in itself and appearance; rather, I present it merely as a metaphor and simile, as a figurative expression of the matter . . . in order to make the matter comprehensible."[97] To do this, he continued, requires the use of an intuitive schema that has space and time as its form, but neither of these *a priori* forms literally applies to the intelligible character. He also defended his analysis of compassion along the same lines. Thus he told Becker that he might say that "compassion along with all the virtues flowing from it are egoistical . . . because it depends on the cognition of my own essence in another. But this rests solely on your wanting to take the phrase 'I once more' literally, whereas it is just a figurative turn of expression. For 'I' in the proper sense of the term refers exclusively to the individual and not the metaphysical thing in itself which *appears* in individuals, but which is directly unknowable."[98]

These admissions to Schopenhauer's philosophically skilled apostle were significant, because seldom in his philosophy did he ever directly fess up that some of his doctrines were expressed figuratively.[99] Indeed, his official stance was that all meaningful discourse must ultimately be

---

[96] See Schopenhauer, ibid., pp. 540–42 for summaries of the philosophical contents of Becker's letters and for Schopenhauer's replies; see his letters to Becker, 3 August 1844, 23 August 1844, 21 September 1844, and 10 December 1844, ibid., pp. 213–22.

[97] Ibid., p. 217, Schopenhauer to Becker, 21 September 1844.

[98] Ibid., p. 220f., Schopenhauer to Becker, 10 December 1844.

[99] See G. Steven Neeley's *Schopenhauer: A Consistent Reading* (Lewiston, NY: Edwin Mellen Press, 2003), pp. 64–71 for a discussion of Schopenhauer's use of metaphor.

based on intuition: that is, ultimately on experience. The sharp distinction between religion and philosophy, both of which, Schopenhauer claimed, sought a metaphysical explanation of a world seeped in suffering and death, balanced on his claim that religion expressed its truth allegorically, whereas philosophy had to present its truths *sensu stricto et proprio*. It now appears that Schopenhauer was made to realize that his use of metaphor signified that he was also attempting to advance our cognitive stock through some other means. After their initial exchange of letters, Schopenhauer must have decided that, for the time being, Becker needed to read the second edition of his principal work. He sent the lawyer, as a well-meaning gift, the proof sheets for the second edition: "sized and bound they will give you a copy just like the others."[100] Becker and Schopenhauer remained friends for life. And when Becker became a district judge in 1850 at Mainz, Becker would frequently visit the philosopher and the philosopher would visit the lawyer. Quite naturally, and especially after the death of his friend and lawyer, Martin Emden, Becker was his primary source of legal advice.

Technically, the second edition of *The World as Will and Representation* did not bring Becker to Schopenhauer, because he read its first edition. It did draw another lawyer into his fold. The twenty-six-year-old Munich lawyer Adam Ludwig von Doß discovered Schopenhauer's masterpiece quite accidentally in a Passauer bookstore in 1846. It is not known whether, like Nietzsche's allegedly serendipitous discovery of Schopenhauer in Rohn's bookstore in 1865, a demon also bid him to purchase the work, but he bought it nevertheless.[101] Its effect, though, was comparable to that experienced by the young Nietzsche – it made an overpowering and life-altering impression on the young lawyer, and, as with Nietzsche, Schopenhauer's philosophy resonated in his own pessimistic temperament and with his own metaphysical need to understand the meaning of life. Indeed, in 1849, when Doß first visited the man almost all of the early followers referred to as "master," he reported that "Sch. compared the

---

[100] Schopenhauer, *Gesammelte Briefe*, p. 222, Schopenhauer to Becker, 10 December 1844.

[101] For Nietzsche's October 1865 discovery of Schopenhauer in Rohn's bookstore, see *Nietzsche: Werke in drei Banden*, ed. Karl Schlechta (Munich: Hanser Verlag, 1954–6), Vol. 3, pp. 133–4. Johann Figl makes a convincing case that Nietzsche had already studied some Schopenhauer that summer in Bonn; see Figl's "Nietzsches Begegnung mit Schopenhauers Hauptwerk. Unter Heranziehung eines frühen veröffentlichten Exzerptes," in *Schopenhauer, Nietzsche, und die Kunst*, ed. Wolfgang Schirmacher (Vienna: Passagen Verlag, 1991), pp. 89–100.

responsive, pessimistic mood in which I came to his work to a dry land responsive to rain."[102] Doβ had such passion for his "master's" views that the philosopher called Doβ a "fanatic." And although Schopenhauer appreciated his fanaticism and his comprehension of his philosophy, Doβ never became an evangelist. He referred to Doβ as "John the Apostle," however, and Schopenhauer told Frauenstädt that Doβ "is a writing apostle, writing letters to people whom he did not know, telling them that they should read me."[103]

Schopenhauer encouraged the fanatic's study of Buddhism and directed his readings in the subject. He also encouraged him to correspond and meet with his other disciples. Playfully and ironically, when reporting to Frauenstädt a meeting between Becker and Doβ and then one between the old Dorguth and Doβ, Schopenhauer paraphrased Matthew 18:30: "Where two of you gather in my name, I am there with you."[104] As was his wont with his other followers, Schopenhauer also used Doβ to run errands, once having him deliver a copy of *The Two Fundamental Problems of Ethics* to Ignaz Perner, the founder of the Munich Union against Cruelty to Animals, to whom he would later refer in a footnote in the same book. Schopenhauer, of course, was not beyond offering Doβ advice concerning his love life. When a thirty-year-old Doβ confided that he was in love and was contemplating marriage, Schopenhauer could not restrain himself: "Young friend . . . do not marry! Take my warning. Marry not! Let science be your beloved and wife. You will find yourself a thousand times better off."[105] He told the lovestruck lawyer that he knew woman's love, and told him how his mother entertained as his sick father received care from their maid. When it became apparent that the young man would not heed his advice, Schopenhauer recommended that he at least marry a rich woman, suggesting that his apostle could find a rich woman in Brussels or Hamburg.[106] Three years after Schopenhauer's warnings about the

[102] Schopenhauer, *Gespräche*, p. 142.
[103] Ibid., p. 149.
[104] Ibid., p. 139.
[105] Ibid., p. 151.
[106] Schopenhauer jokingly told a friend, in English, that he could marry ". . . if you can get a girl with at least 30,000 Rth [*Reichstaler*]." He also offered him "a sound maxim of my own making, though it's in English: 'Matrimony = war & want. Single blessedness = peace & plenty,'" Schopenhauer, *Gesammelte Briefe*, p. 438, Schopenhauer to David Asher, 4 November 1858. David Asher was a linguist, writer, Jewish activist, and a teacher of English in Leipzig, whose monograph "Open Letter to the Highly-Learned Mr. Doctor Schopenhauer"

evils of marriage, Doβ married his beloved, Anna Wepfer, who was not rich, in 1853. Schopenhauer did not hold this folly against his apostle. The married lawyer would continue to regularly visit Schopenhauer through 1857, and he maintained contact with him up to the philosopher's death.

The net of Schopenhauer's philosophy never hauled in twelve apostles, but eight by his own reckoning.[107] He never drew a Paul, but he never attracted a Judas.

The Sovereign *Canaille*

Politics interested Schopenhauer little, and this lack of interest is reflected in his philosophy. There is no sustained reflection on political philosophy, and whatever he wrote on this subject was simply an afterthought. It is as if this lack of interest is but a corollary of the philosopher's life. The staunch republican Heinrich Floris dragged his family away from Danzig to avoid Prussian control. The five-year-old Arthur was towed along. During the grand European tour of 1803 and 1804, the family took great pains to avoid Napoleon's mischief. While in France at that time, the family visited sights associated with the French Revolution, an event both Heinrich Floris and Johanna celebrated, but this was done as if these sites were but tourist attractions. When Schopenhauer fled Berlin for the first time in 1813, he did so fearing military conscription, and he sought the peaceful village of Rudolstadt to write his dissertation, in which he did not feel to be a man of his times. Schopenhauer's ultimate attitudes toward contemporary political and social events were analogous to his attitudes toward the various philosophical fashions and fads of his time – relative indifference, unless they personally concerned him. His concern was the universal, the unchanging, the eternally true, and what remains the same behind fleeting and changing circumstances. History only shows more of the same, he argued, *eadem, sed aliter*, "the same but otherwise." Human

---

[*Offenes Sendschreiben an den hochgelehrten Herrn Dr. Arthur Schopenhauer*, Leipzig: Dyk, 1855] led to a letter exchange between the two men that lasted until Schopenhauer's death. Schopenhauer tried unsuccessfully to have Asher translate his works; see Schopenhauer ibid., p. 439, Schopenhauer to Asher, 3 January 1859.

[107] In addition to Dorguth, Frauenstädt, Becker, Doβ, and Asher, Schopenhauer counted the Berlin doctor J. Kormann, the Frankfurt bank employee August Gabriel Kilzer, and the editor of the Berlin *Vossischen Zeitung*, Ernest Otto Linder, as his apostles.

misery, despair, and suffering were a function of the essence of life, of will, and social change simply developed new channels for the expression of the same despair. Politics just did not matter in the larger scheme of life.

But as much as Schopenhauer attempted to turn his back on social and political events, he could not escape the revolutionary year of 1848, as progressive, liberal forces attempted to shove democratic reform onto recalcitrant German lands. In that same year, Marx and Engels urged working men of all countries to unite in *The Communist Manifesto*, exaggerating the extent to which the communist specter haunted Europe. But the spirit-seeing Schopenhauer was haunted and made fearful that social upheaval and the rule of the mob would rob him of his wealth. He began to manage his money even more carefully, and he economized on his expenses, even canceling book orders, a particularly drastic move for a bibliophile.

In September 1848, violence erupted in Frankfurt. General Hans Jakob von Auerwald and Prince Felix Lichnowsky, two Austrian representatives of the status quo, were brutally murdered. Street fights broke out, roads were barricaded, and lead flew throughout the air. On 18 September the view from Schopenhauer's second floor apartment on the Schöne Aussicht was not beautiful. The philosopher observed a disorderly crowd of people armed with poles, pitchforks, and rifles pour across the bridges from Sachsenhausen. Snipers assumed strategic positions in the streets, busily firing away. As Schopenhauer observed the chaotic events from the safety of his rooms, he heard loud voices and banging on his locked and barred doors. He feared it was the "sovereign *canaille*," as he wrote Frauenstädt. He prepared for the worst, although he did not mention whether he grabbed his ever-present pistols. His maid, who appeared to be braver than the philosopher, informed her employer that it was Austrian troops causing the commotion. "Immediately I opened the door to these worthy friends," he wrote his arch-evangelist: "20 stout Bohemians in blue pants rushed in to shoot at the sovereign *canaille* from my window. Soon, however, they thought better of it and went to a neighboring house. From the first floor the officer reconnoitered the crowd behind the barricade. Immediately, I sent him my big, double opera glasses. . . ."[108]

---

[108] Ibid., p. 234, Schopenhauer to Frauenstädt, 2 March 1849. In this letter, Schopenhauer reminded Frauenstädt that the double opera glasses that he sent to the Austrian officer were

The conservative Schopenhauer was reported as saying that Robert Blum, one of the leaders of the rebellion, should have been hanged and not shot, and his loud, heartfelt support for Prince Alfred C. F. Windischgrätz for restoring order drew a rebuke even from aristocratic officers who dined with him at the Englischer Hof.[109] Schopenhauer, however, despite his fear and his opposition to the democratic forces, escaped the upset of 1848, minus only some books and his opera glasses. He gained, moreover, far more than he lost. The failure of the revolutionary years of 1848 and 1849 helped to shape a culture and social mood more receptive to his philosophy. For Schopenhauer, as with many others, the Hegelian faith in inevitable social progress to the type of state in which genuine, concrete human freedom would blossom was reconceptualized by the materialists among the Young Hegelians, and promised to deliver a dream. But this proved to be a pipe dream. The true content of European history, the philosopher told Frauenstädt, is nothing but a "brawl," a series of cat-fights. When there seems to be progress, there is always a counterbalancing retrogression and a relapse into barbarism. This was what the brawls of 1848 made clear. But even if, the philosopher continued, history would ultimately deliver a heaven on earth, this could not bring any consolation to those who suffered along the way and were now deep in their graves. "The human race," Schopenhauer said at another time in his resolute pessimism, "is at once determined by their nature to misery and ruin. If, however, injustice and need would be put to an end through the state, what would occur would be a type of sluggard's life. Humans would fight among themselves out of boredom, falling upon one another, or overpopulation would exterminate them through starvation."[110] Human oppression and exploitation were not mere functions of inhumane social conditions; not a landlord, factory owner, or king that made life miserable – it was king will and redemption was only possible by its denial.

---

the same ones Frauenstädt used to observe the launch of Charles George Green's balloon in Frankfurt during the summer of 1847.

[109] See Schopenhauer, *Gespräche*, p. 222, remarks reported by Robert von Hornstein; also see Safranski, *Schopenhauer and the Wild Years of Philosophy*, p. 323.

[110] Ibid., p. 113. Schopenhauer did not claim that by altering social conditions you could not lessen some types of human suffering, but that the basis of human misery is due to humans' essence as will, something never changed by altered social conditions. For Marxist criticisms of Schopenhauer; see György Lukács, *The Destruction of Reason*, trans. Peter Palmer (London: Merlin, 1979), Chap. 4, and Bernard Bykhovsky, *Schopenhauer and the Grounds of Existence*, trans. Philip Moral (Amsterdam: Gruner, 1984), esp. Chaps. 9 and 10.

Lapses into barbarism, cruelty, violence, and madness were inevitable, Schopenhauer thought, because they expressed ineradicable dispositions found in human nature. Whereas Schopenhauer argued that theoretical egoism or solipsism was a stance only maintained by those in a madhouse, where its advocate needed a cure rather than a philosophical refutation, most people were practical egoists and lived as if only their interests and well-being mattered. "Egoism is colossal," Schopenhauer argued, "it towers above the world; for if every individual were given the choice between his own destruction and the rest of the world, I need not say how the decision would go in the vast majority of cases."[111] To express the idea of the dominance of egoism in human behavior and the horrid behavior it engendered, the philosopher searched for a hyperbole. That many a man would be capable of slaying another to smear his boots with the victim's fat seemed to hit the nail on the head, he thought, but then he wondered "whether it was really a hyperbole."[112] The rebellions of 1848 threatened the state, and without the state, egoism is given free reign. Without the state, human life would be, to use Hobbes' phrase, a *"bellum omnium contra omnes,"* a war of all against all.[113]

And continuing on Hobbesian lines, Schopenhauer argued that the state sprang from mutual fear of mutual violence, which made it in each person's self-interest for there to be a central power, institutionalized in the state, to provide protection from fellow citizens and the aggression of foreign powers. *Homo homini lupus*, man is the wolf to man, Schopenhauer was fond of observing, and the state serves to muzzle the wolf of egoism. Through criminal laws and criminal sanctions, egoism itself curbed the deleterious effects of egoism. Fear of punishment checked egoism and led to right and just conduct: that is, conduct that did not harm others. Unlike Kant, whose retributive view of punishment struck Schopenhauer as a disguised form of revenge, Schopenhauer justified punishment on the basis of its deterrent effect: its ability to prevent future crimes. The state, consequently, is not a vehicle for moral reform or improvement – it only alters behavior; the moral quality of a person is a function of one's inner disposition, according to Schopenhauer, and this is a function of one's character and one's will, and, as such, is innate, unchangeable,

---

[111] Schopenhauer, *On the Basis of Morality*, 132/*Sämtliche Werke*, Vol. 4, p. 197.

[112] Ibid., p. 134/ibid., Vol. 4, p. 198.

[113] See Schopenhauer, ibid., p. 133/ibid., Vol. 4, p. 198. Schopenhauer is quoting from Thomas Hobbes, *Leviathan* (Amsterdam: 1670), Bk. 1, Chap. 13.

and individual: "The wicked man is born with his wickedness as much as the serpent is with its poisonous fangs and glands; and he is as little able to change his character as the serpent its fangs."[114] A serpent can be muzzled, but it is always disposed to strike, and the same was true of humankind.

On 26 June 1852, Schopenhauer added an amendment to his will, leaving the bulk of his estate not to the blue-trousered Bohemians who rushed his apartment, but to "the fund established in Berlin for the support of the Prussian soldiers who fought for the maintenance and restoration of legal order in Germany and who became invalids in the battles of riot and rebellion in the years 1848 and 1849 as well as for the survivors of those killed in battle."[115] It is not likely that Heinrich Floris would have approved his son's generosity toward the Prussians – it was Prussia that made the family flee Danzig – and it is even more unlikely that he would have embraced his son's support for a hereditary monarchy.[116]

A Philosophy for the World

If the revolutionary year of 1848 fueled Schopenhauer's natural inclination for paranoia, 1849 brought great sadness to the philosopher. His sister died, robbing him of the only person to whom he could freely express his innermost feelings and from whom he received sympathetic understanding. He was, however, affected even more deeply by the death of a being that gave him unconditional love. In a conversation with Frauenstädt, he once told his devoted follower that if there were no dogs, he would have preferred not to live. "I have lost my loyal, loving, great poodle," he lamented to his arch-evangelist; "He died before the infirmities of old age, not quite 10 years old. This seriously depressed me for a long time."[117] Schopenhauer could not obtain another sister, but he

---

[114] Ibid., p. 187/ibid., Vol. 4, p. 249.

[115] Hugo Busch, *Das Testament Arthur Schopenhauer* (Wieshaden: Brockhaus, 1950), p. 8, quoted in Hübscher, *Sämtliche Werke*, Vol. 1, p. 118.

[116] See Schopenhauer, *The World as Will and Representation*, Vol. 2, p. 595/*Sämtliche Werke*, Vol. 3, p. 683f., where Schopenhauer also discusses protection from the protector of all; that is, protection for the hereditary monarch. This, he argued, is accomplished by providing the king with so much power, wealth, security, and absolute inviolability that he is no longer under the sway of egoism.

[117] Schopenhauer, *Gesammelte Briefe*, p. 240, Schopenhauer to Frauenstädt, 9 December 1849; see Schopenhauer, *Gespräche*, p. 100 for Schopenhauer's remark about wishing not to live, had there been no dogs.

immediately bought another poodle, and although this poodle was brown and not white like the last one, he also named it "Atma" – as if he would never lose his beloved dog.

After the failure of the second editions of his dissertation and principal work, Schopenhauer developed a new strategy to cultivate a readership. In June 1850, he once more approached Brockhaus, but now with a prospectus for *Parerga and Paralipomena*, a massive two-volume work of 986 pages. He had been laboring on the book for six years, following the second edition of *The World as Will and Representation*, and it constituted, as he told Brockhaus, the completion of his miscellaneous philosophy: that is, his reflections on subjects that could not find their way into his systematic philosophy. He suggested that this could be the end of his writing career: "I think that after this I will have nothing more to write, because I will be on guard against bringing forth weak children of old age, who indict their father and detract from his fame."[118] Here he was thinking, perhaps, of his heroes Kant and Goethe, both of whom he accused of prattling in their works of old age. Because this work was slanted to a general audience, he assumed that it would be popular, and so, unlike the second edition of his principal work, he requested a modest honorarium for his efforts.

This time Brockhaus was not buying what Schopenhauer was selling. The publisher had been burned twice by his systematic philosophy, and so Brockhaus had even less interest in his miscellany. Schopenhauer was advised to publish the work on his own. Instead of letting the matter drop, Schopenhauer asked Brockhaus to help secure a publisher. Embedded in this odd request was another attempt to sell his book. He was willing to wave the honorarium, he told the publisher, and he warned Brockhaus that it would be a mistake to decline the work. Think of him as you will, Schopenhauer wrote, but he was not the only person who thought that his writings were the best produced during this century. He was also confident that this book would overcome the "passive resistance" by the "guild of professors of philosophy," because he had written a "philosophy for the world," and so he promised the reluctant publisher that it would be popular.[119] Brockhaus declined to aid the philosopher in securing a publisher, as well as Schopenhauer's second sales pitch.

[118] Ibid., p. 242, Schopenhauer to Brockhaus, 26 June 1850.
[119] Ibid., p. 247, Schopenhauer to Brockhaus, 3 September 1850.

Schopenhauer approached Friedrich Emil Suchsland, the Frankfurt publisher who had accepted *The Two Fundamental Problems of Ethics* and the second edition of his dissertation. Suchsland, however, did not think that the world was ready for his philosophy. This judgment was also shared at the Dieterich'sche Buchhandlung in Göttingen. A frustrated Schopenhauer turned to his arch-evangelist Frauenstädt for help, but first he complained bitterly about Brockhaus for publishing "Hegelian twaddle" such as Heinrich Moritz Chalybäus' *Ethics: On the Family, State, and Religious Morals* [*Ethik, über die Familie, den Staat und die religiöse Sitte*, 1850] and Karl Rosenkranz' *System of Science* [*System der Wissenschaft*, 1850]. Even Herbart's works received a twelve-volume edition, Schopenhauer sneered. Even worse, he continued, the dancer and mistress of Ludwig I of Bayern, Lola Montez, was writing her memoirs, and English publishers were rumored to have offered her large sums of money for her book. Schopenhauer also provided Frauenstädt with the terms he required for the publication of his philosophy for the world. It had to appear in German (*Frakturschrift*) and not Latin type; he must receive proof-sheets; 750 copies needed to be produced; he needed to evaluate and approve a test copy of the book; he was to receive ten copies bound in high-quality paper; and he had to retain the rights for a second edition. He did not, however, require an honorarium.[120] Frauenstädt piqued the interest of the Berlin publisher Adolf Wilhelm Hayn. Schopenhauer appointed Frauenstädt his agent and advised him to "Read aloud to Hayn the conditions for the contract with a thundering voice. I will not deviate from them."[121] The arch-evangelist must have thundered sufficiently, because Hayn agreed to Schopenhauer's terms. The "philosophy for the world" appeared in 1851.

Parerga and Paralipomena

Schopenhauer insisted that his philosophy for the world bear a Latin title, because it was written for scholars. The unwieldy title, *Parerga and Paralipomena*, was descriptive, meaning literally "subordinate work and things left out" of his philosophy proper. In the preface, Schopenhauer claimed that some of his essays would have found their place in his

---

[120] Ibid., p. 247, Schopenhauer to Frauenstädt, 16 September 1850.
[121] Ibid., p. 248, Schopenhauer to Frauenstädt, 30 September 1850.

earlier books, had they not come so late. Others, due to their subject matter, would not have been placed in his systematic works. In any case, Schopenhauer assured his readers that all of the essays would be interesting and comprehensible to those unfamiliar with his earlier works – except for a few passages. The essays "left out" of his systematic works would further additional explanations for his ideas, the philosopher explained, and the "subordinate essays" would also help elucidate his philosophy, as he put it, because everything that emanated from his mind helped to illuminate his philosophy.

Six essays compose the first volume, the *Parerga*, and the first two, "Sketch of a History of the Ideal and Real" and "Fragments for the History of Philosophy," serve as glosses on modern philosophy and the history of Western philosophy. The first essay details Schopenhauer's analysis of what he found to be the major problem in philosophy from Descartes down to that of his own, the relationship between our perceptions of things and things in themselves. Surveying the philosophies of Descartes, Nicholas de Malebranche, Spinoza, Leibnitz, Locke, Berkeley, Hume, and Kant on this issue, the philosopher immodestly concluded that his philosophy alone solved this problem by showing that the ideal or the representation and the real or the represented thing are will. To show his contempt for his contemporaries, the "three sophists" in particular, Fichte, Schelling, and Hegel, he cast their views outside the course of philosophical development, by treating their views on this issue in a hypercritical appendix to this essay. In the second essay, Schopenhauer integrated his philosophy into the Western philosophical tradition, putting it in the very tradition from which professors of philosophy tried to exclude it. In its fourteenth section, "Some Observations on My Own Philosophy," he recounted the Kantian basis of his philosophy, highlighted its consistency, and endeavored to show, due to his own Kantian roots, why it might appear that his thought had some kinship to Fichte and Schelling. Nevertheless, just as he had at the beginning of his philosophical career, he also confronted the same charge at the end; "Noak [sic.] says . . . that I had stolen everything from Fichte and Schelling."[122] The upshot of both of his essays was to

---

[122] Ibid, p. 460, Schopenhauer to Linder, 21 November 1859. Ludwig Noack had emphasized Fichte and Schelling's influence on Schopenhauer in *Schelling und die Philosophie der Romantik*, 2 vols. (Berlin: Mittler, 1859), Vol. 2, pp. 360–75.

show that the philosophical outsider was the most faithful player within the mainstream Western philosophical tradition, with his philosophy representing its very highest development.

The third essay, "On Philosophy at the University" was a harsh polemic against academic philosophy and professors of philosophy, in which he decried the state of philosophy in German universities. Given the state of German academic philosophy, taught by those who lived by and not for philosophy, mere minions of the state and church, Schopenhauer called for the abolition of philosophy in the universities. All students really needed was a one-term, descriptive course on the history of philosophy and a course in logic. These courses would prepare students for their own, self-directed course of study, which should consist of reading original works of genuine philosophers.

The fourth and fifth essays, "Transcendent Speculations on the Apparent Deliberateness in the Fate of Individuals" and "Essay on Spirit Seeing and Everything Connected Therewith," are curious writings. The former was a "metaphysical fantasy," an attempt to explain what appears as a form of supernatural guidance of the events in an individual's life. This groping around in the dark led Schopenhauer to formally violate his commitment to develop a completely immanent philosophy, one that would not transcend the bounds of experience. Cautiously and circumspectly, Schopenhauer advanced a transcendent claim by suggesting that each individual's life receives invisible guidance that seems to direct a person's will to turn away from life. The "Essay on Spirit Seeing" articulated the philosopher's deep interest in occult phenomena and his idealistic account of the metaphysics of ghosts, which was discussed earlier.

The last two essays showed Schopenhauer speculating and opining in ways he would not have done in his systematic works. The sixth essay, the concluding essay of the first volume of *Parerga and Paralipomena*, "Aphorisms on the Wisdom of Life," even formally suspended "the higher metaphysical-ethical standpoint" of his philosophy proper, which concludes that nonexistence is preferable to existence, in order to develop an eudaemonism, instructions for living as pleasantly as possible.[123] This essay was the heart of his philosophy for the world, and it was the most popular of all of his essays. A relatively happy, that is, a not unhappy, life

---

[123] Schopenhauer, *Parerga and Paralipomena*, Vol. 1, p. 313/*Sämtliche Werke*, Vol. 5, p. 333.

was derived from three sources: what a person is; what a person has; and what a person represents – how a person is regarded by others. Ultimately, Schopenhauer concluded that central to living well is what a person is, and he recommended that one needs to know oneself, one's own deepest tendencies and character, and to mold a life most suitable for one's own personality. This essay represented an idealized description of how Schopenhauer attempted to live, even if he often fell short of his own ideals.

The second volume of this work, the so-called *"Paralipomena,"* consists of thirty-one chapters and concludes with a set of poems drawn primarily from Schopenhauer's early years. The first sixteen chapters supplement his systematic writings, covering topics as diverse as philosophy and its method, observations on the antithesis of the thing in itself and appearances, ethics, philosophy and science, color theory, remarks on the vanity of existence, suicide, and religion.[124] The remaining fifteen chapters are more obliquely related to his philosophy and represent some of the philosopher's far-flung interests. He included chapters on his observations on Sanskrit literature, archaeology, mythology, literary criticism, scholars and scholarship, language and words, reading, education, physiognomy, and noise, among other subjects. The twenty-seventh chapter is his infamously misogynistic essay, "On Women." Although Schopenhauer knew that he was a philosopher and not a poet, he concluded his "last book" with a group of poems, doing so to more freely and openly express his feelings in a personal and very human way, something he did to provide his readers with a more personal acquaintance with the author of his philosophy – as if Schopenhauer the man was not stamped all over his philosophy. This, however, was a significant change of heart for the old philosophical warrior. He viewed his philosophy as the purpose of his life, and he thought his philosophy stood on its own merits, the recognition of which did not require knowledge of its author, but now he was becoming

---

[124] Schopenhauer begins the fifteenth chapter of ibid., Vol. 2, "On Religion," with a dialogue between Demopheles and Philalethes, a dialogue which, according to Philip Rieff, Freud read closely and which served as a model for the dialogue in Freud's *The Future of an Illusion*, trans. James Strachery (New York: W.W. Norton, 1963). Freud, like Schopenhauer, held that religious beliefs were recognized as absurd by rational people, but Freud was more optimistic about the ability of science to displace religion; see *Freud: The Mind of the Moralist*, Philip Rieff, pp. 294–97.

personal. For a man who saw philosophy itself in Hobbesian terms as a "war of all against all," closing with poetry signified an act of peace.[125]

[125] In "Philosophy and Its Method," Schopenhauer argued that there can be thousands of good poems but only one true philosophy. Therefore he claimed that philosophy is always polemical and that philosophical systems stand in a Hobbesian *bellum omnium contra omnes*: "Thus . . . works of poets pasture peacefully side by side like lambs, those of philosophy are born beasts of prey and, even in their destructive impulse, they are like scorpions, spiders, and the larvae of some insects and are turned primarily against their own species," *Parerga and Paralipomena*, Vol. 2, p. 5/*Sämtliche Werke*, Vol. 6, p. 5.

11

The Dawn of Fame and the End of Life

" **I** AM QUITE GLAD to experience the birth of my last child through which I see my mission to the world completed," Schopenhauer told Frauenstädt. "Actually, I now feel a heavy burden that I have borne and felt since my twenty-fourth year to have been lifted. No one can imagine what that means."[1] Schopenhauer's last child did not fall stillborn from the press like its earlier siblings.

Parerga and Paralipomena drew a readership. The arch-evangelists did their part. Dorguth, Frauenstädt, and Kilzer wrote flattering pieces in praise of their master.[2] Anonymous and generally positive reviews appeared in the Hamburg-based *Seasons* [*Jahreszeiten*, December 1851], the *Literary Central Newspaper for Germany* [*Litterarisches Centralblatt für Deutschland*, January 1852], and on 1 April 1852, Schopenhauer received his first review outside of Germany, when a three-page criticism appeared in the British *The Westminster Review* – it was no April Fool's joke. In a short year, the unknown British critic would play a decisive role in the reception of Schopenhauer's thought. Schopenhauer was thrilled by the review in *Seasons*: "It is laudatory throughout, almost enthusiastic, and very well composed . . . The time of barking dogs and tub-thumpers is past."[3] He was even amused when a critic referred to him as "deceased."[4]

---

[1] Schopenhauer, *Gesammelte Briefe*, p. 251, Schopenhauer to Frauenstädt, 23 October 1850.

[2] See Dorguth's *Miscellaneous Remarks on Schopenhauer's Philosophy. A Letter to the Master* [*Vermischte Bemerkungen ueber die Philosophie Schopenhauers, Ein Brief an den Meister*, Magdeburg: Heinrichshofen, 1852]. Frauenstädt's review appeared in the *Pages for Literary Diversion* [*Blätter für litterarische Unterhaltung*], No. 9, March 1852; and Kilzer's review appeared in the Frankfurt *Didaskalia*, 14 April 1852.[Author: For consistency, add Kilzer to bibliography?]

[3] Schopenhauer, *Gesammelte Briefe*, p. 274, Schopenhauer to Frauenstädt, 11 January 1852.

[4] Ibid., *Gesammelte Briefe*, p. 311, Schopenhauer to Linder, 9 May 1853.

As *Parerga and Paralipomena* began to make waves in the wider intellectual world, professors of philosophy were gradually breaking their silence. The Heidelberg philosopher Karl Fortlage discussed Schopenhauer extensively in his *Genetic History of Philosophy since Kant* [*Genetische Geschichte der Philosophie seit Kant*, 1852], and Fichte's son, Immanuel Hermann, did so from Tübingen in his *System of Ethics* [*System der Ethik*, 1853], and the journal he co-edited with Hermann Ulrici from Halle contained frequent references to Schopenhauer. The Hegelian from Halle, Johann Eduard Erdmann, whom Schopenhauer quoted and used as an example of young professors of philosophy who were ignorant of Kant, contrasted "Schopenhauer and Herbart" (1853) in the young Fichte's journal, drawing a postscript from the editor. Erdmann, who made a genuine effort to understand Schopenhauer and who would later share an awkward dinner with the philosopher, included thirty-seven pages on Schopenhauer in his *Development of German Speculation since Kant* [*Die Entwicklung der deutschen Speculation seit Kant*, 1853]. Schopenhauer himself wrote the "Notice on My Life" that appeared in the Halle professor's book.[5]

Schopenhauer, of course, enjoyed the attention paid to him by academic philosophers, but he also enjoyed complaining about the quality of his commentators' work. He did not, however, confront his critics publicly. Indeed, with the exception of the early incident with Beneke and his seething criticism of the poor judgment of the Royal Danish Society, he shied away from such intellectual catfights. He did complain to his disciples privately, encouraging his evangelists to defend him. Although he credited Fortlage for his judicious selection of passages from his books, Schopenhauer found just the opposite of an advanced position in the judgments of the Heidelberg professor, which he called "false, distorted, and bad." He also viewed Fortlage's book itself to be simply a "hasty product of the mania to publish books." Always keen to hurl an *ad hominem*,

---

5 See ibid., pp. 260–61, Schopenhauer to Erdmann, 9 April 1851, for Schopenhauer's biographical notice. Schopenhauer described the awkward dinner with Erdmann at the Englischer Hof – a "farce," as he called it in a letter to Frauenstädt, 11 May 1854; see ibid., p. 340. Schopenhauer found Erdmann incapable of putting together a coherent series of thoughts, and he was relieved that a third party at the table engaged in conversation with the young professor. Schopenhauer exploited the opportunity to quickly polish off his half a chicken and to leave abruptly, after expressing his pleasure at meeting Erdmann and requesting him to convey his greetings to Frauenstädt when he returned to Berlin.

Schopenhauer told Frauenstädt that Fortlage was "*a priori dumb*."[6] He was harsher about the younger Fichte. Fichte's book was "a web of lies from beginning to end," and Schopenhauer judged Fichte's system of ethics a "system of the most vulgar philistinism." Sarcastically, he even claimed that the junior Fichte presented a challenge to Schopenhauer's own theory that children inherit their characters from their fathers. Fichte senior was a "windbag," but he did possess some talent and understanding. The son, however, was simply a "liar."[7] Erdmann's essay on Schopenhauer and Herbart had correctly depicted Herbart as his opposite, he told Frauenstädt, but not, as the Halle professor argued, from their starting from different points in Kant, but because the false is the contradictory of the true. As for the earth man's treatment of him in his book, Schopenhauer thought that the first ten pages of the thirty-seven were good, but they were simply an overview of his treatment of the four roots of the principle of sufficient reason. Otherwise, he said, Erdmann's work was cursory, confused, and ignored his fundamental doctrines. Consequently, Erdmann was unable to appreciate how he was different from others, and so Erdmann treated him "just like one snake among other snakes." He could only detect two outright lies, he said to Frauenstädt. He had not said that Leibniz was a mathematician and a polymath, but not a philosopher. He had merely said he was more of a mathematician and polymath than a philosopher. He did not say that Hegel was "a simpleton of our times"; rather, he said this of Hegelians.[8] To detect "lies," Schopenhauer certainly cut fine distinctions!

While Schopenhauer was gathering a small and enthusiastic group of followers, and as some professors of philosophy deemed his philosophy to be worthy of note, and as *Parerga and Paralipomena* slowly drew readers, the anonymous British reviewer once again spoke in *The Westminster Review* in April 1853. Unlike his three-page lukewarm review of *Parerga and Paralipomena*, this time, in twenty pages, headed by a listings of all of Schopenhauer's books, with the exception of *On Vision and Colors*, this review, "Iconoclasm in German Philosophy," which meant only to describe Schopenhauer's philosophy and only to praise his style without accepting his "ultra-pessimism," lauded Schopenhauer's philosophical

---

[6] Schopenhauer, *Gesamelte Briefe*, p. 283, Schopenhauer to Frauenstädt, 10 June 1852.

[7] Ibid., p. 300, Schopenhauer to Frauenstädt, 22 November 1852.

[8] Ibid., p. 326, Schopenhauer to Frauenstädt, 2 November 1853.

attitude, his perseverance through the decades of secreting against his philosophy, and the clarity and power of his thought, painting the author in heroic and deeply inviting terms:

Few, indeed, we venture to assert, will be those of our English readers who are familiar with the name Arthur Schopenhauer. Fewer still will there be who are aware of this mysterious being owning that name has been working for something like forty years to subvert the whole system of German philosophy which has been raised by university professors since the decease of Immanuel Kant, and that, after his long labor, he has just succeeded in making himself heard – wonderfully illustrating that doctrine in acoustics which shows how long an interval may elapse between the discharge of the cannon and the hearing of the report. And even still fewer will there be who are aware that Arthur Schopenhauer is one of the most ingenious and readable authors in the world, skillful in the art of theory building, universal in attainments, inexhaustible in the power of illustration, terribly logical and unflinching in the pursuit of consequences, and – a most amusing qualification to everyone but the persons "hit" – a formidable hitter of adversaries.[9]

Schopenhauer's lawyer and friend, Martin Emden, alerted him to the second *Westminster* review after he quite accidentally came across a reference to it in the British commercial weekly, *The Economist*. Schopenhauer notified his young friend Linder, who found and sent a copy to the philosopher. The life-long Anglophile was pleased by the review, reading it three times – as he told Linder. Schopenhauer understood the author's claim of not endorsing his philosophy simply as a ploy to avoid "appearing as a partisan of one such heretic, atheist, and diabolical man."[10] He was pleased, moreover, with the reviewer's knowledge of Kant and by his recognition of the obscurity and apparent meaninglessness of Hegel's philosophy. The review also contained translations of three lengthy passages from his works, and he was particularly impressed with the quality of their rendering into English.[11] He was also delighted by the selection of a passage from

[9] John Oxenford, "Iconoclasm in German Philosophy," pp. 388–407; reprinted in *Zwölftes Jahrbuch der Schopenhauer-Gesellschaft für die Jahre 1923–1925*, pp. 117–407. This quotation is found on pp. 117–18 of the reprint.
[10] Schopenhauer, *Gesammelte Briefe*, p. 311, Schopenhauer to Linder, 9 May 1853.
[11] Oxenford translated two passages from *The World as Will and Representation*, Vol. 1, pp. 36–37, 105/*Sämtliche Werke*, Vol. 2, pp. 43–4, 125f. (the second passage was Schopenhauer's grand cosmic analogy where he extended the will discovered in self-conscious to all representations), and one passage for *The Fourfold Root of the Principle of Sufficient Reason*, pp. 57–9/*Sämtliche Werke*, Vol. 1, pp. 37–9. These passages are found, respectively, on pp. 397–8, 402, and 399–400 in the original review and pp. 124–5, 129, and 126–7 in the reprint. Schopenhauer told Asher, whom he tried to convince to translate his works into English, that he was astonished

the second edition of *The Fourfold Root*, one in which Schopenhauer raked "German professors of philosophy" for ignoring Kant and for attempting to ride a disguised form of the cosmological argument to the "Absolute," a word that "has a foreign, decent, and aristocratic ring; and we know best what can be done with Germans by assuming an air of superiority." The review then offered a description of Schopenhauer's writing style, one that assuaged the philosopher: "It shows that odd mixture of sarcasm, invective, and common-sense argument, which constitutes the polemic style of Schopenhauer, and, at the same time, allows that private pique, which is never wholly forgotten, to appear in the form of bitter irony."[12] It is curious that Schopenhauer regarded as the very best thing in the review the author's use of the word "nothing" three times in regard to the type of response to his books by German professors of philosophy.[13]

   Although Schopenhauer was thrilled by the review, he did not think its presentation of his philosophy was complete. He thought it short-changed his ethics, failed to convey the unity and completeness of his philosophy, and did not mention his key doctrine of the primacy of the will and the secondary status of the intellect. Nor was he happy with its closing reference to him as "this misanthropic sage of Frankfort."[14] He could accept the designation "sage" but not "misanthropic." His philosophy was "philanthropic": an act of abstract love for humankind. By solving the ever-disquieting problem of existence, and by explaining the significance and meaning of living in a world in which suffering and death follows from the very essence of the world, he was trying to provide metaphysical comfort for humankind – even if he found it difficult to concretely love particular human bipeds. It may have been this final reference to him as a misanthrope that led him to believe that the anonymous reviewer was William Smith, a popularizer of Fichte. Only later would he discover that its true author was John Oxenford, poet, author, theater critic, and the

---

by Oxenford's ability to "not simply reflect the sense, but also the style, mannerisms and gestures [of his writing] as in a mirror," *Gesammelte Briefe*, p. 420, Schopenhauer to Asher, 22 October 1857.

[12] Oxenford, "Iconoclasm in German Philosophy," p. 400f.; reprint, p. 127.

[13] See Schopenhauer, *Gesammelte Briefe*, p. 311, Schopenhauer to Linder, 9 May 1853. Oxenford only used "nothing" twice, to describe the response, first, to Schopenhauer's dissertation, and second, to his principal work. To the response to *The Two Fundamental Problems of Ethics*, Oxford claimed that there was "no report at all"; see "Iconoclasm in German Philosophy," pp. 389–90; reprint, 116–17.

[14] Oxenford, ibid., p. 407; reprint, p. 134.

translator of Goethe's autobiography, *Truth and Poetry*. Oxenford had also written the first notice in *The Westminster Review*.

Schopenhauer convinced Linder to have his English-born wife translate Oxenford's review into German, but he asked her to omit the reference to him as "misanthropic." Later, however, when he read the translation against the original, among the changes that he made, he restored the omitted word. "I have even myself wrote in [misanthropic] again," he told Linder: "one must translate faithfully and honestly."[15] The translation would appear June 1853 in the *Voss Journal* (*Vossische Zeitung*) and Frauenstädt would include it in what would be the first detailed interpretation of his master's system, *Letters on the Schopenhauerian Philosophy* [*Briefe über die Schopenhauersche Philosophie*, Leipzig: F. A. Brockhaus, 1854]. Even a metareview, a review of Oxenford's review, was published as "A. Schopenhauer, a German Philosopher Celebrated in England," in the Berlin-based *Magazine for Foreign Literature* [*Magazin für die Litteratur des Auslandes*, 1854]. Karl Rosenkranz, however, was skeptical. He thought that Oxenford's review was written in Germany by one of Schopenhauer's devotees.[16]

Following the activity of Schopenhauer's evangelists, positive popular reviews of *Parerga and Paralipomena*, and the notice of a few professors of philosophy, the German translation of Oxenford's review served as a flashpoint to ignite interest in Schopenhauer's philosophy. With his increased popularity, Schopenhauer was able to convince Suchsland to issue a second edition of *On the Will in Nature* and Hartknoch to do the same for *On Vision and Colors*, both in 1854. Brockhaus printed both books, the latter in a run of 1,050 copies. The Catholic priest Beda Weber felt compelled to warn his parishioners about the philosopher who recognized "no personal God, no personal freedom, and no existence after death for the individual" in the *Frankfurt Catholic Church Newspaper* [*Frankfurter Katholische Kirchenzeitung*, November, 1854].[17] In Zurich, a group of German political exiles were still licking their wounds from the drubbings of 1848 and 1849, "ultra-democrats" busily reading and discussing

---

[15] Schopenhauer, *Gesammelte Briefe*, p. 313, Schopenhauer to Linder, 9 June 1853. In a letter to Linder, 9 May 1853, Schopenhauer had asked Linder to remove "misanthropic" from the translation; see ibid., p. 312.

[16] See Karl Rosenkranz, "Zur Charakteristik Schopenhauers," note 63. Also see Hübscher, *The Philosophy of Schopenhauer in Its Intellectural Context*, pp. 509, 517.

[17] Schopenhauer, *Gesammelte Briefe*, p. 593.

the conservative philosopher. One such refugee, the Hungarian student, Franz Bizonfy, wrote to the philosopher, inviting him to come to Zurich for a few days or weeks, not to meet just him but "many others, who will give you more pleasure than all the professors of two centuries, join me in my request."[18] Schopenhauer declined the invitation, as he told a friend: "The Hungarian, along with a complete cadre of wits, who are banned [from Germany] earnestly requested that I should travel to Zurich this December, in order to satisfy their curiosity; I answered politely, friendly, and briefly, . . . that I no longer travel."[19]

Two of the "wits" mentioned by Bizonfy were the poet Jörg Herwegh and the composer Richard Wagner, who found it expedient to flee from Dresden to Switzerland in the summer of 1849 to avoid the fate of his anarchist friend and the later founder of the First International, Michael Bakunin. As the forty-one-year-old Wagner was being introduced to Schopenhauer's *The World as Will and Representation* by Herwegh in the autumn of 1849, Bakunin was introduced to a German prison. Wagner's experience of Schopenhauer was life-transforming. As he would write to the great pianist and composer Franz Liszt, whose daughter, Cosima, Wagner would later steal from Hans von Bülow, Schopenhauer's philosophy " . . . has come to me in my loneliness like a gift from heaven."[20] Derisively, Nietzsche, who always seemed to kill whoever he once loved, summed up the relationship: "The benefit Schopenhauer conferred on Wagner is immeasurable. Only the *philosopher of decadence* gave to the artist of decadence – *himself.*"[21]

Wagner returned a gift to the philosopher. In December 1854, Schopenhauer received in the mail, quite unexpectedly, a handsomely bound, privately-printed copy of *The Nibelung's Ring* [*Der Ring der Niebelung*], which was printed on heavy paper. The composer was too

---

[18] Quoted in Hübscher, *The Philosophy of Schopenhauer in Its Intellectual Context*, p. 427.

[19] Schopenhauer, *Gesammelte Briefe*, p. 357, Schopenhauer to Frauenstädt, 30 December 1854.

[20] Quoted in Hübscher, *The Philosophy of Schopenhauer in Its Intellectual Context*, p. 429. Wagner was writing the second and third acts of *The Valkyrie* [*Die Walküre*], the second of the four operas in the *Ring* cycle; see Bryan Magee, *The Philosophy of Schopenhauer* (New York: Oxford University Press, 1997), p. 331. My understanding of Wagner's relationship to Schopenhauer is greatly indebted to Magee's fine work.

[21] Friedrich Nietzsche, *The Case of Wagner*, Sect. 4. In the preface to this book, Nietzsche interprets his infatuations with both Schopenhauer and Wagner as revealing his own decadence, and he claims that by overcoming these two antipodes, he was able to become himself and also to overcome modernity.

timid to include a letter. Under the title, he simply wrote "from respect and gratitude." Schopenhauer did not respond to the author, preferring instead to fill the manuscript with snide remarks, critical observations, question marks, underlingings, and exclamations marks. Frequently, he was offended by Wagner's language – it hurt his ears: "He has no ears, this deaf musician."[22] To a stage instruction, indicating that the curtain was to close quickly, Schopenhauer quipped, "Since it is high time." At the close of the first act of *The Valkyrie*, the incestuous and adulterous love scene between Siegmund and Sieglinde, Schopenhauer, who himself would sometimes suspend sexual morality, was appalled: "One can forget about morality occasionally, but one should not slap it in the face." Words of praise or signs of enjoyment are curiously absent in Schopenhauer's marginalia. He tells his friend Frauenstädt, "[this] is probably the genuine artwork of the future. It appears to be very rambling."[23]

Wagner would learn Schopenhauer's judgment about *The Nibelung's Ring* indirectly. A member of the composer's Zurich circle, the Swiss journalist Franz Arnold Wille, called on Schopenhauer in April 1855. Quite naturally their conversation turned to Wagner. "Convey to your friend Wagner my gratitude for sending me his *Nibelung*," the philosopher intoned; "but tell him that he should stop writing music. His genius is greater as a poet. I, Schopenhauer, remain faithful to Rossini and Mozart."[24] Wagner was disappointed by Schopenhauer's "gratitude" for his gift. He thought his character of Wotan represented the breaking of the will, but without the intervention of some higher grace. "I am convinced that Schopenhauer would have been annoyed that I discovered this before I knew of his philosophy," he told his wife Cosima in 1878, and he intimated that he had anticipated Schopenhauer's reaction. "I, a political refugee, the indefensibility of whose theory had been proved by his disciple Kossack on the basis of his philosophy, since my music was

[22] Schopenhauer, *Der handschriftliche Nachlaß*, Vol. 5, p. 436, which includes Schopenhauer's marginalia and his highlights of Wagner's 159-page text. Wagner had fifty copies of the book produced for distribution to his friends.

[23] Schopenhauer, *Gesammelte Briefe*, p. 357, Schopenhauer to Frauenstädt, 30 December 1854. Schopenhauer mentions here both the dedication and the fact that Wagner included no letter with *The Nibelung's Ring*. Schopenhauer's copy of this book is in the Houghton Library, at Harvard University. Also see Karl S. Guthke, "The Deaf Musician: Arthur Schopenhauer Reads Richard Wagner," *Harvard Magazine*, Vol. 99, no. 1 (Sept.–Oct. 1996) for a description of Schopenhauer's reception of Wagner's gift.

[24] Schopenhauer, *Gespräche*, p. 199.

supposed to have no melody. But that was not very nice. It is the way
Goethe treated Kleist, who he should have acclaimed. . . . "[25]

Karl Ludwig Ernst Kossak was not one of Schopenhauer's disciples.
The very alive philosopher was amused when the music and theater
critic once referred to him as "dead." Schopenhauer had read, however, Kossak's polemic against Wagner and he endorsed it: "The aesthete
Kossak . . . made a very fitting use of my views against Wagner and quite
rightly. Bravo!"[26] Schopenhauer had attended a performance of Wagner's
The Flying Dutchman [*Der Fliegende Holländer*] and found it overdone and
too busy. Indeed, music stood at the pinnacle of Schopenhauer's hierarchy
of the arts, because it expresses in tone the inner essence of existence, will.
All other arts remain on the level of appearances. Wagner's total work of
art was predicated on the reciprocal interaction between music, action,
word, and scene, where, ultimately, music requires word and image and
where poetry seems to take the leading role. This linking, synthesizing
the arts, hearkens back to the Romantics, and Schopenhauer valued pure
instrumental music as the ultimate art. Not to recognize this was, for
Schopenhauer, a failure to recognize that music is an unconscious exercise in metaphysics. As Schopenhauer had Wille convey to Wagner, he
was more of a poet than a musician. For Schopenhauer, Wagner's music
did not convey will; it buried it.

When the composer gifted the philosopher with the libretto for *Tris-
tan and Isolde*, in 1858, Schopenhauer did not respond at all. But, despite
the philosopher's coldness, Wagner's enthusiasm for Schopenhauer never
abated. The composer continued to promote Schopenhauer for his entire
life, and his activity on Schopenhauer's behalf may have done more to
enhance Schopenhauer's popularity than the activities of the philosopher's evangelists. And, as Bryan Magee has suggested, Schopenhauer's
effect on Wagner "is probably the outstanding instance in our culture of a great artist's work being importantly influenced by a great

---

[25] Quoted in Magee, The Philosophy of Schopenhauer, p. 338, Cosima Wagner's Diaries,
Vol. 2, p. 52.

[26] Schopenhauer, *Gesammelte Briefe*, p. 343, Schopenhauer to Frauenstädt, 22 May 1854. Two
days earlier, he told Becker that in the *Berlin Music – Newspaper Echo [Berliner Music – Zeitung
Echo*, 7 and 14 May 1854] an article appeared "in which passages on music from my writings
were used polemically against the operas of Rich. Wagner as if they were oracular decrees,"
ibid., p. 341. Kossak's article was titled "*Aphorisms to the More Recent Musical Literature*"
[*Gedanken-Späne zur Neueren Musikalischen Litteratur*].

philosopher's."[27] Nevertheless, it was best to love Schopenhauer at a distance. When Wagner was in Frankfurt in 1860, he did not even consider visiting the old philosopher.

But if Wagner was too demure to attempt to have a word with his philosophical hero, the composer's hero was also too demure to have a word with his musical hero. When Schopenhauer directed Wille to tell Wagner that he remained loyal to Rossini and Mozart, it was not coincidental that he mentioned the Italian composer first. Gioachino Antonio Rossini's music embodied all the virtues that Wagner's music lacked. By not forcing music to attach itself to words, and by not forcing it to mold itself according to events, Rossini, Schopenhauer argued, was not trying to have his music speak a foreign language: "His [Rossini's] music speaks its own language so distinctly and purely that it requires no words at all, and therefore produces its full effect even when rendered by instruments alone."[28] Schopenhauer was said to roll his eyes upwards to the heavens, when he spoke of Rossini, and he regularly blew his flute to Rossini's music, all of which he had arranged for the flute. When the Italian composer stopped in Frankfurt in September 1856, Schopenhauer arranged with the owner of the Englisher Hof to reserve two seats near his hero. But he never said a word to the Italian. Later, he told Robert von Hornstein that "I did not want to make his [Rossini's] acquaintance."[29] He did not, however, tell Hornstein why this was the case. Perhaps Schopenhauer was like Wagner, too shy and intimidated by his idol. Perhaps, however, he was also like Wagner, too proud, fearful of not receiving the type of reception that he thought he deserved.

Søren Kierkegaard privately noted Schopenhauer's popularity in his journals, the very same year Wagner found his philosophical mentor. "There can be no doubt that the position in Germany is this," the Dane reflected, "that – it is easy to see because all the literary gossips, journalists and authorlings have begun to busy themselves with S[chopenhauer] – that he is now to be dragged forward on the scene and

[27] Magee, *The Philosophy of Schopenhauer*, p. 379. Magee deftly analyzes Wagner's reception of Schopenhauer in pp. 326–78 of this work.

[28] Schopenhauer, *The World as Will and Representation*, Vol. 1, p. 262/*Sämtliche Werke*, Vol. 2, p. 309.

[29] Schopenhauer, *Gespräche*, p. 220. Shemann reported that "Schopenhauer was too proud to intrude upon the famous guest." Ibid., p. 221.

proclaimed."[30] Kierkegaard appreciated the philosopher's writing style and irony, and agreed with his complaints against professors of philosophy. Naturally, Kierkegaard maliciously enjoyed Schopenhauer's abuse of Hegel, and he envied the Germans for having the word "windbag," a word, he noted, that Schopenhauer made excellent use of as both a noun and an adjective. Like Nietzsche later, however, the great Dane questioned Schopenhauer's "pessimism," a term, however, that the philosopher never used to describe his philosophy in any of the books that he prepared for publication.[31] He evinced too much joy as he thundered his scorn down upon German professors of philosophy. He desired fame and renown. Had he been a true pessimist, he would have invited scorn, and he would have scorned fame. The master of irony, moreover, could not help but note that despite Schopenhauer's heaping abuse on the heads of his contemporaries, he sounded very much the professor: "Not without great self-satisfaction he [Schopenhauer] says; he is the first who has designated a place for asceticism in a system. Yes, that is completely the talk of a professor. I am *the first....* "[32] Indeed, Kierkegaard was amazed that the philosopher was so pleased by having his essay on the freedom of the will crowned by the Royal Norwegian Society and that he was upset that Kierkegaard's own home town society, the Royal Danish Society, withheld from Schopenhauer the same honor for his essay on morality. He should have laughed at being crowned and at not being crowned, Kierkegaard concluded. Yet, despite complete disagreement with his thought, the Dane was astonished by how deeply the "thundering Jupiter" touched him.

---

[30] Søren Kierkegaard, *The Journals of Kierkegaard*, trans. Alexander Dru (New York: Harper Row, 1959), p. 237.

[31] I could find Schopenhauer referring only once to his philosophy as "pessimistic." In a note from 1828, in a contrast between his philosophy and pantheism, he referred to the latter as optimistic, remarking that "my doctrine is pessimistic." Schopenhauer would use most of this note in the second volume of *The World as Will and Representation*, dropping the reference to his views as "pessimistic." It is likely that he did not accept this as a description of his philosophy due to his use of "optimism" and "pessimism" to signify the most important difference between types of religions. Unlike religion, his philosophy did not conceal the true in myths and allegories and, for this reason, he may have thought that this term had no application to his philosophy: see, Schopenhauer, *Manuscript Remains*, Vol. 3, pp. 504-6/ *Der handschriftliche Nachlaß*, Vol. 3, pp. 463-5 and *The World as Will and Representation*, Vol. 2, pp. 642-6/*Sämtliche Werke*, Vol. 3, pp. 736-41. As we have seen on numerous occasions, Schopenhauer called himself a pessimist and had no problem with others calling him one.

[32] Kierkegaard, quoted in *Über Arthur Schopenhauer*, ed. Gerd Haffmans (Zurich: Diogenes, 1977), p. 209.

As Kierkegaard and Wagner were having their different reactions to Schopenhauer, the editor of *Pierer's Universal Lexicon* requested and received from the philosopher a short biographical notice, one of three he would write.[33] Later, when Asher inquired whether someone was writing his biography, the philosopher changed the subject and addressed his autobiography. "I will not serve my private life as a treat for the cold and spiteful curiosity of the public."[34] Two years after his death, Gwinner would publish a biography, one that set off a public spat among his followers, concerning the fate of his private diary "About Myself." Gwinner, who used it for his biography, claimed that he followed Schopenhauer's instructions by destroying it, saying that the philosopher feared the mischief that could be done by the "cold and spiteful public."[35]

And in the fateful year of 1854, the theologist Ludwig Noack, who earlier provided the first presentation of Schopenhauer's metaphysics of music and would later play pop psychologist by arguing that Schopenhauer's misogyny was a symptom of an inclination for pederasty, followed Erdmann's lead and unsuccessfully attempted to synthesize Hegel's development of consciousness into Schopenhauer's account of the development of will.[36] Noack's *Propaedeutic for Philosophy* [*Propädeutik der Philosophie*] struck Schopenhauer as an attempt to square the circle. And, if Noack's self-undermining task displeased the philosopher, he was more than compensated by Alexandre Weill's *Philosophie de la Magic* (*Revue française*, T. VII, 1856), the first French translation of Schopenhauer, drawn from "Animal Magnetism and Magic," that curious chapter from *On the Will in Nature*. It was also during this time that the unskeptical philosopher was

---

[33] In addition to the biographical sketch that Schopenhauer prepared for Erdmann's "The Development of German Speculation since Kant," and *Pierers Universal-Lexikon*, he also wrote a biographical notice for *Meyers Konversations/Lexikon*. See Schopenhauer, *Gesammelte Briefe*, pp. 260–61, 263, and 417.

[34] Ibid., p. 417, Schopenhauer to Asher, 15 July 1857.

[35] Hübscher provides a concise account concerning the controversy surrounding Schopenhauer's private diary, "About Myself," as well as a reconstruction in *Manuscript Remains*, Vol. 4, p. 472–513/*Der handschriftliche Nachlaß*, Vol. 4, 2, pp. 106–27.

[36] Noack's account of Schopenhauer's metaphysics of music is in his *History of Philosophy in a Concise Survey. Textbook for the Use with Academic Lectures and for Self-Instruction* [*Geschichte der Philosophie in gedrängter Übersicht. Lehrbuch zum Gebrauche bei akademischen Vorlesungen und Selbstunterricht*, 1853]. He made the claim about Schopenhauer's inclination towards pedastry in *The Master Woman-Hater and Woman-Glorifier. A Psychological Antithesis between Schopenhauer and Daumer in Frankfurt* [*Die Meister Weiberfeind und Frauenlob. Eine Psychologische Antithese zwischen Schopenhauer und Daumer in Frankfurt*, 1860].

dazzled by the magical miracles executed by the amazing Signor Regazzoni, whom he would immortalize in that very chapter Weill turned into
French. Schopenhauer did not take it well when his dear Frauenstädt
told him that he agreed with Regazzoni's critics; "But, my best one, do
you take me for an old fool, who does not know what he sees?"[37] Wisely,
Frauenstädt did not reply to his master's question. In this instance, he
would have been tempted to say "yes."

Then what would have been hardly imaginable a short decade earlier
occurred. The university at Leipzig sponsored an essay contest in 1856
for the best "explanation and critique of the principles of the Schopenhauerian philosophy." Schopenhauer read about the contest on 5 January
1856 in an announcement in the *Frankfurt Journal* [*Frankfurter Journal*]. At first, he worried whether there would be any entries, because he
thought that the contest was poorly publicized. But after he reflected for
a moment, he then thought that the contest was a setup job, meant to
bash his philosophy. He considered the philosophical faculty at Leipzig
his enemies, especially the Herbartians, Gustav Hartenstein and Moritz
Drobish. That the Hegelian apostate and advocate of Schelling's positive
philosophy, Christian Hermann Weiße, set the question and would sit on
the reading committee with Drobish did little to ease the philosopher's
suspicions.[38] Schopenhauer judged that his doubts about the fairness of
the contest were confirmed when the theology student Rudolf Seydel won
the gold medal with his *Schopenhauer's Philosophical System Explained and
Reviewed* [*Schopenhauer's Philosophisches System dargestellt und beurtheilt*].
Seydel also earned his doctorate with this work.

Seydel's essay was published in June 1857. Becker immediately secured
a copy, reporting to Schopenhauer that the essay was extremely critical
and rife with "insolent misuse of quotations."[39] Schopenhauer's reaction
was more extreme. The very selection of Seydel's essay demonstrated

---

[37] Schopenhauer, *Gesammelte Briefe*, p. 355, Schopenhauer to Frauenstädt, 30 November 1854.
[38] Carl Bähr reported to Schopenhauer that Weiße regularly held discussion groups in which
    students disputed Schopenhauer's philosophy and that the essay contest was inspired by these
    meetings. Although Weiße and Drobisch sat on the reading committee, it is likely that they
    were able to set aside their prejudices against Schopenhauer. It was the Ministry that decided
    the contest; see ibid., 394f, Schopenhauer to Frauenstädt, 6 June 1856 and ibid., pp. 398,
    Schopenhauer to Asher, 20 July 1856, and for a discussion of the essay contest, Max Brahn,
    Arthur Schopenhauer Briefwechsel und andere Dokumente (Leipzig: Insel, 1911).
[39] Schopenhauer, *Gesammelte Briefe*, p. 619, Becker to Schopenhauer, 7 June 1857.

that the faculty at Leipzig had no genuine interest in trying to understand his philosophy. Instead, they merely wanted to tear it down. Had they any interest in his philosophy, he thought, they would have selected the only other essay in the contest; that of Carl Georg Bähr, a twenty-two-year-old law student and the son of Schopenhauer's friend, a professor living at Dresden, Johann Karl Bähr. The title of the younger Bähr's work said it all. His *The Schopenhauerian Philosophy in Its Fundamental Features Explained and Critically Elucidated* [*Die Schopenhauersche Philosophie in ihren Grundzügen dargestellt und Kritisch beleuchtet*, Dresen: Rudolf Kuntze, 1857] sought to explain and elucidate its subject, whereas Seydel sought to explain and negatively criticize. Bähr was interested in the truth, and Seydel was interested in pleasing the anti-Schopenhauer faculty. At least, this is what the Schopenhauer camp maintained.

Schopenhauer found Seydel's use of quotations more than insolent. It was the means through which he generated his many claims that Schopenhauer's thought was contradictory. Seydel's essay, he told Becker, "is a miserable piece of work. A complex of passages are broken off from remote parts of my writings, then they are distorted, misrepresented, falsified, to show that my work is completely full of contradictions. To indicate contradictions is the most infamous and notorious way of refuting an author. One can do this to anyone, because in 99 cases out of 100, the contradiction is merely apparent."[40] Schopenhauer accused Seydel of dishonesty, and he called the theology student "dumb," because he misunderstood a parable that he praised.[41]

By this time Schopenhauer was used to confronting the charge of contradiction. It was a demon that haunted his philosophy from the earliest reviews of his principal work and it is one that endures to the present day. Herbart, Rätze, and Beneke had leveled this damning charge, and shortly before Seydel, Aldolp Cornill, a *Privatdozent* at Heidelberg, and Saint-René[42] Taillandier, a French author and literary historian, raised the

---

[40] Schopenhauer ibid., p. 415, Schopenhauer to Becker, 10 June 1857.

[41] Hübscher notes that Schopenhauer was being unfair to Seydel. He did not imply that the parable of the desert and oasis signified a theodicy, but only that other passages in *Parerga and Paralipomena* suggested such. The parable in question is in Sect. 380 in the second volume of *Parerga and Paralipomena*; see Schopenhauer, *Gesammelte Briefe*, p. 619, note 415.

[42] G. Steven Neely in *Schopenhauer: A Consistent Reading* discusses and replies to many of the charges of inconsistency in Schopenhauer's philosophy.

same devil. Schopenhauer, however, gave them hell, but not in a public forum – he left that to his followers – but in a letter to Frauenstädt. Both Cornill and Taillandier were "blockheads," and "only such blockheads could believe that the spirit of my thought did not observe the simplest of all logical laws, the law of contradiction, or that one could work one's entire life on a system without having a clear image before one's eyes through which the possibility of all contradictions falls away."[43] The failure to grasp the unity of his philosophy, the harmony between his philosophy and the world, became for Schopenhauer the sure sign that one lacked the ability to comprehend his thought. But it was not so much the inability to understand his thought that Schopenhauer condemned as it was how this failure was expressed. If he judged that his critic did so to advance a career, as a means to serve self-interest rather than the truth, then Schopenhauer lost what little philosophical equanimity he possessed. The problem was that he sensed self-serving ends behind the complaints of almost all of his critics. The only exception to this seems to be Becker, who rigorously challenged Schopenhauer's views. Even Frauenstädt, his arch-evangelist, suffered when the philosopher sensed self-interested ends to his challenges. Schopenhauer failed to even consider the possibility that his own commitment to the truth was self-serving. He was so convinced of the truth of his views that an attack on his philosophy was an assault on truth itself.

As much as criticisms by professors of philosophy irritated Schopenhauer, at another level they pleased him. The conspiracy of silence was broken, and bad press was better than no press at all. At least he was being recognized and judged to be significant enough to refute. He also hoped that eventually there would be members of the academy who lived for rather than by philosophy and that these lovers of the truth would find their beloved in his philosophy. When Franz Peter Knooth, theologist and professor of philosophy in Bonn, and G. W. Körber, a *Privatdozent* at Breslau, lectured on his philosophy in 1857, the philosopher believed that academia might one day transform itself. Nevertheless, Schopenhauer recognized that the broad basis of his fame was the educated public, and if members of the philosophy trade noticed him only to condemn him, the genie was out of the bottle. For the time being, he reflected, "After 35 long

---

[43] Schopenhauer, *Gesammelte Briefe*, p. 400, Schopenhauer to Becker, 4 August 1856.

years they [professors of philosophy] have hid my light under a bushel through their silence. Now they employ all of their powers to discredit me, so do [I. M.] Fichte, Michelet, Rosenkranz, Hoffman, Raumer in Erlangen, Ulrici, Bartholoméβ, etc., etc. – they have done the most for me. Now, good luck."[44]

The academy did not transform itself as Schopenhauer had hoped. There never was a school of Schopenhauerian philosophers as there were Kantians, Fichteans, Schellingites, Hegelians, Herbartians, and, later, Neo-Kantians.[45] Schopenhauer remained a philosophical outsider in academic philosophy, in professional philosophy, just as he currently remains as a figure in the philosophical canon, but hardly canonized. In part, this was due to that very work, *Parerga and Paralipomena*, which made him popular. Essays drawn from this work were widely published in Germany, Great Britain, France, Italy, and Russia. These essays, "Aphorisms on the Wisdom of Life," "Essay on Spirit Seeing," "Transcendental Speculation on the Apparent Deliberateness in the Fate of Individuals," the notorious "On Women," and selections from his principal work such as "Metaphysics of Sexual Love" proved very popular and helped make him one of the most widely read philosophers of recent times. The essays did not contain his philosophy proper and were lacking the rigor and argumentation used to establish his basic and most significant philosophical views. For many professional philosophers, Schopenhauer was recognized as a great stylist, a social critic, and a keen observer of human behavior, but as also lacking a sustained and carefully articulated substantive philosophical perspective. Just about everyone had heard of Schopenhauer, but people tended to know, wrongly, more about his life than about his philosophy.[46]

---

[44] Ibid., p. 389, Schopenhauer to Frauenstädt, 21 March 1856. Karl Ludwig Michelet was a "young Hegelian" and a professor of philosophy in Berlin; Franz Hoffman was a professor at Würzburg and a follower of Franz von Baader; Friedrich von Raumer was a professor of history at Breslau, later at Berlin; Hermann Ulrici was a theistic opponent of Hegel and, along with I. M. Fichte, editor of the *Journal for Philosophy and Philosophical Critique* [*Zeitschrift für Philosophie und philosophische Kritik*]; and Christian-Jean-Guillaume was a French historian.

[45] In *German Pessimism & Indian Philosophy: A Hermeneutical Reading* (Frankfurt am Main: Ajanta Publications, 1986), Johann Joachim Gestering identifies Eduard von Hartmann, Philipp Mainländer, and Paul Deussen as "three Schopenhauerian thinkers," but not as Schopenhauerians; see, pp. 67-88.

[46] John E. Atwell observed that "Students of philosophy usually know much more about Schopenhauer than they know about his philosophy," *Schopenhauer: The Human Character*, p. 3.

The Comedy of Fame

Schopenhauer became a friend of a French painter with a German name in the winter of 1854. Jules [Isaac] Lunteschütz dined with the philosopher frequently, and he was his dining partner at the Englischer Hof when Schopenhauer silently observed Rossini. The Frenchman convinced the philosopher to sit for an oil painting, the first of four such portraits, but the only one for which Schopenhauer sat. The painting was displayed at the Frankfurt Exhibition, where the common sentiment was that the artist had masterfully captured his subject. Schopenhauer, Emden, and Kilzer dissented from this judgment, holding that the 1855 rendering failed to capture Schopenhauer's intelligent and intense spirit. Lunteschütz bore all the expenses for the project, and he engaged in the project purely on speculation. It is not known why the philosopher participated, but he may have been motivated by vanity and the hope that its display would advance his fame.

Lunteschütz speculated well, because he sold the painting for a hefty price to the wealthy landowner and Schopenhauer fanatic Carl Ferdinand Wiesike. Schopenhauer was astonished at his worshiper's devotion. "The unheard of thing," a thrilled Schopenhauer wrote to Frauenstädt, "is that he [Wiesike] told me and the painter quite seriously that he wanted to build a house to display the painting! – that will be the first chapel erected for me. *Recitativo*: Yes, Yes! Sarasto rules here."[47] The wealthy landowner also built an altar. Before the portrait, he placed a table holding all of Schopenhauer's books, as if they were holy scripture.

Wiesike's fanaticism was contagious. Admirers searched for the first edition of *The World as Will and Representation* as if it were the holy grail. Others traveled to Rudolstadt in search of the graffiti he left behind in the room in which he wrote his dissertation, treating this scribbling as if it were a "holy relic," as the philosopher once more told Frauenstädt. Lithographs were made of paintings, copies of daguerreotypes, photographs, and sketches of Schopenhauer circulated among the faithful, and it was as if his image became a fetish. The mania that surrounded the philosopher fed into his half-playful and half-serious appropriation

---

[47] Schopenhauer, *Gesammelte Briefe*, p. 370, Schopenhauer to Frauenstädt, 17 August 1855. Schopenhauer quotes, unattributed, from Mozart's *The Magic Flute*, I, 19 at the end of this quotation: "Sarastro rules here."

of religious terms to refer to his philosophy and its reception. Disciples, apostles, evangelists, and arch-evangelists served the metaphysical comfort offered by a secular prophet. Schopenhauer had always emphasized that the truths allegorically expressed in religion were philosophically demonstrated in his philosophy and that, like religion, his philosophy addressed the very human need to come to terms with living in a world steeped in pain and death. And, when it came to his theory of redemption, his doctrine of the denial of the will, where he had reached the limits of meaningful discourse, to give a hint, to indicate a direction for understanding, he had said that the denial of the will, salvation, the appearance of the will's freedom, was not a function of causality, but as Christians would say, was a "rebirth," proceeding from efficacious "grace"; a transcendental change coming immediately, out of the blue, like a bolt of lightning. At times, moreover, he sensed the same source for his more profound insights, which he said "Can be called a *revelation* and inspired by the spirit of *truth*. Even in the fourth book [of *The World as Will and Representation*] there are a few sections that could be regarded as inspired by the *Holy Ghost*."[48]

The ruckus of his fame did not serve to match Schopenhauer's sense of the dignity of his philosophy, nor did it serve to adequately compensate him for the many years of the neglect of his philosophy. He became a minor tourist attraction in Frankfurt. People celebrated his birthday and admirers would send him gifts. They would observe him from a distance during his daily walks with Atma, and poodles became popular in Frankfurt. He was observed dining at the Englischer Hof, where people could observe his famous capacity to eat and where they could hear his frequently loud, animated conversations with his tablemates. He believed, moreover, that his presence at the inn increased its business. People sought his autograph and the lucky ones would receive it, along with some appropriate remark. During a visit by the dramatist Christian Friedrich Hebbel, the philosopher spoke of the "comedy of my fame." His situation was analogous to that of a stage hand, he said, who is busily lighting the stage's candles and is seen scurrying off stage as the curtain rises.[49] And, if this remark shows Schopenhauer's ironic amusement at his fame, his

---

[48] Schopenhauer, *Manuscript Remains*, Vol. 4, p. 366/*Der handschriftliche Nachlaß*, Vol. 4, 2, p. 8.
[49] Schopenhauer, *Gespräche*, p. 306.

private diary records his bitter disappointment with its ultimate effect:
"When one has spent such a long life in insignificance, neglect, and
disdain, then they come at the end with the beating of drums and the
blowing of trumpets, and imagine that this is something."[50] And when,
unexpectedly, Schopenhauer received a letter from Ottilie von Goethe in
which she expressed her joy at observing his achievement of the goal he
had set fifty years earlier of becoming "the philosopher of the nineteenth
century," her old acquaintance from the Weimar years confided, "You
know that I was never very sociable, and I live now as secluded as ever.
A couple of friends come now and then in order to see how I am, and
in summer I receive many visits by strangers from all regions – *Visite di
curiosità*, as Michelangelo called it."[51]

In his letter of reply to Goethe's daughter-in-law, Schopenhauer also
lamented the common and sad experience of old age, that of watching
friends and contemporaries die. Two deaths hit the old philosopher hard.
He learned from Linder, his "Dr. *indefatigablis*," of the death of Heinrich
von Lowtzow, who died impoverished in miserable circumstances. The
baron who steered Schopenhauer into a disastrous investment in Mexican
bonds was regarded by the philosopher as a loyal and supportive friend. He
was deeply saddened by Lowtzow's death. But even more devastating for
the seventy-year-old philosopher was the death of his friend, the Jewish
lawyer Martin Emden. This time, Schopenhauer reported the death to
Linder: "Alas, today my best friend for many years, Dr. Emden has died.
I am in deep sadness, due to this irreparable loss."[52]

Schopenhauer's relationship to Emden was curious, as was his earlier
relationship to the Jewish Berlin student Josef Gans. He also respected
his "apostle" David Asher, who was active in his faith and in Jewish
social causes. Although it could be said that Schopenhauer's philosophy
expressed an abstract love for humankind and that he found it personally
difficult to have real love for particular people, it could also be said that he
had an abstract hatred for Judaism as well but he could value highly individual Jews. His contempt for Judaism was philosophical, directed at its
early biblical form, where it appeared to have no doctrine of immortality

---

[50] Schopenhauer, *Manuscript Remains*, Vol. 4, p. 517/*Der handschriftliche Nachlaß*, Vol. 4, 2,
p. 126.

[51] Schopenhauer, *Gesammelte Briefe*, p. 476, Schopenhauer to Ottilie von Goethe, 22 April 1860.

[52] Ibid., p. 437, Schopenhauer to Linder, 3 November 1858, and p. 383, Schopenhauer to
Linder, 11 February 1856 (Schopenhauer's response to Lowtzow's death).

for the faithful, a doctrine he thought essential for a religion. His disdain was enhanced by viewing Judaism as expressing realism and optimism, a false metaphysics and a pernicious attitude toward a world doomed to suffering and death. He found the creation story in Genesis to be absurd, because it posited a God summoning the world out of nothing and endorsing creation by calling it "good." The first claim was logically impossible, he argued, and the second was contradicted by the wretchedness of the world. Last, he argued that Judaism radically separated humans from other living beings by claiming that only humans were created in God's image.[53] In several regards, Schopenhauer's hatred of Judaism paralleled his hatred of Hegel's philosophy: a hatred of a false worldview whose doctrines actually made life worse for its followers. So great was his disgust for Judaism, however, that he would claim to smell a *"Foetur judaicus,"* a Judaic stench, to any view he sensed as descending from Judaism.[54] He would never reject a perspective due to its "Hegelian stench."

[53] Schopenhauer's attitudes toward Judaism and his view of Jews were colored by and helped to foster anti-Semitic trends in German cultural and political life. He argued that it was a mistake to simply think of Jews as a religious group: they should be considered a homeless, nationalistic race, whose monotheism was deeply ethnocentric. Although he decried the barbaric treatment of Jews in Europe, and although he argued they should be granted civil rights and be allowed to marry Christians, he also said that Jews should not be allowed to participate in the governance of Christian countries, that intermarriage would diminish the number of Jews, and that they live parasitically on other nations. Within a discussion of what he regarded as the worst side of religion, namely, that believers regard themselves as divinely justified in treating outsiders with extreme wickedness and merciless cruelty, Schopenhauer attempted to account for the historical basis of Exodus by appealing to the Roman historians Tacitus and Justin, both of whom mentioned that the Jews were despised. Schopenhauer conjectured that the fact that they were despised "may be due partly to the fact that they were the only people on earth who did not credit humans with an existence beyond this life and were, therefore, regarded as cattle, as dregs of humanity – but great masters of lies," *Parerga and Paralipomena*, Vol. 2, p. 357fn./*Sämtliche Werke*, Vol. 6, p. 379fn. Hitler, who claimed to have carried five volumes of Schopenhauer during the first world war, quoted the concluding phrase of this passage, "great masters of lies" twice in *Mein Kampf*, conveniently forgetting that this remark was made in a context in which Schopenhauer was denouncing fanatical cruelty, such as that of "Christians against Hindus, Mohammedans, American natives, Negroes, Jews, heretics and others," ibid., Vol. 2, p. 358/ibid, Vol. 6, p. 379. Nevertheless, Schopenhauer concluded that this systematic cruelty resulted only from monotheistic religions, Judaism and its branches, Christianity and Islam, suggesting that Jewish monotheism was the source of its own woes. Wolfgang Weimer, "Der Philosoph und der Diktator: Arthur Schopenhauer und Adolf Hitler," *Schopenhauer-Jahrbuch*, Vol. 84 (2003), pp. 157–67 carefully analyzes Hitler's relationship to Schopenhauer.

[54] Schopenhauer also claimed to detect a *"foetor judaicus"* in Spinoza's philosophy. He had, however, great admiration for Spinoza himself, and praised the great monist for his intellect and integrity. He praised Spinoza for living for and not by philosophy, something Schopenhauer saw in Spinoza's willingness to grind lenses for a living instead of accepting an academic appointment, which, Spinoza himself believed, could have cost his intellectual freedom. He

Schopenhauer's friendship with Emden did nothing to alter his harsh attitude toward Judaism. The effects of his popularity, however, may have moved him to alter his view of women. The old misogynist became enchanted by the twenty-six-year-old Elisabeth Ney, who came to Frankfurt to carve Schopenhauer's bust. The vivacious and intelligent sculptress impressed the philosopher by her artistic talents, and despite the fact that she was a buxom blonde and not a brunette, he was delighted when the grandniece of Marshal Michel Ney (who was executed at Waterloo) sent the old man a photograph of her standing by the bust as it was on display in Hannover, where she went to sculpt King Georg V. Schopenhauer's close association with Ney, along with the number of women who were keen to discuss his philosophy, may have led the philosopher to waver in his belief that women lacked the intellect and objectivity to meaningfully engage in science or philosophy. Malwida von Meysenbug, Wagner's friend and an acquaintance of Nietzsche, gave hearsay evidence for this possibility by reporting that a female friend told her that the old philosopher said to her, "Oh, I have still not said my final word about women."[55] If Schopenhauer did change his mind about women, he did not live to publish his final words on the subject. He just left Meysenbug's friend with the tantalizing possibility that his view would change, telling her that when a woman succeeds in raising herself above the crowd, she grows ceaselessly and greater than a man.

No Will, No Representation, No World

Schopenhauer enjoyed relatively good health in his later years, the product, he held, of continued movement and fresh air. He continued his daily walks, no matter the weather. To an ailing Doβ he dispensed advice: "Go walking daily, quickly for 2 hours, that will help you more than all baths and it costs nothing. Without my promenades, I would not be at 72 years so perfectly healthy, hale and hearty, as I am and as I remain."[56] He

also admired Spinoza's commitment to the truth of his views, which led to his expulsion from the synagogue. Nevertheless, Schopenhauer decried what he regarded as Spinoza's optimistic pantheism and his deification of the world by calling it "God." Indeed, he attributed almost all of the defects in Spinoza's philosophy to the unconscious intrusion of Jewish theology into his thoughts; see, for example, *Parerga and Paralipomena*, Vol. 1, pp. 70–74, esp. p. 73/ *Sämtliche Werke*, Vol. 5, pp. 76–81, esp. p. 78.

[55] Schopenhauer, *Gespräche*, p. 376.

[56] Schopenhauer, *Gesammelte Briefe*, p. 472. Schopenhauer to von Doβ, 1 March 1860.

took great pride in his ability to read without glasses and his well-known appetite persisted until the end. He continued to blow his flute daily, making sure that he had a proper night's rest. When Doβ told his "master" that his life was so hectic, he had to sacrifice sleep to read, Schopenhauer advised against such a practice: "Sleep is the source of all health and energy, even of the intellectual sort. I sleep 7, often 8 hours, sometimes 9."[57] The well-rested peripatetic remained intellectually alive; reading, corresponding with his disciples and admirers, and adding reflections to his manuscript books, material for future publications. Just three weeks before his death, Schopenhauer wrote a lucid letter to two military cadets, carefully explaining how their worry that the denial of will entailed the end of the world involved an "amphiboly of concepts."[58] He prepared a third edition of his principal work and Brockhaus eagerly published it (1859). *The World as Will and Representation* had finally become a "good deal" for the Leipzig publishing house. Schopenhauer tried to arrange with Brockhaus the publication of his collected works, but with his books held by six publishers, the legal complexities prevented this project during the philosopher's life. It would not be until 1873 that Frauenstädt edited and Brockhaus published a six-volume *Collected Works*.[59] A short time before Schopenhauer's death, the second edition of his *The Two Fundamental Problems of Ethics* appeared in 1860, and in the preface to the second edition, the philosopher was still cursing those he believed wronged him by not awarding him the gold medal for his essay on morality.

Although the old Schopenhauer enjoyed relatively good health, this is not to say that he escaped the Buddha's "evil" of old age. In the mid-1850s, he developed rheumatism in his feet, which he treated with brandy and salt. His hearing continued to decline, a problem that plagued him as a youth. By 1823 he lost hearing in his left ear, and by 1856 he was suffering hearing loss in his good ear. He stopped attending the theater and only attended farces. He feared that ultimately he would only be able to attend operas, a prospect that distressed him. Oddly, the philosopher who was especially sensitive to noise and railed against it in "On Din and Noise" in the second volume of *Parerga and Paralipomena* did not

---

[57] Ibid., p. 425, Schopenhauer to von Doβ, 4 March 1858.
[58] Ibid., pp. 482–3, Schopenhauer to Sikič and Schramek, 1 September 1860.
[59] Frauenstädt's *Arthur Schopenhauer's Sämmtliche Werke* is the ancestor of Hübscher's historical and critical edition of the *Sämtliche Werke*.

view his immunity to cracking whips, barking dogs, hammering, and banging, which had been "throughout my life a daily torment to me," as compensation for the loss of the theater.[60] In 1860, he moved from Schönen Aussicht 17 to 16, a ground floor apartment, out of fear that he could not move quickly enough to escape fire.

In April 1860, as he returned home from the Englischer Hof, he found it difficult to walk at his normal brisk pace, and he suffered shortness of breath and heart palpitations. These symptoms persisted through the summer. The obstinate philosopher paid no heed to his doctor or his friends' advice to alter his lifestyle, except to cut short his daily walks. On 9 September he became extremely ill with "inflammation of the lungs," and he thought that he would die. But in a few days, he recovered sufficiently to leave his bed and to entertain visitors. Gwinner was the last of Schopenhauer's friends to record his visits with the dying philosopher.[61] On 19 September, Gwinner visited his hero for the last time. Although the philosopher complained about palpitations and spoke in hushed tones, the two men talked until twilight.

Gwinner and Schopenhauer discussed Baader's commentary on Saint-Martin's writings and the significance of Jakob Böhme. The philosopher was reading Isaac D'Israeli's *Curiosities of Literature* (1834) and joked that he could have almost been included in the author's discussion of the secret history of authors who had ruined their booksellers. He expressed concern that he would die before he was able to include some important additions to *Parerga and Paralipomena*, and he expressed pride in the fact that additions he made to *The World as Will and Representation* were as fresh and flowed with the same vivacity as his early writings, but with even greater clarity. The philosopher who always held that his philosophy provided metaphysical comfort for his readers expressed the hope that in an age suffering a loss of faith, his irreligious doctrines would fill this void and become the source of inner peace and satisfaction.

The philosopher who wrote so powerfully, extensively, and profoundly on death faced his own demise well. In a soft voice and in poignant terms, he told Gwinner "That soon his body would be gnawed by worms did not anger him. On the contrary, he thought with horror on how his spirit

---

[60] Schopenhauer, *Parerga and Paralipomena*, Vol. 2, p. 643/*Sämtliche Werke*, Vol. 6, p. 679.

[61] See Gwinner, *Arthur Schopenhauer aus personlichem Umgange dargestellt*, pp. 195–204, for an account of Schopenhauer's final days and funeral.

would be abused by the hands of 'professors of philosophy.'"[62] He told his old friend that he would die with a clear intellectual conscience and that "it would only be a blessing for him to attain absolute nothingness, but unfortunately death offered no such prospect."[63] It is not clear whether Schopenhauer was joking with this last remark, whether Gwinner misreported it, or whether the philosopher had forgotten that he had already argued against some "absolute nothing," a *nihil negativum*, in the concluding section of the first edition of his principal work.

Gwinner would never again see the living philosopher. On 20 September, the philosopher fell after rising from his bed and absorbed a nasty blow to his forehead. Nevertheless, he slept well that night, and arose from his bed the next morning without incident. He followed his daily practice of washing with cold water and taking breakfast. The maid opened the windows to Schopenhauer's room, letting in the fresh air the philosopher viewed as so conducive to his health. She left the room a few minutes before Schopenhauer's doctor arrived. The fresh air failed the old man, who was found dead, slumped in the corner of the sofa. He appeared as if he had fallen asleep. There were no signs of agony. The day Schopenhauer died, 21 September 1860, was a Friday, the same day of the week on which he was born.

No autopsy was conducted on Schopenhauer's body, and his corpse, crowned with a wreath of laurel leaves, lay longer than was customary in the cemetery's mortuary (the philosopher feared being buried alive). With the exception of the laurel crown, all of this was done according to Schopenhauer's directions. On a rainy Wednesday, 26 September a small private funeral was conducted to lay the philosopher in a grave marked by a flat, dark marble slab that bore simply the name "Arthur Schopenhauer." Becker, Kilzer, Hornstein, Gwinner, and a Lutheran minister, Dr. Basse, accompanied Schopenhauer's decaying corpse to the graveyard (like his idealist hero George Berkeley, Schopenhauer knew that five days in the mortuary would provide olfactory proof of death). The minister delivered an evangelical service. Gwinner gave a brief and heartfelt eulogy. Schopenhauer's first biographer praised the philosopher's unswerving commitment to the truth, the loneliness of his pursuit of that coy mistress, and Schopenhauer's fervent desire to deserve the inheritance that

[62] Ibid., p. 197.
[63] Ibid., p. 200.

enabled him to pursue his calling without being hampered by the burdens of the world. Gwinner noted that the laurel leaves that crowned Schopenhauer's brow had come late in life, a confirmation of his unshakeable certainty in his destiny. Gwinner closed his oration with a quotation that would have pleased the philosopher: "Great is the power of truth and it will be victorious."[64] This quotation from the book of Ezra had served as the motto for *The Two Fundamental Problems of Ethics*, the second edition of which appeared a few weeks before its author's death.

The philosopher of will and of compassion had provided his own reflection on his life a few years earlier, one delivered from the perspective of a life lived rather than from a perspective of a life observed, like Gwinner's eulogy. "[I have always hoped to die easily]," Schopenhauer reflected in his private diary; "for whoever has been lonely all his life will be a better judge than others of this solitary business. Instead of going out amid the nonsense and foolishness calculated for the impoverished capacity of human bipeds, I will end joyfully conscious of returning to the place where I started out so highly endowed and of having fulfilled my mission."[65] Schopenhauer had returned home.

[64] Ibid., p. 203.

[65] Schopenhauer, *Manuscript Remains*, Vol. 4, p. 517/*Der handschriftliche Nachlaß*, Vol. 4, 2, p. 127.

Works Cited

Allison, Henry. *Kant's Theory of Freedom.* Cambridge: Cambridge University Press, 1993.

Ameriks, Karl. *The Cambridge Companion to German Idealism.* Cambridge: Cambridge University Press, 2000.

Anquetil-Duperron, Abraham Hyacinthe (trans.). *Oupnek'hat (id est, secretum tegendum)* . . . , 2 vols. Argentorati: Levrault, 1801.

Anscombe, G. E. M. "Modern Moral Philosophy," *Philosophy*, Vol. 33 (1958): 1–19.

Apel, Johan August and Friedrich Laun (eds). *Das Gespensterbuch.* Leipzig: G. J. Göschen, 1811-17.

App, Urs. "Notes and Excerpts by Schopenhauer Related to Volumes 1–9 of the Asiatick Researches," *Schopenhauer-Jahrbuch*, Vol. 79 (1998): 1–33.

———. "Notizen Schopenhauer zu Ost-, Nord-und Südostasien vom Sommersemester 1811," *Schopenhauer-Jarhbuch*, Vol. 84 (2003): 21–39.

———. "Schopenhauer's Initial Encounter with Indian Thought," *Schopenhauer-Jahrbuch*, Vol. 87 (2006): 35–76.

———. "Schopenhauers Begegnung mit dem Buddhismus," *Schopenhauer-Jahrbuch*, Vol. 79 (1998): 11–33.

Asendorf, Kurt. "Altes und Neues zur Schopenhauer-Genealogie," *Schopenhauer-Jahrbuch*, Vol. 69 (1988): 609–13.

Asher, David. *Offenes Sendschreiben an den hochgelehrten Herrn Dr. Arthur Schopenhauer.* Leipzig: Dyk, 1855.

———. "Schopenhauer and Darwin," *Journal of Anthropology*, Vol. 1 (1866): 312–32.

Atwell, John E. *Ends and Principles in Kant's Moral Thought.* Dordrecht: Martinus Nijhoff, 1986.

———. *Schopenhauer on the Character of the World: The Metaphysics of the Will.* Berkeley: University of California Press, 1995.

———. *Schopenhauer: The Human Character.* Philadelphia: Temple University Press, 1990.

Bachmann, C. F. "Idealismus," in *Allgemeine Encyklopädie der Wissenschaft und Künste.* Leipzig: Brockhaus, 1838.

Bähr, Carl Georg. *Die Schopenhauer'sche Philosophie in ihren Grundzügen dargestellt und kritisch beleuhtet.* Dresden: Rudolf Kuntze, 1857.

Bartholmèβ, Christian. "Herbart et Schopenhauer," in *Histoire critique des doctrines religieuses de la philosophie monderne*. Paris: Meyrueis, 1855.

Baumgarten, Alexander Gottlieb. *Metaphysica*. Magdeburg: Hemmerde, 1757.

Beck, Lewis White. "From Leibniz to Kant," in *The Age of German Idealism*, eds. Robert C. Solomon and Kathleen M. Higgins. London/New York: Routledge, 1993.

Beneke, Friedrich Eduard. "Antwort des Rezensensenten," *Intelligenblatt der Jenaischen Allgemeinen Litteratur-Zeitung*, No. 10 (February 1821).

————. *Neue Grundlegung zur Metaphysik*. Berlin: Mittler und Sohn, 1822.

————. Review of *Die Welt als Wille und Vorstellung*, in *Jenaische Allgemeine Litteratur-Zeitung*, Nos. 226–9 (December 1820); reprinted in the *Sechstes Jahrbuch der Schopenhauer-Gesellschaft* (1917): 118–49.

Berger, Douglas L. *The Veil of Māyā: Schopenhauer's System and Early Indian Thought*. Binghamton, NY: Global Academic Publishing, 2004.

Bergmann, Ulrike. *Johanna Schopenhauer: 'Lebe und sei so glücklich als du kannst.'* Leipzig: Reclam, 2002.

Birnbacher, Dieter. "Induktion oder Expression?" *Schopenhauer-Jahrbuch*, Vol. 69 (1988): 7–40.

————. "Schopenhauer und die ethische problem des Selbstmordes," *Schopenhauer-Jahrbuch*, Vol. 66 (1985): 115–30.

Bloch, Iwan. "Schopenhauer's Krankheit im Jahre 1823," *Medizinische Welt* (1906).

Boas, Elizabeth. "Wieland's *Musarion* and the Rococo Verse Narrative," in *Periods in German Literature*, ed. James M. Ritchie, Vol. 2. London: Wolff, 1968,

Bohlen, Peter von. *Die Genesis historisch-kritisch erläutert*. Königsberg: Bornträger, 1835.

Brahn, Max. *Arthur Schopenhauer Briefwechsel und andere Dokumente*. Leipzig: Insel, 1911.

Breazeale, Daniel. "Fichte and Schelling: The Jena Period," in *The Age of German Idealism*, eds. Robert C. Solomon and Kathleen M. Higgins. London: Routledge, 1993.

Bridgwater, Patrick. *Arthur Schopenhauer's English Schooling*. London/New York: Routledge, 1988.

Büch, Gabriele. *Alle Leben ist Traum: Adele Schopenhauer, eine Biographie*. Berlin: Aufbau Taschenbuch Verlag, 2002.

Büchner, Ludwig. *Kraft und Stoff*. Frankfurt: Meidinger Sohn & Comp., 1855.

Burckhardt, Jacob. *Weltgeschichtliche Betractungen*. Stuttgart: Kröner, 1955.

Busch, Hugo. *Das Testament Arthur Schopenhauer*. Wieshaden: Brockhaus, 1950.

Bykhovshy, Bernard. *Schopenhauer and the Grounds of Existence*, trans. Philip Moral. Amsterdam: Gruner, 1984.

Cassina, Ubaldo. *Analytischer Versuch über das Mitleiden*, trans. K. F. Pokkels. Hannover: Ritscher, 1790.

Cartwright, David E. "Compassion and Solidarity with Sufferers: The Metaphysics of *Mitleid*," *European Journal of Philosophy*, Vol. 16, No. 2 (2008): 292–310.

————. "Locke as Schopenhauer's (Kantian) Philosophical Ancestor," *Schopenhauer-Jahrbuch*, Vol. 84 (2003): 147–56.

_____. "Nietzsche's Use and Abuse of Schopenhauer's Moral Philosophy," in *Willing and Nothingness: Schopenhauer as Nietzsche's Educator*, ed. Christopher Janaway. Oxford: Clarendon Press, 1998.

_____. "Reversing Silenus' Wisdom," *Nietzsche-Studien*, Vol. 20 (1991): 309–13.

_____. "Schopenhauer on Suffering, Death, Guilt, and the Consolation of Metaphysics," in *Schopenhauer: New Essays in Honor of His 200th Birthday*, ed. Eric von Luft. Lewiston, NY: Edwin Mellen Press, 1988.

_____. "Schopenhauer's Narrower Sense of Morality," in *The Cambridge Companion to Schopenhauer*, ed. Christopher Janaway. Cambridge: Cambridge University Press, 1999.

_____. "The Last Temptation of Zarathustra," *Journal of the History of Philosophy*, Vol. 31 (1993): 49–69.

_____. "Two Senses of 'Thing-In-Itself' in Schopenhauer's Philosophy," *Idealistic Studies*, Vol. 31 (2001): 31–53.

Chalybäus, Heinrich Moritz. *Ethik über die Familie, den Staat und die religiöse Sitte*, 2 vols. Leipzig: Brockhaus, 1850.

Claudius, Matthias. *Asmus omnia sua portans, oder sämtliche Werke des Wandsbecker Bothen*. Hamburg: Bode et al., 1775–90.

_____. *An meinen Sohn H.* Hamburg: Perthes, 1799.

Cornill, Adolf. *Arthur Schopenhauer, als Uebergangsformation von einer idealistischen in eine realistischen Weltanschauung*. Heidelberg: I. C. B. Mohr, 1856.

Darwin, Charles. *On the Origin of Species by Means of Natural Selection, or the Preservation of Favored Races in the Struggle for Life*. London: John Murray, 1859.

_____. *The Descent of Man, and Selection in Relation to Sex*, 2 vols. London: John Murray, 1874.

_____. *The Expression of the Emotions in Man and Animals*. Chicago: University of Chicago Press, 1965.

De Cian, Nicoletta and Marco Segla, "What Is Will?" *Schopenhauer-Jahrbuch*, Vol. 83 (2002): 13–42.

Decher, Friedhelm. "Das bessere Bewuβtsein: Zur Funktion eines Begriff in Genese der Schopenhauerschen Philosophie," *Schopenhauer-Jahrbuch*, Vol. 77 (1996): 65–83.

Deetjen, Werner. "Aus dem Weimarer Schopenhauer-Kreise," *Jahrbuch der Schopenhauer-Gesellschaft*, Vol. 12 (1925): 96–100.

Descartes, René. "Meditations on First Philosophy," in *The Philosophical Works of Descartes*, trans. E. S. Haldane and G. R. T. Ross, Vol. 1. Cambridge: Cambridge University Press, 1972.

Deussen, Paul. "Schopenhauers Leben," *Sechstes Jahrbuch der Schopenhauer-Gesellschaft*, Vol. 6 (1917):3–46.

Dorguth, Friedrich. *Kritik des Idealismus und Materialismus zur Grundlage des apodiktischen Realrationalismus*. Magdeburg: Heinrichshofen, 1837.

_____. *Vermischte Bemerkungen ueber die Philosophie Schopenhauers, Ein Brief an den Meister*. Magdeburg: Heinrichshofen, 1852.

Dürr, Thomas. "Schopenhauers Grundlegung der Willensmetaphysik," *Schopenhauer-Jahrbuch*, Vol. 84 (2003): 91–119.

Eckermann, Johann Peter. *Gespräche mit Goethe in den letzten Jahren seines Lebens*, ed. Heinrich Hubert Houben. Leipzig: Klinkhardt & Biermann, 1909.

Erdmann, Johann Eduard. *Entwicklung der deutschen Spekulation seit Kant*. Leipzig: Vogel, 1853.

————. "Schopenhauer and Herbart," *Zeitschrift für Philosophie und philosophische Kritik*. Neue Folge, Vol. 21 (1852).

Fichte, Immanuel Hermann. *System der Ethik*. Leipzig: Dyk, 1850–53.

Fichte, Johann Gottlieb. *Das System der Sittenlehre nach den Principien der Wissenschaftslehre*. Jena/Leipzig: Gabler, 1798.

————. *Die Wissenschaftslehre in ihrem allgemeinen Umrisse dargestellt*. Berlin: J. E. Hitzig, 1810.

————. *Gesamtausgabe der Bayerischen Akademie der Wissenschaften*, 24 vols, ed. Lauth, Fuchs, Gliwitzky, Stuggart/Bad Cannstatt: Frommann, 1964–.

————. *Grundlage des Naturrechts nach Principien der Wissenschaftslehre*. Jena/Leipzig: Christian Ernest Gabler, 1796.

————. "Review of Aenesidemus," in *Fichte: Early Philosophical Writings*, ed. and trans. Daniel Breazeale. Ithaca, NY: Cornell University Press, 1988.

————. *The Science of Knowledge*, trans. Peter Heath and John Lachs. Cambridge: Cambridge University Press, 1982.

Fiebiger, Otto. "Neues über Friedrich Müller von Gerstenbergk," *Jahrbuch der Schopenhauer-Gesellschaft*, Vol. 12 (1922): 68–95.

Figl, Johann. "Nietzsches Begegnung mit Schopenhauers Hauptwerk. Unter Heranziehung eines frühen veröffentlichten Exzerptes," in *Schopenhauer, Nietzsche, und die Kunst*, ed. Wolfgang Schirmacher. Vienna: Passagen Verlag, 1991.

Fischer, Kuno. *Schopenhauers Leben, Werke, und Lehre*. Zweite neu bearbeitete und vermehrte Auflage. Heidelberg: Winter, 1898.

Flourens, Marie-Jean-Pierre. *De la vie et de l'intelligence*. Paris: Garnier frères, 1858.

Foot, Phillippa. "Morality as a System of Hypothetical Imperatives," *Philosophical Review*, Vol. 8 (1972): 305–16.

Fortlage, Carl. *Genetische Geschichte der Philosophie seit Kant*. Leipzig: Brockhaus, 1852.

Franks, Paul. "All or Nothing: Systematicity and Nihilism in Jacobi, Reinhold, and Maimon," in *The Cambridge Companion to German Idealism*, ed. Karl Ameriks. Cambridge: Cambridge University Press, 2000.

Frauenstädt, Julius *Briefe über die Schopenhauer'sche Philosophie*. Leipzig: F. A. Brockhaus, 1854.

————. *Das Sittliche Leben, Ethische Studien*. Leipzig: Brockhaus, 1866.

————. *Der Materialismus. Seine Wahrheit und sein Irrthum. Eine Erwiderungen auf Dr. Louis Buchner's "Kraft und Stoff."* Leipzig: F. A. Brockhaus, 1856.

————. Review of *Parerga and Paralipomena* in *Blätter für litterarische Unterhaltung*, No. 9 (March 1852): 677–80.

Feuerbach, Ludwig. *Das Wesen des Christenthums*. Leipzig: Otto Wigand, 1841.

Freud, Sigmund. *Civilization and Its Discontents*, trans. James Strachery. New York: W. W. Norton, 1961.

_____. *The Future of an Illusion*, trans. James Strachery. New York: W. W. Norton, 1963.

Frommann, Hermann. *Arthur Schopenhauer, Drei Vorlesungen*. Jena: Friedrich Frommann, 1872.

Gestering, Johann Joachim. *German Pessimism and Indian Philosophy: A Hermeneutic Reading*. Frankfurt am Main: Ajanta Publications, 1986.

Gilleir, Anke. *Johanna Schopenhauer und die Weimarer Klassik: Betrachtungen über die Selbstpositionierung weiblichen Schreibens*. Hildesheim: Olms-Weidmann, 2000.

Gillies, A. "Herder and Goethe," in *German Studies: Presented to Leonard Ashley Willoghby by Pupils, Colleagues and Friends*. Oxford: Basil Blackwell, 1952.

Goethe, Johann Wolfgang von. "Lähmung," in *Goethes Gedichte*, Part 2. Stuttgart/Tübingen: J. G. Cotta 1815.

_____. *Letters from Goethe*, trans. M. von Herzfeld and C. Melvilsym. Edinburgh: Edinburgh University Press, 1957.

_____. *Sämtliche Werke*, 45 vols., ed. Peter Boerner. Munich: Deutscher Taschenbuch Verlag, 1961–3.

_____. *Tagebücher 1810–1832*, ed. Peter Boerner. Munich: Deutscher Taschenbuch Verlag, 1963.

_____. *The Autobiography of Johann Wolfgang von Goethe*, trans. John Oxenford. Chicago: The University of Chicago Press, 1974.

_____. *Theory of Colours*, trans. Charles Eastlake. London: 1840.

Goldschmidt, Hermann Levin. *Pestalozzis unvollendete Revolution: Philosophie dank der Schweiz von Rousseau bis Turel*. Vienna: Passagen, 1995.

Gracián, Baltasar, *Gracians Handorakel und Kunst der Weltklugheit*, trans. Arthur Schopenhauer. Leipzig: F. A. Brockhaus, 1862.

Gräf, Hans Gerhard. *Goethes Ehe in Briefen*. Leipzig: Rütten & Loening, 1972.

Gruber, Robert, "Die Familie Schopenhauer und der Ausgleich Muhls," in *Suddeutsche Monatshefte*, Vol. 30 (May 1933): 492–505.

Guthke, Karl S. "The Deaf Musician: Arthur Schopenhauer Reads Richard Wagner," *Harvard Magazine*, Vol. 99, No. 1 (Sept.-Oct. 1996).

Guyer, Paul. "Schopenhauer, Kant, and the Methods of Philosophy," in *The Cambridge Companion to Schopenhauer*, ed. Christopher Janaway. Cambridge: Cambridge University Press, 1999.

Guyon, Jeanne-Marie Bouvier de la Motte. *La vie de Madame de la Motte Guyon*. Cologne: J. de la Pierre, 1720.

_____. *Les opuscules spirituels*, new ed., 2 vols. Paris: Libaires associés, 1790.

Gwinner, Wilhelm. *Arthur Schopenhauer aus persönlichem Umgange dargestellt: Blick sein Leben, seine Charakter und sein Leben*, ed. Charlotte von Gwinner. Leipzig: Brockhaus, 1922.

_____. *Schopenhauers Leben*, 3rd ed. Leipzig: Brockhaus, 1910.

Haffmans, Gerd (ed.). *Über Arthur Schopenhauer*. Zurich: Diogenes, 1977.

Hamlyn, D. W. "Why Are There Phenomena?" in *Zeit der Ernte: Studien zum Stand der Schopenhauer-Forschung. Festschrift für Arthur Hübscher zum 85. Geburtstag*, ed. Wolfgang Schirmacher. Stuttgart/Bad Cannstatt: Frommann-Holzboog, 1982.

Hardy, Robert Spence. *A Manuel of Buddhism, in Its Modern Development*. London: Partridge and Oakey, 1853.

―――. *Eastern Monachism: An Account of the Orgins, Laws, Discipline of the Order of Mendicants Founded by Gôtama Buddha*. London: Partridge and Oakey, 1850.

Hartenstein, Gustav. Unsigned review of the second edition of *Die Welt als Wille und Vorstellung*, in *Leipziger Repertorium der deutschen und ausländischen Litteratur*, Vol. 3 (1844): 91–3.

Hartmann, Eduard von. *Die Gefühlsmoral*, ed. Jean-Claude Wolf. Hamburg: Felix Meiner, 2006.

―――. *Philosophy of the Unconscious: Speculative Results According to the Inductive Method of Physical Science*, trans. WilliamCoupland. New York: Harcourt, Brace & Company, 1931.

―――. *Schelling's positive Philosophie als Einheit von Hegel und Schopenhauer*. Berlin: Otto Loewenstein, 1869.

Haβargen, Hermann. "Die Danziger Vorfahren Arthur Schopenhauers," in *Heimatblätter des Deutschen Heimatbundes*. Danzig, 1928.

Hecker, Jutta. *Wieland: Die Geschichte eines Menschen in der Zeit*. Stuttgart: Mellinger, 1971.

Hegel, Georg Wilhelm Friedrich. *Hegel's Logic*, trans. William Wallace. Oxford: Clarendon Press, 1975.

―――. *Hegel's Philosophy of Mind*, trans. William Wallace. Oxford: Clarendon Press, 1971.

―――. *Hegel's Philosophy of Nature*, trans. A. V. Miller. Oxford: Clarendon Press, 1970.

―――. *Phenomenology of Spirit*, trans. A. V. Miller. Oxford: Oxford University Press, 1981.

―――. *Philosophy of Right*, trans. T. M. Knox. Oxford: Oxford University Press, 1967.

―――. *Reason in History*, trans. Robert S. Hartman. Indianapolis/New York: Bobbs-Merrill, 1953.

―――. *Science of Logic*, 2 vols., trans. W. H. Johnson and L. G. Struthers. London: Allen and Unwin, 1929.

―――. *The Letters*, trans. Clark Butler and Christiane Seiler. Bloomington, IN: Indiana University Press, 1984.

―――. *The Philosophy of History*, trans. J. Sibree. New York: Dover, 1956.

Heisenberg, Werner. "Die Goethesche und die Newtonsche Farbenlehre im Lichte der modernen Physik," in *Wandlungen in der Grundlagen der Naturwissenschaft*. Leipzig, 1943.

Helvétius, Claude-Adrien. *De l'espirt*, 2 vols. Paris: Durand, 1758.

Herbart, Johann Friedrich. *Hauptpuncte der Metaphysik*. Göttingen: Justus Friedrich Danckwerts, 1808.

―――. Review of *The World as Will and Representation* in *Hermes oder kritisches Jahrbuch der Litteratur*, No. 3, 1820; reprinted in *Sechstes Jahrbuch der Schopenhauer – Gesellschaft*, Vol. 6 (1917): 89–115.

Herder, Johann Gottfried, *Ideen zur Philosophie der Geschichte der Menschenheit*. Riga/Leipzig: Johann Friedrich Hartknoch, 1784–91.

———. *Verstand und Erfahrung. Ein Metakritik zur Kritik der reinen Vernunft*. Leipzig: Johann Friedrich Hartknock, 1799.

Herschel, John F. W. *A Treatise on Astronomy*, new ed. London: Longman, Rees, Orme, Brown, Green, and Longman, 1833.

Hillebrand, Karl. Review of Friedrich Nietzsche's "Schopenhauer als Erzieher," in the *Allgemeine Zeitung Augsburg* (18 December 1874).

Hobbes, Thomas. *Elementa philosophica de Cive*. Amsterdam: L. Elzevir, 1647.

———. *Leviathan, siva, De material, forma et poteste civitatis ecclesiasticae et civilis*. Amsterdam:L. Elzevir, 1670.

Hoffbauer, Johann Christoph. *Analytik der Urtheile und Schlüsse*. Halle: Schwetschke, 1792.

Hoffmann, Paul. "Schopenhauer und Hamburg," *Jahrbuch der Schopenhauer-Gesellschaft*, Vol. 19 (1932), pp. 207–51.

Holtman, Robert B. *The Napoleonic Revolution*. Philadelphia/New York/Toronto: Lippincott, 1967.

Horstmann, Rolf-Peter. "The Early Philosophy of Fichte and Schelling," in *The Cambridge Companion to German Idealism*, ed. Karl Ameriks. Cambridge: Cambridge University Press, 2000.

Hübscher, Arthur. "Adele an Arthur Schopenhauer. Unbekannte Briefe 1," *Schopenhauer-Jahrbuch*, Vol. 58 (1977): 133–86.

———. "Arthur Schopenhauer: Ein Lebensbild," in *Arthur Schopenhauer: Sämtliche Werke*, 7 vols., ed. Arthur Hübscher, Vol. 1. Mannheim: F. A. Brockhaus, 1988.

———. (ed.). *Arthur Schopenhauer: Gespräche*. Stuttgart/Bad Cannstatt: Frommann-Holzboog, 1971.

———. "Drei Tanten Schopenhauers," *Schopenhauer-Jahrbuch*, Vol. 61 (1980): 127–50.

———. "Ein vegessener Schulfreund Schopenhauers," *Schopenhauer-Jahrbuch*, Vol. 46 (1965): 130–52.

———. "Eine verschollene Arbeit Schopenhauers," *Schopenhauer-Jahrbuch*, Vol. 22 (1935): 239–441.

———. *Schopenhauer-Bibliographie*. Stuttgart/Bad Cannstatt: Frommann-Holzboog, 1981.

———. *Schopenhauer-Bildnisse: Eine Ikonographie*. Frankfurt am Main: Kramer, 1968.

———. *The Philosophy of Schopenhauer in Its Intellectual Context: Thinker against the Tide*, trans. Joachim Baer and David E. Cartwright. Lewiston, NY: Edwin Mellen Press, 1989.

———. "Zwei Hamburger Jugenfreunde," *Schopenhauer-Jahrbuch*, Vol. 51 (1970): 38.

Hühn, Lore. "Die intelligible Tat, zu einer Gemeinsamkeit Schellings und Schopenhauer," in *Selbstbesinnung der philosophischen Moderne*, eds. C. Iber and R. Pocai. Dartford: T. Junghans Verlag, 1998, 55–94.

Hume, David. *A Treatise of Human Nature*, 2 vols. London: 1739.

――――. *Dialogues Concerning Natural Religion*, 2nd ed. London: 1779.

――――. *Essays Moral, Political and Literary*. Indianapolis: Library Fund, 1987.

――――. *History of Great Britain from the Invasion of Julius Caesar to the Revolution of 1688*, 6 vols. London: Andrew Millar, 1754–62.

――――. "The Natural History of Religion," in *Four Dissertations*. London: A. Murray and Son, 1757.

Jacobi, Friedrich Heinrich. *David Hume über den Glauben oder Idealismus und Realismus. Ein Gespräche*. Breslau: Gottlieb Loewe, 1787.

――――. *Jacobi an Fichte*. Hamburg: Friedrich Perthes, 1799.

――――. *The Main Philosophical Writings and the Novel Allwill*, trans. and ed. George di Giovanni. Montreal: McGill–Queens University Press, 1994.

――――. *Von den Göttlichen Dingen und ihrer Offenbarung*. Leipzig: Fleischer d. Jung, 1811.

Jacquette, Dale. "Schopenhauer on the Ethics of Suicide," *Continental Philosophy Review*, Vol. 33 (2000): 43–58.

――――. "Schopenhauer's Circle and the Principle of Sufficient Reason," *Metaphilosophy*, Vol. 23 (1992): 279–87.

――――. *The Philosophy of Schopenhauer*. Chesham: Acumen, 2005.

Jaeger, Werner. *Paideia: The Ideals of Greek Culture*. Oxford: Oxford University Press, 1933–44.

Jakob, Ludwig Heinrich. *Grundriß der allgemeinen Logik*. Halle: Francke and Bispisch, 1788.

Janaway, Christopher. "Nietzsche, the Self, and Schopenhauer," in *Nietzsche and Modern German Thought*, ed. Keith Ansell-Pearson. New York: Routledge, 1991.

――――. *Self and World in Schopenhauer's Philosophy*. Oxford: The Clarendon Press, 1989.

――――. "Schopenhauer as Nietzsche's Educator," in *Willing and Nothingness: Schopenhauer as Nietzsche's Educator*, ed. Christopher Janaway. Oxford: The Clarendon Press, 1998.

――――. "Will and Nature," in *The Cambridge Companion to Schopenhauer*, ed. Christopher Janaway. Cambridge: Cambridge University Press, 1999.

Kamata, Yasuo. *Der junge Schopenhauer: Genese des Grundgedankens der Welt als Wille und Vorstellung*. Munich: Alber, 1988.

Kant, Immanuel. *Critique of Judgment*, trans. J. C. Meredith. Oxford: The Clarendon Press, 1952.

――――. *Critique of Practical Reason*, trans. Lewis White Beck. Indianapolis: Bobbs-Merrill, 1956.

――――. *Critique of Pure Reason*, trans. Paul Guyer and Allen W. Wood. Cambridge: Cambridge University Press, 1998.

――――. *Gesammelte Schriften*, ed. by the Prussian Academy. Berlin: Walter de Gruyter, 1902 –.

――――. *Groundwork for the Metaphysics of Morals*, trans. H. J. Paton. New York: Harper and Row, 1964.

_____. *Kant's Sämtliche Werke*, 12 vols., ed. Karl Rosenkranz and Schubert. Leipzig: Leopold Voss, 1838–42.

_____. *Logik*. Königsberg: Jäsche, 1800.

_____. *Prolegomena to Any Future Metaphysics*, trans. Lewis White Beck. Indianapolis: Bobbs-Merrill, 1950.

_____. *Träume eines Geistersehers, erlautert durch Träume der Metaphysik*. Königsberg: Johann Jakob Kanter, 1766.

_____. *Über die von der Königl. Akademie der Wissenschaften zu Berlin für das Jahr 1791 ausgesetzte Preisfrage: Welches sind die wirklichen Fortschritte, die die Metaphysik seit Leibnitzens und Wolf's Zeiten in Deutschland gemacht hat*. Königsberg: Goebbels and Unzer, 1804.

Kantorowiez, Hermann. "Schopenhauer's akademische Erfahrungen," *Frankfurter Zeitung*, 28 May 1929; excerpted in *Kantstudien*, Vol. 34, 516–17.

Kerner, Justinus. *Die Seherin von Prevost. Eröffnung über da innere Leben des Menschen and uber das Hereinragen einer Geisterwelt in die unsere*. Stuttgart: J. G. Cotta, 1837.

Kierkegaard, Søren. *Attack upon 'Christendom'*, trans. Walter Lowie. Boston: The Beacon Press, 1960.

_____. *The Journals of Kierkegaard*, trans. Alexander Dru. New York: Harper & Row, 1959.

Kiesewetter, Johann Gottfried Carl Christian. *Grundriß einer reinen allgemeinen Logik nach Kantischen Grundsätzen, zum Gebrauch für Vorlesungen*. Berlin: F. T. Lagarde, 1802/1806.

Kilpatrick, William. *The Education of Man – Aphorisms*. New York: Philosophical Library, 1951.

Knox, Vicesimus. *Liberal Education*. London: C. Dilly, 1788.

Köppen, Carl Friedrich. *Die Religion des Buddha und ihre Entstehung*. 2 vols. Berlin: Schneider, 1857–9.

Kosack, Carl Rudolf. *Beiträge zu einer systematischen Entwickelung der Geometrie aus der Anschauung*. Nordhausen: Eberhardtsche Buchdruckerei, 1852.

Koßler, Matthias. "Empirischer und intelligibler Charackter: Von Kant über Fries und Schelling zu Schopenhauer," *Schopenhauer-Jahrbuch* 76 (1995): 195–201.

Krause, Karl Christian Friedrich. *Anschauungen oder die Lehren und Entwürfe zur Höherbildung des Menschenlebens. Aus der handschriftlichem Nachlaß des Verfassers*, ed. Paul Hohfeld and August Wünsche. Leipzig,: Dieterische Verlagsbuchhandlung Theodor Weicher, 1891.

Krug, Wilhelm Traugott. Review of *Die Welt als Wille und Vorstellung* in *Leipziger Litteratur-Zeitung*, No. 21 (24 January 1821); reprinted in *Sechstes Jahrbuch der Schopenhauer-Gesellschaft* (1917): 158–75.

Kuehn, Manfred. *Kant: A Biography*. Cambridge: Cambridge University Press, 2001.

Lambert, Johann Heinrich. *Neues Organon, oder Gedanken über die Erforschung und Bezeichnung des Wahren und dessen Unsheidung vom Irrthum und Schein*. Leipzig: Wendler, 1764.

Lampert, Laurence. *Nietzsche's Teaching: An Interpretation of "*Thus Spoke Zarathustra." New Haven, CT: Yale University Press, 1986.

Lauxtermann, Paul F. H. "Hegel and Schopenhauer as Partisans of Goethe's Theory of Color," *Journal of the History of Ideas*, Vol. 50 (1990): 588–624.

———. *Schopenhauer's Broken World-View: Colours and Ethics between Kant and Goethe*. Dordrecht: Kluwer Academic Publishers, 2000.

Leibniz, Gottfried Wilhelm. *Epistolae ad Diversos, Theologici, Juridici, Medici, Philosophici, Mathematici, Historici, et Philologici*. Vol. 1. Bern: Christoph Breitkoph, 1734.

Leip, Hans. *Die Lady und die Admiral*. 1933.

Linder, Ernest Otto and Julius Frauenstädt. *Arthur Schopenhauer. Von ihm. Über ihn.* Berlin: A. W. Hayn, 1863.

Locke, John. *An Essay concerning Human Understanding, in Four Books*. 14th ed. London: S. Birt, 1753.

Lovejoy, Arthur O. "Schopenhauer as an Evolutionist," *Mind*, Vol. 21 (1911): 116.

Lukács, György, *The Destruction of Reason*, trans. Peter Palmer. London: Merlin, 1979.

Lütkehaus, Ludger (ed.), *Die Schopenhauers: Der Familien Briefwechsel von Adele, Arthur, Heinrich Floris und Johanna Schopenhauer*. Zurich: Haffmans Verlag, 1991.

Maass, Johann Gebhard Ehrenreich. *Grundriß der Logik zum, Gebrauche bei Vorlesungen*. Halle: Ruff, 1793.

Machtaler, Hildegard von. "Lorenz Meyers Tagebücher," *Schopenhauer-Jahrbuch*, Vol. 49 (1968) : 95–111.

Maimon, Salomon. *Versuch einer neuen Logik oder Theorie des Denkens*. Berlin: Felisch, 1794.

Magee, Bryan. *Misunderstanding Schopenhauer*. London: Institute of Germanic Studies, University of London, 1990.

———. *The Philosophy of Schopenhauer*. New York: Oxford University Press, 1997.

Majer, Friedrich. "Das Bhaguat-Geeta, oder Gespräche zwischen Kreeshna und Arjoon," in *Asiatisches Magazin*, Vols. 1 and 2 (1802).:412–453; 105–35.

———. *Zur Kulturgeschichte der Völker, historische Untersuchungen*. Leipzig: J. F. Hartknoch, 1798.

Malter, Rudolf. *Arthur Schopenhauer: Transzendental Philosophie und Metaphysik des Willens*. Stuttgart/Bad Cannstatt: Frommann, 1991.

———. *Der eine Gedanke: Hinführung zur Philosophie Arthur Schopenhauers*. Darmstadt: Wissenschaftliche Buchgesellschaft, 1988.

———. (ed.), *Faksimilenachdruck der I. Auflage der Welt als Wille und Vorstellungen*. Frankfurt am Main: Insel, 1987.

Mann, Thomas. *Schopenhauer*. Stockholm: Bermann-Fischer Verlag, 1938.

Mannion, Gerard. *Schopenhauer, Religion, and Morality: The Humble Path to Ethics*. Burlington, VT: Ashgate, 2003.

Martensen, Hans L. *Between Hegel and Kierkegaard: Hans L. Martensen's Philosophy of Religion*. trans., with an introduction by Curtis Thompson. Atlanta: Scholars Press, 1997.

Marx, Karl. *Capital*, trans. Samuel Moore and Edward Aueling, Vol. 1. New York: International Publishers, 1974.

McCarthy, John A. *Christoph Martin Wieland*. Boston: Twayne, 1979.

McCleland, Charles E. *State, Society, and University in Germany: 1700–1914*. Cambridge: Cambridge University Press, 1980.

McGill, V. J., *Schopenhauer: Pessimist and Pagan*. New York: Haskell House, 1971.

Mendelssohn, Moses. "Morgenstunden, oder Vorlesungen ueber das Dasein Gottes,".in *Gesammelte Schriften*, Vol. III/2. Leipzig : F. A. Brockhaus, 1843.

Muscheler, Karl-Heinz. *Die Schopenhauer-Marquet-Prozesse und das Preußische Recht*. Tübingen: J. C. B. Mohr, 1996.

Neeley, G. Steven. *Schopenhauer: A Consistent Reading*. Lewiston, NY: Edwin Mellen Press, 2003.

Nicholls, Moira. "The Influence of Eastern Thought on Schopenhauer's Doctrine of the Thing-in-Itself," in *The Cambridge Companion to Schopenhauer*, ed. Christopher Janaway. Cambridge: Cambridge University Press, 2000.

Nietzsche, Friedrich. *Beyond Good and Evil*, trans. Walter Kaufmann. New York: Vintage, 1966.

———. "David Strauss, the Confessor and Writer," in *Untimely Meditations*, trans. R. J. Hollingdale. Cambridge: Cambridge University Press, 1983.

———. *Daybreak: Thoughts on the Prejudices of Morality*, trans. R. J. Hollingsdale. Cambridge: Cambridge University Press, 1982.

———. *Human, All Too Human*, trans. R. J. Hollingdale. Cambridge: Cambridge University Press, 1986.

———. *Nietzsche: Werke in drei Banden*, Vol. 3, ed. Karl Schlechta. Munich: Hanser Verlag, 1954–6.

———. *Nietzsche: Kritische Gesamtausgabe*, Vol. 5, eds. G. Colli and M. Montinari. Berlin: de Gruyter, 1971.

———. *On the Genealogy of Morality*, trans. Maudemarie Clark and Alan Swensen. Indianapolis: Hackett, 1998.

———. "Schopenhauer as Educator," in *Untimely Meditations*, trans. R. J. Hollingdale. Cambridge: Cambridge University Press, 1983.

———. *The Gay Science*, trans. Walter Kaufmann. New York: Vintage, 1974.

Noack, Ludwig. *Schelling und die Philosophie der Romantik*, 2 vols. Berlin: Mittler, 1859.

Oettingen, Wolfgang von (ed.). "Aus Ottilie von Goethe's Nachlaß. Briefe von ihr und an sie 1806–1822," in *Schriften der Goethe-Gesellschaft*, Vol. 27, (1912).

———. (ed.). "Aus Ottilie von Goethes Nachlaß. Briefe von ihr und an sie bis 1833," in *Schriften der Goethe Gesellschaft*, Vol. 28 (1913).

Oxenford, John. "Iconoclasm in German Philosophy," *The Westminster Review* New Series III (1 April 1853): p. 388–407; reprinted in *Zwölftes Jahrbuch der Schopenhauer-Gesellschaft für die Jahre 1923–1925*.

Paul, Jean (Johann Paul Friedrich Richter). *Vorschule der Ästhetik*, 2 vols. Breslau: Josef Max und Komp, 1825.

Pinkard, Terry. *German Philosophy 1760–1860: The Legacy of Idealism*. Cambridge: Cambridge University Press, 2002.

_____. *Hegel: A Biography*. Cambridge: Cambridge University Press, 2000.

Platner, Ernst. *Philosophische Aphorismeus, nebst einigen Anleitungen zur philosophischen Geschichte*. Leipzig: Schwickert, 1782–4.

Plato. *The Collected Dialogues*, eds. Edith Hamilton and Huntington Cairns. Princeton, NJ: Princeton University Press, 1973.

Pleticha, H. (ed.), *Das Klassische Weimar: Texte und Zeugnisse*. Munich: Deutscher Taschenbuch Verlag 1983.

Polier, Louis Henri de. *Mythologie des Indous*. Rudolstadt/Paris: Schoel, 1809.

Räsänen, Petri. *Schopenhauer and Kant's Transcendental Idealism*. Tampere: Tampere University Press, 2005.

Rauschenberger, Walther. "Nachträge zu Schopenhauers Ahnentafel," *Jahrbuch der Schopenhauer-Gesellschaft*, Vol. 24 (1937) : 153–56.

_____. "Schopenhauers Ahnen," *Jahrbuch der Schopenhauer-Gesellschaft*, Vol. 21 (1934): 131–49.

Reimarus, Hermann Samuel. *Die Vernunftlehre, als eine Anweisung zum richtigen Gebrauch der Vernunft in der Erkenntniß der Wahrheit, aus zwoen ganz natürlichen Regeln der Einstimmung und des Widerspruch hergeleitet*, 5th ed. Hamburg: Bohn, 1790.

Reinhold, Carl Leonhard. *Briefe über die kantische Philosophie*. Leipzig: Georg Joachim Göschen, 1790

_____. *Ueber das Fundament des philosophischen Wissens*. Jena: Mauke, 1790; reprint, Hamburg: Felix Meiner, 1978.

_____. *Versuch einer Neuen Theorie des Menschlichen Vorstellungsvermögens*. Darmstadt: Wissenschftliche Buchgesellschaft, 1963: reprint of the 1781 edition, Widtmann and Mauke, Prague and Jena.

Riedinger, Franz. "Die Akten über Schopenhauers Doktorpromotion," *Jahrbuch der Schopenhauer-Gesellschaft*, Vol. 11 (1924): 98.

Rieff, Philip. *Freud: The Mind of the Moralist*. Chicago: University of Chicago Press, 1979.

Rosenkranz, Karl. *George Wilhelm Friedrich Hegels Leben*. Berlin: Duncker and Humbolt, 1844.

_____. "Zur Charakteristik Schopenhauer," *Deutsche Wochenschrift*, No. 22, ed. Karl Gödeke. Hannover: Rümpler, 1854.

Roy, Rām Mohan. *Translation of Several Principal Books, Passages, and Texts of the Vedas*. London: Parbury, Allen & Co., 1832.

Ruhl, Ludwig Sigismund. *Eine Groteske* .Cassel: Krieger, 1882.

Safranski, Rüdiger. "Hoch auf dem Berge und – entronnen! Schopenhauers bessere Bewußtsein: Ekstase des Sehers," *Lutherische Monatshefte*, Vol. 28 (1989): 267–71.

_____. *Schopenhauer and the Wild Years of Philosophy*, trans. Ewald Osers. Cambridge, MA: Harvard University Press, 1990.

Salaquarda, Jörg. "Der Antichrist," *Nietzsche Studien*, Vol. 2 (1973): 90–136.

Sartre, Jean-Paul. *Existentialism and Human Emotions*. New York: Citadel Press, 2000.

Schacht, Richard. *Nietzsche*. London: Routledge and Kegan Paul, 1983.

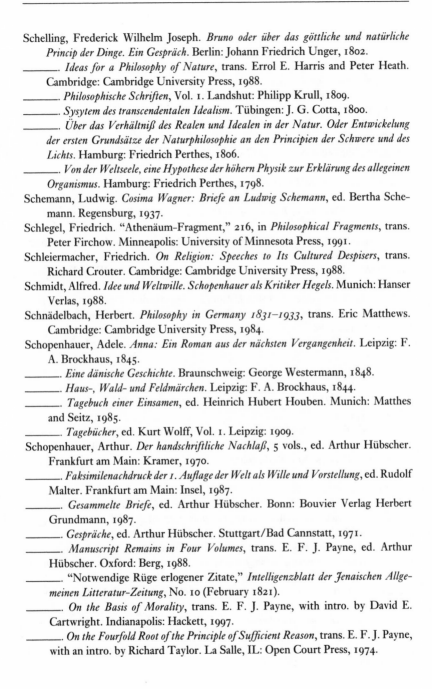

Schelling, Frederick Wilhelm Joseph. *Bruno oder über das göttliche und natürliche Princip der Dinge. Ein Gespräch.* Berlin: Johann Friedrich Unger, 1802.

———. *Ideas for a Philosophy of Nature,* trans. Errol E. Harris and Peter Heath. Cambridge: Cambridge University Press, 1988.

———. *Philosophische Schriften,* Vol. 1. Landshut: Philipp Krull, 1809.

———. *Sysytem des transcendentalen Idealism.* Tübingen: J. G. Cotta, 1800.

———. *Über das Verhältniß des Realen und Idealen in der Natur. Oder Entwickelung der ersten Grundsätze der Naturphilosophie an den Principien der Schwere und des Lichts.* Hamburg: Friedrich Perthes, 1806.

———. *Von der Weltseele, eine Hypothese der höhern Physik zur Erklärung des allegeinen Organismus.* Hamburg: Friedrich Perthes, 1798.

Schemann, Ludwig. *Cosima Wagner: Briefe an Ludwig Schemann,* ed. Bertha Schemann. Regensburg, 1937.

Schlegel, Friedrich. "Athenäum-Fragment," 216, in *Philosophical Fragments,* trans. Peter Firchow. Minneapolis: University of Minnesota Press, 1991.

Schleiermacher, Friedrich. *On Religion: Speeches to Its Cultured Despisers,* trans. Richard Crouter. Cambridge: Cambridge University Press, 1988.

Schmidt, Alfred. *Idee und Weltwille. Schopenhauer als Kritiker Hegels.* Munich: Hanser Verlas, 1988.

Schnädelbach, Herbert. *Philosophy in Germany 1831–1933,* trans. Eric Matthews. Cambridge: Cambridge University Press, 1984.

Schopenhauer, Adele. *Anna: Ein Roman aus der nächsten Vergangenheit.* Leipzig: F. A. Brockhaus, 1845.

———. *Eine dänische Geschichte.* Braunschweig: George Westermann, 1848.

———. *Haus-, Wald- und Feldmärchen.* Leipzig: F. A. Brockhaus, 1844.

———. *Tagebuch einer Einsamen,* ed. Heinrich Hubert Houben. Munich: Matthes and Seitz, 1985.

———. *Tagebücher,* ed. Kurt Wolff, Vol. 1. Leipzig: 1909.

Schopenhauer, Arthur. *Der handschriftliche Nachlaß,* 5 vols., ed. Arthur Hübscher. Frankfurt am Main: Kramer, 1970.

———. *Faksimilenachdruck der 1. Auflage der Welt als Wille und Vorstellung,* ed. Rudolf Malter. Frankfurt am Main: Insel, 1987.

———. *Gesammelte Briefe,* ed. Arthur Hübscher. Bonn: Bouvier Verlag Herbert Grundmann, 1987.

———. *Gespräche,* ed. Arthur Hübscher. Stuttgart/Bad Cannstatt, 1971.

———. *Manuscript Remains in Four Volumes,* trans. E. F. J. Payne, ed. Arthur Hübscher. Oxford: Berg, 1988.

———. "Notwendige Rüge erlogener Zitate," *Intelligenzblatt der Jenaischen Allgemeinen Litteratur-Zeitung,* No. 10 (February 1821).

———. *On the Basis of Morality,* trans. E. F. J. Payne, with intro. by David E. Cartwright. Indianapolis: Hackett, 1997.

———. *On the Fourfold Root of the Principle of Sufficient Reason,* trans. E. F. J. Payne, with an intro. by Richard Taylor. La Salle, IL: Open Court Press, 1974.

————. *On the Will in Nature: A Discussion of the Corroborations from the Empirical Sciences That the Author's Philosophy Has Received Since Its First Appearance*, trans. E. F. J. Payne, edited with an intro. by David E. Cartwright. Oxford: Berg, 1992.

————. *On Vision and Colors*, trans. E. F. J. Payne, edited with an intro. by David E. Cartwright. Oxford: Berg, 1994.

————. *Parerga and Paralipomena*, 2 vols., trans. E. F. J. Payne. Oxford: Clarendon Press, 1974; reprint, 2001.

————. "Philosophie de la magie," trans. Alexandre Weill, *Revue française*, T. VII, 1856.

————. *Philosophische Vorlesungen aus dem handschriftlichen Nachlaß*, 4 vols., ed. Volker Spierling. Munich: R. Piper, 1984–6.

————. *Prize Essay on the Freedom of the Will*, trans. E. F. J. Payne, with an intro. by Günter Zöller. Cambridge: Cambridge University Press, 1999.

————. *Reisetagbücher aus den Jahren 1803–1804*, ed. Charlotte von Gwinner. Leipzig: F. A. Brockhaus, 1923.

————. *Sämtliche Werke*, 6 vols., ed. Julius Frauenstädt. Leipzig: F. A. Brockhaus, 1873/4.

————. *Sämtliche Werke*, 16 vols., ed. Paul Deussen. Munich: Piper, 1911–1942.

————. *Sämtliche Werke*, 7 vols., ed. Arthur Hübscher, 4th ed. Mannheim: F. A. Brockhaus, 1988.

————. *Schopenhauer's Early Fourfold Root*, trans. F. C. White. Aldershot: Avebury, 1997.

————. *The World as Will and Presentation*, Vol. 1, trans. Richard E. Aquila with David Carus. New York: Pearson/Longman, 2008.

————. *The World as Will and Representation*, 2 vols., trans. E. F. J. Payne.New York; Dover, 1969.,.

————. *Two Essays. I. On the Will in Nature. II. On the Fourfold Root of the Principle of Sufficient Reason*, trans. Mme. Karl Hillebrand. London: G. Bell, 1889; reprint Cosimo Classics, New York, 2007.

————. *Werke in zehn Bänden*, 10 vols., ed. Arthur Hübscher. Zurich: Diogenes, 1977.

Schopenhauer, Johanna. *A Lady Travels: The Diaries of Johanna Schopenhauer*, trans. Ruth Michaelis and Willy Merson. London: Routledge, 1988.

————. *Carl Ludwig Fernows Leben*. Tübingen: Cotta, 1810.

————. *Gabriele: Ein Roman*. Leipzig: F. A. Brockhaus, 1819.

————. "Jugenderinnerungen" in *Johanna Schopenhauer: Im Wechsel der Zeiten, im Gedränge der Welt*, ed. Rolf Weber. Munich: Winkler, 1986.

————. *Jugendleben und Wanderbilder*, ed. Adele Schopenhauer, 2 vols. Braunschweig: Westermann, 1839.

————. *Jugendleben und Wanderbilder*, ed. Willi Drost. Barmstedt Holstein: Velox-Verlag, 1958.

————. *Sämtliche Schriften*, 24 vols. Leipzig: F. A. Brockhaus, 1st ed, 1830–31; 2nd ed., 1834.

Schröder, William von. "Der Frankfurter Skandal um den Magnetiseur Ragazzoni," *Frankfurter Allgemeine Zeitung* (31 December 1957).

Schulze, Gottlob Ernst. *Aenesidemus, oder über die Fundamente der von dem Herrn Professor Reinhold in Jena gelieferten Elementar-Philosophie. Nebst einer Vertheidigung des Skepticismus gegen die Anmaassungen der Vernufikritik.* [Helmstädt]: 1792.

_____. *Grundsätze der allgemeinen Logik.* Helmstädt: Fleckeisen, 1810.

_____. *Kritik der theoretischen Philosophie,* 2 vols. Hamburg: Carl Ernst Bohn, 1801.

Segala, Marco. *I fantasmi, il cervello, l'anima Schopenhauer, l'occulto e la scienza.* Florence: Leo S. Olschki, 1998.

_____. *Schopenhauer, la filosofia, le scienze.* Pisa: Scuola Normale Superiore, 2009.

Seydel, Rudolf. *Schopenhauers philosophisches System, dargestellt und beurteilt.* Leipzig: Breitkopt and Härtel, 1857.

Sheehan, James. *German History: 1720–1866.* Oxford: Oxford University Press, 1989.

Silber, K. *Pestalozzi: The Man and His Work.* London: Routledge & Kegan Paul, 1965.

Singer, Peter. *Animal Liberation: A New Ethics for Our Treatment of Animals.* New York: Avon Books, 1975.

Sober, Elliot and David Sloan Wilson. *Unto Others: The Evolution of Unselfish Behavior.* Cambridge, MA: Harvard University Press, 1998.

Spinoza, Benedict de. *Ethics,* trans. R. H. M. Ewes. New York: Dover, 1955.

Stadler, Peter. *Pestalozzi: Geschichte Biographie von der alten Ordnung zur Revolution, 1746–1797.* Zurich: Neu Zürcher Zeitung, 1988.

Steinmetz, Max (ed.), *Geschichte der Univesität Jena.* Jena: VEB Gustav Fischer, 1958.

Sterne, Laurence. *The Life and Times of Tristram Shady, Gentleman.* Altenberg: G. E. Richtert, 1772.

Stoetzer, O. Carlos. *Karl Christian Friedrich Krause and His Influence in the Hispanic World.* Cologne: Böhlau, 1998.

Strauss, David Friedrich. *Der alte und neue Glaube.* Stuttgart: Kröner, 1872.

_____. *Das Leben Jesu kritisch Bearbeitet.* Tübingen: C. F. Oslander, 1838-39.

Taylor, Richard. *Virtue Ethics: An Introduction.* Interlaken, NY: Linden Books, 1991.

Varner, G. E. "The Schopenhauer Challenge in Environmental Ethics," *Environmental Ethics,* Vol. 7 (1985): 209–29.

Wackenroder, Wilhelm Heinrich. *Confessions and Fantasies,* trans. Mary Hurst Schubert. University Park, PA/London: The Pennsylvania State University Press, 1971.

Weimer, Wolfgang. "Der Philosoph und der Diktator: Arthur Schopenhauer und Adolf Hitler," *Schopenhauer-Jahrbuch,* Vol. 84 (2003): 157–67.

White, Lynn Jr. "The Historical Roots of Our Ecological Crisis," *Science,* Vol. 155 (1967): 1203–07.

Wicks, Robert. *Schopenhauer.* Malden, MA:Blackwell, 2008.

Wieland, Martin. *Geschichte der Abderiten,* 2 vols. Karlsruhe: Schmieder,1774-81.

_____. *Musarion, oder die Philosophy der Grazien* Karlsbad: G. Braun,. 1768

Wittgenstein, Ludwig. *Philosophical Investigations,* trans. G.E.M. Anscombe. New York: Macmillan, 1966.

————. *Remarks on Colour*, trans. G. E. M. Anscombe. Berkeley and Los Angeles: University of California Press, 1978.

————. *Tractatus Logico-Philosophicus*, trans. C. K. Ogden. London: Routledge & Kegan Paul, 1922.

Wolff, Christian. *Philosophia prima, sive Ontologia methodo scientifica pertractata, qua omnis cognitionis humanae principia continentur*. Francof. et Lips, 1736.

Young, Christopher and Andrew Brook. "Schopenhauer and Freud," in *International Journal of Psychoananlysis*. Vol. 75 (1994): 101–18.

Young, Julian, *Schopenhauer*. London: Routledge, 2005.

————. "Was Schopenhauer an Irrationalist?" *Schopenhauer-Jahrbuch*, Vol. 69 (1988): 85–100.

————. *Willing and Unwilling: A Study in the Philosophy of Arthur Schopenhauer*. Dordrecht: Nijhoff, 1987.

Zentner, Marcel. *Die Flucht ins Vergessen:Die Anfänge der Psychoanalyse Freuds bei Schopenhauer*. Darmstadt: Wissenschaftliche Buchgesellschaft, 1995.

Zimmern, Helen. *Arthur Schopenhauer, His Life and His Philosophy*. London: Longmans, Green and Co., 1876.

Zint, Hans. "Schopenhauer und seine Schwester, Ein Beitrag zur Lebensgeschichte des Philosophen," *Sechstes Jahrbuch der Schopenhauer-Gesellschaft* Vol. 6 (1917): 179–250.

————. "Schopenhauers Philosophie des doppelten Bewuβtsein," *Schopenhauer-Jahrbuch*, Vol. 10 (1921): pp. 3–45.

Ziolkowski, Theodore. *German Romanticism and Its Institutions*. Princeton, NJ: Princeton University Press, 1990.

Zöller, Günter. "German Realism: The Self-limitation of Idealist Thinking in Fichte, Schelling and Schopenhauer," in *The Cambridge Companion to German Idealism*, ed. Karl Ameriks. Cambridge: Cambridge University Press, 2000

————. "Kichtenhauer: Der Ursprung von Schopenhauers Welt als Wille und Vorstellung in Fichtes Wissenschaftslehre 1812 und System der Sittenlehre," in *Die Ethik Schopenhauer im Ausgang von Deutschen Idealismus*, ed. Lore Hühn with Philipp Schwab. Würzburg: Ergon, 2006.

Index